The
TRAVELING
MARATHONER
by Elise Allen

Fodor's

A Complete Guide to Top U.S. Races
and Sightseeing on the Run

Fodor's Travel Publications
New York • Toronto • London • Sydney • Auckland

www.fodors.com
www.travelingmarathoner.com

MAR   2006

THE TRAVELING MARATHONER

EDITOR: Laura M. Kidder
EDITORIAL PRODUCTION: Linda K. Schmidt
MAPS: David Lindroth, Inc., and Ed Jacobus, *cartographers;* Bob Blake and Rebecca Baer, *map editors*
DESIGN: Tigist Getachew
PRODUCTION/MANUFACTURING: Robert B. Shields

Copyright
Copyright © 2006 by Fodor's Travel, a division of Random House, Inc.

Fodor's is a registered trademark of Random House, Inc.

All rights reserved under International and Pan-American Copyright Conventions. Published in the United States by Fodor's Travel, a division of Random House, Inc., and simultaneously in Canada by Random House of Canada Limited, Toronto. Distributed by Random House, Inc., New York.

No maps, illustrations, or other portions of this book may be reproduced in any form without written permission from the publisher.

ISBN: 1-4000-1459-X
ISBN-13: 978-1-4000-1459-0

Library of Congress Cataloguing-in-Publication data available upon request

Photo Credits
Cover photo: Brian Sytnyk/Masterfile. Disney Chapter Title: Elise Allen. Disney Profile: James Crigler. New Orleans Chapter Title: Marathon Foto. New Orleans Profile: Paul and Lydia Cowlishaw. Los Angeles Chapter Title: Marathon Foto. Los Angeles Profile: Jeremy N. C. Newman. Boston Chapter Title: Fay Foto, used with permission of the Boston Athletic Association. Boston Profile: Elise Allen. Boston Qualifying Charts: used with permission of the Boston Athletic Association. Cincinnati Chapter Title: Michael Anderson. Cincinnati Profile Photo: Joyce Tucker. Cincinnati Profile Excerpt: Cynthia Wheeler. Newport Chapter Title and Profile: Adrenaline Event Photography. Salt Lake City Chapter Title: *Deseret Morning News.* Salt Lake City Profile: Robert H. Harmon. Grizzly Chapter Title: Grizzly Activities, Inc. Grizzly Profile: Christine A. McCormick. Stowe Chapter Title: Don Landwehrle and LL Photo. Stowe Profile: Connor Polow. Chicago Chapter Title: LaSalle Bank Chicago Marathon. Chicago Profile: Omar Angeles. New York City Chapter Title: New York Road Runners. New York City Profile: Edward Ines. Honolulu Chapter Title: Honolulu Marathon. Honolulu Profile: Mike Burrill, Jr. Back Cover: Randy Nellis.

Special Sales
This book is available for special discounts for bulk purchases for sales promotions or premiums. Special editions, including personalized covers, excerpts of existing books, and corporate imprints, can be created in large quantities for special needs. For more information, write to Special Markets/Premium Sales, 1745 Broadway, MD 6-2, New York, New York 10019, or e-mail specialmarkets@randomhouse.com.

PRINTED IN THE UNITED STATES OF AMERICA

10 9 8 7 6 5 4 3 2 1

THE TRAVELING MARATHONER

In 2006, upward of a half-million people will complete a U.S. marathon. Of those, only the teeniest sliver of a percentage have the slightest chance of finishing within sight of the victors, never mind actually breaking the tape and winning the race. Why, then, do the rest of us do it? After all, it's not like it's easy. It's 26.2 miles. They say Phidippides, the first person to ever run the marathon, *died* when he finished. Where exactly is the upside here?

Amazingly enough, there are a lot of upsides. There's the camaraderie of everyone on the course, all striving for the same incredible goal. There's the satisfaction of running for a charity, digging deep and pouring your own sweat equity into a worthy cause. There's the spectacle of the big-city races: fireworks, and bands, and crowds of screaming spectators. There's the intimacy of running through a city or region, getting to know it in a way you can't from inside a car. Yet the greatest upside to running a marathon is accomplishing what seems impossible. Whether you race through the course in 2 hours and 45 minutes or walk through it in 9 hours and 15, you'll have achieved something magnificent, and the elation you'll feel is unlike anything else in this world. It's magical . . . and it's addictive.

I say that from experience: I went from scoffing at runners to becoming a marathon junkie. By publication date I'll have run seven of them (rather slowly, I might add), and I don't see myself stopping. And although I enjoy my hometown marathon, I really love traveling to races. I'll go with my running partners, our families and friends, and make a vacation of it—a bizarre vacation in which the centerpiece is a 26.2-mile run. But planning these vacations isn't easy. I could usually find information on the marathon and its host city, but I could find nothing that wed the two. What were the closest hotels to the marathon expo and starting line? What were the best local restaurants for a prerace carbo load? Where should my family and friends go to cheer me on? And when the race was over, what was the best way to take in a city when my knees wouldn't bend?

I never did find a resource that could give me all the answers, so I set out to find them myself. This book is the result: my picks for the most outstanding U.S. race of each month of the year, and a complete guide filled with all the information you need. It's a perfect resource for marathoners, marathoners' cheering sections, and anyone intrigued by the idea of tackling 26.2 miles (check out the *Anyone Can Run a Marathon* profiles in each chapter for quick shots of inspiration). Flip to any chapter, and you'll learn the best way to devour that marathon city or town—on the run.

CONTENTS

Maps

HOW TO USE THIS BOOK

Before we start in on the races, I want to give you a quick overview of how the book works. It's divided into 12 chapters, each chapter highlighting the most outstanding race for that particular month. So no matter what time of year you'd like to run your next race, there's a great marathon at your disposal.

"'The most outstanding race,' huh?" you might say. "Isn't that a little subjective?"

Admittedly, it is. And the one-race-per-month format by nature omits a lot of fantastic races, especially in prime marathon months like October and November. Still, I believe each race I chose stands out within its particular month because of its exciting location, its history, its character, or a mix of all three. Taken as a whole, the 12 also represent a solid mix of marathon types and locales. Run every race in this book, and you'll traipse all over the country, experiencing everything from the Big Apple to Big Sky Country.

This book is written *by* a traveling marathoner, *for* traveling marathoners, their spectators, and all those intrigued by the idea. As such, it's a little different from regular guidebooks. The following is an outline of a basic chapter. Within it, I have laid out what to expect from each section, as well as any assumptions I've made or marathon terms that first-timers might not know.

One more thing, just for the record—no marathon or property has paid to be included in this book. If they're in here, it's only because I think they're worthwhile options. So, without further ado...

Chapter Outline

Each chapter begins with a brief blurb about the race: a paragraph or two to give you its overall feeling. A couple of things apply throughout each chapter:

TOP CHOICES: Places marked with 🏃, the **Marathoner's Choice** symbol, offer the best blend of quality, convenience to race events, specific marathoner amenities, and (often) runner discounts. **Starred properties (★)** are simply outstanding places, well worth your patronage whether or not you're running a marathon.

CREDIT CARDS: AE, D, DC, MC, and V following lodging or restaurant listings indicate that American Express, Discover, Diners Club, MasterCard, and Visa are accepted.

So You're Running . . .

Here you'll get a snapshot of the race's city, town, or region. In large cities this includes a breakdown of the major neighborhoods and their basic layouts. Look here for area maps as well as visitor information.

Race Basics

This is where you'll get the nuts and bolts of the race, including when to register, the cost, and any hoops you'll need to jump through (qualifying for Boston, the New York City Marathon lottery). Although I always recommend you register online, those without Web access can get an application by calling the race; look for the number in this section. Since so many people are online, I discuss the marathon Web site and what it offers. Also look for information on special divisions for which you need to sign up specifically, such as team challenges, Hercules (Clydesdale) and Athena divisions for heavier runners, and wheelchair divisions.

As I discuss these races, readers new to marathoning might by thrown by terms like "PR." This stands for personal record, or your best marathon time. Mine, for instance, is 4:47 (and I'm pretty psyched about it), which is not a time of day, but an elapsed marathon time of 4 hours and 47 minutes. Also please note that when I say "runner" in this book, I mean any marathoner, whether you're an actual runner, a walker, or a wheelchair athlete.

HOTELS

Within Race Basics you'll also find a list of recommended hotels. These places—whether homey bed-and-breakfasts, mom-and-pop motels, grand inns, or luxury resorts—are the cream of the crop in each price and lodging category. *Book early*—as soon as you know you're running the race. Cities fill up at marathon time. Plus, the earlier you book, the better the deal you'll get.

I made a point to note all the marathoner specials and amenities that the hotels offer, but such things change regularly, so call and check. Note also that some hotels have no specific marathon policies but will go out of their way to help you once they know you're running the race. Within hotel listings, note the following:

BATHS: You'll find private bathrooms unless noted otherwise.

CLOSINGS: Assume that lodgings are open all year unless otherwise noted.

FACILITIES: I list what's available, but I don't always specify what costs extra. When pricing accommodations, always ask what's included. The term *hot tub* denotes hot tubs, whirlpools, and Jacuzzis. Assume that lodgings have phones, TVs, and air-conditioning and that they permit smoking and kids, unless I note otherwise. Specifically for marathoners and their entourages, I've added extra facilities information you won't necessarily find in other Fodor's guides:

Wake-up Calls and/or Alarm Clocks: For most races, you'll need to wake up early.

24-hr. Room Service: So you know if you can get a meal before an early morning race.

Coffeemakers: Some runners can't do without coffee before a race. You know who you are.

Robes: After 26.2 miles (or even before), you deserve all creature comforts.

Newspapers: Meaning the papers are delivered to your room.

Wi-Fi: Noted only if Wi-Fi is actually in the rooms, not just in public areas.

24-Hour Gym: Just in case you want to warm-up or cool down at an off hour.

PRICES: Price categories are based on the price range for a standard double room at high season, excluding service charges, tax, and marathoner discounts. Price categories for all-suite properties are based on prices for standard suites.

WHAT IT COSTS

$$$$	over $350
$$$	$276–$350
$$	$201–$275
$	$125–$200
¢	under $125

And You're Off!

This section goes through the marathon events of race weekend (I say "weekend," even though some races, like Boston, take place during the week), starting with:

THE EXPO/PACKET PICKUP: All races in this book have either an expo or packet pickup, which all runners must attend. Bring your photo ID and any confirmation card the race sent you (not all races send these). At the expo/packet pickup, you'll get your bib number, a goodie bag filled with flyers and swag from race sponsors, and if your race uses chip timing, a ChampionChip. These devices attach to your shoelaces and time your race. This is especially important in larger races, where there can be upward of a half-hour between the time the race begins and the time the back of the pack crosses the starting line. Some smaller races don't bother with chip timing because it's too expensive and not necessary for making the race a Boston qualifier. Every race in this book is certified and can be used to qualify for the Boston Marathon.

NIGHT–BEFORE PASTA DINNER: This section provides an overview of the marathon-sponsored pasta dinner (if there is one) and cites recommendations for local pasta spots. If you want to eat in a restaurant, be sure to book well in advance—even before you leave for your trip.

THE COURSE: On this basic tour of the marathon course, I'll tell you about entertainment, amenities, and great things to look for along the way. Unless otherwise stated, there will be a baggage check at the race start, so you can leave extra gear and pick it up after the race. Since many races begin early, it can be cold at the starting area. A great plan is to wear cheap throwaway sweats and discard them just before the race starts. Marathons collect these discarded clothes and donate them to charity. Also in this section, I give the number of hours the course is open before roads re-open to traffic. Unless otherwise stated, you can continue the marathon after this point, but you must move to the side of the street and obey traffic laws. If you think you'll be a late finisher, carry a water belt stocked with fluid and energy gels, since aid stations might close.

SPECTATING: I discuss the best race-day strategies for your fans. Make sure you tell them your expected pace so they can figure out when to be at each cheering spot. Also make plans about where you'll meet after the race. Marathons with family-reunion areas post letters of the alphabet under which people can reconnect; to avoid confusion, confirm your letter with your friends before the race begins. Chances are your friends and family will have some downtime between bouts of screaming your name as you race on by; I always recommend a few terrific breakfast places.

CELEBRATE: When applicable, this section covers the marathon-sponsored post-race party.

ANYONE CAN RUN A MARATHON: These sections form the true heart of the book. Each chapter profiles an average runner who has tackled that chapter's race, giving you the story and insights on what 26.2 miles means to him or her.

Beyond the Finish Line

Here's where you'll find out more about the town or city hosting the marathon, including:

REPLACING 2,620 CALORIES: That's a rough approximation of what you burn during a marathon, and you deserve to replenish it with the best the area offers. I make a point of including local food-lovers' hot spots as well as neighborhood favorites, including cheaper as well as more expensive options.

DRESS: Jackets or ties are not required for men unless otherwise noted.

MEALS AND HOURS: Assume that restaurants are open for lunch and dinner unless otherwise noted. I always specify days closed and meals not available.

RESERVATIONS: They're always a good idea, but I don't mention them unless they're essential or are not accepted.

PRICES: The price categories listed are based on the cost per person for a main course at dinner or, when dinner isn't available, the next most expensive meal.

WHAT IT COSTS

$$$$	over $35
$$$	$26–$35
$$	$16–$25
$	$5–$15
¢	under $5

SIGHTSEEING ON (AND OFF) YOUR FEET: This section lists the best sights in town, grouped according to how good your post-race legs need to feel in order to enjoy them. Also in this section is the self-explanatory box "Forget Sightseeing. Get Me to a Spa!" Note that it's wise to book spa appointments well in advance of your trip.

SHOP TILL YOU DROP and **I LOVE THE NIGHTLIFE** give you a heads-up to each area's best shopping and nightlife options.

Helpful Info

Details about transportation and other logistical information conclude each chapter. Be sure to check Web sites or call for particulars.

An Important Tip

All prices, opening times, and other details in this book are based on information I researched at press time, but changes constantly occur in the travel world, especially in seasonal destinations. Fodor's cannot accept responsibility for facts that become outdated or for inadvertent errors or omissions. Always confirm information when it matters, especially if you're making a detour to visit a specific place.

Let Me Hear from You

Keeping a travel guide fresh and up-to-date is a big job, and I welcome any and all comments. I'd love to have your thoughts on places I've listed, and I'm interested in hearing about your special finds. Contact me via e-mail at elise@travelingmarathoner.com or via snail mail care of *The Traveling Marathoner* at Fodor's, 1745 Broadway, New York, NY 10019.

Also, please visit www.travelingmarathoner.com. Not only is it filled with great information and links to other marathon resources, but it's also a true runners community—a place to join other marathoners, spectators, and those considering 26.2 through message boards where you can share your thoughts, exchange tips, and even look for running buddies for specific races.

I look forward to hearing from you. And in the meantime, have a great race!

—Elise Allen

CHAPTER 1

JANUARY

Walt Disney World Marathon, Orlando, FL

It may be a small world after all, but it won't feel that way when you're on Mile 20 of the Walt Disney World Marathon. This race twists along the Mouse's Orlando turf, running through all four major parks: Epcot, the Magic Kingdom, Disney's Animal Kingdom, and Disney–MGM Studios.

There are many reasons that this marathon is a standout: the flat course, the unique route, and the impeccable Disney attention to detail. But I've run this race, and I can tell you that what truly makes it special is its magic. I don't care how big a cynic you are, you can't help but get a huge grin on your face when you run through Cinderella Castle—music from your favorite Disney movies ringing in your ears, spectators cheering you on—and then fall into Winnie the Pooh's arms for a big hug before zooming off again. It hits your inner child in a very profound and fundamental way, even if you think you have no inner child.

VISITOR INFO

General Info
☎
407/824-4321
🌐
www.disneyworld.com
•
Dining Info
☎
407/WDW-DINE
•
Resort Info
☎
407/W-DISNEY

And if you're at all a Disney fan, you must do this race once. At least once.

So, You're Running Disney . . .

Disney World is titanic; it occupies 30,000 acres—twice the size of Manhattan—near Kissimmee, Florida. Only 107 of those acres make up the Magic Kingdom, which is what most people imagine when they hear "Walt Disney World." The rest includes Epcot, a combination science exploratorium and world's fair; Disney–MGM Studios, devoted to the world of film and TV entertainment; and Disney's Animal Kingdom, showcasing creatures both real and fantastical. Add to these two water parks, more than two dozen hotels, a sports complex, and countless shops, restaurants, and nightspots—you get the idea. There's a lot to see.

The good news is that when you come to Disney World for the marathon, you'll have the time of your life. The bad news is you'll pay more for a marathon trip than you ever thought possible. Don't get me wrong—there are plenty of ways to economize, but you can't get past the basic fact that after you finish, say, the Boston Marathon, you don't have to pay to walk around the city. How then can you do this race without going completely broke? You choose your admission-ticket package (⇨ Sightseeing, *below*) and your hotel and dining options wisely. There are high-quality choices at every price point, so set a budget and plan accordingly.

SPORTS ENTHUSIASTS

Want to experience the Disney Marathon without breaking a sweat? Volunteer your time as a Sports Enthusiast. As such you can work at any marathon weekend event and get such perks as marathon discounts, free food and beverages, a commemorative windbreaker, and a one-day theme-park ticket good at Epcot, Magic Kingdom, Animal Kingdom, or Disney–MGM Studios.

To register, go to www.disneyworldsports.com, click on "Sports Enthusiasts" (along the left side of the screen), then choose an event. You'll see a list of positions, and can check the one you prefer. Organizers try to honor requests but make no guarantees. Like the race itself, volunteer spots fill up quickly, so sign up early. As marathon weekend nears, you'll get your volunteer schedule in the mail. You'll need to pick up a confirmation packet at Disney's Wide World of Sports.

RACE BASICS

The Walt Disney World Marathon began in 1994, and immediately captured the imagination of many runners, several of whom became regulars. As of 2005, there's a list of 129 "Perfect 12s," people who have run all 12 Disney World marathons. What keeps them coming back? This is a race to which you can bring your entire family, knowing that everyone will have a fantastic time. The course is also a draw: you storm through Epcot before it's even open, you're regaled with entertainment that's pure Disney magic, and in the end you get a medal shaped like Mickey Mouse. In addition to the big race, marathon weekend also sees a half-marathon, a 5K family fun run, and a series of kids' races, including a diaper dash for children 12 months and under.

Registration

Sign up early; this race is first-come, first-served, and it always sells out. Registration for next year's race opens the day after this year's is run, and the best way to register is through the marathon Web site. It's light on marathon weekend specifics, but registered runners get more detailed information around October, in the form of a very comprehensive race program. What the site does have is plenty of registration data, a course map, and a merchandise store selling official Disney Marathon training gear.

Registration costs $95 and includes the excellent race program, a T-shirt, and entry into the post-race party at Disney's Pleasure Island. The fee is nonrefundable. If you know in advance that you can't do the race, contact the organizers about running the next year's marathon; you'll have to pay to register again, but you'll be guaranteed a spot.

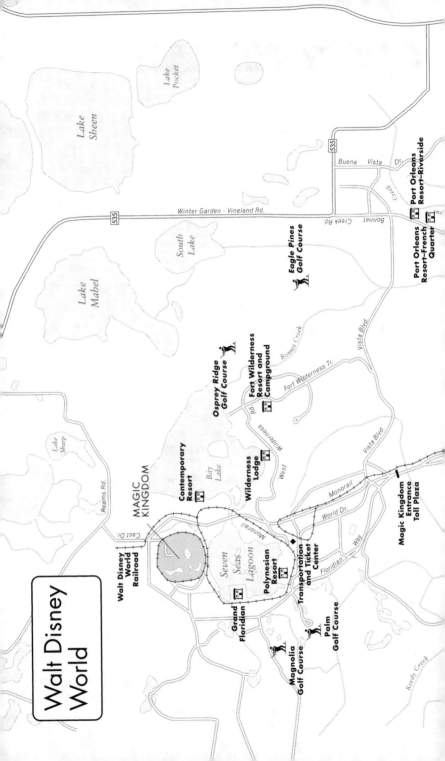

Special divisions for this race include wheelchair and military. If you register online you can request that Disney contact you about rooms, airfare, and/or car rental. You can also make an optional donation to the Leukemia and Lymphoma Society, the main race beneficiary.

You can also run as part of a team of three to five people. Each member must sign up individually, then the group pays an additional $35 fee and submits a registration form on which it cites the team name, declares a captain, states the team category (men, women, mixed, masters, military, and so on), and lists its members. Teams get a special check-in area at the expo and a separate reunion area at the finish.

Hotels to Consider

You might think staying off Disney property is a good way to economize. Bad idea. It's a million times easier to get around if you're staying on-site, as all the hotels are linked to the parks and each other via the free transit system. In addition to cutting down on transportation hassles, an on-site stay saves you the cost of a rental car and parking fees. The Disney hotels are also equipped to meet runners' needs. They greet you with an in-room race information letter, offer wake-up calls, and provide reliable transportation to the starting area. Many also offer runner-friendly specials in their restaurants, stock their stores with energy bars and other marathoner fuel, and/or open a store or restaurant early so you can grab a snack before heading to the race.

RACE CONTACTS

Walt Disney World Marathon

☎
407/986-1160

🌐
www.disneyworldmarathon.com
•
Disney Sports Travel

☎
407/939-7810

As an added convenience, Disney hotels allow you to charge purchases made anywhere on the property to your room. You also qualify for the Extra Magic Hour perk that lets you enter a certain park an hour before the official opening time or remain up to three hours after closing each day.

Each Disney hotel is impeccably designed according to a theme, and there are no bad on-site properties. That said, some are more exceptional and/or offer more marathon perks than others. Disney divides its hotels into three price categories: Value ($77–$131), Moderate ($134–$209), and Deluxe ($199–$870). There are also several resorts that are part of the Disney Vacation Club (Disney's version of a time-share program, but different: check out dvc.disney.go.com/dvc/index for details), though you can also reserve rooms at them on a nightly basis. The ultimate budget option is the Fort Wilderness Campground, which can accommodate RVs as well as tents.

The hotel selection below is by no means comprehensive; rather it's a list of a few standouts. For details on all the Disney properties check out www.disneyworld.com. Click "Plan All Your Vacation Details," and then "Find the Perfect Resort." When you know what you want, book it through Disney Sports Travel (⇨ Race Contacts, *above*). Booking through them is not only convenient, but also the best way to get any available marathoner discounts on hotels and/or park tickets.

A PERFECT 12

Jakson Badenhoop is a member of the Perfect 12, someone who has, as of this writing, run all 12 Walt Disney World Marathons. Jakson has run more than 100 marathons and is himself a race director for Performance MultiSports (www.performacemultisports.com), so he's very critical of other races. Disney is the only marathon he runs consistently every year.

Jakson stresses that he's "*not* a Disney fanatic." He tends to enjoy the stretches *between* the parks, where he can simply run and concentrate on form. But every year, when he passes through Cinderella Castle, over the moat—with Disney music playing and characters and spectators cheering—he's moved. "I guess maybe it's a vestige of childhood, but it's a special moment," he says. "I wasn't prepared to get emotional." But he does, every year. And he has no intention of stopping.

The Magic Kingdom

With the exception of the Wilderness Lodge, these resorts are all on the monorail line, making them especially convenient for runners and their fans. The monorail runs between the resorts, the Magic Kingdom, and the Transportation and Ticket Center (TTC), where you can catch another line to Epcot. The monorail is the simplest way for spectators to reach several viewing stations along the marathon route. After the race, runners staying at these resorts can also hop the monorail to get back to their rooms quickly, avoiding the sometimes very long wait for buses.

🏃 **CONTEMPORARY RESORT.** Looking like an intergalactic docking bay, this 15-story, flat-topped pyramid bustles from dawn to after midnight. Upper floors of the main tower (where rooms are more expensive) offer a great view of the Magic Kingdom. The best reason to stay? Location. The monorail runs *through* the tower lobby, so it takes just minutes to get to the Magic Kingdom and Epcot. ☎ 407/824-1000 ✒ 983 rooms, 25 suites ☁ 3 restaurants, snack bar, 24-hr room service, wake-up calls, alarm clocks, coffeemakers, newspapers, cable TV, in-room data ports, some refrigerators, in-room safes, golf privileges, 6 tennis courts, 3 pools, wading pool, gym, hair salon, 2 hot tubs, massage, beach, boating, marina, waterskiing, basketball, volleyball, 2 lobby lounges, video game room, shops, babysitting, children's programs (ages 4–12), playground, laundry facilities, laundry service, concierge, concierge floor, business services, convention center, meeting rooms, no-smoking floors ▤ AE, D, DC, MC, V $$–$$$$.

🏃 **GRAND FLORIDIAN RESORT & SPA.** The Grand Floridian is Disney's flagship resort—no other has better amenities. Yet you won't look out of place walking through the lobby in flip-flops. This Victorian-style property on the shores of the Seven Seas Lagoon is all delicate gingerbread, rambling verandas, and brick chimneys. You can spend more in a weekend here than on an average mortgage payment, but you'll have the memory of the best that Disney offers. ☎ 407/824-3000 ✒ 900 rooms, 90 suites ☁ 5 restaurants, snack bar, 24-hr room service, wake-up calls, alarm clocks, coffeemakers, newspapers, cable TV, in-room data ports, in-room safes, golf privileges, 2 tennis courts, 3 pools, wading pool, gym, hair salon, massage, spa, beach, boating, marina, waterskiing, croquet, shuffleboard, volleyball, 4 lounges, video game room, babysitting, children's programs (ages 4–12), playground, laundry facilities, laundry service, concierge, concierge floor, business services, convention center, meeting rooms, no-smoking floors ▤ AE, D, DC, MC, V $$$-$$$$$.

🐾 **POLYNESIAN RESORT.** If it weren't for the kids in Mickey Mouse caps, you'd think you were in Fiji. The lobby is a three-story tropical atrium. Orchids bloom alongside coconut palms and banana trees, and water cascades from volcanic-rock fountains. A mainstay here is the evening luau (Wednesday–Sunday), in which Polynesian dancers perform before a feast with Hawaiian-style roast pork. Rooms sleep five, since they all have two queen-size beds and a daybed. Lagoon-view rooms—which overlook the Electrical Water Pageant show—are the most peaceful and the priciest. ☎ 407/824-2000 ⇆ 853 rooms, 5 suites ♨ 4 restaurants, snack bar, room service, wake-up calls, alarm clocks, coffeemakers, newspapers, cable TV, in-room data ports, in-room safes, golf privileges, 2 pools, wading pool, gym, hair salon, massage, beach, boating, volleyball, bar, lobby lounge, video game room, babysitting, children's programs (ages 4–12), playground, laundry facilities, laundry service, concierge, concierge floors, business services, no-smoking floors ▤ AE, D, DC, MC, V $$$-$$$$.

★ **WILDERNESS LODGE.** The architects outdid themselves with this hotel modeled after the majestic turn-of-the-20th-century lodges of the American Northwest. The five-story lobby, supported by towering tree trunks, has an 82-foot-high fireplace made of rocks from the Grand Canyon and lighted by enormous tepee-shape chandeliers. Two 55-foot-tall hand-carved totem poles complete the illusion. Rooms have leather chairs, patchwork quilts, and cowboy art. Each has a balcony or a patio. The hotel's showstopper is its Fire Rock Geyser, a faux Old Faithful, near the large pool, which begins as an artificially heated hot spring in the lobby. ☎ 407/824-3200 ⇆ 728 rooms, 31 suites ♨ 3 restaurants, some room service, wake-up calls, alarm clocks, coffeemakers, newspapers, cable TV with movies, in-room data ports, pool, wading pool, 2 hot tubs, beach, boating, bicycles, 2 lobby lounges, video game room, babysitting, children's programs (ages 4–12), laundry facilities, laundry service, concierge, concierge floor, business services, no-smoking floors ▤ AE, D, DC, MC, V $-$$$$.

Epcot

The BoardWalk Inn and the Beach and Yacht Club resorts are on the marathon course. Stay in one of these places and your cheering section can easily roll out of bed to root for you.

★ **BEACH AND YACHT CLUB RESORTS.** These properties on Seven Seas Lagoon seem straight out of a Cape Cod summer. The five-story Yacht Club has hardwood floors, a lobby full of gleaming brass and polished leather, an oyster-gray clapboard facade, and evergreen landscaping; there's even a lighthouse on its pier. At the Beach Club, a croquet lawn and cabana-dotted white-sand beach set the scene. Stormalong Bay, a 3-acre water park with slides and whirlpools, is part of this club. ☎ 407/934-8000 Beach Club, 407/934-7000 Yacht Club ⇆ 1,213 rooms, 112 suites ♨ 4 restaurants, snack bar, room service (24-hr in Yacht Club), wake-up calls, alarm clocks, coffeemakers, in-room data ports, in-room safes, newspapers, cable TV with movies, golf privileges, 2 tennis courts, 3 pools, gym, hair salon, massage, sauna, beach, boating, bicycles, croquet, volleyball, 3 lobby lounges, video game room, babysitting, children's programs (ages 4–12), laundry service, concierge, business services, convention center, no-smoking floors ▤ AE, D, DC, MC, V $$$-$$$$.

FEELING GOOFY?

Marathon not daunting enough for you? Try Goofy's Race and a Half Challenge. Disney's half-marathon used to run concurrently with the marathon. In fact, if you couldn't handle the marathon, you could always peel off with the half-marathoners en route to an earlier finish. Sure, you'd miss out on a Mickey medal, but you'd get a Donald Duck medal, which is almost as impressive. Now the half-marathon occurs the day before the marathon, affording a fantastic, albeit slightly insane, proposition: run both races and snag a Donald, a Mickey, and a Goofy.

The fee for the Race and a Half Challenge is $180, the sum of the marathon and half-marathon fees. Enter and your marathon program will come with *two* race number pick-up cards. At the expo you check in at a special booth, where you get two race numbers, two ChampionChips, two T-shirts, and a wristband. Wear that band for Saturday's half-marathon. When you finish and get your Donald, go to the Race and a Half Challenge booth to get a second wristband. Wear that band for the marathon. When you finish and get your Mickey, go to the Race and a Half Challenge booth again to collect your Goofy—because you have to be seriously goofy to run 39.3 miles in two days.

★ **BOARDWALK INN AND VILLAS.** Architectural master Robert A. M. Stern designed the crowning jewel of the BoardWalk to mimic 19th-century New England building styles. A 200-foot waterslide in the form of a classic wooden roller coaster cascades into the pool area. And there's plenty to do on the lakeside BoardWalk: ride surrey bikes, watch a game at the ESPN Sports Club, or dine in some of Disney's better restaurants. Rooms overlooking Crescent Lake and the BoardWalk cost the most and are the noisiest. ☎ 407/939–5100 inn, 407/939–6200 villas 🔁 370 rooms, 19 suites, 526 villas ⚓ 4 restaurants, room service, wake-up calls, alarm clocks, coffeemakers, newspapers, in-room data ports, in-room safes, golf privileges, miniature golf, tennis court, pool, gym, fishing, croquet, lobby lounge, nightclub, video game room, babysitting, children's programs (ages 4–12), laundry facilities, laundry service, concierge, business services, convention center, no-smoking floors ▤ AE, D, DC, MC, V $$$–$$$$.

CARIBBEAN BEACH RESORT. Awash in dizzying Caribbean colors, six palm-studded "villages" share 45-acre Barefoot Bay and its white-sand beach. A promenade circles the lake, and bridges over it connect to a 1-acre play and picnic area called Parrot Cay. You can rent boats for a tour on the lake, or rent bikes for a ride around the property. The Old Port Royale complex, decorated with pirates' cannons, tropical birds, and statues, has a food court, a lounge, and a pool with waterfalls and a big slide. ☎ 407/934–3400 🔁 2,112 rooms ⚓ Restaurant, food court, room service, wake-up calls, alarm clocks, coffeemakers, in-room data ports, in-room safes, newspapers, cable TV with movies, golf privileges, 7 pools, wading pool, hot tub, beach, boating, bicycles, lobby lounge, video game room, babysitting, playground, laundry facilities, laundry service, no-smoking floors ▤ AE, D, DC, MC, V $–$$.

CORONADO SPRINGS RESORT. It's popular with families, who come for its casual southwestern architecture; its lively Mexican-style Pepper Market food court; and its elaborate swimming pool complex, which has a Mayan pyramid with a big waterslide. There's a full-service health club that offers massage, and if you like jogging, walking, or biking, you're in the right place—a sidewalk circles the property's 15-acre lake. ☎ 407/939–1000 ⟫1,967 rooms ♿2 restaurants, food court, room service, wake-up calls, alarm clocks, coffeemakers, newspapers, cable TV with movies, in-room data ports, in-room safes, golf privileges, 4 pools, gym, massage, hair salon, boating, bicycles, bar, video game room, babysitting, playground, laundry service, business services, convention center, no-smoking floors ▭ AE, D, DC, MC, V $–$$.

Animal Kingdom

ALL-STAR SPORTS, ALL-STAR MUSIC, AND ALL-STAR MOVIES RESORTS. If you want to save money, these resorts are your best bets. In the Sports resort, 30-foot tennis rackets strike balls the size of small cars; in the Music resort you'll walk by giant bongos; and in the Movies resort, huge characters like *Toy Story*'s Buzz Lightyear frame each building. Rooms have two double beds, a closet rod, an armoire, and a desk. The food courts sell standard fast food, and you can have pizza delivered to your room. Don't take a room near the food courts or pools if a little noise bothers you. ☎ 407/939–5000 Sports, 407/939–6000 Music, 407/939–7000 Movies ⟫1,920 rooms at each ♿3 food courts, room service, wake-up calls, alarm clocks, cable TV with movies, in-room data ports, in-room safes, golf privileges, 6 pools, 3 bars, video game rooms, babysitting, playground, laundry facilities, laundry service, no-smoking floors ▭ AE, D, DC, MC, V ¢–$.

POST-RACE MASSAGE

Sign up at the expo for a finish-area massage. The cost is just $10, which goes to the Leukemia and Lymphoma Society.

Downtown Disney

SARATOGA SPRINGS RESORT & SPA. A cluster of three- and four-story buildings, decorated in and out to look like 19th-century resorts from upstate New York, overlook a giant pool with man-made hot springs surrounded by faux boulders. Standard rooms include microwaves and refrigerators; suites have full kitchens. Three-bedroom family suites, occupying two levels, have dining rooms, living rooms, and four bathrooms. Dark-wood, early-American–style furniture and overstuffed couches make things homey. Stay here and you don't have to travel anywhere for a post-race spa treatment. ☎ 407/934–7639 ⟫552 units ♿Restaurant, snack bar, wake-up calls, alarm clocks, coffeemakers, newspapers, cable TV with movies, in-room data ports, in-room safes, microwaves, golf privileges, 2 tennis courts, 2 pools, gym, 4 hot tubs, spa, boating, bicycles, basketball, shuffleboard, lobby lounge, theater, video game room, business services, no-smoking floors ▭ AE, D, DC, MC, V $$–$$$$.

THE GRATEFUL DEADS

If you're even thinking about running the Walt Disney World Marathon and you have e-mail, join the Disney Deads (www.disney-deads.com), an online group whose only requirement for membership is an interest in the Walt Disney World Marathon—be it as a runner, a walker, or a supporter. The Deads offer the perfect place to find answers to any and all of your Disney marathon questions. Many people on the list have run this race several times; quite a few have run *every* Disney World Marathon.

The Deads are also a fantastically supportive running community, sharing training and race reports, cheering one another's successes, and buoying each other up after setbacks. Come marathon weekend, the Deads move beyond the virtual, with encounters like a Friday morning fun run, a group pasta dinner, a post-race "bragathon," and a Monday morning jog. ("Jog" is used very loosely. "Stagger," "limp," or "crawl" can be equally appropriate). After the Deads return home from Disney and type up their race reports, they continue the camaraderie, offering advice and encouragement as they all prepare for the next year's Disney World Marathon.

AND YOU'RE OFF . . .

The Expo

The expo is held at Disney's Wide World of Sports Complex the three days before the race: half a day on Thursday and all day Friday and Saturday. Buses to the expo are available from all resorts as well as Disney–MGM Studios. They start running every 45 minutes to an hour before the expo opens, and stop an hour after closing. When you go, be sure to bring the official race number pick-up card you received with your race program. All participants must also sign a waiver. Your goodie bag will include an event guide and final race instructions.

You won't need more than an hour to tour this midsize event, the highlight of which is the official Walt Disney World Marathon merchandise store. If you're interested in seminars and celebrity speakers, check the marathon Web site in December for a schedule. Speaker information is also e-mailed to participants and posted at the expo itself. To avoid crowds try to hit the expo on Thursday, first thing Friday morning, or late Friday or Saturday.

Race Day

The Course

Set your alarm *and* request a wake-up call, because you're getting up early. Buses from the resorts to the staging area begin running at 3 AM; the last ones leave at 4 AM. It's usually cold, so bundle up. Although people on the buses often speak in voices hushed by nerves and the unreal hour, things spring to life the minute you step into the Epcot parking lot. Hordes of runners and spectators pour out of bus after bus, following a red carpet to the banks of spotlights slicing through the sky at the staging area.

Look up and you see the giant dome of Epcot's Spaceship Earth, glowing purple and blue against the night sky. All around you people swarm, illuminated by bright lights and energized by a live band. There are prerace snacks for sale (expect a line) as well as marathon merchandise. There's also a baggage check and an insane number of portable toilets. A race organizer announces the time as it ticks by.

WEATHER THE RUN

There's nothing reliable about weather here: it can be cold, rainy, hot—sometimes all three in just a few hours. Temperatures are usually in the 50s or 60s, but watch the forecasts.

At about 4:30 AM, organizers start herding you toward the starting line, a little more than a half mile away. Expect this walk to feel long; it often takes about 20 minutes. When you arrive, enter the corral that corresponds to the letter on your bib number, stretch, maybe make another bathroom run. You still have time before the race begins. Finally, the real race emcee takes the stage: Mickey Mouse. He wishes you luck, music plays, and then, with a burst of fireworks, you're off—zooming toward Epcot through predawn light. Just after Mile 2, you storm through the park itself, which twinkles with lights and hums with music. The park won't officially open for three hours, so you have it all to yourself while pounding through Future World and one side of the World Showcase as the sun rises.

After you leave Epcot, there's a 6-mile-or-so stretch with very little to see except scattered on-course entertainment. At Mile 10 you enter the Magic Kingdom, the most spectacular part of the course. It's impossible not to be overcome by childlike awe as you enter this Technicolor dreamworld. Music seems to come from the very air, and as you pour onto Main Street, U.S.A., you're met by the cheers and whoops of a sea of spectators. Let their adulation carry you up Main Street and around to Fantasyland, where you'll pass the carousel, run through the back of Cinderella Castle, then burst out through its main entrance and over the moat, where spectators still roar.

Characters offer hugs and photo ops before you veer toward Adventureland and out of the park, legs reinvigorated by the joy of the Magic Kingdom. Savor the energy, because there's now a 5-mile stretch with little to see before you enter Disney's Animal Kingdom. By the time back-of-the-packers hit this park, it's open to the public, so the course takes a less obtrusive spin through its grounds. When you leave this park, you begin the third, and final, fairly empty stretch, running all the way to the Wide World of Sports Complex, then doubling back, peeling off just before Mile 22 to head to

NIGHT-BEFORE PASTA DINNER

There's no official pasta party, but resorts offer pasta specials, and Disney World teems with unique restaurants perfect for carbo-loads. Many are in the theme parks, which means paying park admission as well as the dinner tab—an excellent reason to consider a Park Hopper pass (⇨ Sightseeing, *below*). Call 407/WDW–DINE in advance for priority seating.

★ **L'ORIGINALE ALFREDO DI ROMA RISTORANTE.** Waiters skip around singing arias, a show in itself. Their voices and the restaurant's namesake dish, made with mountains of imported Italian butter, account for its popularity. Runners who won't fare well with heaps of Alfredo in their system can also choose from lighter pasta dishes. Other options include roasted grouper with a white wine sauce or slow-roasted chicken served with polenta. Desserts include a good tiramisu and an even better cannoli. ⊠ Epcot World Showcase, Italy ▭ AE, D, DC, MC, V $$–$$$.

MAMA MELROSE'S RISTORANTE ITALIANO. Wood-fired flatbreads with hearty toppings such as chicken and Italian cheeses make great starters before the arrival of such main courses as eggplant Parmesan and grilled salmon with sun-dried tomato pesto. The sangria, available by the carafe, flows generously. Cappuccino crème brûlée is a great dessert. If you're not turning in too early, ask for the *Fantasmic!* dinner package to get priority seating for the show. ⊠ Disney–MGM Studios, Street of America ▭ AE, D, DC, MC, V $–$$.

PORTOBELLO YACHT CLUB. This option is not in a theme park, and its northern Italian cuisine is uniformly good. The spaghettini alla Portobello (with scallops, clams, and Alaskan king crab) is outstanding, as are the charcoal-grilled rack of lamb served with creamy risotto cake and the rigatoni alla Calabrese, with sausage, mushrooms, tomatoes, and black olives. There's always a fresh-catch special, as well as tasty wood-oven pizza. ⊠ Pleasure Island ▭ AE, D, DC, MC, V $$–$$$$.

TONY'S TOWN SQUARE RESTAURANT. Inspired by *Lady and the Tramp*, the adorable Tony's offers everything from spaghetti and meatballs to wood-oven pizza and a very decent pork osso buco. Portions are large, and include plenty of bread—a carbo-loading dream. Come with your sweetie and try to resist the urge to lovingly roll a meatball his or her way with your snout. Don't miss the tiramisu for dessert. ⊠ The Magic Kingdom, Main St., U.S.A., Liberty Sq. ▭ AE, D, DC, MC, V $$.

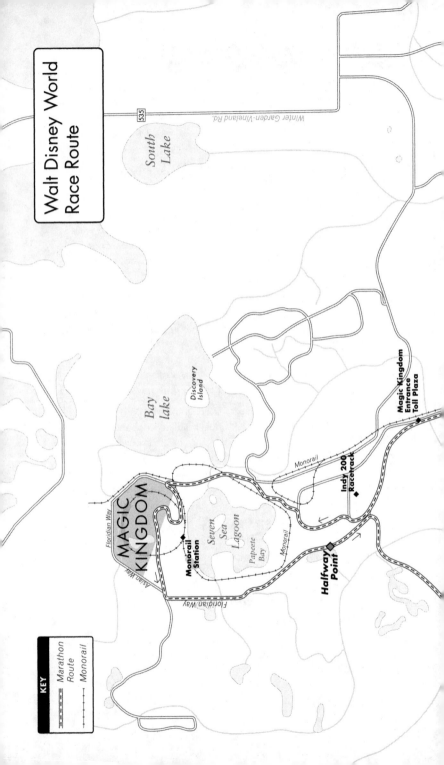

Walt Disney World Race Route

KEY
≡≡≡ Marathon Route
─┼─ Monorail

South Lake

Winter Garden-Vineland Rd.

535

Bay lake

Discovery Island

Magic Kingdom Entrance Toll Plaza

Monorail

Indy 200 Racetrack

MAGIC KINGDOM

Floridian Way

Asian Way

Monorail Station

Seven Sea Lagoon

Papeete Bay

Monorail

Floridian Way

Halfway Point

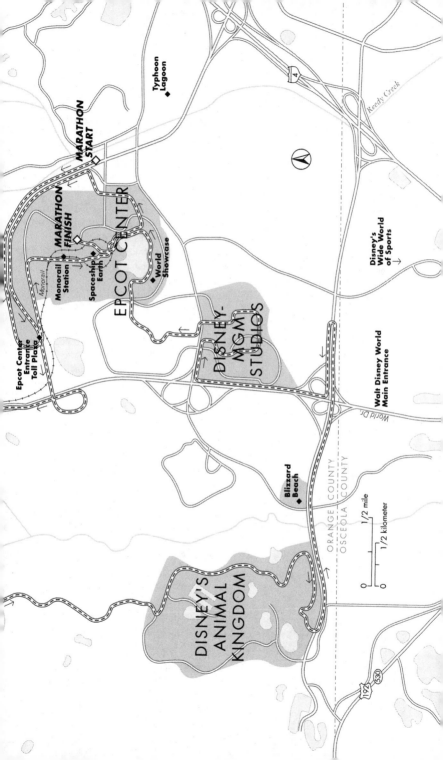

Disney–MGM Studios. Here you'll take in New York Street and the giant Sorcerer Mickey hat before cruising by Hollywood Boulevard, out the main gates, and on to the homestretch.

From here on out, the eye candy doesn't stop. You run along the water through the Beach and Yacht Club resort, then reenter Epcot's World Showcase, passing all the countries of the world (and feeling as if you've run through all the countries of the world). You then shoot out of the park to the cheers of spectators and . . . is that Minnie Mouse? It is! Minnie, Mickey, Donald, Pluto, Goofy—any or all of them could be there, jumping up and down and clapping for you as you blow past and cross the finish line.

Keep moving forward through the finishers' chute, where someone gives you your well-earned (and well-eared) Mickey medal, someone else removes your ChampionChip, and still another someone hands you a Mylar blanket. Beyond this are the refreshment and baggage areas. Refreshments include energy drinks, water, fruit, bagels, and other food. Once you have everything you need, head to the family reunion area to reconnect with your cheering section. If you have trouble finding your fans, you can always leave messages for people at the family reunion tent or information booth.

HANDLED WITH CARE

The course is well manned. There are 22 water stations, 13 first-aid stations, 3 fruit stations, an energy gel station, a candy station, and a sponge station.

Those staying on the monorail route will likely have the shortest wait for transport back to the hotel, though lines can get very long. Buses from Epcot to the resorts are notoriously slow on marathon morning, especially if you finish early. Don't be discouraged; a bus will eventually come.

Everyone must finish the race in seven hours. If you can't keep up a 16-minute-mile pace, you'll be picked up and driven to the finish line.

Spectating

If you *really* want to show your support, prepare to wake up early, bundle up, and board the buses to the staging area with your favorite runner. You can hang together until the marathoners head to the start corrals, at which point you'll follow the large signs pointing spectators through a small copse of trees, over a bridge, and to the road along the first mile of the race. Here you'll catch the whole field, everyone looking fresh and excited. Bring something waterproof to sit on while you wait.

Next you have the opportunity to enjoy the defining moment of the Walt Disney World Marathon: the run through the Magic Kingdom. From Epcot, hop a monorail to the Magic Kingdom, and stake out a spot along Main Street, U.S.A. to join masses of other spectators, as well as several Disney characters. Be part of the magic when the runners enter the Magic Kingdom (at about Mile 10), zoom up Main Street, curve out of sight into Fantasyland, then burst through Cinderella Castle. It's an absolute must-see.

Other spots to watch runners include the Transportation and Ticket Center (Mile 9), the Contemporary Resort (just before Mile 10), the Grand Floridian (Mile 12), Floridian Way (Miles 12.7 to 13), the Polynesian Resort (just before Mile 13), Disney's Animal Kingdom (Miles 16.5 to 17.3), Disney–MGM Studios (Miles 23 to 23.5), the Beach and Yacht Club

BREAKFAST SPOTS

Many hotels open their restaurants or convenience stores early for runners and spectators. The most convenient breakfast options for spectators include the following, all within the ¢–$$ price range:

MAIN STREET BAKERY. This small grab-and-go coffee shop on Main Street, U.S.A. opens early so you can grab a hot beverage and choose from among delicious baked goods while you wait for the marathon field to storm through. ⊠ Magic Kingdom, Main Street, U.S.A. ⊟ AE, D, DC, MC, V.

RAINFOREST CAFÉ. You don't have to pay park admission to dine at the Rainforest Café. Breakfast is served beginning at 7:30, so hit it either before or after you watch the runners go by. Enjoy standbys like eggs and waffles, or try a Mexican breakfast-style pizza. ⊠ Disney's Animal Kingdom ☎ 407/938–9100 ⊕ www.rainforestcafe.com ⊟ AE, D, DC, MC, V.

YACHT CLUB GALLEY. It's a great choice if you want to see the marathoners run by the water. The buffet is an all-you-can-eat feast of several Continental choices, as well as frittatas, eggs, bacon, sausage, and potatoes. From an à la carte menu consider oatmeal brûlée, crab cake Benedict, or a Mickey waffle. ⊠ Disney's Yacht Club Resort ⊟ AE, D, DC, MC, V.

Resorts (between Miles 24 and 25), Epcot Center (Miles 25 to 25.9), and the finish line, at the Epcot parking lot.

The viewing sites you choose are a matter of personal preference. Just be aware that if you want to see the runners go through Disney–MGM Studios, Disney's Animal Kingdom, or Epcot Center, you'll need to pay park admission (or have a Park Hopper Pass; ⇨ Sightseeing, *below*) to do so. Admission isn't necessary to watch the field run through the Magic Kingdom; this occurs before the park opens. Also keep in mind that Disney buses are on a regular schedule for the marathon, meaning that by the time they start running to Disney–MGM Studios and Disney's Animal Kingdom, particularly fast runners may have already blown through.

To help you plan, the official race program has a whole section dedicated to spectators, and gives the exact time frame in which runners will be at each viewing spot. Whatever your spectating schedule, don't be discouraged if you can't actually see your favorite runners cross the finish line, since the area gets very crowded. Instead, cheer them on in the final stretch just outside Epcot Center, then proceed to the family reunion area and enjoy a DJ, music, and a video screen with a live feed of the finish while you wait.

Celebrate!

You might want to nap after the race, because from 7 PM to 2 AM you're invited to a blowout post-race party at Pleasure Island in Downtown Disney. Pleasure Island is home to seven unique clubs. The BET SoundStage Club pays tribute to all genres of African-American music through videos, live performances, and shows by BET's own dance troupe. As the evening progresses, tunes shift from Top 10 to old R&B to hip-hop. The 8TRAX dance club brings back the '70s, complete with lava lamps, disco balls, and lots of Donna Summer. The techno dance palace Mannequins has a revolving dance floor, elaborate lighting, and special effects (think bubbles and snow). At Motion, it's all about a young, hip clientele. The dance music varies, but it's a good bet that whatever you hear is hot *now*. The Adventurers' Club hosts an audience participatory comedy show. Meanwhile, over at the Comedy Warehouse, actors improvise sketches based on audience suggestions. Lines for the shows start forming roughly 45 minutes before curtain.

Finally, there's the Rock & Roll Beach Club, where you can dance to rock from the '50s to today, or play pool, pinball, foosball, darts, or video games. Although your celebration will no doubt sprawl all over Pleasure Island, the Rock & Roll Beach Club hosts the official post-race festivities, which run until 10 PM. Every night is New Year's Eve on Pleasure Island, so be sure to head outside as the clock nears 12 for a countdown and fireworks.

BATHROOM BREAK

There are plenty of portable toilets on the course, but if you're looking for something more appealing, use the restrooms in the parks.

Normally, one admission fee gives access to all Pleasure Island's clubs. This holds true on marathon night, except for one thing: runners don't pay a single penny to enter. Show your race number at the ticket counter, and you get in for free. You can also buy up to three tickets at half price. Even kids can enjoy the party, as long as they're accompanied by an adult and don't enter the clubs Motion, Mannequins, or BET SoundStage.

BEYOND THE FINISH LINE

Replacing 2,620 Calories

Whatever you're craving, you'll find it somewhere at Walt Disney World—from elegant foreign cuisine to burgers and fries, from an impeccable chocolate souffle to a ridiculously loaded ice cream sundae. The listings below are my picks. To see all on-property restaurants, go to www.disneyworld.com (click on "Dining Finder"). To dine in theme park restaurants, you need to pay park admission or have a Park Hopper Pass (⇨ Sightseeing, *below*). It pays to get priority seating for all but the fast-food places. To do so, call 407/WDW–DINE (939–3463) up to several weeks in advance. Disney restaurants accept all major credit cards, or you can charge meals to your Disney resort room.

Disney–MGM Studios

'50S PRIME TIME CAFÉ. Who says you can't go home again? If you grew up in middle America in the 1950s, just step inside. While *I Love Lucy* and *The Donna Reed Show* play on a television screen, your waitstaff (a.k.a. "Mom," "Big Sister," or another family member) brings you meat loaf, pot roast, fried chicken, or other comfort food favorites, all served on a Formica tabletop. Add a thick milk shake, available in chocolate, strawberry, vanilla, even peanut butter and jelly, then follow it up with apple pie à la mode or s'mores. ✉ Echo Lake $–$$.

Epcot

★ **BISTRO DE PARIS.** The great secret in the France pavilion—and, indeed, in all of Epcot—is the Bistro de Paris. The sophisticated menu changes regularly and reflects cutting-edge French with pan-seared lobster, roasted rack of venison with black-pepper sauce, and seared scallops with truffle-potato purée. Save room for the Grand Marnier flambéed crepes. Come late, ask for a window seat, and linger to watch IllumiNations, which usually starts around 9 PM. Moderately priced French wines are available by the bottle and the glass. ✉ World Showcase, France $$$–$$$$.

★ **CORAL REEF RESTAURANT.** One wall is made entirely of glass and looks directly into the 6-million-gallon Living Seas aquarium. And with a three-tiered seating area, everyone has a good view. Edible attractions include salmon stuffed with basil; ahi tuna lightly grilled; and Dublin mussels and clams steamed in a Harp beer broth. Crab fritters with spicy marinara sauce make a great appetizer. You might finish off with Kahlua tiramisu in raspberry sauce. ✉ The Living Seas $$$–$$$$.

Downtown Disney

FULTON'S CRAB HOUSE. Set in a faux riverboat docked in a lagoon between Pleasure Island and the Marketplace, this fish house offers fine, if expensive, dining. The signature seafood is flown in daily. Dungeness crab from the Pacific coast, Alaskan king crab, Florida stone crab: it's all fresh and delicious, and portions are large. Start with the crab and lobster bisque, then try one of the many combination entrées like the Gulf shrimp and Dungeness crab cake platter. The sublime cappuccino ice-cream cake is $13, but one order is easily enough for two. ✉ Downtown Disney MarketPl. $$–$$$$.

Resort Hotels

ARTIST POINT. If you're not a guest at the Wilderness Lodge, come for a meal to see the giant totem poles and huge rock fireplace. The specialty is cedar-plank salmon and mashed potatoes with roasted fennel and truffle butter. Another good option: grilled buffalo sirloin with sweet potato–hazelnut gratin and sweet-onion jam. For dessert, try the wild berry cobbler or the flourless chocolate–whiskey cake with pecans and raspberry sorbet. Wine pairings for the meal cost $18 to $23 per person. ✉ Wilderness Lodge ⟁ Reservations essential $$–$$$.

BEACHES & CREAM SODA SHOP. Located poolside at the Beach Club, this old-fashioned soda shop serves all-American favorites: burgers, sandwiches, fries, and shakes. Customize your sodas with a variety of syrups, and absolutely save room for dessert. Sundaes are large and decadent, and include the classic banana split and the fudge mud slide, piled on a gooey brownie. To truly reward yourself for running a marathon, dive into the Kitchen Sink (scoops of vanilla, chocolate, strawberry, coffee, and mint chocolate chip ice cream, smothered in every topping on the menu). ✉ Disney's Beach Club $.

While trying to stay awake in a college class, Shymeka Hunter started making a list of everything she wanted to accomplish in her life. She scrawled down books she wanted to read, places she wanted to visit, her career goals, then finally "run a marathon." There. Now it was down on paper. Now she'd do it. But not yet. She was still an undergrad; she had plenty of time to tackle the marathon later.

Then she went to law school. Who has time to train for a marathon while in law school? She'd wait, she figured. There'd be plenty of time to tackle the marathon later.

Then Shymeka got a high-pressure job as a lawyer at a prestigious firm in Atlanta. Who could possibly train for a marathon while working those kind of hours? Besides . . . plenty of time.

But when Shymeka was 28, her boyfriend James proposed. And as she says: "Something about knocking on 30 and planning a wedding made me feel like time was no longer on my side, at least not when it came to running 26.2 miles. I didn't think I would ever be in better shape, nor did I think that my time would be my own as much as it was [that] year." So when her coworkers (who had recently run the Chicago marathon) promised they'd do the 2005 Disney World half-marathon if Shymeka did the full, she agreed and signed up, despite the fact that she hadn't exercised regularly for a few years. After all, the race was six and a half months away; there was plenty of time to train.

Yet despite Shymeka's best intentions, she never quite got to the training. Work kept her busy 65 to 70 hours a week, and the rest of her time was devoted to her wedding: a 200-guest affair in Savannah, every detail of which was planned by her alone. Before she knew it, the race was just over two months away, and she hadn't even begun to train. Quitting wasn't an option. She said she'd run a marathon; she was going to run a marathon. She desperately sought out a schedule that would get her from 0 to 26.2 miles in no time at all, and a runner friend came through. Suddenly Shymeka was hitting the road at least five days a week, rotating between short and long runs, and often starting before 6 AM. "It sounds crazy," she says, "but it was actually wonderful to watch the sun rise as I ran. I felt a great sense of accomplishment knowing that I began the day that way. It was kind of like those military commercials—I did more before 9 AM than most people did all day. Very motivating." Shymeka did have some trouble with her knees, and suffered a 10-day setback about four weeks before the race, but weight training helped, and by marathon day she felt ready to go . . . kind of.

"I don't think I have ever been more nervous for anything in my life—not even taking the bar exam or getting married!" Shymeka says of waiting at the starting line. "I think it was because I didn't know if my knees would hold up or if I would finish in less than seven hours, which I needed to do to receive a medal." Standing with the other back-of-the-packers, Shymeka felt the frizzle of everyone's energy as they anxiously waited for their turn to cross the starting line. "By the time I actually started," she laughs, "the leaders were already at Mile 2!"

I asked Shymeka what stood out most for her during the race itself. She didn't hesitate: it was Mile 18. "I will never forget Mile 18," she says. "I wanted to quit at Mile 18. My left knee had started to hurt really badly. I had no choice but to pull over and stretch it out. I was in pain, I was tired, and I had no idea if my knee could stand any more pressure. To make matters worse, my fiancé, who had been taking shuttles to meet me at various checkpoints, called my cell phone to say he wasn't going to make it to Mile 18 but would try to meet me at Mile 24. Mile 18 also represented the farthest distance I had run during my training. My friends insisted that if I could run 18 miles in training, I could run 26.2 on race day. So I was in uncharted territory. I think stopping to stretch my knee only made it worse, because I seemed to be in more pain from that moment on. I had every reason to quit, but I just couldn't let myself be a quitter. I chanted, I prayed, I thought about the less fortunate, I chastised myself for complaining about a knee injury when there were 60- and 70-year-olds out there finding a way to keep moving. I kept moving. My friends who ran the half met me at Mile 23 and finished the race with me. They talked to me the whole time to keep my mind off the pain. My fiancé also showed up at Mile 24, so there was definitely no stopping me from there!"

Shymeka finished the race in 6:44 clock time, about 6:30 chip time. Well within the time frame to get her Mickey medal. Looking back, what she relishes most about her experience is the knowledge that her body will do whatever she pushes it to achieve. Despite the pain, despite the nagging urge to quit, "my previous accomplishments and everything I had learned from others who have overcome adversity was there to inspire me. All I had to do was keep running. The ability to win the battle of mind over matter was awesome." And for anyone out there who still thinks there's no way they could run a marathon, Shymeka disagrees. "It's really just a mind game. If you think you can, you can. If you think you can't, you can, but you probably won't." Her biggest piece of advice?

"Take at least three months to train." ■

CHARACTER DINING

If your kids want to eat with their favorite characters, try these options. Call 407/WDW–DINE for exact times. It's best to book early (some experiences can fill up more than 60 days in advance).

BREAKFAST

Mary Poppins presides at 1900 Park Fare Restaurant in the Grand Floridian for a daily **Character Breakfast Buffet** (☎ $17.99 adults, $10.99 children ages 3–11). At the Contemporary Resort, **Chef Mickey's Buffet** (☎ $17.99 adults, $9.99 ages 3–11) offers character fun daily. Main Street, U.S.A.'s **Crystal Palace Buffet** (☎ $17.99 adults, $9.99 ages 3–11) has breakfast with Winnie the Pooh and friends daily. Donald Duck and his friends are at **Donald's Prehistoric Breakfastosaurus** (☎ $17.99 adults, $9.99 ages 3–11) daily in the Animal Kingdom. Join Chip 'n' Dale, Minnie, and Goofy every morning at **Goofy's Beach Club Breakfast Buffet** (☎ $17.99 adults, $9.99 ages 3–11). The Polynesian Resort's **'Ohana Character Breakfast with Mickey and Friends** (☎ $17.99 adults, $9.99 ages 3–11) runs daily. Cinderella herself hosts the **Once Upon a Time Character Breakfast** (☎ $21.99 adults, $11.99 ages 3–11) every day at Cinderella Castle in the Magic Kingdom. This is *extremely* popular. Book 90 days in advance. The **Princess Storybook Breakfast** (☎ $21.99 adults, $11.99 ages 3–11) is set in Restaurant Akershus, a Norwegian castle in Epcot's Norway Pavilion. Snow White, Sleeping Beauty, and at least three other princesses join kids for all-American fare every morning.

LUNCH

Winnie the Pooh, Tigger, and Eeyore come to the **Crystal Palace Buffet** (☎ $19.99 adults, $10.99 ages 3–11) on Main Street, U.S.A. daily. The Once Upon a Time Breakfast has been expanded into **A Fairytale Lunch at Cinderella's Royal Table** (☎ $21.99 adults, $11.99 ages 3–11). Book 90 days in advance; it's the only way to get in. Join Mickey, Pluto, and Chip 'n' Dale at the **Garden Grill Restaurant Character Experience** (☎ $20.99 adults, $10.99 ages 3–11) in The Land pavilion at Epcot. The **Princess Storybook Lunches** (☎ $23.99 adults, $12.99 ages 3–11) with Snow White, Sleeping Beauty, and at least three other princesses are held at Epcot in Restaurant Akershus in the Norway Pavilion.

AFTERNOON SNACKS

The **Garden Grill Ice Cream Social** (☎ $6.99) at the Land in Epcot has seatings at 3 PM, 3:10 PM, and 3:20 PM. Mickey comes around to visit, and it's usually not crowded. If you really want to go extravagant, check out **My Disney Girl's Perfectly Princess Tea Party** (☎ $200 plus tax), in the Garden View Lounge of the Grand Floridian, Sunday, Monday, and Wednesday through Friday from 10 AM to noon. The basic fee is for one adult and one child, both of whom get "tea" (kids get apple juice) and a small luncheon plate. In addition, your child gets a special meet-and-greet with Princess Aurora, a My Disney Girl doll, a tiara, and other goodies. It's a splurge, but if your little girl is into the Disney princesses, she'll absolutely love it. During the **Wonderland Tea Party** (☎ $28.17) at the Grand Floridian Resort, Alice and other Wonderland characters preside over afternoon tea on weekdays from 1:30 PM to 2:30 PM. With the cast's help, children ages 3 to 10 can bake their own cupcakes to eat at the party.

DINNER

Every night at 8 (7 in winter), near Fort Wilderness's Meadow Trading Post, there is a **Character Campfire** with a free sing-along. There are usually around five characters there, with Chip 'n' Dale frequent attendees. The Contemporary Resort hosts the wildly popular **Chef Mickey's Buffet** (☎ $26.99 adults, $11.99 ages 3–11), starring the head honcho himself. Winnie the Pooh and friends appear nightly at the **Crystal Palace Buffet** (☎ $22.99 adults, $10.99 ages 3–11) on Main Street, U.S.A. **Cinderella's Gala Feast** (☎ $27.99 adults, $12.99 ages 3–11) buffet is held at the Grand Floridian's 1900 Park Fare. Farmer Mickey appears at Future World's **Garden Grill Restaurant Character Experience** (☎ $22.99 adults, $10.99 ages 3–11). At the Walt Disney World Swan, you can dine with *Lion King* characters Monday and Friday at **Gulliver's Grill**. Gulliver's hosts Goofy and Pluto the other five nights of the week. Meals are à la carte—an adult dinner runs $18 to $30 and a child's meal $4 to $10. The **Liberty Tree Tavern Character Dinner with Minnie and Friends** (☎ $22.99 adults, $10.99 ages 3–11) includes a feast of smoked pork, turkey, carved beef, and all the trimmings. It's served nightly in the Magic Kingdom's Liberty Square. The **Princess Storybook Dinner** (☎ $27.99 adults, $12.99 ages 3–11) with Snow White, Sleeping Beauty, and at least three other princesses is held at Epcot Center in Restaurant Akershus in the Norway Pavilion.

★**CALIFORNIA GRILL.** The view of the surrounding Disney parks from this rooftop restaurant is as stunning as the food, and you can watch the nightly Magic Kingdom fireworks from the patio. Start with the brick-oven flatbread with grilled duck sausage or the *unagi* (eel) sushi. For a main course, try the oak-fired beef fillet with three-cheese potato gratin and tamarind barbecue sauce. Good dessert choices include the orange crepes with Grand Marnier custard, raspberries, and blackberry coulis; and the butterscotch, orange, and vanilla crème brûlée. ⊠ Contemporary Resort $$-$$$$.

JIKO—THE COOKING PLACE. The specialty here is African-style cooking, such as seared jumbo scallops with spicy Chaka-Laka sauce and mealie corn pap. The menu changes but typically includes such entrées as roasted chicken with mashed potatoes, and pomegranate-glazed quails stuffed with saffron basmati rice. For dessert, go crazy with a flourless chocolate cake or the cheese selection. ⊠ Disney's Animal Kingdom Lodge ⌂ Reservations essential $$–$$$.

SPOODLES. The international tapas-style menu here draws on the best foods of the Mediterranean, from tuna with sun-dried tomato couscous to Italian fettuccine with rich Parmesan cream sauce. Oak-fired flatbreads with such toppings as roasted peppers make stellar appetizers. For an unusual entrée, try the Spanish peppers stuffed with roasted vegetables and chickpeas, and served with almond pilaf, spicy onion-and-tomato relish, and manchego cheese. For dessert, try the cheesecake with banana slices or go for a sampler from the dessert tower. There's also a walk-up pizza window if you prefer to stroll the BoardWalk. ⊠ Disney's BoardWalk $$–$$$.

★**VICTORIA & ALBERT'S.** Servers work in man-woman pairs, reciting specials in tandem. It's one of the plushest fine-dining experiences in Florida: a regal meal in a lavish, Victorian-style room. The seven-course, prix-fixe menu ($95; wine is an additional $50) changes daily. Appetizers might include Iranian caviar, veal sweetbreads, or artichokes in a mushroom sauce; entrées may be Kobe beef with celery-root purée or veal tenderloin with cauliflower-and-potato purée. There are two seatings, at 5:45 and 9. The chef's table dinner event is $115 to $162 (with wine pairing) per person. ⊠ Grand Floridian ⌂ Reservations essential ⌂ Jacket required ⊙ No lunch $$$$.

Sightseeing on (and off) Your Feet

You're at Walt Disney World, so you'll most likely want to hit at least some of the parks. Here are a few suggestions on what to tackle, depending on how you feel.

I FEEL GREAT! Touring the parks requires strong legs—not only for all the walking involved but also for standing in line. If you're feeling great you should have no problem wandering at will through the four majors or checking out the water parks.

I FEEL PRETTY GOOD. You can probably take on Disney–MGM Studios, the park with the most long-duration shows and theater-style attractions. Or rent a canoe, rowboat, pedal boat, or other vessel and sail around one of the bodies of water that often surround the resort hotels. Rentals are approximately $6.50 per half hour.

LET'S TAKE IT SLOWLY. Go easy with some shopping at Downtown Disney (⇨ Shop Around), or play video games at the DisneyQuest arcade. Alternatively you could go for a slow stroll along the BoardWalk. Consider dining with Disney characters at a resort. In the evening, consider a dinner show.

OW! NO. The resorts have beautiful, themed pools—many with Jacuzzis. A little swimming or water-walking might help your muscles feel human again. Try to attend a Cirque du Soleil performance in the evening.

Tickets & Admission

You can buy individual or multiday tickets at disneyworld.com and many Disney Stores. You can also book your tickets through Disney Sports as part of your whole travel package (⇨ Race Contacts box *under* Race Basics, *above*).

The basic park ticket is called Magic Your Way and allows you to enter one park a day (you choose which park), each day of your ticket. Prices change often, but as of this writing, a one-day Magic Your Way ticket costs $48 for kids 3–9 (kids under 3 enter for free) and $59.75 for ages 10 and over. For $35 more (price based on a one-day ticket), you can add the Park Hopper option, which allows you to hop in and out of all four major parks at will. I highly recommend this, as it gives you the freedom to move through the parks readily—handy for both marathon cheering and enjoying prerace and celebratory meals in park restaurants.

Add another $45 to your ticket price (again based on a one-day ticket), and you'll get the Magic Plus Pack, which adds the water parks, Pleasure Island, or other Disney attractions to your Park Hopper. Another $10 to $100 on top of that (depending on the length of your pass—it's not applicable to one-day passes) makes your ticket a no-expiration one.

It can add all up quickly. The more days you stay, however, the greater your per-day savings. For example, a one-day adult Magic Your Way base ticket costs $59.75, but the four-day version costs $185, or $46.25 a day.

FASTPASS

To experience theme-park attractions with little or no wait, feed your ticket into a Fastpass machine and book a reservation-time "window." Return to bypass the regular line.

Transportation

Disney's free buses, trams, monorail trains, and boats can take you wherever you want to go on Disney property. Boats run between the Magic Kingdom and the Magic Kingdom resorts and between the Magic Kingdom and the Transportation and Ticket Center. They also run between the Epcot resorts (except Caribbean Beach), Epcot, and Disney–MGM Studios. From Port Orleans and Old Key West, you can take a boat to Downtown Disney. Buses provide direct service from every on-site resort to the major and minor theme parks; express buses run directly between the major theme parks. One monorail line links the Magic Kingdom; the Transportation and Ticket Center; and the Contemporary, Grand Floridian, and Polynesian resorts. A second line links the Transportation and Ticket Center and Epcot. In general, allow an hour to travel between sites on Disney property.

Parks & Other Activities

THEME PARKS

- **DISNEY–MGM STUDIOS.** It's a gauzy look at Hollywood with such highlights as the Twilight Zone Tower of Terror, a chilling ride through a haunted hotel, during which you experience a free fall that isn't: you're dropped partway, then lifted back up several times, and the number of times this happens changes with each ride, so you never know how long it'll be before you finally fall 130 feet to the bottom. The indoor Rock 'n' Roller Coaster Starring Aerosmith has a high-speed start, corkscrews, hairpins, loops, and eye-popping scenery. Oh yeah, and Aerosmith blares in your ears the whole time—too cool. And no Muppet fan should miss Jim Henson's *Muppet*Vision 3-D*.

DISNEY'S ANIMAL KINGDOM. This celebration of all animals—real, extinct, and purely fanciful—is split into "lands," each with a distinct personality. Don't miss Kilimanjaro Safaris, where you'll see rhinos, hippos, antelope, wildebeests, giraffes, zebras, elephants, lions, and more as you lurch and bump over some 100 acres of savanna, forest, rivers, and rocky hills. To get the most from your adventure, do this early in the day or in the late afternoon, when the animals are awake. Kali River Rapids is a thrilling, jouncing, churning raft ride. Be prepared: you *will* get wet. The 3D movie *It's Tough to Be a Bug!*, starring Flik from *A Bug's Life*, is whimsical, clever, and filled with surprises. Expedition: EVEREST is a roller-coaster ride on a quest for the infamous yeti.

EPCOT. It's a park in two parts: Future World, with pavilions demonstrating technological advances, and World Showcase, with microcosms of 11 countries from four continents. Highlights include Soarin', a simulator ride that makes you feel like you're hang gliding over California; Test Track, a fast (up to nearly 60 mph), bumpy ride in which you help put a car through its paces; and Mission: SPACE, which simulates a flight to Mars (be warned: there's a reason it's equipped with airsickness bags). Kids will enjoy the Imagination pavilion and its 3D movie *Honey I Shrunk the Audience*.

THE MAGIC KINGDOM. The heart and soul of Disney opens onto that quintessential vista: Main Street, U.S.A. leading up to Cinderella Castle. Thrill rides include the log flume Splash Mountain; the roller-coaster ride through blackest space that is Space Mountain; and Big Thunder Mountain Railroad, a comparatively tame but still rollicking roller coaster. In Toontown kids can meet many of their favorite characters. Fantasyland is home to It's a Small World, that nauseatingly cute boat ride that kids love and adults love to hate (but often secretly love). In the excellent 3D movie musical *Philharmagic* Donald Duck has a misadventure with Mickey's sorcerer's hat and stumbles through several Disney movies. And don't forget the standbys: the Haunted Mansion, Pirates of the Caribbean, and the Country Bear Jamboree never seem to get old.

Try to stick around until after dark. There's a certain feeling in the air when Cinderella Castle is bathed in purple and blue, lights twinkle along Main Street, U.S.A., and Disney music plays lightly. It's truly something special.

WATER PARKS
BLIZZARD BEACH AND TYPHOON LAGOON. The theme of Blizzard Beach is a ski resort meltdown. Typhoon Lagoon exists in the wake of—you guessed it—a huge typhoon. If the weather's warm enough, either park is a great choice, though one will always be closed for refurbishment during marathon time. ☉ Winter hours usually 10–5 ☞ $28–$34; admission can also be part of some Park Hopper passes.

REST OF THE WORLD
DISNEYQUEST. This five-story interactive games arcade in Downtown Disney West Side is a virtual kingdom of attractions and adventures split into four zones: the Explore Zone, a virtual adventureland of exotic and ancient locales; the Score Zone, where you can match wits and gaming skills against supervillains; the Create Zone, a studio of expression and in-

Stop! Don't even *think* about changing that diaper in a bathroom.

The major theme parks all have Baby Care Centers, or as I called them when I park-hopped with my four-month-old: oases of joy, tranquillity, and all things good. Large, padded changing tables are cleaned by an attendant after each use, almost any forgotten supply is available, and nursing moms can lounge on comfy rockers. The centers are rarely crowded, and the buzz of the park seems a million miles away. The center in Epcot is especially plush; you'll almost look forward to a poopy diaper.

Almost.

vention where you might create your own animated character or produce your own hit song; and the Replay Zone, where classic games like Skeeball have futuristic twists.

To avoid crowds, arrive at opening time, usually 11:30 AM. One price ($28–$34) gains admission to the building and entrance to all the attractions, excluding prize play games. Plan to stay for at least four hours to get the most of your admission (DisneyQuest usually closes at 11 PM or midnight). The Cheesecake Factory Express restaurant is inside so you can have lunch or dinner and then get back to the virtual fun.

DISNEY'S BOARDWALK. If you have fond memories of strolling along an Atlantic boardwalk, hearing the bumpity-bump of bicycle tires on the boards, smelling fresh-baked pizza, and watching lovers stroll hand in hand, you're in for a heaping dose of nostalgia at Disney's BoardWalk in the Epcot resort area. You can rent a bicycle for two or a cycling surrey. A DJ runs the party nightly at the Atlantic Dance hall, with its spacious dance floor and waterfront balcony. At Jellyrolls, you can sing along with dueling pianos (there's a $7 cover charge after 7 PM).

RICHARD PETTY DRIVING EXPERIENCE. Drive or ride along in a NASCAR-style stock car at speeds of 145 mph and up. Passengers must be at least 16 and don't need reservations. Drivers must be at least 18, have a valid driver's license, and know how to drive a manual transmission car. Reservations are a must. Experiences include anything from 8 to 30 laps around the track. 🎫$105–$1,330 🕐Daily 9–5, weather permitting; call ahead ☎800/BE–PETTY ⊕ www.1800bepetty.com.

Shop Around

Main Street, U.S.A., Magic Kingdom

The street is lined with shops. The Chapeau sells those classic monogrammed mouse ears, and Main Street Market House has items for foodies (think Mickey waffle irons). At Uptown Jewelers artists sketch Disney characters and themes that are then transferred to the faces of one-of-a-kind Citizen watches ($200–$350). Serious memorabilia collectors should also stop at the Main Street Gallery, where limited-edition sculptures, dolls, posters—even park signs—are sold. But the big daddy of all Magic Kingdom shops is the 17,000-square-foot Emporium stocked with thousands of Disney character products, from sunglasses to stuffed animals. It's perpetually crowded—absolutely mobbed at closing time—but it's the best place for souvenirs.

Epcot World Showcase

Each country represented has at least one gift shop loaded with goods, many of which are authentic imported handicrafts. Taste some wine at Les Vins de France, and then pick up a bottle of your favorite. Explore the open-air market in Morocco, or shop for kimonos in Japan. Italy's Il Bel Cristallo sells chic Italian handbags and accessories, and Germany's Der Teddybar has unique teddy bears and other toys. At the Village Traders in the Saluting Africa Outpost, wood carvers from Kenya whittle animals while you watch. China's Yong Feng Shangdian has exquisite furniture with heavy lacquer and beautiful inlays as well as hand-painted figurines, hand-carved chess sets, and traditional clothing.

Downtown Disney

Stores in this shopping mecca are in two areas. The Marketplace is home to the LEGO Imagination Center as well as Once Upon A Toy—a fusion of Disney and Hasbro with such things as Princess Monopoly and the Pirates of the Caribbean Game of Life. Pin Traders has an enormous Disney pin selection, plus many limited-edition, hard-to-find items. In the West Side, the second shopping area, Guitar Gallery sells guitars priced at $89 to $20,000. Magnetron has magnets in every shape, size, and color imaginable. Starabilia's is all about pop memorabilia. Candy Cauldron is filled with chocolate, fudge, hard candy, and other wholesome foods. Celebrity Eyeworks sells replicas of glasses worn by characters in popular films. Mickey's Groove carries hip lamps, posters, greeting cards, and souvenirs inspired by The Mouse. Hoypolloi adds art to the mix, with sculptures in various media—glass, wood, clay, and metals.

I Love the Nightlife

The hottest nightlife spot at Disney World is Pleasure Island, home of the post-race party. There are other options, however, among them bars on the BoardWalk (⇨ Disney's Board-Walk *above*) and dazzling fireworks displays, parades, and shows at the theme parks. These often happen around closing time, but schedules can vary, so check in advance.

Fireworks & Parades

ILLUMINATIONS: REFLECTIONS OF THE EARTH. Epcot's light and fireworks show takes place over the reflective World Showcase lagoon. As orchestral music fills the air, accompanied by the whoosh and boom of lasers and pyrotechnic bursts, a 30-foot globe on a barge floats across the water, revealing the wonders of the seven continents on its curved LED screens. Meanwhile, each of the World Showcase pavilions is illuminated with more than 26,000 feet of lights. Fireworks bring the show to a crescendo.

SPECTROMAGIC. First, a nostalgic sigh for the Main Street Electrical Parade, which this replaced. Just make it a quick sigh because SpectroMagic is just as impressive as its pred-

FORGET SIGHTSEEING. GET ME TO A SPA!

Disney has two on-property spas, both perfect for aching post-race muscles. Just make sure to schedule your appointments in advance.

GRAND FLORIDIAN SPA & HEALTH CLUB. Almost as soon as you enter this spa you can feel the stress melt away. Arrive early for a soak in the hot tub, then indulge in a sports massage, which incorporates heat packs to ease sore muscles, or a personalized massage, in which the therapist takes his or her cues from you, concentrating on whatever you need most. Prices range from $110 to $125 for a 50-minute massage. ☎ 407/824–2332 ☉ Daily 8–8.

THE SPA AT DISNEY'S SARATOGA SPRINGS. Healing spring waters of turn-of-the-20th-century Saratoga, New York, inspired the theme for this spa. Consider a hydromassage (45 minutes, $105) for deep tissue penetration, or the Adirondack stone-therapy massage (80 minutes, $175) in which hot rocks add to your relaxation. If you want to concentrate on your aching feet, a reflexology massage (50 minutes, $120) is perfect. Kids can get a "My First" facial, manicure, or pedicure. ☎ 407/827–4455 ☉ Daily 8–8.

ecessor, a luminescent parade that runs down Main Street in the Magic Kingdom. It's filled with fun, beautiful floats, and a complete lineup of favorite Disney characters.

WISHES. Fireworks accompanied by Disney melodies are launched from 11 locations around the park. The displays recall scenes from Disney films in which the fairy-tale characters' wishes really do come true. The best place to watch the show is on Main Street; try to snag seats on the second floor of the train station.

Shows

CIRQUE DU SOLEIL–*LA NOUBA.* This surreal show by the world-famous circus company starts at 100 mph and accelerates from there through 90 minutes of extraordinary acrobatics, avant-garde stagings, costumes, choreography, and a finale that makes you doubt Newton's law of gravity. Hints: reserve tickets well in advance to get good seats, and hire a babysitter if necessary (admission is charged for children, including infants). ✉ Downtown Disney, West Side ☎ 407/939-7600 reservations ⊕ www.cirquedusoleil.com 🖰 Premium seats (center section) $65-$87; Category 2 seats (to the side and the back) $56-$75; Category 3 seats (to the far sides and very back) $44-$59 ☉ Performances Tues.–Sat. 6 and 9 PM.

FANTASMIC! Disney–MGM's blockbuster after-dark show is held once nightly in a 6,500-seat amphitheater. Mickey Mouse, in the guise of the Sorcerer's Apprentice, goes on a gripping adventure full of song and dance, pyrotechnics, and superlative special effects. No mere description does this show justice; you have to see it. (One caveat: if you've seen the show at Disneyland, you'll be a bit disappointed—this one isn't quite as impressive as its West Coast sister.) Arrive an hour in advance for the best seats, 20 minutes if you don't mind sitting to the side of the stage. Alternatively, make dinner reservations at the Studio's Brown Derby, Hollywood & Vine, or Mama Melrose restaurants and get early seating as part of a package.

HELPFUL INFO

Air Travel

Orlando International Airport (MCO) is served by most major airlines. From the airport, take a Mears Shuttle ($12 round-trip) to your Disney World hotel. Call or go online to make your reservation, then catch the shuttle outside the airport terminal. Call Mears again at least 24 hours in advance to schedule a shuttle for your return to the airport.

INFORMATION

🚋 **Mears Shuttle** ☎ 407/423-5566 ⊕ www.mearstransportation.com. **Orlando International Airport** ☎ 407/825-2001 ⊕ www.orlando-mco.com.

Disabilities & Accessibility

Many attractions are accessible to guests using wheelchairs, and most are accessible to people with some mobility impairments. Guide dogs and service animals are permitted, unless a ride or special effect could spook the animal. At attractions, guests with mobility, hearing, and visual disabilities use accessible entrances; to find out where to enter, see any host or hostess.

WDW's "Guidebook for Guests with Disabilities" is available at the main visitor information desks in every park. You can also get cassette tapes and portable players that provide audio narration for most attractions (no charge, but refundable deposit required), as well as wireless handheld captioning devices. There are also wheelchair rentals in every park, and services that include American Sign Language interpretation.

Emergencies

In an emergency, call 911 from any Disney property phone. For in-room medical care, call 407/238-2000. First-aid stations are in every theme park, and have the same hours as that park. Disney provides complimentary transportation to the Florida Hospital Centra Care walk-in centers, which are open 8 AM to midnight weekdays and 8 to 8 on weekends. Turner Drugs will deliver prescriptions to your room for a $5 fee.

🚋 **DOCTORS Florida Hospital Centra Care Walk-In Urgent Care Centers** ☎ 407/239-6463.

🚋 **HOSPITALS Orlando Regional Medical Center** ✉ 1414 Kuhl Ave., Orlando ☎ 407/841-5111. **Sand Lake Hospital** ✉ 9400 Turkey Lake Rd., Orlando ☎ 407/351-8500.

🚋 **PHARMACY Turner Drugs** ☎ 407/828-8125.

CHAPTER 2
FEBRUARY

Mardi Gras Marathon, New Orleans, LA

It seems counterintuitive to pair "Mardi Gras"—that

raucous, hedonistic, pre-Lenten blowout—with "marathon"—that exercise in extreme discipline. Or maybe not. The New Orleans Track Club has always bent over backward to make the Mardi Gras Marathon a celebration—a 26.2-mile party. Expect aid stations manned by boisterous revelers in costume, a flat course, and an anything-but-flat post-race celebration in this city that's always ready to revel. You can't help but have a fantastic time. And when it's all over and you're back home, you will indeed know what it means to miss New Orleans.

YOU SAY TOMATO . . .

Despite clear diction in that song about missing New Orleans, you'll sound more like a local if you meld the words together and say, "N'awlins."

So You're Running New Orleans . . .

First a word about this fantastic city, and the hardships it recently endured. I'm writing this in December 2005, just a few months after the devastation of Hurricane Katrina. By the time the book comes out, the 2006 Mardi Gras Marathon will have already been run along a slightly altered course—one that doesn't begin and end in the damaged Superdome. The New Orleans Track Club hopes, however, to be back in a rebuilt Dome by 2007 and to again start and finish the race there.

I fell in love with this city and its marathon when I visited and have high hopes that both will come back even stronger than before. I am, therefore, assuming in this chapter that the 2007 race will be back in the Superdome and run the same route it has followed for years. I make my recommendations and course descriptions accordingly. As for the city itself, there's no denying that the face of New Orleans has changed, and it's impossible to know for sure what will or won't be back. Just in case, call before your trip to double-check that the sights, restaurants, and clubs that interest you are up and running.

New Orleans is unlike any city in the world. You'll sense this while sipping a drink and listening to live jazz, while gorging on food so decadently delicious it's almost criminal, and while strolling the timeworn streets of the French Quarter or the Garden District. You'll drink deeply of this city every second you're there and still leave craving more.

New Orleans covers approximately 365 square miles of flat, drained swampland that extends between the Mississippi River and Lake Pontchartrain. The city has a small-town atmosphere, with neighborhoods in many cases populated by families who have lived within the same blocks for decades. Its main sections include the following:

THE FRENCH QUARTER. The Vieux Carré, or just "the Quarter" as it's often called, is a 6-by-12-block rectangle along the Mississippi River where the city was first established by the French in 1718. The streets are lined with beautifully restored structures containing shops, restaurants, offices, and homes. Except for Bourbon Street, a world-famous entertainment strip, the French Quarter has no neon signs, and its buildings conform to the architectural styles of the late-18th to mid-19th century. Artists, street performers, and visitors gravitate to Jackson Square at the Quarter's very heart.

FAUBOURG MARIGNY & BYWATER. The predominantly residential area to the northeast of the Quarter is a haven for bohemians. It has the beautiful campus of the New Orleans Center for the Creative Arts (NOCCA) as well as colorful low-lying cottages and sprawling warehouses—some converted, some abandoned. Although bars, scenic walks, and local color are the mainstays of a foray here, a growing number of galleries and ever-increasing cultural activity are promising diversions. With several excellent clubs, Frenchmen Street is a top place for live music.

CENTRAL BUSINESS DISTRICT (CBD). Adjacent to the Quarter, the CBD encompasses impressive office buildings, courthouses, hotels, malls, and the Louisiana Superdome. The district extends to the foot of Canal Street, home of the Aquarium of the Americas and the ferry to Algiers Point.

WAREHOUSE DISTRICT. Once an industrial district it's now a trendy destination for loft-style living, museum and gallery hopping, shopping, and fine dining. Julia Street, the center, is the site of monthly gallery openings and Emeril Lagasse's flagship restaurant. A cluster of museums, including the National D-Day Museum and the Contemporary Arts Center, form another focal point. The district's riverfront property is claimed by the Riverwalk, a half-mile marketplace of more than 200 shops.

THE GARDEN DISTRICT. Settled by Americans who made their fortunes in New Orleans after the 1803 Louisiana Purchase, this wealthy neighborhood is renowned for its sumptuous antebellum homes (many in the Greek Revival style with lovely ironwork) surrounded by gardens. The Garden District begins where St. Charles Avenue crosses Jackson Avenue. It's bordered to the south by the Magazine Street shopping area and claims one of the city's grandest restaurants, Commander's Palace.

UPTOWN. This area stretches from the Garden District, past Tulane and Loyola universities, and to the end of the St. Charles Avenue streetcar line. Uptown has many mansions, several good music venues, and the Riverbend and Maple Street shopping areas. Across from the universities is Audubon Park, a former plantation that now has a zoo, a golf course, winding lagoons, and miles of trails.

MID–CITY. This working-class neighborhood north of the French Quarter and south of Lake Pontchartrain is home to the Fair Grounds, the nation's third-oldest racetrack and site of the annual New Orleans Jazz & Heritage Festival.

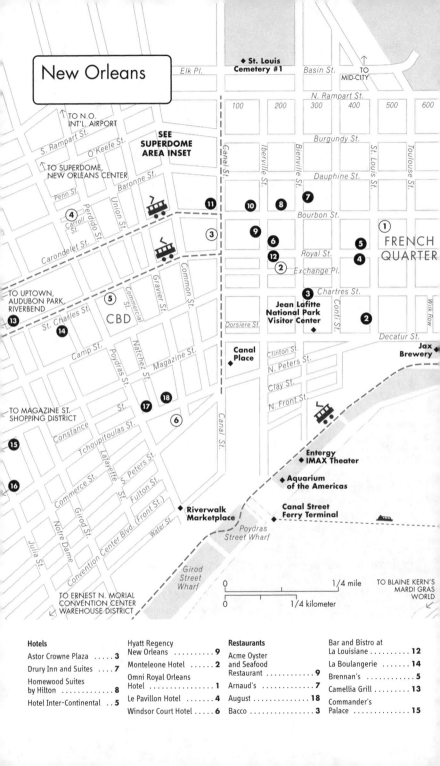

New Orleans

St. Louis Cemetery #1

SEE SUPERDOME AREA INSET

TO N.O. INT'L. AIRPORT

TO SUPERDOME, NEW ORLEANS CENTER

TO MID-CITY

FRENCH QUARTER

CBD

TO UPTOWN, AUDUBON PARK, RIVERBEND

TO MAGAZINE ST. SHOPPING DISTRICT

Canal Place

Jean Lafitte National Park Visitor Center

Jax Brewery

Entergy IMAX Theater

Aquarium of the Americas

Canal Street Ferry Terminal

Riverwalk Marketplace

Poydras Street Wharf

Girod Street Wharf

TO BLAINE KERN'S MARDI GRAS WORLD

TO ERNEST N. MORIAL CONVENTION CENTER WAREHOUSE DISTRICT

0   1/4 mile
0   1/4 kilometer

Hotels

Astor Crowne Plaza **3**
Drury Inn and Suites **7**
Homewood Suites by Hilton **8**
Hotel Inter-Continental . . **5**

Hyatt Regency New Orleans **9**
Monteleone Hotel **2**
Omni Royal Orleans Hotel **1**
Le Pavillon Hotel **4**
Windsor Court Hotel **6**

Restaurants

Acme Oyster and Seafood Restaurant **9**
Arnaud's **7**
August **18**
Bacco **3**

Bar and Bistro at La Louisiane **12**
La Boulangerie **14**
Brennan's **5**
Camellia Grill **13**
Commander's Palace **15**

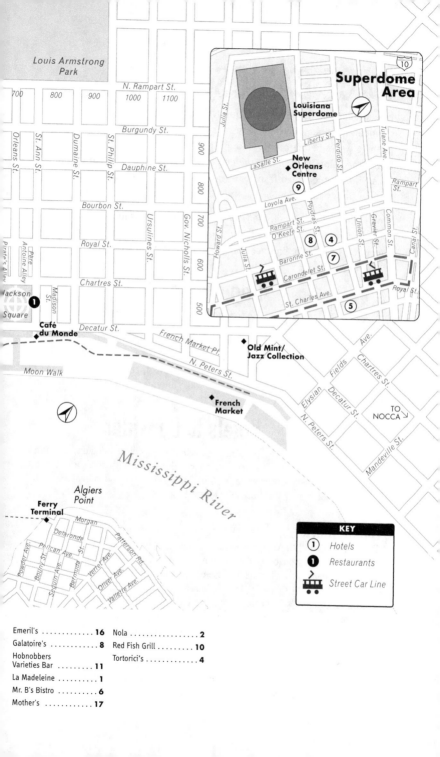

Louis Armstrong Park

700 | 800 | 900 | 1000 | 1100

N. Rampart St.

Burgundy St.

Orleans St.
St. Ann St.
Dumaine St.
St. Philip St.

Dauphine St.

900

800

Bourbon St.

Ursulines St.

Gov. Nicholls St.

Royal St.

700

600

Chartres St.

Pirate's Alley
Père Antoine Alley

Madison St.

Jackson Square

1

Café du Monde

Decatur St.

French Market Pl.

N. Peters St.

Moon Walk

500

Superdome Area

Julia St.

Louisiana Superdome

Liberty St.

Tulane Ave.

LaSalle St.

New Orleans Centre

9

Loyola Ave.

Howard St.

Poydras St.

Perdido St.

Rampart St.

Gravier St.

Common St.

Rampart St.

Union St.

Rampart St. O'Keefe St.

8 **4**

Baronne St.

7

Julia St.

Carondelet St.

St. Charles Ave.

Royal St.

5

Old Mint/ Jazz Collection

French Market

Fields

Chartres St.

Elysian

Decatur St.

N. Peters St.

TO NOCCA →

Mandeville St.

Mississippi River

Algiers Point

Ferry Terminal

Morgan

Delaronde

Pelican Ave.
Powder Ave.
Bouny St.
Seguin St.
Bermuda St.

Verret Ave.
Patterson Rd.

Oliver Ave.
Vallette Ave.

KEY	
1	Hotels
1	Restaurants
🚋	Street Car Line

RACE BASICS

Like Mardi Gras, which changes from year to year based on the Lenten calendar, the marathon date varies. It's always on a Sunday, and always two to three weeks before or after Mardi Gras. This usually places it in February, but on occasion it will fall at the end of January. If the race is after Mardi Gras, you get the added festivity of race-route trees draped with beads thrown from parade floats.

Along with the marathon, the New Orleans Track Club sponsors a 5K, held the day before the main event, and a half-marathon, which runs concurrently with the big race and gives you a taste of its flavor.

RACE CONTACT

Premier Event Management

✉

3829 Veterans Blvd.,
Suite 102,
Metairie, LA 70002

☎

866/454-6561 or
504/454-6561

⊕

www.mardigrasmarathon.com or
www.pem-usa.com

Registration

Registration opens in late spring or early summer, and fees are $65 before early October, $75 before late December, $90 by late January, and $100 at the expo. The simplest way to register is online. The official Web site is simple to navigate and fairly comprehensive in terms of both race and travel information.

Hotels to Consider

You absolutely want to be within walking distance of the Superdome, which means staying in either the CBD or the part of the French Quarter closest to the CBD. The marathon is held in high season for New Orleans; book as early as November for the best rates.

French Quarter

ASTOR CROWNE PLAZA. This luxury hotel combines a French Quarter atmosphere with a location that's a reasonable walk to or from the Dome. Enjoy its Sleep Advantage program, which provides the ultimate in plush bedding, an eye mask, lavender spray, and a relaxation CD. ✉ 739 Canal St., French Quarter, 70130 ☎ 504/962-0500 ⊕ www. astorcrowneplaza.com 🛏 689 rooms, 28 suites 🍴 Restaurant, 24-hr room service, wake-up calls, alarm clocks, coffeemakers, newspapers weekdays, robes, cable TV with movies and video games, in-room data ports, in-room safes, pool, sauna, gym, bar, concierge, concierge floor, meeting rooms, no-smoking rooms $$.

★ **MONTELEONE HOTEL.** This hotel is the farthest from the Superdome of all those I recommend, but given its grandeur, it's worth the walk. The 1886 grande dame has a baroque facade, liveried doormen, shimmering lobby chandeliers, plus all the same appointments as its brand-new competitors. Rooms are extra large and luxurious, with rich fabrics. The hotel is also known for being haunted—check out its Web site for ghost stories. ✉ 214 Royal St., French Quarter, 70130 ☎ 504/523–3341 or 800/535–9595 ⊕ www. hotelmonteleone.com 🛏 570 rooms, 28 suites 🍴 3 restaurants, room service, wake-up calls, alarm clocks, coffeemakers, robes, cable TV with movies and video games, in-room data ports, in-room safes, minibars, pool, gym, spa, bar, concierge, business services, meeting rooms, no-smoking rooms ▭ AE, D, DC, MC, V $-$$$.

OMNI ROYAL ORLEANS HOTEL. Sconce-enhanced columns, gilt mirrors, fan windows, and three magnificent chandeliers re-create the atmosphere of old New Orleans. Service is impeccable, and rooms are well appointed and spacious, with marble baths and marble-top dressers and tables. Enjoy the rooftop pool, and check out the viewing deck for a terrific French Quarter vista. One small detraction—there's a flight of stairs to the lobby. If you can't take them, you'll find that the entrance for people with disabilities isn't as accessible as it should be. ✉ 621 St. Louis St., French Quarter, 70140 ☎ 504/529–5333 or 800/843–6664 ⊕ www.omnihotels.com 🛏 321 rooms, 25 suites 🍴 Restaurant, 24-hr room service, wake-up calls, alarm clocks, coffeemakers, newspapers weekdays, robes, cable TV with movies and video games, in-room data ports, in-room safes, minibars, free Wi-Fi, pool, gym, hair salon, 3 lounges, shops, babysitting, concierge, business services, meeting room, parking (fee), no-smoking floor ▭ AE, D, DC, MC, V $$$-$$$$.

CBD

DRURY INN AND SUITES. From the outside, this onetime home of the Bell South phone company looks like nothing. Step inside, however, and you'll be amazed. The lobby is old-school ornate, with large chandeliers, upholstery in rich reds and blacks, and a sitting room complete with a piano. Breakfast is complimentary, as are evening beverages and snacks. Rooms have a sophisticated, upscale feel. It's not a luxury hotel, but you do get a lot for the price. ✉ 820 Poydras St., CBD, 70112 ☎ 504/529–7800 ⊕ www.druryhotels.com 🛏 156 rooms 🍴 Wake-up calls, alarm clocks, coffeemakers, cable TV, in-room data ports, microwaves, refrigerators, pool, 24-hr gym, hot tub, dry cleaning, laundry facilities, no-smoking floors ▭ AE, D, DC, MC, V ¢-$.

HOMEWOOD SUITES BY HILTON. It has so much New Orleans ambience that you'll find it hard to believe that this hotel, just a short walk from the Superdome, is part of a chain. Bay windows and high ceilings lend spaciousness to rooms that are already on the large side. Complimentary breakfast is served every morning, and the manager's reception Monday through Thursday evenings has light snacks and beverages. The indoor pool is huge and beautiful. You'll be hard-pressed to get more for your money anyplace else. ✉ 901 Poydras St., CBD, 70112 ☎ 504/581–5599 ⊕ www.homewoodsuites.com 🛏 166 suites 🍴 Wake-up calls, alarm clocks, coffeemakers, newspapers weekdays, cable TV with video games, in-room data ports, kitchens, microwaves, refrigerators, free Wi-Fi, indoor pool, 24-hr gym, hot tub, shop, laundry facilities, concierge, business services, no-smoking floors ▭ AE, D, DC, MC, V $.

HOTEL INTERCONTINENTAL. In this modern rose-granite structure overlooking St. Charles Avenue, public spaces include a spacious, inviting second-floor lobby and a peaceful sculpture garden. Rooms are large and well lighted, with matching quilted spreads and draperies. The VIP level contains some of the city's finest suites. The health club and pool feature complimentary fresh fruit. ⊠ 444 St. Charles Ave., CBD, 70130 ☎ 504/525–5566 or 800/445–6563 ⊕ www.intercontinental.com ⇨ 449 rooms, 30 suites ⚱ 3 restaurants, 24-hr room service, wake-up calls, alarm clocks, coffeemakers, newspapers, robes, cable TV with movies, in-room data ports, in-room safes, minibars, pool, 24-hr gym, lounge, shop, dry cleaning, laundry service, concierge, concierge floor, business services, parking (fee), no-smoking floors ▭ AE, D, DC, MC, V $-$$.

⚡ **HYATT REGENCY NEW ORLEANS.** This hotel sustained a great deal of damage in Katrina and will remain closed until early 2007. Yet when it re-opens, this luxury hotel will be the perfect marathon locale as it's right next to the Superdome (before the hurricane it was connected to the Dome via a glass atrium). Call for updates. ⊠ 500 Poydras Plaza, CBD, 70113 ☎ 504/561–1234 or 800/233–1234 ⊕ www.hyatt.com ⇨ 1,136 rooms, 48 suites ⚱ 2 restaurants, room service, wake-up calls, alarm clocks, coffeemakers, cable TV with movies, in-room data ports, Wi-Fi (fee), pool, hot tub, gym, sports bar, lounge, dry cleaning, concierge, concierge floor, business services, meeting rooms, parking (fee), no-smoking floors ▭ AE, D, DC, MC, V $$.

★ **LE PAVILLON HOTEL.** "Lush" and "magnificent" are the words that immediately spring to mind when you enter the lobby of this hotel dating from 1907. It's just down the street from the Superdome, and its guest rooms have high ceilings and traditional decor; suites are particularly luxurious. Every night from 10 to 11, all guests are invited to the lobby for a late-night snack: peanut butter and jelly sandwiches with milk or hot chocolate. Book early for excellent rates. ⊠ 833 Poydras St., CBD, 70112 ☎ 504/581–3111 or 800/535–9095 ⊕ www.lepavillon.com ⇨ 226 rooms, 14 suites ⚱ Restaurant, 24-hr room service, wake-up calls, alarm clocks, newspapers, robes, cable TV, in-room data ports, in-room safes, free Wi-Fi, pool, gym, hot tub, bar, laundry service, concierge, meeting rooms, parking (fee), no-smoking rooms ▭ AE, D, DC, MC, V $.

★ **WINDSOR COURT HOTEL.** Exquisite, gracious, elegant, eminently civilized—these all describe Windsor Court yet still fail to capture its essence. From Le Salon's scrumptious afternoon tea, served daily in the lobby, to the unbelievably large rooms, this is one of *the* places to stay in New Orleans. Plush carpeting, canopy and four-poster beds, stocked wet bars, marble vanities, oversize mirrors, and dressing areas are just some of the pampering touches. ⊠ 300 Gravier St., CBD, 70130 ☎ 504/523–6000 or 800/262–2662 ⊕ www.windsorcourthotel.com ⇨ 58 rooms, 266 suites, 2 penthouses ⚱ 2 restaurants, 24-hr room service, wake-up calls, alarm clocks, newspapers weekdays, robes, cable TV, in-room VCRs, in-room data ports, in-room safes, minibars, pool, gym, hot tub, massage, sauna, steam room, lounge, laundry service, babysitting, concierge, business services, parking (fee), no-smoking floors ▭ AE, D, DC, MC, V $$-$$$.

NIGHT-BEFORE PASTA DINNER

There's no marathon-sponsored pasta dinner. Why? Because no one would go! Restaurants in New Orleans are too good to pass up. That said, New Orleans isn't known for health food. Even steamed vegetables are likely made with a butter-and-flour roux. But don't despair: the following places offer terrific dishes that won't leave you logy.

BACCO. Though many dishes are too rich for runners, the roast chicken and *stracci* ("pasta rags" with chicken, basil, spinach, and tomato sauce) will fuel you up without weighing you down. ✉ 310 Chartres St., French Quarter ☎ 504/522-2426 ⊕ www.bacco.com ▤ AE, D, DC, MC, V $$-$$$.

TORTORICI'S. Piano music accompanies your meal at the Quarter's oldest Italian restaurant. The menu has everything from traditional pastas to New Orleans–style barbecue shrimp, served with extra bread to sop up the sauce. ✉ 441 Royal St., French Quarter ☎ 504/522-4295 ⊕ www.tortoricis.com ▤ AE, D, DC, MC, V $$-$$$.

AND YOU'RE OFF . . .

The Expo

The expo is held at the Superdome Friday afternoon and evening and all day Saturday before the race. Transportation is simple: walk. All the hotels I recommend are within walking distance of the Dome, and the jaunt is a great way to stretch your legs before the race. The expo is relatively small but still has any last-minute gear you might need.

Race Day

The Course

The race begins at the Superdome at 7 AM, so you need to set out early from your hotel. The Dome is in a rather safe area, and the closer you get to it, the more fellow runners will be by your side. Still, this is a city, so use common sense and be vigilant.

In the Dome, you'll find baggage check, as well as plenty of space to stretch, warm up, and mingle with runners and spectators (all are welcome) as you listen to prerace announcements. Water, Gatorade, and energy gel are available, and there are usually one or two expo booths selling last-minute provisions. You can even check out the finish line, also inside the Dome. And the best part of starting here? Real toilets. There are large restrooms at Gate A, on your way in from the Poydras Street entrance. Lines will be long, so leave yourself plenty of time.

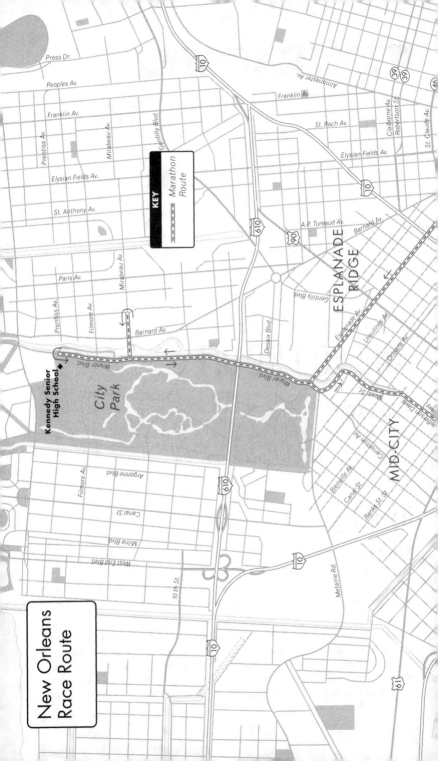

New Orleans Race Route

KEY

Marathon Route

Press Dr.

Peoples Av.

Franklin Av.

Prentiss Av.

Mirabeau Av.

Gentilly Blvd.

Elysian Fields Av.

St. Anthony Av.

Paris Av.

Mirabeau Av.

Prentiss Av.

Filmore Av.

Barnard Av.

Kennedy Senior High School

Wisner Blvd.

City Park

Filmore Av.

Argonne Blvd.

Canal St.

Milne Blvd.

West End Blvd.

10th St.

Franklin Av.

Almonaster Av.

St. Roch Av.

Claiborne Av.

Robertson St.

St. Claude Av.

Elysian Fields Av.

A.P. Tureaud Av.

Barnard Av.

ESPLANADE RIDGE

Gentilly Blvd.

Desaix Blvd.

Esplanade Av.

Ursulines Av.

Orleans Av.

Moss St.

Jefferson Davis Hwy.

MID-CITY

Carrollton Av.

Bienville Av.

Cana St.

Banks St. St.

Metairie Rd.

At 6:45 AM, everyone lines up outside the Dome, where runners are seeded according to projected finish times. Then, at exactly 7 AM, the race begins, leading you on a perfectly choreographed journey past New Orleans's most famous sites. In just a few hours, you'll get to know the city better than you would in several days as a regular tourist. You start in the CBD, then cut through the Warehouse District en route to the French Quarter. After running past the Quarter's wrought-iron-balconied buildings, you zoom up Esplanade alongside columned mansions. From the northernmost point of your race, just after Mile 7, you turn and dart back through Mid-City.

At Mile 13 half-marathoners are diverted back to the Superdome to finish their race. Full marathoners head back through the CBD and then to the Garden District, filled with the grand houses that spring to mind when you think about New Orleans. You run all the way to Audubon Park before turning and retracing your steps to the Superdome for the big finish.

The course is remarkably flat, and you'll enjoy entertainment from a few bands along the route, plus support from 13 aid stations, some of which you'll hit twice. Stations are stocked with water, Gatorade, and energy bars, and there are also portable toilets. Expect something special at each station. There's a contest every year for the station with the best theme, and volunteers go all out to try to win. Although there could always be an upset, look for the best station to be that sponsored by the New Orleans Hash House Harriers, usually around Mile 23. According to the Harriers' Web site, they're "the drinking club with a running problem." Don't worry, you won't miss them. Look for the crowd of women and men decked out in red dresses, screaming encouragement and offering beer.

PRERACE TIP

Often, the second-floor restrooms are open and have shorter lines than those on the first floor. Pop up the escalators by the Poydras Street entrance to beat the crowds.

The course stays open for seven hours, after which the roads reopen and runners must move to the sidewalks. Late aid stations do tend to stay open, as does the finish line.

Spectating

There are many races where the streets are lined with spectators, beginning to end.

The Mardi Gras Marathon is not one of them, which means that everyone who *does* come out to cheer is all the more appreciated.

If you want to support a runner, join him or her at the starting line. You can hang out together in the Superdome until 6:45 AM, when you can either head outside and stand right next to the line of runners, or stay inside the Dome and take the escalators by the Poydras Street entrance. Head up two flights, then exit onto the bridge that crosses Poydras. It's the perfect place to watch the whole sea of runners slowly make their way to the starting line, then break free to begin the race.

After the start, the Superdome remains your perfect spectator base. Slip behind it (to the building's west side) to catch your favorite runner at the halfway point. Then, when your runner's set to finish, head back inside to cheer his or her moment of victory.

Celebrate!

Pound through the finish line inside the Superdome, and you'll find yourself in the middle of a party. A live band plays, and the Dome teems with people. Get your medal, get your ChampionChip removed, and enjoy yourself—whether it's getting a massage or downing a piece of king cake (a Mardi Gras tradition). Although spectators can join the festivities, a large section of the Superdome is cordoned off for runners only. Show your bib number to get inside, and enjoy free snacks, sandwiches, smoothies, and all the beer you can drink.

The marathon party is a fine event, but don't think it's the end of your post-race celebration. New Orleans is made for revelry, so plan to spend the evening out on the town, rejoicing in your accomplishment (⇨ "I Love the Nightlife," below for the best nightspots).

BEYOND THE FINISH LINE

WEATHER THE RUN

The average marathon day low is 42°F and the average high is 64°F— great running weather.

Replacing 2,620 Calories

People in New Orleans don't eat to live, they live to eat. Food and drink here aren't just fuel, they're social lubrication, and meals are meant to be *savored*. After the race, you might have enough time to play at the post-race party, get back to your hotel, shower, change, and hit that most glorious of traditions in New Orleans: Sunday brunch. Take a few hours to digest, maybe grab a po'boy sandwich to tide you over, and then head out to another glorious New Orleans tradition: a long, leisurely dinner. Wherever you go, count on food that's unique, rich, and delicious.

CBD & Warehouse District

★ AUGUST. Glossy woods and thick brocades lend romance, and servers are perfectly attentive but not pushy. Chef John Besh's dazzling, modern technique informs every plate on the contemporary menu. The prime beef and lamb dishes could hardly be improved; tiny soft-shell crabs crackle with sea flavors; and lumps of back-fin crabmeat and pillows of springy gnocchi glisten in truffle oil. Dessert is no less divine, so save room. The restaurant is closed Sunday, so you can't come the evening of the race, but do try to get here at some point. ✉ 301 Tchoupitoulas St., CBD ☎ 504/299-9777 ⊕ www.rest-august. com ▭ AE, D, DC, MC, V ⊗ Closed Sun. No lunch Sat. $$–$$$.

EMERIL'S. Celebrity chef Emeril Lagasse's flagship is always jammed. A wood ceiling in an oversize basket-weave pattern muffles much of the clatter and chatter. In a far corner, the food bar framed by glass-encased spices and legumes seats nine guests who desire special attention from the chef de cuisine. The ambitious menu gives equal emphasis to creole and modern American cooking. Desserts, such as the renowned banana cream pie, verge on gargantuan. Service is meticulously organized, and the wine list's depth and range should pop the eye of the most persnickety imbiber. ⊠ 800 Tchoupitoulas St., Warehouse District ☏ 504/528-9393 ⊕ www.emerils.com ⌦ Reservations essential ⊟ AE, D, DC, MC, V ⊗ No lunch weekends $$-$$$$.

HOBNOBBERS VARIETIES BAR. Small, easy-to-miss Hobnobbers is the real deal when it comes to po'boys and other creole food for lunch. Mother's attracts the tourists, but *this* is where the locals go. Miss Mary will treat you right, with huge portions of barbecue ribs, stuffed pork chops, chicken wings, or the po'boys. ⊠ 139 Carondelet St., CBD ☏ 504/525-5428 ⌦ Reservations not accepted ⊟ No credit cards ⊗ No dinner ¢-$.

MOTHER'S. People line up for down-home eats at this island of blue-collar sincerity amid downtown's glittery hotels. Mother's dispenses delicious baked ham and roast beef po'boys (ask for "debris" on the beef sandwich, and the bread will be slathered with meat juices and shreds of meat), home-style biscuits and jambalaya, and a very good chicken gumbo in a couple of bare-bones dining rooms. Breakfast eggs and coffee are sometimes cold, but that doesn't seem to repel the hordes fighting for seats. Service is cafeteria-style, with a counter or two augmenting the tables. ⊠ 401 Poydras St., CBD ☏ 504/523-9656 ⌦ Reservations not accepted ⊟ AE, MC, V $-$$.

French Quarter

ACME OYSTER AND SEAFOOD RESTAURANT. This classic, no-nonsense seafood eatery at the entrance to the Quarter is a prime source for cool, salty oysters on the half shell; shrimp, oyster, and roast beef po'boys; and state-of-the-art red beans and rice. Expect lengthy lines at the marble-top oyster bar. Crowds lighten in the late afternoon. ⊠ 724 Iberville St., French Quarter ☏ 504/522-5973 ⊕ www.acmeoyster.com ⌦ Reservations not accepted ⊟ AE, D, DC, MC, V $-$$.

ARNAUD'S. The grande dame of classic creole restaurants still sparkles. In the main dining room, where jackets are requested, ornate etched glass reflects light from the charming old chandeliers while the late founder, Arnaud Cazenave, gazes from an oil portrait. The overflow spills into a labyrinth of plush banquet rooms and bars. Always reliable are cold shrimp Arnaud, in a superb rémoulade, and creamy oyster stew, as well as the fish in crawfish sauce, beef Wellington, and crème brûlée. ⊠ 813 Bienville St., French Quarter ☏ 504/523-5433 ⊕ www.arnauds.com ⌦ Reservations essential ⊟ AE, D, DC, MC, V ⊗ No lunch Sat. $$-$$$$.

★ **BAR AND BISTRO AT LA LOUISIANE.** Established in 1881, this restaurant was for years the place to see and be seen in New Orleans, hosting such luminaries as William Randolph Hearst, Al Jolson, and Harry Houdini. The atmosphere is inviting, and the food is delicious—the gumbo is among the best in the city. Don't miss the "Diamond Jim" special cocktail or the sticky cake—both are magnificent. And check out the first-floor bathrooms; their one-way mirrors allow you to look out into the bar. Once you get over the gnawing feeling that you're performing for an audience, you might just settle in and people-watch. ⊠ 725 Iberville, French Quarter ☏ 504/378-8200 ⊕ www.lalouisiane.com ⊟ AE, D, DC, MC, V $$-$$$.

BREAKFAST SPOTS

Whatever your runner's speed, you'll have time between rounds of cheering. What's the best thing to do with extra time in New Orleans? Eat. Here are some options (all in the ¢ to $ category) reasonably close to the race route.

★ **CAFÉ DU MONDE.** No trip to New Orleans is complete without a cup of chicory-laced café au lait and a few sugar-dusted beignets (funnel cakes meet doughnuts—sort of) from Café du Monde. If you go just after the race starts, you'll easily find an empty table—a rarity. Sit on the covered patio to feast on the delicacies and the views of Jackson Square. ⊠ 800 Decatur St., French Quarter ☎ 504/525-4544 ⊕ www.cafedumonde.com ⊟ No credit cards.

LA BOULANGERIE FRENCH BAKERY. An upstairs loft filled with couches makes this bakery the perfect place to relax with a newspaper, hot beverage, and pastry. It's a reasonable walk from the Superdome, and is fairly empty marathon morning. ⊠ 625 St. Charles Ave., CBD ☎ 504/569-1925 ⊟ D, MC, V ⤱ No smoking.

LA MADELEINE. Though it's part of a chain, it's filled with French country charm—a perfect fit for the Vieux Carré. Floor-to-ceiling windows open onto outdoor dining areas. Order at the counter, then sit and enjoy coffee and a pastry, quiche, or omelet. ⊠ 547 St. Ann St., French Quarter ☎ 504/568-0073 ⊕ www.lamadeleine.com ⊟ AE, D, DC, MC, V.

★**BRENNAN'S.** Come for breakfast, come for brunch, or come for dinner; just come, and come hungry. Relish your traditional creole meal; Brennan's will never hurry you. Lavish breakfasts of elaborate poached-egg dishes are what first put Brennan's on the map, and they're still a major draw. Dinners are also a delight, with rich treats like a shrimp-and-crabmeat crepe; or three tournedos of beef, each in a different sauce. Don't even think of leaving without having the bananas Foster—invented here and made to perfection. ⊠417 Royal St., French Quarter ☎504/525-9711 ⊕www.brennansneworleans.com ⤳Reservations essential ⊟AE, D, DC, MC, V $$$-$$$$.

★**GALATOIRE'S.** It's the epitome of the French-creole bistro; indeed, many of the recipes date from1905. Fried oysters and bacon en brochette are worth every calorie, and the brick-red rémoulade sauce sets a high standard. Other winners include veal chops in béarnaise sauce and seafood-stuffed eggplant. The narrow downstairs dining room is lighted with glistening brass chandeliers; bentwood chairs at the white-cloth tables lend timelessness. The din of the regulars, however, sometimes inhibits conversation. Reservations are accepted for the upstairs dining rooms only. ⊠209 Bourbon St., French Quarter ☎504/525-2021 🏛Jacket required ⊟AE, DC, MC, V ⊘ Closed Mon. $-$$$.

MR. B'S BISTRO. The energy rarely subsides, with servers darting between the wood-and-glass screens that reduce the vastness of the dining room. Brunch is highly touted, but any meal here features a dependable contemporary creole menu centering on meats and seafood from a grill fueled with aromatic woods. Pasta dishes, especially the pasta jambalaya with andouille sausage and shrimp, are fresh and creative. The bread pudding with Irish-whiskey sauce is excellent, too. Lunchtime finds most of the tables taken up by locals, who adore the countrified chicken-andouille gumbo and the distinctly local version of barbecue shrimp. ⊠ 201 Royal St., French Quarter ☎ 504/523–2078 ⊕ www. mrbsbistro.com ⊟ AE, D, DC, MC, V $$–$$$.

NOLA. Fans of chef Emeril Lagasse who can't get a table at Emeril's have this sassy French Quarter restaurant as an alternative. Lagasse hasn't lowered his sights with Nola's menu, as lusty and rich as any in town. The appetizers are as freewheeling as Lagasse's television personality, with Vietnamese stuffed chicken wings listed beside steak tartare. A main-course redfish is swathed in a horseradish-citrus crust before it's plank-roasted in a wood oven. Duck arrives glistening with a whiskey-caramel glaze. The combinations seem endless. For dessert, try the coconut-cream or apple-buttermilk pie. ⊠ 534 St. Louis St., French Quarter ☎ 504/522–6652 ⊕ www.emerils.com ⚖ Reservations essential ⊟ AE, D, DC, MC, V ☾ No lunch Sun. $$$–$$$$.

RED FISH GRILL. A high energy level and a riotous color scheme put this big, bouncy, seafood place in tune with Bourbon Street. "Casual" is the byword in the central dining space, edged on three sides by banquettes, smaller rooms, and a huge oyster bar, all festooned with images reflecting the menu's focus on seafood. The kitchen's handiwork includes hefty po'boys, a seafood gumbo with alligator sausage, grilled fish with buttery sauces, and grilled oysters with lemon and garlic. The signature dessert is a variation on bananas Foster. ⊠ 115 Bourbon St., French Quarter ☎ 504/598–1200 ⊕ www.redfishgrill.com ⊟ AE, DC, MC, V $–$$.

Garden District/Uptown

CAMELLIA GRILL. Every diner should be as classy as Camellia Grill, a one-of-a-kind, truly American eatery that deserves its following. Locals vie until the early-morning hours for one of the 29 stools at the gleaming counter, each place supplied with a large, fresh linen napkin. The hamburger—4 ounces of excellent beef on a fresh bun with any number of embellishments—is one of the best in town. Other blue-ribbon dishes are the chili, the chicken salad sandwiches, the pecan and meringue pies, and the omelets. Everything's made on the premises and served by bow-tied, white-waistcoated waiters with the fastest feet in the business. At this writing the Camellia Grill was closed, and there was no news about when it would re-open. Fingers-crossed that it does; it's such a classic. ⊠ 626 S. Carrollton Ave., Uptown ☎ 504/866–9573 ⊟ No credit cards $.

★ **COMMANDER'S PALACE.** The second you decide you're running the marathon, call and make reservations here for Sunday brunch—a creole experience not to be missed. Strolling jazz musicians serenade you as you dine on a three-course meal including such entrées as New Orleans French toast with peaches, bourbon whipped cream, and cham-

EAT, DRINK, AND BE MERRY

Forget *Essence of Emeril.* If you want to learn to cook New Orleans–style, grab a seat in chef Kevin Belton's class at the New Orleans School of Cooking. Picture the charm and storytelling ability of Bill Cosby, toss in a sprig of *Seinfeld*'s Kramer, fold in the culinary know-how of Julia Child, then blow the package up to 6 feet 9 inches and 400 pounds, and you've got Chef Kevin, a.k.a. Big Kevin. He's made numerous TV appearances, has his own brand of spices, and by all rights should be an international superstar. It will happen sooner or later; best to catch Big Kevin in person while you still can.

Kevin owns the school and is one of a handful of chefs who teach there. The others may be great, but they can't possibly compare with Big Kevin. Make reservations early, and request his class. From the minute you enter the classroom and grab a seat at one of the eight tables of eight, Kevin has you laughing and learning. His station is on a dais, and mirrors above the counter and range show exactly what he's doing. There isn't a bad seat in the house.

The first thing Kevin asks is if you're hungry. And if you are? "Shame on you." As Kevin tells it, "You come to New Orleans to fill your head with music and your belly with food." But the New Orleans love affair with food isn't about gluttony, he says, it's about being social. Folks here visit over food. And when you take Kevin's class, that's exactly what you do.

In a two-hour class, Kevin teaches you how to make a three-course meal. In my case, it was corn-and-crab bisque, shrimp creole, and fresh pralines. As Kevin cooks, he tells stories—about being large, about his kids, about living in New Orleans, about cooking. And much as you'll love his stories, you'll really love it when they stop because that's when you get to eat, doctoring your food with Kevin's brand of spices and washing it all down with free Abita beer. Kevin's ebullient charm is infectious, and you'll find yourself chatting with the strangers at your table like old friends. When you've licked your plate clean, class empties out into the Louisiana General Store, where you can stock up on all things Cajun and creole—including more fresh pralines. ⊠ New Orleans School of Cooking, 524 St. Louis St., French Quarter ☎ 504/525–2665 ⊕ www. nosoc.com ⊑ 3-hr class, $27 per person; 2-hr class, $22 per person ⊙ Classes daily 10–1 or 2–4.

pagne syrup; or pecan-crusted Gulf fish with lump crabmeat. The entire meal is a show, with servers putting each course down in front of everyone at your table before lifting the plate covers in exact unison. Don't skimp on dessert; the bread pudding soufflé is unbelievable, as is the creole cheesecake. ⊠ 1403 Washington Ave., Garden District ☎ 504/899–8221 ⊕ www.commanderspalace.com ⌂ Reservations essential ▭ AE, D, DC, MC, V $$$–$$$$.

The sign above the expo table made me laugh out loud: 50 STATES MARATHON CLUB—RUN ALL 50 STATES! Yeah, right. I had completed four marathons and felt like Xena: Warrior Princess. Fifty? You'd have to be an Olympian. Or one of those gazelles who can roll out of bed and qualify for Boston. Or a Kenyan.

But the couple manning the desk didn't seem to fit any of these categories. She looked like a normal midwestern mom. And him? With his thin-rimmed glasses and long, wild strands of gray hair, he looked a lot like Eugene Levy's "Mitch" at the end of A Mighty Wind. So I had to ask: had they run in all 50 states?

They had. And then some.

Between them, Steve and Paula Boone have run more than 400 marathons. They even met at a marathon, the first time Paula qualified for Boston. It was her fourth race and Steve's 106th. He had done Boston before and offered to show her around. They became best friends immediately and married a year later. Steve promised her their lives would never be boring, and he didn't lie. The two are on the road most of the year except summertime (the marathon low season), seeing the country together as they hop from race to race. Along the way, they started seeing the same faces and grew close with many in the marathon community. A lot of runners, Paula and Steve realized, were pursuing the goal of a race in all 50 states, but they were doing it without support or recognition for their Herculean efforts. So in 2001 Steve and Paula formed the nonprofit 50 States Marathon Club.

To become a member you must complete a marathon in 10 states. From there the group will support you in your quest for 50, celebrate your accomplishments, and cheer you on as you strive for your next goal—whether it's reaching the 100-marathon mark, participating in a marathon on each continent, or just continuing to run regularly. The group has its own Web site and newsletter detailing member accomplishments, and Steve and Paula do their best to make sure crowds show up at members' milestone races. The two have also secured member discounts on entry fees at many marathons and have even launched races in states without them, just so members could achieve their goals.

Steve and Paula share a lust for life that's infectious, a buzzing vibrancy that's directly tied to following their passion. Talk to them for more than a minute about marathons, and you'll want to be part of their world. And the beauty is, you can. As Steve says, there's a special camaraderie among marathoners. It's the only sport in the world where rank amateurs compete against the best in the sport. "You walk out there, and you stand next to the fastest people in the world . . . and they kick your butt, but there's always the chance you can beat 'em."

And technically, Steve did. He finished the Boston Marathon in a year when one of the elite male athletes dropped out partway through the race. The next year, when he saw that elite runner signing autographs at the expo, Steve called, "Hey—I beat you last year!" The elite runner agreed—yes, he had. And a whole line of autograph seekers were suddenly staring at Steve, wondering who he was and how he had beat one of the world's fastest runners.

That's the real glory of the marathon. Fast or slow, elite or back-of-the-pack, all runners are sharing a singular experience. No matter what your finishing time, you're all in the trenches together. And the minute you hit the starting line of your first race, you're part of a very special community.

The day I met Paula and Steve was the day before the 2005 Mardi Gras Marathon, which Paula was about to run for the first time. After hearing their story, it was tough to imagine that running was ever *not* a part of their lives. But for Paula, it wasn't for many years. She ran some in high school but stopped entirely after graduation. Two children and several pounds later, she felt terrible about her body and knew she needed to take action. She tried the gym, but the scale didn't budge. Remembering how much she had enjoyed running as a teen, she decided to try it again. At first she could only walk with a friend, but slowly she progressed to running. When she ran her first 5K and didn't come in dead last, she was hooked, and ran her first marathon less than a year later.

I asked Paula what advice she would give to people considering tackling the marathon for the first time. "Be prepared for a life-changing experience," she said. "If you are well trained and prepared, the marathon is a party to celebrate your accomplishment. The training is the hard part—the marathon is fun! For your first marathon, just stick with what you know works. Don't try anything new—no new clothes, no new shoes, no new food, no gimmicks you picked up at the expo (there is no magic). Remember that your first marathon will be a personal record for that distance no matter when you finish. 'Run when you can, walk when you have to, finish no matter what' is my mantra. There is nothing like crossing that finish line. You will have accomplished something that most people haven't done (but just about anyone can)." ∎

Sightseeing on (and off) Your Feet

I Feel Great!

GO GHOST-HUNTING. Many parts of the French Quarter are believed to be haunted. If your legs are feeling strong, take a walking tour devoted to this dark side of New Orleans life to learn more about its best ghost stories, as well as the practice of voodoo. Cemetery tours are popular in New Orleans thanks to unique aboveground tombs. The most famous, St. Louis Cemetery No. 1, is just outside the Quarter. It's best (read: safer) to visit it on a tour. **Haunted History Tours** (☎ 888/644–6787 or 504/861–2727 ⊕ www.hauntedhistorytours.com) offers several tours through the Quarter and the Garden District. They're conducted during the day and at night, and most cost $20 per person. **Magic Walking Tours** (☎ 504/588–9693 ⊕ www.neworleansmagicwalkingtours.com) conducts cemetery tours for $18. Reservations are a must. **New Orleans Spirit Tours** (☎ 504/566–9877 ⊕ www.neworleanstours.net) offers two-hour walking tours for $18. They leave at 10:30 AM, 1:15 PM, or 8:15 PM. The evening tour is perfect for the subject at hand. Make reservations for the **Save Our Cemeteries** (☎ 888/721–7493 or 504/525–3377 ⊕ www.saveourcemeteries.org) cemetery tours, which cost $12.

TOUR THE TOWN. Docents associated with the **Friends of the Cabildo** (☎ 504/523–3939 ⊕ www.friendsofthecabildo.org ✉ $12) give two-hour general history walking tours of the Quarter, beginning at the 1850 House Museum Store at 523 St. Ann Street on Jackson Square at 10 AM and 1:30 PM every day but Monday, when only the afternoon tour is offered. The price includes admission to the 1850 House and Madame John's Legacy (a colonial creole home). No reservations are necessary; just arrive 15 minutes before the tour starts.

Several companies offer specialized walking tours on specific aspects of the French Quarter. Some accommodate as few as two people. **Heritage Tours** (☎ 504/949–9805), for example, leads general literary tours as well as those focusing on either William Faulkner or Tennessee Williams. Rangers from the **Jean Lafitte National Park** (✉ 419 Decatur St., French Quarter ☎ 504/589–2636 ⊕ www.nps.gov/jela/jelaweb.htm) give free 1½-hour general history tours of the French Quarter daily at 9:30 AM. Tours are limited to 25 people. You must pick up a ticket in person the morning of the tour at the Jean Lafitte Visitor Center in the Quarter.

I Feel Pretty Good

ALGIERS POINT. Climb the stairs (there's a ramp for wheelchair access) near the Spanish Plaza and the Riverwalk shopping area and board the Canal Street Ferry to get to Algiers Point. The trip takes about 10 minutes; ferries leave on the hour and half hour from the east bank and on the :15 and :45 of every hour on the west bank and run from 5:45 AM to midnight. Check with the attendants if you're crossing in the evening, as hours vary and it's no fun to be stranded on the other side.

The best way to experience Algiers Point is by walking along its quiet streets, admiring the architecture and savoring its small-town feel. Because it's isolated, take the usual precautions for personal safety. A one-man Algiers Point welcoming and information service is provided by Russell Templet at his **Hair and Style Shop** (✉ 143 Delaronde St., Algiers Point ☎ 504/368-9417) a half block on the right from the ferry landing. Drop in and say hello.

The big attraction on Algiers Point is **Blaine Kern's Mardi Gras World** (✉ 233 Newton St., Algiers Point ☎ 504/362-8211 ⊕ www.mardigrasworld.com). Blaine Kern is the best-known artist and creator of Mardi Gras floats; he often personally conducts tours through this one-of-a-kind facility. You can watch the artists and builders at work, view a film about Mardi Gras, and buy Carnival memorabilia in the gift shop. A photo of yourself with one of the giant figures used on the floats makes a terrific souvenir, and there's a chest full of costumes for children to try on. You can get here from the ferry landing in a free shuttle or on an enjoyable 10-minute walk along the levee. The museum is open daily 9:30-4:30, and the $13.50 admission includes cake and coffee.

★ **AQUARIUM OF THE AMERICAS.** Katrina devasted the aquarium but it hopes to re-open in summer 2006. In this marvelous family attraction more than 7,000 aquatic creatures swim in 60 displays. Each of the four major exhibit areas—the Amazon Rain Forest, the Caribbean Reef, the Mississippi River, and the Gulf Coast—has fish and animals native to that environment. An exhibit called Beyond Green houses more than 25 frog species. The aquarium's design allows you to feel part of the watery worlds by providing close-up encounters with the inhabitants. A gift shop and café are on the premises. Woldenberg Riverfront Park, which surrounds the aquarium, is a tranquil spot with a view of the Mississippi. Package tickets for the aquarium and a river cruise are available outside the aquarium. You can also combine tickets for the aquarium and the Entergy IMAX Theater, a river cruise, and the Audubon Zoo. ✉ 1 Canal St., French Quarter ☎ 504/581-4629 or 800/774-7394 ⊕ www.auduboninstitute.org ✉ Aquarium $14; combination ticket with IMAX $18; combination ticket for aquarium, zoo, and round-trip cruise $32.50 ☉ Aquarium Sun.–Thurs. 9:30-6 (last ticket sold at 5), Fri. and Sat. 9:30-7 (last ticket sold at 6).

★ **AUDUBON PARK** is a large, lush stretch of green between St. Charles Avenue and Magazine Street, continuing across Magazine Street to the river. It contains the Audubon Zoo; a 1.7-mile track for running, walking, or biking; picnic and play areas; a golf course; riding stables; a tennis court; and a river view. Calm lagoons wind through the park, harboring egrets, catfish, and other indigenous species.

If you'd like, you can venture beyond the zoo, cross the railroad tracks, and stroll along Riverview Drive, a long stretch of land on the levee overlooking the Mississippi River. This area is referred to as "The Fly" by locals and is a popular place for picnics and pickup sports. The river lookout includes a landscaped walkway and Audubon Landing, where the John James Audubon cruise boat (nicknamed "the zoo cruise") docks. ✉ 6500 Magazine St., Uptown ☎ 504/586-8777 ⊕ www.auduboninstitute.org ✉ Park free; zoo cruise $16.50, combination ticket for cruise, zoo, and aquarium $32.50 ☉ 7-mi river ride to French Quarter and Canal St. daily at 11, 1, 3, and 5.

Let's Take It Slowly

★ **JACKSON SQUARE.** Surrounded by historic buildings and filled with plenty of street life, this park is at the heart of the French Quarter. Originally called the Place d'Armes, the square was founded in 1718 as a military parade ground. It was also the site of public executions carried out in various styles, including burning at the stake, beheading, breaking on the wheel, and hanging. A statue of Andrew Jackson, victorious leader of the Battle of New Orleans in the War of 1812, commands the square's center; the park was renamed for him in the 1850s.

Among the square's notable buildings are the St. Louis Cathedral and Faulkner House. Two Spanish colonial-style buildings, the Cabildo and the Presbytère, flank the cathedral. The handsome rows of brick apartments on either side of the square are the Pontalba Buildings. The park is landscaped in a sun pattern, with walkways set like rays streaming out from the center. This was a popular garden design in the royal court of King Louis XIV, the Sun King. In the daytime, dozens of artists hang their paintings on the park fence, work on canvases, or offer to draw portraits of passersby. These artists are easy to engage in conversation and are knowledgeable about New Orleans. You can also catch musicians, mimes, tarot-card readers, and magicians who perform on the flagstone pedestrian mall surrounding the square, many of them both day and night.

LOUISIANA CHILDREN'S MUSEUM. Why not let your kids move around while you rest up? Favorite activities include a minigrocery store, a giant bubble station, and a minifitness center with a kid-size stationary bicycle and rock-climbing wall. An indoor playground is reserved for toddlers age three and under. Art teachers lead classes daily, a theater hosts morning programs, and special activities such as jewelry making and storytelling are held each week. Most exhibits are accessible to children with disabilities, and some are aimed directly at increasing a healthy awareness of the disabilities of others. ⊠ 420 Julia St., Warehouse District ☎ 504/523-1357 ⊕ www.lcm.org ☑ $6 ⊙ Late Aug.–early June, Tues.–Sat. 9:30–4:30, Sun. noon–4:30; early June–late Aug., Mon.–Sat. 9:30–4:30, Sun. noon–4:30 (last ticket sold at 4).

★ **NEW ORLEANS JAZZ COLLECTION.** Housed in the Old Mint building and part of the Louisiana State Museum, the collection provides a brief but evocative tour of the history of traditional New Orleans jazz. Among the gems are the soprano saxophone owned by Sidney Bechet, the trumpets of Pops Celestin and Dizzy Gillespie, and the cornet given to Louis Armstrong at the juvenile home where he spent much of his youth. Sadly, the Old Mint was extensively damaged in Hurricane Katrina and is closed as of this writing. Call for updates. ⊠ 400 Esplanade Ave., French Quarter ☎ 504/568-6968 ☑ $5 ⊙ Tues.–Sun. 9–5.

Ow! No.

RIDE A STREETCAR. This is a great way to see the city while staying off your feet. The riverfront streetcar covers a 2-mile route along the Mississippi, connecting major sights from the end of the French Quarter (Esplanade Avenue) to the New Orleans Convention Center (Julia Street). Eight stops en route include the French Market, Jackson Brewery, Canal Place, the World Trade Center, the Riverwalk, and the Hilton Hotel. This streetcar operates 7 AM until 11 PM, passing each stop every 20 minutes. Unlike the historic St. Charles Avenue streetcar, the riverfront and Canal Street streetcars are wheelchair accessible.

The St. Charles Avenue streetcar runs the 5 miles from the CBD to the bend in the river at Carrollton Avenue (and beyond to the intersection of Carrollton and Claiborne) 24 hours

FORGET SIGHTSEEING. GET ME TO A SPA!

ARIA. It's an oasis of pampering tucked into the Monteleone hotel. Candles and fragrance aid in your relaxation. Massages run from 30 to 90 minutes, and a 60-minute pedicure promises relief for your feet. Costs range from $55 to $110. ✉ 214 Royal St., French Quarter ☎ 504/523–3341 ⊕ www.hotelmonteleone.com.

★ **MISS CELIE'S SPA ORLEANS** is part of Miss Celie's Olde Victorian Inn, a bed-and-breakfast whose only downside for runners is its distance from the Superdome. The spa has not only typical Swedish and deep-tissue massages, but also the very New Orleans past-life-regression massage. Costs range from $75 to $120. Finish up in the VooBrew coffeehouse by having a psychic read your future in coffee grounds. And say hello to the spa manager—a bulldog named Sadie Chanel. ✉ 914 N. Rampart St., French Quarter ☎ 504/522–7288 ⊕ www.spaorleans.com.

SPA AT THE RITZ CARLTON. Let your aches melt away in the sauna, steam, and elegant relaxation rooms. Indulge in signature treatments like the Essence of Magnolia—a milky, magnolia-scented bath followed by a hot oil Swedish massage. Costs range from $100 to $150. If you make a day of it, grab a bite in the Spa Cafe, where robes are the attire de rigueur. Reserve treatments at least a week in advance. ✉ 921 Canal St., French Quarter ☎ 504/670–2929 ⊕ www.ritzcarlton.com.

a day. Cars pass every 10 minutes 7 AM–8 PM, every half hour 8 PM–midnight, and every hour midnight–7 AM. It's a great way to explore Uptown and the Garden District. A third streetcar line runs along Canal Street, starting several blocks from the river and continuing all the way to City Park.

One-way streetcar fare is $1.25 (exact change); one-day and three-day VisiTour passes are available at $5 and $12, respectively, for unlimited rides on streetcars and RTA buses. The one-day pass is available from streetcar operators. Note that streetcar service may be interrupted the morning of the race. For information on schedules and passes check information centers at hotels and stores or contact the **Regional Transit Authority** (RTA; ☎ 504/248–3900, 504/242–2600 automated information ⊕ www.norta.com).

SAIL OLD MUDDY. Want to sightsee without moving a muscle? Try a riverboat cruise. **New Orleans Paddlewheels** (☎ 504/524–0814 or 800/445–4109 ⊕ www.neworleanspaddlewheels.com) has several paddle-wheel and riverboat cruises, including a battlefield cruise, dinner jazz cruise, and harbor cruise. Prices range from $15 to $53, depending on the cruise and if you order a meal. The ticket office is near the Riverwalk.

The **New Orleans Steamboat Company** (☎ 800/233–2628 or 504/586–8777 ⊕ www.steamboatnatchez.com ✉ $18.50–$54, depending on the cruise) offers two-hour narrated and jazz cruises up and down the Mississippi on the *Natchez,* an authentic paddle wheeler. Ticket sales and departures for the *Natchez* are at the Toulouse Street Wharf behind Jackson Brewery.

Shop Around

Store hours are generally from 10 to 5:30 or 6 PM Monday through Saturday and noon to 5 on Sunday. At malls and in areas with active nightlife, such as the French Quarter, many stores stay open until 7 PM and beyond.

Areas

CBD & WAREHOUSE DISTRICT. Amid the high-tech and boutique hotels that fill the CBD, you'll find tony malls, middle- and high-end chain stores, and artisans' studios. Nearby, in the heart of the Warehouse District, art and crafts galleries line Julia Street, the premier avenue of the arts for New Orleans, and spill over into the adjoining areas.

FRENCH QUARTER. In these blocks lined with narrow storefronts, the shopping experience is as much a treasure hunt as a well-scripted scenario. Stores selling fine art and photography, made-to-order perfumes, or custom-made hats may well sit beside those selling used CDs (and even records), feather boas and Mardi Gras masks, toy soldiers, or books on voodoo. The Quarter is also well known for its fine antiques shops, most of which are on Royal and Chartres streets. Stroll at will. And don't feel compelled to rush: a bistro, café, or coffee shop is always nearby. The **Royal Street Guild** (☎ 504/524–1260 ⊕ www.royalstreetguild.com), a merchants' association, distributes informative brochures in shops and hotels. **Macon Riddle** (☎ 504/899–3027 ⊕ www.neworleansantiquing.com) is a one-woman antiques and collectibles encyclopedia. She shares her expertise in half- or full-day shopping expeditions tailored to your needs.

MAGAZINE STREET. Named for the French word for shop (*magasin*), this street's 6-mile stretch includes dozens of intriguing antiques and jewelry shops, bric-a-brac vendors, and art galleries. Bus 11 runs here from Canal, and the St. Charles streetcar stops within blocks of the district. The most convenient way to shop, however, is by car, because of the length of the district and the fact that some blocks are residential. The **Magazine Street Merchants Association** (☎ 800/387–8924 ⊕ www.magazinestreet.com) publishes a free brochure with maps and store descriptions. You'll find it in most hotels.

MAPLE STREET/RIVERBEND. This area exudes an old-fashioned, small-town feeling. On Maple Street stores run for six blocks, from Carrollton to Cherokee Street; in Riverbend, they dot the streets surrounding the shopping center on Carrollton. To reach the Riverbend from downtown, take the streetcar until St. Charles Avenue runs into Carrollton Avenue. (Be sure to look for the Camellia Grill; ⇨ Replenishing 2,620 Calories, *above*.) The streetcar's next stop is at the corner of Maple Street and Carrollton.

Markets & Malls

CANAL PLACE. At the river end of Canal Street and the edge of the French Quarter, this upscale mall has more than 60 shops, mostly national chains, including Saks Fifth Avenue, Gucci, Williams-Sonoma, Pottery Barn, Banana Republic, Ann Taylor, and Brooks Brothers. It also has a movie theater that screens independent films and a repertory theater that stages local productions. ✉ 333 Canal St., CBD ☎ 504/522–9200 ⊕ www.theshopsatcanalplace.com.

FRENCH MARKET. The market's sounds, colors, and smells are alluring: street performers, ships' horns on the river, pralines, muffulettas, sugarcane. The extravaganza stretches along Decatur and North Peters streets from Café du Monde to the edge of the Quarter. In the Farmers' Market pavilion the seasonal produce includes pecans, mirlitons, creole tomatoes, strawberries, and okra. Garlic wreaths hang from the rafters of the building where the great chefs of New Orleans shop for their kitchens. After a block or so the produce gives way to a flea market, filled with bargain collectibles, jewelry, posters, CDs, and handicrafts. ☎ 504/522–2621 ⊕ www.frenchmarket.org ◷ Daily 7–7; hrs vary depending on season and weather.

JAX BREWERY. A historic building that once was a factory for Jax beer now is the anchor for connected indoor malls with a mix of local shops and national chains. The Brewhouse is home to a Virgin Megastore, plus stores that sell locally inspired fashions and souvenirs. ✉ 600 Decatur St., French Quarter ☎ 504/566–7245 ⊕ www.jacksonbrewery.com.

NEW ORLEANS CENTRE. National chains are represented with Macy's, Ann Taylor, Ashley Stewart, Foot Locker, and others, but there also are tourist-oriented souvenir spots, including Mardi Gras Madness, N'Awlin's Gifts, and Crescent City Collectables. ✉ 1400 Poydras St., CBD ☎ 504/568–0000.

RIVERWALK MARKETPLACE. Once the site of the 1984 World's Fair International Pavilion, Riverwalk provides a scenic view of the Mississippi from its long balcony and a half-mile stretch of shops and restaurants that include local businesses such as Café du Monde and souvenir-laden stores as well as such national chains as Abercrombie & Fitch, Gap, Banana Republic, and Bebe. ✉ 1 Poydras St., Warehouse District ☎ 504/522–1555 ⊕ www.riverwalkmarketplace.com.

I Love the Nightlife

There's no better place to be decadent than the Big Easy, even on a post-marathon Sunday. In New Orleans, Sunday night is as good as any other for some of the best live music, dancing, drinking, and just generally letting loose you'll find anywhere.

Absolutely see a live music show. Music has a rich tradition here. This is the city that cradled jazz and helped birth the blues. Louis Armstrong, Louis Prima, Harry Connick Jr., and Dr. John all played in the small, cramped clubs of New Orleans before hitting it big. Members of the Marsalis and Neville families are popular regulars on the entertainment circuit. Head to the Quarter or the Marigny, where sets start as early as 6 PM and can go on all night. To find out who's playing where, catch the music calendar that's broadcast daily at the top of each odd hour on WWOZ, 90.7 FM. There are also music listings in the *Times-Picayune* daily paper and in *Gambit*, the alternative weekly that appears on Sunday and is carried free in many bars, cafés, and stores. The monthly *OffBeat* magazine has in-depth music coverage and listings and is available in many spots. As the month goes on, however, its listings become less reliable.

Wherever you go, bring cash. You might have to pay a cover, you'll certainly want to buy drinks, and not all places take credit cards. And remember that in New Orleans, it's legal to carry open drinks on the street as long as they're in plastic containers (look for "go cups" at the doors of clubs and bars). The only thing to stop you from taking your beverage from one club to the next will probably be a bouncer. Clubs want you to buy drinks from their own bars rather than sip something from a competitor.

French Quarter

The classic place to go is Bourbon Street, the only place in the Quarter where you'll find neon, which lends the street a Las Vegas–meets-frat-party feel. Sure, it can be tacky and trashy. Yes, there are strip clubs. But it's still a great place to find live bands performing music of every type. Listen for the styles that you like best, then pop in and enjoy.

CAROUSEL REVOLVING BAR. A veritable institution, this piano bar in the Monteleone Hotel has a revolving carousel that serves as a centerpiece, with the bar stools revolving around the service area. The weak of stomach can opt for stationary seating beyond the carousel. On nights when the pianist is on duty, be prepared to join in the sing-alongs. ⊠ 214 Royal St., French Quarter ☎ 504/523-3341.

★ **DONNA'S BAR & GRILL.** Donna's is a great place to hear traditional jazz, R&B, and the city's young brass bands in an informal neighborhood setting. On Monday night many of the city's top musicians stop by after their regular gigs to sit in for the diverse sets of drummer Bob French; free red beans and rice are served. ⊠ 800 N. Rampart St., French Quarter ☎ 504/596-6914 ⊕ www.donnasbarandgrill.com.

FUNKY BUTT AT CONGO SQUARE. Named after jazz pioneer Buddy Bolden's signature tune and housed in art deco splendor, this club is a top spot for contemporary jazz. Local talent and local connoisseurs are both plentiful; Jason Marsalis, of the local musical dynasty, often plays here. ⊠ 714 N. Rampart St., French Quarter ☎ 504/558-0872 ⊕ www.funkybutt.com.

NAPOLEON HOUSE BAR AND CAFE. This vintage watering hole has long been popular with writers, artists, and other free spirits. Locals who wouldn't be caught dead on Bourbon Street come to this shrine of faded grandeur. Murmuring ceiling fans, diffused light, and a tiny patio create a timeless escapist mood. The house specialty is a Pimm's Cup cocktail; a menu including sandwiches, soups, salads, and cheese boards is also available. Come for late-afternoon people-watching, an evening nightcap, or the beginning of an up-until-dawn bender. ⊠ 500 Chartres St., French Quarter ☎ 504/524-9752.

PALM COURT JAZZ CAFÉ. Banjo player Danny Barker immortalized this restaurant in his song "Palm Court Strut." The best of traditional New Orleans jazz is presented in a classy setting with tile floors, exposed brick walls, and a handsome mahogany bar. There are decent creature comforts; regional cuisine is served, and you can sit at the bar and rub elbows with local musicians. ⊠ 1204 Decatur St., French Quarter ☎ 504/525-0200.

PAT O'BRIEN'S. One of the biggest tourist spots in town is home to the oversize alcoholic beverage known as the Hurricane. Many take their glass home as a souvenir; be aware that the deposit charged at the time of purchase should be refunded if you opt to leave yours behind. Actually five bars in one, Pat O's claims to sell more liquor than any other establishment in the world. The bar on the left through the entrance is popular with Quarterites, the patio in the rear draws the young (and young at heart) in temperate months, and the piano bar on the right side of the brick corridor packs in raucous celebrants year-round. ✉ 718 St. Peter St., French Quarter ☎ 504/525-4823 ⊕ www.patobriens.com.

★ **PRESERVATION HALL.** The jazz tradition that flowered in the 1920s is enshrined in this cultural landmark by a cadre of distinguished musicians, most of whom were schooled by an ever-dwindling group of elder statesmen who actually played with Louis Armstrong et al. There's limited seating on benches—many patrons end up squatting on the floor or standing in back—and no beverages are served or allowed, but an evening here is an essential New Orleans experience. ✉ 726 St. Peter St., French Quarter ☎ 504/522-2841 or 504/523-8939 ⊕ www.preservationhall.com.

Faubourg Marigny

One of the hippest places for live music is Frenchmen Street in the Marigny. You can easily spend the whole night there, grabbing food and listening to incredible jazz, blues, zydeco, or whatever else might be playing. Although the area where the clubs are is safe enough, getting there from your hotel on foot isn't. Take a cab.

★ **SNUG HARBOR.** This intimate club just outside the Quarter is one of the city's best rooms for soaking up modern jazz, blues, and R&B. It's the home base of such esteemed talent as vocalist Charmaine Neville and pianist-patriarch Ellis Marsalis (father of Wynton and Branford). The dining room is known for its burgers. Budget-conscious types can listen to bands through speakers in the bar to avoid paying the rather high cover. ✉ 626 Frenchmen St., Faubourg Marigny ☎ 504/949-0696 ⊕ www.snugjazz.com.

★ **SPOTTED CAT.** One of the more pleasant places to hear music is on the rattan furniture at the front window of this comfortable little bar. Two bands play per night, and the music ranges from contemplative jazz to sweaty salsa. The vibe varies accordingly. ✉ 623 Frenchmen St., Faubourg Marigny ☎ 504/943-3887.

Elsewhere

CIRCLE BAR. In the tiny living room at this intimate club on Lee Circle, jazz, blues, funk, and experimental groups play just about every night. ✉ 1032 St. Charles Ave., Warehouse District ☎ 504/588-2616.

MICHAUL'S LIVE CAJUN MUSIC RESTAURANT. Michaul's has a huge dance floor on which patient teachers give free Cajun dance lessons until around 11 PM every night but Sunday, mostly to visitors. The Cajun food is authentic if not inventive. ✉ 840 St. Charles Ave., Warehouse District ☎ 504/522-5517 ⊕ www.michauls.com.

★ **MID-CITY BOWLING LANES ROCK 'N' BOWL.** The phrase "Only in New Orleans…" applies to this combination bowling alley and music club. Dancers may spill over into the lanes when a favorite band such as zydeco legend Boozoo Chavis takes the stage. Blues, R&B, rock, swing, and Cajun music are all presented. Thursday is zydeco night, bringing the best musicians in from rural Louisiana. Be sure to ask club owner

John Blancher for a dance lesson. ⊠ 4133 S. Carrollton Ave., Mid-City ☎ 504/482–3133 ⊕ www.rocknbowl.com.

MULATE'S. Across from the convention center, this large restaurant seats 400, and its dance floor swells with couples twirling and two-stepping to authentic Cajun bands. Regulars love to drag first-timers to the floor for impromptu lessons. The home-style Cajun cuisine is good, and the bands play until 10:30 or 11 PM. ⊠ 201 Julia St., Warehouse District ☎ 504/522–1492 ⊕ www.mulates.com.

TIPITINA'S. The original Tip's was founded in the mid-1970s as the home base for Professor Longhair, the pioneering rhythm-and-blues pianist and singer who died in 1980; the club takes its name from one of his most popular songs. A bust of "Fess" stands near the front door; first-timers should place their hand upon his bald head upon entering in a onetime homage. Tip's hosts a variety of local and global acts. For about a decade Bruce Daigrepont has played a weekly Cajun dance on Sunday, 5 PM–9 PM; free red beans and rice are served. ⊠ 501 Napoleon Ave., Uptown ☎ 504/895–8477 ⊕ www.tipitinas.com.

HELPFUL INFO

Air Travel

Louis Armstrong New Orleans International Airport (MSY) is 15 miles west of the city. It's an hour-long drive on the I–10 Expressway during rush hour, about 30 minutes at other times. A cab to uptown or downtown New Orleans costs $28 for the first two passengers, then $12 for each additional passenger. There may be an additional charge for extra baggage. Pickup is on the lower level, outside the baggage-claim area.

Shuttle-bus service between the airport and downtown hotels is available through New Orleans Tours Airport Shuttle. Buses leave regularly from the ground-floor level near the baggage claim. To return to the airport, call 24 hours in advance of flight time. The cost one-way is $13 per person, and the trip takes about 40 minutes.

🚩 **Louis Armstrong New Orleans International Airport** ⊠ 900 Airline Dr., Kenner ☎ 504/464–0831. **New Orleans Tours Airport Shuttle** ☎ 504/522–3500.

Bus & Streetcar Travel

Greyhound has one terminal in the city, in the Union Passenger Terminal in the CBD. Check with your local Greyhound ticket office for prices and schedules.

The RTA operates public buses and streetcars with interconnecting lines throughout the city. Vehicles are generally clean and on time. Buses and streetcars run 24 hours a day, though waits can be as long as an hour or more in the earliest hours. Smoking, eating, and drinking are not permitted on RTA vehicles. Those who violate this rule may pay a hefty fine or get pulled off the bus and arrested. Buses and streetcars are wheelchair accessible, with the exception of the St. Charles streetcar line.

Bus and streetcar fare is $1.25 exact change plus 25¢ for transfers. Senior citizens 65 or over who have a valid Medicare ID card may ride public transit for only 40¢. Unlimited passes cost $5 for one day, $12 for three days, and $55 for a month. The daily passes are available from streetcar and bus operators; three-day passes are available at many hotels; monthly passes must be purchased from official vendors, including all local Whitney Banks.

✈ **Greyhound** Union Passenger Terminal, ⊠ 1001 Loyola Ave. ☎ 800/231-2222 ⊕ www. greyhound.com. **RTA** ☎ 504/248-3900, 504/242-2600 automated information ⊕ www. norta.com.

Car Travel

You really don't need to rent a car, because it's so easy to get around town on foot, by public transportation, or by cab. If you do have a car, carefully read street signs in the French Quarter and CBD; tickets are quickly written. Parking is fairly easy everywhere but the Quarter, where meter maids are plentiful and tow trucks are eager. If in doubt about a space, pass it up and pay to use a lot. Avoid spaces at corners and curbs: less than 15 feet between your car and the corner will result in a ticket.

I-10 runs from Florida to California and passes directly through the city. To get to the CBD, exit at Poydras Street near the Louisiana Superdome. For the French Quarter, look for the Orleans Avenue/Vieux Carré exit.

Disabilities & Accessibility

Curbs are cut on most corners in the French Quarter and CBD. In the Garden District the terrain is flat, but not all curbs are cut and the sidewalks are badly cracked by the roots of the many live oaks. Audubon Zoo, the Aquarium of the Americas, and the riverboats are all accessible. Gray Line has tour buses that accommodate visitors with mobility, hearing, and visual impairments.

✈ **LOCAL RESOURCES Advocacy Center for the Elderly and Disabled** ☎ 800/960-7705 [also TTY], 504/522-2337 [also TTY] ⊕ www.advocacyla.org. **Easter Seals Society of Louisiana for Children and Adults with Disabilities** ☎ 800/695-7325 [also TTY], 504/ 523-7325 [also TTY] ⊕ www.louisiana.easterseals.com. **Gray Line** ☎ 800/535-7786 or 504/587-0861 ⊕ www.graylineneworleans.com.

Emergencies

✈ **DOCTORS & DENTISTS Charity Hospital & Medical Center of Louisiana** provides 24-hour dental emergency treatment (⇨ Hospitals). For referrals, contact the **New Orleans Dental Association** ☎ 504/834-6449 ⊕ www.nodental.org. **Touro Infirmary** ☎ 504/ 897-7777 has a physician-referral service available weekdays 8-5 (⇨ Hospitals).

✈ **HOSPITALS Charity Hospital & Medical Center of Louisiana** ⊠ 1532 Tulane Ave. ☎ 504/903-3000. **Touro Infirmary** ⊠ 1401 Foucher St. ☎ 504/897-7011 or 504/897-8250. **Tulane University Medical Center** ⊠ 1415 Tulane Ave. ☎ 504/588-5711.

◪ **PHARMACIES Royal Pharmacy** ✉ 1101 Royal St., French Quarter ☎ 504/523–5401. **Walgreens** ✉ 900 Canal St., French Quarter ☎ 504/568–1271 ✉ 1801 St. Charles Ave. [24-hr pharmacy], Garden District ☎ 504/561–8458.

Taxis

Cabs are metered at $2.50 minimum for two passengers, plus $1 for each additional passenger and $1.60 per mile. It's very difficult to hail a cab. Either catch one outside a hotel or call one. United Cabs is your best bet, but be aware that they often get swamped with calls and you might get repeated busy signals. Keep trying.

◪ **CAB COMPANY United Cabs** ☎ 504/522–9771.

Train Travel

Three major Amtrak lines arrive at and depart from New Orleans's Union Passenger Terminal. The *Crescent* makes daily runs from New York to New Orleans by way of Washington, D.C. The *City of New Orleans* runs daily between New Orleans and Chicago. The *Sunset Limited* makes the two-day trip from Los Angeles to New Orleans en route to Orlando. It departs from New Orleans traveling westward on Monday, Wednesday, and Friday and leaves Los Angeles on Sunday, Wednesday, and Friday. Trains arrive at and depart from New Orleans's Union Passenger Terminal in the heart of the CBD.

◪ **TRAIN INFORMATION Amtrak** ☎ 800/872–7245 ⊕ www.amtrak.com. **Union Passenger Terminal** ✉ 1001 Loyola Ave. ☎ 504/524–7571.

CHAPTER 3

MARCH

City of Los Angeles Marathon

Think of Los Angeles, and you think of the beach, Rodeo Drive, movie stars, and Hollywood.

You get none of that in the L.A. Marathon.

Check that—you may well get movie stars. Several have run or otherwise been involved with the L.A. Marathon. Dennis Quaid and Scott Bakula have both raced, and Halle Berry volunteered at an aid station in 2005.

The possibility of a celebrity running mate aside, there's not much glitz at

VISITOR INFO

L.A. Inc./The Convention
and Visitors Bureau

☎

213/624-7300 or
800/228-2452

⊕

www.lacvb.com

the city's major racing event. The course starts downtown—not the hub it is in most cities—and loops through many areas that would never make it onto any self-respecting sightseeing tour. The starting queue is crowded, the temperatures can be high, and the 8-ish start can push slower runners into the day's worst sun. This race has its flaws, which might be why elite runners don't flock here the way they do to Boston or Chicago.

But the L.A. Marathon isn't made for the elites. It's made for the pack. There's a palpable energy shared among the runners, volunteers, and spectators. Entertainment and aid stations remain open until everyone has finished, whether it's in 3:35 or 8:14. Instead of "movie star" L.A., the race showcases "real" L.A.: a smorgasbord of ethnic communities, each pouring into the streets to cheer with its own flair. In this sprawling town of fiercely individual interests, the marathon creates a community, and for one day it feels like the whole town has a single, uniting goal.

It's a shame it happens only once a year.

So You're Running Los Angeles . . .

Welcome! As an L.A. transplant of 12 years now (long enough to consider myself a native), I promise you'll love it here . . . if you rent a car.

It's best to stay downtown for the marathon and its ancillary events. This area has a lot to offer, but you'll miss out on a great deal if you don't venture farther afield. L.A. has something for everyone: the beach, Griffith Park, and the Santa Monica Mountains for outdoors lovers; television tapings, the HOLLYWOOD sign, and the Walk of Fame for the starstruck; Rodeo Drive for shopaholics. Foodies get a whole host of restaurants, from the swanki-

WEB WISDOM

The City of Los Angeles site (⊕ www.lacity.org) has various entertainment and cultural links. Other helpful sites include ⊕ www.beverlyhillsbehere.com, the site of the Beverly Hills Conference and Visitors Bureau; ⊕ www.santamonica.com, site of the Santa Monica Convention & Visitors Bureau; and ⊕ www.visitwesthollywood.com, site of the West Hollywood Convention and Visitors Bureau.

est hot spots to the yummiest greasy spoons. There's even Disneyland, the happiest place on Earth! All these phenomenal places scream "L.A." (OK—Disneyland's actually in Orange County), but they're nowhere near one another. Reaching them all via public transportation would be a nightmare, so budget for a rental car.

Dorothy Parker described Los Angeles as "72 suburbs in search of a city." It's tough, if not impossible, to define the "true" Los Angeles; your best bet is learning a little about the individual areas that make up this sprawling behemoth.

DOWNTOWN. The multicultural pockets, museums, and historic buildings of downtown make it worth a visit. You'll get the basic flavor as you run the race, but spots such as Olvera Street and the Walt Disney Concert Hall deserve even greater attention.

HOLLYWOOD. If you're expecting the glamour of the film industry's golden days, you'll be disappointed. That said, Hollywood has a new-mixed-with-vintage flavor all its own. The Walk of Fame, Grauman's Chinese Theatre, the Hollywood Bowl, El Capitan Theatre, and the Capitol Records Tower are reminders of the neighborhood's romantic past, and stabs at revitalization continue to bring interesting new things to the area.

WEST HOLLYWOOD & WESTSIDE. Drive into Beverly Hills, Bel Air, Brentwood, Westwood, and West L.A., and you'll discover that just looking good isn't enough—looking prosperous is the name of the game. Shop Rodeo Drive, head to Sunset Boulevard or Santa Monica Boulevard in West Hollywood to find hot new restaurants and clubs, or soak up some culture at the dazzling Getty Center.

BEACH CITIES. No matter how far up the Pacific Coast Highway you drive, you're assured dramatic views. Locals flex their muscles, play, and perform on the Venice boardwalk; Santa Monica and Pacific Palisades draw beach lovers; and Malibu is where the rich and famous hide away in their "colony."

SAN FERNANDO VALLEY. Referred to simply as "the Valley," the San Fernando Valley, northwest of L.A., has a mix of income levels and ethnic groups. The main sightseeing draws are Universal Studios Hollywood, studio tours at Warner Brothers, and TV tapings at NBC.

SAN GABRIEL VALLEY. A visit to Pasadena, in San Gabriel Valley northeast of L.A., is a step back to the early 20th century, when wealthy Easterners built fabulous winter homes here. Old Pasadena, restored and revitalized, is lively. The gardens and art collections at the Huntington estate in San Marino make it a premier destination.

ORANGE COUNTY & CATALINA ISLAND. Southeast of L.A., "the O.C." is home to Disneyland as well as beach and harbor towns such as Huntington Beach, Newport Harbor, the Balboa Peninsula, Laguna Beach, and Dana Point. A short boat ride away is Catalina Island, with its pocket-size town and large nature preserve.

JUST ANOTHER RUNNER

Make no mistake, Scott Bakula is a celebrity. His leading roles on the TV shows *Quantum Leap* and *Enterprise* have earned him legions of fans. Yet in March 2005, Scott was just another runner embarking on the 26.2-mile trek that is the Los Angeles Marathon.

Scott had toyed with the idea of the marathon for years, but something—work, injuries, lack of time—had always gotten in the way. When his 50th birthday started to loom large, though, he began to think about racing again. Training for a marathon would be something new—something that would shake up his metabolism and help him stay in shape. He bought Jeff Galloway's book *Marathon*, which promotes staying injury-free using a run-walk system. The book quickly became Scott's bible, and he and his friend Keith used it to prepare for their first race: the 2004 Rock 'n' Roll Marathon in San Diego.

Though Scott had been a runner in the past, he fell in love with the sport all over again. He found running meditative and loved the time on his own to just think. He'd laugh to himself when he saw other runners carrying cell phones—didn't they *ever* get away from it all? He noticed that the longer he ran, the harder it was to hang onto anger or frustration. "Eventually," he says, "you just run it out." And although running alone was a joy, he also loved his long runs with Keith, their "therapy sessions" talking about their kids and relationships.

The Rock 'n' Roll Marathon was a huge success for Keith and Scott. They stuck to Galloway's program and had a blast. Probably the roughest part was letting go of their egos during their early walk breaks, when it seemed like the whole pack was rushing by. "You get over it," Scott says, especially when the results are so fantastic. He and Keith finished in 4:08, and Scott felt strong enough for a dip in the ocean (the cold water was bliss on his muscles), a swim in the pool with his kids, and a walk to a celebratory dinner. The experience was so stellar that Scott knew immediately he'd tackle the distance again. He and Keith realized they wanted more than just to finish another marathon; they wanted to chase a time. Specifically, they wanted to break 3:45. Maybe even 3:35, which would qualify them for Boston. The race for this challenge? The Los Angeles Marathon.

All through that winter, Scott trained hard. It was a brutal season, filled with torrential downpours that flooded out swaths of L.A. County, including Griffith Park, Scott's training ground of choice. He ran anyway; he needed to know that he could handle hours in the rain, just in case. Sloshing through the deserted park felt like running in an altered world. Although he worked hard to prepare for the race, he's quick to point out that he wasn't alone. Everyone in his life helped by encouraging him to carve out the time he needed to train. By March he felt prepared to meet his goal.

For the first 16 miles of the 2005 L.A. Marathon, everything went according to plan. Scott and Keith cruised, hitting Mile 16 in 2:14—right on target. Scott even did an interview for NBC as they ran. No sweat; he felt great. Then came Mile 18 . . . and Keith started to live the marathoner's nightmare: his body locked up. Stabbing cramps crippled one calf, then the other, then both quads, until finally all these muscles seized at once, hobbling him in his tracks. Looking back, Scott realizes they should have seen it coming. Keith had been fighting a bronchial infection the past several weeks; he'd been flying constantly for work; he'd just moved. This wasn't the time to push for a PR. But here they were at Mile 18, and Keith could barely continue, certainly not at the pace they'd been running. He could have stopped; he must have thought about stopping. But there's a momentum to being in the pack of a marathon, everyone moving inexorably forward toward the finish. Even if you need to slow down, even if you need to walk instead of run, or shuffle instead of walk, you can't help but want to keep moving forward. Keith wanted to keep moving forward. Besides, his kids were waiting for him at the finish. Despite his pain, he was determined to grind it out. With Scott encouraging him and remaining by his side, Keith walked, he jogged, he walked again. He pushed himself through those last 8 miles, and both men crossed the finish line in 4:10.

For Scott, Keith's courageous struggle to finish the race despite the torture in his legs exemplifies the marathon's simple beauty. It's a microcosm of life, both intensely personal and thrillingly communal. When you run this race, you're truly competing with yourself. "We're all doing that every day," Scott says, "competing with growing old, gaining weight, whatever's personal to you." At the same time, even as you tackle this personal challenge, you're part of something bigger, surrounded by people of all ages, all backgrounds, and all body types, all striving for the same goal without (except for the elites) competition. There's no discrimination in the pack, no I'm-better-than-you. "It's a huge communal ideal," Scott says, "everybody for everybody. I don't know where else that exists."

RACE BASICS

L.A. is the country's fourth-largest marathon, with approximately 20,000 runners, 1 million spectators, and 12,000 volunteers. Yet among big-city races, it's still fairly new. It started in 1986, when it drew 10,868 runners (as opposed to the 127 runners who entered New York City's first marathon in 1970). From the first, organizers strived to make the race fun and exciting for everyone. In 1995 they introduced the pre-race Bike Tour, which allows cyclists to ride the marathon course free of auto traffic. In 2005 those who

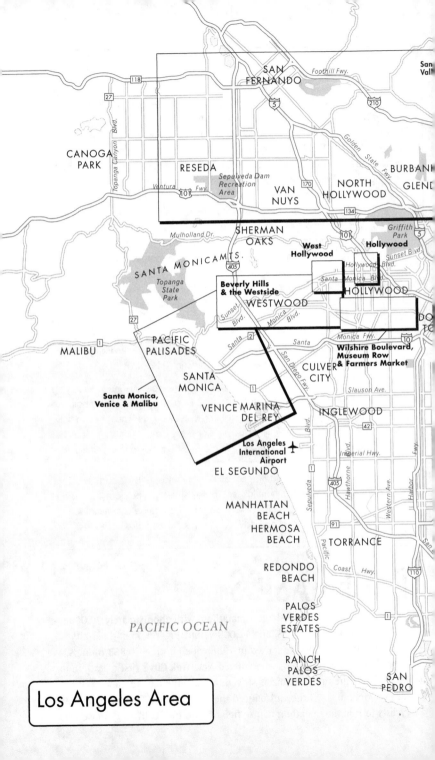

Los Angeles Area

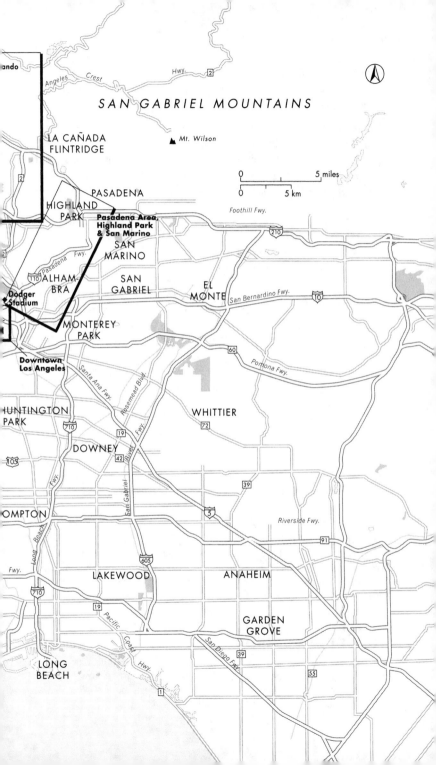

participated in this event *and* the marathon were transported from the cycling finish line to the marathon starting line in the Spa On Wheels, a bus-turned-spa complete with music, snacks, water, and mini-massages.

The 2003 race saw the addition of personalized bibs, so spectators can (and do!) cheer for runners by name. In 2004 the elite women were given just enough of a head start to allow them to finish with the elite men. Since the first person to cross the finish line wins both a hefty bonus and a car, this adjustment makes for a nail-biting climax.

Registration

Registration opens around June 1 the year before each race. Fees are $75 for early registration (until around November 1); $85 from then until mail-in and online registration close (sometime in February); and $95 at the expo. If you want a personalized bib, you must register before December 31. There's no registration cap. The marathon Web site is comprehensive and easy to navigate, with extras like virtual training programs.

RACE CONTACT

Los Angeles Marathon, Inc.

✉
11110 West Ohio Ave.,
Suite 100,
Los Angeles, CA 90025

☎
310/444–5544

🌐
www.lamarathon.com

There are a variety of divisions: runner/walker, wheelchair (open, quad, or crank chair), or racewalker. If you plan to walk or run/walk the course, note that it's not the same as *racewalking*. Those registered in that division must abide by official racewalking rules.

If you've run a marathon in less than five hours in the 12 months before the race, you're eligible for one of three special corrals (sub-3, sub-4, and sub-5 hour) set up for faster nonelites. Send or fax proof of your time to the marathon office within a week of registering for the race. You must register by December 31 to request one of these corrals. The Corporate Competition is open to teams from any industry. There's no limit to the number of full-time employees to a team, though each team must have at least four members.

If you register by the end of February or so, you'll get a confirmation postcard in the mail with your name, bib number, address, division, sex, and age group; contact the marathon about mistakes. (You'll need this postcard and a photo ID to get your bib number at the expo.) You'll also receive marathon newsletters about twice a year. Provide an e-mail address, and you'll get "blasts" filled with race info about 15 times a year.

Hotels to Consider

The only logical place to stay is downtown, where the hotels are within walking distance of the expo and the start and finish lines. If you extend your trip beyond marathon weekend, consider moving to a hotel in the part of L.A. that interests you most. (Check out www.fodors.com for hotel recommendations in other parts of the city.)

THE WHEEL DEAL

The L.A. Marathon's wheelchair division attracts a large field: 56 athletes in 2005. What are the wheelchair divisions? There are differences among races, but in L.A. they break down as follows:

OPEN. Open to paraplegics of all ages in pushrim wheelchairs. The division is separated into Men's and Women's.

QUAD. Open to quadriplegics in pushrim wheelchairs. All ages and both sexes are combined for this division.

CRANK CHAIR. It's often referred to as the Handcycle Division. Athletes in this division race in a machine more similar to a bicycle than a wheelchair. It uses a chain and gears but is operated with the upper body as opposed to the lower. Handcycles are used for the "bike" portion of wheelchair triathlons, and pushrim chairs for the "run."

In some races, both paraplegic and quadriplegic divisions are broken down further (i.e., Quad T1, Quad T2) to ensure that athletes with similar functionality are racing against one another. And "In a perfect world," says a representative of the L.A. Marathon, "we would offer master and senior divisions."

★ **THE DOWNTOWN L.A. STANDARD.** It's designed to amuse with a splashy, tongue-in-cheek style. The large guest rooms have orange built-in couches, windows that actually open, and platform beds. Some have a 2-foot-tall plush toy in the shape of a foot, just to keep you on your toes. Bathrooms have extra-large tubs (which you can fill with Mr. Bubble from the minibar) and are separated from sleeping areas by curtains instead of doors. The rooftop lounge, surrounded by skyscrapers, is downtown's most happening bar. The nighttime bar scene and daytime traffic make many rooms noisy; ask for a room on an upper floor away from the lounge. Special marathoner rates are available. ✉ 550 S. Flower St., Downtown, 90071 ☎ 213/892–8080 ⊕ www.standardhotel.com ⇌ 205 rooms, 2 suites ♿ Restaurant, 24-hr room service, wake-up calls, alarm clocks, robes, cable TV with movies and video games, in-room data ports, in-room safes, minibars, pool, 24-hr gym, massage, 2 bars, lobby lounge, dry cleaning, laundry service, concierge, business services, meeting rooms, parking (fee), some pets allowed, no-smoking floors ▭ AE, D, DC, MC, V ¢–$.

FIGUEROA HOTEL. On the outside, it's Spanish Revival; on the inside, this 1926, 12-story hotel is a mix of Southwestern, Mexican, and Mediterranean styles, with earth tones, hand-painted furniture, and wrought-iron beds. You can lounge around the pool and bubbling hot tub surrounded by greenery and in the shadow of skyscrapers. A soothing beverage from the back patio bar completes the L.A. experience. Since it's reasonably priced and next to the convention center and Staples Center, this hotel books up months in advance of major events. ✉ 939 S. Figueroa St., Downtown, 90015 ☎ 213/627–8971 or 800/421–9092 ⊕ www.figueroahotel.com ⇌ 278 rooms, 8 suites ♿ Restaurant, café, wake-up calls, some fans, cable TV, in-room data ports, refrigerators, Wi-Fi (fee), pool, outdoor hot tub,

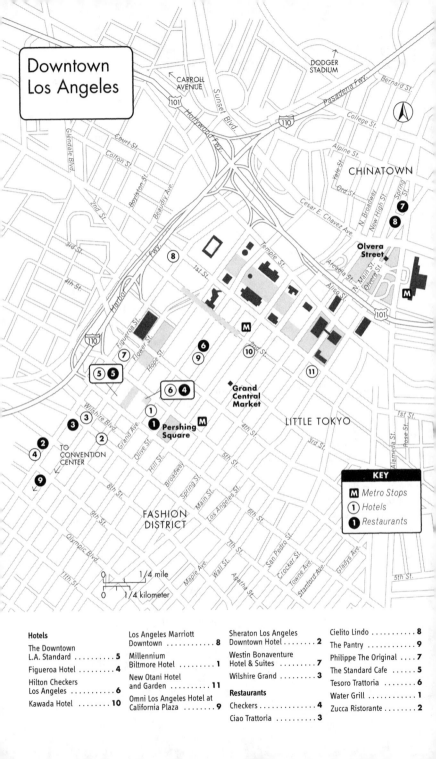

Downtown Los Angeles

CARROLL AVENUE

DODGER STADIUM

CHINATOWN

Olvera Street

Grand Central Market

LITTLE TOKYO

Pershing Square

TO CONVENTION CENTER

FASHION DISTRICT

0   1/4 mile
0   1/4 kilometer

KEY

M Metro Stops
① Hotels
❶ Restaurants

2 bars, dry cleaning, laundry facilities, concierge, parking (fee), no-smoking rooms ▭AE, DC, MC, V $.

★ **HILTON CHECKERS LOS ANGELES.** Opened in 1927, Checkers retains much of its original character. Rooms are various sizes and have period details as well as such modern essentials as pillow-top mattresses, ample lighting, large mirrors, granite-top desks, and cordless phones. A rooftop pool deck overlooks the historic L.A. library and nearby office towers. The plush lobby bar and lounge look as if they belong in a private club, with comfy leather chairs and a large plasma-screen TV. In the mornings, take advantage of complimentary car service to travel anywhere within a 1-mile radius. Marathoners can enjoy high-carb options on all hotel menus. ⊠ 535 S. Grand Ave., Downtown, 90071 ☎ 213/624-0000 or 800/445-8667 ⊕ www.hiltoncheckers.com ⟿ 183 rooms, 5 suites ⚘ Restaurant, 24-hr room service, wake-up calls, alarm clocks, coffeemakers, newspapers weekdays, robes, cable TV with movies and video games, in-room data ports, minibars, pool, 24-hr gym, outdoor hot tub, sauna, spa, steam room, bar, dry cleaning, laundry service, concierge, business services, meeting room, parking (fee), some pets allowed (fee), no-smoking floors ▭AE, D, DC, MC, V $-$$$.

KAWADA HOTEL. This eclectic, four-story redbrick hotel is near the Music Center and local government buildings. Immaculate guest rooms are on the small side but have two phones and a wet bar. ⊠ 200 S. Hill St., Downtown, 90012 ☎ 213/621-4455 or 800/752-9232 ⊕ www.kawadahotel.com ⟿ 116 rooms ⚘ 3 restaurants, room service, wake-up calls, alarm clocks, cable TV, in-room data ports, in-room VCRs, some kitchenettes, refrigerators, laundry facilities, laundry service, concierge, business services, meeting room, parking (fee); no smoking floors ▭AE, D, DC, MC, V ¢.

LOS ANGELES MARRIOTT DOWNTOWN. Very close to the marathon starting and finish lines, the 14-story, glass-walled Marriott has large guest rooms with marble baths and huge windows. If you've grown weary of standard breakfast fare, the Japanese buffet (miso soup and salmon) puts a spin on the morning meal. Marathoners will enjoy "carbed-up" menus in the hotel restaurants and room service, plus free bottled water in the hotel driveway on both pre-race mornings (for early morning runs) and on marathon day. ⊠ 333 S. Figueroa St., Downtown, 90071 ☎ 213/617-1133 or 800/228-9290 ⊕ www.marriott.com ⟿ 400 rooms, 69 suites ⚘ 3 restaurants, room service, wake-up calls, alarm clocks, coffeemakers, newspapers, robes, cable TV with movies, in-room data ports, in-room safes, minibars, pool, 24-hr gym, bar, piano bar, cinemas, laundry service, concierge, concierge floors, business services, meeting rooms, parking (fee), no-smoking floors ▭AE, D, MC, V $$.

✦ **MILLENNIUM BILTMORE HOTEL.** Built in 1923, this beaux-arts masterpiece has a storied past. The lobby (formerly the Music Room) was the headquarters of JFK's presidential campaign, and the ballroom hosted some of the earliest Academy Awards. Guest rooms are classically styled with upholstered headboards, shuttered windows, and marble bathrooms. They also have such high-tech amenities as CD players and cordless phones. Marathoner perks include a night-before pasta buffet and marathon morning "carbo bags" (each has a bagel, cream cheese, a banana, and a bottle of water) that go on sale as early as 6 AM. ⊠ 506 S. Grand Ave., Downtown, 90071 ☎ 213/624-1011 or 866/866-8086 ⊕ www.millennium-hotels.com ⟿ 655 rooms, 28 suites ⚘ 2 restaurants, café, 24-hr room service, wake-up calls, alarm clocks, coffeemakers, cable TV with movies and video games, in-room data ports, in-room safes, minibars, indoor pool, gym, hot tub, spa, bar, lobby lounge, sports bar, shops, babysitting, laundry service, concierge, concierge floor, business services, meeting rooms, car rental, parking (fee), no-smoking floors ▭AE, D, DC, MC, V $–$$.

NEW OTANI HOTEL AND GARDEN. On the edge of Little Tokyo, the New Otani isn't as race-convenient as some hotels, but it's truly unique, and it offers excellent marathon discounts. The Japanese Experience rooms have tatami mats, futon beds, extra-deep tubs, and shoji window screens. The American-style rooms are somewhat plain, but you can liven things up with a tea service and shiatsu massage. The hotel also provides marathoners with complimentary bottled water. Two restaurants serve authentic Japanese cuisine; a third has Continental fare. If you want a contemplative pre-race moment, there's a ½-acre Japanese garden on the roof. ✉ 120 S. Los Angeles St., Little Tokyo, 90012 ☎ 213/629–1200 or 800/639–6826 ⊕ www.newotani.com ⋗ 414 rooms, 20 suites ♨ 3 restaurants, room service, wake-up calls, alarm clocks, coffeemakers, newspapers, cable TV with movies, in-room data ports, in-room safes, minibars, gym, hot tub, spa, 2 bars, shops, dry cleaning, laundry service, concierge, business services, meeting rooms, car rental, parking (fee), no-smoking rooms ▭AE, D, DC, MC, V $$.

OMNI LOS ANGELES HOTEL AT CALIFORNIA PLAZA. The 17-story Omni is steps from the Museum of Contemporary Art and the Los Angeles Philharmonic's new home, the Disney Hall. Rooms are airy and have a cheery, California-casual look. Ask for a western view to take full advantage of the floor-to-ceiling windows. A free town car takes you anywhere within a 3-mi radius. Ask about Get Fit rooms, with such amenities as portable treadmills and healthful minibar snacks. Even better, schedule a post-race deep-tissue or hot-stone treatment. ✉ 251 S. Olive St., Downtown, 90012 ☎ 213/617–3300 or 800/442–5251 ⊕ www.omnihotels.com ⋗ 439 rooms, 14 suites ♨ 2 restaurants, 24-hr room service, wake-up calls, alarm clocks, coffeemakers, newspapers, robes, cable TV with movies and video games, in-room data ports, minibars, free Wi-Fi, pool, gym, hot tub, massage, bar, shops, babysitting, dry cleaning, laundry service, concierge, concierge floor, business services, meeting rooms, car rental, parking (fee), some pets allowed (fee), no-smoking floors ▭AE, D, DC, MC, V $$.

SHERATON LOS ANGELES DOWNTOWN HOTEL. Windows with dramatic city views jazz up the mahogany- and cherrywood-filled rooms at this hotel near the convention center and Staples Center. It's also close to the race start and finish lines, and marathoners get a special room rate. Concierge-level guests will enjoy a complimentary Continental breakfast and evening hors d'oeuvres. ✉ 711 S. Hope St., Downtown, 90017 ☎ 213/488–3500 ⊕ www.starwoodhotels.com ⋗ 444 rooms, 41 suites ♨ 2 restaurants, room service, wake-up calls, alarm clocks, coffeemakers, cable TV, in-room data ports, refrigerators, gym, hot tub, lounge, dry cleaning, laundry service, concierge, concierge floor, business services, meeting rooms, car rental, parking (fee), some pets allowed (fee), no-smoking floors ▭AE, D, DC, MC, V $$$.

WESTIN BONAVENTURE HOTEL & SUITES. L.A.'s largest hotel is very close to the marathon start. It has five towers—each one mirrored, cylindrical, and 35 stories tall. Inside the futuristic lobby are fountains, a lake, a track, and 12 glass elevators. Color-coded hotel floors and numerous signs help you navigate. Standard rooms are small but have floor-to-ceiling windows, many with terrific views. Ask for maps by *Runner's World*, which show 3- and 5-mile routes from the hotel. ⊠ 404 S. Figueroa St., Downtown, 90071 ☎ 213/624–1000 or 800/937–8461 ⊕ www.westin.com ⬎ 1,218 rooms, 135 suites ◬ 17 restaurants, 24-hr room service, wake-up calls, alarm clocks, coffeemakers, in-room data ports, newspapers weekdays, robes, cable TV with movies, in-room safes, pool, 24-hr gym, spa, hair salon, 5 bars, shops, laundry service, concierge, business services, meeting rooms, airport shuttle, car rental, travel services, parking (fee), some pets allowed (fee), no-smoking rooms ⊟ AE, D, DC, MC, V $–$$.

✹ **WILSHIRE GRAND HOTEL & CENTRE.** The official hotel of the Los Angeles Marathon is wedged in among the other high-rises at the start of Wilshire Boulevard, just two blocks from the Staples Center and the convention center. The independently operated, 16-story hotel prides itself on extraordinary service. The Kyoto restaurant serves Japanese cuisine, and Seoul Jung has Korean barbecue. Point Moorea, the lower-lobby bar, makes good martinis and attracts a lively after-work crowd. ⊠ 930 Wilshire Blvd., Downtown, 90017 ☎ 213/688–7777 or 888/773–2888 ⊕ www.wilshiregrand.com ⬎ 866 rooms, 34 suites ◬ 4 restaurants, café, room service, wake-up calls, alarm clocks, cable TV with movies and video games, in-room data ports, free Wi-Fi, pool, 24-hr gym, hair salon, outdoor hot tub, bar, shops, dry cleaning, laundry service, concierge, concierge floor, business services, meeting rooms, car rental, travel services, parking (fee), no-smoking floors ⊟ AE, D, DC, MC, V $$.

AND YOU'RE OFF . . .

The Expo

The expo is held at the L.A. Convention Center for three days before the race and is touted on the marathon Web site as "the largest marathon expo in the world." Music fills the room as you enter, and huge booths vie for your attention: rows of cars from Honda, a pavilion of hot new gadgets from HP, a climbing wall sponsored by the U.S. Army. Walking the aisles is like shopping a giant discount bazaar. It seems like any product you could dream up is here: sports drinks, running gear, massage chairs . . . even cutlery and dog food. Come hungry since you'll end up sampling nuts, energy bars and drinks, rice dishes—the list goes on. Prepare for crowds; the expo attracts more than 80,000 people. Visit Thursday or early Friday to miss the mob.

Expo seminars are terrific. Notable ones have been "Overcoming Adversity" conducted by Jeremy Newman, a wheelchair marathoner and world-class triathlete (⇨ Anyone Can Run a Marathon, *below*); "Improving Your Race Day Performance" led by Olympic gold medalist Joan Benoit Samuelson; and, my favorite, "Training with Your Dog" by pet nutrition expert Lisa Dunn. Seminar schedules are posted on the marathon Web site a few weeks before the race, and the marathon office can e-mail or fax you a copy. The schedule is also printed in the expo program, which you pick up as you enter the hall.

If you want to hit a certain race time, look into the Clif Bar Pace Team (www.clifbar.com). Pace group leaders run the marathon in anywhere from 3:10 to 5:30, with eight increments in between. There's no cost to join a group, and you can do so at the expo or online. Check out the Clif Bar Web site and/or stop by the pace team booth at the expo to talk to the leaders—all experienced athletes with a healthy sense of fun. Note that signing up online gets you swag: a free training kit with product samples and conditioning tips.

Race Day

The Course

The race begins at Sixth and Figueroa, right by the famous Bonaventure Hotel (a great place for a pit stop if you want to avoid the portable toilets, though expect a wait). The opening corrals are crowded and seem to stretch forever, but everything is well organized, so it's not hard to get where you need to go.

READY, SET . . . STOP?

Be sure the starter gun is really a starter gun. In 1989, a balloon popped, and the whole field took off early. Incredibly, officials wrangled everyone back for the *real* start.

As you stand in your corral, shoulder to shoulder with hordes of other runners, all bubbling with excitement, the other divisions begin. First the pushrim wheelchair athletes, then the elite women, followed by the hand-crank wheelchair athletes. Then, at around quarter after eight, you'll hear the *crack* of a starter gun, the blaring lilt of Randy Newman's "I Love L.A." . . . and you're off, making your way past throngs of cheering spectators as you begin your 26.2-mile journey.

The first 9 miles are mostly downhill. You'll find ups and downs from Mile 9 to 15, but nothing too arduous. Although the last 11.2 miles are essentially uphill, the slope is gradual, and several downhill patches ease the way. As I've mentioned, the L.A. Marathon takes you nowhere near the most famous sights. You won't see the beach, you won't see Hollywood, you won't see Rodeo Drive. You *will*, however, see many landmarks that are just as iconic in their own way.

Soon after the start you'll whip past the Staples Center, home of the L.A. Lakers and Clippers. Around Mile 10 you'll reach "Gospel Road," a stretch of Crenshaw about a half mile long, lined with gospel choirs who come out in force to inspire you. On a good day you can catch a glimpse of the HOLLYWOOD sign around Mile 11. Look up and to the right—it's to the northeast, up in the hills.

As you turn between Miles 11 and 12 and start heading west, the marathon media guide says you can see "a panoramic view from the Hollywood Hills past the Century City skyline to the sea." That sounds lovely, but don't expect to hear waves crashing; you're very much inland. Around Miles 18 and 19, you have a view of the La Brea Tar Pits, where replicas of woolly mammoths and other ancient creatures sit in the mire. Soon after, you enter the homestretch back to downtown, passing the old mansions of Hancock Park, then Koreatown.

NIGHT-BEFORE PASTA DINNER

Carbo-load-dinner tickets are $20, and as there are only 1,500 available, it's best to buy them when you register for the race. The all-you-can-eat dinner in the ballroom of the Wilshire Grand includes salad, chicken, pasta dishes, breakfast cereals, and desserts. While you eat enjoy live entertainment and video highlights from past races. Seatings are at 5 PM and 6:30 PM. There are also great downtown pasta restaurants, including:

CIAO TRATTORIA. A full menu of Italian classics, including such pre-race-friendly fare as capellini *con pollo e pomodoro* (with chicken breast in a fresh tomato and basil sauce). They add wheat pastas to the menu at marathon time. Non-pasta entrées include veal, chicken, and fish dishes, such as halibut seared and roasted on a bed of steamed vegetables. ⊠ 815 W. Seventh St., Downtown ☎ 213/624–2244 ⊕ www.ciaotrattoria.com ▤ AE, DC, MC, V $–$$$.

TESORO TRATTORIA. Although many of the pasta options here are made with cream sauce, there are a few lighter options, such as angel hair pasta with fresh tomatoes, basil, and garlic. If you aren't carbo loading, there are plenty of other options, including lamb chops, filet mignon, or seafood. ⊠ 300 S. Grand Ave., Downtown ☎ 213/680–0000 ⊕ www.tesorotrattoria.com ▤ AE, D, DC, MC, V $–$$$.

ZUCCA RISTORANTE. Here superchef-restaurateur Joachim Splichal turns his attention to Italian cuisine, leavening sophistication with earthy flavors. The exquisite Murano glass chandeliers and mural of a Venetian carnival scene energize the seductive, albeit noisy, dining room. Consider such dishes as pumpkin tortelloni—*zucca*, after all, is "pumpkin" in Italian—with butter-sage sauce, osso buco, and a lovely *branzino* (striped bass) from the wood-burning oven. The restaurant also offers many healthful pasta options for pre-race carbo-loads. ⊠ 801 S. Figueroa St., Downtown ☎ 213/614–7800 ⌬ Reservations essential ▤ AE, D, DC, MC, V ⊘ Closed Sun. No lunch Sat. $$–$$$.

But it's not the scenery that makes this marathon so great. It's the people. The support for this race is fantastic. About a million spectators pour into the streets to cheer you on. Volunteers man 25 water stations. Starting at Mile 3 sports drinks are available at every other station. There are two energy-gel zones, one at Mile 10, the other at Mile 18. And at Mile 19, as you near "the wall," you'll find a pain-relief zone, where volunteers spray aching runners with topical analgesic. If you need more serious treatment, there are eight medical vans along the course as well as medical tents and another pain-relief zone at the finish area. Portable toilets appear at every mile.

When it comes to entertainment, Tinseltown doesn't disappoint. There are 10 major entertainment centers on the course, each showcasing a different culture. Recent centers

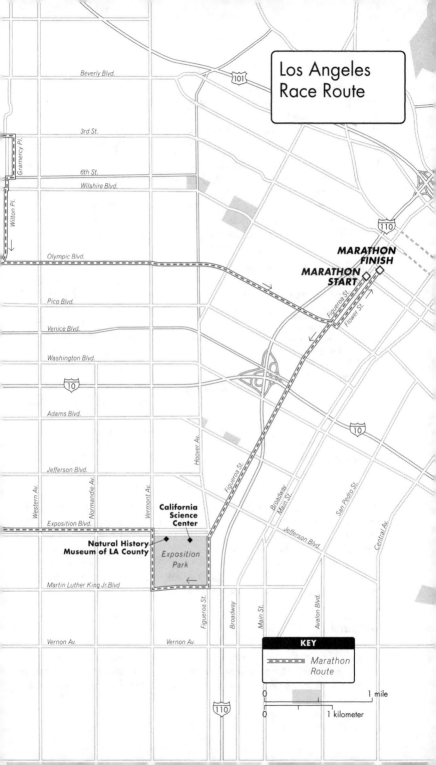

were brought to life by the Japanese, Chinese, Mexican, Ecuadoran, and Guatemalan communities, just to name a few. They attract huge crowds, and stay open until the early evening. You'll also find upward of 85 smaller entertainment sites along the way, many with music from local bands and radio stations. Moreover, thousands of cheerleaders from middle- and high-school squads all over L.A. County dot the course, competing to bring the most spirit to the race as part of the L.A. Marathon Cheer Competition.

There's no course time limit, and the goal is to keep everything going until the last walker treads across the finish line. In practice, things don't quite work out that way, but they come close. Streets reopen and smaller stages shut down about the time that 13-minute-milers pass them. Slower participants must move to the side of the road and obey traffic signs. Although six water stations between Mile 15 and the finish remain open late, the marathon recommends that walkers and slower runners wear waist packs with water bottles to be sure they stay well hydrated.

At the end of the race, you're swept through the finishers' area, where you get your chip removed and receive your medal and Mylar blanket. Water, juice, sports drinks, energy bars, and baked goods are all available to help you recharge. Emerge at the family reunion area, where massage therapists offer their services for free. There are medical tents at the finish line and family reunion area.

TRAINING TUNES

Wish you could spend more time listening to the race-day entertainment? Download a course-music CD from the marathon Web site—great for training runs!

Spectating

If you really want to see the race start, go for a bird's-eye view. Head into the Bonaventure Hotel and look for the Union Bank Bridge on Level 4. (A warning—the Bonaventure towers are giant circles; it's very easy to lose your sense of direction inside.) Stand on the bridge, and you're directly over the starting corrals. Alternatively, follow the bridge to the restaurant-lined plaza across the road where you'll find several more great places to watch the whole pack of runners stream over the starting line.

Another great option is to watch the race start on Figueroa, between 6th and 9th streets. Decide in advance which side of the street you'll be on and your runner can veer to that side. After the start grab a bite, then make your way to the finish line (very crowded) or head to Figueroa and Olympic, between Miles 25 and 26. Here you have a great shot at connecting with your favorite runner as you cheer him or her on in the final stretch. Afterward, take Figueroa to Third Street and make a right; the family reunion area and Finish Line Festival are on Third, just east of Figueroa.

Celebrate!

After the race, enjoy the Finish Line Festival, a giant block party filled with music and food. A huge screen broadcasts TV coverage of the race, and live bands play all through the afternoon. Booths sell kettle corn, pizza, lemonade, and beer, among other treats. Hang out at this much-deserved party as long as you want, basking in the glory of your accomplishment.

Feeling particularly motivated as a spectator? Consider signing up for the 5K Run/Walk. It begins an hour after the marathon, giving you time to watch its start before heading to your own starting line at the Staples Center. (Or just hang at the Staples Center—the marathon runs right by.) The 5K ends just a short walk from Olympic and Figueroa, which is a great place to watch the elite marathoners zoom toward their finish line.

BEYOND THE FINISH LINE

Replacing 2,620 Calories

As someone who lives in Los Angeles, I can assure you: the food is excellent. It's also eclectic: where Chicago has its deep-dish pizza and Cincinnati has its chili, Los Angeles doesn't have a signature delicacy. All kinds of restaurants scream L.A., from delicious dives to celebrity-studded gourmet eateries. After your race you deserve to treat yourself, so here are my top picks. Enjoy!

Downtown

★ **CIELITO LINDO.** When it comes to the *taquito* stands on downtown's Olvera Street, everyone swears their favorite is the best. But unless they say Cielito Lindo, they're wrong. The taquitos and guacamole sauce here are far superior to any others. Order at the window, grab one of the four tables, and enjoy. Try Combination 1: three taquitos with guacamole sauce, beans, and cheese. Add some hot sauce, and you'll be in gustatory heaven. ⊠E-23 Olvera St., Downtown ☎213/687-4391 ⊕www.cielitolindo.org ▭No credit cards ♡ Closed Sun. ¢–$.

★ **PHILIPPE THE ORIGINAL.** L.A.'s oldest restaurant (1908) is reputedly where the French Dip sandwich originated. Here you can get one made with beef, pork, ham, lamb, or turkey on a freshly baked roll; the house hot mustard is as famous as the sandwiches. Philippe earns its reputation by maintaining its traditions, from sawdust on the floor to long, communal, wooden tables. The home cooking includes hearty breakfasts, chili, pickled eggs, and an enormous pie selection. The best bargain: a cup of java for only 9¢. ⊠1001 N. Alameda St., Downtown ☎213/628-3781 ⚐Reservations not accepted ▭No credit cards ¢–$.

★ **WATER GRILL.** Chef Michael Cimarusti has turned this lively, swank dining room into the city's premier seafood restaurant, netting the finest fish from around the world. With heavyweight mentors like Alain Ducasse and Paul Bocuse, it's no surprise that many of Cimarusti's dishes have French influences. But you'll also find Japanese inspirations as in the marvelous sashimi. Enticing entrées include Icelandic char with beets and horseradish cream, and wild Copper River salmon with applewood-smoked bacon and salsify puree. ⊠544 S. Grand Ave., Downtown ☎213/891-0900 ⚐Reservations essential ▭AE, DC, MC, V ♡No lunch weekends $$$–$$$$.

Hollywood

MUSSO & FRANK GRILL. Liver and onions, lamb chops, goulash, shrimp Louis, salad—you'll find all the old favorites here in Hollywood's oldest restaurant. A film-industry hangout since it opened in 1919, Musso & Frank still welcomes the working studio set to its maroon, faux-leather booths. Come before 3 PM for the kitchen's famous "flannel cakes" (pancakes). ⊠ 6667 Hollywood Blvd., Hollywood ☎ 323/467-7788 ▤ AE, DC, MC, V ☉ Closed Sun. and Mon. $-$$$.

PINK'S HOT DOGS. Orson Welles ate 18 of these hot dogs in one sitting (purportedly the record) and you, too, will be tempted to order more than one. The chili dogs are the main draw, but the menu has expanded to include such creations as the Ozzy Osbourne Dog (with cheese, grilled onions, guacamole, and tomatoes). Angelenos and tourists alike have lined up at all hours ('til 3 AM on weekends) since 1939 to plunk down some modest change for one of the greatest guilty pleasures in L.A. ⊠ 709 N. La Brea Ave., Hollywood ☎ 323/931-4223 ⌖ Reservations not accepted ▤ No credit cards ¢-$.

WEATHER THE RUN

Start-time temps average 59°F, but things can get hot, especially for slower runners. Hydrate intelligently, use sunscreen, and consider wearing a brimmed hat that breathes.

Westside

A.O.C. Named for the French initialism for *Appellation d'Origine Contrôlée*, the regulatory system that ensures the quality of local wines and cheeses, trendy A.O.C. upholds the standard of excellence. It's dominated by a long, candle-laden wine bar serving more than 50 vintages by the glass. There's also an L.A. rarity: a charcuterie bar. The small-plates menu is perfectly calibrated to the wine list; you could pick a salt cod–potato gratin, or an indulgent slab of pork rillettes, or just plunge into one of the city's best cheese selections. ⊠ 8022 W. 3rd St., south of West Hollywood ☎ 323/653-6359 ⌖ Reservations essential ▤ AE, MC, V ☉ No lunch $-$$.

★ **THE APPLE PAN.** I'm positive I ran a PR in the L.A. Marathon because I knew my husband would treat me to a meal here at the end. Since 1947, this unassuming joint with a horseshoe-shape counter—no tables here—has turned out amazing burgers. Try the one topped with Tillamook cheddar or the hickory burger with barbecue sauce. You'll also find fab fries and an apple pie good enough to name a restaurant after (although many regulars would argue the banana cream deserves the honor). Be prepared to wait for a seat. ⊠ 10801 W. Pico Blvd., West L.A. ☎ 310/475-3585 ⌖ Reservations not accepted ▤ No credit cards ☉ Closed Mon. ¢-$.

CRUSTACEAN. Exotic fish swim in a floor-to-ceiling aquarium and through a glass-topped "river" that meanders through the marble floor toward the bar. The French-influenced Southeast Asian menu might include lemongrass-scented bouillabaisse or salmon in a ginger emulsion. From the restaurateur's "secret kitchen," in which only family members are allowed, come colossal tiger prawns and whole Dungeness crab simmered in sake, chardonnay, and cognac. ⊠ 9646 Santa Monica Blvd., Beverly Hills ☎ 310/205-8990 ⌖ Reservations essential ▤ AE, DC, MC, V ☉ Closed Sun. No lunch Sat. $$-$$$$.

HUGO'S. It has a huge, eclectic menu filled with fresh, excellent fare. Breakfast is always served; look for such unique dishes as the oatmeal frittata (an egg-white frittata made

BREAKFAST SPOTS

While your runner tackles 26.2, you'll have time for a bite. Here are some breakfast spots (all in the ¢ to $ category) close to the starting line.

CHECKERS. Instead of plain waffles, there are apple waffles with praline butter; instead of plain pancakes, cornmeal pancakes with cinnamon pecan butter and strawberries. Those seeking savory dishes will be pleased by Tuscan-style eggs with wild mushrooms and tomatoes, among others. ⊠ Hilton Checkers, 535 S. Grand Ave., Downtown ☎ 213/624–0000 ▭ AE, D, DC, MC, V.

★ THE PANTRY. The marathon runs right past this institution, so after the pack takes off, follow the trail of confetti for just a few blocks. Though it's open 24 hours (has been since 1924), breakfast is the thing. Think Formica counters, old photos, and huge portions of diner food. Sourdough bread is a must. There *will* be a line, but it's worth the wait. ⊠ 877 S. Figueroa St., Downtown ☎ 213/ 972–9279 ▭ No credit cards.

★ THE STANDARD CAFE. A funky, swanky, *yellow* coffee shop. Enjoy breakfast comforts like steak and eggs, French toast, and omelets or such unique choices as eggsadilla (eggs, guacamole, cheese, and pico de gallo in a flour tortilla). You can celebrate that you're *not* running a marathon with a drink from the full bar. ⊠ Downtown L.A. Standard, 550 S. Flower, Downtown ☎ 213/892–8080 ▭ AE, D, DC, MC, V.

with whole-grain hot cereal and topped with applesauce and cottage cheese—odd but addictive). For lunch there's everything from your typical burger or salad to hummus-avocado wraps. It's often crowded during the midday meal, but when it's busy, the possibility of spotting a celebrity is higher. There's also a branch in the Valley. ⊠ 8401 Santa Monica Blvd., West Hollywood ☎ 323/654–3993 $–$$.

★ IN-N-OUT BURGER. I swear, this is no ordinary burger joint. Pop into In-N-Out at any but the most off hour, and you're sure to find a line. Wait. It's worth it. The menu is simple as can be: hamburger, cheeseburger, double-double (2 patties, 2 slices of cheese), fries, shakes. Everything is made with the freshest ingredients, and will spoil you for all other fast food. Check out the Web site for the inside scoop on their "secret menu." There are several branches throughout the L.A. area. ⊠ 922 Gayley Ave., Westwood ☎ 800/786– 1000 (all branches) ⊕ www.in-n-out.com ¢.

★ MATSUHISA. Freshness and innovation are the hallmarks of this flagship restaurant of superchef Nobu Matsuhisa's growing empire. The surprisingly modest-looking place draws crowds (and celebrities) with its stellar menu. Look for caviar-capped tuna stuffed with black truffles, foie gras sushi, and monkfish liver pâté wrapped in gold leaf. Regulars ask for the *omakase* (chef's choice), assured of an amazing experience, and then steel

Before May 24, 1997, if you'd asked Jeremy Newman what his life was like, he knows exactly what he would have said. "My life," he'd have beamed, "is *extraordinary*." And he'd have been telling the truth. After all, he was young and athletic, working as a personal trainer and running marathons; he had a lot of money; he lived a life of extreme adventure, going bungee jumping and cliff diving; and he was juggling five or six girlfriends. Was he happy? C'mon—he was living the dream.

But then came The Accident, which deserves those capital letters because it changed absolutely everything. That day in May, Jeremy went sky diving with a guy who was far more experienced. When the more experienced jumper made a faster acceleration toward the drop zone, Jeremy's ego couldn't take it. He purposely collapsed the end cells (the outermost edges) of his parachute to fall faster. It helped, but it didn't get him moving fast enough to catch the other guy. The solution? Jeremy collapsed the next row of cells, only to see his entire canopy collapse, rendering the parachute useless.

Instead of immediately deploying his reserve shoot, Jeremy again listened to his ego, which swore he could fix the problem on his own. He struggled and twisted, trying to get the canopy to fill, but it was no use. And by the time he realized this, it was too late for the reserve chute to help. Jeremy remembers every second as he plummeted through the sky from 1,200 feet, then smacked onto the unforgiving ground.

The effects were devastating: Jeremy's aorta ruptured in three places. Doctors said he would die, or at best be on a ventilator for the rest of his life. Yet miraculously Jeremy improved, albeit with one exception: he was paralyzed from the waist down.

For a guy with a life like Jeremy's, paralysis was inconceivable. He was infuriated by his condition, and took out his frustration on everyone around him, pushing them away. Then his mother intervened. She sat on his hospital bed and pointedly said, "You have a choice. You can either lie in bed and be bitter and angry and alone, or you can choose to use what you have and inspire people." It was a lovely message, but not one Jeremy wanted to hear. He asked his mom to leave.

By the next morning, he was even angrier. He had no control over his bodily functions and woke up a mess. He had to call a nurse to clean him, and the burn of humiliation as she did her job was unbearable. He kept rushing her, rudely needling her until she stood up, said, "I don't have to put up with this," and strode from the room, leaving Jeremy alone . . . and still soiled. As he was lying there, his mother's words rang in his head. She was right. He had a choice to make. And in that moment he chose to turn away from anger and solitude. He would make the most of what he had, and use it to make a difference in other people's lives.

Jeremy was in the hospital for 2½ months. The day after he got out, he went back to work as a personal trainer, pushing people toward their goals. He pushed himself even harder, immediately training for his first 5K as a wheelchair athlete, which he completed only about a month after his release. Soon after that, friends invited him to join them in a triathlon relay: Jeremy would take the swim. Even as an able-bodied athlete, he'd been intimidated by the triathlon. His friends wanted him to try it *now*?

But the doubt was only fleeting. Ever since his epiphany in the hospital, Jeremy felt his mission was to be living proof that you can't give up in the face of adversity. And that meant he could handle the ocean swim: even though it was never his sport; even though he couldn't use his legs; even though he'd be the only physically challenged athlete in the race. He drove himself hard, training in the pool five days a week for several weeks until he thought he was ready.

The day of the race, Jeremy swam into the ocean, along with all the other athletes. Quick reality check: for those who don't know, an ocean swim is a challenge for any athlete. You have to fight your way through the breakers, which are often choppy and disorienting. The water is usually cold, the current tugs at you, you're engulfed in a mass of thrashing arms and legs as everyone battles for position, and it's all you can do to maintain your stroke and breathing. Many people find it too hard to take; some even disqualify themselves rather than struggle through. Now imagine tackling all that when you can't use your legs. Being in the ocean at all is terrifying, never mind in race conditions. Of course Jeremy was scared, but dropping out wasn't an option. He drove on.

As he continued to race, tackling marathons and triathlons (full triathlons, not just relays), Jeremy was often the only physically challenged athlete on the course. His competitors always supported him, congratulating him as they passed on their bikes (wheelchair triathletes use a handcrank chair for the bike portion of the race) or cheering him as he whipped by them in his racing chair during the run. Their sportsmanship brought tears to his eyes, but one woman made him see there was something more to it. At the end of a race, she caught up with him in the transition area and thanked him. "You passed me on the run and I was done—I couldn't go any farther," she said. "But you looked at me and said, 'You can do it,' and I started running again and finished the race." Simply by being out there on the course defying his own limitations, he was motivating people to dig deeper, push harder, and achieve more.

That's when racing changed for Jeremy. Before the accident, it was all about his ego—being the best, beating other people. But now, "I don't care if I'm the last person across the finish line," he told me. "I'm the first person in [spectators' and other athletes'] heads when they think about what's not satisfying them in life." Inspiring others has become Jeremy's true passion, one he lives out not only in his racing life, but also in his careers as a trainer and motivational speaker, and in his volunteer work with the Big Brothers Big Sisters organization. Now when Jeremy looks back on the "extraordinary" life he led before the accident, he sees someone who was terribly unhappy. Everything he did was for himself; the revolving door of girlfriends was just a way to keep anyone from getting too close. Where once relying on others seemed like a blow to his independence, now it's his greatest joy. "I'm nothing without other people," he proclaims. "Other people is where I get my strength."

And what Jeremy gets, he gives back a million times over. He's living proof that nothing is impossible. Since his accident, he has done seven L.A. Marathons; nearly three dozen triathlons; and many duathlons and 5K and 10K races. He's one of a very few wheelchair triathletes, and was one of only two such athletes selected to represent the United States in the 2002 World Triathlon Championships. He spits in the face of adversity daily, and in doing so reminds the rest of us that we have the power to change our lives.

Now Jeremy is tackling his greatest challenge yet. He's trying to walk again. After years of numbness, he recently regained sensitivity in his legs. *Hyper*sensitivity. The slightest touch, the gentlest brush felt as if someone was flaying the skin from his body. Maybe it should have been thrilling, but it only made him mad. He had come so far, and now he had to live in pain? Yet true to his philosophy, he didn't wallow. He pushed through the pain, and eventually it subsided, leaving just normal sensation, and a chance for something truly miraculous. After eight years of dormancy, Jeremy's legs are learning to walk again, little by little.

If you've ever spoken to Jeremy, you know that not only will he get back on his feet, but he'll also be running marathons on them.

And if he can do it, anyone can. ■

themselves for a daunting tab. ⊠ 129 N. La Cienega Blvd., Beverly Hills ☎ 310/659-9639 ⚜ Reservations essential ▤ AE, DC, MC, V ⊙ No lunch weekends $-$$$.

MULBERRY STREET PIZZERIA. Hands down it's the best pizza in L.A. Owned by Cathy Moriarty and her ex-boyfriend Richie Palmer, Mulberry serves thin-crust pizza that rivals even the top pies in New York. Slices are large and toppings generous. Check out the walls covered with celebrity signatures and movie posters. While you're enjoying your slice, soak up even more Manhattan flavor with the *New York Post,* always out and available. There's another branch in Beverly Hills (on South Beverly Drive) as well as one in the Valley. ⊠ 347 N. Cañon Dr., Beverly Hills ☎ 310/247-8998 ▤ AE, DC, MC, V ¢-$.

SPAGO BEVERLY HILLS. Wolfgang Puck's casually elegant contemporary restaurant centers on an outdoor courtyard shaded by 100-year-old olive trees, from which you can glimpse the exhibition kitchen and, on occasion, the affable chef-owner greeting his famous friends. The daily-changing menu is likely to offer several renditions of foie gras as well as such dishes as pan-roasted halibut in a saffron-champagne sauce, tandoori lamb, and some traditional Austrian specialties. Look for incredible finales from acclaimed pastry chef Sherry Yard. ⊠ 176 N. Cañon Dr., Beverly Hills ☎ 310/385-0880 ⚜ Reservations essential ▤ AE, D, DC, MC, V ⊙ No lunch Sun. $$$-$$$$.

Beach Cities

GLADSTONE'S. It's one of the most popular restaurants along the Southern California coast. The food is notable mostly for its Brobdingnagian portions: giant bowls of crab chowder, mounds of steamed clams, and the famous mile-high chocolate cake, which could easily feed a small regiment. The real reason to visit Gladstone's is the glorious vista of sea, sky, and beach. If you have to wait for a table, munch on peanuts from the giant barrels in the foyer. ⊠ 17300 Pacific Coast Hwy., at Sunset Blvd., Malibu ☎ 310/454-3474 ▤ AE, D, DC, MC, V $$-$$$.

★ **MÉLISSE.** In a city where informality reigns, this is one of L.A's dressier—but not stuffier—restaurants. A crystal chandelier hangs above well-spaced tables that are topped with flowers and Limoges china. The garden room loosens up with a stone fountain and a retractable roof. Chef-owner Josiah Citrin enriches his modern French cooking with sea-

FOOD FOR FITNESS

When you're training for a marathon, it's not always simple to find the delicious, healthful food your body needs—especially if you're eating out.

Unless you're in L.A.

In 2005 the marathon partnered with area fast-food chains and fine-dining establishments alike to institute special Fitness Training Menus that offer a healthful mix of carbohydrates and protein—the perfect fuel. From early January to Marathon Sunday, participating restaurants carried the menus to show their support for L.A. runners. The marathon hopes to continue this partnership; check the race Web site for details.

sonal California produce. Consider roasted beets and cheese drizzled with a 50-year-old sherry vinegar emulsion, lobster Thermidor, or wild Scottish partridge with truffle puree in a rich *albufera* sauce. The cheese cart is loaded with domestic and European selections. Jackets may not be absolutely required, but they are preferred. ⊠ 1104 Wilshire Blvd., Santa Monica ☎ 310/395-0881 ⏦ Reservations essential ▤ AE, D, DC, MC, V ⊘ No lunch Sat.-Tues. $$$-$$$$.

RÖCKENWAGNER. Local celebrity chef Hans Röckenwagner's restaurant, in a Frank Gehry-designed building, delivers warmth and finesse in its casual brasserie and its smaller, more formal dining room. Hit the brasserie for hearty veal goulash with spaetzle and braised pork belly with red cabbage. The other space cleaves to the contemporary cooking that made Röckenwagner's reputation; its two tasting menus could list crab soufflé with papaya, Thai-inspired bouillabaisse, or a salmon Napoléon with basil sauce. ⊠ 2435 Main St., Santa Monica ☎ 310/399-6504 ⏦ Reservations essential ▤ AE, DC, MC, V ⊘ No lunch $$-$$$.

EL TEXATE. It's a hole-in-the-wall, but the incredible Oaxacan food is the real thing. For a real treat, have the mole *negro*; its rich complexity will have you grabbing the corn tortillas to sop up every drop. Combine it with a margarita on the rocks for the perfect meal. ⊠ 316 Pico Blvd., Santa Monica ☎ 310/399-1115 ▤ AE, D, DC, MC, V $.

Sightseeing on (and off) Your Feet

This is where it gets crazy. Maybe I'm biased because I live here, but there are so many things to see and do in L.A. that it's absolutely staggering. You can't fit everything in, so figure out what excites you most about the city—the entertainment industry, the outdoors, the culture—and pursue it full force. Depending, of course, on how you feel . . .

I Feel Great!

★ **HIT THE STRAND.** This 22-mi concrete route runs along the Pacific from Will Rogers State Beach to Torrance Beach. It attracts legions of cyclists, joggers, rollerbladers, skaters, skateboarders, and walkers. In some places, bikes have their own parallel path. Along stretches where everyone shares the way, be considerate—if you're moving slowly, keep right.

If you start on the Strand in Santa Monica and head south, you'll first pass the Santa Monica Pier before cruising along to the eclectic show that is Venice. Next is Marina del Rey, where you'll leave the beach for a bit to roll through the streets of town, a park, and the marina itself. Once you're back on the beach, there's nothing but deserted sand and ocean for what seems like ages—until you come to Manhattan and Hermosa beaches. Drool over the beautiful beachfront houses and the beautiful beachfront bodies lounging on patios, playing volleyball, or heading out to catch a wave. Going south from Hermosa Beach, you'll again veer away from the ocean, following the bike path through town until Redondo Beach, when you're in sight of the waves once again.

To rent a bike or skates, drive to Santa Monica or Venice to hit **Perry's Cafe and Sports Rentals** (⊠ 1200 The Promenade, Santa Monica ☎ 310/458-3975 ⌂ 2600 Ocean Front

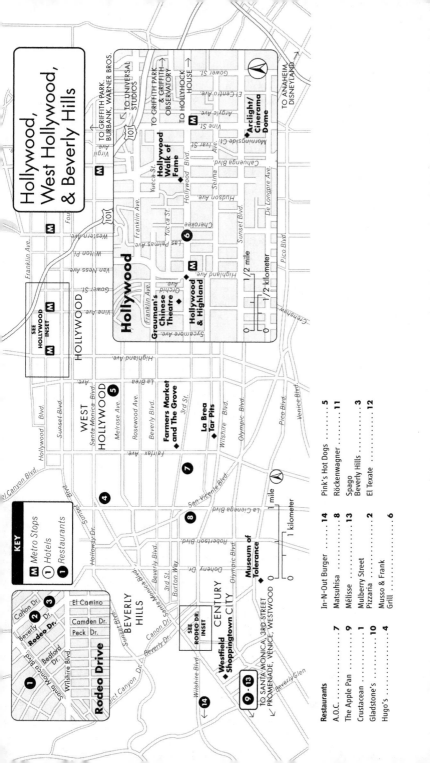

Hollywood, West Hollywood & Beverly Hills

KEY

- Ⓜ Metro Stops
- ① Hotels
- ❶ Restaurants

TO GRIFFITH PARK,
BURBANK, WARNER BROS.

TO UNIVERSAL
STUDIOS

TO GRIFFITH PARK
& GRIFFITH
OBSERVATORY →

TO HOLLYHOCK
HOUSE →

TO ANAHEIM
DISNEYLAND →

Hollywood

Walk of Fame

Grauman's
Chinese Theatre

Hollywood
& Highland

Arclight/
Cinerama
Dome

Cherokee ❻

½ mile

½ kilometer

WEST HOLLYWOOD

Farmers Market
and The Grove ❺

La Brea
Tar Pits

❼

❹

❽

SEE
HOLLYWOOD
INSET

Museum of
Tolerance

BEVERLY HILLS

CENTURY CITY

SEE
RODEO DR.
INSET

Westfield ◆
Shoppingtown
❾ - ⓭

TO SANTA MONICA, 3RD-STREET
PROMENADE, VENICE, WESTWOOD

El Camino

Camden Dr.

Peck Dr.

Rodeo Drive

❶ ❷ ❸

⓮

Restaurants

A.O.C. 7
The Apple Pan 9
Crustacean 1
Gladstone's 10
Hugo's 4

In-N-Out Burger 14
Matsuhisa 8
Mélisse 13
Mulberry Street
Pizzaria 2
Musso & Frank
Grill 6

Pink's Hot Dogs 5
Röckenwagner 11
Spago
Beverly Hills 3
El Texate 12

Walk, Venice ☎310/584-9306 ✉2400 Ocean Front Walk, Venice ☎310/372-3138), **Sea Mist Rentals** (✉1619 Ocean Front Walk, at the Santa Monica Pier, Santa Monica ☎310/ 395-7076), **Boardwalk Skates** (✉201½ Ocean Front Walk, Venice ☎310/450-6634), or **Venice Bike and Skate** (✉21 Washington Blvd., just east of the Strand, Venice ☎310/ 301-4011)

For a snack along the way, try **GoodStuff Hermosa Beach** (✉1286 The Strand, Hermosa Beach ☎310/374-2334), which has a huge array of healthful, delicious food. The **Beach Hut** (✉1342 Hermosa Ave., Hermosa Beach ☎310/376-4252) serves cheap, no-frills, but very yummy Hawaiian fare.

★ **HIKE A CANYON.** There's a fine trail a surprisingly short hop away from just about any point in L.A. My favorites are Runyan Canyon, high above Hollywood, and Temescal Canyon, which has a waterfall as well as stunning city and ocean views. Take plenty of water and don't forget the sunblock.

The **Sierra Club** (☎213/387-4287 ⊕www.sierraclub.org) conducts several guided treks, including evening jaunts. **Local Hikes** (⊕www.localhikes.com) lists an almost impossible number of terrific L.A. hikes and gives detailed information about the trails, levels of difficulty, directions to the trailheads, and reviews.

I Feel Pretty Good

★ **HUNTINGTON LIBRARY, ART COLLECTIONS, AND BOTANICAL GARDENS.** The Huntington was built in the early 1900s as the home of railroad tycoon Henry E. Huntington. He and his wife, Arabella, collected rare books and manuscripts, botanical specimens, and 18th-century British art. The institution they established is one of the world's most extraordinary cultural complexes. The Huntington Gallery holds the world-famous collection of British paintings; American art is displayed in the Virginia Steele Scott Gallery of American Art. The Huntington Library contains more than 600,000 books and some 300 manuscripts, including such treasures as George Washington's genealogy in his own handwriting and unrivaled early editions of Shakespeare.

The stunning Huntington Botanical Gardens includes a 12-acre Desert Garden, with the world's largest group of mature cacti and other succulents, arranged by continent. The Japanese Garden holds traditional Japanese plants, stone ornaments, a drum bridge, a Japanese house, a bonsai court, and a Zen rock garden. The 3-acre rose garden is displayed chronologically, so you can see the development leading to today's strains. On the grounds is the charming Rose Garden Tea Room, where traditional high tea is a must; call for reservations. There are also herb, palm, and jungle gardens, plus a Shakespeare garden, which blooms with plants mentioned in Shakespeare's works. Docents lead 1¼-hour guided tours at posted times, and you can pick up a free brochure with a map and highlights at the entrance pavilion. ✉1151 Oxford Rd., San Marino ☎626/405-2100 ⊕www.huntington. org 🎫$15 adults; free 1st Thurs. of the month ⏰Tues.-Fri. noon-4:30, weekends 10:30-4:30.

OLVERA STREET. This busy pedestrian block tantalizes with piñatas, mariachis, and fragrant Mexican food. As the oldest section of the city, known as El Pueblo de Los Angeles, Olvera Street represents the city's rich Mexican heritage. Vendors sell puppets, sandals, serapes, and handicrafts from stalls that line the center of the narrow street. On weekends restaurants are packed as musicians play in the central plaza. For information, stop by the **Olvera Street Visitors Center** (✉ 622 N. Main St., Downtown ☎ 213/628-1274 ⊕ - www.olvera-street.com), open Tuesday–Saturday 10-3. Free 50-minute walking tours leave here at 10, 11, and noon Tuesday–Saturday.

HOLLYWOOD WALK OF FAME. On this mile-long stretch of Hollywood Boulevard, names are embossed in brass, each at the center of a pink star embedded in dark-gray terrazzo. They're not all screen deities; many stars memorialize people who worked in technical fields. To aid in the identification, stars have one of five logos: a motion-picture camera, a radio microphone, a television set, a record, and a theatrical mask. Contact the **Hollywood Chamber of Commerce** (✉ 7018 Hollywood Blvd., Hollywood ☎ 323/469-8311 ⊕ www.hollywoodcoc.org) for celebrity-star locations and information on future installations.

★ **GETTY CENTER.** With its curving walls and isolated hilltop perch, the Getty Center resembles a pristine fort. Its architecture, gardens, and city views are as stunning as its art collections. Five pavilions surround a central courtyard and are bridged by walkways. From the courtyard, plazas, and walks, you can survey the city from the San Gabriel Mountains to the ocean. Inside the pavilions, galleries contain European paintings, drawings, sculpture, illuminated manuscripts, and decorative arts as well as American and European photographs. The Getty also presents lectures, films, concerts, and special programs for kids and families. The complex includes a restaurant (reservations required), two cafeterias, and two outdoor coffee bars. ✉ 1200 Getty Center Dr., Brentwood ☎ 310/440-7300 ⊕ www.getty.edu 💲 Free; parking $7 ⊙ Tues.–Thurs. and Sun. 10-6, Fri. and Sat. 10-9.

SANTA MONICA PIER. Eateries, souvenir shops, a small aquarium, an arcade, and Pacific Park—an amusement park full of rides—are all part of this truncated pier at the foot of Colorado Boulevard below Palisades Park. The pier's trademark 46-horse Looff carousel, built in 1916, has appeared in many films, including *The Sting.* ✉ Colorado Ave. and the ocean, Santa Monica ☎ 310/458-8900 pier, 310/260-8744 Pacific Park, 310/393-6149 aquarium ⊕ www.santamonicapier.org or www.pacpark.com 💲 Pacific Park rides: $2–$6, day passes $19.95-$21.95. Carousel: $1. Aquarium: $5 suggested ($1 minimum) ⊙ Pacific Park hrs vary, call ahead. Carousel: Mon.–Thurs. 11-5, Fri.–Sun. 11-7. Aquarium: Tues.–Fri. 2-6, weekends 12:30-6.

UNIVERSAL STUDIOS HOLLYWOOD. Take the famous tram ride and experience special effects like the parting of the Red Sea, an avalanche, and an earthquake. You'll also meet King Kong and get attacked by the ravenous killer shark of *Jaws* fame. Tram tours last 45 minutes and run all day long. You can also enjoy attractions based on Universal films and TV shows. Highlights include *Terminator 2: 3D,* mixing 3-D with virtual reality and live action; *Jurassic Park—The Ride,* a flume ride through a jungle full of dinosaurs and with an 84-foot drop; and *Back to the Future—The Ride,* a flight simulator showcasing excellent special effects. The adjacent CityWalk is a separate venue with shops, restaurants, nightclubs, and movie theaters—including IMAX 3-D. ✉ 100 Universal City Plaza, Universal City ☎ 800/UNIVERSAL ⊕ www.universalstudios.com 💲 Packages vary ($43 and up). Parking: $10-$17 ⊙ Hrs vary but are roughly mid-June–early Sept., daily 8 AM–10 PM; early Sept.–early June, daily 10 AM-6 PM.

★ **DISNEYLAND.** One of the biggest misconceptions people have about Disneyland is that they've "been there, done that" if they've visited the more mammoth Disney World. But Disneyland came first, and there's plenty here that you won't find there, such as New Orleans Square; the Indiana Jones Adventure ride; and a far-superior version of the spectacular laser/fire/water/live show, *Fantasmic!* I could easily fill a whole book on Disneyland without even touching Disney's California Adventure theme park or Downtown Disney. Suffice it to say that if you're really interested, extend your trip a couple of days, splurge on the stunning Grand Californian hotel, buy a Park Hopper Pass, and enjoy. If you want to devote only a few hours to the Mouse, stick with Disneyland. It's truly magical, particularly after dark when it's all lighted up. Stay late enough and you might catch fireworks. ⊠ 1313 Harbor Blvd., Anaheim ☎ 714/781-4565 ⊕ www.disneyland.com ☑ $56 for an adult, 1-day, 1-park ticket; check Web site for other ticketing options ⊙ Daily, year-round; call for specific times.

Let's Take It Slowly

GRIFFITH OBSERVATORY. High on a hill overlooking the city, the Griffith Observatory is one of L.A.'s most celebrated icons, as much for the views as for academic astronomy shows in the planetarium theater, the free telescope viewings, and astronomy exhibits in the Hall of Science. You might recognize the observatory and grounds from such movies as *Rebel Without a Cause* and *The Terminator.* As of this writing, the Observatory is closed for renovation, but is expected to reopen in May 2006. ⊠ 2800 E. Observatory Rd., Griffith Park ☎ 323/664-1191 ⊕ www.griffithobservatory.org.

LA BREA TAR PITS AND PAGE MUSEUM. La Brea Tar Pits contained the largest collection of Pleistocene, or Ice Age, fossils ever found at one location: more than 600 species of birds, mammals, plants, reptiles, and insects. More than 100 tons of fossil bones have been removed in excavations over the last seven decades, making this one of the world's most famous fossil sites. The Page Museum at the La Brea Tar Pits displays fossils from the tar pits. ⊠ 5801 Wilshire Blvd., Miracle Mile (an area just south of Hollywood) ☎ 323/934-PAGE ⊕ www.tarpits.org ☑ $7 ⊙ Weekdays 9:30-5, weekends 10-5.

★ **MUSEUM OF TOLERANCE.** Using interactive technology, this important museum (part of the Simon Wiesenthal Center) challenges you to confront bigotry and racism. One of the most affecting sections covers the Holocaust, with film footage of deportation scenes and simulated sets of concentration camps. You're issued a "passport" bearing the name of a child whose life was dramatically changed by Nazi rule and World War II; as you go through the exhibit, you learn the fate of that child. Anne Frank artifacts are part of the permanent collection. Interactive exhibits include the "Millennium Machine," which asks you to suggest solutions to human rights abuses around the world, and the "Point of View Diner," where video jukeboxes in red diner booths present controversial topics for you to discuss. To ensure a visit to this popular museum, make reservations (especially for Friday, Sunday, and holidays) and plan to spend at least three hours. Museum entry stops two hours before closing time. A photo ID is required for admission. ⊠ 9786 W. Pico Blvd., just south of Beverly Hills ☎ 310/553-8403 ⊕ www.museumoftolerance.com ☑ $10 ⊙ Nov.-Mar., Sun. 11-7:30, Mon.-Thurs. 11:30-6:30, Fri. 11:30-3; Apr.-Oct., Sun. 11-7:30, Mon.-Thurs. 11:30-6:30, Fri. 11:30-5.

FORGET SIGHTSEEING. GET ME TO A SPA!

Ready to indulge after your run? Consider these downtown havens.

BONAVENTURE CLUB. The Bonaventure hotel's spa offers shiatsu or Swedish massage treatments ranging from $75 for 45 minutes to $198 for 120 minutes. Use of the sauna, steam room, and outdoor pool is included. ⊠ 404 S. Figueroa St., Blue Tower, 3rd Level, Downtown ☎ 213/629–0900 ⊕ www.bonaventureclub.com ☉ Daily 11 AM–11:30 PM.

CHECKERS SPA. This downtown rooftop spa has such delights as the Lower Leg and Feet Treat ($75 for 45 minutes): a mineral bath, scrub, and massage that's sure to ease your marathon woes. Pair it with a Checkers Sports Massage ($110–$210 for 60–120 minutes) for full-body relief. ⊠ 535 S. Grand Ave., Downtown ☎ 213/624–0000 ⊕ www.hiltoncheckers.com ☉ Daily 9–9.

SANWA HEALTH SPA. On the 4th floor of the New Otani hotel, this low-key health spa specializes in Japanese shiatsu, a massage that works with your body's energy flow. Prices range from $53 for 45 minutes to $100 for 90 minutes and include use of the sauna. ⊠ 120 S. Los Angeles St., Downtown ☎ 213/687–4597 ⊕ www.sanwahealth.com ☉ Mon.–Sat. 2–11, Sun. noon—9.

★**WARNER BROS. STUDIOS.** Two-and-a-quarter-hour tours travel the lot via large golf carts, visiting the sets and sound stages, where you might spot a celeb or see a shoot in action. Tours change from day to day, depending on what's shooting on the lot. They include a stop at the Warner Bros. museum, with its collection of costumes, props, and scripts. Tickets are sold on the day of your tour, first come, first served. Tours are given every half hour. Arrive 20 minutes before your tour. Children under 8 aren't admitted. ⊠ 4301 W. Olive Ave., Burbank ☎ 818/972-8687 ⊕ www2.warnerbros.com/vipstudiotour 💲 $39 ☉ Tours Oct.–Apr., weekdays 9-3; May–Sept., weekdays 9-4.

Ow! No.

ATTEND A TV SHOW TAPING! Book well in advance. The three to four hours spent as part of a studio audience will give you a new appreciation for the half-hour final product. Hide a snack in your pockets and make sure to bring a photo ID for admittance. **Audiences Unlimited** (☎ 818/753-3470 ⊕ www.tvtickets.com) is the best source for tickets to many television shows. For tickets and information about *The Tonight Show with Jay Leno,* contact **NBC** (☎ 818/840-7500 ⊕ www.nbc.com). For Paramount shows, contact **Paramount Studios** (☎ 323/956-1777 ⊕ www.paramountshowtickets.com). For *Jeopardy* and *Wheel of Fortune* tickets, get in touch with **Sony Studios** (☎ 800/482-9840). To get tickets to *The Price Is Right,* contact **CBS** (☎ 323/575-2458).

SEE A MOVIE! But not just anywhere. L.A. has several notable theaters:

Arclight/Cinerama Dome. The geodesic Cinerama Dome has a giant curved screen—a must for any major blockbuster. Other theaters in its complex also have spacious seating and souped-up audio and visual technology. Seats are pre-assigned by general area (front, middle, or back). Expect to pay for the luxe experience: tickets can be as much as $14. ⊠ 6360 Sunset Blvd., at Vine St., Hollywood ☎ 323/464-4226 ⊕ www.arclightcinemas.com.

Grauman's Chinese Theatre. This fantasy of Chinese pagodas and temples is famous for its courtyard filled with iconic concrete hand- and footprints. This tradition is said to have begun at the theater's opening in 1927, with the premiere of Cecil B. DeMille's *King of Kings,* when actress Norma Talmadge accidentally stepped into wet concrete. Now more than 160 celebrities have contributed imprints of their appendages for posterity. There are a few oddballs, like the one of Jimmy Durante's nose. ⊠ 6925 Hollywood Blvd., Hollywood ☎ 323/461-3331 ⊕ www.manntheaters.com/chinese.

Pacific's El Capitan. In this art deco masterpiece meticulously renovated by Disney, first-run movies alternate with Disney revivals. The theater also often presents live stage shows in conjunction with its features. ⊠ 6838 Hollywood Blvd., Hollywood ☎ 323/467-7674 ⊕ disney.go.com/disneypictures/el_capitan.

Silent Movie Theater. This is a treasure. Thursday through Sunday it screens exclusively the cream of the pre-talkies era with live musical accompaniment, plus shorts before the films. It's one of the only theaters of its kind. ⊠ 611 N. Fairfax Ave., Fairfax District ☎ 323/655-2520 ⊕ www.silentmovietheater.com.

LOUNGE ON THE BEACH. L.A.'s beaches are an integral part of the Southern California lifestyle. From downtown, hit the coast by taking the Santa Monica Freeway (I–10) due west. Once you reach the end of the freeway, I–10 runs into the famous Highway 1, better known as the Pacific Coast Highway, or PCH. L.A. County beaches (and state beaches operated by the county) have lifeguards on duty year-round. Public parking is usually available, though fees can be as much as $8; in some areas, it's possible to find free street and highway parking. One caveat: after a rain, certain strands become very polluted. Call ahead for **Beach Conditions** (☎ 310/457-9701 Malibu, 310/578-0478 Santa Monica, 310/379-8471 South Bay area). The following are some choice beach options, listed north to south.

Zuma Beach. Zuma, 2 miles of white sand usually littered with tanning teenagers, has it all: from fishing and diving to swings for the kids to volleyball courts. ⊠ 30050 PCH, Malibu ☞ Parking, lifeguard (year-round, though as needed in winter), restrooms, food concessions.

Will Rogers State Beach. This clean, sandy, 3-mile beach, with volleyball nets, gymnastics equipment, and playground equipment for kids, is an all-around favorite. ⊠ 17700 PCH, 2 mi north of Santa Monica pier, Pacific Palisades ☞ Parking, lifeguard (year-round, though as needed in winter), restrooms.

Santa Monica State Beach. It's the first beach you'll hit after the Santa Monica Freeway (I–10) runs into PCH. ⊠ 1642 Promenade (PCH at California Incline), Santa Monica ☞ Parking, lifeguard (year-round), restrooms, showers.

Venice City Beach. The main attraction here is the boardwalk scene, but the surf and wide stretches of sand are great as well. ⊠ West of Pacific Ave., Venice ☞ Parking, playground, restrooms, showers, food concessions.

Manhattan Beach. A wide, sandy strip with good swimming and rows of volleyball courts, this is the preferred destination of muscled, tanned young professionals and dedicated bikini-watchers. ⊠ Manhattan Beach Blvd. and North Ocean Dr., Manhattan Beach ☞ Parking, lifeguard (year-round), restrooms, showers, food concessions.

Hermosa Beach. South of Manhattan Beach, Hermosa Beach has all the amenities of its neighbor, but it attracts more of a college party crowd. ⊠ Hermosa Ave. and 33rd St., Hermosa Beach ☞ Parking, lifeguard (year-round), restrooms, showers, food concessions, wheelchair access to pier, walkway.

Shop Around

★ **FARMERS MARKET AND THE GROVE.** The European-style open-air market at Third Street and Fairfax Avenue is an institution, with 110 stalls, 20-plus counter-order restaurants, and a landmark 1941 clock tower. Don't miss Loteria for Mexican food or Bennett's Ice Cream. Attached to the Farmers Market is The Grove, home to chains like Banana Republic, Crate & Barrel, and the various Gaps. Los Angeles history gets a nod with the electric Red Car Trolley that winds through both venues. ⊠ 6333 W. 3rd St., Fairfax District (south of Hollywood) ☎ 323/933-9211 market, 888/315-8883 or 323/900-8080 The Grove ⊕-www.farmersmarketla.com; www.thegrovela.com ⊗ Farmers Market: weekdays 9–9, Sat. 9–8, Sun. 10–7. The Grove: Mon.–Thurs. 10–9, Fri. and Sat. 10–10, Sun. 11–7.

> ### THE PERFECT BREAK
>
> While shopping, duck into **The Coffee Bean & Tea Leaf** (☎ 800/832-5323 ⊕ www.coffeebean.com), with branches all over town, for an Iced Blended in one of many yummy flavors.

GRAND CENTRAL MARKET. Handmade white-corn tamales, warm olive bread, dried figs, Mexican fruit drinks . . . hungry yet? The city's largest and most active food market is a testament to Los Angeles's diversity. Butcher shops display everything from lambs' heads to pigs' tails; produce stalls are piled high with locally grown avocados and heirloom tomatoes. Even if you don't buy anything, the market is a delightful place to browse and people-watch. ⊠ 317 S. Broadway, Downtown ☎ 213/624-2378 ⊕ www.grandcentralsquare.com ⊗ Daily 9–6.

HOLLYWOOD & HIGHLAND. This megamillion-dollar hotel-retail-entertainment complex (which includes the Kodak Theatre, home of the Academy Awards) makes a swaggering play to bring back the glitz Hollywood lacked for years. Does it succeed? You be the judge. ⊠ Hollywood Blvd. and Highland Ave., Hollywood ⊕ www.hollywoodandhighland.com ⊗ Mon.–Sat., 10–10, Sun. 10–7.

MELROSE AVENUE. Melrose Avenue has a split personality: part bohemian-punk shopping district (from North Highland to Sweetzer) and part upscale art and design mecca (upper Melrose Avenue and Melrose Place). The bohemian-punk part, however, is its true claim to fame—tons of funky and fun vintage clothing shops that are always worth at least a browse.

RODEO DRIVE. Window-shop at Tiffany & Co., Gucci, Armani, Hermès, Harry Winston, Lladró, and other places. Several nearby restaurants have patios where you can sip a drink while watching fashionable shoppers saunter by. At the southern end of Rodeo Drive (at

Wilshire Boulevard) is Via Rodeo, a curvy cobblestone street designed to resemble a European shopping *via*. ⊠ Beverly Hills.

THIRD STREET PROMENADE. Stretch your legs along this pedestrian-only three-block strip of Third Street, just a whiff away from the Pacific. Look for outdoor cafés, pushcart vendors, movie theaters, and street musicians. Come Wednesday or Saturday morning for the Farmers Market. ⊠ 3rd St. between Wilshire Blvd. and Broadway, Santa Monica ⊕ www.downtownsm.com.

WESTFIELD SHOPPINGTOWN CENTURY CITY. It's a mall without a roof—a great open-air place to shop in upscale stores, grab a bite, or see a movie. ⊠ 10250 Santa Monica Blvd., Century City ☎ 310/277–3898 ⊕ www.westfield.com/centurycity.

I Love the Nightlife

From the überhip and trendy to the low-key and casual, L.A.'s nightlife has a little something for everyone. The *Los Angeles Times* (⊕ www.latimes.com) has coverage of arts, events listings, movie reviews, and the like. Pick up the paper or click on the Web site, which links to the CalendarLive section (⊕ www.calendarlive.com). The *LA Weekly* (⊕ www.laweekly.com), a free publication found all over the city, maintains a hip site with lively features and insiders' guides to dining, the arts, and nightlife.

Downtown

BONAVISTA LOUNGE. This cocktail lounge on the 34th floor of the Bonaventure Hotel offers a panoramic view of the city and completes a 360° revolution every hour. ⊠ 404 S. Figueroa St., Downtown ☎ 213/624–1000.

★ **DOWNTOWN L.A. STANDARD.** It has a groovy lounge, with pink sofas and chill-beat DJs, and an all-white restaurant that looks like something out of *2001: A Space Odyssey*. But it's the rooftop bar (with an amazing view of illuminated skyscrapers, a heated swimming pool, and private, pod-like water-bed tents) that has become almost impossible to get into, especially on weekends. ⊠ 550 S. Flower St., Downtown ☎ 213/892–8080.

★ **WALT DISNEY CONCERT HALL.** The home of the Los Angeles Philharmonic and the Los Angeles Master Chorale is a sculpture of gleaming, curved steel. The 2,265-seat theater also has a public park, gardens, and shops as well as two amphitheaters for children's and preconcert events. ⊠ 151 S. Grand Ave., Downtown ☎ 323/850–2000 ⊕ www.musiccenter.org.

Hollywood

BEAUTY BAR. You can get manicures and makeovers along with perfect martinis here. But those who flock to this retro salon-bar (the little sister of the Beauty Bars in N.Y.C. and San Fran) don't really need the cosmetic care—this is where the edgier beautiful people hang. ⊠ 1638 Cahuenga Blvd., Hollywood ☎ 323/464–7676.

LARGO. Musician-producer Jon Brion (Fiona Apple, Aimee Mann) shows off his ability to play virtually any instrument and any song in the rock lexicon—and beyond—as host of a popular evening of music every Friday at Largo. Other nights, low-key rock and singer-songwriter fare is offered at this cozy supper club–bar. Reservations are required for tables, but bar stools are open. ✉ 432 N. Fairfax Ave., Hollywood ☎ 323/852–1073.

LUCKY STRIKE LANES. It's a swanky, retro bowling joy, with great food, great drinks, and 12 great lanes. It's in the Hollywood & Highland hotel-retail-entertainment complex. ✉ Hollywood Blvd. and Highland Ave., Hollywood ☎ 323/467–7776 ⊕ www.bowlluckystrike.com.

VINE STREET LOUNGE. It's fast becoming one of the hottest clubs in town, especially since Jamie Foxx had an Oscar party here. Enjoy live music Sunday, DJ and dancing Tuesday through Saturday. ✉ 1708 N. Vine St., Hollywood ☎ 323/464–0404 ⊕ www.vinestreetlounge.com ⊘ Closed Mon.

West Hollywood

RAGE. This gay bar is a longtime favorite—and practically an institution—with DJs following a different musical theme every night of the week (alternative rock, house, dance remixes, etc.). The cover is free to $10. ✉ 8911 Santa Monica Blvd., West Hollywood ☎ 310/652–7055 ⊕ www.ragewesthollywood.com.

ROXY. A Sunset Strip fixture for decades, the Roxy hosts local and touring rock, alternative, blues, and rockabilly bands. It's not the comfiest club around, yet it is the site of many memorable shows. ✉ 9009 Sunset Blvd., West Hollywood ☎ 310/276–2222 ⊕ www.theroxyonsunset.com.

SKYBAR. To enter Skybar, the poolside bar at the Hotel Mondrian, patrons—including many celebrities—must have a Mondrian room key, screen credit, or spot on the guest list. The view is as fabulous as the clientele. ✉ 8440 Sunset Blvd., West Hollywood ☎ 323/650–8999 ⊕ www.mondrianhotel.com.

TROUBADOUR. One of the most comfortable clubs in town has weathered the test of time since its '60s debut as a folk club. It now books alternative rock acts. ✉ 9081 Santa Monica Blvd., West Hollywood ☎ 310/276–6168 ⊕ www.troubadour.com.

WHISKY-A-GO-GO. It has to be the most famous rock-and-roll club on the Strip. It's where, back in the '60s, Johnny Rivers cut hit singles and the Doors cut their musical eye-teeth. It's still going strong, with up-and-coming alternative, hard rock, and punk bands. Monday sees L.A.'s cutting-edge acts. ✉ 8901 Sunset Blvd., West Hollywood ☎ 310/652–4202 ⊕ www.whiskyagogo.com.

Elsewhere

Both of the following clubs are in Los Feliz, just a few minutes northeast of Hollywood, and well worth seeking out.

DERBY. Come to this spacious, elegant club with a 360-degree brass-railed bar and plush-velvet curtained booths on Sunday when the emphasis is on swing and jazz. There are free dance lessons at 8 PM, live music begins at 9:30 or 10, and the cover ranges from free to $10. ✉ 4500 Los Feliz Blvd., Los Feliz ☎ 323/663–8979 ⊕ www.the-derby.com.

★ **DRESDEN ROOM.** A '40s-style loungey bar immortalized in the film *Swingers*, the Dresden Room is a must. It's a popular hangout with old-timers and Gen X lounge lizards alike. Marty and Elayne (also seen in the film) perform nightly, except Sunday, 9 PM–1:15 AM, and burn up the joint with inimitable covers of "Staying Alive," "Livin' La Vida Loca," and "Muskrat Love." (Elayne does an unbelievable muskrat impression.) There's no cover, but there is a two-drink minimum. ⊠ 1760 N. Vermont Ave., Los Feliz ☎ 323/665-4294 ⊕ www.thedresden.com.

HELPFUL INFO

Air Travel

American Airlines is the official carrier of the Los Angeles Marathon. Check with the marathon for the latest discount codes. The major gateway is Los Angeles International Airport (LAX). Smaller airports include Ontario International Airport (ONT), about 35 mi east of Los Angeles, Burbank/Glendale/Pasadena Airport (BUR) in the San Fernando Valley, and Long Beach Airport (LGB), at the southern tip of Los Angeles County.

🛃 **American Airlines** ☎ 800/433-1790 ⊕ www.aa.com. **Burbank/Glendale/Pasadena Airport** ⊠ 2627 N. Hollywood Way, Burbank ☎ 818/840-8830 or 818/840-8847 ⊕ www. burbankairport.com. **Long Beach Airport** ⊠ 4100 Donald Douglas Dr. ☎ 562/570-2600 ⊕ www.lgb.org. **Los Angeles International Airport (LAX)** ☎ 310/646-5252 ⊕ www.lawa. org. **Ontario International Airport** ⊠ Airport Dr. and Vineyard Ave. ☎ 909/937-2700 ⊕ www.lawa.org.

AIRPORT TRANSFERS

LAX provides free bus service from one terminal to another, and the car rental companies also have gratis shuttles to their nearby branches. It can take at least 45 minutes to drive downtown via the 105 East to the 110 North.

Taxis cost $38 between downtown L.A. and LAX, plus a $2.50 surcharge. Taxis to and from Ontario Airport can cost up to $40 or $50, depending on traffic. Taxis between downtown and the Burbank airport run $35 to $40. From Long Beach Airport, trips to downtown L.A. are roughly $60.

For two or three travelers, shuttle services are economical at $12–$20 per person, though the ride is generally longer than a cab ride. These big vans typically circle the airport repeatedly to fill up with passengers. Your travel time will be determined in part by how many other travelers are dropped off before you. At LAX, Prime Time and SuperShuttle allow passengers without prior reservations; otherwise, you'll need to make a reservation at least 24 hours in advance for a ride either to or from an airport.

🛃 **SHUTTLE OPERATORS Prime Time** ☎ 800/RED-VANS ⊕ www.primetimeshuttle.com. **SuperShuttle** ☎ 800/BLUE-VAN ⊕ www.supershuttle.com. **Xpress Shuttle** ☎ 800/I-AR-RIVE ⊕ www.expressshuttle.com.

🄳TAXIS Bell Cab ☎888/235-5222 ⊕www.bellcab.com. Checker Cab ☎800/300-5007. Independent Cab Co. ☎800/521-TAXI ⊕www.taxi4u.com.

Bus Travel

The only Greyhound terminal is in an industrial area of downtown, off Alameda Street. Taxis serve it. Greyhound has dozens of daily trips in and out of Los Angeles. Buy tickets by phone, on the Greyhound Web site (at least two hours before departure), or at the terminal.

🄳BUS INFORMATION Greyhound ✉1716 E. 7th St., Downtown ☎213/629-8405 or 800/231-2222 ⊕www.greyhound.com.

Car Travel

Finding your way can be a piece of cake or a nightmare. Your best bet is simply to get clear directions and stick to them. The *Thomas Guide*, a hefty, spiral-bound, super-thorough street guide and directory (with L.A. and Orange County versions), is published annually and is sold in book, drug, and grocery stores.

Traffic can be ugly in L.A., but you can make it more palatable by avoiding rush hours. That said, when traffic is good, the dad in *Clueless* is right: "Everywhere in L.A. takes 20 minutes." Here's a quickie guide to the major freeways:

U.S. ROUTE 101: connects the Valley and downtown, running north–south on a diagonal, so you might see it called the 101 North and South or the 101 East and West. Just know that, with the 101, "west" really means "north."

STATE ROUTE 134: runs east–west through Burbank, Glendale, and Pasadena.

INTERSTATE 5: runs north–south from Sacramento to San Diego, cutting through downtown on its way.

INTERSTATE 10: runs east–west all the way across the country, cutting through downtown on its way to Santa Monica, where it ends at the beach.

INTERSTATE 405: runs north–south, connecting the airport, the Westside, and the Valley. No freeway is pretty during rush hour, but the 405 can be a special kind of nightmare, and the 405/101 interchange is often cited as the country's worst.

INTERSTATE 105: heads east from LAX.

INTERSTATE 110: connects Pasadena and downtown.

🄳MAJOR RENTAL AGENCIES Alamo ☎800/327-9633 ⊕www.alamo.com. Avis ☎800/331-1212 ⊕www.avis.com. Budget ☎800/527-0700 ⊕www.budget.com. Dollar ☎800/800-4000 ⊕www.dollar.com. Hertz ☎800/654-3131 ⊕www.hertz.com. National Car Rental ☎800/227-7368 ⊕www.nationalcar.com.

Disabilities & Accessibility

Check LA Tourist.com for excellent information on accessibility throughout the city.

🄳LA Tourist.com ⊕www.latourist.com/accessible.htm.

Emergencies

🚩 **HOSPITALS Cedars–Sinai Medical Center** ✉ 8700 Beverly Blvd., Westside ☎ 310/4–CEDARS ⊕ www.cedars-sinai.edu. **USC Medical Center** ✉ 1200 N. State St., Downtown ☎ 323/226–2622 ⊕ www.usc.edu.

🚩 **PHARMACIES Rite Aid** ⊕ www.riteaid.com.

Metro Travel

The Metro Red Line starts downtown and can take you to Hollywood, Pasadena, or the Valley. Fares are $1.25 per boarding or $3 for a day pass. The Metropolitan Tranportation Authority (MTA) has route maps and more information.

🚩 **MTA** ☎ 800/COMMUTE ⊕ www.mta.net

Train Travel

Downtown's beautiful art deco Union Station is one of the grande dames of railroad stations. The interior is well kept and includes comfortable seating, a restaurant, and snack bars. As the city's rail hub, it's the place to catch an Amtrak train.

🚩 **TRAIN INFORMATION Amtrak** ☎ 800/872–7245 ⊕ www.amtrak.com. **Union Station** ✉ 800 N. Alameda St., Downtown ☎ 213/683–6979.

CHAPTER 4

APRIL

Boston Marathon

The buzz began as soon as I got on the Jetway for the flight from LAX to Boston. I heard it from all sides:

"We have to start off slow. Easy eight-minute miles."

"Last year I died on Heartbreak Hill."

"Did you remember the body glide?"

Nearly every person was on his or her way either to run the Boston Marathon or to cheer a runner on.

And the energy was palpable.

Boston is the most prestigious marathon around, bar none. People travel from all over the world to make the 26.2-mile trek from Hopkinton, Massachusetts, to Boylston Street, and thus earn the awe and admiration of anyone even remotely involved with the sport. I'm serious: tell a fellow marathoner that you've done Boston, and you'll see the change in his or her eyes. Not only does it carry the cachet of being the nation's longest-running marathon (circa 1897), but it's also the only one (aside from Olympic and Olympic trials marathons) that requires you to qualify for participation. Even the most casual marathoner is inspired by the dream of one day qualifying for Boston.

Bostonians themselves take enormous pride in their marathon, as they do about everything else in this town. (Don't even start about the Red Sox.) Spectators come out in droves to line the route and cheer their lungs out.

So You're Running Boston . . .

Boston is a very accessible city and quite safe. (Just use common sense.) In decent weather, it's very much a walking town. In inclement weather you can always hop a cab or take the T—the fantastic subway system. Even far-flung areas are rendered close via the T, so there's no need to rent a car.

BACK BAY. This is the place to stay during marathon weekend. It's close to expo transportation and starting area shuttles as well as the finish line. In American lore, the Back Bay stands with New York's Park Avenue and San Francisco's Nob Hill as a symbol of high social standing. You'll also find lots of great shopping and dining.

BEACON HILL. Beacon Hill is Boston at its most Bostonian. The redbrick elegance of its narrow, cobbled streets transports you back to the 19th century. This beautiful neighborhood is very close to the Back Bay, and during the day you can walk from one to the other through Boston Common, the country's oldest public park. By sunrise on nice days it's filled with joggers and walkers, and throughout the day people come to run, bike, rollerblade, or just relax and feed the ducks in the pond.

SAINT RALPH

The Boston Marathon has always held great significance for its participants, but never so much as in the movie *Saint Ralph*, in which a 14-year-old boy becomes convinced that if he can win the Boston Marathon, it will be miracle enough to help save his ailing mother. The writer and director of the movie, Michael McGowan, is a marathoner himself. He won the 1985 Detroit Marathon, and was a contender for the Canadian Olympic team in 1996.

Given the subject of his movie, it's clear that marathoning had a profound impact on McGowan's life. I asked how the sport had changed him, and he said it gave him a sense of perspective. More than anything, the marathon clearly showed him the arbitrariness between success and failure. You spend months and months training and can do everything right, yet in the end it comes down to your race-day performance, which can be affected by a million things beyond your control. "The marathon is really 26.2 miles of potential disaster," he says, and no matter how hard you train, you can't control its outcome. You might not win; you might not get the time you want. And that has to be OK. Marathoners learn that failing doesn't make you a failure, just as winning doesn't make you a winner.

In the movie, Ralph makes a journey familiar to all first-time marathoners. By taking on the challenge of 26.2 miles, he reaches for something seemingly well beyond his grasp, and his determination flies in the face of all logic. As McGowan himself says, "It makes no logical sense for anyone to want to run 26.2 miles," and yet people push themselves to try nonetheless. That in itself is a triumph of the human spirit, and one celebrated by McGowan's film.

No longer a competitive runner, McGowan now puts the lessons he learned from marathoning to use in his life as a filmmaker. Both pursuits involve "chasing after miracles": putting in the effort day after day, with no guarantee of success. Instead of logging daily miles, McGowan now logs words, but the goal is the same: the pursuit of a dream, an effort that allows people to transcend the mundane. "There is nothing more boring than training for a marathon," McGowan says, "but the sublime of a beautiful effort in the marathon is worth it. There's something miraculous in that quest." And as Campbell Scott's character in *Saint Ralph* says, "If we're not chasing after miracles, what's the point?"

GOVERNMENT CENTER & THE NORTH END. Heading northeast from the Back Bay, you come to Government Center, home to city hall. Abutting Government Center is the North End. Although it's one of the country's oldest neighborhoods, what you see today is almost entirely a creation of the late 19th century, when brick tenements filled up with European immigrants. You'll find dozens of old-world–style groceries, bakeries, churches, and cafés, plus authentic Italian restaurants. Carbo-load dinner, anyone?

DOWNTOWN. The Financial District—what Bostonians call "downtown"—is just a short T ride (or a long walk) from the Back Bay. There's little logic to the streets here; they were,

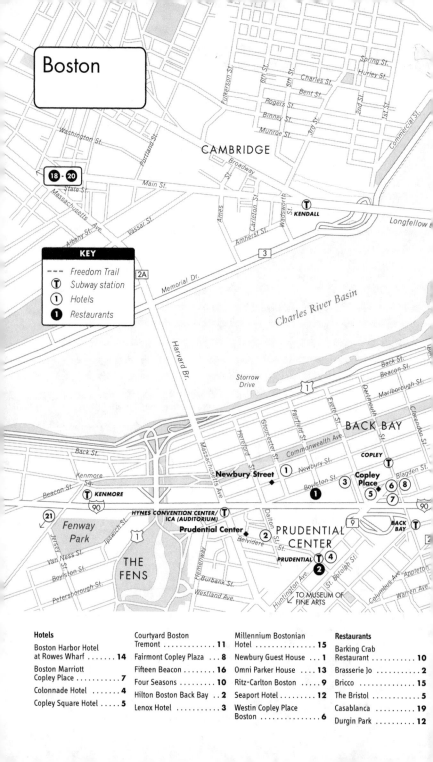

Boston

KEY

- - - Freedom Trail
T Subway station
① Hotels
❶ Restaurants

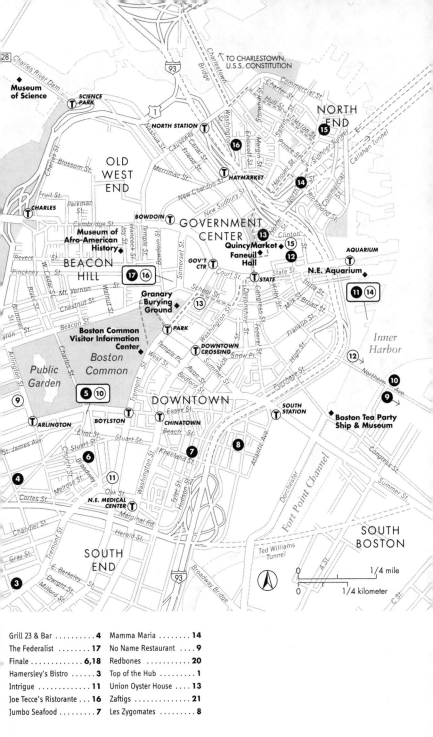

after all, village lanes that now happen to be lined with 40-story office towers. Downtown is home to some of Boston's most idiosyncratic districts. The Leather District directly abuts Chinatown, which is also bordered by the Theater District farther west. Head east to hit the Inner Harbor and Waterfront, an area coming into its own.

SOUTH END. The South End has gone through many incarnations over the years. Today it's in fashion with ethnic enclaves, upscale eateries, and redbrick row houses in various states—from refurbished splendor to genteel decay. It's also known for its large, well-connected gay community, which started the area's gentrification more than two decades ago and has brought with it a neighborly feel.

THE FENS. Two quirky institutions give this area its character: Fenway Park, no longer a monument to perennial heartbreak, and the Isabella Stewart Gardner Museum, the legacy of a 19th-century bon vivant Brahmin. Kenmore Square, a favorite haunt of college students, adds a bit of funky flavor to the mix.

CAMBRIDGE. Pronounced with either prideful satisfaction or a smirk, the nickname "The People's Republic of Cambridge" sums up this independent city of nearly 100,000 over the Charles River from Boston. Cambridge is not only the home of two great educational institutions, Harvard University and the Massachusetts Institute of Technology, but also has a long history as a haven for freethinkers, writers, and activists of every stamp.

VISITOR INFO

Greater Boston Convention
and Visitors Bureau
🌐
www.bostonusa.com
•
Massachusetts Office of
Travel and Tourism
☎
617/973-8500 or
800/227-MASS
🌐
www.massvacation.com

RACE BASICS

The marathon is run each year on Patriots' Day, the third Monday in April. Never heard of Patriots' Day? I hadn't either, so you're not alone. The holiday commemorates the beginning of the Revolutionary War, and is celebrated only in Maine and in Boston, a city that takes its patriots as seriously as its marathons. There are many Patriots' Day traditions, but perhaps none so revered as the early Red Sox game at Fenway Park (usually against the despised New York Yankees), timed perfectly so fans can emerge from the stadium and cheer for the marathoners as they run by.

A citywide long weekend, a wicked-awesome baseball game, and arguably the country's greatest marathon. Is it any wonder the whole town feels like a party on race day?

DO I REALLY HAVE TO QUALIFY?

The basic answer is "yes"; the Boston Marathon prides itself on being a qualifying race. As with every rule, however, there are exceptions—three of them in this case, two of which are legitimate.

DO THE RIGHT THING. Every year 16 charities get a total of 1,200 bib numbers, which go to people running to raise money for the charities. An official-charity runner need only be able to finish the race in six hours. If you want to run for charity, check with the BAA after the Labor Day prior to the marathon for the list of official charities. Then contact those charities directly and ask them about their Boston Marathon program.

BE AN EXCEPTION TO GET AN EXCEPTION. Each year a couple hundred bib numbers are reserved for "special circumstance" cases. A special circumstance can be a soldier who was overseas and didn't get the chance to run his or her qualifying race; a marathoner who has run Boston 10 years in a row, desperately wants to keep his or her streak going, but couldn't qualify due to injury; or even a friend of someone in the BAA who has always wanted to do the race but couldn't make the time. These exceptions are handled case by case, and make up a minuscule percentage of the official runners.

BE A BANDIT. No, I'm not telling you to rob a bank. Every year, 1,500 to 3,000 people (depending on the weather) run the marathon unofficially, as "bandits." Although the bandits have become part of the character of the race, I can't recommend going this route, especially as a traveling marathoner. It's incredibly difficult to get to Hopkinton from Boston without a bib number and a ride on an official shuttle; you start the race well after all the official participants; and if you finish, you don't even get an official race time or medal for your efforts. Besides, the BAA works hard to make the entire marathon weekend an experience of a lifetime, and you just can't get that experience unless you enter the race legitimately.

Qualifying

As mentioned, one of the thrills (or horrors, if you're a slower runner like me) of Boston is that you have to qualify for it. The qualifying time is valid only if it's in a certified marathon, which most races are. (Contact individual races to be sure.) You must qualify within 18 months before your attempt at Boston. In other words, to run Boston 2007, you need to qualify sometime after September 2005. Check out the charts to see if you've made the cut. Note that the age refers to how old you'll be the day of the Boston Marathon.

In addition to the qualifying times cited in the charts, there are time requirements for visually impaired athletes, who must have a qualifying race of no more than five hours.

CLASS	AGE	MEN	WOMEN
	18–34	3 hrs, 10 mins	3 hrs, 40 mins
	35–39	3 hrs, 15 mins	3 hrs, 45 mins
	40–44	3 hrs, 20 mins	3 hrs, 50 mins
	45–49	3 hrs, 30 mins	4 hrs, 00 mins
	50–54	3 hrs, 35 mins	4 hrs, 05 mins
	55–59	3 hrs, 45 mins	4 hrs, 15 mins
	60–64	4 hrs, 00 mins	4 hrs, 30 mins
	65–69	4 hrs, 15 mins	4 hrs, 45 mins
	70–74	4 hrs, 30 mins	5 hrs, 00 mins
	75–79	4 hrs, 45 mins	5 hrs, 15 mins
	80 and over	5 hrs, 00 mins	5 hrs, 30 mins

Athletes who, "because of the nature of their disability, have difficulty ambulating" must have a qualifying time of six hours, and athletes who, "because of the nature of their disability, need mobility aids such as prosthetics, leg braces, or crutches to ambulate" must have a qualifying time of eight hours.

The folks in Boston are pretty generous with their seconds. In other words, if you're a 50-year-old guy who runs the Chicago Marathon in 3:35:59, you still qualify for Boston. But add just one more second, you're out of luck and cursing that blasted potty break.

The Boston Marathon doesn't mess around much. But that's part of what makes it so special.

If you've already qualified, or feel that with a little effort you can qualify, fantastic! Make it happen, and kick some serious Boston butt. If you do well, you can even use your time to qualify for the next year's Boston Marathon. If, however, those qualifying times bring on a slight migraine, don't feel bad. I'm a woman in my early 30s, who's in reasonable shape and has run seven marathons. Using my best finishing time ever, I'd still have to be 70–74 years old to qualify for Boston.

Registration

You can register roughly six months before the race, sometime in September. Register the minute you qualify, and get a jump on planning your trip; the city books up fast. Registration costs $95 if you live in the United States and $125 if you live abroad. The fee covers your entry, transportation from Boston to the Hopkinton starting line, and admission for one to the prerace pasta party and the official after party.

Online registration is easy. After you've registered, you'll get a welcome book (via e-mail and/or snail mail) that tells you everything you need to know about the race, the course, the expo, and all the other marathon events.

The official Web site has great information about the race, its history, the course, and Patriots' Day weekend in Boston. It's not, however, the easiest site to navigate. If you're looking for something specific, you may be scrolling and clicking through several screens before you find it.

Hotels to Consider

Your best bet for this marathon is to stay in the Back Bay, within walking distance of the marathon shuttles and the finish line. Other hotel options are just a quick T or cab ride away. A great way to get deals on hotels is booking through **MARATHON TOURS** (☎ 617/242–7845 or 800/444–4097 ⊕ www.marathontours.com).

Back Bay

🏃 **BOSTON MARRIOTT COPLEY PLACE.** Enter this megahotel through a street-level lobby, a glass sky bridge from the Prudential Center/Hynes Auditorium, or from the Copley Plaza shopping mall. Guest rooms have French colonial–style dark-wood furniture and burgundy-and-green color schemes. Some look out toward Boston Harbor or the Charles. The location is very convenient for marathoners, as are the health club's hot tub, sauna, and massage services. Starbucks opens early marathon morning, so runners can grab food on their way to the shuttles. ✉ 110 Huntington Ave., Back Bay, 02116 ☎ 617/236–5800 or 800/228–9290 ⊕ www.marriott.com 🛏 1,100 rooms, 47 suites 🍴 4 restaurants, coffee shop, 24-hr room service, wake-up calls, alarm clocks, coffeemakers, newspapers,

Wheelchair Qualifying Times

CLASS	AGE	MEN	WOMEN
Open (Classes 3 & 4)	18–39	2 hrs, 00 mins	2 hrs, 25 mins
	40–49	2 hrs, 15 mins	2 hrs, 40 mins
	50 and over	2 hrs, 30 mins	2 hrs, 55 mins
Quad (Classes 1 & 2)	18–39	2 hrs, 45 mins	3 hrs, 10 mins
	40–49	3hrs, 00 mins	3 hrs, 25 mins
	50 and over	3 hrs, 15 mins	3 hrs, 40 mins

cable TV with movies and video games, in-room data ports, in-room safes, refrigerators, indoor pool, 24-hr gym, hot tub, massage, sauna, 2 bars, lounge, shop, dry cleaning, laundry service, concierge, concierge floor, business services, meeting rooms, car rental, parking (fee), no-smoking rooms ▭ AE, D, DC, MC, V Ⓜ Back Bay $$–$$$$.

★ **COLONNADE HOTEL.** Modern angles and clean lines greet you as you enter and extend to the well-appointed rooms. In-room amenity baskets include water, snacks, and historical information on the marathon. Room service and Brasserie Jo offer healthful pasta specials the three days before the race. There's also a Marathon Monday To-Go Breakfast in the lobby from 6 AM to 9:30 AM. ✉ 120 Huntington Ave., Back Bay, 02116 ☎ 617/424-7000 or 800/962-3030 ⊕ www.colonnadehotel.com ⇗ 273 rooms, 12 suites ⚙ Restaurant, 24-hr room service, wake-up calls, alarm clocks, newspapers, robes, cable TV with movies, in-room data ports, in-room safes, minibars, Wi-Fi (fee), pool, gym, bar, babysitting, dry cleaning, laundry service, concierge, business services, meeting rooms, airport shuttle, parking (fee), some pets allowed, no-smoking floors ▭ AE, D, DC, MC, V Ⓜ Prudential $$$–$$$$.

COPLEY SQUARE HOTEL. Built circa 1891, this hotel has a quirky turn-of-the-last-century charm. It also has a convenient location and discounted rates for marathoners. The property is busy yet comfortable, with winding corridors and repro-antique furniture. Rooms are idiosyncratic; some have couches. Complimentary afternoon tea is served daily in the lobby. On marathon morning, runners can have breakfast early at the hotel or grab a boxed breakfast and go. ✉ 47 Huntington Ave., Back Bay, 02116 ☎ 617/536-9000 or 800/225-7062 ⊕ www.copleysquarehotel.com ⇗ 142 rooms, 6 suites ⚙ 2 restaurants, room service, wake-up calls, alarm clocks, coffeemakers, cable TV with movies, in-room safes, free Wi-Fi, 24-hr gym, 3 bars, dry cleaning, laundry service, concierge, business services, parking (fee), no-smoking floors ▭ AE, D, DC, MC, V Ⓜ Copley $$$.

🏃 **FAIRMONT COPLEY PLAZA.** Not only is it near the shuttles to Hopkinton *and* the finish line, but it's also marathon headquarters. The 1912 landmark hotel feels ornate and imposing, with high gilded and painted ceilings, mosaic floors, and marble pillars, but the staff is absolutely welcoming and accommodating, and the rooms are very comfortable. ✉ 138 St. James Ave., Back Bay, 02116 ☎ 617/267-5300 or 800/441-1414 ⊕ www.fairmont.com ⇗ 366 rooms, 17 suites ⚙ Restaurant, 24-hr room service, wake-up calls, alarm clocks, newspapers, robes, cable TV with movies, in-room data ports, minibars, gym, bar, shop, babysitting, dry cleaning, laundry service, concierge, concierge floor, business services, meeting rooms, parking (fee), some pets allowed, no-smoking floors ▭ AE, D, DC, MC, V Ⓜ Copley, Back Bay $$$$.

★ **FOUR SEASONS.** The location is great, and nowhere else will you find such luxury, comfort, and service. Marathoners get a small welcome gift, such as a granola bar or energy drink. After the race, look for complimentary fruit, water, and chilled towels in the lobby as well as energy bars and drinks in the fitness center. The hotel's excellent spa staffs extra therapists for the post-race rush. Relax your aching legs in the hot tub or the 51-foot lap pool, both of which offer amazing Public Garden views. ✉ 200 Boylston St., Back Bay, 02116 ☎ 617/338-4400 or 800/332-3442 ⊕ www.fourseasons.com ⇗ 201 rooms, 72 suites ⚙ 2 restaurants, 24-hr room service, wake-up calls, alarm clocks, robes, cable TV with movies, in-room data ports, in-room safes, minibars, indoor pool, 24-hr gym, hot tub, spa, bar, lounge, babysitting, dry cleaning, laundry service, concierge, business services, meeting rooms, parking (fee), some pets allowed, no-smoking rooms ▤AE, D, DC, MC, V Ⓜ Arlington $$$$.

HILTON BOSTON BACK BAY. Rooms here have oversize showers and wall-to-wall windows that overlook the Back Bay and Fenway Park. If you crave fresh air, request one of the older rooms, which have windows that open and balconies. On Marathon Monday, the lobby lounge opens at 5:30 AM and is stocked with fruit, pastries, coffee, and the like for purchase; there's also a water station in the lobby. Discounted rates are available for marathoners. ⊠40 Dalton St., Back Bay, 02115 ☎617/236–1100 or 800/874–0663 ⊕ www.hilton.com ↪375 rooms, 10 suites ♨Restaurant, room service, wake-up calls, alarm clocks, coffeemakers, newspapers weekdays, robes, cable TV with movies and video games, in-room data ports, minibars, Wi-Fi (fee), indoor pool, 24-hr gym, hot tub, lounge, dry cleaning, laundry service, shop, concierge, concierge floor, business services, meeting rooms, parking (fee), no-smoking rooms ▤AE, D, DC, MC, V Ⓜ Hynes Convention Center $$–$$$$.

LENOX HOTEL. It's right on the finish line, runners get discounts, the restaurant opens early on Marathon Monday, and there are also boxed breakfasts to go. The archways, elaborate moldings, and other period details in this 1900 building are quite handsome. Twelve of the airy, spacious corner rooms have working fireplaces. All rooms have such modern touches as custom-made furnishings and marble baths; some rooms also have walk-in closets. ⊠61 Exeter St., Back Bay, 02116 ☎617/536–5300 or 800/225–7676 ⊕ www.lenoxhotel.com ↪210 rooms, 4 suites ♨2 restaurants, room service, wake-up calls, alarm clocks, newspapers weekdays, robes, in-room data ports, cable TV with movies, in-room fax, free Wi-Fi, 24-hr gym, 2 bars, dry cleaning, laundry service, concierge, business services, meeting rooms, parking (fee), no-smoking rooms ▤AE, D, DC, MC, V Ⓜ Copley $$$.

★**NEWBURY GUEST HOUSE.** This elegant redbrick-and-brownstone 1882 row house is a wildly successful bed-and-breakfast on Boston's most fashionable shopping street. Many marathon guests return year after year, so be sure to book a few months ahead. Rooms, which have queen-size beds, natural pine floors, and elegant reproduction Victorian furnishings, open off an oak staircase. Prints from the Museum of Fine Arts adorn the walls. Some rooms have bay windows; others have decorative fireplaces. Breakfast is served early for runners on Marathon Monday, and if post-race legs are too sore to climb stairs, there's an elevator. ⊠261 Newbury St., Back Bay, 02116 ☎617/437–7666 or 800/437–7668 ⊕ www.newburyguesthouse.com ↪32 rooms ♨Wake-up calls, alarm clocks, robes, cable TV, in-room data ports, free Wi-Fi, concierge, parking (fee) ▤AE, D, DC, MC, V ⅠⓄⅠCP Ⓜ Copley, Hynes Convention Center $.

RITZ-CARLTON BOSTON. The interior is a vision in white. It's just across from the Public Garden and convenient to the Hopkinton shuttles and the finish line, and like all Ritz hotels, it's dedicated to pampering its guests. Free bottled water is available at the entrance every morning. There's no spa, but massage therapists are available upon request. ⊠15 Arlington St., Back Bay, 02116 ☎617/536–5700 or 800/241–3333 ⊕ www.ritzcarlton.com ↪237 rooms, 35 suites ♨2 restaurants, 24-hr room service, wake-up calls, alarm clocks, newspapers, robes, cable TV with movies and video games, in-room data ports, in-room safes, minibars, 24-hr gym, massage, bar, lounge, babysitting, laundry service, concierge, concierge floor, business services, meeting rooms, parking (fee), some pets allowed, no-smoking floors ▤AE, D, DC, MC, V Ⓜ Arlington $$$–$$$$.

WESTIN COPLEY PLACE BOSTON. From the windows of this 36-story hotel you can gaze at the Charles River, Copley Square, the South End, or the Back Bay. Rooms are done in fresh beige and dark green. The lobby has abundant chairs, freestanding reading lamps, lots of large plants, and a comforting fireplace. The hotel is close to the Hopkinton shuttles and the finish line; the Grettacole spa is just off the lobby. Area running maps from *Runner's World* are available for warm-up or cool-down jaunts. ⊠ 10 Huntington Ave., Back Bay, 02116 ☎ 617/262-9600 or 800/937-8461 ⊕ www.westin.com/copleyplace 659 rooms, 141 suites ♿ 5 restaurants, coffee shop, 24-hr room service, wake-up calls, alarm clocks, coffeemakers, newspapers weekdays, robes, cable TV with movies and video games, in-room data ports, in-room safes, minibars, refrigerators, indoor pool, 24-hr gym, hair salon, hot tub, spa, bar, shop, dry cleaning, laundry service, concierge, business services, meeting rooms, airport shuttle, car rental, parking (fee), some pets allowed, no-smoking rooms ⊟ AE, D, DC, MC, V Ⓜ Back Bay $$$-$$$$.

Beacon Hill

★ **FIFTEEN BEACON.** Old-school cage elevators meld with modern art and comforts in this stylish boutique hotel. Fresh flowers and fruit and Italian-made 300-thread-count sheets add luxury to every room. All bathrooms have heated towel racks, and some have whirlpool tubs—a real treat after the race. The night before the run, marathoners receive an amenity basket with fruit, energy bars, water, and a note wishing them luck. If you'd rather not walk several blocks to the shuttles on race morning, prearrange a complimentary ride with the hotel's Mercedes service. ⊠ 15 Beacon St., Beacon Hill, 02108 ☎ 617/670-1500 or 877/982-3226 ⊕ www.xvbeacon.com 45 rooms, 15 suites ♿ Restaurant, 24-hr room service, wake-up calls, newspapers, robes, cable TV, in-room data ports, in-room fax, in-room safes, minibars, 24-hr gym, bar, dry cleaning, laundry service, concierge, meeting room, parking (fee), some pets allowed, no-smoking rooms ⊟ AE, D, DC, MC, V Ⓜ Park Street, Downtown Crossing $$$$.

Downtown

★ **BOSTON HARBOR HOTEL AT ROWES WHARF.** If you have to stay beyond walking distance of the shuttles to Hopkinton and the finish line, stay at this harborside property. Marathoners get reduced rates; other perks include water-shuttle service to and from Logan Airport and spacious rooms with 360-thread-count sheets and down comforters. There's also a light-fare spa menu, free water in the lobby on race day, and free transportation to the starting area shuttles. Consider a massage in the hotel's phenomenal health club. ⊠ 70 Rowes Wharf, Downtown, 02110 ☎ 617/439-7000 or 800/752-7077 ⊕ www.bhh.com 203 rooms, 27 suites ♿ 2 restaurants, 24-hr room service, wake-up calls, alarm clocks, coffeemakers, newspapers, robes, cable TV with movies and video games, in-room data ports, minibars, indoor pool, health club, hot tub, sauna, spa, steam room, marina, bar, shop, babysitting, dry cleaning, laundry service, concierge, business services, meeting rooms, airport shuttle, parking (fee), some pets allowed, no-smoking floors ⊟ AE, D, DC, MC, V Ⓜ Aquarium, South Station $$$-$$$$.

MILLENNIUM BOSTONIAN HOTEL. It's a large luxury hotel with the intimacy of a much smaller property. It also goes out of its way for runners: special room rates and runner-friendly choices on room-service and restaurant menus. In the lobby on marathon day, look for complimentary sunblock and ice buckets filled with free bottled water. Between the oversize tubs in many rooms and the spa services at the neighboring health club (to which you have free access), you'll have no trouble relaxing after the race. There are also free freshly baked cookies in the lobby each afternoon—go ahead and indulge; you've earned it. ✉ 26 North St., at Faneuil Hall Marketplace, Downtown, 02109 ☎ 617/523-3600 or 800/343-0922 ⊕ www.millennium-hotels.com ➥ 187 rooms, 14 suites ⚴ Restaurant, 24-hr room service, wake-up calls, alarm clocks, newspapers, robes, cable TV with movies, in-room data ports, in-room safes, minibars, 24-hr gym, lounge, shop, babysitting, laundry service, concierge, business services, meeting rooms, airport shuttle, car rental, parking (fee), no-smoking floors ⊟ AE, D, DC, MC, V Ⓜ Government Center, Haymarket $–$$$$.

OMNI PARKER HOUSE. For a true taste of historic Boston, you can't beat the Parker House, America's oldest continuously operating hotel. Charles Dickens had his first reading of *A Christmas Carol* here, and JFK proposed to Jackie in the Parker House Restaurant, whose famous rolls Franklin and Eleanor Roosevelt adored. Gorgeous chandeliers and original woodwork lend majesty and history, yet the place still seems homey. It's just a few blocks from the Hopkinton shuttles and the finish line. Runners are treated to welcome packets in their rooms, and the lobby's snack cart is open early on race day. Runner-friendly items are added to the dinner menu, and a post-race runners' lounge just off the lobby provides water, snacks, and a great place to stretch. ✉ 60 School St., Downtown, 02108 ☎ 617/227-8600 or 800/843-6664 ⊕ www.omnihotels.com ➥ 530 rooms, 21 suites ⚴ Restaurant, 24-hr room service, wake-up calls, alarm clocks, coffeemakers, newspapers weekdays, robes, cable TV with movies and video games, in-room data ports, minibars, 24-hr gym, 2 bars, dry cleaning, shop, concierge, business services, meeting rooms, parking (fee), some pets allowed, no-smoking rooms ⊟ AE, D, DC, MC, V Ⓜ Park Street $–$$$.

Theater District

COURTYARD BOSTON TREMONT. Known for attracting an international crowd, the comfortable Tremont is a convenient home away from home for marathoners. It's within walking distance of the shuttles to Hopkinton and the finish line. ✉ 275 Tremont St., Theater District, 02116 ☎ 617/426-1400 or 800/331-9998 ⊕ www.marriott.com ➥ 322 rooms ⚴ Restaurant, wake-up calls, alarm clocks, coffeemakers, newspapers, cable TV with movies, in-room data ports, gym, lounge, dry cleaning, concierge, business services, meeting rooms, parking (fee), no-smoking floors ⊟ AE, D, DC, MC, V Ⓜ Boylston, New England Medical Center $$–$$$.

Waterfront

SEAPORT HOTEL. This hotel puts you right next to Boston's World Trade Center, a major plus when the expo is held there. Rooms are huge and have handcrafted cherry furniture, waterfront views, and marble bathrooms. Check out the excellent spa and health club, where the heated lap pool has music piped underwater. ✉ 1 Seaport La., World Trade Center, Waterfront, 02110 ☎ 617/385-4000 or 877/732-7678 ⊕ www.seaporthotel.com ➥ 396 rooms, 30 suites ⚴ Restaurant, café, 24-hr room service, wake-up calls, alarm clocks, coffeemakers, newspapers, robes, cable TV with movies and video games, in-room data ports, in-room safes, minibars, indoor pool, gym, spa, lounge, shop, babysitting, laundry service, concierge, business services, convention center, meeting rooms, airport shuttle, parking (fee), some pets allowed; no smoking ☱AE, D, DC, MC, V Ⓜ World Trade Center $$–$$$$.

AND YOU'RE OFF . . .

The Expo

The expo occurs the Saturday and Sunday before the race, from morning until early evening, and, as befits such a prestigious race, it's fantastic. It has more than 150 vendors showcasing and selling all kinds of food, drinks, clothing, books, equipment, and other merchandise. Anything a runner could possibly want or imagine is here. Even your nonrunning friends and family will enjoy checking out the booths, trying the free food and juice samples, and entering prize drawings. The expo also attracts excellent speakers; look for lectures on such topics as nutrition, running form, and even conquering the Boston course. Check your welcome book for the schedule of speakers.

CRUISE THE COURSE

For $25, you can tour the marathon course before the race. Contact **Marathon Tours** (☎ 800/444–4097 or 617/242–7845 ⊕ www.marathontours.com) for info and reservations.

The expo draws monumental crowds, especially on Sunday afternoon. Your best bet is to go early on either day. No matter when you go, set aside plenty of time to look around. Just scanning every booth could easily take an hour, and you'll need more time if you want to catch some speakers or take advantage of discount shopping.

Past expos have been held at the Hynes Convention Center in the Back Bay and the World Trade Center in the South Boston/Seaport district. You can easily get to either on foot or via the T, depending on where you're staying. Although the expo will most likely continue to bounce between these two venues, consult the Web site and/or your welcome book for the exact location.

Race Day

The Starting Area

The Boston Marathon starts in Hopkinton, Massachusetts; you'll be staying in Boston. How, then, do you get to the start? The BAA makes it simple with shuttle buses that pick you up in the Back Bay area, on the Tremont Street side of the Boston Common. The shuttles leave between 6:30 and 8:30 and carry only registered runners with bib numbers. Wheelchair racers should look at their bib number pick-up card for transportation information.

NIGHT-BEFORE PASTA DINNER

The prerace pasta buffet dinner, held in huge tents in Government Center's City Hall Plaza, is free to every marathoner. Friends and family are also welcome and can buy tickets at the expo for $15 each. The meal runs from about 4:30 to 8:30 and marathoners are encouraged to go during the assigned window of time based on their bib number, though that rule is rarely enforced. Expect a line to get into the tents, and enjoy live entertainment while you wait; more live entertainment plays in side. Give a wave to the mayor; he attends the dinner every year.

If you'd rather try something local before the race, bring your cheering section to the North End, filled with excellent Italian restaurants, including:

BRICCO. It's a sophisticated but unpretentious enclave of nouveau Italian. The velvety butternut-squash soup alone is argument for a reservation. Runners will enjoy the homemade pastas; nonrunners might gravitate to such simple but balanced main courses as roasted rabbit loin in pancetta. The room is conducive to relaxation, with its warmth and floor-to-ceiling windows. ✉ 241 Hanover St., North End ☎ 617/248–6800 ⊕ www.bricco.com ⌂ Reservations essential ⊟ AE, D, DC, MC, V Ⓜ Haymarket $$–$$$.

JOE TECCE'S RISTORANTE. Some find this North End landmark too touristy; others absolutely swear by the food and the prices. Joe Tecce's has been in business since 1948, and remains family owned. The decor is kicky and fun, the cuisine is genuine Neapolitan, and the portions are large. It's terrific for families. ✉ 61 N. Washington St. (Joe Tecce's Way), North End ☎ 617/742–6210 ⊕ www.joeteccees.com ⌂ Reservations essential ⊟ AE, DC, MC, V Ⓜ Haymarket $–$$.

MAMMA MARIA. Don't let the clichéd name fool you: Mamma Maria is one of the North End's most elegant restaurants. Runners will enjoy all the pasta and protein options, including the couple of extra pasta dishes added just for marathon time. Nonrunners will find plenty to love as well, from the innovative sauces and entrées to the daily tiramisu and other dessert specials. ✉ 3 North Sq., North End ☎ 617/523–0077 ⊕ www.mammamaria.com ⊟ AE, D, DC, MC, V ⊗ No lunch Ⓜ Haymarket, North Station, Government Center, Aquarium $$–$$$.

In the long hours between the first shuttle departure at 6:30 and the noon starting time, runners wait in Athletes' Village, less than a mile from the starting line in Hopkinton. The village has a tented hangout area, food, a stage with entertainment (local bands or speakers such as famous marathoners), free minimassages and of course, portable toilets. Around 11, runners start moving from the village into the actual start corrals.

Beginning in 2006 the Boston Marathon will implement a two-wave start. The waves will be determined by speed and will divide the field approximately in half. To accommodate this, the Athletes Village will be expanded, with a separate section for each wave, from which runners will be led to their starting corrals at the proper time.

With the new system in place, starting times for the marathon will run approximately as follows: 10 AM for some mobility-impaired athletes, 11:25 AM for wheelchair athletes, 11:31 AM for elite women, noon for elite men and the first wave of runners, and 12:30 PM for the second wave. Since runners (except prize-money winners) will be scored and ranked by net (chip) time, a second-wave start has no negative impact.

The Course

First, as you tromp over the starting line, take a moment to look down. Every year it's hand-painted by Jack LeDuc, who has taken it upon himself to turn it into a small work of art. He never uses the same pattern twice, and in case he's tempted to cheat, he actually destroys the stencil after the painting is complete. The result is a masterpiece on asphalt.

WEATHER THE RUN

Watch the forecasts: recent race temperatures have ranged from comfortable 50s to sweltering 80s. Early-morning temps at Athletes' Village are much cooler; layer for the morning wait.

From Hopkinton you'll run through the suburbs of Ashland, Framingham, Natick, Wellesley, and Newton, before finishing in the heart of Boston itself: Boylston Street by Copley Square, in front of the Boston Public Library. Water, energy drinks, and first aid stations appear approximately every mile, and there's a gel station around Mile 17.

Most of the route is lined with fans, which makes it a little easier to forget the aches in your legs. Just before Mile 13, you'll pass Wellesley College, an all-women's school with a tradition of turning out en masse to cheer. You'll hear the roar a good half mile before you see the women, and several marathoners claim that giant wall of sound literally pulls them through to the halfway point.

As for the lay of the land, the good news is that the marathon is almost all downhill. The bad news is that word "almost." Things get dicey in Newton. That's when you hit the foothills, which are only a prelude to the three larger hills, the third and largest of which bears the deservedly terrifying name Heartbreak Hill. This hill is brutal, and you may well want to rip out your quadriceps before it's over (far less painful than actually continuing to run with them), but once you've crested it, the last 5 miles are all downhill.

The course remains open until 6:30 PM, though early aid stations will start to close well before that. When you finish the race, to the adulation of the crowd, you get to savor a major accomplishment, and you get some well-deserved treats: the official finisher's medal, a Mylar blanket, musical entertainment, and lots of post-race-appropriate snacks. If you need a massage, there are roughly 200 therapists on hand in John Hancock hall, at the corner of Stuart and Berkeley. There will be a line and the massage will be short, but it will also be an oh-so-sweet way to kick-start your recovery. If your aches and pains need more than just a massage, there's also a large medical tent.

Spectating

Plenty of people cheer the start of the race. As a "traveling" spectator, however, you won't get to do so. Only runners are allowed on the buses to Hopkinton, so there's no good way

THE LEGEND OF JOHNNY KELLEY

You can't discuss Heartbreak Hill without mentioning Johnny Kelley (1907–2004), a two-time Olympian (1936, 1948) and Boston Marathon icon. Since 1928, Kelley had run this race 58 times, finishing in the top ten 18 times. Legend has it that Heartbreak Hill got its name in 1934, when its rigor made Kelley lose a gripping, race-long struggle for first place. Marathoners are reminded of Kelley's tenacity with *Young at Heart,* a statue at the bottom of the hill depicting a younger and an older Kelley holding hands as they cross the finish line.

for you to get there and see the race begin. That's the bad news. The good news is that while your favorite runners are getting up before dawn to hurry up and wait for several hours in Athletes' Village, you can sleep in and enjoy Boston until it's time to cheer them in the city.

The marathon's recommended cheering sites are all easily accessible by T:

WOODLAND: Mile 16.8, off the Green Line D.

BOSTON COLLEGE: Mile 21.4, off the Green Line B.

CLEVELAND CIRCLE: Mile 22.4, off the Green Line C.

KENMORE SQUARE: One mile to go, off the Green Line B, C, or D.

FINISH LINE: Boylston Street in the Back Bay.

If you have time, grab breakfast before you head off to cheer. If you eat in the city, just hop the appropriate Green Line when you're finished. If you want to skip out of town and breakfast at Zaftigs (⇨ "Breakfast Spots" box), take the C branch of the Green Line to Coolidge Corner. From there, according to Zaftigs' Web site, you exit the train and turn right onto Harvard Street, heading toward the Coolidge Corner cinema. Zaftigs is two blocks along on your right. Enjoy your breakfast, then check your time to see which cheering station to head to. For Woodland, take the T back five stops to Kenmore, switch to the D line, and take it 12 stops. For Boston College take the C line back to Kenmore, then switch to the B line and ride it to the end. For Cleveland Circle, take the C to the end of the line.

Marathon Monday is Patriots' Day, so generally allow more time for travel on the T and to find a good vantage point at often crowded cheering areas. Post-race, look for your runner at the family meeting area along Clarendon and St. James Avenue.

Celebrate!

In the evening, the BAA sponsors a dance party at a nightclub, usually in the Theater District or behind Fenway Park in the Kenmore Square area. Check the Web site and/or welcome book for details. Your friends and family can buy tickets at the door for $10 each. There's generally a cash bar, and sometimes a marathon sponsor will provide free beer. The party is a great way to celebrate your victory—and you never know, dancing may just loosen up your legs enough so that you can actually walk in the morning!

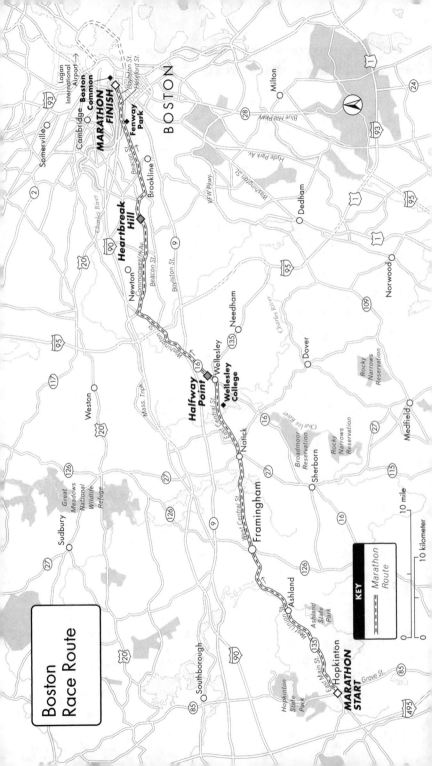

Boston
Race Route

BOSTON

MARATHON FINISH

Boston Common
Logan International Airport →
Cambridge
Somerville
Boylston St.
Hereford St.
Fenway Park
Brookline
Beacon St.

Heartbreak Hill
Newton
Commonwealth Av.
Boylston St.
Beacon St.
Charles River

Washington St.
Halfway Point
Wellesley
Wellesley College
Mass. Tnpk.
Weston

Natick
East Central St.
Central St.
West Central St.
Framingham

Ashland
Ashland State Park
West Union St.
East Main St.
Hopkinton
Grove St.
MARATHON START
Hopkinton State Park

Southborough
Sudbury
Great Meadows National Wildlife Refuge

Milton
Blue Hill Pkwy.
Hyde Park Av.
Washington St.
Dedham
Norwood
Needham
Dover
Charles River
Rocky Narrows Reservation
Sherborn
Broadmoor Reservation
Charles River
Rocky Narrows Reservation
Medfield

VFW Pkwy.

KEY
Marathon Route

0   10 mile
0   10 kilometer

2   93   20   90   9   16   16   27   135   126   27   95   109   28   11   24   93   1   95   95   117   27   85   85   495   126

TEAM HOYT

While running the course, keep an eye out for Team Hoyt, the incredible father-and-son team that's run 24 straight Boston Marathons, more than 200 triathlons, over 20 duathlons, and countless other races. The team's fastest marathon time is 2:40:47, a fantastic accomplishment made all the more stunning when you consider that half of this team can neither walk nor talk.

The Team Hoyt Web site tells their amazing story. When Rick Hoyt was born, his umbilical cord wrapped around his neck, cutting off oxygen to his brain and impairing his development. Though Rick can communicate only through a computer he controls with slight head movements, typing out letters of the alphabet, he's quite intelligent and defies all doctors' early expectations for him.

Dick and Rick have been racing together since 1977. In running matches, Dick pushes Rick's wheelchair; when cycling, Rick rides in a seat attached to the front of Dick's bike; during swims, Rick sits in a boat tethered to Dick's waist. The two are a fixture at the Boston Marathon, and have made remarkable strides in raising the profile of the physically challenged. For their full amazing story and information on the Hoyt Fund (a charity geared toward "enhancing the lives and mobility of people with disabilities"), check out their Web site: www.teamhoyt.com.

BEYOND THE FINISH LINE

Replacing 2,620 Calories

You've finished the marathon, and now you deserve to indulge. Boston can oblige. Whether you crave new and challenging flavors, comfort food, or a traditional New England lobster dinner, it's right here for the scarfing.

Back Bay/Beacon Hill

★ **THE FEDERALIST.** At this sophisticated restaurant in the swanky Fifteen Beacon hotel, Chef David Daniels's menu is a melding of modern and traditional, driven by local ingredients; look for such dishes as native quail breast with foie gras. The wine list, with more than 1,000 entries, is an impressive but expensive proposition. ⊠ Fifteen Beacon hotel, 15 Beacon St., Beacon Hill ☎ 617/670–2515 ⊕ www.xvbeacon.com ⊘ Reservations essential ☰ AE, D, DC, MC, V Ⓜ Park Street, Downtown Crossing $$$–$$$$.

★ **FINALE.** It's a restaurant whose main aim is to provide decadent desserts. What could possibly be bad? If you insist on eating more than just dessert, you can order from the "prelude" menu of appetizers to whet your appetite for the true main course—dessert. Chocolate Bliss, Fantasia, Molten Chocolate ... even the names are luscious. And it's all guilt-free for anyone who has just run a marathon. ⊠ One Columbus Ave., Back Bay ☎617/423-3184 ⊕ www.finaledesserts.com Ⓜ Arlington ⊠ 30 Dunster St., Cambridge ☎617/441-9797 Ⓜ Harvard Square ⚛ Reservations not accepted ☰ AE, D, DC, MC, V ⊘ No lunch weekends $$-$$$.

★ **GRILL 23 & BAR.** Pinstriped suits, dark paneling, comically oversize flatware, and waiters in white jackets give this steak house a posh, men's-club ambience. The menu is anything but predictable, with dishes such as rotisserie tenderloin with Roquefort mashed potatoes. Seafood plates such as grilled Maine salmon give beef sales a run for their money. Desserts, like the wonderfully tangy lemon cheesecake and the super-rich fallen chocolate soufflé cake, are far above average. ⊠ 161 Berkeley St., Back Bay ☎617/542-2255 ⊕ www.grill23.com ⚛ Reservations essential ☰ AE, D, DC, MC, V Ⓜ Arlington ⊘ No lunch $$-$$$.

TOP OF THE HUB. Sure, the food and drinks are pricey, but the view is simply not to be believed. On the 52nd floor of the Prudential Tower, the restaurant offers panoramas of Boston. If you come for dinner, classic American preparations of beef sirloin, lamb, swordfish, or, of course, lobster accompany the views. If a meal is too pricey, come for drinks and hang out in the cocktail lounge, where live jazz groups play nightly. Business casual dress is encouraged, but you won't get thrown out if you're not in a blazer and tie. ⊠ 800 Boylston St., Prudential Tower, 52nd fl, Back Bay ☎ 617/536-1775 ⊕ www.selectrestaurants.com ⚛ Reservations essential Ⓜ Prudential $$-$$$.

GETTING AROUND

The Copley T station is closed Marathon Monday. Instead, use Arlington, Back Bay, Prudential, or Hynes Convention Center/ICA (Auditorium). All are a short walk from Copley.

Cambridge/Somerville

CASABLANCA. Long before *The Rocky Horror Picture Show*, Harvard and Radcliffe types would don trench coats and head to the Brattle Theatre to see *Casablanca*, rising to recite the Bogart and Bergman lines in unison. Then it was on to this restaurant for more of the same. The path to this local institution is still well worn, thanks to phyllo-wrapped shrimp and grilled quail with almond-honey butter. ⊠ 40 Brattle St., Cambridge ☎617/876-0999 ⊕ www.casablanca-restaurant.com ☰ AE, D, DC, MC, V Ⓜ Harvard Square $$.

REDBONES. It's a bit out of the city (take the Red Line to Davis Square), but this southern food joint is highly touted. There's nothing fancy, just massive portions of delicious food. Get your ribs prepared in the style of Memphis, Texas, Arkansas, or St. Louis. If you're really hungry, add on corn pudding, candied yams, or hush puppies. Still have room? Try the sweet-potato pie. Be prepared to wait; while away the time with a microbrew from the long list. ⊠ 55 Chester St., Somerville ☎617/628-2200 ⊕ www.redbonesbbq.com ⚛ Reservations not accepted ☰ No credit cards Ⓜ Davis Square $-$$.

Downtown/Chinatown

JUMBO SEAFOOD. Although this Cantonese/Hong Kong–style restaurant has much to be proud of, it's happily unpretentious. Try a whole sea bass with ginger and scallion; nonoceanic plates are equally good. The Hong Kong influence results in a lot of fried food; crispy fried calamari with salted pepper is a standout. The waiters are very understanding,

BREAKFAST SPOTS

Several hotel restaurants have good morning meals (¢–$$). Those willing to venture farther afield can have a fantastic breakfast at Zaftigs in Brookline.

BRASSERIE JO. This restaurant in the Colonnade Hotel has a wonderful French brasserie feel. Its menu choices range from the all-American eggs, bacon, and toast to more unique crepes, two types of croque madame, and chocolate French toast with almonds. ✉ 120 Huntington Ave, Back Bay ☎ 617/425–3240 ⊕ www.colonnadehotel.com ▭ AE, D, DC, MC, V Ⓜ Prudential.

THE BRISTOL. This beautiful Four Seasons restaurant has windows overlooking the Public Garden. Look for dishes with a New England spin, such as lobster frittata with asparagus and goat cheese. All the breakfast standards are available, some with exciting twists like the rum-glazed banana French toast with spiced pecan butter. ✉ 200 Boylston St., Back Bay ☎ 617/338–4400 ⊕ www.fourseasons.com ▭ AE, D, DC, MC, V Ⓜ Arlington.

INTRIGUE. In the Boston Harbor Hotel, Intrigue offers a small but delicious breakfast menu. Enjoy the waterfront view through floor-to-ceiling glass doors. Indulge in something sweet, like the sour cream and raspberry pancakes with Vermont maple syrup. Savory dishes include the three-egg omelet with a choice of crabmeat, tomato, mushroom, broccoli, or cheddar cheese. ✉ 70 Rowes Wharf, Downtown ☎ 617/439–7000 ⊕ www.bhh.com ▭ AE, D, DC, MC, V Ⓜ Aquarium, South Station.

★ ZAFTIGS. As the Web site says, "This ain't your grandma's deli." Zaftigs has made a name for itself as a contemporary version of a Jewish deli. You can get all the deli standbys: lox and a bagel, fried matzo, eggs. You can also get banana-stuffed French toast in a bourbon-vanilla batter with date butter or a McIntosh apple and Vermont sharp cheddar omelet. You'll be so excited, you'll schvitz. ✉ 335 Harvard St., Brookline ☎ 617/975–0075 ⊕ www.zaftigs. com ▭ AE, D, DC, MC, V Ⓜ Coolidge Corner.

---

though some don't speak English fluently. ✉ 7 Hudson St., Chinatown ☎ 617/542-2823 ▭ AE, MC, V Ⓜ South Station $-$$$.

★ LES ZYGOMATES. *Les zygomates* is the French expression for the muscles on the human face that make you smile—and this combination wine bar/bistro inarguably lives up to its name, with classic French bistro fare that is both simple and simply delicious. Prix-fixe menus are available at lunch and dinner and could include oysters by the half dozen or pancetta-wrapped venison with roasted pears. ✉ 129 South St., Downtown ☎ 617/542-5108 ⊕ www.winebar.com ⚲ Reservations essential ▭ AE, D, DC, MC, V ☉ Closed Sun. No lunch Sat. Ⓜ South Station $$-$$$.

Bob Magnan has run the Boston Marathon 24 times.

Long and lanky with an unassuming smile, he's humble about his accomplishment. In fact, he'd be the first to tell you that he's nothing special; just a schoolteacher and a guy who was lucky enough to find and marry Cindy, the love of his life. But because he knew I was coming over to talk about the race, his dining room table was spread thick with memorabilia: finishers' and volunteer medals from years of Boston Marathons, newspaper clippings, photographs—even a painting, the significance of which I wouldn't learn about until later.

Bob isn't the kind of marathoner who travels all over the world, chasing the biggest, most unusual races. For him it's only about Boston, and his love of the race runs deep. He's been involved since his childhood in Hopkinton: he played trombone for the school band, and every year they'd perform the "Star Spangled Banner" before the opening gun. Years later Bob became a teacher in Hopkinton, and when he took over as band director, he also led a fresh crop of kids to the starting line every year. Still, he had no intention of running the marathon himself. His athletic dreams had always leaned toward those of most kids who grow up in Boston: he wanted to play for the Red Sox in Fenway Park.

The Sox never called, but by 1979 he had heard people say, "You're from Hopkinton? Have you run the marathon?" too many times. They always seemed a little disappointed when he replied "no." Clearly he had to give it a try, just so he could finally say yes and be done with it.

So Bob joined up with his friend Rick, and they trained to tackle the race. They jumped in as bandits, but back then the race was smaller and bandits weren't such a problem, so they still received medals. Bob swears he would have been fine ending his marathon career right there, but Rick was hooked, and he wanted company. Again and again, Rick goaded Bob into the race, until finally Bob caught the bug on his own. He started wearing a Superman T-shirt every year, and basked in the shouts from the sideline, "Go, Superman!" "Superman! Yeah!" His students also piled along the course to cheer him on, easing the way in those early miles.

Before long, the marathon became an essential part of Bob's year. Since he began, he has missed only three races: 1993 and 1994 when he was teaching overseas, and 2004, when neck disc surgery forced him to sit out. He ran in cold weather; he ran in the heat. He ran for fun, and he ran for causes, raising money for the Lions Club, the Birmingham Teachers' Association, and to start a scholarship fund in honor of a murdered ex-student. He ran after a bee flew in his mouth, and spent the next several miles imagining it stinging the inside of his throat again and again and again. . . before, amazingly, it flew out again. He ran after spending the night before the race so sick he could barely function. He ran after pulling a hamstring, a jolt that "felt like someone had just taken a rifle and shot me, right in the leg." He ran after his feet broke out in blisters so painful that he had to hobble into an aid station for help. "When they were treating me," he says, "I felt like they were branding me with a branding iron." And yet he put his sneakers back on and ran to the end.

Over the years, Bob has been a regular customer at the post-race medical tent. In fact, that's how his parents first saw his racing prowess. They were sitting at home in Hopkinton, only half paying attention to the TV's marathon coverage as they went about their day. By chance, his mother happened to look up just as the on-air reporter grimly described runners "suffering everything from blisters and cramps to severe dehydration." And there, on the screen, was Bob, lolling in a chair, barely conscious, the Superman emblem standing out ironically from his deflated chest. Within seconds Bob's image disappeared and the newscaster chirped on to happier stories, but Bob's parents were a mess, convinced the marathon had killed their son.

After another harsh race, Bob lay in the medical tent when an old man was helped into the cot beside him. It was none other than Johnny Kelley, Boston Marathon legend. Bob worried about Kelley. Sure, the man had run this marathon more times than Bob could count, but he was in his eighties, and lying there on the cot, he didn't look so good. But seemingly within minutes, Kelley was back on his feet, fully refreshed and rarin' to go. And Bob? Still too wasted to move.

This encounter wasn't the first time Bob had had the honor of meeting Johnny Kelley. During his years of consistently running the hometown marathon, Bob had become friendly with several of the race's organizers, and would meet with them every year after the race to drink beer, eat pizza, and swap war stories about the run. Kelley joined the party on occasion, and Bob got the honor of hearing *his* war stories. Once, Kelley even invited Bob out to his house on Cape Cod, where he showed Bob all his old medals from the 1936 Olympics, blackened with age. Painting was apparently a hobby of Kelley's, and Bob liked his works so much he bought one (that would be the painting laid out among Bob's marathon memorabilia). For his part, Kelley signed a jacket of Bob's, and a pair of his running shoes—mementos Bob still holds dear today.

The Boston Marathon is steeped in tradition. It's always run on Patriots' Day, and the course hasn't changed in years. Even some of the people stay the same, and to a regular like Bob, they're as familiar as characters on a favorite sitcom. There's the guy who dresses up as and walks just like Groucho Marx for the entire course. And the guy who runs backward, navigating with a mirror. And the guy who runs while pushing his son, who uses a wheelchair.

Then there are the other characters, who only come out once but who make a real splash. Like the guy who wore a suit made entirely of pennies. Or the one dressed as a tree. And then there was the year Bob found himself passing the Old North Church. Not the famous Boston landmark, but literally a guy running the marathon dressed up as the Old North Church.

Speak with Bob at any length about the marathon, and you begin to understand that it draws you into a community, something far bigger than any individual runner. Talk to him, and you'll want to run it too. When we spoke, he got misty. It was 2004, two days before the race. He was still recovering from neck-disc surgery, and the doctor had forbidden him to run. This would be the first Boston Marathon Bob would miss in nine years. The more he delved into stories, the hungrier he became for the taste of that race, and I could see his wife, Cindy, getting antsy. "Maybe I could still run it this year," he mused, but Cindy was adamant. The doctor said no. Cindy would she'd tie him down if she had to, but he was not running the race. Bob sighed, then smiled wistfully as the memories played in his head. "There's something about that marathon," he said. "I remember a couple times I was crying coming down the finish line, 'cause I couldn't believe I got there, couldn't believe it was almost over. There's no high like it." He gazed at Cindy and gave her a reassuring smile. "That's why I'm going to miss it this year." ∎

SOMETHING TO WINE ABOUT

After finishing a marathon, what better way to celebrate than with delectable food matched perfectly to a fine glass of wine? Boston has two restaurants ready to delight your palate in just that way. Granted, you might have to extend your long marathon weekend to enjoy them, but you'll find the experience well worth it.

Although **Les Zygomates** (⌂ 129 South St., Downtown ☎ 617/542–5108 ⊕ www.winebar.com Ⓜ South Station) is always a great choice for dinner, on Tuesday at 6 PM and 8 PM it becomes something special. Up to 40 people gather in a private room to eat, drink, learn about wine, and get a little irreverent. As their sommelier Geoffrey Fallon says, "Wine should be fun. The best way to learn about wine is by drinking it." Fallon, an ex-stand-up comic, keeps the room laughing as he teaches you to ferret out the subtler tones, body, and flavors of four to five wines. Every tasting has a theme: Chic Cali Chardonnays, Affordable Burgundy, Just Desserts. Les Zygomates also serves free appetizers that pair perfectly with each glass. And every tasting includes a cooking demonstration, at which chef Ian Just prepares one of the night's appetizers table-side. Tastings cost $25 (all major credit cards accepted), and reservations are essential.

For another marriage of delicacies and wines, head to Boston Harbor Hotel's **Meritage** (⌂ Rowes Wharf at the Boston Harbor Hotel, Downtown ☎ 617/439–3995 ⊕ www.bhh.com ⊗ No lunch. Closed Mon. Only brunch Sun. ⊟ AE, D, DC, MC, V Ⓜ Aquarium, South Station) restaurant. The menu is organized not by meat, fish, and poultry, but by sparklers, light whites, full-bodied whites, fruity reds, spicy/earthy reds, and robust reds. Lists of appropriate dishes appear under each wine category. Each dish is available as either a small plate ($15) or large plate ($29). Even the cocktails are matched perfectly to food. Periodically, the restaurant offers such events as the Eight Minute Wine Pairing, a tasting at which participants get to experience a new pour of wine and ideally matched tasting spoon every eight minutes; or the Wine School, which pairs wines with food in a five-course dinner. Even if no special programs are available during the marathon, the impeccable blend of food and wine offered by Meritage provides a truly unique dining experience.

Government Center

DURGIN PARK. You should be hungry enough to cope with enormous portions, yet not so hungry you can't tolerate a long wait. Durgin Park was serving its same hearty New England fare (Indian pudding, baked beans, corned beef and cabbage, and a prime rib that hangs over the edge of the plate) back when Faneuil Hall was a working market instead of a tourist attraction. The service is famously brusque bordering on rude bordering on good-natured. ⌂ 340 Faneuil Hall Market Pl., North Market Bldg., Government Center ☎617/227–2038 ⊕ www.durgin-park.com ▭AE, D, DC, MC, V Ⓜ Haymarket, Copley $–$$.

UNION OYSTER HOUSE. Established in 1826, this Fanueil Hall–area spot is Boston's oldest continuing restaurant. Consider having what Daniel Webster had—oysters on the half shell at the ground-floor raw bar, which is the oldest and best part of the restaurant. The rooms at the top of the narrow staircase are dark and have low ceilings—very Ye Olde New England—and plenty of nonrestaurant history. Uncomfortably small tables and chairs tend to undermine the simple, decent, but pricey food. ✉ 41 Union St., Government Center ☎617/227–2750 ⊕www.unionoysterhouse.com ▭AE, D, DC, MC, V Ⓜ Government Center, Haymarket $$–$$$.

South End

★**HAMERSLEY'S BISTRO.** Gordon Hamersley has earned a national reputation, thanks to such signature dishes as a grilled mushroom-and-garlic sandwich, duck confit, and souffléed lemon custard. His place has a full bar, a café area with 10 tables for walk-ins, and a larger dining room that's a little more formal and decorative. ✉ 553 Tremont St., South End ☎617/423–2700 ⊕ www.hamersleysbistro.com ▭AE, D, DC, MC, V Ⓜ Back Bay/South End, Copley Square $$–$$$.

Waterfront

BARKING CRAB RESTAURANT. It is, believe it or not, a seaside clam shack plunk in the middle of Boston, with a stunning view of the downtown skyscrapers. An outdoor lobster tent in summer, in winter it retreats indoors to a warmhearted version of a waterfront dive, with chestnuts roasting on a cozy woodstove. Look for the classic New England clambake—chowder, lobster, steamed clams, corn on the cob—or the spicier crab boil. The fried food lags. ✉ 88 Sleeper St. (Northern Ave. Bridge), Waterfront ☎617/426–2722 ⊕-www.barkingcrab.com ▭AE, DC, MC, V Ⓜ South Station $–$$.

NO NAME RESTAURANT. Famous for not being famous, the No Name sits right on the fish pier and has been serving fresh seafood, simply broiled or fried, since 1917. ✉ 15¹/₂ Fish Pier, off Northern Ave., Waterfront ☎617/338–7539 or 617/423–2705 ▭No credit cards Ⓜ World Trade Center $–$$.

Sightseeing on (and off) Your Feet

Boston is far older than the republic its residents helped create. The most famous buildings aren't merely civic landmarks but national icons. Local heroes are known to the nation: John and Samuel Adams, Paul Revere, John Hancock, and many more who live at the crossroads of history and myth.

At the same time, Boston is a contemporary center of high finance and high technology, a place of granite-and-glass towers rising along what once were rutted lanes. Its many

THE CURSE IS REVERSED!

You can't go to Boston without visiting **Fenway Park,** which has changed little since its construction in 1912. It has seen no shortage of heroics: Babe Ruth pitched here when it was new; Ted Williams and Carl Yastrzemski had epic careers here. Spectators can catch the Patriots' Day game against the Yankees, then pour out to see marathoners pass. If you're running, try to catch a game in the days before or after the race. ✉ 4 Yawkey Way, between Van Ness and Lansdowne Sts., Fens ☎ 617/267–1700, 617/267–8661 recorded information ⊕ www.redsox.com/fenway 🎫 Ticket prices vary Ⓜ Kenmore, Fenway.

students, artists, academics, and professionals have made the town a haven for the arts, international cinema, late-night bookstores, ethnic food, alternative music, and unconventional politics.

The following sights will give you a great taste of the city. Where should you go first? It all depends on how you're feeling.

I Feel Great!

BIKE THE CHARLES. You've seen greater Boston from the marathon route, but you can get even better views of the city itself on the Dr. Paul Dudley White Bikeway. This course is approximately 18 miles long, and follows both banks of the Charles River as it winds from Watertown Square to the Museum of Science. **Community Bicycle Supply** (✉ 496 Tremont St., at E. Berkeley St., South End ☎ 617/542-8623 Ⓜ Arlington, Back Bay) rents cycles from April through September, at rates of $20 for 24 hours or $5 per hour (minimum two hours).

BLACK HERITAGE TRAIL. Until the end of the 19th century, Beacon Hill's north side was home to many free people of color. The 1½-mile Black Heritage Trail celebrates that community, stitching together 14 Beacon Hill sites. Tours guided by National Park Service rangers meet at the Shaw Memorial on the Beacon Street side of the Boston Common, but you must call to make reservations at marathon time. You can also take a self-guided tour. For maps and historical information, visit the Museum of Afro-American History or contact the National Park Service. ✉ Museum: 46 Joy St., Beacon Hill ☎ Museum: 617/725-0022. National Park Service: 617/742-5415 ⊕ www.afroammuseum.org/trail.htm; www.nps.gov/boaf ⊗ Museum: Mon.–Sat. 10–4; reservations required for trail tours Labor Day–Memorial Day Ⓜ Park Street, Bowdoin Street.

★ **FREEDOM TRAIL.** It's literally a red line on the ground delineating a 2½-mile walking tour of the sights of the American Revolution, including the State House, the Old State House, the Paul Revere House, the Old North Church, and the Bunker Hill Monument. Your tour can be anywhere from an aerobic 90 minutes to a leisurely full day. You can follow the trail on your own using the maps available at the Boston National Historical Park Visitor Center or the Visitor Information Center on Boston Common, or you can rent an audio tour with excellent historical information and entertaining characters, sound effects, and celebrities. Either option allows you the freedom to make the tour your own, enjoying certain sights more deeply or stopping for a snack. You can also take a 90-minute tour guided by a costumed historical character; such tours leave from the Visitor Information Center on Boston Common every day at 11 AM, noon, and 1 PM. ☎ 617/357-8300 ⊕ www.thefreedomtrail.org ▱ Audio tour $15, character tour $12 Ⓜ Park Street (for beginning of trail and Boston Common).

I Feel Pretty Good

BOSTON TEA PARTY SHIP AND MUSEUM. At this writing, the site is closed for renovations. It's scheduled to reopen in late 2006; check the Web site for updates. ✉ Congress St. Bridge, Downtown ☎ 617/269-7150 ⊕ www.bostonteapartyship.com Ⓜ South Station.

★ **FANEUIL HALL.** Faneuil Hall was erected in 1742 to serve as a place for town meetings and a public market. Inside are the great mural *Webster's Reply to Hayne,* Gilbert Stuart's portrait of Washington at Dorchester Heights, several worthwhile shops in the basement, and, on the top floors, the headquarters and museum of the Ancient and Honorable Artillery Company of Massachusetts, the Western Hemisphere's oldest militia (1638). ✉ Faneuil Hall Sq., Government Center ⊕ www.faneuilhallmarketplace.com ▱ Free ⊙ Daily 9–5 Ⓜ Government Center, State Street.

GRANARY BURYING GROUND. "It is a fine thing to die in Boston," essayist A. C. Lyons once remarked—alluding to Boston's cemeteries, among the most picturesque and historic in America. If you found a resting place here at the Old Granary (as it's affectionately called), chances are your headstone would have been eloquently ornamented and your neighbors would have been mighty eloquent, too: Samuel Adams, John Hancock, Benjamin Franklin's parents, and Paul Revere. ✉ Entrance on Tremont St., Beacon Hill ⊙ Dec.–Apr., daily 9–dusk; May–Nov., daily 9–5 Ⓜ Park Street.

USS *CONSTITUTION.* Better known as "Old Ironsides," the more than two-centuries-old USS *Constitution* is docked at the Charlestown Navy Yard. Launched in 1797, the oldest commissioned ship in the U.S. fleet is from the days of "wooden ships and iron men"—when she and her crew of 200 helped to assert the sovereignty of an improbable new nation. The ship's principal service was in the War of 1812. The adjacent **Constitution Museum** (☎ 617/426–1812) has artifacts and hands-on exhibits. It's open May–October, daily 9–6; November–April, daily 10–5. ✉ Charlestown Navy Yard, off Water St., Charlestown ☎ 617/242-5670 ⊕ www.ussconstitution.navy.mil or or www.ussconstitutionmuseum.org. ▱ Free ⊙ Daily noon–sunset; continuous tour (last one about 15 mins before sunset) Ⓜ Haymarket; then MBTA Bus 92 or 93 to Charlestown City Sq. Or MBTA water shuttle from Long Wharf to Pier 4.

Let's Take It Slowly

★ **BOSTON COMMON.** The nation's oldest public park is also the largest and undoubtedly the most famous of the town commons around which New England settlements were traditionally arranged. As old as the city around it (it dates from 1634) and originally the spot where the freemen of Boston could graze their cattle, the Common contains intriguing sights. On the Beacon Street side is the Robert Gould Shaw Memorial, honoring the 54th Massachusetts Regiment, the first Civil War unit made up of free people of color;

the regiment's stirring saga inspired the 1989 movie *Glory*. Just below the monument is the Frog Pond—a tame and frogless concrete depression, used as a children's wading pool during steamy summer days and for ice-skating in winter. The Central Burying Ground, along the Boylston Street side, is the final resting place of Tories and Patriots, as well as many British casualties of the Battle of Bunker Hill. Take your time to stroll, wander, or simply people-watch as you sit and relax your legs. ⊠ Beacon Hill Ⓜ Park Street, Boylston Street.

★ **BOSTON PUBLIC GARDEN.** The oldest botanical garden in the United States is beloved by Bostonians and visitors alike. The park's pond has been famous since 1877 for its foot pedal–powered Swan Boats, which make leisurely cruises during warm months, starting the week before the marathon. The park's dominant statuary is Thomas Ball's equestrian George Washington (1869); the granite and red-marble Ether Monument, which commemorates the advent of anesthesia at nearby Massachusetts General Hospital; and its charming fountains—though the hands-down favorite sculpture of kids (and many adults) is the *Make Way for Ducklings* bronze group, a tribute to the 1941 classic children's story by Robert McCloskey. If you really want to rest your legs, grab some bread, then head to the pond to sit and feed the ducks and adorable ducklings. The garden gates are always open, but it's not a good idea to visit after dark. ⊠ Beacon Hill ☎ 617/522–1966 or 617/635–4505 ⊕ www.swanboats.com 🎫 Swan Boats $2.50 ☉ Swan Boats mid-Apr.–mid-June, daily 10–4; mid-June–Labor Day, daily 10–5; Labor Day–mid-Sept., weekdays noon–4, weekends 10–4 Ⓜ Arlington.

★ **MUSEUM OF FINE ARTS.** The MFA's holdings of American art surpass those of all but two or three other U.S. museums. There are more than 50 works by John Singleton Copley, Colonial Boston's most celebrated portraitist, plus major paintings by Winslow Homer, John Singer Sargent, and Edward Hopper. Other artists represented include Mary Cassatt, Georgia O'Keeffe, and Berthe Morisot. The museum also has a sublime collection of French impressionists—including the largest collection of Monet's work outside France—and renowned collections of Asian, Egyptian, and Nubian art. Three excellent galleries showcase the art of Africa, Oceania, and the Ancient Americas, expanding the MFA's emphasis on civilizations outside the Western tradition. In the West Wing are changing exhibits of contemporary arts, prints, and photographs. The museum has a gift shop, two restaurants, a cafeteria, and a gallery café. ⊠ 465 Huntington Ave., Fens ☎ 617/267–9300 ⊕ www.mfa.org 🎫 $15; by donation Wed. after 4 ☉ Museum Mon., Tues., and weekends 10–4:45, Wed.–Fri. 10–9:45. West Wing only Thurs. and Fri. after 4:45 Ⓜ Museum of Fine Arts, Ruggles.

MUSEUM OF SCIENCE. With 15-foot lightning bolts in the Theater of Electricity and a 20-foot-high T-rex model, this is just the place to ignite any child's Jurassic spark. The museum, astride the Charles River Dam, has a restaurant, a planetarium, and a theater, all of which will provide an excellent break for aching legs. The Charles Hayden Planetarium, with its sophisticated multi-image system, produces exciting programs on astronomical discoveries. The Mugar Omni Theater has a five-story domed screen and 27,000 watts of power driving its 84 loudspeakers. ⊠ Science Park at the Charles River Dam, Old West End ☎ 617/723–2500 ⊕ www.mos.org 🎫 $15 ☉ Museum July 5–Labor Day, Sat.–Thurs. 9–7, Fri. 9–9; Labor Day–July 4, Sat.–Thurs. 9–5, Fri. 9–9 Ⓜ Science Park.

★**NEW ENGLAND AQUARIUM.** More than just another pretty fish, this aquarium challenges you to really imagine life under (and around) the sea. Seals bark outside the West Wing, its glass-and-steel exterior constructed to mimic fish scales. This facility has a café, a gift shop, and several changing exhibits. Inside the main building are examples of more than 2,000 species of marine life from sharks to jellyfish, many of which make their homes in a four-story ocean-reef tank. Don't miss the five-times-a-day feedings, a fascinating procedure that lasts nearly an hour. Educational programs, like the "Science at Sea" cruise, take place year-round. Sea lion shows are held aboard *Discovery*, a floating marine mammal pavilion; and whale-watching cruises ($29) leave from the aquarium's dock from April to early November. ⊠ Central Wharf (between Central and Milk Sts.), Downtown ☎ 617/973-5200 ⊕ www.neaq.org ⊠ $15.95 ⊙ July–early Sept., Mon.–Thurs. 9–6, Fri.–Sun. 9–7; early Sept.–June, weekdays 9–5, weekends 9–6 Ⓜ Aquarium, State Street.

Ow! No.

★**BOSTON DUCK TOURS.** These fun, 80-minute tours are conducted in World War II amphibious vehicles. They begin on the city's streets and then splash into the Charles River. Tours begin and end at the Huntington Avenue entrance to the Prudential Center, at 101 Huntington Avenue. From April to November, tours leave every half hour from 9 AM until dark; the fare is about $25. Tickets are sold inside the Prudential Center, the Museum of Science, Faneuil Hall, and over the Internet; weekend tours often sell out early. Tours leave from the Museum of Science (Science Park T station) and the Prudential Center (Prudential, Copley, Hynes Convention Center, Back Bay T Stations). ⊠ 3 Copley Pl., Suite 310, Boarding—Museum of Science: Old West End; Prudential Center: Back Bay ☎ 617/267-DUCK ⊕ www.bostonducktours.com.

OLD TOWN TROLLEY TOURS. Old Town Trolley offers one-hour, 40-minute city tours, covering all the major historic sites. Your $29 admission allows you on-and-off privileges, so you can hop off to check something out in more detail, then hop on another trolley to continue your tour. The trolley is closed Marathon Monday, but it's a great way to rest if your legs are still sore Tuesday morning. ⊠ 380 Dorchester Ave., South Boston ☎ 617/269-7010 or 800/868-7482 ⊕ www.trolleytours.com.

Shop Around

Boston shops are generally open Monday–Saturday 9–7 and Sunday noon–6; malls generally have hours Monday–Saturday 9–8 and Sunday noon–6. There's no state sales tax on clothing, but there is a 5% luxury tax on clothes priced higher than $175 per item.

CAMBRIDGE. In Cambridge you'll find eclectic Central Square, which holds a mix of furniture stores, used-record shops, and ethnic restaurants. Harvard Square comprises just a few blocks but contains more than 150 stores selling clothes, books and records, furnishings, and a range of specialty items. Porter Square, on Massachusetts Avenue, has distinctive clothing and home furnishings stores, crafts shops, natural food markets, and restaurants. ⊕ www.centralsquarecambridge.com Ⓜ Central Square.

FORGET SIGHTSEEING. GET ME TO A SPA!

Indulge for an hour; splurge for a day. Many hotels have their own massage or spa services, but Boston also has several day spas:

BELLA SANTE. It's a true getaway. Between treatments, you can lounge on couches, sip drinks from the juice bar, or melt away in the eucalyptus steam room. A sports massage (50–80 minutes; $90–$135) might be just the prescription for post-race pains. ⊠ 38 Newbury St., Back Bay ☎ 617/424–9930 ⊕ www.bellasante.com ☺ Weekdays 9–9, Sat. 9–6, Sun. noon–6.

ÉTANT. This new-agey spa whisks you away from the outside world. Try a sports massage (60–90 minutes; $90–$125) or a four-handed massage, with two therapists at once (one hour for $180). ⊠ 524 Tremont St., South End ☎ 617/423–5040 ⊕ www.etant.com ☺ Weekdays 11–9, Sat. 9–6, Sun. by appt.

GIULIANO. Top picks include the deep-tissue massage (50–80 minutes, $90–$130), an 80-minute deluxe pedicure ($85), or the La Stone Therapy massage (50–80 minutes, $110–$145). ⊠ 338 Newbury St., Back Bay ☎ 617/262–2220 or 800/511–3886 ⊕ www.giulianodayspa.com ☺ Mon.–Wed. 8–8, Thurs. and Fri. 8–9, Sat. 8–6, Sun. 10–6.

GRETTACOLE. It's an independent spa in the lobby of the Westin Copley Place. Try the headache therapy massage (30–60 minutes, $60–$95), sports massage (one hour for $95), or spa pedicure ($75). ⊠ 10 Huntington Ave., Back Bay ☎ 617/266–6166 ⊕ www.grettacole.com ☺ Mon.–Sat. 8:30–8, Sun. 10–6.

COPLEY PLACE AND THE PRUDENTIAL CENTER. Copley Place and the Prudential Center are Back Bay malls connected by a glass skywalk over Huntington Avenue. Copley packs more wallet-wallop, whereas "the Pru" contains moderately priced chain stores. ⊠ 100 Huntington Ave., Back Bay ☎ 617/369–5000 ⊕ www.simon.com (Copley Place); www.prudentialcenter.com Ⓜ Prudential, Copley, Hynes Convention Center, Back Bay.

FANEUIL HALL MARKETPLACE. This historic marketplace (also known as Quincy Market) is an enormous complex that's hugely popular. It combines the familiar with the unique, as chains like the Disney Store and Banana Republic provide the backdrop for street performers and truly great casual dining experiences. ⊠ Faneuil Hall Sq., Government Center ☎ 617/338–2323 ⊕ www.faneuilhallmarketplace.com Ⓜ Government Center, State Street.

NEWBURY STREET. In just eight blocks, Newbury Street in the Back Bay goes from New York's 5th Avenue stylish to SoHo funky, from Armani to The Hempest, a store with a massive selection of hemp clothing and products. While strolling Newbury, you can duck into art galleries, nibble at cafés, or pop by a salon to refresh your look. ⊕ www.newbury-st.com Ⓜ Hynes Convention Center.

I Love the Nightlife

If you don't feel like hitting the marathon after party, or you're traveling with a runner and don't need to rest up before the race, what do you do in Boston at night? Here are some of your best options.

Back Bay

BULL & FINCH PUB. This bar is best known for inspiring the TV series *Cheers*, and in fact now mostly goes by that name. It often attracts long lines of tourists and students. ⊠ 84 Beacon St., Back Bay ☎ 617/227-9605 ⊕ www.cheersboston.com Ⓜ Arlington.

KING'S. Swanky, kicky, and just awesome, King's is a bowling alley with 16 lanes, automatic scoring, and super-cool graphics. Between games, play pool in the billiards lounge, or enjoy food and cocktails from the attached DeVille lounge. After 6 PM, anyone under 21 must be accompanied by a parent or guardian. ⊠ 10 Scotia St., Back Bay ☎ 617/266-BOWL ⊕ www.kingsbackbay.com ⊗ Mon.–Wed. 5 PM–2 AM, Thurs. 4 PM–2 AM, Fri.–Sun. 11:30 AM–2 AM Ⓜ Hynes Convention Center.

SONSIE. At this European-style see-and-be-seen bistro, the bar is full of trendy, cosmopolitan types and professionals. In warm weather, the crowd spills out to sidewalk tables. ⊠ 327 Newbury St., Back Bay ☎ 617/351-2500 Ⓜ Hynes Convention Center.

Government Center

BLACK ROSE. It's an authentic Irish pub that draws as many tourists as locals, but music by contemporary and traditional Irish musicians makes it worth the crowds. ⊠ 160 State St., Government Center ☎ 617/742-2286 ⊕ www.irishconnection.com Ⓜ State Street.

Theater District

ROXY. One of Boston's biggest nightclubs is renowned for theme events. Look for those featuring reggae, salsa, swing, and Top 40. ⊠ 279 Tremont St., Theater District ☎ 617/338-7699 ⊕ www.roxyplex.com Ⓜ New England Medical Center.

The Fens

AVALON. It hosts concerts by alternative, rock, and dance acts and then turns into a dance club. Themes include "Euro Night," Top 40, and techno. ⊠ 15 Lansdowne St., Fens ☎ 617/262-2424 ⊕ www.avalonboston.com Ⓜ Kenmore Square.

BOSTON BEER WORKS. It serves up its own brews to students, young professionals, and baseball fans from nearby Fenway Park. ⊠ 61 Brookline Ave., Fens ☎ 617/536-BEER (2337) ⊕ http://beerworks.net Ⓜ Kenmore Square.

Cambridge

JOHN HARVARD'S BREW HOUSE. This English-style pub dispenses a range of ales, lagers, pilsners, and stouts brewed on the premises. ⊠ 33 Dunster St., Harvard Sq., Cambridge ☎ 617/868-3585 ⊕ www.johnharvards.com Ⓜ Harvard Square.

Improvboston (✉ Back Alley Theater, 1253 Cambridge St., Cambridge ☎ 617/576–1253 ⊕ www.improvboston.com) presents fresh, daring, hysterically funny improv. As they say about their shows, "Ultimately, there are no rules, as the audience and performers share the joy of being perfectly okay not knowing what the '@#$%' is going on." Tickets cost $5–$12, and shows run Wednesday–Saturday nights. Reservations are essential. **Musical Improv Company** (☎ 781/643–2188 ⊕ www.musicalimprovco.com) creates completely improvised, full-length musicals based on audience suggestions. Show times and locations vary, so check the Web or call for details.

LIZARD LOUNGE. One of the area's hottest nightspots presents national and lesser-known folk, rock, acid jazz, and pop bands Wednesday–Saturday. Sunday sees a poetry jam. ✉ 1667 Massachusetts Ave., between Harvard and Porter Sqs., Cambridge ☎ 617/547-0759 Ⓜ Harvard Square.

REGATTABAR. The draws here are top headliners from the world of jazz. Reservations are essential. ✉ Charles Hotel, Bennett and Eliot Sts., Harvard Sq., Cambridge ☎ 617/661-5000 or 617/395-7757 for tickets ⊕ www.regattabarjazz.com Ⓜ Harvard Square.

Elsewhere

SCULLERS JAZZ CLUB. It's in West Boston and nowhere near a T, but the fantastic live jazz shows by top performers and views of Boston's skyline make it well worth the cab ride. Dinner-and-show packages include a three-course meal at the Boathouse Grille. ✉ Doubletree Guest Suites hotel, 400 Soldiers Rd., West Boston ☎ 617/562-4111 ⊕ www.scullersjazz.com.

HELPFUL INFO

Airports & Transfers

Logan International, across the harbor from downtown, receives flights from most major domestic airlines and some carriers from outside the United States. Cabs are available outside each terminal. Fares to and from downtown average about $20 including tip.

The Airport Water Shuttle crosses Boston Harbor in about seven minutes, running between Logan Airport and Rowes Wharf. (A free shuttle bus operates between the ferry dock and airline terminals.) Adult fare is $10 one-way. The Blue Line T from Airport Station is one of the fastest ways to reach downtown from the airport: about 20 minutes. From there, you can reach the Red, Green, or Orange Line, or commuter rail. Shuttles run between airport terminals and the subway.

∎ Airport Water Shuttle ☎800/235-6426. **Logan International** ⊠I-93 N, Exit 24 ☎617/561-1800, 800/235-6426 24-hr information about parking and ground transportation options ⊕ www.massport.com. **Massachusetts Bay Transportation Authority** (MBTA) ☎617/222-3200 or 800/392-6100, 617/222-5854 TTY ⊕ www.mbta.com.

Bus Travel

South Station is the depot for most of the major bus companies that serve Boston. To find out more about buses within the city, contact or look up the MBTA.

∎ BUS INFORMATION South Station ⊠Atlantic Ave. and Summer St. ☎617/345-7451.

∎ MAJOR BUS COMPANIES Bonanza Bus Lines ☎800/556-3815 ⊕ www.bonanzabus. com. **Greyhound** ☎800/231-2222 ⊕ www.greyhound.com. **Peter Pan Bus Lines** ☎413/ 781-2900 or 800/237-8747 ⊕ www.peterpanbus.com.

∎ CITY BUSES MBTA ☎617/222-3200 or 800/392-6100, 617/222-5854 TTY ⊕ www. mbta.com.

Car Travel

Boston isn't an easy city to drive because of the many one-way streets, streets with the same name, streets that abruptly *change* name in the middle, and the many illogical twists and turns. If you must bring a car, bring a good map, keep to the main thoroughfares, and park in lots rather than on the street to avoid tickets, accidents, or theft. Some neighborhoods have strictly enforced residents-only rules, with just a handful of two-hour visitor's spaces.

Interstate 95 (also called Route 128 in some parts) skirts Boston's western edge. Interstate 93 runs north from Boston into New Hampshire. Interstate 90 (a toll road, a.k.a., the Massachusetts Turnpike, "the Mass Pike" or "the Pike") enters the city from the west. Route 9, roughly parallel to I-90, passes through Newton and Brookline on its way into Boston from the west. Route 2 enters Cambridge from the northwest.

PARKING

Major public lots are at Government Center and Quincy Market, beneath Boston Common (entrance on Charles Street), beneath Post Office Square, at the Prudential Center, at Copley Place, off Clarendon Street near the John Hancock Tower, and at several hotels. Smaller lots are scattered throughout downtown. Most are expensive (expect to pay $10 and up for an evening out, $20 and up to park all day). The few city-run garages are a bargain at about $10 per day—but try finding a space in them.

Disabilities & Accessibility

∎ LOCAL/ONLINE RESOURCES Access-Able Travel Source ⊕ www.access-able.com. **Easter Seals Massachusetts** ⊠89 South St. Downtown ☎617/226-2640 ⊕ www. eastersealsma.org.

You can buy (cash only) half-price, same-day dance, music, and theater tickets at BosTix booths in Copley Square and the Faneuil Hall Marketplace. Booths open at 11 AM.

CityPass ($39) is a reduced-fee ticket to six major sights: J.F.K. Library and Museum, Prudential Center Skywalk Observatory, Museum of Fine Arts, Museum of Science, New England Aquarium, and Museum of Natural History. Passes are available at participating attractions or online, at www.citypass.com.

MBTA visitor passes are available for unlimited travel on subway, local bus, and inner-harbor ferry for one-, three-, and seven-day periods ($7.50, $18, and $35 respectively).

Emergencies

⚐ DOCTORS & DENTISTS Dental Referral ☎800/917–6453. Physician Referral Service ☎617/726–5800.

⚐ HOSPITALS Brigham and Women's Hospital ✉75 Francis St., Brookline ☎617/732–5500. Massachusetts General Hospital ✉55 Fruit St., Cambridge ☎617/726–2000.

⚐ PHARMACIES CVS ✉151 Tremont St., Back Bay ☎617/426–5737 ⊕www.cvs.com for other locations. Walgreens ✉841 Boylston St., Back Bay ☎617/236–8130 ⊕www.walgreens.com for other locations.

Subway, Train & Trolley Travel

Boston's public transportation system, the MBTA or "T" for short, is superlative. It operates subways, elevated trains, trolleys, and buses along five lines. T vehicles operate from about 5:30 AM to about 12:30 AM. Fares are $1.25, though an extra fare is required heading inbound from distant Green Line stops and in both directions for certain distant Red Line stops. Refer to the detailed maps at any T station or on the MBTA Web site.

Boston is served by Amtrak at South Station and Back Bay Station, which accommodates frequent departures for and arrivals from New York, Philadelphia, and Washington, D.C. South Station is also the eastern terminus of Amtrak's *Lake Shore Limited*, which travels daily between Boston and Chicago by way of Albany, Rochester, Buffalo, and Cleveland.

⚐ TRAIN INFORMATION Amtrak ☎617/482–3660 or 800/872–7245 ⊕www.amtrak.com. MBTA ☎617/222–3200 or 800/392–6100, 617/222–5854 TTY ⊕www.mbta.com.

Taxis

Cabs are not easy to hail on the street; use a hotel taxi stand or call. Taxis also generally line up in Harvard Square, around South Station, near Faneuil Hall Marketplace, and in the Theater District. A taxi ride within the city of Boston starts at $1.75, plus 30¢ for each

¹/₈ mi thereafter. Companies offering 24-hour service include Boston Cab Association; Checker; Green Cab Association; Independent Taxi Operators Association; Town Taxi; and Cambridge Checker Cab.

🚖 TAXI COMPANIES Boston Cab Association ☎617/536-3200. Cambridge Checker Cab ✉Cambridge ☎617/497-1500. Checker ☎617/536-7000. Green Cab Association ☎617/628-0600. Independent Taxi Operators Association (ITOA) ☎617/426-8700. Town Taxi ☎617/536-5000.

CHAPTER 5

MAY

Cincinnati Flying Pig Marathon, Cincinnati, OH

If Boston is the valedictorian of marathons, then the

Cincinnati Flying Pig is the class clown. Race organizers explain that this is a seriously run marathon that doesn't take itself seriously. At this marathon, spectators are Squealers, volunteers are Grunts, medals are emblazoned with a flying pig, and everyone crossing the finish is greeted (and often hugged) by a pair of genuine winged oinkers out for the occasion. (Okay, they're volunteers in plushy Flying Pig costumes, but you get the idea.)

For all the frivolity, organization is impeccable (impiggable?). You'll be cheered and entertained all along the fast, fairly flat course, as upward of 3,000 Grunts work their curly tails off to make sure you have a fantastic race. As a bonus, when you run The Pig, you not only do something great for yourself, but also help others. The whole outfit is a nonprofit corporation set up to raise money for charities via the race. In 2004, for example, The Pig raised more than 1 million charitable dollars. Check the marathon Web site to see the organizations that benefit in any given year.

VISITOR INFO

Greater Cincinnati Convention
and Visitors Bureau

☎

513/621–2142 or
800/CINCY–USA

🌐

www.cincyusa.com

So You're Running Cincinnati . . .

Actually, you're running both Cincinnati and Kentucky. Cincinnati is just across the Ohio River from Kentucky, and Pig events will take you to both banks. Still, you won't need to rent a car. In decent weather, you can easily make the trek from Kentucky to Ohio and vice versa by strolling across the Roebling Suspension Bridge or the pedestrian walkway known as the Purple People Bridge. If the weather isn't kind, cabs and/or shuttles make it simple to get around.

Downtown Cincinnati feels like a once-thriving metropolis that has passed its prime. It bustles during the workweek, but totally empties out in the evenings and on weekends. Hope of an urban renaissance blooms eternal, however, and some standout sights, ho-tels, and restaurants make time spent downtown well worthwhile.

Beyond downtown, hop a cab or bus to explore Clifton and Mount Adams. Mount Adams is a trendy area uphill from downtown, and home to beautiful Eden Park. It has lots of restaurants, nightclubs, and shops as well as such sights as the Cincinnati Art Museum and the Krohn Conservatory. Clifton, in the northern suburbs, is home to the University of Cincinnati and has many shopping, dining, and nightspots popular with the college crowd.

Across the Roebling Bridge in Kentucky, Covington has several hotels and a convention center, as well as MainStrasse Village, with its charming shops and quality restaurants.

The **Southbank Shuttle** (☎ 859/331–TANK ⊕ www.tankbus.org; click "Southbank Shuttle" under "Routes/Schedules") runs through Newport, Cincinnati, and Covington, hitting all the major tourist areas. The cost is only $1, and shuttles follow one of two routes. One begins in Covington, then travels through Cincinnati to Newport; another does the reverse. Shuttles hit each stop about every 15 minutes, seven days a week. Monday–Thursday they run 6 AM–10 PM, Friday 6 AM–midnight, Saturday 10 AM–midnight, and Sunday 10–10.

Cross into Newport, Kentucky via the Purple People Bridge and you're at Newport on the Levee, a shopping mall next to the Newport Aquarium.

RACE BASICS

The Pig is dedicated to its runners. The course was designed by runners, and has been at least partially tweaked most years in response to participant feedback. The race director (a.k.a., Boss Hog) and his team work hard to bring joy to every aspect of the race, from the Web site to the run itself.

To round out Flying Pig weekend, the day before the main event sees a 10K, 5K, kids' fun run, and diaper dash. For those not up for a whole marathon, The Pig offers a half-marathon on race day, as well as a four-person marathon relay.

Registration

The Pig's Web site is the best marathon site I've ever seen. It instantly draws you into the community, and it's simple to navigate, unbelievably comprehensive, and (in true Pig fashion) a lot of fun. And no race has better merchandise, so check out the e-store. Surf further to learn the race logistics with a very detailed course tour, complete with tips on how to make the most of every section. Training information, tips on area sights, spotlights on race charities, and a spectator guide are also there. Looking for personal stories of other Pig runners? Check out "Pig Tales." If you want still more information, you can subscribe to their free e-mail newsletter, *The Squeal.*

Registration fees are $55 before late January, $65 between then and early April, and $80 after that. Beyond the regular field, runners can register for the wheelchair division, one of two Clydesdale divisions (men 200–219 pounds, men 220+ pounds), or an Athena division (women 140+ pounds). Relay runners can enter either an open four-person event ($220–$260 per team) or the Corporate Challenge ($500 per team). Faster runners can submit previous marathon times to qualify for the elite start area (men under 3:00; women under 3:30). Registration opens in late September; once you've registered, expect a confirmation postcard in the mail.

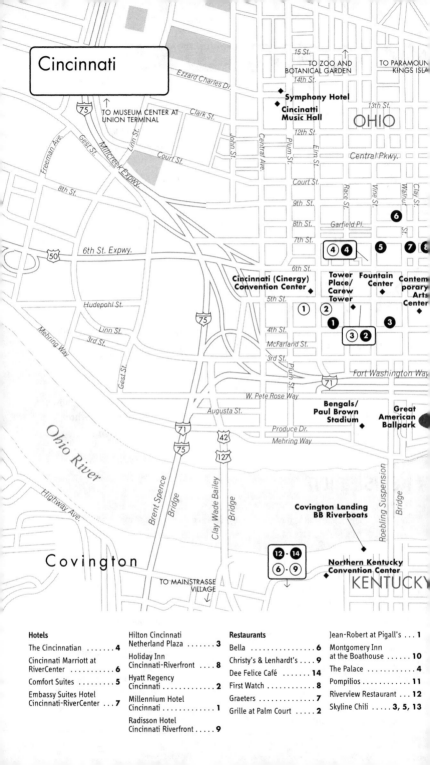

Cincinnati

TO ZOO AND
BOTANICAL GARDEN

TO PARAMOUN
KINGS ISLA

Symphony Hotel

Cincinatti
Music Hall

OHIO

TO MUSEUM CENTER AT
UNION TERMINAL

Central Pkwy.

Tower
Place/
Carew
Tower

Fountain
Center

Contem
porary
Arts
Center

Cincinnati (Cinergy)
Convention Center

Fort Washington Way

Bengals/
Paul Brown
Stadium

Great
American
Ballpark

Ohio River

Covington Landing
BB Riverboats

Covington

Northern Kentucky
Convention Center

TO MAINSTRASSE
VILLAGE

KENTUCKY

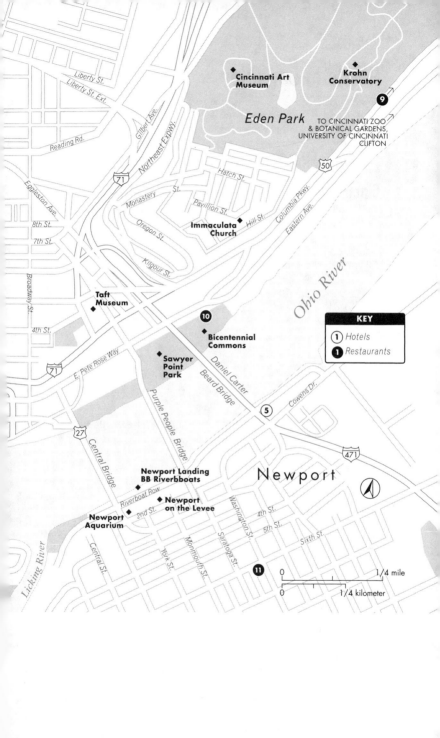

Hotels to Consider

Before you book your hotel, find out the expo location—either in Cincinnati or Covington, Kentucky. If it's in Cincinnati, the hotels there are your best bet. When the new Cincinnati convention center expansion is complete (projected in 2006), most will be connected to the center via skywalk. If the expo is in Covington, both Covington and Cincinnati hotels will be equally race convenient.

Cincinnati

★ **THE CINCINNATIAN.** It was built in 1882 and, roughly 100 years later, gutted entirely—almost. The grand staircase still curls through the hotel. No two rooms are the same, though most are spacious, and deep, inviting bathtubs are standard. Art from all over the world graces the walls. Service is excellent; in the past, the chef has put special dishes on the restaurant menu just for marathoners, who can also preorder race-day boxed breakfasts. This is easily the area's best hotel for understated luxury. ☒ 601 Vine St., Downtown, Cincinnati, OH 45202 ☎ 513/381-3000 or 800/942-9000 ⊕ www.cincinnatianhotel.com ↵ 139 rooms, 7 suites ⚴ Restaurant, 24-hr room service, wake-up calls, alarm clocks, newspapers weekdays, robes, cable TV, in-room data ports, in-room safes, minibars, 24-hr gym, lounge, dry cleaning, laundry service, concierge, business services, meeting rooms, no-smoking floors ⊟ AE, D, DC, MC, V $-$$$$.

<table>
<tr><td>RACE CONTACT</td></tr>
<tr><td>Cincinnati Flying Pig Marathon</td></tr>
<tr><td>☒</td></tr>
<tr><td>644 Linn St.,
Suite 626,
Cincinnati, OH 45203</td></tr>
<tr><td>☎</td></tr>
<tr><td>513/721-PIGS</td></tr>
<tr><td>⊕</td></tr>
<tr><td>www.flyingpigmarathon.com</td></tr>
</table>

🏃 **HILTON CINCINNATI NETHERLAND PLAZA.** Original 1931 Rookwood pottery, Brazilian rosewood, and lots of ornate architectural details make this an art deco stunner. Beds are extremely comfortable. Marathoners enjoy special rates, plus such extras as carb-loading specials at the Palm Court Restaurant and late checkout. The breakfast/coffee to-go station, PC Express, opens at 5 AM on marathon Sunday. Paragon Spa is on-site, and the hotel is convenient to the starting line. It's also attached to Carew Tower, which offers shopping opportunities and some of Cincinnati's best views. ☒ 35 W. 5th St., Downtown, Cincinnati, OH 45202 ☎ 513/421-9100 ⊕ www.cincinnatinetherlandplaza.hilton.com ↵ 500 rooms, 61 suites ⚴ 2 restaurants, room service, wake-up calls, alarm clocks, coffeemakers, newspapers weekdays, cable TV with movies, in-room data ports, indoor pool, gym, lounge, shop, hair salon, dry cleaning, laundry service, concierge, concierge floor, business services, meeting rooms, parking (fee), no-smoking floors ⊟ AE, D, DC, MC, V $-$$$.

HYATT REGENCY CINCINNATI. Just five blocks from the starting line and right by the convention center, this is a top choice for marathoners. Everything is spacious and airy, from the lobby to the guest rooms. Enjoy the pool and hot tub, both housed in a glass-enclosed room that makes you feel as if you're outdoors. ☒ 151 W. 5th St., Downtown, Cincinnati, OH 45202 ☎ 513/579-1234 ⊕ www.hyatt.com ↵ 473 rooms, 15 suites ⚴ Restaurant, room service, wake-up calls, alarm clocks, coffeemakers, newspapers, cable

WHY A FLYING PIG?

Excellent question. I thought the tongue-in-cheek (or jowl) name was just used so race organizers could emblazon the very catchy slogan "I'll Run a Marathon When Pigs Fly" on T-shirts. But there's history behind the Flying Pig. In the 1800s Cincinnati was best known for its slop yards and pork-packing plants. It was once the world's largest pork processor, an accomplishment that led to the affectionate (or not so affectionate) nickname of Porkopolis.

For Cincinnati's 1988 bicentennial, sculptor Andrew Leicester drew on this history, crafting four giant statues of chubby, winged swine to stand proudly over the then-new Bicentennial Park—angelic representatives of the pigs who passed so Cincinnati could live. Despite the earnest message behind the swine, many Cincinnatians were scandalized. Flying pigs? Surely their town should be immortalized with something a little more serious. A battle raged, and happily, goofier minds prevailed. The pigs were erected and quickly became the town's unofficial mascots. Eleven years later, it only seemed right that the city's marathon should bear the name of the Flying Pig, the whimsical yet oddly majestic creature that perfectly encapsulates what this race is all about.

TV with movies, in-room data ports, Wi-Fi (fee), indoor pool, gym, hot tub, sports bar, concierge, concierge floor, business services, meeting rooms, parking (fee), no-smoking floors ▭AE, D, DC, MC, V $-$$.

MILLENNIUM HOTEL CINCINNATI. Right next to the convention center, this is a great choice if the expo is held in Cincinnati. Rooms are comfortable and sophisticated, and many have extra space to spread out. Massage services are available by appointment. ✉150 W. 5th St., Downtown, Cincinnati, OH 45202 ☎513/352-2100 or 866/866-8086 ⊕www.millenniumhotels.com ↩844 rooms, 28 suites ♿Restaurant, room service, wake-up calls, alarm clocks, coffeemakers, robes, cable TV with movies, in-room data ports, minibars, pool, 24-hr gym, massage, bar, babysitting, shop, dry cleaning, laundry service, concierge, concierge floor, business services, meeting rooms, car rental, parking (fee), some pets allowed, no-smoking floors ▭AE, D, DC, MC, V $-$$.

Covington, KY

CINCINNATI MARRIOTT AT RIVERCENTER. Not only is the Marriott surprisingly beautiful and spacious, but it's also attached to the Northern Kentucky Convention Center (the expo's Kentucky home), and a short walk from the Roebling Suspension Bridge. The hotel strives to please marathoners and places welcome letters in their rooms. Should you need a post-race massage, the concierge can arrange for a visit from an area therapist. ✉10 W. RiverCenter Blvd., Covington, KY 41011 ☎859/261-2900 or 800/266-6605 ⊕www.marriott.com ↩317 rooms, 4 suites ♿Restaurant, room service, wake-up calls, alarm clocks, coffeemakers, newspapers, robes, cable TV with movies and video games, in-room data ports, minibars, refrigerators, free Wi-Fi, indoor pool, gym, hot tub, massage, sauna, lounge, shop, babysitting, laundry, dry cleaning, concierge, concierge floor, business services, meeting rooms, parking (fee), no-smoking floors ▭AE, D, DC, MC, V $-$$.

EMBASSY SUITES HOTEL CINCINNATI-RIVERCENTER. You get a lot of space for your money here: accommodations are suites, location is race-convenient, and rates include a cooked-to-order breakfast and an evening reception with beverages. A Continental breakfast of fruit, danish, and bottled water is laid out early for marathoners on race morning. ✉ 10 E. RiverCenter Blvd., Covington, KY 41011 ☎ 859/261-8400 ⊕ www.embassysuites.com ⬌ 227 suites ⌂ Restaurant, room service, wake-up calls, alarm clocks, coffeemakers, newspapers weekdays, cable TV with movies, in-room data ports, microwaves, refrigerators, free Wi-Fi, pool, gym, hot tub, lounge, shop, laundry facilities, business services, meeting rooms, free parking, some pets allowed, no-smoking floors ▭AE, D, DC, MC, V $-$$.

HOLIDAY INN CINCINNATI-RIVERFRONT. This is a solid budget choice, especially when you factor in reduced rates for marathoners. The hotel is convenient to the Northern Kentucky Convention Center and Roebling Bridge, and puts out a large Continental breakfast very early marathon morning, including fresh fruit, hot and cold cereal, yogurt, and beverages. There's also a pasta buffet the night before the race. ✉ 600 W. 3rd St., Covington, KY 41011 ☎ 859/291-4300 ⊕ www.holiday-inn.com ⬌ 156 rooms, 3 suites ⌂ Restaurant, room service, wake-up calls, alarm clocks, coffeemakers, newspapers, cable TV with movies, in-room data ports, free Wi-Fi, pool, 24-hr gym, lounge, laundry service, dry cleaning, concierge floor, business services, free parking, no-smoking floors ▭AE, D, DC, MC, V ¢.

> **IT'S A PIG DEAL**
>
> Check your goodie bag for the Piggy Backer card, which you can show at various restaurants, shops, and attractions to receive discounts. The marathon Web site lists participants.

RADISSON HOTEL CINCINNATI RIVERFRONT. It's a good deal for the money, with amenities like an indoor/outdoor pool and hot tub. Rooms are generally spacious, and the furnishings are comfortable. A 24-hour convenience stand in the lobby sells snacks and toiletries. The hotel is a distance from the Roebling Suspension Bridge, but the distance is walkable. Choose a suite for an in-room hot tub. ✉ 668 W. 5th St., Covington, KY 41011 ☎ 859/491-1200 ⊕ www.radisson.com ⬌ 232 rooms, 4 suites ⌂ Restaurant, room service, wake-up calls, alarm clocks, coffeemakers, newspapers weekdays, cable TV, in-room data ports, free Wi-Fi, indoor/outdoor pool, 24-hr gym, hot tub, lounge, dry cleaning, laundry facilities, shop, concierge, airport shuttle, meeting rooms, free parking, no-smoking floors ▭AE, D, DC, MC, V $.

Newport, KY

COMFORT SUITES. It's about a mile from the Purple People Bridge, so this hotel is less convenient than some, though it's still a viable option. Guest quarters are all suites, and a complimentary "deluxe" Continental breakfast is provided. Presidential suites have whirlpool bathtubs. ✉ 420 Riverboat Row, Newport, KY 41071 ☎ 859/291-6700 ⊕ www.comfortsuites.com ⬌ 124 suites ⌂ Wake-up calls, alarm clocks, coffeemakers, newspa-

NIGHT-BEFORE PASTA DINNER

The Pasta Pig Out costs $15; buy tickets during registration or at the expo. Only 1,000 combined total seats are available for the two seatings (4:30 and 6). They do sell out, so buy early. Though locations vary, it's always themed in full Pig fashion, and includes all-you-can-eat pasta, salads, and desserts, plus beverages (including beer and wine). If you can't get in, or would rather try someplace local . . .

BELLA. Plenty of unique pizza and pasta dishes pepper sophisticated Bella's menu. Other types of entrées put new twists on old standbys: witness the grilled salmon BLT and the Szechuan barbecue pork chops. ✉ 600 Walnut St., Downtown, Cincinnati, OH ☎ 513/721-7100 ⊕ www.bellacincinnati.com ⊙ No lunch weekends ⊟ AE, DC, MC, V $–$$$.

POMPILIOS. Remember in *Rain Man* when all the toothpicks dropped and Dustin Hoffman counted them instantly? That was at Pompilios. This casual neighborhood restaurant (think checkered tablecloths, lotsa pasta, plenty of bread) offers generous portions of classic dishes at reasonable prices. Saturday nights are crowded, so have your prerace meal early. ✉ 600 Washington Ave., Newport, KY ☎ 859/581-3065 ⊟ AE, D, DC, MC, V $.

pers weekdays, cable TV, in-room data ports, in-room safes, microwaves, refrigerators, free Wi-Fi, gym, dry cleaning, laundry service, business services, meeting rooms, free parking, some pets allowed (fee), no-smoking rooms ⊟ AE, D, DC, MC, V ¢–$.

AND YOU'RE OFF . . .

The Expo

The expo is held in either the Northern Kentucky Convention Center in Covington, Kentucky, or the Cincinnati Convention Center in downtown Cincinnati. It's open the Friday (from about noon till early in the evening) and Saturday (late morning into the early evening) before the race. The expo is midsize, but growing every year. Give yourself about an hour to experience it, more if there's a specific presentation you'd like to see. A schedule of speakers is posted on the Web site and is printed in both the expo program and the marathon spectator guide. Previous topics have been led by such notables as Jeff Galloway and have included "Mental Aspects of Marathoning," "Fueling and Hydrating," and advice from the Clif Bar pace-team leaders. (For more on Clif Bar Pace Teams, see the L.A. Marathon chapter of this book.)

At the expo, Clydesdale and Athena runners must weigh in. Tickets are available for the pasta party (if it hasn't sold out), the water taxi from Covington to Cincinnati the morning of the race (⇨ *also* The Course *under* Race Day, *below*), and the *Belle of Cincinnati* breakfast boat (⇨ *also* Spectating *under* Race Day, *below*). Naturally, there's lots of excellent Pig merchandise for sale, so if you happen to be in the market for snouts, you're in luck.

Race Day

The Course

The starting area is at Central Avenue and Mehring Way, by the Paul Brown Stadium. It's well organized, with baggage check and plenty of portable toilets. If you're not partial to portable toilets, duck into the stadium for the real deal. It will be cold this early in the day, so layer accordingly. Getting to the start is a simple walk either from your Cincinnati hotel, over the Roebling Suspension Bridge from Covington (enter the walkway on RiverCenter Boulevard, walk on the west [left] side of the bridge to the stadium—about a mile trip), or over the Purple People Bridge from Newport (enter at the east end of Newport on the Levee; it's about 1.7 miles to the stadium). Another option for those in Covington is a BB Riverboats water taxi. These large boats make three trips from Covington Landing, at 5, 5:30, and 6. Tickets cost $3 round-trip. Although you can wait in line and get them race morning, you're better off buying them in advance at the expo.

WEATHER THE RUN

Temperatures average in the comfortable mid-50s. As of 2005, the lowest race low was 32°F and the highest race high was 73°F.

Runners line up based on projected finish times, and at 6 AM the race begins. It starts out relatively flat, aside from the bridges crossing the Ohio River as you head into and then back out of Kentucky. The toughest section begins after Mile 5, with the steep climb into Eden Park. The view from the park is lovely; keep that reward in mind if you're struggling. The next few miles bring rolling hills, but nothing as steep as the ascent to the park. Around Mile 9 to 9.5, keep an eye out for the residents and staff of St. Margaret Hall, an area nursing home that comes out in force to cheer and ring bells. You can't miss them—just look for the nuns in pig snouts.

There will be a few more light ups and downs before you hit some of Cincinnati's residential neighborhoods, where folks go crazy for The Pig. People come out in their pajamas and have pancake breakfasts, mimosas flow in front yards, and everyone cheers and hollers for the marathoners. In Hyde Park, around the midpoint of the course, upward of 3,000 people gather in the town square, and Mariemont claims to have the whole village out squealing.

At Mile 20 you'll hit Cheerleader Row. Between here and the race finish, several high school squads power you through the Wall. At Mile 23 you'll be inspired by the powerful vocals of a 150-person Christian choir. In all, marathoners are feted at about 58 entertainment zones, including those with local bands, Elvis impersonators, toga parties . . . the list goes on and changes every year as zones compete to be named most popular, an honor posted on the Web site after the race.

Beyond the entertainment, The Pig looks out for its runners with water and energy drinks every mile and an energy gel station between Miles 17 and 18. Portable toilets pepper the course, and first aid is never far, with six medical stations plus EMTs who cycle the course with radios, ready to jump into action if needed.

With so much to see, you won't even notice your hurting legs, and you'll cruise the final 8 or 9 flat miles to . . . the Finish Swine!

Cross it proudly, and be congratulated by one of two Flying Pigs, on hand (on hoof?) to hug, high-five, and otherwise congratulate all finishers. The course is officially open eight hours, but Pig organizers are wonderful about sticking around the Finish Swine until every runner has crossed. After your big pig hug, you'll get your Mylar blanket and very cool finisher's medal, emblazoned with a flying pig. Wear it with pride as you move through the recovery area, helping yourself to energy bars, bagels, bananas, apples, oranges, yogurt, a salty snack, cookies, and ice cream, plus plenty of water and energy drinks.

WHEN TO GO

Hate waiting in portable toilet lines? Wait for the "restroom oasis" of several portable toilets, refreshments, and entertainment at Mile 12.

Spectating

Absolutely check out the spectator guide, available on-line or at the expo. My advice is to begin your spectating at the starting line; there are plenty of great viewing spots along the street. As you cheer the pack, give an extra squeal to the runners in snouts and wings. After all, what better way to race the Flying Pig than as its namesake?

Once the runners are on their way, head north on Central Avenue to Third Street (there's usually a whole crowd doing this) to catch the runners between Miles 3 and 4. Cheer like crazy, then take some time for breakfast before heading to the finish line.

The race finishes on Mehring Way. It's very accessible to spectators, so you'll have a great shot at seeing your favorite runner in that final stretch to the Finish Swine. Head to the family reunion area while your marathoner moves through runner recovery.

Celebrate!

The Sawyer Point victory party is very close to the Finish Swine—just follow the crowd—and has the feel of an outdoor festival: there's a giant stage for bands, rides and activities for kids, and loads of concessions booths. The party runs from 9 AM to 2 PM. When you're partied out, walk or take marathon transportation back to your hotel. Those with tickets can catch water taxis back to Covington; they run every 30 minutes between 10 AM and 2 PM. The race also has shuttles that pick up near the finish line, and drop off at either the Hyatt in Cincinnati, or at several hotels in Kentucky. These shuttles run every 20 minutes from 9 AM to 3 PM, and accommodate spectators as well as runners.

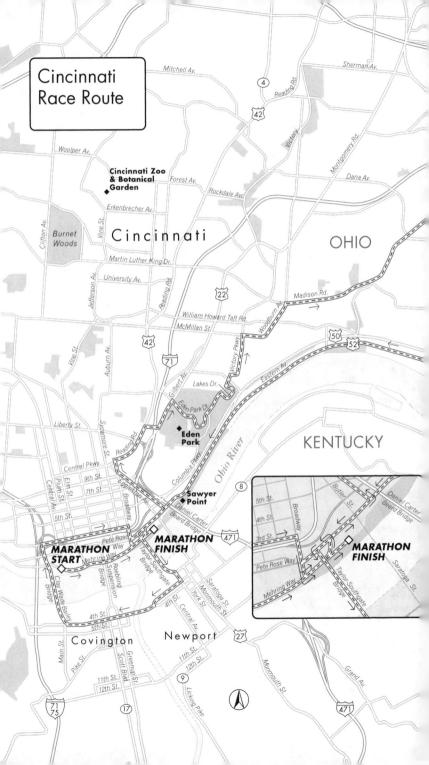

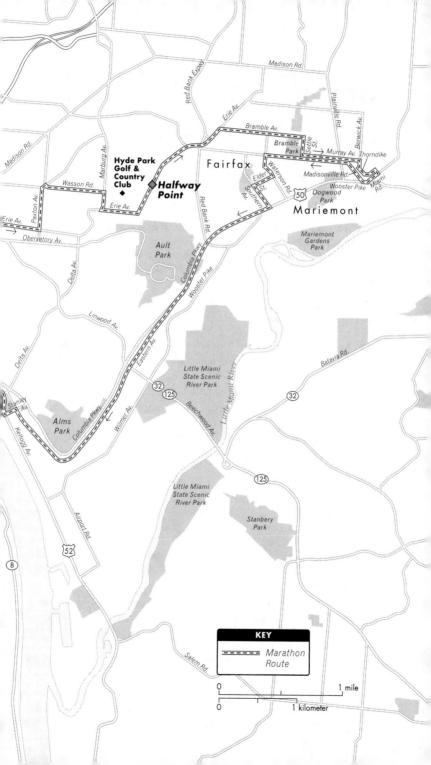

BEYOND THE FINISH LINE

Replacing 2,620 Calories

Cincinnati is famous for its chili, but in fact it offers a variety of tasty treats—everything from incredible barbecue to Oprah Winfrey's favorite ice cream.

Cincinnati

CHRISTY'S & LENHARDT'S. It's a casual place that serves schnitzel, Viennese and Hungarian goulash, sauerbraten, and potato pancakes. Burgers and sandwiches are also available, and hours extend into the late night. The beer garden is a great escape in good weather. ⊠ 151 W. McMillan Ave., Clifton, Cincinnati, OH ☎ 513/281–3600 ⊟ AE, D, MC, V ☉ Closed Sun., no lunch Mon., no lunch Sat. ¢–$.

GRAETERS. Oprah Winfrey was quoted as saying, "You haven't had ice cream till you've had Graeter's." It takes time to make this thick, creamy treat. The outfit uses a French-pot process, making only 2 rich, full flavored gallons at a time. Although every variety is exceptional, try one with chocolate chips, which are more like thick, melt-in-your-mouth chunks. The store isn't open Sunday, so plan accordingly. ⊠ 41 E. 4th St., Downtown, Cincinnati, OH ☎ 513/381–0653 ⊟ AE, D, DC, MC, V ☉ Closed Sun. ¢.

JEAN–ROBERT AT PIGALL'S. Jean-Robert spent seven years as *chef de cuisine* at the Maisonette, Cincinnati's finest (and sadly now closed) restaurant, before striking out on his own. The seasonal French prix-fixe menu and the carefully chosen wine list have garnered local and national attention. Make reservations well in advance; a seat at the chef's table, in an alcove of the kitchen, gives diners the inside scoop. ⊠ 127 W. 4th St., Downtown, Cincinnati, OH ☎ 513/721–1345 ⊕ www.jean-robertatpigalls.com ⌕ Reservations essential ⊟ AE, D, MC, V ☉ Closed Sun. and Mon. No lunch $$$$.

★ **MONTGOMERY INN AT THE BOATHOUSE.** The spicy sauce on the incredible barbecue ribs lingers in your mouth. The ribs pair wonderfully with a baked sweet potato; don't miss the appetizer fried shrimp with plum and mustard sauce. Expect crowds; head to the upstairs sports lounge area to enjoy a fantastic view over the Ohio River while you wait. Request a table by the window to take in the view during your meal. ⊠ 925 Eastern Ave., Downtown, Cincinnati, OH ☎ 513/721–7427 ⊕ www.montgomeryinn.com ⌕ Reservations essential ⊟ AE, D, DC, MC, V ☉ No lunch weekends $–$$$.

THE PALACE. The food at this Cincinatian Hotel restaurant is decadent and delicious. Dinner is expensive, but such dishes as steamed Maine lobster on Asian bamboo-rice risotto won't disappoint. There are more than 350 wine selections, and pastry chef Noreen Nagao's creations aren't to be missed. ⊠ 601 Vine St., Downtown, Cincinnati, OH ☎ 513/381–6006 ⊕ www.cincinnatianhotel.com ⌕ Reservations essential ⊟ AE, D, DC, MC, V $$–$$$$.

SKYLINE CHILI. There are other chili chains in Cincinnati, but this one is tops. The taste is distinct; some Cincinnatians say it takes a few visits to get used to it, then suddenly you find yourself craving it at odd hours of the night. Go for the classic three-way: a huge

BREAKFAST SPOTS

Aside from the *Belle of Cincinnati,* the following are all are in the ¢–$ or $$ range.

BELLE OF CINCINNATI. If you really want to enhance your marathon experience, opt for breakfast aboard the *Belle of Cincinnati* (a.k.a. The Finish Swine Boat). This old paddle wheeler is anchored by the Finish Swine, and offers a fantastic view of the race finale. For $25 you get a full breakfast including omelets, potatoes, sausage, fruit, muffins, and a beverage; there's also a cash bar. Breakfast is served 7–11, and the boat remains open until 1. You can buy tickets at the door, but it's wiser to do so in advance, either through the marathon Web site (download and mail in the order form) or at the expo.

FIRST WATCH. Prices are reasonable, and the food is a cut above your basic diner fare. Healthful options include egg-white scrambles and yogurt parfaits. Or skip the health food and opt for raisin-bread French toast or Belgian waffles. ⊠ 700 Walnut St. (on 7th St. between Walnut and Main), Downtown, Cincinnati, OH ☎ 513/721-4744 ⊠ 50 E. RiverCenter Blvd., Covington, KY ☎ 859/491–0869 ▤ AE, D, DC, MC, V ☺ No dinner.

GRILLE AT PALM COURT. The beautiful dining room in the Hilton Cincinnati Netherland Plaza envelops you in luxury. Relax over a breakfast buffet or order à la carte dishes. For the most healthful options, check out the Heart Healthy Fare menu. ⊠ 35 W. 5th St., Downtown, Cincinnati, OH ☎ 513/421-9100 ▤ AE, D, DC, MC, V.

RIVERVIEW RESTAURANT. The revolving restaurant atop the Radisson hotel stays still during breakfast. You'll find all the basics here, but it's the view that makes this eatery worth the trip. It's a bit of a trek from the race route, so walk here only if your runner is slower-paced; otherwise hop a cab. ⊠ 668 W. 5th St., Covington, KY ☎ 859/491–1200 ▤ AE, D, DC, MC, V.

---

pile of cheddar cheese, over a thick mound of rich beef chili, over a plate of pasta. First timers will want to wear a bib. Expect crowds at lunch. ⊠254 E. 4th St., Downtown, Cincinnati, OH ☎ 513/241-4848 ⊕ www.skylinechili.com ⊠ 643 Vine St., Downtown, Cincinnati, OH ☎ 513/241–2020 ⊠ 617 W. 3rd St., Covington, KY ☎ 859/261-8474 ▤AE, D, MC, V ¢–$.

Covington, KY

★ **DEE FELICE CAFE.** When you've finished running The Pig and hanging at the victory party, *this* is where to come. Make reservations to enjoy a jazz brunch that'll make you feel as if you're in New Orleans. The atmosphere is fun and casual, and both the food and the live music will delight. The restaurant is right in the heart of the charming Main-

Cynthia Wheeler had no intention of running the 2004 Flying Pig Marathon. It's not that she didn't want to run; she just didn't want to run that far. She had trained for the half-marathon. She was ready for the half-marathon. She had traveled from Pittsburgh to Cincinnati for the half-marathon. One problem: in 2004, The Pig *had* no half-marathon.

That left her with three choices: walk away, run only half the race, or do what she actually did, which is throw up her arms and say, "What the heck, I'm going all the way!"

At almost 49, Cynthia had a history of running short distances, but could never get motivated to plunge into longer runs until her sister advised her to not just run, but "run *for* something." That's when Cynthia discovered Team in Training. It's run by the Leukemia and Lymphoma Society and is the world's largest endurance sports training program. Whatever your level of fitness or experience, Team in Training can get you ready for a marathon. They'll coach you for four to five months, giving you tips on nutrition, injury prevention, and tackling races mentally and physically. They'll cover your entry fees, travel to the race, and accommodations. They'll support you during the race, cheering you on at several points. In return for all this, you agree to raise money for their cause: finding a cure for such blood cancers as leukemia, lymphoma, and myeloma.

For Cynthia, getting involved with Team in Training had special resonance. Her mother, Joyce, is a lymphoma survivor, and her older sister, Julie Tucker, was lost to leukemia at age four, a year before Cynthia was born. As part of her fund-raising efforts, Cynthia wrote a heartbreaking letter about Julie, described by their mother as "a brave and beautiful child who only complained in her most dire moments." She also wrote of Joyce's long struggle with lymphoma. Fourteen years later, Joyce remains cancer free and "one of the healthiest, most vibrant 80-year-olds you'll ever meet."

Cynthia put her heart and soul into training for The Pig, and it was this dedication that led her to take on the full marathon. And how did it go? In her own words, from a letter she wrote after the race to her supporters:

"For me, the race was a 26.2-mile party thanks to the revelers, musicians, spectators, and encouragers who lined the course almost every step of the way. I fell in and chatted with other runners along the course, sang to the music, and be-bopped to the beat. The camaraderie with these athletes was so cool. We were fellow marathoners!

"At the 20-mile mark I started noticing spectators waving signs that proclaimed THERE IS NO WALL. Being a novice, I had no idea what they were referring to until I hit the Wall. The final six miles of the race were grueling. Everything from my waist down was hurting. My fingers were numb and without strength. It had been a chilly, rainy race, and I was drenched from start to finish.

I pushed on and began searching the crowds for my mother at the 25-mile mark, calling out, 'Where's my mommy?!' I laughed and cried and danced a jig near the finish line when I finally located my dear 'Mumzie,' who is a brave survivor of lymphoma . . . I finished in 4:36, which, I am told, is pretty darn good by any standards.

"Partying aside, my main purpose for running this race ranks as one of the most honorable endeavors I have ever undertaken. Indeed, I have done something very good for myself. My self-esteem is at an all-time high; I am fit and have never felt better. Far more importantly though, with your generosity, we have helped to fund critical research. . . .

"When I spotted Mom standing there in the cold, waiting for me to appear, I realized that she is my hero . . . I am grateful beyond expression to have honored her by persevering for the duration of the marathon."

When I met up with Cynthia, she had just finished the race, and she was elated. "I can't believe I ran the whole thing," she told me. "I did it. I did it!" Then her eyes welled as she spoke about running with Team in Training. She had raised about $2,000. She had pushed her body to the extreme in honor of her mother and the older sister she'd never met, and the enormity of her achievement moved both her and Joyce to tears.

In the year after her first marathon, Cynthia not only continued working with Team in Training to run two more half-marathons (this time they really *were* half-marathons), but also became a Team in Training mentor. Now she helps coach first timers, and enjoys watching as they get bitten by the bug.

Asked what struck with her most about The Pig, Cynthia said she loved it all, but especially the unique way that each neighborhood came out to show support, giving the runners a true taste of each section of town. The marathon "is a great way to see a place on your feet," she said, and she knows she'll run more in the future.

Yet the best part of marathoning for Cynthia has been the bond that has solidified between her and her mom. Getting involved with Team in Training and raising money to fight the diseases that have caused her family so much heartache has brought them closer than ever before. And for that, Cynthia will always be grateful. ∎

Strasse district in Covington. ⊠610 Main St., Covington, KY ☎859/261-2365 ⊕www.deefelice.com ⊘No lunch ⊟AE, D, DC, MC, V $$.

Sightseeing on (and off) Your Feet

Cincinnati, Covington, and Newport are easy to navigate on foot or via the Southbank Shuttle. For sights outside this area, just grab a cab or city bus.

I Feel Great!

CINCINNATI ZOO AND BOTANICAL GARDEN. The nation's second-oldest zoo (the oldest belongs to my hometown, Philadelphia) is famous for its white Bengal tigers. In 1999 it was one of three facilities outside Florida to be allowed to take in Florida manatees; the mammals can be observed at the Manatee Springs exhibit. The zoo is also home to walruses, lowland gorillas, polar bears, and hundreds of other species, including 3,000 plant varieties. Be sure to wear your sneakers; there are a lot of hills in greater Cincinnati, and they all seem to be here. ⊠3400 Vine St., Clifton, Cincinnati, OH ☎513/281-4700 or 800/944-4776 ⊕www.cincyzoo.org ⊠$12.95 ⊘At marathon time, 9-5 weekdays, 9-6 weekends.

KROHN CONSERVATORY. If plants are more your thing than fish or animals, walk around the Krohn Conservatory in Eden Park. There you'll find a greenhouse and gardens with more than 5,000 species. ⊠Mount Adams, Cincinnati, OH ☎513/421-4086 ⊕www.cinci-parks.org ⊠Free (donations welcomed) ⊘Daily 10-5.

I Feel Pretty Good

CINCINNATI ART MUSEUM. Founded in 1881, the museum explores 5,000 years of art through paintings, sculpture, decorative arts, and special exhibitions from around the world. The Cincinnati Wing traces the history of the city's art, which encompasses ceramics, furniture, metalworks, and sculpture. ⊠953 Eden Park Dr., Mount Adams, Cincinnati, OH ☎513/721-ARTS ⊕www.cincinnatiartmuseum.com ⊠Free ⊘Tues. and Thurs.-Sun. 11-5; Wed: 11-9.

CONTEMPORARY ARTS CENTER. The center presents some of today's most cutting-edge artists. Exhibits showcase photography, film, performance art, and even art that primarily utilizes sound. The UnMuseum is a 7,400-square-foot wonderland for kids and adults; one of the more popular attractions is the robot tree, which responds to your presence by raising or lowering its branches. The youngest children will love the Leaf Lounge, where they take off their shoes and roll in more than 450 large, handmade stuffed leaves on a bed of bouncy foam. ⊠44 E. 6th St., Downtown, Cincinnati, OH ☎513/345-8400 ⊕www.contemporaryartscenter.org ⊠$7.50 ⊘Mon. 10-9, Wed.-Fri. 10-6, weekends 11-6.

MUSEUM CENTER AT UNION TERMINAL. This historic former train station looks like a huge art deco cabinet radio, and houses the Cinergy Children's Museum, an inventive, hands-on museum for children of all ages; the Museum of Natural History and Science, which has a cave with real bats; the Cincinnati History Museum; and the Robert D. Lindner Family Omnimax Theater. ⊠1301 Western Ave., West Downtown, Cincinnati, OH

FORGET SIGHTSEEING. GET ME TO A SPA!

Some hotels can arrange a post-race massage, but for a full spa experience, you'll have to wait until Monday: Downtown Cincinnati and Kentucky's spas aren't open on Sunday.

INNER PEACE HOLISTIC CENTER. The Swedish massage sessions last 30–90 minutes ($30–$85), but the 90-minute hot-stone massages ($90) are tops. The heat of the stones and the scent of the essential oil work together to ease the tightness in your muscles far better than typical massage alone. ✉ 708 Walnut St., Downtown, Cincinnati, OH ☎ 513/784–0403 ⊕ www.innerpeaceholistic.com ⊗ Weekdays 10–9, Sat. 10–7.

PARAGON. Enjoy a one-hour hot-stone ($100) or full-body massage ($65) at this spa in the lower level of the Carew Tower. At $45 for an hour treatment, a sport pedicure is a great way to pamper post-race feet. ✉ 441 Vine St., Downtown, Cincinnati, OH ☎ 513/651–4600 ⊕ www.paragonsalon.com ⊗ Mon. and Thurs. 9–8, Tues. and Sat. 9–5, Wed. and Fri. 9–6.

REVERIE THERAPEUTICS. Massages include deep tissue (30–90 minutes: $50–$100), aromatherapy (30–90 minutes: $50–$110), and guided meditation (90 minutes for $110)—an intriguing way to work those kinks out of your quads. ✉ 520 Main St., Covington, KY ☎ 859/261–5444 ⊗ Tues.–Fri. 10–7, Sat. 10–5.

☎ 513/287–7000 or 800/733–2077 ⊕ www.cincymuseum.com ✉ $7.25 for one attraction, with discounts for combination tickets ⊗ Mon.–Sat. 10–5, Sun. 11–6.

NEWPORT AQUARIUM. Just over the Purple People Bridge from Cincinnati is the Newport Aquarium, with more than 11,000 undersea creatures. Acrylic tunnels give you 360-degree views of ocean life. Also check out the Hidden Treasures of the Rainforest Islands. ✉ One Aquarium Way, Newport, KY ☎ 859/491–FINS ⊕ www.newportaquarium.com ✉ $17.95 ⊗ Daily 10–6.

Let's Take It Slowly

BICENTENNIAL COMMONS. Take an easy walk and check out Bicentennial Commons, a recreation center at Sawyer Point on the Ohio River. The post-race party is in this area, but you might want to head back after the event to look over all the monuments, which tell the story of Cincinnati's origins. And don't forget to salute the flying pigs, without whom this race would have been nowhere near as much fun.

TAFT MUSEUM OF ART. Works by artists from around the globe are displayed in this Federal-period mansion, where William Howard Taft accepted his presidential nomination in 1908. The permanent collections include paintings by Rembrandt, Gainsborough, and Corot; Chinese porcelains; 19th-century American furniture; French Renaissance enameled plaques; sculpture; and jewelry. To rest your legs, visit the lovely tearoom.

✉316 Pike St., Downtown, Cincinnati, OH ☎513/241–0343 ⊕www.taftmuseum.org
🎟$7, free Wed. 🕐Tues., Wed., and Fri. 11–5, Thurs. 11–8, Sat. 10–5, Sun. noon–5.

Ow! No.

BB RIVERBOATS. The company that runs the water taxis for the marathon also conducts sightseeing cruises along the Ohio River. It has several different packages, some of which include food, live music, or both. Call or check the Web site for schedules and costs on marathon weekend. ✉One Madison Ave., Covington, KY ☎859/261–8500 or 800/261–8586 ⊕www.bbriverboats.com.

Shop Around

FOUNTAIN PLACE. Upscale stores include Tiffany & Co. and Brooks Brothers. ✉5th and Race Sts., Downtown, Cincinnati, OH.

MAINSTRASSE VILLAGE. Stroll around this picturesque shopping, dining, and residential district, centered around what was once Covington's German area. Landscaping makes the charming area perfect for walking around, and you can easily duck into art galleries, antiques shops, clothing stores, and restaurants. ⊕www.nkyvillage.com.

NEWPORT ON THE LEVEE. Just over the Purple People Bridge from Cincinnati is Newport on the Levee. Shop stores like American Eagle and Hot Topic, relax at Barnes & Noble, play at GameWorks, or catch a movie at the AMC Newport 20. ✉One Levee Way, Newport, KY ☎859/291–0550 ⊕www.newportonthelevee.com.

TOWER PLACE AT THE CAREW TOWER. This atrium shopping mall has skywalks, three levels of retailers, and a food court. Head up to the tower's observation deck for sweeping views of the city. Skywalks connect Tower Place with **Saks Fifth Avenue** (☎513/421–6800). ✉28 W. 4th St., Downtown, Cincinnati, OH ☎513/241–7700.

I Love the Nightlife

BLIND LEMON. This bar has a courtyard, a funky old interior, and a cozy fireplace. Musicians sometimes set up in a back corner to play. ✉936 Hatch St., Mount Adams, Cincinnati, OH ☎513/241–3885 ⊕www.blindlemoncafe.com.

BOGARTS. Look for performances by local garage bands and college bands, as well as national acts. ✉2621 Vine St., Clifton, Cincinnati, OH ☎513/281–8400 ⊕www.bogarts.com.

JAPPS CIGAR AND MARTINI BAR. The 1800s building was once home to a wig maker. The new, sleek incarnation attracts businesspeople and those in touch with the good life. Don't walk here though; best to take a cab. ✉1134 Main St., Downtown (Over the Rhine), Cincinnati, OH ☎513/684–0007.

JILLIAN'S. It has a hibachi grill restaurant, a bowling alley with a retro lounge, arcade games both old and new, a bar, dance clubs, pool tables, Ping-Pong, darts, and shuffle-

A LITTLE NIGHT MUSIC

Across from the Cincinnati Music Hall is a true find: the **Symphony Hotel** (✉ 210 W. 14th St., Downtown, Cincinnati, OH ☎ 513/721–3353 ⊕ www.symphonyhotel.com). It's been around since 1871, and was once a boardinghouse for students at the College of Music.

Today it's a charming, reasonably priced bed-and-breakfast with four rooms, each honoring a composer: Beethoven, Bach, Mozart, and Schubert. The owners are gracious and helpful, and the resident dog, Chop-Chop, is a big ol' love pig. That said, it's not the best hotel for marathoners: it's far from the expo and the starting and finish lines, and it's in a fairly rough part of town.

Still, put the Symphony Hotel on your list of Cincinnati "must do's," because of its special affiliation with the symphony orchestra. On concert nights, you can enjoy the hotel's dinner–concert package ($135 for 2 people). Chef David Buchman serves a five-course "light French" meal in the intimate dining room. The food is superb, and the menu changes regularly to reflect the season. Meals always include soup, salad, sorbet, and choices for both the entrées and desserts. It's easy to strike up a conversation with fellow symphony goers, and many patrons are regulars.

After dinner, simply cross over to the Cincinnati Music Hall. Built in 1878, it has been transformed over the years into an ideal music venue. The acoustics are amazing, the seats are plush, and the surroundings are elegant. Though you don't have to dress up for a concert here, many people do. Single tickets cost $17.50–$90.50, and the season runs from September into May. To be honest, I'm woefully ignorant about classical music, but conductor Paavo Järvi and the **Cincinnati Symphony Orchestra** (☎ 513/381–3300 ⊕ www. cincinnatisymphony.org), the nation's fifth oldest, blew me away.

The concert began with the world premiere of Jonathan Holland's *Halcyon Sun*. Honestly, it wasn't my thing. But then the orchestra moved on to Beethoven's *Concerto Number 5 in E-Flat Major for Piano and Orchestra,* and my jaw dropped. Guest pianist Andre Watts dazzled with his playing; the entire auditorium was entranced. Even intermission impressed, with excellent Cincinnati-made confections from Divine's European Chocolates (⊕ www.cincinnatichocolates. com). After intermission, Watts, Järvi, and the orchestra continued to stun with Schumann's *Symphony Number 2 in C Major.*

This was an unforgettable evening, and one I strongly recommend to anyone visiting Cincinnati. Dinner at the Symphony Hotel, then a concert by the CSO: a Cincinnati treasure not to be missed.

board. Kids and adults alike can find a lot to love. ⊠ 1200 Jillian's Way, Covington, KY ☎ 859/491–5388 ⊕ www.jilliansbilliards.com.

RHYTHM & BLUES CAFE. Come for the live funk, soul, reggae, and blues bands. ⊠ 1142 Main St., Downtown (Over the Rhine), Cincinnati, OH ☎ 513/684–0080.

HELPFUL INFO
Airport & Transfers
The Cincinnati/Northern Kentucky International Airport is 12 miles south of downtown, off I–275, in Kentucky. It's served by many major airlines. Airport Executive Shuttle runs between the airport and area hotels ($15 one-way, $25 round-trip). Reserve 24 hours in advance, or go to their desk in baggage claim. Taxis downtown cost about $25, plus tip. Hire a cab at the taxi desk in Terminal 3, or use the courtesy phone near the exits of Terminal 1 and 2. It's about a 10-minute drive from the airport to Cincinnati.

🔋 Airport Executive Shuttle ☎ 859/261–8841, 513/352–2135, or 800/990–8841 ⊕ www. executivetranscincy.com. **Cincinnati/Northern Kentucky International Airport** ☎ 859/ 767–3151 ⊕ www.cvgairport.com.

Bus Travel
Cincinnati is served by Greyhound bus; the station is open 24 hours. City buses connect Cincinnati with its suburbs. Bus 1 runs from the Museum Center, through Downtown and Mount Adams to the zoo (and the reverse). The fare is $1 each way, and exact change is required. The Southbank Shuttle connects tourists attractions in downtown Cincinnati, Covington, KY, and Newport, KY. Fares are $1 per trip.

🔋 BUS INFORMATION Greyhound ⊠ 1005 Gilbert Ave., Downtown ☎ 800/231–2222 or 513/352–6012 ⊕ www.greyhound.com. **Southbank Shuttle** ☎ 859/331–TANK ⊕ www.tankbus.org. **Southwest Ohio Regional Transit Authority** ☎ 513/632–7575 ⊕ www.sorta.com.

Car Travel
The major north–south routes through Cincinnati, I–71 and I–75, merge into a single highway downtown. They pass together over the double-decker Brent Spence Bridge, then continue south into Kentucky. I–74 originates in Cincinnati and heads west into Indiana. I–275 circles the city and parts of northern Kentucky. Many Cincinnati streets are one-way, and parking can be difficult.

Disabilities & Accessibility
🔋 LOCAL RESOURCES Inclusion Network ⊠ 312 Walnut St., Suite 1160, Cincinnati, OH ☎ 513/345–1330 or 513/345–1336 (TTY) ⊕ www.inclusion.org. **United Way of Greater Cincinnati** ⊠ 2400 Reading Rd., Cincinnati, OH ☎ 513/762–7100 ⊕ www.uwgc.org.

Emergencies

🚩 HOSPITALS St. Luke East ✉85 Grand Ave., Fort Thomas, KY ☎859/572–3100 ⊕ - www.health-alliance.com/stluke. **University Hospital** ✉234 Goodman St., Clifton, Cincinnati, OH ☎513/584–1000 ⊕ www.health-alliance.com/university.

🚩 PHARMACIES Walgreens ✉ 121 E. 5th St., Downtown, Cincinnati, OH ☎513/721–0840 ⊕ www.walgreens.com for other branches.

Taxis

Cincinnati isn't a place to hail cabs on the street. Look for them outside hotels or call for a pickup. Although cabs will happily take you from Cincinnati to Kentucky and vice versa, you sometimes need to call a Kentucky cab company if you're on that side of the Ohio River, and a Cincinnati cab company if you're on the Ohio side of the river.

🚩 TAXI COMPANIES Community Yellow Cab ☎859/727–2900. **Pure Gold Taxi** ☎513/721–2100.

Train Travel

🚩 TRAIN INFORMATION Amtrak ✉Union Terminal, 1301 Western Ave., Downtown, Cincinnati, OH ☎800/872–7245.

CHAPTER 6

JUNE

Newport Marathon, Newport, OR

Standing amid the greenery of Yaquina Bay State Park, you almost forget you're at the beginning of a marathon. Oh sure, there's the line of people at the portable toilets, the START banner strung up between a large wooden sign and a U-Haul, and the guy in the RACE DIRECTOR cap making announcements into a bullhorn. But there are also dogs romping with their families; small groups of friends casually chatting and laughing; couples holding hands as they peer out over the ocean; and people climbing up to view the historic "haunted" Yaquina Bay Lighthouse.

VISITOR INFO

Greater Newport Chamber
of Commerce

☎

503/265-8801 or
800/COAST44

🌐

www.newportchamber.org

•

Discover Newport

🌐

www.discovernewport.com

There's a tranquility here at the Newport starting line, thanks to the small, 750-runner field. Yet within that field are marathoners of all shapes, sizes, and speeds, many of whom travel to Newport that first Saturday after Memorial Day each year for gorgeous weather; a flat, fast course; and a race that *Runner's World* magazine has called "one of the best-kept marathon secrets."

So You're Running Newport . . .

Coastal Newport is a long, deep breath of fresh ocean air. Wholly unpretentious, the beaches, hiking trails, and oceanfront bed-and-breakfasts embrace you with their charms. Everyone is friendly, and everyone has a story. Many of these stories involve vacationing in Newport, falling in love with the area, settling down, and never looking back. Historic Nye Beach, one of the Oregon coast's first beachside communities, is a magnet for such transplants, who in turn lured upscale restaurants, unique shops, and enticing cafés to the area. The result is an enchanting combination of old and new, an upscale bohemian artists' colony along a beautiful stretch of sand.

RACE BASICS

Most marathons tweak their course several times in the first few years. This one is unchanged since 1999, mainly because so much planning went into making it ideal for both the participants and the community. The route is almost totally flat and run entirely at sea level, so many people come here to

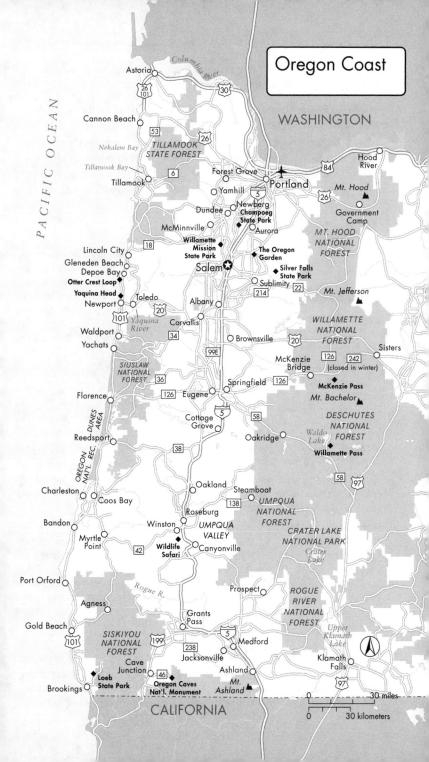

Oregon Coast

PACIFIC OCEAN

WASHINGTON

Astoria
Cannon Beach
Columbia River
26 101
30
Hood River
84
Mt. Hood
26
Government Camp

53
TILLAMOOK STATE FOREST
26
Nebalem Bay
Tillamook Bay
6
Tillamook
Forest Grove
Yamhill
5
Portland
Dundee
Newberg
Champoeg State Park
Aurora
MT. HOOD NATIONAL FOREST

McMinnville
18
Willamette Mission State Park
Salem
The Oregon Garden
Silver Falls State Park
Mt. Jefferson

Lincoln City
Gleneden Beach
Depoe Bay
Otter Crest Loop
Yaquina Head
Newport
Toledo
20
101
Yaquina River
Sublimity
214
22

Waldport
Yachats
34
Albany
Corvallis
Brownsville
20
WILLAMETTE NATIONAL FOREST
Sisters
McKenzie Bridge
126 242
(closed in winter)

SIUSLAW NATIONAL FOREST
36
99E
Springfield
126
McKenzie Pass
Mt. Bachelor

Florence
126
Eugene
Cottage Grove
5
58
DESCHUTES NATIONAL FOREST

OREGON DUNES AREA
OREGON NATL. REC.
Reedsport
38
Oakridge
Waldo Lake
Willamette Pass
58
97

Charleston
Coos Bay
Oakland
Steamboat
138
UMPQUA NATIONAL FOREST
CRATER LAKE NATIONAL PARK
Crater Lake

Bandon
Myrtle Point
42
Winston
Wildlife Safari
Roseburg
UMPQUA VALLEY
Canyonville

Port Orford
Agness
Rogue R.
Prospect
ROGUE RIVER NATIONAL FOREST
Upper Klamath Lake

Gold Beach
101
SISKIYOU NATIONAL FOREST
199
Grants Pass
238
5
Medford
Jacksonville
Ashland
Klamath Falls

Loeb State Park
Cave Junction
46
Oregon Caves Nat'l. Monument
Mt. Ashland
97

Brookings

CALIFORNIA

0   30 miles
0   30 kilometers

set personal records (PRs) or qualify for Boston, which about 25% of the finishers—a staggering number—did in 2003.

The Newport Marathon was set up as a nonprofit fund-raiser for the area's student track-and-field programs, and most of the money raised from registration fees goes directly there. No extra funds are spent on the race; even chip timing is eschewed because of the expense. None of this economy hurts the race. Quite the opposite: it's a high-quality "big city race in a small town setting," where both the first and last finisher are treated with equal care.

Registration

The most important thing to remember about registering for Newport is the entrant cap: 750 runners. The first year of the race there was no cap, and 318 people ran. They gave the course rave reviews, and many promised to return with their entire running club. This was great news, but race director Bruce Durkee worried about his ability to keep things running smoothly if the numbers got too high. So he capped the second year's entries at 600 runners, just in case.

The race sold out in April.

The cap has gradually increased, but 750 is likely as high as it will go, and an April sellout isn't uncommon. For the most part, there are no qualifying times that guarantee you entry; it's first-come, first-served. That said, there are a couple of spots available to last-minute runners who can send Bruce documentation of a time that would make them competitive to win in the open or masters divisions.

To run this race, plan to sign up early. Registration opens in early October, and the best way to register is via the simply laid out yet informative Web site. Take the time to read the FAQs, which cover a wide breadth of topics.

Registration costs $45 before mid-March; $55 between then and mid-April. If there are slots left after mid-April, the registration fee rises to $65. There's no race day registration. On the form, you'll specify whether you're a runner or a walker, and if you're in the Hercules (men over 190 pounds) or Athena (women over 140 pounds) divisions. For an extra $6.50 each, you can also buy tickets for the prerace pasta dinner. If you register online, you'll receive a confirmation number; otherwise your canceled check serves as your receipt and confirmation.

RACE CONTACT

Newport Marathon

✉
1215 N.E. Lakewood Dr.,
Newport, OR 97365

☎
541/265-3446

🌐
www.newportmarathon.org

Hotels to Consider

Newport's best accommodations are either full-service beachside hotels or B&Bs that range from ultraluxurious to ultraquirky. Although only a few lodgings offer marathon discounts, rates overall are reasonable. Book well in advance, especially for B&B stays.

BUMP IN THE NIGHT

The Yaquina Bay Lighthouse was built in 1871 but served only three years before it was decommissioned in favor of the far more prominent Yaquina Head Lighthouse. The structure quickly fell into disrepair, becoming a ripe setting for tales of ghosties, ghoulies, and things that go bump in the night. In 1899 Lischen M. Miller obliged, and the *Pacific Monthly* published his fictional story, "The Haunted Lighthouse," about a sea captain's daughter who entered this lighthouse, never to be seen again. . . .

ELIZABETH STREET INN. The Elizabeth Street offers marathon discounts and is close to the starting line. The free Continental breakfast of bagels, muffins, cereal, juice, and coffee starts early on marathon day so runners can fuel up properly. There's easy ocean access, and all guest rooms and most public areas have water views—there's even an ocean vista from the indoor pool. All rooms have private decks and fireplaces, and some have hot tubs. For the best views, request a corner room. ⚬ Wake-up calls, alarm clocks, coffeemakers, newspapers Sunday, cable TV, microwaves, refrigerators, indoor pool, gym, hot tub, laundry facilities, business services, meeting rooms, free parking, no-smoking rooms. ✉ 232 S.W. Elizabeth St. 97365 ☎ 541/265-9400 or 877/265-9400 ⊕ www.elizabethstreetinn.com ⇗ 68 rooms ▭ AE, D, MC, V $.

EMBARCADERO RESORT. This is marathon headquarters: it's across from the finish line, it's the packet pick-up and award ceremony location, and it offers marathon discounts. The resort sprawls, and most accommodations are privately owned condos—some nicer than others. Suites have one or two bedrooms, a kitchen, a fireplace, and a private balcony. For the race the restaurant adds high-carb specials to its menu. There's also an on-site general store that's open 24 hours. For a unique meal, rent a crab ring, catch your entrée, then use the resort's crab cookers to make your own feast. ✉ 1000 S.E. Bay Blvd., 97365 ☎ 541/265-8521 or 800/547-4779 ⊕ www.embarcadero-resort.com ⇗ 85 units ⚬ Restaurant, room service, wake-up calls, alarm clocks, indoor pool, 24-hr gym, outdoor hot tub, sauna, dock, boating, fishing, bar, shop, laundry facilities, free parking ▭ AE, D, DC, MC, V $.

HALLMARK RESORT NEWPORT. This is a great choice for groups who get special activities such as beach bonfires. All rooms have balconies with ocean views; most have fireplaces. Configurations vary: some have queen-size beds with small sitting areas, others have two queen-size beds with full living rooms and kitchenettes, and still others have three queen-size beds (one in a loft space) or a king-size bed. The race starting line is very close, and the hotel provides shuttles back from the finish line. ✉ 744 S.W. Elizabeth St., 97365 ☎ 888/448-4449 or 541/265-2600 ⊕ www.hallmarkinns.com ⇗ 158 rooms ⚬ Restaurant, room service, wake-up calls, alarm clocks, coffeemakers, newspapers, cable TV, in-room data ports, some kitchenettes, free Wi-Fi, indoor pool, 24-hr gym, hot tub, massage, sauna, horseshoes, volleyball, laundry facilities, free parking, some pets allowed (fee) ▭ AE, D, MC, V ¢–$.

NEWPORT BELLE BED & BREAKFAST. This fully operational stern-wheeler stays permanently moored at the Newport Marina. Five rooms have themes that run from the Australian Outback to Montana's West, and all are light and airy. The main salon is cozy, with hardwood floors, a woodstove, and comfortable furniture plus Internet access, a TV, and a phone. Full breakfast is included in the rate, and the innkeeper leaves fruit out on marathon morning. Enjoy special rates if you book the whole boat. ⊠ H Dock, Newport Marina, 97365 ☎ 541/867-6290 or 800/348-1922 ⊕ www.newportbelle.com ⤙ 5 rooms ⌂ Alarm clocks; no a/c, no room phones, no room TVs, no kids under 7, no smoking ⊟ AE, D, MC, V $$.

NYE BEACH HOTEL. Despite its century-old appearance, the Nye Beach Hotel was built in 1992. It's on a cliff above the beach, and all its kicky rooms have balconies with ocean views, private baths, and fireplaces. The lobby's pastel colors and potted tropical plants evoke Key West. Keep an eye out for the macaw and the African lovebirds. ⊠ 219 Cliff St., 97365 ☎ 541/265-3334 or 866/865-3334 ⊕ www.nyebeach.com ⤙ 18 rooms ⌂ Restaurant, room service, alarm clocks, newspapers (every day but Sun.), cable TV, free Wi-Fi, free parking ⊟ AE, D, MC, V ¢–$.

★ **OCEAN HOUSE.** Marie and Bob Garrard are the gracious hosts of this romantic Cape Cod–style B&B on a bluff overlooking Agate Beach. As Marie says, "Anyone can sell a room; we want to create an experience." And they succeed. The grounds include coastal gardens and a walkway to the beach. All the rooms have romantic furnishings; high ceilings; fine linens; antiques; art; and views of the beach, ocean, and lighthouse. Many also have hot tubs. Full breakfast is included in the rate, and juice, coffee, and water are available on race morning. ⊠ 4920 N.W. Woody Way, 97365 ☎ 541/265-6158 or 800/562-2632 ⊕ www.oceanhouse.com ⤙ 7 rooms, 1 cottage ⌂ Free parking; no room phones, no room TVs, no kids ⊟ AE, D, DC, MC, V ¢–$$.

SYLVIA BEACH HOTEL. In this comfortably worn, 1913 beachfront hotel, antiques-filled rooms are named for famous writers. A pendulum swings over the bed in the Poe room. The luxurious Christie, Twain, and Colette rooms all have fireplaces, decks, and great ocean views. A well-stocked, split-level library has decks, a fireplace, slumbering cats, and all-too-comfortable chairs. A full breakfast is included in the rate, as is the mulled wine that's served nightly at 10. On request, a Continental breakfast of homemade pastries, fruit, and beverages is available before the race. ⊠ 267 N.W. Cliff St., 97365 ☎ 541/265-5428 or 888/795-8422 ⊕ www.sylviabeachhotel.com ⤙ 20 rooms ⌂ Restaurant, wake-up "calls" (they come knock on your door), library, free parking; no room phones, no room TVs ⊟ AE, MC, V ¢–$$.

TYEE LODGE OCEANFRONT BED & BREAKFAST. It's a bit of a drive from the marathon, but worth it. A trail leads from this bluff-top 1940s house to the beach. Rooms all have pine furniture, gas fireplaces, and ocean views through towering spruces. Breakfast (included in the rates) is served family-style in a room with a bay window facing the ocean. The innkeeper takes special food requests and ensures that any food you need is available before you leave for the starting line. ⊠ 4925 N.W. Woody Way, 97365 ☎ 541/265-8953 or 888/553-TYEE (8933) ⊕ www.tyeelodge.com ⤙ 5 rooms ⌂ Alarm clocks, massage, free parking; no a/c, no room phones, no room TVs, no kids under 16, no smoking ⊟ AE, D, MC, V $.

NIGHT-BEFORE PASTA DINNER

The pasta dinner is held from 6 PM to 8 PM at the Newport High School and sponsored by its track-and-field team. Everyone is welcome to enjoy generous portions of pasta with marinara sauce, salad with local shrimp, bread, soft drinks, and pie. If you forgot to buy your $6.50 tickets at registration or packet pickup, you can buy them at the door.

If you'd rather try something local and your prerace stomach can handle it, consider seafood, a specialty in Newport.

★ **SHARKS.** Prepare to eat like you've never eaten before. The place is ridiculously small and it doesn't take reservations, so you might have to wait. Do. Their seafood is steamed or poached. Enjoy it in the restaurant's famous cioppino, in a stew, in bouillabaisse, or on its own with the chef's special sauce. Pasta choices include marinara linguine with three types of seafood, or cioppino and pasta. Keep the carb count going with lots of sauce-sopping fresh bread. ✉ 852 S.W. Bay Blvd. ☎ 541/574–0590 ⊕ www.sharksseafoodbar.com ⇦ Reservations not accepted ▭ D, MC, V $–$$$.

★ **TIDAL RAVES.** The food is stellar at this beachside restaurant about 13 miles north of Newport, and every seat in the house has mesmerizing views of waves crashing on the rocky shore. Warm sourdough bread begins a meal that can range from a simple linguine with your choice of sauce, to a salmon-and-vegetable skewer with steamed peanut rice, to a Parmesan-herb-crusted snapper with shrimp-caper sauce. The apple-pecan cake with warm caramel sauce is astounding. ✉ 279 N.W. Hwy. 101, Depoe Bay ☎ 541/765–2995 ⇦ Reservations essential ▭ MC, V $–$$.

WHALE'S TALE. There's a sense of fun to this long-standing bay-front restaurant; marine kitsch adorns the woody walls and ceilings. The food is tasty, and the portions are generous. Burgers are always a great choice, as is the clam chowder. Marathoners looking for pasta can opt for either regular or vegetarian lasagna or a seafood pasta in marinara sauce. ✉ 452 S.W. Bay Blvd. ☎ 541/265–8660 ▭ AE, D, DC, MC, V $–$$.

AND YOU'RE OFF . . .
Packet Pickup

Packet pickup is at the Embarcadero Resort the day before the race (Friday), from the afternoon into the evening. A few sponsors are on hand to promote and sell their goods, and both pasta dinner tickets and official marathon merchandise are available for purchase. Hercules and Athena runners must weigh in at the pickup to qualify for their divisions. Goodie bags include discounts to area attractions and restaurants.

Race Day

The Course

The race starts by the lighthouse at Yaquina Bay State Park. Walk, drive, or hop the shuttles, which run continuously to the start from the finish area by the Embarcadero Resort from around 6:15 AM to about 6:50 AM. Spectators are allowed on the shuttles but rarely take them, because they don't return to the Embarcadero. If you drive to the start, be aware that you can't park in Yaquina Bay State Park on race morning: it's drop-off only.

The race begins at 7 AM sharp. You loop through Newport, taking in some picturesque neighborhoods and ocean views before heading to the bay front, Newport's tourism and fishing hub. You hit the one and only hill—a short rise of about 40 feet—at Mile 4. The route then follows Yaquina Bay and the river estuary along one lane of a two-lane country road. At Mile 15 you turn around and head back toward town, revisiting the hill at Mile 26 before cruising down to the finish line across from the Embarcadero.

WEATHER THE RUN

There are no hard and fast rules about Oregon coastal weather. Still, the marathon traditionally has great running weather, with temperatures in the 50s or 60s.

The marathon course is truly beautiful. You'll see herons and other wildlife as well as fishermen and crabbers plying their trade. Although spectators are few and far between, the folks manning the aid stations every 2 miles or so are very enthusiastic, and will motivate you along the way. All the stations have water, energy drink, and toilets; some also have fruit and/or energy gel. But there's one thing you'll find at an aid station that makes the Newport Marathon stand out from all other races:

Oyster shooters.

Really. Because what's every runner truly craving at Miles 11 and 19? Raw oysters! They're served in small disposable "shooter cups," and you can enjoy them with or without Oregon Oyster Farms' special cocktail sauce. Come on, you know you're tempted. And if you want bragging rights, don't have just one. A woman in the 2004 race shot down 26 of 'em—one for every mile.

At the finish line you'll receive your medal, then proceed to the adjacent recovery area to get your finisher T-shirt (late registrants' shirts will be mailed), and lots of refreshments, including fruit, cookies, bagels, chips, and salsa. You'll also get a "food bag" of water, an energy drink, an energy bar, and coupons for free clam chowder and beer at the finish-area concession stand. The course and finish area remain open for seven hours. Though lanes reopen to traffic after five hours, there's plenty of paved shoulder to run on.

Don't be surprised, though, if you finish sooner than you imagined. The course is very fast, giving many runners a PR, and one a world record. In 2004 Herb Phillips set a record for 63-year-old males with a finishing time of 2:47:28. The previous record had been held

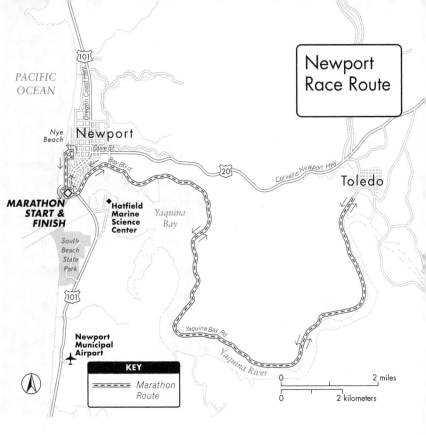

Newport Race Route

PACIFIC OCEAN

Nye Beach

Newport

Olive St.

Bay Blvd

MARATHON START & FINISH

Hatfield Marine Science Center

Yaquina Bay

South Beach State Park

Corvallis-Newport Hwy.

Toledo

Newport Municipal Airport

Yaquina Bay Rd.

Yaquina River

KEY

===== Marathon Route

0   2 miles

0   2 kilometers

for 25 years by Clive Davies, considered one of the greatest senior marathoners of all time. "Pretty cool!" said race director Bruce Durkee when he told me about the accomplishment. "I guess we really do have a fast course!"

Spectating

The best places to watch are the starting and finish lines. After the start, don't move. The runners will do a 2.8-mile loop before zooming right back through the starting area. Once the pack passes, you have some time, so grab breakfast before heading to the finish line, right across the street from the Embarcadero Resort, at the corner of Bay Boulevard and John Moore Road and on the Newport bay front. Note that if you're driving, you'll probably have to park three or four blocks away.

Celebrate!

There's no post-marathon party, but at this race the awards ceremony comes close. It takes place at the Embarcadero around 2:30 PM. Not only will the top three division winners get awards, but all registered marathoners who show up with their bibs are eligible for door prizes such as trophies, plaques, and cool swag from local businesses and sponsors. Plus there's the post-race camaraderie: where else will you find people who want to swap stories about chafing, lost toenails, and bloody nipples?

BEYOND THE FINISH LINE
Replacing 2,620 Calories

Amazing seafood abounds here, especially when it's made into a chowder, deep-fried, or covered in a creamy sauce—delicious but not exactly health food. Stroll the bay front, and you'll swear every restaurant has a clipping in the window naming its clam chowder the best. Want a fun way to recoup all those lost calories? Try 'em all and decide for yourself who's right.

★ **APRIL'S AT NYE BEACH.** The place glows with sophistication and is booked solid most nights. The food matches the ambience, blending Northwest fish, meat, and produce with Mediterranean flavors. Dishes are impeccable, and the service is attentive and gracious but not overbearing. Come at sunset to enjoy the ocean view. ✉ 749 N.W. 3rd St. ☎ 541/265-6855 ⛴ Reservations essential ▤ AE, D, DC, MC, V ⊘ Closed Mon. and Tues. $-$$.

★ **KAM MENG'S CHINESE.** Kam Meng and his wife, Huiya, have a dazzling array of choices on their menu, but you might want to skip right to the Dungeness crab specialties, which can be prepared eight ways. Alternatively, the clay-pot dishes meld flavors perfectly; try the one with garlic, ginger, and seven kinds of seafood. Vegetarian food is another specialty: the vegetable broth is homemade, and you can substitute tofu for meat in any dish. The produce is always fresh, and 90% of the seafood is caught locally. ✉ 837 S.W. Bay Blvd. ☎ 541/574-9450 ▤ D, MC, V ⊘ Closed Wed. $-$$.

MO'S. Mo's has hosted a slew of celebrities, but it remains humble: a joint on the bay where folks hang out and eat fish. Clam chowder is the signature dish; have it with bread and a delicious side salad, chock-full of shrimp and cabbage in a ranch dressing. Mo's Annex, just across the street, hangs out over the bay, offering great views and occasional live music. ✉ 622 S.W. Bay Blvd. ☎ 541/265-2979 ✉ 657 S.W. Bay Blvd. ☎ 541/265-7512 ⊕ www.moschowder.com ▤ AE, D, DC, MC, V ¢-$.

★ **PANINI BAKERY.** The young couple that operates this local favorite bakery and espresso bar takes pride in their home-roasted meats, delicious pizzas, hand-cut breads, and friendly service. Just about everything is made from scratch. The coffee is organic, the eggs free range, and the orange juice fresh squeezed. In good weather, the street-side tables are a great place to take in the Nye Beach scene. ✉ 232 N.W. Coast Hwy. ☎ 541/265-5033 ▤ No credit cards ⊘ Closed Tues. and Wed. ¢-$.

QUIMBY'S. Don't let the boxy exterior fool you; this is a fantastic place for a post-race brunch. The food is not only delicious but also a little adventuresome. Three different types of French toast share the menu with creole crab cakes Benedict and a slew of scrambles

BREAKFAST SPOTS

If you're staying at a Newport B&B, don't even think of going anywhere else for breakfast—their morning meals are exceptional. Otherwise try one of these options in the ¢–$ or $$ range.

★ **CAFE STEPHANIE.** Breakfast specials rotate daily, and you can't go wrong. The pastries, quiches, and crepes are made on-site. The crustless quiche with sausage, sun-dried tomato, and spinach is light and savory, and the banana pecan waffles are sweet without being overpowering. Crusty scones come with each meal, and there's a full espresso bar. Indoor seating is limited; on a nice day grab a picnic table. ⊠ 411 N.W. Coast St. ☎ 541/265–8082 ▭ AE, D, DC, MC, V ☉ No dinner.

GEORGIE'S BEACHSIDE GRILL. Its beachside location elevates this low-key diner up a notch. Georgie's surprises with creative takes on seafood, even at breakfast. The coastal stuffer combines crabmeat and shrimp with potatoes, scrambled eggs, and vegetables—drizzled with hollandaise sauce and served in a sourdough bread bowl. Sweet choices include croissant French toast in a custard batter or a Belgian waffle loaded with pecans. ⊠ Hallmark Hotel, 744 S.W. Elizabeth St. ☎ 541/265–9800 ⊕ www.hallmarkinns.com ▭ AE, D, DC, MC, V.

Other breakfast options include **Whale's Tale** (⇨ Night-Before Pasta Dinner) and **Quimby's** (⇨ Replacing 2,620 Calories).

---

and omelets. Sun-dried tomatoes and capers bring tuna melts to zesty life. And the clam chowder is tops. Portions are huge, and don't even think about counting fat grams here: even less decadent dishes are labeled—with a nudge and a wink—"*almost* heart healthy." ⊠ 740 W. Olive St. ☎ 541/265-9919 or 866/QUIMBYS (784-6297) ⊕ www.quimbysrestaurant.com ▭ AE, D, DC, MC, V $-$$$.

SAFFRON SALMON. As you'd expect, seafood is featured prominently. Enjoy a shrimp- or crab-cocktail appetizer, then move on to a panfried Chinook salmon fillet or grilled jumbo prawns. Meat eaters will also find much to enjoy at this upscale spot, including rack of lamb. ⊠ 859 S.W. Bay Blvd. ☎ 541/265-8921 ⚐ Reservations essential ▭ MC, V ☉ Closed Wed. $$-$$$.

SWAFFORD'S CHAMPAGNE PATIO. Chef Christina Swafford cooks up specials that might one day be Mexican in origin, the next Swedish; she also bakes breads and prepares desserts daily. The restaurant serves wine that comes from the adjoining shop, operated by Joe Swafford, who pens a column on wine in the local weekly. ⊠ 1630 N. Coast Hwy. ☎ 541/265-3044 ▭ AE, D, MC, V ☉ No dinner. Closed Sun. and Mon. $.

TABLES OF CONTENT. The well-plotted prix-fixe menu at this restaurant in the Sylvia Beach Hotel changes nightly. Chances are the main dish will be seafood, perhaps a moist grilled salmon fillet in a sauce Dijonnaise served with sautéed vegetables, fresh-baked bread, and rice pilaf. Desserts are decadent. The interior is functional and unadorned, with

Ever wanted your spouse to give you a really unique present?

How about a marathon?

Race director Bruce Durkee would never have founded the Newport Marathon if it weren't for the inspiration and grit of his wife, Deborah. In 1994, Debi was a casual runner who had dabbled in the sport for more than a decade, entering the occasional 5K or 10K, doing just enough to keep in shape. Yet as she approached 40, those claws of "I'm getting old" started scratching at the back of her neck. She needed a goal to keep her on track and settled on the marathon, declaring to all who would listen that when she turned 40, she'd run the Portland Marathon. She started training for the race and felt fantastic. In fact, she felt so strong that she expanded her goal. Not only would she run a marathon at age 40, but she'd also run a total of *50* marathons by the time she turned 50.

Many people would throw down that gauntlet only to withdraw it within the hour, laughing it off as the result of a crazy endorphin surge. Not Debi. When she sets a goal, nothing gets in her way; she knew the minute the words left her mouth that she'd follow through. What she couldn't know was how great an impact her decision would have not just on her, but on the entire town of Newport.

From the start, her quest wasn't easy. She tore her meniscus in August, but still completed Portland two months later, following it with Honolulu. In 1995, '96, and '97 she tackled six marathons a year, traveling as far away as the Médoc region in southwest France for the Marathon du Médoc—a true 26.2-mile party where runners often wear costumes (Debi was Wilma Flintstone) and enjoy wine-tasting stops and heaps of local delicacies along the way. Though late 1997 brought a stress fracture that put Debi out of commission and threatened her 50-before-50 goal, she doggedly pushed herself back on track a year later, squeezing in three more marathons before the end of 1998.

Throughout this time, Debi trained primarily on Bay Road, which runs along the Yaquina Bay estuary in Newport. The views, the wide shoulders, and the turnouts made for pleasant, easy runs. As she gained marathon experience she realized that Newport would make an excellent race location, an idea she discussed with Bruce, who was intrigued. Until this point, he had attended marathons primarily to cheer on his wife. Now he began to look at each event from a race-director perspective. What would he copy? What pitfalls would he avoid?

One shortcoming Bruce and Debi saw at several races was the lack of attention paid to slower runners. Bruce was determined that at his marathon, the last finisher would get as much care as the first. He and Debi also wanted a nonprofit Newport Marathon, that would benefit the entire community. Not only could it boost the local economy by luring tourists during a slow time of year, but Debi suggested it could also raise much-needed money for track-and-field programs at the local high school, where she volunteered as a running coach. Bruce spent about six months gathering local support and sponsors before contacting the USATF to get his course certified. By June 1999, the race was ready to go.

And what of Debi and her goal?

She sped forward, finishing seven races in 1999, including the very first Newport Marathon. Yet when she trained her eye more closely on her hometown, she realized there was something missing. The local running club had all but collapsed, and without it there was no running community to speak of. She restarted and revitalized the club until in no time it was not only meeting regularly, but also sponsoring three popular annual 5K and 10K races to fund youth running programs. To show their appreciation, club members secretly nominated Debi to be a torchbearer for the 2002 Olympics—and she was selected. She carried the torch for 0.2 mile and says of the incredible experience, "It went by so fast, so unlike the last 0.2 of a marathon!"

Between 2000 and 2003, Debi ran five marathons a year, timing things perfectly to reach her goal at Newport. The running club was out in full force to cheer her on and run the last few hundred yards with her, toting a banner that read: CONGRATULATIONS DEBI—50 MARATHONS BEFORE AGE 50. The emotion was almost overwhelming when she crossed the finish line. Not only had she met her goal, but she had done so a solid 18 months *before* her 50th birthday.

Debi now knows from experience that anyone can run a marathon. To those who doubt she says, "It really is a mental thing. It is [also] amazing what a body can do with training. Whatever you start out at, the next time you can do it plus 10% more, and you just keep building from there."

And although Debi's goal has been realized, its impact continues. Newport now has a true runners' community: her running club and its fund-raising events are thriving. The Newport Marathon reaches capacity every year, luring people and revenue into town. Moreover, as of its eighth year, the marathon had raised more than $180,000 for local school district track-and-field programs. All this because one highly determined woman got a little nervous about the approach of middle age.

Kinda makes you wonder what she'll decide to do next. ■

family-size tables. Come for the food and the conversation, not the furnishings. ✉ 267 N.W. Cliff St. (from U.S. 101 head west on 3rd St.) ☎ 541/265-5428 ⊕ www. sylviabeachhotel.com ⚓ Reservations essential ▭ AE, MC, V ⊙ No lunch $$.

Sightseeing on (and off) Your Feet

Newport is relatively small, with a population of about 10,000. U.S. 101, running north-south, is the main thoroughfare through town. On a map Newport's shape recalls a long-necked decanter. If you're driving south along the Oregon coast, you enter town through the decanter's top, skinny part. Here the notable sights are along the ocean, including the amazing Yaquina Head Outstanding Natural Area. Head south a few miles and you'll come to Agate Beach, home of the Ocean House and Tyee B&Bs.

Keep heading south to the decanter's bulbous portion—the town proper. Here U.S. 101 moves slightly inland to make way for the charming Nye Beach area. If you continue south on U.S. 101, you'll be heading for Yaquina Bay. Before the bay, Elizabeth Street, home to several beachfront hotels, is to the west. Just off it is Yaquina Bay State Park, the marathon's starting point. To the east of U.S. 101 is Newport's historic bay front. It's home to an active fishing industry as well as restaurants, shops, and such touristy kitsch as *Ripley's Believe it or Not.* If you stay on U.S. 101, you'll cross the Yaquina Bay Bridge, passing the Oregon Coast Aquarium.

On such a drive through the town, you're bound to see something you'd like to do. Decide how your legs feel, then take your pick of Newport's highlights.

I Feel Great!

KAYAK YAQUINA BAY. Rent a kayak at the **Embarcadero Resort General Store** (✉ 1000 S.E. Bay Blvd. ☎ 541/265-8521 ⊕ www.embarcadero-resort.com) and explore Yaquina Bay. Rentals require a $250 deposit, plus the rental fee of $15 an hour (there are discounts for long rentals). Rental is open to both guests and nonguests of the resort. For safety reasons, you must stay within the bay and within sight of the Embarcadero during your time on the water.

★**YAQUINA HEAD OUTSTANDING NATURAL AREA.** If you're up for some major walking, this is must. Start at the **Yaquina Head Lighthouse,** the Oregon coast's tallest lighthouse at 93 feet, and consider a guided morning tour. Look out to the water and you'll see Colony Rock, where thousands of birds—cormorants, gulls, common murres, pigeon guillemots—make their homes.

Trek through Yaquina Head and find all kinds of treasures, such as natural and man-made tide pools (the latter engineered to be accessible to people with disabilities) crawling with life. Cobble Beach is a stretch of round basalt rocks believed to have originated from volcano eruptions 14 million years ago in the Columbia Gorge 300 miles away. Look to the ocean around here and you'll see Seal Island, often filled with seals sunning themselves. Throughout the area, trails wind through fields of sea grass and wildflowers, leading to spectacular views. There's also an interpretive center, where you can view a short video about the area, read old lighthouse logbooks, and listen to the songs of seabirds and whales.

FORGET SIGHTSEEING. GET ME TO A SPA!

Many hotels and B&Bs have arrangements with massage therapists. Ask about and make arrangements for in-room treatments when you book, or try one of the following day spas:

DESERT SPRINGS NATURAL HEALING SPA. Desert Springs is about healing the mind, body, and spirit. Prices are very reasonable; consider a 90-minute sports, Swedish, or deep-tissue massage ($75). Spa packages include an hour-long massage with foot-renewal treatment and scalp massage—all for $120. ⊠ 422 S.W. 10th St. ☎ 541/574–9887 ⊕ www.dshealing.com ☉ Mon.–Sat. 10–5; evenings and Sun. by appt.

JERILYN & COMPANY. Prices are fantastic: for the cost of an hour-long massage at a big-city hotel, you can get a half-day spa package that includes a one-hour massage, spa manicure, spa pedicure, shampoo, and style ($135). Massage choices include deep tissue, hot stone, and relaxation (30–90 minutes; $35–$75). Opt for a 90-minute version; you deserve it. ⊠ 145 N. Coast Hwy., Suite F ☎ 541/265–7792 or 541/265–5182 ⊕ www. jerilynandcompany.com ☉ Mon. and Fri. 7–7; Tues.–Thurs. 8–7; Sat. 7–4; additional times by appt.

⊠ 750 N.W. Lighthouse Dr. ☎ 541/574–3100 🚗 $5 per vehicle (9 passengers or fewer) ☉ Daily dawn–dusk.

I Feel Pretty Good

HATFIELD MARINE SCIENCE CENTER. Interactive and interpretive exhibits at Oregon State University's science center, which is connected by a trail to the Oregon Coast Aquarium, explain current marine research from satellite, bird's-eye, eye-level, and microscopic perspectives. The star of the show is a large octopus in a touch tank near the entrance. She seems as interested in humans as they are in her; guided by a staff volunteer, you can sometimes reach in to stroke her suction-tipped tentacles. ⊠ 2030 S. Marine Science Dr., Heading south from Newport, cross Yaquina Bay Bridge on U.S. 101 S and follow signs ☎ 541/867–0100 ⊕ http://hmsc.oregonstate.edu 🎟 Suggested donation $4 ☉ Memorial Day–Sept., daily 10–5; Oct.–Memorial Day, daily 10–4.

★ **OREGON COAST AQUARIUM.** This 4½-acre complex has re-creations of Pacific marine habitats, all teeming with life: playful sea otters, comical puffins, fragile jellyfish, and even a 60-pound octopus. There's North America's largest seabird aviary and an interactive area for children. Permanent exhibits include Passages of the Deep, a trio of tanks linked by a 200-foot underwater tunnel with 360-degree views of sharks, wolf eels, halibut, and other sea life. You can watch large coho salmon and sturgeon in a naturalistic setting through a window wall 9 feet high and 20 feet wide. ⊠ 2820 S.E. Ferry Slip Rd., Heading south from Newport, go over Yaquina Bay Bridge, turn right, and follow signs ☎ 541/867–3474 ⊕ www.aquarium.org 🎟 $12 ☉ Daily 9–6.

Let's Take It Slowly

★ **ENJOY THE BEACHES.** Wander Nye Beach, Agate Beach, or Newport's other sandy strips, taking it as easy as you'd like. Explore tide pools and dip your feet in the water (June in Oregon is too cold for a swim, but hey, maybe that's just me), or just bring a picnic lunch and watch the waves.

MARINER SQUARE. This spot on the historic bay front has several attractions that are cheesy but fun in their own way, especially on a rainy day. **Ripley's Believe It or Not** has strange but true exhibits. At **Undersea Gardens** look for scuba-diving shows, marine plants, and animal exhibits. As its name suggests, **Wax Works** has wax-figure exhibits of famous people. ⊠ 250 S.W. Bay Blvd. ☎ 541/265–2206 ⊕ www.marinersquare. com 🎫 $8.95 for 1 attraction, discounts for additional attractions ☉ May and Sept., daily 10–5; June and Oct., daily 10–6; July and Aug., daily 9–8.

Ow! No.

DRIVE THE COAST. If even the thought of walking makes you wince, why not head out on a drive? Take Highway 101 either north or south. It mostly hugs the ocean, and the views are gorgeous. Be sure to pull over periodically and take it all in.

★ **MARINE DISCOVERY TOURS.** Two-hour whale-watching cruises with this operation may well be the highlight of your trip (it was for me). The outfit's bilevel, 65-foot, wheelchair-accessible excursion boat *Discovery* departs from Newport's bay front each morning and afternoon (weather permitting). The guides are personable and knowledgeable. The best viewing is March–October, though tours run year-round. Although there's no guarantee you'll see a whale, 95% of the outings are successful in this regard. There's a resident population of gray whales in Newport year-round, including young mothers with calves who feed less than a mile from shore. In summer they often come right up to the boat. In the bay you'll likely spot sea lions. Just remember to bundle up; June weather feels quite cold when you're zipping along the water. ⊠ 345 S.W. Bay Blvd. ☎ 541/265–6200 or 800/903–2628 ⊕ www.marinediscovery.com 🎫 $30.

Shop Around

Market

Shop for fresh-baked goods, local produce, plants, crafts, and homemade dog goodies at Newport's **SATURDAY FARMER'S MARKET** (⊠ U.S. 101 in Armory parking lot ☎ 541/574–4040 ⊕ www.newportfarmersmarket.org), open 9 to 1 May through October.

Specialty Shops

MAINSALE (⊠ 338 S.W. Bay Blvd. ☎ 541/265–3940) stocks marine- and nature-related gift items. **OREGON OYSTER FARMS** (⊠ 6878 Yaquina Bay Rd. ☎ 541/265–5078) raises and sells many kinds of oysters, and also sells shucking knives, sauces, and T-shirts. Search for that out-of-print classic or that slightly used best-seller at **NYE BEACH BOOK HOUSE** (⊠ 727 N.W. 3rd St. ☎ 541/265–6840), where three rooms are lined floor-to-ceiling with tomes. The **NYE BEACH GALLERY** (✉ 715 N.W. 3rd St. ☎ 541/265–3292) features fine wines and artisanal cheeses. On Saturday, stop by for samples and to admire (or buy) Lon Brusselback's bronze sculptures.

The boutique **TOUJOURS** (✉ 704 N.W. Beach Dr. ☎ 541/574–6404) carries natural-fiber women's wear, shoes, jewelry, unique hair accessories, purses, and a line of Brighton watches and sunglasses. **THE WOOD GALLERY** (✉ 818 S.W. Bay Blvd. ☎ 541/265–6843 or 800/359–1419) sells wood crafts and paintings.

I Love the Nightlife

BLU CORK WINE BAR. Sip wine, munch tapas, and splurge on desserts in a trendy atmosphere, all while listening to jazz. ✉ 613 N.W. 3rd St. ☎ 541/265–2257.

MOBY DICK'S. There's karaoke Sunday through Thursday, live music Friday and Saturday, and all-you-can-eat fish-and-chips daily. Play billiards, play video games, or watch your favorite sports on one of several TVs, including a 61-incher. ✉ 448 S.W. Coast Hwy. ☎ 541/265–7847 ⊕ www.mobydicksseafood.com.

NEWPORT PERFORMING ARTS CENTER. The Oregon coast's only such facility hosts performers from all over the world and showcases local theater companies. On any given evening, a performance may include tango dancers, a reading by nationally known actors and actresses, or a symphony concert. The center also hosts an international film series. ✉ 777 W. Olive St. ☎ 541/265–2787 ⊕ www.coastarts.org.

ROGUE ALES PUBLIC HOUSE. Once the Rogue Brewery, this bay-front location has a bar, pool tables, a golf video game, and a casino room with video poker machines and blackjack tables (gaming is legal here). Enjoy fish-and-chips, pizza, pasta, and, of course, Rogue beer Sunday–Thursday till 1 AM and Friday–Saturday till 2 AM. ✉ 748 S.W. Bay Blvd. ☎ 541/265–3188 ⊕ www.rogue.com.

HELPFUL INFO

Air Travel

Fly to Portland International Airport (PDX), then rent a car (there are several major agencies at the airport) and drive to Newport. It's about a three-hour trip. Head south from Portland on I-5, then west on Route 20, which takes you right into Newport, or go south on I-5, west on Route 22 (at about Lincoln City) to the coast, then pick up Route 101. PDX is served by most major airlines.

🛪 AIRPORTS **Portland International Airport** (PDX,) ☎ 503/460–4234 or 877/739–4636 ⊕ www.flypdx.com.

🛪 CAR RENTAL AGENCIES **Avis Rent-a-Car** ☎ 503/249–4950 ⊕ www.avis.com. **Budget Rent-a-Car** ☎ 503/249–4556 ⊕ www.budgetrentacar.com. **Dollar Rent-a-Car**

☎ 503/249-4793 ⊕ www.dollar.com. **Enterprise Rent-a-Car** ☎ 503/692-8400 ⊕ www.enterprise.com. **Hertz Rent-a-Car** ☎ 503/249-8216 ⊕ www.hertz.com.

Bus Travel

Greyhound provides bus service between Newport and Portland, Albany, Corvalis, Bend, and Salem.

🚋 **Greyhound Newport** ✉ 956 S.W. 10th St. ☎ 800/231-2222 or 541/265-2253 ⊕ www. greyhound.com.

Car Travel

You absolutely want to have a car in Newport. Navigating the area is simple: U.S. 101 runs through Newport all the way to Yaquina Bay Bridge at the town's southern limits. To the west of U.S. 101 are Newport's beaches; to the east of it is Newport's bay front. The east-west streets that cross U.S. 101 are numbered more or less sequentially. Heading north over the Yaquina Bay Bridge, you'll first cross Bay Boulevard before curving through the city center and passing 2nd Street, 3rd Street, and so on to northernmost 60th Street.

In northern Newport, U.S. 101 hugs the coast. To keep to the coast as you drive south, branch off onto Ocean View Drive. It will turn into Spring Street, Coast Street, and Elizabeth Street before curling around by Yaquina Bay and to the bay front.

Disabilities & Accessibility

🚋 **Newport Chamber of Commerce** ☎ 541/265-8801 or 800/262-7844 ⊕ www. newportchamber.org.

Emergencies

🚋 **HOSPITALS Pacific Communities Hospital** ✉ 930 S.W. Abbey ☎ 541/265-2244 ⊕ www.samhealth.org.

🚋 **PHARMACIES Wal-Mart** ✉ 160 N.W. 25th St. ☎ 541/265-6560 ⊕ www.walmart.com.

Taxis

You need to call for taxis, which are metered and start at $2.75, then cost $3.50 a mile thereafter.

🚋 **CAB COMPANY Newport Express/Yaquina Cab Company, Newport** ☎ 541/265-9552.

CHAPTER 7

JULY

KJZZ TV/*Deseret Morning News* Marathon, Salt Lake City, UT

As the sun breaks over a high mountain top, a lone

bagpiper plays, heralding the beginning of the KJZZ TV/*Deseret Morning News* marathon, a race notable not only for its singular start, but also for the truly unique way it ties into its city's culture. The marathon takes place on July 24, also known as Pioneer Day—a major Utah holiday commemorating the day in 1847 that Brigham Young and his band of fellow Mormons (also called Latter-day Saints, or LDS) first arrived in the Salt Lake Valley after an arduous trek through the Rockies. The marathon course roughly follows Young's descent into the valley, beginning at the top of Big Mountain at sunrise, then winding through town to Liberty Park, the perfect place to join pretty much everyone in town for the Pioneer Day celebrations.

AND ON THE SEVENTH DAY . . .

If July 24 falls on a Sunday, the marathon (and all Pioneer Day events) is held on Monday the 25th.

So You're Running *Deseret* . . .

Salt Lake City is a great walking city, with wide thoroughfares and lots of green spaces. If you want to go beyond walking distance, count on the city's efficient mass transit, or call a cab. You won't need a rental car if you're staying in the city your whole trip, though you might consider one for side trips out of town.

Salt Lake City's layout is based on a grid devised by Brigham Young. Most street names have a directional and a numerical designation that describes their location in relation to one of two axes. Streets with "east" or "west" in their names are east or west of (and parallel to) Main Street, which runs north–south. Streets with "north" and "south" in their names run parallel to South Temple. The numbers tell how far the streets are from the axes (e.g., 200 East Street is two blocks east of Main Street). Addresses typically include two directional and two numerical references: 320 East 200 South, for instance, is in the east 300 block of 200 South Street. This all sounds disturbingly complicated, but it becomes second nature quickly; it's remarkably easy to find your way around.

DOWNTOWN & TEMPLE SQUARE. Downtown's core is a compact, six-block area that includes three large malls, numerous historic buildings, and several entertainment venues. Temple Square, the headquarters of the Mormon Church, has buildings ranging from the Tabernacle (1860s) to the Conference Center (2000). North Temple, South Temple, and West Temple streets run parallel to the square's north, south, and west borders. Main Street borders the square's east side.

CAPITOL HILL, MARMALADE HILL HISTORIC DISTRICT & THE AVENUES. These three neighborhoods overlook the city from the foothills north of downtown. Capitol Hill is named for the state capitol. The Marmalade Hill Historic District surrounds the capitol on three sides. The Avenues run along the foothills, north of South Temple, and extend from Capitol Hill on the west to the University of Utah on the east.

EASTSIDE & UNIVERSITY OF UTAH. East of downtown is the University of Utah, the oldest university west of the Mississippi. There's plenty to see and do here, much of it outdoors. Hike trails in the foothills above campus; visit Red Butte Garden and Arboretum or This Is the Place Heritage Park; shop for Utah souvenirs in centers like Foothill Village, Trolley Square, or Sugar House.

THE SUBURBS. Salt Lake City proper ends at 3300 South Street. The suburban area below this line is home to Gardner Village, a collection of pioneer period houses used as specialty shops. For more international flavor, drive along 3500 South Street and Redwood Road to sample authentic Latin American, Asian, or Polynesian cuisine.

RACE BASICS

VISITOR INFO

Salt Lake Convention and
Visitors Bureau

☎

801/521-2822

🌐

www.saltlake.org

•

Utah Travel Council

☎

801/538-1030 or
800/200-1160

🌐

www.utah.com

Not so long ago, the *Deseret Morning News* Marathon was considered a lost cause: organization was poor, participation was down, and its prospects were grim. Then came new race director Bob Wood, a titan in the running world. He has been a runner, a coach, a race organizer, and an agent to many of the world's top racers; he was also the head official for the U.S. Olympic Marathon trials and the Olympic Games. This is a man who knows the sport cold, and he had a vision of what this sleeping giant of a race could become. Immediately he changed the course, cutting out a large hill to attract runners hoping for a PR. He expanded the expo, improved organization a millionfold, and worked tirelessly to turn a troubled race into something truly special. In addition to the marathon, KJZZ TV and the *Deseret Morning News* sponsor a 5K walk and a popular 10K run, both also on Pioneer Day.

Registration

Registration, which costs $50, opens around the first of the year and must be in by about a week before the race. Register online, by mail, or in person at the offices of the *Deseret Morning News* during business hours. On the registration form, specify if you want to enter the Clydesdale or Athena divisions (for men over 200 pounds or women over 140 pounds,

PIONEER DAY & THE DAYS OF '47

Pioneer Day in Salt Lake City is huge. It's in fact too huge to be contained in one day, and instead spreads across the "Days of '47," after the year (1847) in which Brigham Young and his followers made it to the Salt Lake Valley. The Days of '47 kick off around mid-May, but really get rolling in July, with several events each week. Look for the following when you're in town for the race:

CELEBRATION OF UTAH'S CULTURES. Although the Days of '47 and Pioneer Day began as Mormon celebrations, the LDS have made it their business to honor the pioneering spirit of all cultures. This event, usually held just before Pioneer Day, showcases artisans, musicians, dancers, and cuisines from all over the world. Fireworks add an exciting grand finale.

LANDSCAPE ART SHOW. This is a weeklong event to showcase landscape painting in the state of Utah.

NATIVE AMERICAN CELEBRATION. This celebration of the Native American community takes place in Liberty Park, which is where the marathon ends. The festival includes an intertribal competition powwow, food, arts and crafts, storytelling, live music, and fireworks. ☎ 801/533–9503 ⊕ www. nativeamericancelebration.com.

PIONEER DAY PARADE. Running since 1849, it's touted as one of the country's largest and oldest parades. Floats range from the simple to the surprisingly intricate and are complemented by bands, horses, clowns, and local celebrities. It seems like every man, woman, and child in Salt Lake lines the parade route.

PIONEER DAY SUNRISE SERVICE. Marathoners would already be on the course, but their friends and families could experience this hour-long Pioneer Day kickoff.

PIONEER FESTIVAL AND TERRITORIAL FAIR. This is usually held on Pioneer Day and the day before at This Is the Place Heritage Park, a living history recreation of a Utah settlement circa 1847–1869. Celebrate with the pioneers and participate in gunnysack races, arm wrestling, stick pulling, and other period contests.

WORLD CHAMPIONSHIP RODEO. It's the real deal. Contestants are professionals vying to improve their world standings. Events include bareback riding, barrel racing, bull riding, tie-down roping, saddle bronc riding, steer wrestling, and team roping. The rodeo is held annually at the Delta Center the week leading up to Pioneer Day, with the final day falling on the holiday itself.

YOUTH PARADE AND FESTIVAL. The nation's largest youth parade (almost 5,000 participants) is held just before Pioneer Day. At the end of the parade route is the kid-friendly Youth Festival, with games, crafts, obstacle courses, bouncers and inflatable slides, entertainment, and food.

With the exception of the rodeo and the festival at This Is the Place, all the events are free. Most are organized by **The Days of '47 Inc.** (⊕ www. daysof47.com), so check their Web site for specific venues, dates, and times. Check local newspapers for other municipal celebrations, such as fireworks.

respectively), and which shuttle you'd like to take to the race starting line. Since you'll be staying downtown, opt for the shuttle leaving from the Delta Center. The marathon Web site is clean, easy to navigate, and full of race information. There are also training recommendations which are geared toward faster runners.

Hotels to Consider

It's best to stay downtown and within walking distance of the Delta Center, one of the marathon shuttle pick-up and drop-off points. With the exception of the Radisson, the marathon's official hotel, race awareness among the hotels is low, with few marathon discounts.

> **RACE CONTACT**
>
> KJZZ TV/*Deseret Morning News* Marathon
>
> ⊠
> 30 E. 100 South St.,
> Downtown,
> Salt Lake City, UT 84111
>
> ☎
> 801/333–7473
>
> ⊕
> www.desnews.com/run

CRYSTAL INN. Just south of the heart of downtown, this contemporary hotel has spacious guest rooms with sitting areas. A morning buffet is included in the room rate. With a little notice, the staff can have a Continental breakfast ready for you the morning of the marathon. A small on-site convenience store is open 24 hours. ⊠230 W. 500 South St., Downtown, 84101 ☎801/328–4466 or 800/ 366–4466 ⊕www.crystalinns.com ↬159 rooms, 16 suites ♘Wake-up calls, alarm clocks, coffeemakers, newspapers, cable TV with movies and video games, in-room data ports, microwaves, refrigerators, free Wi-Fi, indoor pool, gym, hot tub, sauna, ski storage, dry cleaning, laundry facilities, airport shuttle, free parking ▤AE, D, DC, MC, V ¢–$.

★ **GRAND AMERICA HOTEL.** I've visited a staggering number of hotels for this book; the Grand America is among the best. It dominates the skyline with its white, Bethel-granite exterior and its 24 stories. Beyond the beveled-glass and brass doors is a world covered in Italian marble and adorned with English wool carpets, French furniture and tapestries, and Murano-glass chandeliers. Guest rooms average 700 square feet, and most have views and small balconies. The spa and outdoor pool are the city's best. Service throughout is impeccable. ⊠555 S. Main St., Downtown, 84111 ☎801/258–6000 or 800/ 621–4505 ⊕www.grandamerica.com ↬775 rooms ♘2 restaurants, 24-hr room service, wake-up calls, alarm clocks, newspapers, robes, cable TV with movies and video games, in-room data ports, in-room safes, minibars, 2 pools (1 indoor), gym, hair salon, outdoor hot tub, spa, lounge, babysitting, shops, concierge, concierge floor, laundry service, business services, meeting rooms, car rental, airport shuttle, parking (fee) ▤AE, D, DC, MC, V $$–$$$$.

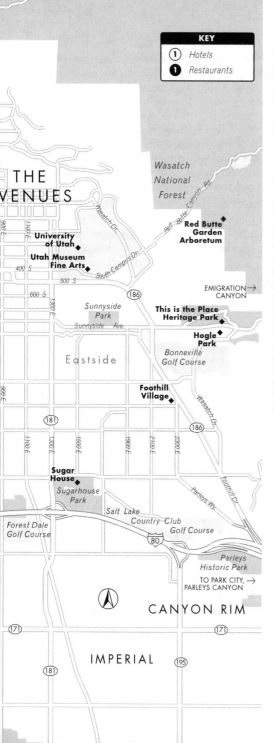

KEY

① *Hotels*

❶ *Restaurants*

★ **HOTEL MONACO.** The exterior of this hotel used to house a bank; the interior is sophisticated, eclectic, and upbeat. Rooms have lots of pillows, big fringed ottomans, oversize framed mirrors, and pet goldfish (upon request). If you need to stretch, ask for a complimentary yoga kit and turn on the 24-hour yoga channel. Gather in the lobby between 5 PM and 6 PM to enjoy wine as well as, on some nights, a neck/shoulder massage or a palm reading—all for free. ⊠ 15 W. 200 South St., Downtown, 84101 ☎ 801/595-0000 or 877/294-9710 ⊕ www.monaco-saltlakecity.com ⇆ 187 rooms, 38 suites ♨ Restaurant, 24-hr room service, wake-up calls, alarm clocks, coffeemakers, newspapers, robes, cable TV with movies and video games, in-room data ports, in-room safes, minibars, free Wi-Fi, 24-hr gym, massage, ski storage, bar, babysitting, concierge, laundry service, meeting rooms, some pets allowed, no-smoking rooms, parking (fee) ⊟ AE, D, DC, MC, V $-$$$.

★ **LITTLE AMERICA HOTEL.** The prices are lower than those at its sister property across the street yet it offers the same high level of hospitality. What's more, a stay here gets you access to many facilities at the Grand America (and vice versa). Tower rooms are spacious, and garden rooms have private entrances. There's a large indoor-outdoor pool, a lobby fireplace, and such elegant fixtures as deep marble tubs, rich fabrics, and plush seating. ⊠ 500 S. Main St., Downtown, 84101 ☎ 801/363-6781 or 800/453-9450 ⊕ www.littleamerica.com ⇆ 850 rooms ♨ Restaurant, coffee shop, room service, wake-up calls, alarm clocks, newspapers, robes, cable TV with movies and video games, in-room data ports, in-room safes, pool, gym, hair salon, hot tub, sauna, ski storage, piano bar, concierge, dry cleaning, laundry facilities, laundry service, business services, airport shuttle, free parking ⊟ AE, D, DC, MC, V ¢-$.

> ### WEATHER THE RUN
>
> The weather is absolutely a factor, so come prepared. Temperatures atop Big Mountain are usually only in the 40s, but as you descend into the Salt Lake Valley, the mercury can rise into the 70s or 80s.

MARRIOTT CITY CENTER. It's next to Gallivan Center, site of summer concerts. Public areas are upscale and contemporary. Rooms have king-size beds and comfortable seating. ⊠ 220 S. State St., Downtown, 84111 ☎ 801/961-8700 ⊕ www.marriott.com ⇆ 342 rooms, 17 suites ♨ Restaurant, coffee shop, room service, wake-up calls, alarm clocks, coffeemakers, newspapers, robes, cable TV with movies and video games, in-room data ports, in-room safes, pool, 24-hr gym, hot tub, ski storage, lounge, concierge, concierge floor, dry cleaning, laundry service, business services, convention center, airport shuttle, car rental, parking (fee) ⊟ AE, D, DC, MC, V $-$$.

MARRIOTT SALT LAKE CITY DOWNTOWN. It's close to the Salt Palace Convention Center and the Crossroads Mall, and a half block from Temple Square. Rooms are fairly standard; those on higher floors are made more noteworthy by lovely mountain views. There's an inviting indoor-outdoor pool. ⊠ 75 S. West Temple, Downtown, 84101 ☎ 801/531-0800 ⊕ www.marriott.com ⇆ 515 rooms, 6 suites ♨ Restaurant, room service, wake-up calls, alarm clocks, coffeemakers, newspapers weekdays, in-room data ports, indoor-outdoor pool, gym, hot tub, massage, ski storage, bar, concierge, concierge floor, dry cleaning, laundry facilities, business services, airport shuttle, car rental, parking (fee) ⊟ AE, D, DC, MC, V $.

SALT LAKE CITY MARATHON

Salt Lake City actually has two marathons, and they're completely different animals. The *Deseret Morning News* is the more intimate of the races, almost slipping under the radar of a community wrapped up in the excitement of Pioneer Day. The newer **Salt Lake City Marathon** (⊕ www.saltlakecitymarathon.com), however, is a raucous party race with massive community outreach. It's run by Devine Racing, which also organizes the Las Vegas and Los Angeles marathons (⇨ Chapter 3) The Salt Lake City Marathon is held in early June and pulls out all the stops: spectators line the streets; on-course entertainment rocks; and the race hits many of the city's highlights. When thinking of the two races, imagine *Deseret Morning News* as a cool jazz trio and the Salt Lake City Marathon as the Rolling Stones. Both are great at what they do; it just depends on what you want to hear.

★ **PEERY HOTEL.** This lovingly restored boutique hotel, with a grand lobby and wide staircases, has been in operation since 1910. Marble floors, brass chandeliers, and a grand piano are polished to perfection. Each room has a slightly different configuration, but all have lots of natural light, and sheer drapes as bed canopies. Enjoy free coffee, tea, and cocoa in the upstairs sitting area. ⊠ 110 W. Broadway (300 South St.), Downtown, 84101 ☎ 801/521–4300 or 800/331–0073 ⊕ www.peeryhotel.com 🛏 73 rooms ⚘ 2 restaurants, room service, wake-up calls, alarm clocks, robes, in-room data ports, cable TV, free Wi-Fi, 24-hr gym, ski storage, bar, business services, meeting rooms, airport shuttle; no smoking ⊟ AE, D, DC, MC, V ¢–$.

🏃 **RADISSON DOWNTOWN HOTEL.** Here at the official race hotel, you're right next to the Delta Center. Rooms can be small but are comfortable, with armoires and work areas. Excellent discounts are offered to runners, and the hotel restaurant adds several runner-friendly dishes to the menu the night before the marathon to accommodate prerace carbo loads. ⊠ 215 W. South Temple, Downtown, 84101 ☎ 801/531–7500 ⊕ www.radisson.com 🛏 374 rooms, 7 suites ⚘ Restaurant, room service, wake-up calls, alarm clocks, coffeemakers, newspapers weekdays, cable TV with movies, in-room data ports, free Wi-Fi, indoor pool, 24-hr gym, hot tub, sauna, ski storage, bar, shop, dry cleaning, laundry facilities, concierge, business services, convention center, airport shuttle, parking (fee), no-smoking rooms ⊟ AE, D, DC, MC, V ¢–$.

SHERATON CITY CENTRE HOTEL. One of the city's major full-service hotels and convention centers, the Sheraton has a huge lobby with its own Starbucks coffee shop, oversize chairs, and fireplace. Rooms are spacious and tailored, some have balconies, and many offer mountain views. ⊠ 150 W. 500 South St., Downtown, 84101 ☎ 801/401–2000 or 800/364–3295 🛏 312 rooms, 40 suites ⚘ Restaurant, room service, wake-up calls, alarm clocks, coffeemakers, in-room data ports, newspapers weekdays, cable TV with movies, pool, gym, hair salon, hot tub, sauna, ski storage, bar, dry cleaning, laundry facilities, laundry service, business services, convention center, meeting rooms, airport shuttle, parking (fee) ⊟ AE, D, DC, MC, V $.

AND YOU'RE OFF . . .

The Expo

The expo is held on the two days prior to the race (unless the race is on a Monday, in which case the expo runs Friday and Saturday) on the main floor of the ZCMI Center—an easy walk from any downtown hotel. Enjoy free health screenings and browse booths with fitness products. There may also be speakers and/or race clinics, though these are sometimes held at the Radisson hotel instead of at the expo. Check the race Web site for details.

Race Day

NEED A PIT STOP?

There are plenty of portable toilets at the finish line, but Liberty Park's well-maintained public restrooms are much more pleasant.

The Course

Set those alarm clocks and wake-up calls; shuttles to the top of Big Mountain pick up at the Delta Center at 3:45 AM and 4:15 AM. The shuttle ride lasts about a half hour, depositing you atop the mountain before sunrise. It will be cold, so layer accordingly. Baggage check is available, as are portable toilets and free food and drink. As the clock nears 5:30 AM, the sun just begins to peek over the mountains. A lone bagpiper plays: a moment of pure majesty and serenity, capped by the footfalls of 700–800 runners beginning their 26.2 mile journey.

From start to end, the route descends an incredible 3,200 feet, most of it in the stunning first 16 miles, as you run through Emigration Canyon. Some love this; others find it exceptionally tough on the knees. The first 6 meandering miles are entirely downhill. There's a climb after that, before another 7 or so miles of downhill ends outside the canyon near the Hogle Zoo, at Mile 15.5. You'll have a couple out-and-back stretches as you tour through the Eastside, then at Mile 18 you'll encounter the course's most challenging hill. It's not the grade that makes it difficult, simply its placement: by this point in the race your legs are probably toast. You then continue through the heart of downtown Salt Lake and across South Temple, briefly running along the Pioneer Day parade route before cruising to the finish line.

All the miles are clearly marked, and there's one official clock at the halfway point. Aid stations with portable toilets appear every other mile starting with Mile 3. Gel is usually available at Miles 7, 13, and 19. Energy drinks appear at aid stations beginning at Mile 5 and are available at every other station after that. Aid stations are well stocked, but as race temperatures soar, you might want to hydrate more often than every other mile. Consider carrying water. The course closes after six hours; a marathon vehicle will pick up anyone unable to complete the race.

NIGHT-BEFORE PASTA DINNER

There's no marathon-sponsored dinner, but Salt Lake has excellent carb-friendly restaurants, such as these:

BACI TRATTORIA. The dining room has high, arched ceilings and lots of natural light. Pizzas made in the wood-burning oven are great shared starters. Carbo-loaders can opt for spaghettini pomodoro or rigatoni and meatballs. Shellfish lovers should consider the capellini *alla pescatora* (shellfish with angel hair pasta and tomato sauce). ✉ 134 W. Pierpont Ave. (250 South), Downtown ☎ 801/328–1500 ⊕ www.gastronomyinc.com/baci ⊟ AE, D, DC, MC, V ⊘ Closed Sun. $–$$$$.

★ **CUCINA TOSCANA.** This busy trattoria is in a renovated Firestone Tire shop. Enjoy house-made pastas like ravioli with four cheeses and asparagus and gnocchi with sage butter. Main courses include trout grilled Tuscan-style or osso buco with polenta. The pressed-tin ceiling and open kitchen create an urban atmosphere that's complemented by top-notch service, food, and wines. ✉ 307 W. Pierpont Ave., Downtown ☎ 801/328–3463 ⌂ Reservations essential ⊟ AE, D, DC, MC, V ⊘ Closed Sun. $–$$.

HIGH ROCK STEAKHOUSE. In the Radisson, the official marathon hotel, this steak house goes out of its way to offer runner-friendly entrées the night before the marathon. Naturally, it's also a fantastic place for steak. Enjoy patio seating if weather permits. ✉ 215 W. South Temple, Downtown ☎ 801/521–7800 ⊟ AE, D, DC, MC, V $–$$$.

The marathon ends in Liberty Park, where you'll cross the finish line and receive your medal. A band plays from 7 AM to 9 AM, free massages are available for runners, and there's plenty to drink and eat, including bananas, apples, bagels, and yogurt. When you're ready to leave, either walk to your hotel or take a marathon bus. Buses run from 7 AM to 1 PM, picking up runners with bib numbers in Liberty Park along 700 East, and dropping them at the Delta Center, Rice Eccles Stadium, or Research Park.

That said, why leave so soon? Trek deeper into Liberty Park to check out the Native American Celebration. Entertainment usually doesn't begin until around 11 AM, but food booths open as early as 7 AM. You can also catch the Pioneer Day Parade, which begins at 9 AM on South Temple, then meanders down 200 East to 900 South, where it turns and makes its way down 900 South to 600 East, finishing at the park.

Spectating

Spectators can't go to the starting line, so don't worry about waking up insanely early with your favorite runner. Instead, drive or take a cab to the Hogle Zoo, where you can see the runners twice: once when they leave the canyon at Mile 15.5, and again at Mile 18. Once your favorite runner has passed, walk, drive, or hop a cab the 1½ miles to the finish line at Liberty Park. Alternatively, skip the Hogle Zoo and head right to the finish. It's a nice

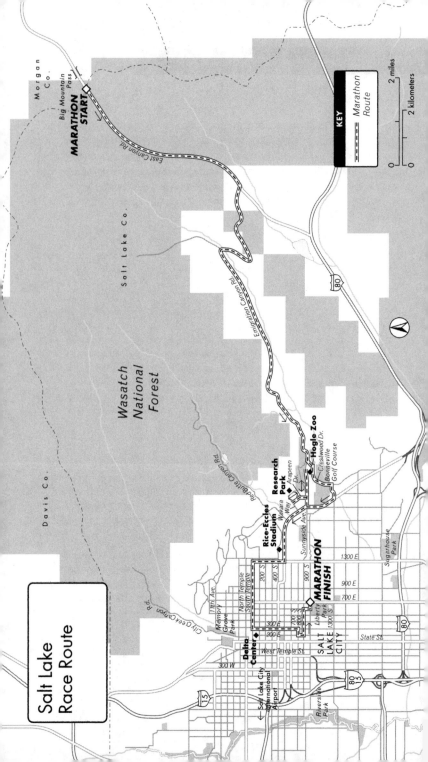

Salt Lake Race Route

KEY

--- Marathon Route

MARATHON START

Morgan Co.

Big Mountain Pass

East Canyon Rd.

Salt Lake Co.

Davis Co.

Wasatch National Forest

Emigration Canyon Rd.

Red Butte Canyon Rd.

City Creek Canyon Rd.

Memory Grove Park

Rice-Eccles Stadium

Research Park

Wakara Way

Arapen Dr.

Crestwood Dr.

Hogle Zoo

Bonneville Golf Course

Sunnyside Ave.

17th Ave.

North Temple
South Temple

200 S
400 S

900 S

300 S
500 S
700 S
800 S

200 E

300 W

West Temple St.

Delta Center

Salt Lake City International Airport

MARATHON FINISH

Liberty Park

1300 S

SALT LAKE CITY

700 E

900 E

1300 E

State St.

Sugarhouse Park

Riverside Park

80

15

80

15

2 miles

2 kilometers

0
0

BREAKFAST SPOTS

If you have a chance to grab breakfast before spectating, consider one of these restaurants (¢–$):

★ **BAMBARA.** Swanky, vibrant Bambara is in what was the lobby of a 1924 bank. Upscale breakfast entrées include a bistro omelet with feta cheese and vegetables, Atlantic smoked-salmon Benedict, and a house-made granola. This is also a terrific place for dinner and/or cocktails. ⊠ 202 S. Main St., Downtown ☎ 801/363–5454 ⊕ www.bambara-slc.com ⊟ AE, D, DC, MC, V.

★ **COFFEE SHOP AT THE LITTLE AMERICA.** Expect comfy booths, generous portions, and a waitstaff that's friendly and ready to kibitz. Regulars are at the door when it opens at 6 AM. As is the case with everything at the Grand and Little America hotels, service is impeccable. Breakfast runs the gamut of basic morning comfort foods: pancakes or French toast, Belgian waffles, steak and eggs, and omelets. ⊠ Little America hotel, 500 S. Main St., Downtown ☎ 801/596–5700 ⊕ www.littleamerica.com ⊟ AE, D, DC, MC, V.

PIASTRA. The menu includes all the basics, plus standouts like oatmeal crème brûlée. There's also a crunchy, surprisingly yummy grilled French toast made with whole wheat bread dipped in cholesterol-free eggs and crushed cornflakes. ⊠ Marriott City Center Hotel, 220 S. State St., Downtown ☎ 801/961–8700 ⊟ AE, D, DC, MC, V.

---

walk to the park from downtown hotels, and along the way you'll witness what seems to be all of Salt Lake sitting curbside for the Pioneer Day Parade.

BEYOND THE FINISH LINE

Replacing 2,620 Calories

There was a time when "cuisine" in Salt Lake City meant just one thing: green Jell-O (a.k.a. Mormon soul food). But all that changed when the city hosted the 2002 Olympic Winter Games. Now you'll find hip eateries with sophisticated chefs and menus, microbreweries known as much for their food as for their brew, superb sushi and other ethnic options, and neighborhood bistros that won't break the bank. It's also easy now to order a cocktail or glass of wine with dinner at almost any restaurant.

★ **AFTERNOON TEA AT THE GRAND AMERICA HOTEL.** Relax in plush armchairs and delight in tea, sandwiches, scones, and other pastries, served from 2 till 5 each day. A harpist and the stunning decor set a tranquil tone. Service is attentive, and the food is

In the cover art of Pamela Hansen's *Running with Angels*, a lone woman runs along a still lake. In the water runs her inverted reflection, followed by the reflection of two skipping children, a boy and a girl, so clearly happy and carefree you can practically hear their giggles.

It's a beautiful image, but once you know Pam's story, it can make you cry. Those children are hers: Emily and Eric, one who lived for only a day after her birth, the other stillborn. They are Pam's angels, born 13 years apart, and bookends to a self-inflicted exile within her own body. The pain of losing one child sent Pam spiraling into morbid obesity as she reached for food to numb the terrible pain. The torture of losing a second propelled her on a journey to do something, anything, to change the way she felt—a journey that culminated in Pam shedding 100 pounds and fulfilling a life-long goal: running the *Deseret Morning News* marathon.

As a teen, Pam volunteered to help at the race one year, and was moved watching the runners. Their looks of triumph even as they struggled was inspiring, and Pam promised herself that one day she'd join them. She figured she'd run the race in a couple of years, but life had other plans. As each training season came and went, something else was already on Pam's agenda: she was studying in Europe, she was getting married, she was pregnant, she was living out of town. By the time baby Emily and her twin sister, Amy, were born, Pam already had a two-year-old boy. Her family was her main focus; the marathon was the farthest thing from her mind.

There's nothing simple about dealing with the loss of a child, and for Pam it was only complicated by the delight she took in her other children. How could she feel joy when her baby was gone? How could she feel grief when holding her wonderful son and daughter? And how could she truly deal with her feelings when there just wasn't enough time in the day? The obvious answer was not to deal with those feelings at all, and push them aside. Food was the only thing that seemed to take the raw edge off Pam's emotions; it was her Novocain. The pounds started to load onto her frame, but for the most part, Pam wouldn't let herself notice. Yes, she was getting heavier; yes, she wanted to do something about it—but not now. Her family needed her now; she'd deal with herself later.

The next several years brought more children, more joys, and more heartache. One daughter received a diagnosis of juvenile rheumatoid arthritis, another the rare and potentially disfiguring Ollier's Disease. Both daughters needed extra care, and with so much on her plate, there was no time for Pam to take care of herself. The one reward, the one comfort she had time for, was food. And as each year passed, the pounds piled on, until Pam was stunned to realize that at 39 years old, she weighed a full 100 pounds more than when she got married.

Although this was a staggering revelation, part of Pam knew it was coming. She felt her body growing larger, saw herself putting aside her attractive clothes in favor of baggy sweats, actively choosing to avoid mirrors. Still, the whole process felt beyond her, like her body was gaining weight of its own volition. Pam loathed her oversize body; she felt like a prisoner trapped inside it.

Then came the stillbirth of Pam's youngest son. Desperate to feel something other than emptiness, she took a walk around a nearby park. At first every fiber of her being rebelled—it wasn't right that she should feel fresh air and sun when her baby was lost. But soon she fought through her grief, and pulled her hulking body around the park: a half mile. She felt wonderful. The sheer joy of being outside and using her body fed her soul in a way that 13 years of constant overeating couldn't. The exercise made her feel alive in a way she hadn't since Emily's death, and the fact that her body could give her this gift made her start to appreciate it, despite its cumbersome size. Her body didn't have to be her prison; it could be her home.

Thus began Pam's weight-loss journey. It wasn't easy. She had to learn ways to cope that didn't involve food. She had to change her relationship with food, and discover the feeling of "satisfied" versus "stuffed." She joined Weight Watchers, and that helped, but she needed something more, a goal that had a greater emotional pull than food. A goal she'd had since that long-ago race during which she'd watched the triumph on all those runners' faces. She would finally run the *Deseret Morning News* marathon.

Even thinking it gave Pam a thrill—and a scare. Could she really do it? She had lost 40 pounds on Weight Watchers, but she had 60 more to go. Could someone in her shape really run a marathon? Pam wasn't sure, but one thing was clear: to even have a shot at it, she'd need to make exercise an inviolable part of her week. With a family of six depending on her, that was easier said than done. With a great deal of trepidation, Pam moved herself up on the priority list. There were new rules in her house: when mom was on the treadmill or out for a run, the older kids were in charge and everyone had to work things out for themselves. Pam was quite positive her family would fall apart without her there 100% of the time. They thrived.

Oh sure, there were hiccups at first, but Pam's kids quickly learned that Mom's a person, too, with her own goals and dreams, a lesson she was especially thrilled to give her daughters. As for Pam herself, the chunk of time she carved out for herself allowed her to return to her family refreshed. It made her a better person and a better mother.

Thus Pam pursued her marathon goals. In the beginning, she was so embarrassed by her size that she would train only in the dark, and her first run lasted a whopping 10 steps. Gradually, however, she built up her distance. Within several months, the exercise plus the change in her diet helped her get close to her goal weight, which is when she began training for the marathon in earnest. She adopted a 16-week schedule that would have her ready for the Pioneer Day race. It was difficult, but she had the support of her friends and family, and their strength and encouragement helped her push forward when she wasn't sure she could do it.

Finally, on July 24, 2002, just 15 months after losing her son Eric, a 100-pounds-lighter Pam Hansen fulfilled her dream and ran the *Deseret Morning News* marathon. She dedicated each mile of the race to one of the "angels" who helped her along the way, including her two lost children. As she ran, she also thought about Brigham Young and the pioneers who founded Salt Lake City, following the very same course she now traveled. In a way, Pam was a pioneer as well, trailblazing a new way of life for herself and her family.

Pam came from a place where even the idea of a marathon was beyond impossible, and yet she did it. To those who view the race as a faraway dream, Pam would say that's not enough. A dream is too ephemeral; it's too easy to let it float above you, never accomplished. If you really want to achieve something, give it importance. Make it a goal. And because the road to a goal is never easy, "surround yourself with angels." Their support will help pull you through.

Running with Angels *by Pamela H. Hansen is available in bookstores or through amazon.com. For more information, visit www.runningwithangels. com.* ■

delicate perfection. ✉555 S. Main St., Downtown ☎801/258-6911 ⊕www.grandamerica. com ⚓Reservations essential ☰AE, D, DC, MC, V $$.

HATCH FAMILY CHOCOLATES. This old neighborhood grocery store has been transformed into an immaculate candy and ice-cream shop. Jerry Hatch uses his mother's secret recipe for creamy caramel, and each piece of chocolate is hand dipped. You can also get espresso, Italian soda, and ice-cream sundaes with homemade caramel sauce. ✉390 E. 4th Ave., The Avenues ☎801/532-4912 ☰AE, D, DC, MC, V ¢.

ICHIBAN. It's set in an old church with exquisite stained-glass windows, vaulted ceilings, and a modern feng-shui–inspired interior. The cuisine is classic sushi as well as multilayered Americanized interpretations. Fine sake is an option, and there's a full bar. ✉336 S. 400 East St., Downtown ☎801/532-7522 ⚓Reservations not accepted ☰AE, MC, V $–$$.

LAMB'S GRILL CAFÉ. One of the city's oldest dining establishments, it's a cozy-mahogany-booth, white-tablecloth kind of place where you can indulge in an old-fashioned lamb shank or fresh trout dinner. The longtime Greek owners have also included such Mediterranean dishes as homemade lemon-rice soup. Don't forget the famous rice pudding for dessert. ✉169 S. Main St., Downtown ☎801/364-7166 ⊕www.lambsgrill.com ☰AE, D, DC, MC, V ⊘Closed Sun. $–$$.

★ **LITTLE AMERICA SUNDAY BRUNCH.** Sunday brunch here is easily the most popular in town, if not the state. Enjoy fresh seafood, plus several carving stations and an omelet station. Fresh breads and salads abound, and the dessert table is filled with decadent treats. ✉500 S. Main St., Downtown ☎801/596-5700 ⊕www.littleamerica.com ⚓Reservations essential ☰AE, D, DC, MC, V $$.

★ **MARKET STREET GRILL.** Seafood's the focus at this local standby in a beautifully restored 1906 building, formerly the New York Hotel. It's a popular breakfast, lunch, and dinner destination where the selections range from fresh seafood to certified Angus beef. Portions are large and include all the side dishes. The atmosphere is usually lively. ✉48 Market St., Downtown ☎801/322-4668 ⊕www.gastronomyinc.com ⚓Reservations not accepted ☰AE, D, DC, MC, V $–$$$.

MARTINE. Part of this romantic café's appeal is its setting in an old brownstone. Meet at the tiny bar, backed by an original bank vault, for a cocktail and appetizer. Ask for a table in the intimate balcony or a booth on the main level. Then settle in for such flavorful (and contemporary) tapas as seared mustard-and-lavender lamb loin with mission fig chutney, or an entrée of halibut with preserved lemon and marjoram. Desserts are original and house made. 22 E. 100 South St., Downtown ☎801/363-9328 ☰AE, D, DC, MC, V ⊘Closed Sun. No dinner Mon. $$.

METROPOLITAN. From its inventive cuisine to its minimalist design, this restaurant oozes chic. Menus veer from Asian-fusion to Rocky Mountain fare. Sit at the curved bar and order from a small bistro menu, or for the full experience, reserve a table and put yourself in the chef's capable hands with the daily tasting menu. Service here borders on choreography—synchronized and unobtrusive. The wine list is excellent. ✉173 W. Broadway, Downtown ☎801/364-3472 ⊕www.themetropolitan.com ☰AE, D, MC, V ⊘Closed Sun. $$–$$$.

★ **ONE WORLD CAFE.** Denise Cerreta believes that if given the chance, people will be trustworthy, and she puts her livelihood on the line to prove it. Her restaurant has no menu: you come in, check out what's on the buffet line, and ask for however little (just a *sliver* of pie) or however much (that entire quiche, please) you like. When you're finished eating, simply deposit what you think is a fair amount in a basket as you leave. The food is very healthful and often vegan friendly. Try the "everything" cookies, made with whatever Denise happens to have on hand that day. ⊠ 41 S. 300 East St., Downtown ☎ No phone ⊟ No credit cards N/A (pay what you wish) ¢–$$$$.

RED IGUANA. It's a bit rough around the edges and on a bleak thoroughfare, but this lively Mexican restaurant is staffed with a warm, accommodating crew and serves the best house-made moles and chile verde in town. Look for premium margaritas, good Mexican beers, and an endless supply of salsa and chips. Expect a wait on weekend nights. ⊠ 736 W. North Temple, Downtown ☎ 801/322–1489 ⊕ www.rediguana.com ⊟ AE, D, DC, MC, V ¢–$.

Sightseeing on (and off) Your Feet

While downtown Salt Lake City has a great deal to offer, you can also take a fantastic day trip to one of Utah's mountain getaways, or to the city's namesake, the Great Salt Lake.

I Feel Great!

IN TOWN

★ **RED BUTTE GARDEN AND ARBORETUM.** The grounds provide many pleasurable hours of strolling. Of special interest are the perennial, fragrance, and medicinal gardens; the daylily collection; the water pavilion; and the children's garden. Trails lead to areas whose pristine vegetation gives you an idea of what northern Utah looked like in the early days. The trails also access nearby mountain terrain. Lectures—on everything from bugs to gardening in arid climates—workshops, and concerts are presented regularly, and a gift shop sells books, soaps, sculptures, and other items. ⊠ 300 Wakara Way, University of Utah ☎ 801/581–IRIS ⊕ www.redbuttegarden.org 🎟 $5 ⊙ May–Aug., Mon.–Sat. 9–9, Sun. 9–5; Sept. and Apr., Mon.–Sat. 9–7:30, Sun. 9–5; Oct.–Mar., daily 10–5.

TRACY AVIARY. This 7½-acre facility has 133 species of birds from around the globe, including emus, bald eagles, flamingos, parrots, and waterfowl. One of the aviary's missions is to educate the public about birds native to Utah and their corresponding ecosystems. There are two free-flight bird shows daily in summer. ⊠ 589 E. 1300 South St., Eastside ☎ 801/596–8500 ⊕ www.tracyaviary.org 🎟 $5 ⊙ Nov.–Mar., daily 9–4:30; Apr.–Oct., daily 9–6.

UTAH'S HOGLE ZOO. The zoo houses more than 1,400 creatures from all over the world. Exhibits present animals in their representative habitats. A children's zoo, interactive exhibits, and special presentations make visits informative and engaging for both adults and children. In summer, youngsters can tour the zoo aboard a miniature train. ⊠ 2600 E. Sunnyside Ave., Eastside ☎ 801/582–1631 ⊕ www.hoglezoo.org 🎟 $8 ⊙ Mar.–Oct., daily 9–5 (grounds open until 6:30); Nov.–Feb., daily 9–4 (grounds until 5:30).

SALT LAKE ENVIRONS

TIMPANOGOS CAVE NATIONAL MONUMENT. Soaring to 11,750 feet, Mt. Timpanogos is the centerpiece of a wilderness area of the same name and towers over Timpanogos Cave National Monument. After a strenuous hike 1½ miles up to the entrance, you can explore three caves filled with stalactites, stalagmites, and other formations and connected by two man-made tunnels. It's a three-hour round-trip endeavor. No refreshments are available, and the year-round cave temperature is 45°F, so bring water and warm clothes. Although there's some lighting, a flashlight comes in handy both in the caves and if you have to head back down the trail at dusk. Note that cave tours often sell out, so buy tickets in advance. ⊠ 36 mi south of Salt Lake City via I–15 and Rte. 92 E ☎ 801/756–5239 cave information, 801/756–5238 advance tickets ⊕ www.nps.gov/tica ☑ Tours $6 ⊙ Early May–Oct., daily 7–5:30.

I Feel Pretty Good

IN TOWN

UTAH MUSEUM OF FINE ART. Because it encompasses 74,000 square feet and more than 20 galleries, you'll be glad this facility has a café and a sculpture court—perfect places to rest. The vast permanent collection includes Egyptian, Greek, and Roman relics; Italian Renaissance and other European paintings; Chinese ceramics and scrolls; Japanese screens; Thai and Cambodian sculptures; African and Latin American artworks; Navajo rugs; and American art from the 17th century to the present. ⊠ 410 Campus Center Dr., University of Utah ☎ 801/581–7332 ⊕ www.umfa.utah.edu ☑ $4 ⊙ Tues., Thurs., and Fri., 10–5; Wed. 10–8; weekends 11–5.

SALT LAKE ENVIRONS

★ **EXPLORE PARK CITY.** Park City, 31 miles east of Salt Lake, offers excellent summer activities. Hiking trails are plentiful. A scenic drive over Guardsman Pass (via a gravel road that's passable for most vehicles) provides incredible mountain vistas. There are some acclaimed golf greens, hot-air ballooning is available, and mountain bikers find the ski slopes and old mining roads truly exceptional pedaling.

In summer, **Park City Mountain Resort** becomes an amusement park. The Alpine Slide begins with a chairlift ride up the mountain, then sliders sled down 3,000 feet of winding concrete and fiberglass track at speeds controlled by each rider. Drivers pay $11, passengers pay $3. The Zip Rider ($19) is 60 seconds of adrenaline rush as riders strap into a harness suspended from a cable for a 500-foot vertical drop spanning 2,300 feet. The Little Miners' Park has children's rides that cost $3 each or $22 for 10 rides. There's also a miniature golf course, climbing wall ($7 for two climbs), horseback riding, and lift-served ($11 for one lift ride, $18 for a day pass) mountain biking and hiking. ⊠ 1310 Lowell Ave., Park City ☎ 435/649–8111 or 800/222–PARK (7275) ⊕ www.parkcitymountain.com ⊙ Late May–early Oct., Mon.–Thurs. 1–6, Fri.–Sun. noon–7.

The **Utah Olympic Park** is the year-round training ground for members of the U.S. Ski Team and other athletes. In summer, check out freestyle ski jumpers doing flips and spins into a splash pool and Nordic jumpers soaring to soft landings on a synthetic outrun. There's also an interactive ski museum and an exhibit on the 2002 Winter Olympics; you can take guided or self-guided tours year-round. Ride a wheeled bobsled ($65), a zipline ($13–$22), an Alpine slide ($13), or an aerial bungee ($8) that lets you flip on a circus-style bungee trampoline. ⊠ 3000 Bear Hollow Dr., Park City ☎ 435/658–4200 or 888/OLY-PARK ⊕ www.utaholympicpark.com ☜ $7 ⊗ Daily 9–5.

Let's Take It Slowly

IN TOWN

THIS IS THE PLACE HERITAGE PARK. Utah's premier historic park includes Old Deseret Village, a re-created 19th-century community. In summer, almost 200 volunteers dressed in period clothing demonstrate what pioneer life was like. You can watch artisans at work and take wagon rides around the compound. ⊠ 2601 E. Sunnyside Ave., Eastside ☎ 801/582–1847 ⊕ www.thisistheplace.org ☜ $6–$8 ⊗ Mon. and Fri., 10–9; Tues.–Thurs. and Sat., 10–6.

SALT LAKE ENVIRONS

FLOAT IN THE GREAT SALT LAKE. It's eight times saltier than the ocean and second only to the Dead Sea in salinity. What makes it so briny? There's no outlet to the ocean, so salts and other minerals carried by rivers and streams become concentrated in this enormous evaporation pond. Ready access to this wonder is possible at **Great Salt Lake State Park** (⊠ Frontage Rd., 2 mi east of I-80 Exit 104, Salt Lake City ☎ 801/250–1898 ☜ Free ⊗ Daily 7 AM–10 PM), 16 miles west of Salt Lake City, on the lake's south shore. Though the lake here is too shallow for floating, you can experience water that won't let you sink by dangling your feet in the lake from the marina, where you can also arrange group or charter sails. Trips take from one to six hours, and there's a range of reasonable prices to match; some include meals. **Salt Island Adventures** (☎ 801/252–9336 ⊕ www.gslcruises.com) runs cruises between March and December.

The best place to float in the Great Salt Lake is at **Antelope Island State Park** (⊠ 4528 W. 1700 South St., Syracuse ☎ 801/773–2941 ☜ $8 per vehicle, $4 per bicycle, including causeway toll ⊗ Daily 7 AM–10 PM), 25 miles north of the city via I-15 and the Antelope Island Causeway. Arrange boat trips at the marina, or float in the lake off one of several beaches, which also have hot showers to remove the chill and the salt. Kite flying is excellent here. Interestingly, the island is home to a herd of more than 600 bison, descended from 12 placed here in 1893.

Ow! No.

CLARK PLANETARIUM. The Hansen Star Theatre here uses state-of-the-art technology to simulate three-dimensional flights through space. The planetarium is also home to the state's only 3-D IMAX theater. Hands-on exhibits and science paraphernalia fill the Wonders of the Universe Science Store. ⊠ 110 S. 400 West St., Downtown ☎ 801/456–STAR ⊕ www.clarkplanetarium.org ☜ $8 ⊗ June–Labor Day: Sun. 10:30–8, Mon.–Thurs. 10:30–9, Fri. and Sat. 10:30 AM–11 PM; Labor Day–May: Sun. 11:30–8, Mon.–Thurs. 11:30–9, Fri. and Sat. 11:30–11.

SALT LAKE TEMPLE. Built in the late 1800s of blocks of granite hauled by oxen and train from Little Cottonwood Canyon, the Mormon Temple took 40 years to complete. Off-

FORGET SIGHTSEEING, GET ME TO A SPA!

AKASHA SPA AND SALON. If you must go somewhere other than The Grand Spa, this is a solid option. Arrive early to enjoy complimentary juice or tea or slip into the coed steam room. Massages include Swedish, deep tissue, and hot stone (25–80 minutes, $45–$110). If the marathon left you feeling great and rarin' for more, Akasha offers exciting packages that begin at the spa with yoga, transport you to a guided hike in the mountains, then return you to Akasha for a massage and spa pedicure. Such packages include energy bars, water, sunscreen, and lunch, and they run from $180 to $190 per person. ⊠ 363 S. 500 East St. ☎ 801/364-3330 ⊕ www.akashaspace.com ⊙ Weekdays 9–9, Sat. 9–7, Sun. noon–6.

★ **THE GRAND SPA.** If you really want to be pampered after the race, there's only one place to go: the Grand Spa at the Grand America hotel. Relax in a eucalyptus steam room or sauna before indulging in one (or several) of the many massages (25–80 minutes, $45–$140) or body treatments (50–80 minutes, $95–$130). Bring a bathing suit to enjoy the huge indoor pool and Jacuzzi, where you can soothe your muscles in perfect tranquillity. Reserve your treatments well in advance. ⊠ Grand America hotel, 555 S. Main St., Downtown ☎ 801/258-6000 ⊕ www.grandamerica.com ⊙ Daily 8 AM to 9 PM.

---

limits to all but faithful Mormons, the temple is used for marriages, baptisms, and other religious functions. You can usually hear the **Mormon Tabernacle Choir** (☎ 801/240-4150 ⊕ mormontabernaclechoir.org) in the tabernacle during rehearsals Sunday morning from 8:15 to 10 or Thursday from 8 PM to 9:30 PM. The choir, which includes men and women of all ages, performs sacred music, with some secular (classical and patriotic) works.

Shop Around

CROSSROADS PLAZA. Among its 140 shops and restaurants are Nordstrom; Mervyn's; and the US Olympic Spirit Store, where you can buy T-shirts, jackets, collectibles, and more—all the while supporting the Olympics. ⊠ 50 S. Main St., Downtown ☎ 801/531-1799 ⊕ www.thedowntownmalls.com.

FACTORY STORES OF AMERICA. These shops east of I-15 in the city's south end offer outlet discounts on everything from cookware and coats to luggage, books, and Doc Martens. ⊠ 12101 S. Factory Outlet Dr., The Suburbs ☎ 801/571-2933.

★ **FARMERS' MARKET.** Every Saturday morning from Memorial Day through Labor Day, check out Pioneer Park, at 300 West and 300 South streets, for its wonderful, sprawling Farmers' Market. You'll find a stunning variety of excellent fresh produce, plus local bakeries and restaurants selling tasty treats ranging from fresh salsa to cinnamon rolls.

FOOTHILL VILLAGE. The neighborhood is upscale, and the shops range from those selling apparel, gifts, and jewelry to those with health and wellness products. You can feast on fast food or fine fare here. ⊠ 1400 S. Foothill Dr., Eastside ☎ 801/582–6085 ⊕ www. foothillvillage.com.

GARDNER VILLAGE. At the behest of Brigham Young, dedicated polygamist Archibald Gardner (11 wives) built a flour mill in 1877. Today you can visit the mill and stroll among more than 30 specialty shops in the adjacent Gardner Village. Items for sale include furniture and collectibles. ⊠ 1100 W. 7800 South St., The Suburbs ☎ 801/566–8903 ⊕ www. gardnervillage.com.

★ **THE GATEWAY.** Some of the stores and eateries are part of national chains, but many, such as Cummings Studio Chocolates, are local enterprises. Don't miss the 76-foot-high climbing wall at Galyan's, which you can climb for $2. ⊠ Between 200 South and 50 North Sts., and 400 West and 500 West Sts., Downtown ☎ 801/456–0000 ⊕ www. shopthegateway.com 🖃 Free ⊙ Mon.–Sat. 10–9, Sun. noon–6.

SUGAR HOUSE. This funky mix of locally owned shops and restaurants includes a large thrift store. ⊠ Between 2100 South and I–15, from 700 East to 1300 East Sts., Eastside.

TROLLEY SQUARE. From 1908 to 1945, this sprawling redbrick structure garaged nearly 150 trolleys and electric trains for the Utah Light and Railway Company. Today it shelters more than 90 boutiques and restaurants. ⊠ 600 S. 700 East St., Eastside ☎ 801/521–9877 ⊙ Mon.–Sat. 10–9, Sun. noon–5.

ZCMI CENTER. Home of the marathon expo, the facade of this mall belongs to the original Zion's Cooperative Mercantile Institution building, organized by Brigham Young to keep the church's resources distributed amongst its members. The mall is still owned by the LDS. Check out the food court, where a wall of glass overlooks the temple grounds. ⊠ 36 S. Main St., Downtown ☎ 801/321–8745 ⊕ www.thedowntownmalls.com 🖃 Free ⊙ Mon.–Sat. 10–6.

I Love the Nightlife

Many people think "Salt Lake City nightlife" is an oxymoron. But this town is becoming increasingly cosmopolitan. Bars and clubs serve cocktails and host live music to meet diverse tastes. That said, the state's quirky liquor laws make for a few surprises. For starters, a place has to be deemed a "private club" to serve alcohol, and since only two private clubs are allowed per block, don't plan to barhop along a street. Last call here is 1 AM, and some bars call it earlier. For info on what's happening around town, pick up a *City Weekly* magazine, available at stands outside restaurants and stores.

BREWVIES. Ever hear of a "cinema pub"? Me neither, until I heard about Brewvies, where you can play pool, grab dinner, drink, and watch independent and second-run films. Pool is free until 5 PM and all night Wednesday, which is also $2 movie night. Even the regular movie price is a bargain, at just $4. ⊠ 676 S. 200 West St., Downtown ☎ 801/ 355–5500 ⊕ www.brewvies.com.

DEAD GOAT SALOON. There's live upbeat music nightly here, and the grill is fired up for lunch and dinner. ⊠ 119 S. West Temple, Downtown ☎ 801/328–GOAT (4628) ⊕ www. deadgoat.com.

PORT O' CALL. This sports bar has 14 satellite dishes and 26 TVs. Expect to wait for a table on weekends. ✉ 78 W. 400 South St., Downtown ☎ 801/521-0589 ⊕ www.portocall.com.

THE RED DOOR. Try a martini at this trendy bar where you'll find an eclectic crowd of T-shirt and jeans meets suit and tie. ✉ 57 W. 200 South St., Downtown ☎ 801/363-6030.

SQUATTERS PUB BREWERY. For beer brewed on the premises, head to Squatters. Sandwiches and pasta dishes are on the menu. ✉ 147 W. Broadway, Downtown ☎ 801/363-2739 ⊕ www.squatters.com.

TAVERNACLE SOCIAL. Dueling pianos battle it out in this smoke-free bar. The name implies the satiric twist that the owners take on the local Mormon culture. ✉ 201 E. 300 South St., Downtown ☎ 801/519-8900.

HELPFUL INFO

Air Travel

Salt Lake City International Airport is 7 miles northwest of downtown. It's served by most major airlines, and all the major car rental agencies have desks at the airport. To drive into downtown, take I-80 east to North Temple, which will take you directly to the city center. A taxi ride from the airport into town will cost about $15. The Utah Transit Authority (UTA) runs buses between the airport and the city center. Most downtown hotels offer guests free shuttle service.

🚩 **Salt Lake City International Airport** ☎ 801/575-2400 or 800/595-2442 ⊕ www.slcairport.com. **UTA** ☎ 801/743-3882 ⊕ www.rideuta.com.

Bus & Train Travel

Greyhound Lines runs several buses each day to the terminal at 160 W. South Temple. Amtrak serves the area daily out of the Amtrak Passenger Station.

Salt Lake has a very workable public transportation system. A Free Fare Zone for travel by bus covers a 15-square-block area in downtown and Capitol Hill. The light-rail system, called TRAX, moves passengers quickly around the city and to the southern suburbs. The north-south route begins at the Delta Center and ends at 9800 South Street; there are 16 stations along the way, and 11 have free park-and-ride lots. The east-west route begins at the University of Utah and ends at Main Street. For $2 you can buy an all-day ticket good for unlimited rides on both buses and TRAX. Note that on Pioneer Day, the buses run on a Sunday schedule; the TRAX runs on a weekday schedule.

🚩 **Amtrak Passenger Station** ✉ 340 S. 600 West St., Downtown ☎ 801/322-3510 or 800/USA-RAIL ⊕ www.amtrak.com. **Greyhound Lines** ✉ 300 S. 600 West St., Downtown ☎ 801/355-9579 or 800/231-2222 ⊕ www.greyhound.com. **UTA** ☎ 801/743-3882 ⊕ www.rideuta.com.

Car Travel

Highway travel around Salt Lake is quick and easy. From I-80, take I-15 north to 600 South Street to reach the city center. Salt Lake's streets are extra wide and typically not congested. Most are two-way. Expect heavy traffic weekdays between 6 AM and 10 AM and again between 4 PM and 7 PM. Parking downtown is simple. Many reasonably priced lots are available, as is metered street parking.

Disabilities & Accessibility

⚠ Access Utah Network ⊠ 155 S. 300 West St., Suite 100, Downtown ☎ 801/533-3968 or 800/333-8824 ⊕ www.accessut.org. **Services for People with Disabilities** ⊠ 655 E. 4500 South St., The Suburbs ☎ 801/264-7620.

Emergencies

⚠ HOSPITALS Salt Lake Regional Medical Center ⊠ 1050 E. South Temple, Downtown ☎ 801/350-4111.

⚠ PHARMACIES Broadway Pharmacy ⊠ 242 E. 300 South St., Downtown ☎ 801/363-3939. **Rite Aid** ⊠ 75 S. Main St., Downtown ☎ 801/531-0583.

Taxis

Taxi fares are low, but cabs can be hard to find on the street. Call if you need one. Yellow Cab provides 24-hour service throughout the Salt Lake Valley; other reliable companies are Ute Cab and City Cab.

⚠ City Cab Company ☎ 801/363-8400 or 801/363-5550. **Ute Cab Company** ☎ 801/359-7788. **Yellow Cab** ☎ 801/521-1862.

AUGUST

Grizzly Marathon, Choteau, MT

Given the name of this race, it's reasonable to ask, "Are there really grizzly bears on the course?"

The short answer? Yup. The marathon runs through a Grizzly Bear Recovery Zone, which means grizzlies do tend to roam the area.

The longer answer involves the town sheriff and several "bear scaring" locals, the fact that bears hate crowds, and the rising heat during the marathon, all of which helps ensure that although bears are often on the Grizzly Marathon course, it's highly unlikely you'll see them while you're running the race. What you will see is the vast beauty of the Rocky Mountain Front and the spirit of the town of Choteau, a small community that pulls together to make all runners feel embraced and supported as they tackle this stunning yet challenging course.

Oh, and bear poop. You'll also see bear poop.

So You're Running the Grizzly . . .

Choteau, Montana, is a small town. If you have a picture in your head of what a small town is, think smaller. Everyone knows everyone in Choteau, and people tend to wear many hats. Race director Dave Hirschfeld, for example, is also a rancher, a lawyer, and the town pastor. Choteau even has a town drunk. His license was suspended, but they let him drive his riding mower. Look for it parked outside one of the local bars.

A huge benefit of a town like Choteau is that it's safe—the kind of community where people feel they can leave their doors unlocked. The last murder in Choteau was in the 1800s, and you can still see the tree where they hanged the killer.

VISITOR INFO

Choteau Acantha

406/466-2403

www.choteauacantha.com

•

Choteau Chamber of Commerce

800/823-3866

www.choteaumontana.com

•

Montana Visitors' Bureau

800/VISIT–MT

www.visitmt.com

•

State of Montana

www.discoveringmontana.com.

Choteau sits northwest of the middle of Montana and is one of many small towns along the Rocky Mountain Front, basically the place where prairie meets mountain. The terrain change is not subtle: the Rockies seem to just pop up from the plains. The Front extends for more than 100 miles and supports an incredibly rich cross section of wildlife.

Choteau itself, is actually one of the *larger* towns along the Front and is home to sprawling ranches. Its downtown of shops, hotels, and restaurants sits mainly along . . . well . . . Main Avenue, also known as Route 89. You can venture outside Choteau to visit Augusta, about

26 miles southwest on Route 287, home to a couple of little shops, a restaurant, and an ice-cream parlor. Or take Route 89 about 18 miles southeast to Fairfield, where you'll find a 9-hole golf course and a park with a swimming pool. If you're looking for something more metropolitan, follow Route 89 even farther (about 53 miles total) to Great Falls, where you can hit the 10-plex, the roller rink, or the children's museum. On the other side of the spectrum is Glacier National Park (⇨ Glacier National Park box), about 85 miles northwest of Choteau. Just take Route 89 to Route 2, then head west.

RACE BASICS

The Grizzly Marathon and half marathon are held on the third Saturday in August, and both run through the eastern edge of the Bob Marshall Wilderness. The unspoiled land here is home to countless species of plants and animals. As you run, you might see elk, bighorn sheep, mountain goats, and, of course, bears—all from a distance, of course.

KEEP IN TOUCH

Stock up on calling cards before you arrive in Choteau. Cell-phone carriers just don't seem to cover this town.

Safety precautions start the day before the race, when all the preparation activity scares much of the wildlife away. On race morning, the sheriff rides ahead of the marathoners, clearing the path of any critters. One year, it was a mama grizzly and two cubs, hanging out between Miles 13 and 14. Adorable? Yes. Better they were scared away before the race? Absolutely.

In addition to the sheriff, area ranchers ride the course in their four-wheelers, concentrating on the spots most prone to grizzly visits. In case the sound of their vehicles isn't enough to keep the bears at bay, they also carry bear spray (similar to pepper spray but more concentrated).

One reason Choteau's citizens are so dedicated to helping with the marathon is that they believe in its cause. The event raises money for two charities very dear to the community: the Montana Hope Project (a.k.a., the Bears that Care), a regional charity similar to the Make-A-Wish Foundation, and the Glacier Fund, which supports nearby Glacier National Park.

Registration

You're encouraged to register via the no-frills, easy-to-navigate Web site, and you'll save $2 by doing so. Fees are $60 before early August of your race year, and $75 after that. While

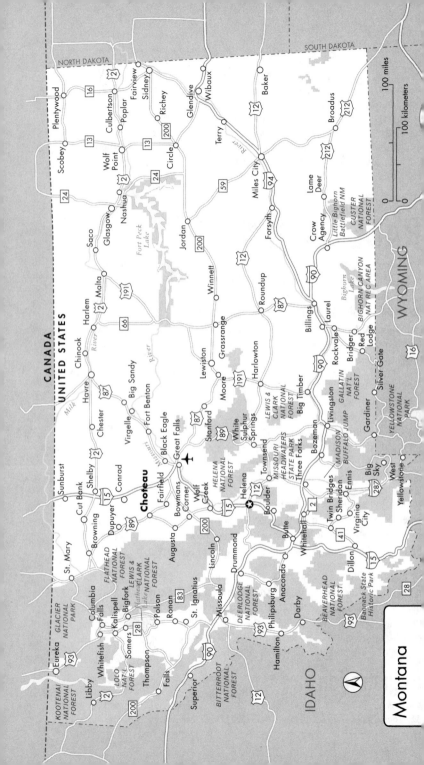

HOME AWAY FROM HOME

Each year, several local families put up runners in their homes. This unique arrangement is managed by Peggy Guthrie, a longtime Choteau resident who assured me the arrangement was actually not so unique at all. "We've done it here for years," she said. "For everyone 60 years old and up, it's second nature."

Peggy took on the challenge of arranging local housing on one condition: there couldn't be a price attached. Locals would open their homes out of the goodness of their hearts, not an ache in their wallets. Every year she puts an ad in the paper: "If you're willing to house a runner, call Peggy." She then gathers a list of willing home owners, how many beds they have available, and any preferences they might have, such as only men or only women. Once the hotels in town are booked, runners can contact Peggy (☎ 406/466–2083), and she'll make a housing match. Although Peggy got her wish and home stays are free, she suggests that guests leave a donation of $25 per person on their pillows when they leave.

Peggy's program has been a major success. In the marathon's second year, 12 homes were filled with a total of about 20 visitors. I spoke to marathoner Merrill Hemming, who came to Choteau with his wife, Alicia, for the race. Peggy offered them a room with locals Caroline and Rod Cole. Merrill and Alicia loved the experience. They were with the Coles for only about 20 hours, but they were treated like family. They also had plenty of privacy and were only a short drive from the marathon starting line. Merrill says he loved getting to know the people of Choteau, an experience he never would have had staying at a hotel. Caroline Cole was equally pleased. Because it was harvest time, she got to spend very little time with the Hemmings, but her daughter Rachel visited with them at length. Both the Coles and the Hemmings have only positive things to say about the lodging experience, and both would repeat it. Merrill even says he'd love a marathon to start near him, so he could open up his own home to visiting runners.

registering, you can buy tickets to the pre-race pasta dinner and/or post-race lunch, and make an optional donation to the official race charities. If you register but can't attend the race, you can opt for a 50% refund, or roll over your application to the next year. Registration for next year's race always opens the day after this year's race is run.

Hotels to Consider

Choteau lodging is very limited; it's not unusual for the whole town to sell out. Book your room by March. If the motels are full, consider camping, arranging a home stay (⇨ Home Away from Home box), or booking at a guest ranch or lodge.

Hotels & Motels

BELLA VISTA MOTEL. The rooms are charming and unpretentious. About half have kitchens with full-size refrigerators, and the cost is the same for rooms with or without the kitchen. ⊠ 614 Main Ave. N, 59422 ☎ 406/466-5711 ♨ Alarm clocks, some kitchens, cable TV ⋑ 15 rooms ☰ D, MC, V ¢.

BIG SKY MOTEL. Small, cozy rooms and attentive management distinguish this downtown motel. It's an easy walk from here to local restaurants and shops. ⊠ 209 S. Main Ave., 59422 ☎ 406/466-5318 ♨ Alarm clocks, cable TV, microwaves, some pets allowed (fee) ⋑ 13 rooms ☰ MC, V ¢.

GUNTHER MOTEL. It's in a residential area just a couple of blocks from downtown. Some rooms have full kitchens. ⊠ 20 7th Ave. SW, 59422 ☎ 406/466-5444 ♨ Alarm clocks, cable TV, microwaves, refrigerators, pets allowed ⋑ 15 rooms ☰ MC, V ¢.

⚔ STAGE STOP INN. This is where you pick up your race packet and catch the shuttles to the starting line, so it's the perfect marathon-weekend home base. Rooms have high ceilings and attractive, rustic details and furnishings. Thoughtful touches include free Continental breakfast, set out early marathon morning, and a small library in the lobby. Bring your bathing suit to take advantage of the indoor pool and hot tub. ⊠ 1005 Main Ave. N, 59422 ☎ 406/466-5900 ⊕ www.stagestopinn.com ♨ Wake-up calls, alarm clocks, cable TV, pool, hot tub, meeting room ⋑ 44 rooms ☰ AE, D, DC, MC, V ¢.

RACE CONTACT

Grizzly Marathon
⌂
Box 7, Choteau, MT 59422
☎
406/466-3333
⊕
www.grizzlymarathon.com

Ranches & Lodges

PINE BUTTE NATURE CONSERVANCY GUEST RANCH. Dinosaur lovers take note: the only way to experience Choteau's Egg Mountain, home to dinosaur-bone excavations, is by staying at this rustic guest ranch and taking the weekly tour. The cabins have fireplaces and handmade wooden furniture. Fresh, healthful meals are served family-style in the main lodge. They're included in the rate, as is transportation to and from Great Falls (home of the airport). What's more, all the profits from this ranch go to the Nature Conservancy, a nonprofit conservation organization. Be aware that there's a one-week minimum stay at this ranch, and weeks go from Sunday to Sunday. ⌂ HC58, Box 34C, 59422 ☎ 406/466-2158 ⊕ www.nature.org/wherewework/northamerica/states/montana/travel ♨ Alarm clocks, dining room, pool, hiking, no room TVs, no room phones ⋑ 10 cabins ☰ AE, V $.

★ SEVEN LAZY P GUEST RANCH. A snug haven in a rugged landscape, this 1,200-acre ranch is surrounded by pines and aspens deep in Teton Canyon, an eastern gateway to the Bob Marshall Wilderness. The duplex cabins are homey, with comfortable furniture, wood-paneled ceilings, rough-hewn wainscoting, and picture windows. Plush sofas and chairs, a large stone fireplace, and more golden wood adorn the main lodge. Three meals daily (included in the rates) are served family-style, and the food is memorable: a sausage-egg-and-cheese bake with homemade muffins for breakfast, grilled lemon-glazed salmon for dinner, and pies just out of the oven. All that food will fortify you for the marathon

NO ROOM AT THE INN

If everything in Choteau is sold out, there are a few options in neighboring communities. (Note that the Hampton Inn in Great Falls has marathon discounts.)

AUGUSTA

Bunkhouse Inn (⌷ 122 Main St., Augusta ☎ 406/562–3387)

FAIRFIELD

Rusty Spur Guest House (⌷ 221 10th La. SW, Fairfield ☎ 406/467–2700). Viewforth Bed and Breakfast (⌷ 4600 Hwy. 287, Fairfield ☎ 406/467–3884 ⊕ www.viewforth.com).

GREAT FALLS

Crystal Inn (⌷ 3701 31st St. SW, Great Falls ☎ 406/727–7788 or 866/727–7788 ⊕ www.crystalinns.com). Best Western Heritage Inn (⌷ 1700 Fox Farm Rd., Great Falls ☎ 406/761–1900 or 800/548–8256 ⊕ www.bestwestern.com). Hampton Inn (⌷ 2301 14th St. SW, Great Falls ☎ 406/453–2675 ⊕ www.hamptoninn.hilton.com). Holiday Inn (⌷ 400 10th Ave. S, Great Falls ☎ 406/727–7200 ⊕ www.holiday-inn.com).
Holiday Inn Express (⌷ 1801 Market Place Dr., Great Falls ☎ 406/455–1000 ⊕ www.holiday-inn.com). LaQuinta Inn (⌷ 600 River Dr. S, Great Falls ☎ 406/761–2600 ⊕ www.lq.com).

---

or a day of hiking, wildlife viewing, or guided horseback riding (also included in the rates). In summer, multiday pack trips offer a glimpse of the Rockies as Lewis and Clark saw them. There is a four-day minimum stay. ⌂ Box 178, 59422 ☎ 406/466–2044 ⊕ www.sevenlazyp.com ↳ 3 rooms, 3 duplex cabins ⚲ Dining room, alarm clocks, coffeemakers, fans, refrigerators, billiards, hiking, horseback riding, piano, airport shuttle, no-smoking rooms; no a/c, no room phones, no room TVs ▤ MC, V ☉ Closed Nov.–Apr. $$$$.

WOLF WILLOW RANCH. There are two cabins—one fully equipped, the other rustic—on a family ranch outside of Bynum, 25 mi northwest of Choteau. Both sit just east of the foot of the mountains, with a view that could inspire you to run a personal best on marathon day. The hiking and bird- and wildlife-watching for which the Rocky Mountain Front is known are right outside the door. One cabin is just like home, with a full kitchen and bath, living room with TV and VCR, and sleeping space (queen and twin beds) for four to six people, depending on how friendly they are. The other cabin has a loft and four bunk beds, a sofa, a propane stove and refrigerator, and an outhouse (in other words, no running water). Read the guest books in the cabins—many veterans of the Grizzly Marathon have stayed here. ⌷ Bynum, 59419 ☎ 406/469–2231 ↳ 2 cabins ▤ No credit cards $.

Campgrounds

CHOTEAU CITY PARK AND CAMPGROUND (⌂ Box 619, 59422 ☎ 406/466–2510 ⊕ www.visitmt.com). This campground ($8 per night) is in the center of Choteau, right by a park and playground. There aren't any RV hookups, but water, fire pits, and restrooms are available. Just be warned—the restrooms aren't the most appealing. If you really can't take it, Main Street Express convenience store is about two blocks away and has nicer facilities. **KOA KAMPGROUND** (✉85 Hwy. 221, 59422 ☎406/466-2615 ⊕www.koa.com) is less than a mile from downtown. KOA provides RV hookups as well as tent sites, and the cabins have heat and lights and sleep four in a double bed and bunk. There are bathrooms (with showers) on the property, plus mini golf and firewood for an added fee. Rates range from $17 to $30 per night.

AND YOU'RE OFF . . .

Packet Pickup

Packet pickup is at the Stage Stop Inn the day before the race or very early on race morning. This is also where you can sign up for starting-line shuttles. Expect cool goodie-bag swag: in past years it has included gourmet coffee, pens and pencils, notebooks—even a Grizzly Marathon watch. You won't however, get a ChampionChip. The race is certified by the USATF and professionally timed, but it doesn't use the expensive chip system.

Race Day

The Course

The race starts at 6:30 AM about 12 miles outside Choteau. If you're driving, try to be at the starting line by 6 AM, as the roads will be closed soon afterward. Take Highway 89 north about 4.5 miles. Turn left on Teton Canyon Road and follow it for about ½ mile. Note that more detailed instructions appear on the race Web site; there will also be signs along the way. Alternatively, hop a shuttle leaving from the Stage Stop Inn at 5:30 AM, and arriving at the start around 6:10 AM. (Be sure to sign up for shuttle service when you pick up your race packet.) Spectators are welcome to join runners at the starting line.

Though the Stage Stop Inn's Continental breakfast is technically for guests, it's put out early for runners looking to fuel up. Head to the drive-through espresso bar at **WINGS AND WILD THINGS** (✉219 N. Main Ave. ☎406/466-5990 ⊕www.wingsandwildthings. com) race morning for excellent coffee drinks.

At exactly 6:30 AM the race begins, and make no mistake: it's not easy. First, there's the altitude. You begin at 4,830 feet above sea level and run to a low of 4,110 feet before climbing again to 4,930 feet. Another challenge is the terrain, which is mostly gravel, rather than asphalt, and ranges from hard-packed to rocky. Spectators are few, and the heat can get brutal. Then there are the hills. Though the course starts off downhill, by Mile 8 you're

NIGHT-BEFORE PASTA DINNER

Your best bet is the pasta party thrown by the local 4-H Club at the Choteau Pavilion. Go east at the town's only stoplight, and the pavilion is a couple of blocks along on your right. Dinner is served from 6 PM to 8 PM, and tickets are only $7.50 for all-you-can-eat spaghetti, sauce with or without meat, rolls made by the Hutterites (a local Amish-like community known for its bread), and dessert. Get your tickets early; there's room for only about 150 people. Otherwise grab some pasta at the Log Cabin Cafe (⇨ Replacing 2,620 Calories).

on rolling hills. These segue into a long, gradual climb until about Mile 18.5, when you hit it:

Hillis Horribilis.

Named after the Latin term for grizzly bear, *ursus arctos horribilis*, this hill is the marathon's way of kicking you when you're down. It isn't that long, but it's very steep, and after nearly 19 miles of running, it's devastating. Happily the folks behind the race know this hill is a bear (so to speak), so they do what they can to make it easier (more bearable?). Every year, the Choteau High School cheerleaders line the hill and do their best to motivate you to the top. If you make it up the hill without stopping and reach the top less than three hours after the race, you receive the special Hillis Horribilis pin.

There are 16 volunteer-run aid stations (12 distinct ones; a few you hit twice), each with a theme and each competing with the others to be the best on the course. In past years, there have been Hawaiian-themed stations and those disguised as oases; there was even one manned by a giant grizzly bear with sneakers dangling from its mouth. All the stations have water, sports drinks, and portable toilets; five also offer bagels, oranges, bananas, and/or sport gel. Though the course is officially open for 7 hours, stations stay open until every runner has passed.

Cross the finish line to cheers from the Choteau High School girls' volleyball team, whose members hand out medals to every finisher. Enjoy free fruit and bagels, or pay $7.50 for a barbecue plate or burger, a side, and a drink (you can prepay for this meal with race registration). A local band plays at the finish area, and there's medical assistance as well as a search-and-rescue unit—just in case. Also take advantage of the massage therapists, who offer their services for a small fee. Choteau doesn't have a slew of day spas, so this is your best bet for a shot of much-needed post-race pampering. If you need a lift back to town, shuttles are available, usually taking off around 1 PM.

Spectating

There are three places where spectators can catch the marathon field: the starting line, Mile 7.5, and the finish line. Get up early to drive your runner to the start: you need to get there by 6 AM, before the roads close. Alternatively, you can hop on a race shuttle at 5:30 AM. Shuttles won't return people to Choteau until 1 PM, but race volunteers drive back and forth, so you can probably catch an earlier ride. Keep in mind that after the race starts, you won't be able to drive back to town for at least an hour and 15 minutes, when the roads open to vehicles again.

Catching the race at Mile 7.5 means you don't have to wake up quite so early. To get there, drive toward the race start. When you reach the closed road, park and prepare to cheer. If you want to make it a truly leisurely morning, sleep in and grab a bite at the Log Cabin Cafe, John Henry's, or the Outpost Deli (⇨ Replacing 2,620 Calories, *below*) then head to the finish line. If you're planning to watch the start or Mile 7.5 then wait around for the finish, consider buying picnic provisions the night before at **REX'S MARKET** (⊠ 29 1st St. NE ☎ 406/466-2927), just off the main drag. On Friday night it's open till 9. Bring cash to the finish area; like marathoners, spectators can buy a hot meal there for just $7.50.

BEYOND THE FINISH LINE

The temperature at the start is usually in the upper 50s. The mercury can rise to 80°F or even 90°F by noon.

Replacing 2,620 Calories

Choteau has just a few restaurants, and they offer straight-forward American cuisine. That said, the food is good, and the prices are as reasonable as you get.

ELK COUNTRY GRILL. Broiled halibut steaks, grilled shrimp over mixed greens, substantial burgers, and everything in between—the Grill serves an ample selection in a bright dining room that draws lots of local families. ⊠ 925 N. Main Ave. ☎ 406/466-3311 ▭ MC, V $.

JOHN HENRY'S. Craving onion rings fried a golden brown? Aching for pizza dripping with cheese? Hungering for a steak sandwich sizzling off the grill? John Henry's offers delicious greasy-spoon fare in a sit-down family-style restaurant. It's also one of the few places in town with a liquor license. ⊠ 215 N. Main Ave. ☎ 406/466-5642 ▭ MC, V $.

★ **LOG CABIN CAFE.** For breakfast, lunch, or dinner, this is your best bet for a sit-down meal. The building is indeed a log cabin, and the inside lives up to all the homey connotations. The menu includes fish, pasta, burgers (beef or buffalo), steaks, and other American classics. ⊠ 102 S. Main Ave. ☎ 406/466-2888 ▭ D, MC, V $-$$.

MEETING GROUNDS. Breakfast options include waffles, French toast, and breakfast sandwiches. At lunch there's a salad bar and a menu of soups and sandwiches. Baked goods, a selection of tea, and coffee and espresso drinks are always available. ⊠ 202 N. Main Ave. ☎ 406/466-2667 ▭ MC, V ◷ No dinner. Closed Sun. ¢-$.

OUTPOST DELI. Come for the simple, high-quality food and the comfortable environment. Enjoy egg dishes for breakfast or burgers and sandwiches for lunch. For dessert there's pie, or you can step into the ice-cream parlor. ⊠ 819 N. Main Ave. ☎ 406/466-5330 ▭ D, MC, V ◷ No dinner ¢-$.

TRADING POST. In the back of this store is a small café with just a few tables. Look for sandwiches and daily soup, plus specials such as bratwurst with sauerkraut. Finish with

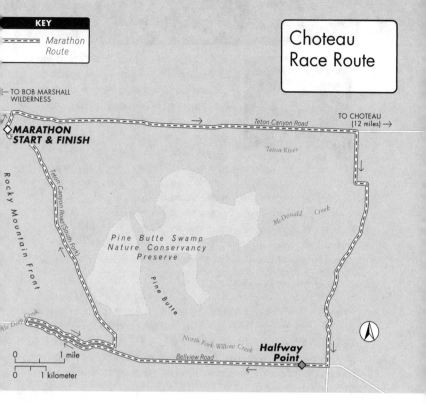

Choteau
Race Route

KEY

===== Marathon Route

← TO BOB MARSHALL WILDERNESS

◇ **MARATHON START & FINISH**

Teton Canyon Road

TO CHOTEAU (12 miles) →

Teton River

Teton Canyon Road (South Fork)

Rocky Mountain Front

McDonald Creek

Pine Butte Swamp Nature Conservancy Preserve

Pine Butte

Little Ditch Creek

North Fork Willow Creek

Bellview Road

Halfway Point ◇

0   1 mile

0   1 kilometer

---

a cookie, a bowl of ice cream, or a slice of cake or pie. Though it's open until 4 PM, the kitchen usually runs out of food well before that; arrive by 2 PM. ⊠ 106 N. Main Ave. ☎ 406/466-5354 ▤ MC, V ⊗ No dinner. Closed weekends ¢.

Sightseeing on (and off) Your Feet

The real joy of visiting Choteau is the great outdoors, which you can experience on foot, on horseback, or while standing in waders and casting a fishing line (though the fishing can be hit-or-miss).

I Feel Great!

TAKE A HIKE. The **Montana Wilderness Association** (☎ 406/443-7350 ⊕ www. wildmontana.org) sponsors free guided treks all over the state throughout the year. It also publishes a free book with trailheads, trail lengths, degrees of difficulty, and other hike info. Call ahead for the book and for hike reservations. The **Montana Wilderness Association Rocky Mountain Front Office** (⊠ Russell Building, 17 3rd St. NE, Choteau ☎ 406/466-2600 ⊕ www.wildmontana.org) publishes a free book of hikes. Some hotels,

In his mid-twenties, Sean McCormick was out of shape and had never run more than a couple of miles at a stretch. Now in his early thirties, Sean has run not only 24 marathons, but also 13 ultramarathons, including four 30-milers, five 50-milers, and four 100-milers. It's easy to hear statistics like that and just shake your head, muttering, "Yeah, but he's not like me. He's one of those guys who was born to do this—a natural runner." But then consider Sean's finishing times. His average marathon time is four hours—respectable, but far from elite. Sean is simply a guy who found the drive to push himself beyond his perceived limits. In doing so, he has kindled a true passion in life and opened the door to a world of new experiences.

They say watching too much TV has turned many of us into couch potatoes, but had Sean not been glued to the tube, he might never have become a runner. Granted, he wasn't watching reruns of *Welcome Back Kotter;* he was glued to the Eco-Challenge Adventure Race and the Ironman Triathlon. Watching those athletes made him antsy, and he couldn't shake the urge to push himself in a similar way. The mental challenge intrigued him as much as the physical one. What kind of mind-set did it take to drive your body to such extremes?

Before he could find out, Sean had to tackle a much more basic challenge—that of getting his butt off the couch, into a pair of running shorts, and out the door. His first few running attempts were horrible, but he kept at it. The more he ran, the more he saw progress, and he was soon ready to shoot for the marathon. He signed up for a race in Columbus, Ohio, not far from his hometown of Cincinnati . . . and proceeded to make every novice mistake in the book. Like his training: 10 miles was his longest pre-race run. Then there was his pace—way too fast. By Mile 16 he slammed hard into the wall, gritting his teeth and dragging himself the last 10 miles on sheer will alone. "I hobbled over to the side of the road and actually cried because of the pain," he says. "I swore to myself right away that I was going to do better in May of '99 at my next marathon [the first Flying Pig], and I trained better, smarter, and harder with a set marathon training schedule, and finished in 3:30."

Thus began a new lifestyle for Sean. These days his favorite thing to do is take out his pop-up camper and travel to marathons. He loves arriving early to go hiking or exploring, but the real sightseeing always happens during the race. "What better way to see a place you've never been than to run 26.2 miles through it?" he asks. On what fuels his passion for running, Sean says, "I think it involves many aspects: the drive of pushing yourself to a distance; the ability to set a goal, train for it, and complete it; the beauty of the places you're running; the way everything feels better when you run, both mentally and physically; and the great people you meet—people with whom you think you're just running a marathon but by the end you call them 'friend.' "

Sean points to the Grizzly Marathon as one of the highlights of his 2004 racing season. And it was actually something of an afterthought—an addendum to camping in Glacier National Park. He liked the idea of running a race while in Montana, as one of his goals is to run a marathon in all 50 states. He had read great reviews of the first Grizzly Marathon, so he drove to Choteau the day before the race. Sean was charmed by the town and enjoyed strolling its main street and ducking into the Old Trail Museum. He opted for the prerace pasta party, which he loved for its good food and the chance to meet fellow runners.

Race morning brought added excitement for the marathoners: a grizzly was spotted on the course. Everyone was warned to keep their eyes peeled during the race. "I never saw the bear," Sean says, "but even the thought of one made it a whole lot more interesting." Above and beyond the promise of grizzly sightings, Sean was thrilled to run in such a beautiful part of the country and to get to know it in such an intimate way. He was also impressed by the community of Choteau. The aid stations were filled with volunteers. Kids, families, ranchers in their cowboy boots and hats . . . they all took time out to cheer and hand water to runners. In fact there were so many volunteers, Sean felt like he was getting individual service.

Sean would recommend the Grizzly Marathon to other runners, but with a word of advice—train on hills. The course is tough, so don't think about a PR. Instead, just enjoy the extra time on the course, and let yourself be dazzled by the spectacular scenery of the Rocky Mountain Front. ∎

such as the Stage Stop Inn, may also have a copy that you can borrow. The **U.S. Forest Service, Rocky Mountain Ranger District** (✉ 1102 Main Ave. NW, Choteau ☐ Box 340, Choteau 59422 ☎ 406/466-5341) has a free booklet on Rocky Mountain Front hikes, which you can get at its office (open weekdays 8-5), across from the Stage Stop Inn. Alternatively, call the office and ask someone to send you a copy.

I Feel Pretty Good

RIDE THE RANGE. If you're staying at a guest ranch, chances are it offers horseback riding. The Seven Lazy P Guest Ranch and Pine Butte Nature Conservatory Guest Ranch (⇨ Ranches & Lodges *under* Hotels to Consider, *above*) have the best locations for getting into the Bob Marshall Wilderness on horseback, and their riding tours, open only to guests, are highly regarded. Seven Lazy P also offers 6- to 10-day pack trips: for about $250 a day, you get everything you need, including complete campsites, plenty of food, a cook, a guide, and, of course, the horse. Contact the ranch for schedules. **Sun Canyon Lodge** (☐ Box 327, Augusta ☎ 888/749-3654 or 406/562-3654 ⊕ www.suncanyonlodge.com) allows nonguests to ride. Sign up for two-hour ($20 per person), half-day ($40), or full-day ($65) tours of the Bob Marshall Wilderness. Call for schedules and reservations, which are essential.

TEE OFF. The **Choteau Country Club** (✉ Airport Rd. ☎ 406/466-2020 ☺ Summer, daily 7 AM–11 PM; winter, daily noon–5) has a 9-hole course as well as a driving range and putting green. Greens fees are $13 for 9 holes and $22 for 18 holes weekdays; $16 for 9 holes and $24 for 18 holes weekends. If miniature golf is more to your liking, head to the **KOA Kampground** (✉ 85 Hwy. 221, Choteau ☎ 406/466-2615 ⊕ www.koa.com), where you can play for $1.50 and enjoy free ice cream when you're finished.

Let's Take It Slowly

OLD TRAIL MUSEUM. The Old West and prehistory mingle in this fascinating museum. Its cluster of frontier-period cabins is loaded with artifacts. Many exhibits focus on the area's dinosaur discoveries. ✉ 823 N. Main Ave. ☎ 406/466-5332 ◨ $2 ☺ May–Sept., daily 9–6; Oct.–Apr., Tues.–Sat. 10–3.

Ow! No.

GLIDE ALONG THE GIBSON. Pontoon-boat trips on the Gibson Reservoir (water level permitting) are offered by **Sun Canyon Lodge** (✉ Box 327 Augusta ☎ 406/562-3654 or 888/749-3654 ⊕ www.suncanyonlodge.com). Trips in the 28-foot-long vessels last two hours ($20 per person), a half day ($40), or a full day ($65). Call for schedules and reservations, which are essential.

Shop Around

The spice store **ALPINE TOUCH** (✉ 714 N. Main Ave. ☎ 406/466-2063 ⊕ www.alpinetouch.com) has its own custom blends. **GRANDMA'S ATTIC** (✉ 308 N. Main Ave. ☎ 406/466-3669) is a charming antiques store with Montana's largest collection of De-

GLACIER NATIONAL PARK

Glacier National Park is only an hour or so from Choteau. Its coniferous forests, thickly vegetated stream bottoms, and green-carpeted meadows and basins provide homes to and sustenance for all kinds of wildlife. Here you can see some of the Rockies' oldest geological formations and numerous rare species of mammals, plants, and birds. The narrow Going-to-the-Sun Road, snaking through Glacier's precipitous center, is one of the continent's most dizzying rides. The park encompasses more than 1 million acres (1,563 square miles) of untrammeled wilds. Along the 720 miles of trails are 37 named glaciers, 200 lakes, and 1,000 miles of streams.

Motorized access to Glacier is limited, but its few roads take you from densely forested lowlands to craggy heights. Touring cars can take you along Going-to-the-Sun Road while a driver interprets. Shuttle services can drop you off and pick you up at many trailheads—useful, as parking at many is limited. Remember that weather in the mountains can change quickly; snow can fall even in August. Be prepared with extra layers, a hat, and rain gear. ⊠ Glacier National Park Headquarters, West Glacier ☎ 406/888–7800 ⊕ www.nps.gov/glac ⌨ $10 per person or $20 per vehicle for a 7-day permit ☉ Park year-round. Parts of Going-to-the-Sun Road close in winter; check Web for details. Visitor centers open all summer; hours vary in winter; check Web for details.

pression glass. **OASIS BOOKS** (⊠820 N. Main Ave. ☎406/466–2800) specializes in books on the American West, including first editions, but has a selection wide enough to satisfy any reading runner who's ready to put her feet up and browse post-marathon. At the **TRADING POST** (⊠ 106 N. Main Ave. ☎406/466–5354) most of the goods have a Western feel. Shop for men's, women's, and kids' clothes, as well as toys and souvenirs. **WINGS AND WILD THINGS** (⊠219 N. Main Ave. ☎406/466–5990 ⊕www.wingsandwildthings. com) has birding, camping, and hiking gear, along with a mix of toys, books, and gifts, plus a fantastic espresso bar.

I Love the Nightlife

Bowl into the night at the **ALLEY CAT** (⊠427 Main Ave. S ☎ 406/466–2818). Though it's technically open daily 3 PM to midnight, staffers will keep things open until 2 AM if people are having fun. While you bowl, enjoy beer and wine or soda, as well as snacks like pizza, corn dogs, barbecue sandwiches, and chicken nuggets. It costs $10 an hour to rent a lane, or you can pay by the game ($2); a pair of shoes runs $1. Everything is cash-only. **JOHN HENRY'S** (⊠215 N. Main Ave. ☎ 406/466–5642) has a bar with a large-screen TV, pool tables, and keno and poker machines (gambling is legal in Montana). The **ROXY THEATER** (⊠25 N. Main Ave. ☎ 406/466–2413) has been around since 1946, and though its marquee looks old-school, it shows first-run movies (evenings only).

HELPFUL INFO

Air Travel

The closest airport to Choteau is Great Falls International Airport, about an hour's drive away on Route 89N. Great Falls International Airport is served by Big Sky Air, Delta (via Sky West), Horizon Air, Northwest Airlines, and United Airlines.

🛈 **AIRLINES & CONTACTS Big Sky** ☎ 800/237-7788 ⊕ www.bigskyair.com. **Delta** ☎ 800/221-1212 ⊕ www.delta-air.com. **Horizon** ☎ 800/547-9308 ⊕ www.horizonair.com. **Northwest** ☎ 800/225-2525 ⊕ www.nwa.com. **United** ☎ 800/864-8331 ⊕ www.ual.com.

🛈 **AIRPORT INFORMATION Great Falls International Airport** ✉ 2800 Terminal Dr., Great Falls ☎ 406/727-3404 ⊕ www.gtfairport.com.

Car Rental

Great Falls International Airport is served by Avis, Budget, Enterprise, Hertz, National, and Rent-a-Wreck. National is the marathon's official car-rental agency and offers a discount. Check the race Web site for the promotional code.

🛈 **Avis Rent-a-Car** ☎ 406/761-7610 or 800/230-4898 ⊕ www.avis.com. **Budget Rent-a-Car** ☎ 406/454-1001 or 800/527-0700 ⊕ www.budget.com. **Enterprise Rent-a-Car** ☎ 406/761-1600 or 800/325-8007 ⊕ www.enterprise.com. **Hertz Rent-a-Car** ☎ 406/761-6641 or 800/654-3131 ⊕ www.hertz.com. **National Car Rental** ☎ 406/453-4386 or 800/CAR-RENT ⊕ www.nationalcar.com. **Rent-a-Wreck** ☎ 406/761-0722 or 800/944-7501 ⊕ www.rent-a-wreck.com.

Disabilities & Accessibility

If you're interested in national parks like Glacier, consider a Golden Access Passport from the National Park Service. This free, lifetime admission pass grants park access to U.S. citizens or permanent residents who have documentation of blindness or permanent disability. Passes must be picked up in person at a National Park Service office or other federal area (see Web site for details).

🛈 **National Park Service** ☎ 888/467-2757 ⊕ www.nps.gov/fees_passes.htm.

Emergencies

🛈 **HOSPITAL Teton Medical Center** ✉ 915 4th St. NW, Choteau ☎ 406/466-5763 ⊕ www.tetonmedicalcenter.net.

🛈 **PHARMACY Choteau Drugs** ✉ 102 Main Ave. N, Choteau ☎ 406/466-2700

CHAPTER 9

SEPTEMBER

Stowe Marathon, Stowe, VT

Ever been traveling and found a cute hotel that's not

in the guidebooks (except Fodor's, of course)? So you try it, and the rooms are spacious and airy, the grounds lush and manicured, the service impeccable, and you can't believe that this amazing place is totally off most people's radar. And you're so excited because it feels like your own hideaway, reserved just for you and the few others resourceful enough to have found it.

That's kind of what it feels like to run the Stowe Marathon on the second Sunday of September. The area is stunningly beautiful, the course is well supported, and the pre- and post-race amenities are superb. And though I'm spilling the secret, race director Peter Wright assures me that, for now, he intends to keep the race small, capping registration at about 1,000 people. This way he can guarantee a high-quality event and maintain that feeling of a "boutique" marathon, catering to a savvy few.

So You're Running Stowe . . .

Stowe is adorable. Smack in the middle of Vermont's northern third, Stowe Village sits beneath Mt. Mansfield, the state's highest peak at 4,395 feet, and the area is known as an East Coast skiing mecca.

You'll want a car for this trip. Route 100 is the main road into Stowe, which is tiny: just a few blocks of shops and restaurants clustered around a picture-perfect white church with a lofty steeple. The village serves as the anchor for the other main thoroughfare, Mountain Road (Route 108), which winds north past restaurants, lodges, and shops on its way to the fabled slopes. In summer Stowe's delights move beyond the slopes and include horseback riding, hiking, canoeing, and kayaking, all in a truly beautiful setting.

Nearby towns worth a visit include Burlington, a community of about 40,000 people roughly 35 miles west of Stowe. It sits on Lake Champlain and offers cycling, boating, and the historic Church Street Marketplace, a charming pedestrian shopping area. Another option is Waterbury, a town of about 5,000 people 10 or so miles southwest of Stowe, just down Route 100. Foodies will find it worth a visit, since it's home to both the Cold Hollow Cider Mill and the very popular Ben & Jerry's Ice Cream plant.

RACE BASICS

The Stowe Marathon was started in 2000 to raise funds for two local charities: the not-for-profit Copley Hospital and CREW, a community sports facility. In the race's second year the entire field was only 39 runners; now 15 times that number come regularly to enjoy this high-quality event that truly showcases Stowe's beauty and charm. Weekend runs include a half-marathon and a kids' race as well as the main event. In 2004, the Stowe Marathon became a Boston Marathon qualifier, an exciting milestone for this New England gem.

Registration

Registration opens in May. Although there's currently no online registration, the form is on the race Web site; submit it via mail or fax. The Web site is small, but it's well laid out and has all the info you need. The posted course map is hand drawn and a little difficult to follow, but if you read "The Route" next to it, you'll get the gist of how it flows. (Note that mile numbers aren't printed on the map; the circled numbers you see represent legs of the team relay.)

> **RACE CONTACT**
>
> Stowe Marathon
> ☏
> Box 1182, Morrisville, VT 05661
> 📠
> 802/888-8301
> 🌐
> www.stowemarathon.com

Registration costs $60 and includes the prerace pasta dinner and the post-race barbecue. It also includes your race T-shirt, but only if you register before the shirts are ordered, about three weeks before the event. Register later and your T-shirt costs an extra $10.

If running all 26.2 miles seems daunting, consider joining with one, two, or three others and forming a relay team. A team of two runners pays a $95 registration fee; a team of three pays $115; and a team of four pays $130. All members register using one form, on which they cite the team name.

You should receive a confirmation letter by August 1. If you register after that, your credit card statement or canceled check is your proof of registration. There are no refunds for bowing out of the race, but if you let race director Peter Wright know in advance, not only will you be guaranteed entry into next year's event, but your registration fee will roll over to cover that race.

Hotels to Consider

Your best bet is to stay at Topnotch Resort, the marathon hub. Its race-special package sells out early, so reserve your room as soon as possible. If you can't stay at Topnotch, Stowe has a bevy of charming inns, lodges, and bed-and-breakfasts.

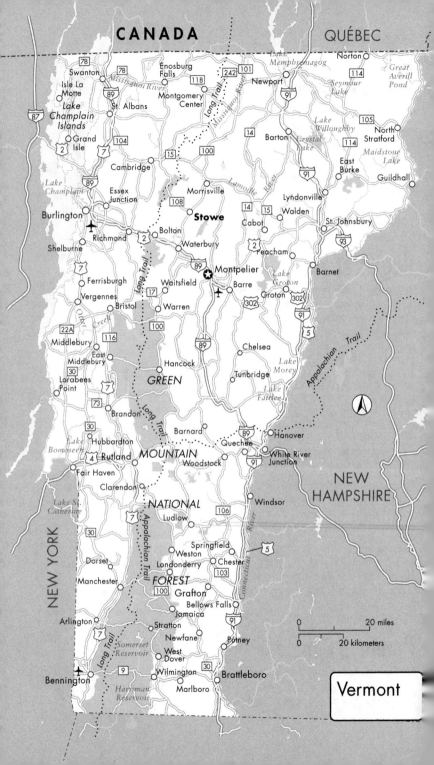

Vermont

GREEN MOUNTAIN INN. This classic redbrick inn has an outdoor heated pool that's open year-round. Rooms in the main inn and annex have early-American design schemes. Two new buildings contain luxury rooms, suites, and town houses. Some deluxe rooms have double hot tubs, fireplaces, and other amenities. In the afternoon, enjoy complimentary cider and cookies in the lobby. ⊠ 18 Main St., 05672 ☎ 802/253-7301 or 800/253-7302 ⊕ www.greenmountaininn.com ↝ 105 rooms ♿ 2 restaurants, wake-up calls, alarm clocks, cable TV, pool, hot tub, massage, sauna, badminton, volleyball, recreation room, shops, some pets allowed ⊟ AE, MC, V $.

INNSBRUCK INN. This hotel offers spectacular discounts for marathoners ($89 per night in past years). Rooms aren't luxurious, but they're large and very comfortable. Some have hot tubs, but any guest can sit in the outdoor whirlpool and enjoy the scenery. A breakfast buffet (set out early on marathon morning) of fruit and baked goods is included in the rates, as is an afternoon tea with refreshments. In-room massage is available by appointment. ⊠ 4361 Mountain Rd., 05672 ☎ 802/253-8582 or 800/225-8582 ⊕ www.innsbruckinn.com ↝ 19 rooms, 5 suites, 1 chalet ♿ Restaurant, wake-up calls, alarm clocks, coffeemakers, robes, cable TV, some in-room hot tubs, refrigerators, free Wi-Fi, pool, exercise equipment, outdoor hot tub, sauna, paddle tennis, playground, some pets allowed; no smoking ⊟ AE, D, DC, MC, V $.

STONE HILL INN. Each elegant (and soundproof) room has a king-size bed, sitting area, and two-person whirlpool bath in front of a fireplace. Common areas include a sitting room and a games room, and the 10 acres of grounds have gardens and waterfalls. Hot and cold beverages are available 24 hours. Choose from three breakfast options (included in the rates), and enjoy complimentary evening hors d'oeuvres. A movie library lets you get the most out of your room VCR. Take advantage of massages, either in your room or in the gazebo. ⊠ 89 Houston Farm Rd., 05672 ☎ 802/253-6282 ⊕ www.stonehillinn.com ↝ 9 rooms ♿ Alarm clocks, robes, cable TV, in-room safes, in-room VCRs, free Wi-Fi, golf privileges, outdoor hot tub, hiking, tobogganing, recreation room, laundry facilities; no room phones, no kids, no smoking ⊟ AE, D, DC, MC, V $$$-$$$$.

STOWE MOTEL & SNOWDRIFT. This motel sits on 16 acres across the river from the Stowe Recreation Path. Accommodations range from one-room studios with small kitchenettes to modern two-bedroom fireplace suites with hot tubs. A variety of bikes and helmets are available for use during your stay. You also get a free Continental breakfast of cereals, fruit, pastries, yogurt, and beverages. ⊠ 2043 Mountain Rd., 05672 ☎ 802/253-7629 or 800/829-7629 ⊕ www.stowemotel.com ↝ 52 rooms, 4 suites ♿ Wake-up calls, alarm clocks, coffeemakers, cable TV, some kitchenettes, refrigerators, tennis court, 2 pools, outdoor hot tub, bicycles, mountain bikes, croquet, recreation room, some pets allowed (fee) ⊟ MC, V ¢-$.

STOWEFLAKE MOUNTAIN RESORT & SPA. Accommodations at this lovely luxury resort range from standard hotel rooms to plush suites with fireplaces, refrigerators, and whirlpool tubs. One- to three-bedroom town houses sit on the resort's perimeter. The spa overlooks an herb labyrinth and is connected to the fitness center via a faux covered bridge. ✉ 1746 Mountain Rd., 05672 ☎ 802/253-7355 or 800/253-2232 ⊕ www.stoweflake.com ↩ 94 rooms, 30 town houses ♿ 2 restaurants, 24-hr room service, wake-up calls, alarm clocks, coffeemakers, robes, cable TV, in-room data ports, some kitchenettes, some microwaves, driving range, putting green, 2 tennis courts, pool, gym, hair salon, sauna, spa, bicycles, sleigh rides, business services, meeting rooms ▤ AE, D, DC, MC, V $-$$$.

🐾 **TOPNOTCH AT STOWE RESORT AND SPA.** Stay here. End of story. The race begins and ends at Topnotch. It offers marathon discounts. Packet pickup, the prerace pasta dinner, and the post-race barbecue are all here; so is an excellent spa. Moreover, it's one of the state's poshest resorts. Floor-to-ceiling windows, a freestanding metal fireplace, and heavy stone walls distinguish the lobby, where you'll enjoy free afternoon tea and cookies. The spacious rooms will make you feel like you're in your own private chalet. My favorite amenity? In-room massages for your dog. ✉ 4000 Mountain Rd., 05672 ☎ 802/ 253-8585 or 800/451-8686 ⊕ www.topnotchresort.com ↩ 77 rooms, 13 suites, 30 town houses ♿ 2 restaurants, room service, wake-up calls, alarm clocks, coffeemakers, newspapers, robes, cable TV, WiFi (fee), 10 tennis courts (4 indoors), 2 pools (1 indoors), sauna, gym, spa, horseback riding, sleigh rides, bar, video game room, some pets allowed, no-smoking rooms ▤ AE, D, DC, MC, V $$-$$$$.

TOWN AND COUNTRY RESORT AT STOWE. Marathoners get excellent discounts here ($89 in recent years). The resort is actually three buildings spread out over 10 acres. A full breakfast is included in the cost of your room, and you can book fly-fishing lessons through the resort. ✉ 876 Mountain Rd., 05672 ☎ 802/253-7595 or 800/323-0311 ⊕ www. townandcountrystowe.com ↩ 45 rooms, 1 cottage ♿ Restaurant, wake-up calls, alarm clocks, cable TV, in-room data ports, tennis court, 2 pools (1 indoors), hot tub, sauna, bar ▤ AE, D, DC, MC, V $-$$.

TRAPP FAMILY LODGE. This Tyrolean lodge was built by the von Trapp family, of *Sound of Music* fame. Stay in the main lodge or guesthouses. Several common rooms and libraries offer space to sprawl and relax. All guest rooms have panoramic mountain views. Opt for the von Trapp suite and stay in the onetime residence of Baroness Maria von Trapp; then try to stop yourself from warbling a constant refrain of "Do Re Mi." ✉ 700 Trapp Hill Rd., 05672 ☎ 802/253-8511 or 800/826-7000 ⊕ www. trappfamilylodge.com ↩ 96 rooms, 100 guesthouses ♿ 3 restaurants, room service (breakfast only), wake-up calls, alarm clocks, cable TV, free Wi-Fi, 2 pools, gym, massage, sauna ▤ AE, D, DC, MC, V $$.

TWO DOG LODGE. There are four innkeepers, two of whom happen to be yellow labs. Every room has a dog bed and bowls, and breakfast is included for both you and your pooch, who also gets a special treat at turndown. Rooms are comfortable, with views of the woods or mountains. Some have robes, and two rustic cabins have their own decks, grills, and fireplaces. There's a dog park as well as doggie day care. ✉ 3576 Mountain Rd., 05672 ☎ 802/253-8555 or 800/339-2364 ⊕ www.twodoglodge.com ↩ 17 rooms, 2 cabins ♿ Alarm clocks, cable TV, in-room data ports, exercise equipment, pool, hot tub, sauna, dog park, pets very much allowed; no smoking ▤ AE, D, DC, MC, V ¢-$.

NIGHT-BEFORE PASTA DINNER

The high-quality, all-you-can-eat pasta buffet at Topnotch is included in the registration fee and well worth attending. It runs from 5:30 PM to 8 PM, and everyone is welcome. Extra tickets are available at the door for $15. Seating is
first-come, first-served, but things don't tend to get overcrowded. If you'd rather
try a local restaurant . . .

★ **FOXFIRE INN AND ITALIAN RESTAURANT.** The restaurant tucked inside
this B&B has a homey, open feel. Large windows look out to the front, where
white lights flicker in the trees after dark. Complimentary homemade bread
sticks come to the table hot and speckled with chunks of garlic—completely addictive. Pasta dishes include lasagna, baked penne, or spaghetti in marinara or
homemade pesto sauce. (You can substitute whole-wheat angel hair for any
pasta.) The menu also has a variety of excellent veal, chicken, beef, and
seafood dishes. ✉ 1606 Pucker St. ☎ 802/253–4887 ⊕ www.foxfireinn.
com ⚑ Reservations essential ▤ AE, D, MC, V ⊗ No lunch $–$$.

★ **PIE IN THE SKY.** Spaghetti, fettuccine, penne, or tortellini come in any of
nine different sauces, so you can create your own pasta feast. The real thrill,
however, is the pizza. Choose thick or thin, white or wheat crust, then check
out the toppings—all 39 of them—to make the pizza of your dreams. Traditional toppers like pepperoni and mushrooms share the list with sliced apple,
jalapeño peppers, and asiago cheese. Your work of edible art is cooked in a
wood-fired oven and brought to your table piping hot. ✉ 492 Mountain Rd.
☎ 802/253–5100 ⊕ www.pieintheskyvt.com ▤ MC, V $.

TRATTORIA LA FESTA. Everything about this restaurant feels old-school Italian,
even though it sits in an old Vermont farmhouse right next to the Topnotch Resort.
The food is authentic and fresh, the portions are large, and the service makes
you feel like a relative rather than just a customer. Enjoy homemade crusty
bread with garlic butter, both basic and specialty pastas, and entrées such as
veal with a mushroom and brandy reduction or sirloin steak with capers,
onions, tomatoes, pepperoncini, and olive oil. Save room for dessert. ✉ 4080
Upper Mountain Rd. ☎ 802/253–9776 or 800/245–5118 ⊕ www.
trattorialafesta.com ▤ AE, MC, V ⊗ Closed Sun. No lunch $–$$.

AND YOU'RE OFF . . .

Packet Pickup

Packet pickup is a low-key affair with just a few sponsors promoting their goods. It takes
place in tents set up in the fields of the Topnotch Resort on Friday evening, all day Sat-

urday, and early on race day morning. Last-minute entrants can register anytime. Check the marathon-weekend schedule before you go: at three points there will be a course briefing first-time Stowe Marathoners shouldn't miss. Race timing is handled manually, so don't expect a chip.

Race Day

The Course

The starting line is in the fields of Topnotch Resort. Topnotch guests will head down the resort driveway, cross Route 100, and follow the Stowe Recreation Path about a half mile. If you're not staying at Topnotch, park at the Topnotch fields or along Route 108; you can walk to the race area from either location.

The starting area is abuzz early, with last-minute packet pickup and race registration. Runners can enjoy bagels, water, and sports drinks and make use of portable toilets until 8:15, when...you're off!

The race begins with a gentle downhill along the Stowe Recreation Path, before you veer onto Mountain Road. Along the way you pass Little River, wooded areas, and meadows before running through oh-so-quaint (and oh-so-small) Stowe Village. Beyond town the terrain remains manageable, maybe with a slight upgrade, until about Mile 9, when you begin the trek to the Trapp Family Lodge. I won't sugarcoat it—the hill is brutal. According to the official race-elevation map, you go from 750 feet at Mile 9 to 1,360 feet at Mile 12. Stick it out. Views from the Trapp Family Lodge are breathtaking, and once you've reached the summit, you can rest easy knowing you've tackled the only major hill.

Next, you veer onto a dirt road that runs steeply downhill, through woods and pastures, before dropping you on a small country lane. The course flattens out as you visit the small village of Moscow, then take another dirt road back into Stowe. After this second jaunt through the village, you run back up the Stowe Recreation Path (now open to the public), on a gradual ascent to Topnotch and the finish line.

For teams, the marathon is broken into four relay segments. Teams decide which member runs which segment or segments; all the race director needs to know is who's crossing the finish line. There are race officials at each relay station, and team members must slap hands before the next leg can start.

Aid stations appear every 2 miles, right around the even mile markers, and provide water, sports drinks, and fruit. There are also two medical stations along the way, and bike marshals patrol the route until every runner is finished. That said, the course does officially close after six hours, at which point aid stations start to shut down.

This isn't a big city–style race. You won't be running with throngs of people. You won't be knee-deep in spectators, though you'll get tons of support from aid station volunteers and those who gather toward the top of that massive hill. You *will* get up to six hours

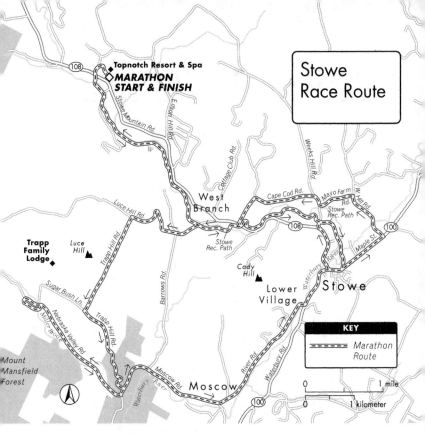

with nothing to do except run, breathe in the clean Vermont air, and enjoy breathtakingly beautiful vistas.

After you cross the finish line, you'll get a medal, a cold cloth, fruit, and plenty of fluid, as well as the attention of nurses from Copley Hospital, if needed.

Spectating

This is a great race for spectators, primarily because the start/finish area is so accessible. Absolutely join your runner at the start of the race. Stowe Village is also a great viewing spot; runners come through at Miles 5 and 21. Try to get to to the Trapp Family Lodge at about the halfway point of the race. It's atop a steep hill, and runners can use your encouragement as they slog toward its peak. Besides, the views from here are spectacular. When you're ready, head back to Topnotch to catch the finish line.

Celebrate!

The Stowe Marathon throws an absolutely fantastic post-race barbecue, which kicks off at noon by the finish line. A DJ plays music, free massages are available, and there's an all-you-can-eat buffet of freshly made burgers and dogs, plus tons of salads and ice cream. The celebration lasts for two to three hours and is included in the registration fee. Friends and family are also welcome and can buy tickets there for $10 each.

BEYOND THE FINISH LINE

Replacing 2,620 Calories

First, check out two places that are fully reviewed elsewhere in the chapter: the Dutch Pancake Cafe (⇨ Breakfast Spots), where you can get a 1-foot-diameter crepelike pancake loaded with sweet or savory deliciousness, and Pie in the Sky (⇨ Night-Before Pasta Dinner), where the pizzas can be topped with just about anything you can imagine—and lots of it. As for other options:

BLUE MOON CAFÉ. It looks rustic and simple, but looks can be deceiving. The creative menu changes weekly to showcase local produce and top-quality meat, seafood, and poultry. Dishes are so elegantly presented, they're works of art. Possible appetizers include a red-wine-poached pear served with local cheese and toasted walnuts; entrées might include salt-crusted scallops with crème fraîche and cucumbers. ⊠ 35 School St. ☎ 802/253-7006 ⊟ AE, D, DC, MC, V ⊘ No lunch $$–$$$.

★ MES AMIS. Locals queue up at this small bistro thanks to such specialties as fresh oysters, lobster bisque, braised lamb shanks, roast duck (secret recipe), and bananas Foster. You can eat in the candlelighted dining room or on the patio, especially appealing on a warm summer's night. ⊠ 311 Mountain Rd. ☎ 802/253-8669 ⊟ AE, D, DC, MC, V ⊘ Closed Mon. $$.

MICHAEL'S ON THE HILL. Chef Michael Kloeti's four-course prix-fixe menus highlight European cuisine such as roasted rabbit with mirepoix or ravioli with braised autumn vegetables. ⊠ 4182 Stowe-Waterbury Rd. (Rte. 100), Waterbury Center, 6 mi south of Stowe ☎ 802/244-7476 ⊟ AE, D, MC, V ⊘ Closed Tues. No lunch $$$–$$$$.

RED BASIL. The traditional Thai entrées here are enhanced with fresh cilantro, Kaffir lime leaves, lemongrass, and ginger. The panang curry is smooth, just a bit hot, and delicious; you can also order from the sushi bar. The martini bar has 18 varieties of James Bond's favorite libation. ⊠ 294 Mountain Rd. ☎ 802/253-4478 ⊟ AE, MC, V $–$$.

Sightseeing on (and off) Your Feet

Though Stowe is best known as a skiers' haven, there's just as much to do here in late summer and fall. What should you choose? It all depends on how you feel.

I Feel Great!

HIKE MT. MANSFIELD. An ascent of Mt. Mansfield makes for a scenic day hike. Trails lead from Mountain Road to the summit ridge, where they meet the north-to-south Long Trail. Views from the summit take in New Hampshire's White Mountains, New York's Adirondacks across Lake Champlain, and southern Québec. For a free hiking guide, call or visit the **Stowe Area Association** (⊠ 51 Main St. ☎ 877/GO-STOWE).

BREAKFAST SPOTS

The following options are in the ¢ to $$ range:

★ **THE DUTCH PANCAKE CAFE.** "The world's most decadent breakfast," claims the menu (a quote from the *New York Times*), and it's absolutely true. Dutch pancakes are a full foot in diameter, with a crepelike consistency, and toppings run the gamut from tame (apple cinnamon), to sinful (banana, chocolate, and coconut), to outrageous (apple, shredded potato, pineapple, raisins, ham, cheddar cheese, and curry). ⊠ Grey Fox Inn, 990 Mountain Rd. ☎ 802/253–5330 or 800/544–8454 ⊕ www.dutchpancake.com ☺ No lunch or dinner ⊟ AE, D, MC, V.

MAXWELL'S. This restaurant at Topnotch serves an excellent breakfast. Sunday sees a $15 brunch buffet, including eggs, bacon, sausage, oatmeal, fruit—all your basic favorites. You can also order from the à la carte menu, which includes such spa cuisine options as egg-white omelets, nondairy buckwheat pancakes, and waffles with berries. ⊠ Topnotch Resort, 4000 Mountain Rd. ☎ 802/253–8585 ⊕ www.topnotchresort.com ⊟ AE, D, DC, MC, V.

MCCARTHY'S. This local favorite breakfast and lunch café offers a variety of breakfast pastries and entrées. Build-your-own-omelets come with nut toast, and fillings range from seven different cheeses and typical meats and veggies, to black beans, artichokes, and roasted red peppers. Waffles, pancakes, and breakfast wraps are also available. ⊠ 454 Mountain Rd. ☎ 802/253–8626 ☺ No dinner ⊟ AE, D, DC, MC, V.

PADDLE AROUND. Umiak Outdoor Outfitters (⊠ 849 S. Main St., just south of Stowe Village ☎ 802/253-2317 ⊕ www.umiak.com) rents canoes and kayaks for half- or full-day trips. Rates run from $35 to $45.

★ **TAKE THE STOWE RECREATION PATH** (☎ 877/GO-STOWE). You ran it in the marathon, so you know how beautiful it is. If you'd like to check out this 5½-mile greenway at a more leisurely pace, consider strolling, biking, or rollerblading it. **Boots 'n Boards** (⊠ 430 Mountain Rd. ☎ 800/298-5574 ⊕ www.bootsnboards.com) rents bikes and Rollerblades ($7-$8 for one hour; hourly rates drop as your rental time increases). **Mountain Sports and Bike Shop** (⊠ 580 Mountain Rd. ☎ 802/253-7919 ⊕ http://bikestowe.com) rents bikes ($11 for two hours; per-hour prices drop as your rental time increases). Check its Web site for recommended rides.

I Feel Pretty Good

BEN & JERRY'S ICE CREAM FACTORY. Welcome to ice-cream Nirvana—a 30-minute tour of the Ben & Jerry's plant culminating in free samples. Tours are first-come, first-served, and run every 10 minutes. They include a movie about Ben and Jerry and a look at the ice-cream factory in action (on production days; otherwise there's a video of the

The older you get, the more time seems to race by. We've all experienced it. How many autumns have you paused in your check writing, stunned and reeling: "October? How can it possibly be October? It was January, like, yesterday!"

But David Polow has found a way to slow that zooming clock, and it's something anyone can do.

Run marathons.

David, who lives in Vermont, was never one for running. He kept fit by playing tennis and mountain biking—even commuting 5½ miles to work on his bike most of the year. Running, however, held absolutely no appeal. It was only when he reached his forties, when Hannah, his then-tween daughter, took up running in school, that he figured he'd give it a try. He entered a local 5K—and adored it. Running quickly went from an idiosyncrasy in others to his own passion. He loved training, he loved racing, and he especially loved that he could share this passion with his family. His wife Bridget is also a runner, and the three of them would occasionally race together in area 5Ks (David's son was too young to join in). It was fantastic, but as the years went by, David felt a tug to push harder and try something more. He set his sights on the 2002 Philadelphia Marathon, and was thrilled when his finishing time was good enough to qualify for Boston: he signed up right away. He was hooked. Three years after that first race, David has run nine marathons, and made the Stowe Marathon an annual event.

David admits that the hardest part of becoming a marathoner was finding the time to train. He's a lawyer, he has a family—he's a busy guy. He was sure the long hours of marathon training would eat into his already full schedule. Even so, he dedicated himself to the training, and something amazing happened. Far from gobbling up precious spare time, becoming a marathoner gave David *more* time. His long runs brought the normal sprint of the clock to a crawl, and he started using them to do all those things he hadn't had the chance to do before. Now there was time to listen to his favorite music without distraction. Now there was time for continuing legal education; he simply downloaded the courses onto his iPod. Now there was extra time to spend with Bridget: she'd join him for the middle of his long runs, and their conversations would help pull him through.

Like his long training runs, the Stowe Marathon offers a serenity that David can't find in bigger races, and it's what keeps him coming back year after year. Though he's usually alone for the bulk of the race, he's never bored. He simply lets time slow down and takes in the awe-inspiring beauty of the course. Although he lives only 8 miles from Stowe and has seen the vistas countless times, they always amaze. And when he's at the tail end of the marathon and could use a little distraction from his solitude, he reaches his favorite stretch: the climb up the Stowe Recreation Path. Though the path is closed to nonmarathon traffic when the race begins, by the end it's open to the public and alive with kids on trikes, rollerbladers, elderly couples shuffling arm in arm—a true cross section of humanity—some cheering for the runners, others oblivious to the fact that there's a marathon going on at all. It's the perfect point in the race for a little excitement, and the fun of people-watching while dodging through the crowds takes David's mind off any aches and pains.

Marathoning has given David not only the gift of time, but also of confidence. There's nothing simple about running 26.2 miles, and he's had races where it's tantamount to torture. Once he was struck by a migraine just after the starting gun. He ran as long as he could, then slowed to a walk, struggling with every fiber to force one foot in front of the other until he made it to the end. By comparison, being a marathoner has made everything else in life seem easy. Well, almost everything else. You know how people say running a marathon is like going through labor? David disagrees. "I've watched childbirth twice," he says. "For any women out there who've had a baby, the marathon is nothing." ■

process). And for dessert? Bring on the samples! ⊠ Rte. 100, 1 mi north of I–89, Waterbury ☎ 866/BJ–TOURS or 802/882–1240 ⊕ www.benjerry.com 🎫 $3 🕙 Late Oct.–May, daily 10–6; June, daily 9–6; July–late Aug., daily 9–9; late Aug.–late Oct., daily 9–7.

GO HORSEBACK RIDING. Guided trail rides for all riding levels are available through **Edson Hill Manor** (⊠ 1500 Edson Hill Rd. ☎ 802/253–8954 ⊕ www.edsonhillmanor. com). Rides are $35 for an hour; reservations are necessary. Extended treks can be arranged in advance. For kids under 10, 20-minute pony rides are available for $15.

TAKE A SWING. The **Stowe Country Club** (⊠ 744 Cape Cod Rd. ☎ 802/253–4893) has a scenic 18-hole, par-72 course; a driving range; and a putting green. Greens fees are $25–$75; cart rental is $20.

Let's Take It Slowly

ALPINE SLIDE. A chairlift takes you to the top of this 2,300-foot slide that runs down Spruce Peak. You control the speed, which helps mitigate any fear factor. ⊠ 5781 Mountain Rd. ☎ 802/253–3500 or 800/253–4754 🎫 $14 🕙 Weekends 10–5.

COLD HOLLOW CIDER MILL. See cider being pressed, see bees making honey (behind glass—no worries), then wander through the store trying samples of jellies, applesauce, fudge, and other delights. Rest up at the Donut Counter with a cider doughnut and coffee, then check out the fudge-making facilities and the winery, where you can try local wine and hard cider. Tours are free. ⊠ 3600 Waterbury-Stowe Rd. (Rte. 100), Waterbury Center ☎ 802/244–8771 or 800/3-APPLES ⊕ www.coldhollow.com 🕙 Daily 8–6.

Ow! No.

FLOAT ON THE BREEZE. Above Reality (☎ 802/899–4007 or 877/FUN–RISE ⊕ www. balloonvermont.com) offers sunrise and sunset hot-air balloon rides that take off from points about 35 to 45 minutes from Stowe. The experience costs $225–$275 per person, and lasts from three to four hours, with about an hour of actual flight time. Reservations are highly recommended.

GLIDE THROUGH THE AIR. Stowe Soaring (⊠ 2305 Laporte Rd., Morrisville ☎ 802/ 888–7845 or 800/898–7845 ⊕ www.stowesoaring.com) takes you high above Stowe in a glider. Choose from a variety of different rides. Your pilot will act as a tour guide, pointing out the highlights of the vistas below. Rates range from $79 to $189, and flights are first-come, first-served.

HANG OUT ON MT. MANSFIELD. The **Gondola at Stowe Mountain Resort** (⊠ 5781 Mountain Rd. ☎ 802/253–3500) carries you to the top of Mt. Mansfield in comfort. The cost is $16, and the gondola operates daily 10–5. Before you descend, enjoy great views and a meal at the **Cliff House Restaurant** (☎ 802/253–3665).

Shop Around

Stowe's Main Street is lined with charming shops that bring to mind New England in the early 1900s. In **THE DEPOT SHOPS AT THE GREEN MOUNTAIN INN** don't miss

FORGET SIGHTSEEING. GET ME TO A SPA!

Many Stowe resorts have spa facilities or at least offer massage. Two spas, however, stand out from the crowd.

★ SPA AT STOWEFLAKE. The aqua solarium alone makes this a must-try. Bring a bathing suit to soak in the Bingham hydrotherapy waterfalls, a 12-foot-high massaging cascade. Also try the soaking pool, featuring mineral salts from Hungary. Enjoy complimentary tea, juice, and fruit in the men's and women's lounges. Women can take advantage of a private sunning deck. Signature massage treatments include LaStone therapy (80 minutes, $155) and a thera-peutic sports massage (25–50 minutes, $65–$105) consisting of assisted stretching and compression of major muscle groups. Traditional massages are also available. ⊠ 1746 Mountain Rd. ☎ 802/760–1083 or 800/253–2232 ⊕ www.stoweflake.com ☉ 8–8.

TOPNOTCH SPA. It's beautiful, with steam rooms, saunas, hot tubs, and spacious lounges with free fresh fruit. The sports massage (80 minutes, $150) is great for marathoners, though the spa also recommends Thai massage (50–80 minutes, $100–$140), which involves a therapist helping you stretch by placing you in various yoga positions. June Jacobs's foot rescue products are available for sale. ⊠ Topnotch Resort, 4000 Mountain Rd. ☎ 802/253–6463 or 800/451–8686 ⊕ www.topnotchresort.com ☉ Daily 6:30 AM–8 PM.

Stowe Mercantile (☎ 802/253–4554), an old-time country store with clothing, stuffed animals, and a slew of specialty foods to sample. South of Waterbury, don't miss the fresh-baked, maple-glazed sticky buns at the **RED HEN BAKING COMPANY** (⊠ 4278 Rte. 100 ☎ 802/244–0966 ⊕ www.redhenbaking.com).

I Love the Nightlife

CHARLIE B'S PUB AND RESTAURANT (⊠ Stoweflake Mountain Resort & Spa, 1746 Mountain Rd. ☎ 802/253–7355) has a festive atmosphere, stays open until 1 AM, and has live music Friday and Saturday night. The **MATTERHORN NIGHT CLUB** (⊠ 4969 Mountain Rd. ☎ 802/253–8198 ⊕ www.matterhornbar.com) is open Thursday–Satur-day nights at marathon time and offers live music and dancing. The special martini bar evokes the Rat Pack days. The **RUSTY NAIL** (⊠ 1190 Mountain Rd. ☎ 802/253–6245 or 877/253–6245 ⊕ http://rustynailbar.com) rocks to live music on weekends and has a late-night menu.

HELPFUL INFO

Air Travel

Continental, Delta, JetBlue, Northwest, United, and US Airways fly into Burlington International Airport (BTV), about 35 miles west of Stowe. From the airport, take I–89 south to Route 100 north.

⁊ AIRPORT INFORMATION Burlington International Airport ⊠ Airport Dr., 3 mi east of Burlington ☎ 802/863–1889 ⊕ www.burlingtonintlairport.com.

Car Travel

Avis, Enterprise, Hertz, and National/Alamo all operate out of Burlington International Airport. Two major interstates run through Vermont: I–91 and I–89. I–91 stretches from Connecticut and Massachusetts to Québec along Vermont's eastern border. I–89 runs from New Hampshire to Québec, cutting through central Vermont. You can get a free state highway map from the Vermont Department of Tourism and Marketing. The *Vermont Atlas and Gazetteer,* sold in many bookstores, shows nearly every road in the state. For current road conditions, call 800/429–7623.

⁊ RENTAL AGENCIES Avis ☎ 800/331–1212 ⊕ www.avis.com. **Enterprise** ☎ 802/864–1111 or 800/261–7331 ⊕ www.enterprise.com. **Hertz** ☎ 802/864–7409 or 800/654–3131 ⊕ www.hertz.com. **National/Alamo Car Rental** ☎ 802/864–7441 or 800/227–7368 ⊕ www.nationalcar.com, www.alamo.com.

Disabilities & Accessibility

The helpful staffers at the Stowe Area Association have accessibility information on many shops, hotels, restaurants, and sights.

⁊ Stowe Area Association ☎ 877/GO-STOWE.

Emergencies

⁊ HOSPITAL Copley Hospital ⊠ 528 Washington Hwy., Morrisville ☎ 802/888–4231.

⁊ PHARMACY Heritage Pharmacy ⊠ 1878 Mountain Rd. ☎ 802/253–2544.

CHAPTER 10

OCTOBER

LaSalle Bank Chicago Marathon

"Check it out! It's Cher!"

That was my friend Michelle, one of the three training buddies who ran the 2000 Chicago Marathon with me—a first for all of us. We were just about at Mile 8 and running down a gorgeous brownstone-lined street, when I followed Michelle's advice and looked up to see . . .

. . . well, not the diva herself, but a pretty close facsimile. In honor of the marathon, a giant stage had been erected, and a major drag show was in full swing for both the runners and spectators, who seemed to line the street several deep. As we glided ahead, buoyed by the surge of energy from the crowd, "Cher" belted out (okay, lip-synched out) a mean "Believe," and blew kisses to every runner. Nearly everyone hooted back, and we all grinned, any worries about the next 19 miles momentarily forgotten.

That's the best thing about the Chicago Marathon: the support. With the possible exception of New York, no other city embraces the marathon like Chicago. People from every neighborhood pour into the streets to sweep the runners all the way to the finish line on a wave of encouragement and excitement. Add in the rather flat course and the usually great running weather, and you end up with an ideal race for a first-timer, someone striving to qualify for Boston, or anyone looking to run a personal best.

If you run just one marathon in this book, make it this one. It'll get you hooked for more.

So You're Running Chicago . . .

Getting around Chicago is easy. It's a great walking city, plus taxis are readily available, and the city's network of buses and rapid transit service is extensive. The Chicago Transit Authority (CTA) is even a marathon partner and works closely with the race to help spectators navigate the marathon route (⇨ Spectating, *below*). The upshot of all this is that you can readily explore this toddlin' town, and all its varied neighborhoods.

DOWNTOWN SOUTH. It's a mixed bag, a once down-and-dirty area that has (mostly) been revitalized. People are drawn by its ethnic mix, its proximity to the Loop and Museum Campus, and its growing community feeling. Here you'll find the Hilton Chicago, the official headquarters hotel of the marathon. If your main concern is convenient access to the starting and finish lines, there's no better area in which to stay.

THE LOOP. Stay in this neighborhood and you'll be very close to the starting and finish lines. Here you'll find noisy, mesmerizing trading centers; gigantic department stores; and such globally known institutions as the Art Institute. And rattling overhead is the train Chicagoans call the El. Why is this called the Loop? It's thanks to the cable cars of the 1880s, which "looped" around the area. The Loop also encompasses Millennium Park, the Sears Tower, and the shopping opportunities on State Street (which I dare you to say without bursting into song Sinatra-style and adding, "that great street").

MUSEUM CAMPUS. South of the Loop's architectural displays, three of Chicago's best-known and best-loved museums reside on the shores of Lake Michigan in the park known as Museum Campus. The Field Museum, the Shedd Aquarium, and the Adler Planetarium & Astronomy Museum cover the bases of the natural sciences, underwater life, and the solar system in a masterful triple play.

NEAR NORTH. This is the part of the city most folks imagine when they think about Chicago. It's home to the Navy Pier Ferris wheel, the John Hancock Building, museums and galleries, and the Magnificent Mile, filled with shops in which you could blow a few (or thousands of) dollars. Some of Chicago's finest hotels also line the Magnificent Mile, and they're fun choices for marathon weekend if you really want to splurge.

GOLD COAST. This posh pocket wears Chicago's great-est treasure—the Lake Michigan shoreline—like a gilded necklace. Made fashionable after the Great Chicago Fire of 1871 by the social-climbing industrialists of the day, today's Gold Coast neighborhood is still a ritzy place to live, work, shop, and mingle.

RIVER NORTH. River North is a vibrant neighborhood of galleries, shops, and restaurants appealing to the artsy and young urban professional crowds. The area's most charming feature is the almost complete absence of con-temporary construction; the handsome buildings are vir-tually all renovations of properties nearly a century old.

WICKER PARK & BUCKTOWN. Creative types cluster in Wicker Park and Bucktown, a hip, somewhat grungy en-clave centered on Milwaukee, Damen, and North avenues. The area is an intriguing mix of nightclubs, cafés, the-aters, coffeehouses, cutting-edge galleries, and a bizarre bazaar of shops. It may well have the best people-watching in the city. When *The Real World* came to Chicago, the room-mates lived here.

VISITOR INFO

Chicago Convention &
Tourism Bureau
☎
877/CHICAGO or
312/567-8500
🌐
www.choosechicago.com or
www.877chicago.com
•
Chicago Office of Tourism
☎
312/744-2400
🌐
www.cityofchicago.org

LINCOLN PARK. Both the park and the neighborhood around it share the name. The city's first public playground was established in 1864 and named after the then recently as-sassinated president. The surrounding neighborhood has unique shops, hot restaurants, and clubs where lines form on weekends. It also has some of the city's loveliest residen-tial streets.

WRIGLEYVILLE & LAKE VIEW. Wrigleyville and Lake View are barely distinguishable from each other; even locals can't figure out where one ends and the other begins. Mostly the differences are a matter of character: Wrigleyville, anchored by Wrigley Field, is where you find the sports bars; Lake View is where you find a mix of gay bars and shops cater-ing to young professionals.

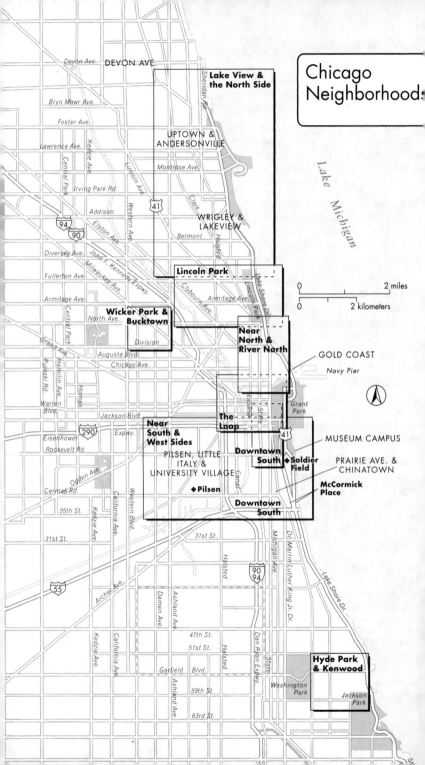

Chicago
Neighborhoods

Lake View &
the North Side

UPTOWN &
ANDERSONVILLE

WRIGLEY &
LAKEVIEW

Lincoln Park

Wicker Park &
Bucktown

Near
North &
River North

GOLD COAST

Navy Pier

The
Loop

MUSEUM CAMPUS

Near
South &
West Sides

Downtown
South

Soldier
Field

PRAIRIE AVE. &
CHINATOWN

PILSEN, LITTLE
ITALY &
UNIVERSITY VILLAGE

◆ Pilsen

McCormick
Place

Downtown
South

Hyde Park
& Kenwood

Lake Michigan

0   2 miles
0   2 kilometers

DEVON AVE.

Devon Ave.

Bryn Mawr Ave.

Foster Ave.

Lawrence Ave.

Kedzie Ave.

Central Park

Irving Park Rd.

Addison

Western Ave.

Lincoln Ave.

Montrose Ave.

Clark

Halsted

Belmont

Sheridan Rd.

Diversey Ave.

Fullerton Ave.

Armitage Ave.

Elston Ave.

John F. Kennedy Expwy.

Milwaukee Ave.

North Ave.

Central Park

Grand Ave.

Division

Augusta Blvd.

Chicago Ave.

Pulaski Rd.

Hamlin Ave.

Homan

Clybourn Ave.

Armitage Ave.

Lincoln Park

Lake Shore Dr.

Warren
Blvd.

Jackson Blvd.

Eisenhower

Roosevelt Rd.

Expwy.

Ogden Ave.

Cermak Rd.

25th St.

31st St.

Kedzie Ave.

California Ave.

Western Ave.

California Blvd.

Canal

Halsted

31st St.

Archer Ave.

Damen Ave.

Ashland Ave.

Kedzie Ave.

California Ave.

Ashland Ave.

47th St.

51st St.

Garfield   Blvd.

59th St.

63rd St.

Halsted

Dan Ryan Expwy.

State

Michigan Ave.

Dr. Martin Luther King Jr. Dr.

Lake Shore Dr.

Washington
Park

Jackson
Park

Grant
Park

Dearborn

State

Cermak

PRAIRIE AVENUE & CHINATOWN. In the 1800s, Prairie Avenue was lined with grand old Victorian homes, a few of which remain. Nearby is Chinatown, whose restaurants, groceries, and food-processing factories still offer first-job opportunities to many Chinese immigrants. Tour the historic commercial district on Wentworth Avenue and you might just forget you're in a Midwestern city.

PILSEN, LITTLE ITALY & UNIVERSITY VILLAGE. The South Side enclave of Pilsen is home to the Midwest's largest Mexican community and is known for its dramatic, colorful murals. To the north of Pilsen is Chicago's Little Italy. It has been encroached upon by the expansion of the nearby university in recent years, but there are still Italian restaurants, bakeries, groceries, and sandwich shops. University Village is an up-and-coming area that's home to the University of Illinois at Chicago.

RACE BASICS

The Chicago Marathon is run on one of the world's fastest courses: at this writing runners have set world records here four times. Elite athletes are actively courted by an impressive purse, including $125,000 for the first-place winner and such prizes as a new Volkswagen to the first male and female to break the existing world record.

RACE CONTACT
LaSalle Bank Chicago Marathon
✍
Box 5709, Chicago, IL 60680–5709
☎
312/904-9800
⊕
www.chicagomarathon.com

But it's not just about the elites; upward of 35% of the field usually consists of debut marathoners. Spectators are also given the royal treatment in Chicago, which is why it's not unusual for more than a million people to line the streets and cheer for all the runners, no matter what their speed.

In short, the Chicago Marathon is a giant party to which everyone is invited—a party you don't want to miss.

Registration

Registration opens January 1 of the race year and remains open until mid-August, or when the cap of 40,000 entrants is reached, whichever comes first. Don't drag your feet—the cap is always reached well before August. The simplest way to register is online. Entry fees are $90 for U.S. residents and $100 for foreigners, and include admission to the post-race party, plus two free drink tickets.

On your registration, you'll specify if you're a wheelchair athlete, or if you qualify for a competitive or preferred starting position. To qualify you must show proof that within the two and a half years before the race, you've run a half-marathon faster than 1:45 (pre-ferred start) or 1:30 (competitive start), or a marathon faster than 3:45 (preferred start) or 3:15 (competitive start). If you scored those times in a LaSalle Bank Chicago Marathon, no proof is needed, just let the marathon know. If you do qualify, there's no guarantee you'll secure a spot in these corrals, since space is limited.

After you've registered, you'll get a postcard in the mail, followed in September by a full confirmation brochure. Don't lose the brochure: not only is it an excellent resource, packed with vital race weekend information, but it also holds your confirmation ticket, which you must present at the expo to get your bib number.

While you wait for the race, stay psyched by cruising the Web site. It's one of the best: easy to navigate, and overflowing with information. Debut marathoners have their own section, as do spectators, who can join the "26.2 Curb Crew." This free club offers added motivation to spectators, including expo gifts and special contests. The training section of the website is incredibly comprehensive, and the interactive marathon map is impressive. With the click of a mouse, it plots every relevant marathon location, from race route aid stations to popular restaurants, on a map of Chicago.

Hotels to Consider

The minute you know you're running the race, check the marathon Web site for a full list of affiliated hotels and book your room. Prime spots can sell out their marathon room blocks as early as May. Since the race starts and ends at Grant Park, it makes sense to stay in Downtown South or the Loop. Near North hotels are also close enough to be a strong option, though the ones along the Magnificent Mile are expensive.

Downtown South

ESSEX INN. The Essex's location, just a quarter mile from the start/finish area, along with its more reasonable prices, make it a solid choice. The hotel caters to marathoners: it has a carb dinner the night before the race, it opens its restaurant at 5 on race morning, and staffers hand out towels to runners as they leave for the start. Many basic rooms have nice views of Grant Park. ⊠ 800 S. Michigan Ave., Downtown South, 60605 ☎ 312/939-2800 or 800/621-6909 ⊕ www.essexinn.com ⇄ 241 rooms, 13 suites ⟁ Restaurant, room service, wake-up calls, alarm clocks, coffeemakers, cable TV, in-room data ports, Wi-Fi (fee), indoor pool, gym, sauna, bar, dry cleaning, business services, meeting rooms, parking (fee), no-smoking rooms ⊟ AE, D, DC, MC, V $.

🏃 **HILTON CHICAGO.** Marathoners are royalty here at the headquarters hotel. A letter welcomes runners, runner-friendly dishes are added to all the menus, the official pasta dinner is here, and the lounge opens at 4:30 AM race morning to sell coffee, bananas, and other pre-race fuel. The health club has extended hours for those needing a post-race hot tub or massage, and a late checkout is provided. Best of all, the start and finish lines are right out the front door. As with many older hotels, guest rooms differ in size and style. Families should ask for one with two double beds and two baths. ⊠ 720 S. Michigan Ave., Downtown South, 60605 ☎ 312/922-4400 or 800/445-8667 ⊕ www.hilton.com ⇄ 1,477 rooms, 67 suites ⟁ 2 restaurants, room service, alarm

GO TEAM!

Love to run with friends? Make it official by entering the Chicago Marathon's Team Challenge. Any group of three to five registered participants can become a team in either the corporate or open divisions; just pay an additional $125 (total, not per person), and fill out a second registration form, usually available around June. Team members don't have to stick together on the course. Each person gets a score based on his or her finishing place within the appropriate age group, and the official team score is calculated from those.

"But I'm already paying to run the marathon," you might protest. "Why would I pay more to be on a team?" Lots of reasons. For starters, the marathon provides special awards for Team Challenge participants, so you gain the camaraderie of working together for a common goal. Then there are the race-day perks. Before and after the race, teams enjoy a special hospitality tent with such amenities as gear check, a changing area, toilets, massage therapists, and post-race food, beer, and other beverages. Teams also get a free team photo, their own runner update area, and their own family and friends reunion tent. In a field of almost 40,000 runners, this is a great way to avoid crowds and lines, and add a little VIP treatment to your marathon experience.

---

clocks, coffeemakers, newspapers weekdays, cable TV with movies and video games, minibars, Wi-Fi (fee), indoor pool, gym, hair salon, hot tub, massage, sauna, billiards, pub, shop, dry cleaning, laundry service, concierge, concierge floor, business services, meeting rooms, helipad, parking (fee), some pets allowed, no-smoking floors ⊟AE, D, DC, MC, V $-$$$.

HOLIDAY INN & SUITES DOWNTOWN CHICAGO. Just a mile from the start/finish area, this Holiday Inn is convenient to race activities. There's a rooftop pool, and the comfortable guest rooms have Nintendo. ⊠ 506 W. Harrison St., Downtown South, 60607 ☏ 312/957-9100 or 800/HOLIDAY ⊕ www.hidowntown.com ⇌ 145 rooms, 27 suites ♻ Restaurant, room service, wake-up calls, alarm clocks, coffeemakers, newspapers weekdays, cable TV with movies and video games, in-room data ports, free Wi-Fi, pool, gym, lounge, video game room, shop, dry cleaning, laundry facilities, laundry service, concierge, business services, meeting rooms, parking (fee), no-smoking floors ⊟AE, D, DC, MC, V $-$$.

HYATT REGENCY MCCORMICK PLACE. This hotel is connected via an enclosed walkway to the vast McCormick Place Convention Center, home of the race expo. It's 1½ miles from the start/finish area. Rooms have basic, modern furnishings. The jogging and biking path along Lake Michigan is steps away; museums, Grant Park, and Soldier Field are also nearby. For the marathon, they stock their coffee bar area with energy bars and drinks. ⊠ 2233 S. Martin L. King Dr., Near South, 60616 ☏ 312/567-1234 or 800/233-1234 ⊕ www.mccormickplace.hyatt.com ⇌ 752 rooms, 48 suites ♻ Restaurant, coffee shop, 24-hr room service, wake-up calls, alarm clocks, coffeemakers, newspapers, cable TV with movies, in-room data ports, indoor pool, gym, sauna, shop, dry cleaning, laundry service, concierge, business services, convention center, meeting rooms, parking (fee), no-smoking rooms ▤AE, D, DC, MC, V $–$$.

The Loop

FAIRMONT. About a mile from the start/finish, this 45-story pink granite tower is a standout. Rooms have marble bathrooms with oversize tubs and separate shower stalls. Say you're a marathoner and the hotel will bend over backward to help you. "If you believe garlic brings you luck, we'll have garlic in the room," says the public relations director. Marathoners enjoy special runner-friendly menu items plus complimentary in-room bottled water and energy drinks. Post-race in-room massage and mineral mud baths are available. Runners are also usually placed on the same floor to avoid possible loud guests and ensure a good night's sleep. ⊠ 200 N. Columbus Dr., Loop, 60601 ☎312/565–8000 or 800/526–2008 ⊕ www.fairmont.com ⇄ 626 rooms, 66 suites ⟂ Restaurant, 24-hr room service, wake-up calls, alarm clocks, newspapers, robes, cable TV with movies, in-room data ports, minibars, bar, babysitting, shop, dry cleaning, laundry service, concierge, business services, meeting rooms, parking (fee), some pets allowed, no-smoking floors ▤AE, D, DC, MC, V $–$$$$.

HARD ROCK HOTEL. This link in the upscale chain plays up Chicago's musical heritage. Music fills a lobby done in black and silver, and filled with portraits of rock stars. Modern rooms, adorned with rock-and-roll paraphernalia, have flat-screen TVs. Those in the tower offer striking views of Michigan Avenue, Millennium Park, and the river. In-room massage is available. A stay at the Hard Rock puts you a half mile from the marathon start/finish area. ⊠ 230 N. Michigan Ave., Loop, 60601 ☎ 312/345–1000 or 877/762–5468 ⊕ www.hardrock.com ⇄ 369 rooms, 12 suites ⟂ Restaurant, 24-hr room service, wake-up calls, alarm clocks, coffeemakers, newspapers, robes, cable TV with movies, in-room data ports, in-room safes, minibars, 24-hr gym, massage, bar, shop, laundry service, concierge, business services, meeting rooms, parking (fee), some pets allowed, no-smoking floors ▤AE, D, DC, MC, V $$–$$$$.

★ HOTEL ALLEGRO CHICAGO. Throughout this hip, art deco structure are bold patterns and splashes of color. Marathoners get a special in-room amenity, as well as a late checkout. Room service menus add a special carb menu the night before the race, and the lobby breakfast bar opens at 5 AM race morning. All guests enjoy a complimentary yoga basket, free Tootsie Rolls at the front desk, a free lobby wine reception every evening, and a full menu of in-room massages, facials, or hand and foot treatments. The hotel is 1½ miles from the start/finish area. ⊠ 171 W. Randolph St., Loop, 60601 ☎312/236–0123 or 800/643–1500 ⊕ www.allegrochicago.com ⇄ 451 rooms, 32 suites ⟂ Room service, wake-up calls, alarm clocks, coffeemakers, newspapers, robes, cable TV with movies, in-room data ports, minibars, free Wi-Fi, 24-hr gym, hair salon, massage, bar, lounge, shop, concierge, business services, meeting rooms, parking (fee), some pets allowed, no-smoking floors ▤AE, D, DC, MC, V $$$.

HOTEL BURNHAM. This intimate hotel, 1½ miles from the start/finish area, was built in 1895 and retains such original details as Carrara marble wainscoting and ceilings, terrazzo floors, and mahogany trim. Guest rooms average 400 square feet. Enjoy complimentary evening wine receptions and a "pillow menu" with eight options to ensure a good night's sleep. In-room massage and other spa treatments are available. On marathon morning, the restaurant opens at 6 AM to offer a runner-friendly buffet. ⊠ 1 W. Washington St., Loop, 60602 ☎ 312/782-1111 or 877/294-9712 ⊕ www.burnhamhotel.com ⤴ 103 rooms, 19 suites ⟑ Restaurant, 24-hr room service, wake-up calls, alarm clocks, coffeemakers, newspapers, robes, cable TV, in-room data ports, minibars, 24-hr gym, massage, bar, dry cleaning, concierge, business services, parking (fee), some pets allowed, no-smoking floor ⊟ AE, D, DC, MC, V $$-$$$.

★ **HOTEL MONACO.** Enjoy complimentary morning coffee and a nightly wine reception. On race day the restaurant opens at 6 AM to serve a runner-friendly buffet. In brightly colored guest rooms, turndown is accompanied by such surprise amenities as Pixy Stix candy. Ask about in-room spa services, including massage. The hotel is 1½ miles from the start/finish area. ⊠ 225 N. Wabash Ave., Loop, 60601 ☎ 312/960-8500 or 866/610-0081 ⊕ www.monaco-chicago.com ⤴ 170 rooms, 22 suites ⟑ Restaurant, 24-hr room service, wake-up calls, alarm clocks, coffeemakers, newspapers, robes, cable TV, in-room data ports, in-room safes, minibars, free Wi-Fi, 24-hr gym, massage, bar, dry cleaning, laundry service, concierge, business services, meeting rooms, parking (fee), some pets allowed, no-smoking floors ⊟ AE, D, DC, MC, V $$-$$$.

HYATT REGENCY CHICAGO. Ficus trees, palms, and fountains fill the two-story greenhouse lobby of one of the world's largest hotels. There's also a bar called Big and illuminated signs that guide you through the labyrinth of halls and escalators throughout the two towers. A full spa offers massage, pedicures, and salon services. In the comfortably sized guest rooms, black-and-white photographs of Chicago landmarks add to the contemporary look. The hotel is 1½ miles from the start/finish area. ⊠ 151 E. Wacker Dr., Loop, 60601 ☎ 312/565-1234 or 800/233-1234 ⊕ www.hyatt.com ⤴ 2,019 rooms, 175 suites ⟑ 3 restaurants, café, 24-hr room service, wake-up calls, alarm clocks, coffeemakers, newspapers, robes, cable TV with movies, in-room data ports, in-room safes, Wi-Fi (fee), gym, hair salon, spa, 2 bars, dance club, shops, dry cleaning, laundry service, concierge, concierge floor, business services, convention center, meeting rooms, parking (fee), no-smoking floors ⊟ AE, D, DC, MC, V $$-$$$$.

PALMER HOUSE HILTON. This landmark in the heart of the Loop is the essence of grand style. Ornate, elegant public areas include the lobby, with its ceiling murals. Rooms are less spectacular, with reproduction antiques; some rooms are rather small. This hotel is a 5-10 minute walk from the start/finish area, and it offers massage. ⊠ 17 E. Monroe St., Loop, 60603 ☎ 312/726-7500 or 800/HILTONS ⊕ www.hilton.com ⤴ 1,551 rooms, 88 suites ⟑ 4 restaurants, room service, wake-up calls, alarm clocks, coffeemakers, newspapers weekdays, cable TV, in-room data ports, minibars, indoor pool, gym, hair salon, massage, sauna, steam room, billiards, bar, shops, dry cleaning, laundry service, concierge, concierge floor, business services, meeting rooms, parking (fee), some pets allowed, no-smoking floors ⊟ AE, D, DC, MC, V $-$$$$.

RENAISSANCE CHICAGO HOTEL. Plush floral carpets, tapestry upholstery, crystal-bead chandeliers, and French provincial furniture make public areas rich. Rooms have sitting areas and rounded windows with spectacular river views. The hotel is a mile from the start/finish area, and adds pasta specials to its menus on marathon weekend. A small on-site spa offers massage and other services. ⊠ 1 W. Wacker Dr., Loop, 60601 ☎ 312/372-7200

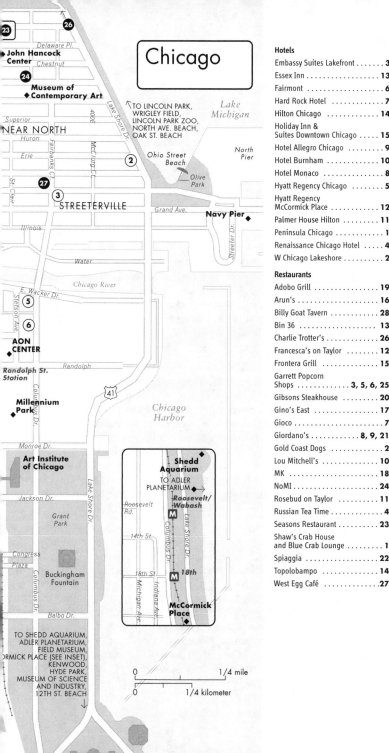

Chicago

TO LINCOLN PARK, WRIGLEY FIELD, LINCOLN PARK ZOO, NORTH AVE. BEACH, OAK ST. BEACH

TO SHEDD AQUARIUM, ADLER PLANETARIUM, FIELD MUSEUM, ORMICK PLACE (SEE INSET), KENWOOD, HYDE PARK, MUSEUM OF SCIENCE AND INDUSTRY, 12TH ST. BEACH

or 800/468-3571 ⊕ www.marriott.com ⌨ 513 rooms, 40 suites ⚬ 2 restaurants, café, 24-hr room service, wake-up calls, alarm clocks, coffeemakers, newspapers, robes, cable TV with movies and video games, in-room data ports, minibars, indoor pool, 24-hr gym, hair salon, hot tub, sauna, spa, bar, lounge, shops, babysitting, dry cleaning, laundry service, concierge, concierge floor, business services, meeting rooms, car rental, parking (fee), no-smoking floors ▤ AE, D, DC, MC, V $$-$$$$.

Near North

EMBASSY SUITES LAKEFRONT. Every guest in this all-suites hotel has views of either Lake Michigan or the Chicago skyscrapers. Rooms have separate bedrooms and living rooms. The sleek, glass atrium bustles during the complimentary cooked-to-order breakfast and evening manager's reception. The night before the race, the hotel offers a special pasta buffet. The marathon start/finish area is 1½ miles away. ✉ 511 N. Columbus Dr., Near North, 60611 ☎ 312/836-5900 or 888/903-8884 ⊕ www.chicagoembassy. com ⌨ 455 suites ⚬ Restaurant, room service, wake-up calls, alarm clocks, coffeemakers, newspapers weekdays, cable TV with movies and video games, in-room data ports, minibars, microwaves, refrigerators, Wi-Fi (fee), indoor pool, gym, hot tub, sauna, bar, cinema, shop, dry cleaning, laundry facilities, concierge, business services, meeting rooms, airport shuttle, parking (fee), no-smoking rooms ▤ AE, D, DC, MC, V $-$$$.

★ **PENINSULA CHICAGO.** If you really want to pamper yourself post-race, this is the place to stay. Free water and bananas are provided marathon morning in the lobby, as is transportation to the starting line. Post-race, you'll love the large glass-enclosed shower and deep soaking tub, above which is a steam-free TV with a DVD player. Make reservations well in advance for a massage at the stunning Peninsula Spa, featuring breathtaking city views. Therapists can also come to your room and provide either massage or a special milk bath in that heavenly tub. ✉ 108 E. Superior St., Near North, 60611 ☎ 312/337-2888 or 866/288-8889 ⊕ www.chicago.peninsula.com ⌨ 291 rooms, 48 suites ⚬ 4 restaurants, 24-hr room service, wake-up calls, alarm clocks, newspapers, robes, cable TV with movies, in-room data ports, in-room safes, minibars, free Wi-Fi, indoor pool, gym, hot tub, spa, bar, dry cleaning, laundry service, concierge, business services, meeting rooms, parking (fee), no-smoking floors ▤ AE, D, DC, MC, V $$$$.

W CHICAGO LAKESHORE. This hotel is just under 2 miles from the start/finish area, and adds pasta dishes to its menus on marathon weekend. Before the race, a "grab'n'go" station is available for runners to buy bananas, water, and other snacks. Comfortable rooms have bathrooms with Aveda bath products and shutters that open for constant views of either downtown or the lake. The hotel's "whatever/whenever" desk is at your service 24 hours a day. In-room massage is available, or check out Bliss, the full-service spa. ✉ 644 N. Lake Shore Dr., Near North, 60611 ☎ 312/943-9200 or 888/627-9034 ⊕ www.starwood. com/whotels ⌨ 490 rooms, 30 suites ⚬ Restaurant, 24-hr room service, wake-up calls, alarm clocks, coffeemakers, newspapers weekdays, robes, cable TV with movies, in-room data ports, in-room safes, minibars, indoor pool, 24-hr gym, hair salon, spa, bar, lobby lounge, babysitting, dry cleaning, laundry service, concierge, business services, meeting rooms, airport shuttle, parking (fee), some pets allowed (fee), no-smoking floors ▤ AE, D, DC, MC, V $-$$$.

AND YOU'RE OFF . . .

The Expo

With more than 150 exhibitors, the Chicago Marathon Health and Fitness Expo is massive. You'll find any running item you could possibly want, plus plenty you never knew you wanted. Look for lectures on topics like tackling the course, preventing injury, tips for debut marathoners, and marathon recovery. Speakers have included such running luminaries as Frank Shorter and Hal Higdon.

If you have a time goal for your race, or you don't want to get caught up in the excitement and start too fast, join one of the New Balance pacing teams (look for the booth at the expo). These are led by experienced marathoners, who can finish in a set time. Pace leaders will run anywhere from a 3:00 race to a 5:45 race, with 13 increments in between. There's no cost to join; just sign up at the expo to get your pace-team bib emblazoned with your goal time (e.g., 4:30), then meet your group at the starting line.

The expo runs all day Friday and Saturday before the race. To avoid crowds, try to go early Friday. The expo is at the McCormick Place Convention Center, and free shuttle buses run regularly between it and several Chicago locations from 8:30 AM to 8:30 PM both Friday and Saturday. Check your confirmation brochure for shuttle stops. Alternatively, consider an easy stroll to and from the expo along Lake Michigan. It's a trek from some hotels, but the views are lovely, and you might find it's a great way to get in some light prerace exercise.

Race Day

The Course

The Chicago Marathon starts and finishes in Grant Park, along Columbus Drive. The area has all the amenities you'll need both before and after the race, including information kiosks in case you get lost. Gear check opens at 5:30 AM, the wheelchair marathon begins at 7:55, and the rest of the field starts at 8. Arrive in time to check your gear, grab free water and sports drinks, use the portable toilets, and enter your starting corral. Corrals are color-coded, matching the color on your bib, and separate the field into five groups: elite, sub-elite, competitive, preferred, and open. (Wheelchair marathoners have their own corral off to the side.) The open corral is further divided by pace per mile (8-minute mile, 10:30-minute mile, etc.); make sure you line up with your expected race pace.

At 8 AM, Sinatra's "My Kind of Town" and "Chicago" blare from loudspeakers, and you're off and zooming through River North and Old Town. You then continue north to Lincoln

Chicago
Race Route

Lake Michigan

West Addison St.

♦ **Wrigley Field**

Western Av.
Damen Av.
Ashland Av.
Clark St.
Broadway
N. Lake
Lake Shore Drive

W. Belmont Av.

Lincoln Park

Racine Av.
Halsted Av.
Diversey Pkwy.
Lincoln Av.

Fullerton Av.

Cannon Dr.

Armitage Av.

Stockton Dr.

Damen Av.

90 94

La Salle Dr.

North Av.

Division St.

41

Chicago St.

Orleans St.
La Salle St.
State Pkwy.
Michigan Av.

Grand St.

Grand St.

Lake St.

Washington Blvd.
Halfway Point

Adams St.
290

Jackson Blvd.

◇ **MARATHON START**

Eisenhower Expwy.
Harrison St.

Ogden Av.

Taylor St.
Roosevelt Rd.

MARATHON FINISH

◇

♦ **Field Museum of Natural History**

Grant Park

90 94

Canal St.
Chicago River
State St.
Michigan Av.

Burnham Park

18th St.

Western Av.

Morgan St.
Canalport Av.

Archer Av.

Cermak Rd.

55

KEY
= = = = *Marathon Route*

26th St.

Archer Av.

31st St.

Halsted St.

33rd St.

Wentworth Av.
La Salle St.
Dr. Martin Luther King Jr. Dr.

35th St.

55

41

0 _____ 1 mile

0 _____ 1 kilometer

NIGHT-BEFORE PASTA DINNER

The official prerace pasta dinner is held at the Hilton Chicago, race headquarters. Tickets cost $25, and only 2,000 are available, so order yours when you register for the race. The sit-down three-course dinner includes salad, rolls, pasta, and dessert. Drink options include water, beer, or wine. There's only one seating, usually at 6 PM.

Of course, with 40,000 race participants and only 2,000 dinner seats, lots of people will be turning instead to Chicago's fantastic restaurants, such as these:

FRANCESCA'S ON TAYLOR. It's a standout among the many Italian places on this stretch of Taylor Street. You might find ravioli stuffed with a spinach-and-artichoke mix or blue marlin with sea scallops and roasted peppers. Veal is usually the only meat on the menu, but all your basic pastas are available, plus fish and chicken dishes. ⊠ 1400 W. Taylor St., Near South ☎ 312/829–2828 ⊕ www.miafrancesca.com ☰ AE, D, DC, MC, V ⊘ No lunch weekends $–$$.

GIOCO. The decor is distressed-urban, with plaster-spattered brick walls and well-worn hardwood floors, but the menu is country-Italian, with rustic fare like homemade penne with prosciutto, grilled lamb chops, and sausage with beans. The Speakeasy Room, a private dining space with its own rear-alley entrance, is an homage to the building's colorful past during Prohibition. ⊠ 1312 S. Wabash Ave., Near South ☎ 312/939–3870 ⊕ www.gioco-chicago. com ☰ AE, D, DC, MC, V ⊘ No lunch weekends $–$$$$.

ROSEBUD ON TAYLOR. This extremely busy restaurant specializes in old-fashioned southern Italian cuisine. It has one of the best red sauces in town, and the roasted peppers, homemade sausage, and exquisitely prepared pastas aren't to be missed. Some dishes have heavy sauces—order carefully so you don't weigh yourself down for the race. Come early to beat the crowds. ⊠ 1500 W. Taylor St., Near South ☎ 312/942–1117 ⊕ www.rosebudrestaurants. com ☰ AE, D, DC, MC, V ⊘ No lunch Sun. $–$$$$.

Park, passing one of the nation's oldest zoos, and Wrigleyville, home of the Chicago Cubs' Wrigley Field. Turning south, you'll cruise through the gorgeous area of Lake View, home to the Mile 8 aid station, sponsored by Frontrunners/Frontwalkers Chicago, a gay and lesbian running club. Their aid station attracts huge, exuberant crowds, it's always fully themed (e.g., "Hairspray" in 2005, the "Cher" show I caught in 2000), and it's a definite course highlight.

Leaving Lake View, you continue back through many of the neighborhoods you passed before, until you reach Greektown and a chorus of "Opaa!" from the spectators. From Greece you head to Italy—Chicago's Little Italy—where it's not uncommon to see dancers and bands playing old Italian songs. As you cross into Pilsen, note the colorful murals, a nod to the Hispanic community here. Chinatown is your next destination; run through its gate and marvel at a Chinese lion dancing in the street. By now you're at Mile 22 and in the homestretch—just push yourself through Bridgeport and the South Loop (where you'll recognize McCormick Place, home of the expo), before zooming back to the finish line in Grant Park.

At no point will you be lacking entertainment. Spectators' cheers will buoy your every step. Cheerleading squads compete to be the best motivators. Vote online for your favorites after the race; the winning squad collects $1,000. Live bands play nearly every mile, plus you'll see dancers, DJs, and huge entertainment zones hosted by marathon sponsors. With practically the whole city cheering for you, your spirit will be well tended. But what about your body? Not to worry: 17 aid stations provide water, sports drinks, toilets, and medical assistance, plus there's energy gel at Mile 17.

When you cross the finish line, just keep moving. Someone will remove your ChampionChip, someone else will give you a Mylar blanket, and another fabulous someone will drape a medal around your neck. You'll be directed to the runner refreshment area and its bagels, bananas, and beverages, then you'll emerge into the main start/finish area. Expect organized chaos: live music, plus swarms of spectators and runners. If you plan to meet someone, head to the runner reunion area around Buckingham Fountain (or the team reunion area if you're with a team), then enjoy the finish-area amenities: the beer tent (free beer for runners!), runner-update tent (where you can check other runners' progress), massage tent (free massages for runners—well worth the long waits), and merchandise booths.

The course remains open for 6½ hours, and transportation to the finish line is available for runners who can't make it to the end. Those who do finish the race within 6½ hours will receive a results postcard, a finisher's certificate, and the official race results book. Runners who finish in three hours or less also become members of the New Balance Three Hour Club, and receive a special gift from New Balance in the mail.

Spectating

The marathon truly caters to spectators, even working with the CTA to print the excellent "Spectator and Transportation Guide." It lists 11 viewing areas along the course, and how best to reach them via public transportation. Look for the guide at the CTA expo booth, at downtown stores and hotels, on the marathon Web site, and at Starbucks branches throughout the city. As a marathon partner, many Starbucks branches are race-day Hot Spot Runner Update Centers, where you can get computer updates on your favorite runner's progress. The centers are mapped out in the spectator guide, online, and in the race confirmation booklet.

There are so many spectating options, it can be tough to pin down a plan of action. I'll suggest a couple of itineraries, both of which involve a terrific breakfast and a good deal of walking. Naturally, you can pick and choose from among the cheering spots I suggest, use public transportation to get to them, or use the marathon's course map and spectator guide to plan your own route.

One possibility is to watch the race start, then walk west on Jackson to State, where you can catch the runners just after Mile 2. Cheer your brains out, then continue west on Jackson to Lou Mitchell's restaurant. After breakfast simply head north a block or so to Adams,

BREAKFAST SPOTS

These restaurants are in the ¢–$$ range, though breakfast at the Seasons Restaurant may run a little higher.

★ **LOU MITCHELL'S.** Shelve your calorie and cholesterol concerns; Lou Mitchell's warrants it. Breakfast here is not to be missed. Start the day with double-yolk eggs and homemade hash browns by the skillet. Though out-the-door waits are common, tables turn rapidly and staffers dole out doughnut holes and Milk Duds to pacify pangs. ⊠ 565 W. Jackson Blvd., West Loop ☎ 312/939-3111 ▤ No credit cards ⊗ No dinner.

SEASONS RESTAURANT. This beautiful restaurant sits high above the Magnificent Mile within the Four Seasons hotel, and offers beautiful city views. The opulent room is uncommonly comfortable and perfectly suited to both power brokers and families. Enjoy an early breakfast or make reservations for one of Chicago's best Sunday brunches. ⊠ Four Seasons Hotel, 120 E. Delaware Pl., Near North ☎ 312/280-8800 ▤ AE, D, DC, MC, V.

WEST EGG CAFE. Near the Magnificent Mile and Navy Pier, this is a fantastic place for creative egg dishes like the Bleu Bayou: an egg, blue cheese, spinach, bacon, and tomato scramble. Or try Fitness French Toast, made with bagel slices dipped in egg whites and served with apple compote. ⊠ 620 N. Fairbanks Ct., Near North ☎ 312/280-8366 ▤ AE, D, DC, MC, V.

---

where you'll see the runners at just about the halfway point. Then make your way several blocks southwest to Halsted and Taylor to watch them at Mile 17, before heading back east to the finish area.

Alternatively, skip the very crowded start and catch your runner just before Mile 1, at Columbus and Grand. From there you can easily walk to the West Egg Cafe (north on Columbus, which becomes North Fairbanks Court), or walk farther to the Seasons Restaurant (north on Columbus/Fairbanks to Ohio, make a left to go west to Michigan Avenue, then make a right to go north about eight blocks to Delaware Court, where you'll make a left and quickly see the Four Seasons hotel). After breakfast, walk southwest to Wells and Hubbard, just before Mile 12, to cheer your runner again. Continue south on Wells to Roosevelt, then walk west on Roosevelt to Halsted. Go north on Halsted a block or so, and you're in the perfect spot to catch your favorite runner just after Mile 17. From here, you can head east to the finish area.

If you really want a prime spot for the race finish, consider 26.2 Curb Crew Advantage tickets. They're $75 each and get you special seating at the finish area, plus access to the 26.2 Curb Crew Advantage tent, which offers a Continental breakfast, portable toilets, computer access to check runners' progress, and a feed of the marathon TV broadcast. Ticket holders have unlimited in-and-out access to the seating area and tent from 7 AM to 2 PM. If you're interested, buy right away. There are only 600 tickets; they go on sale through the marathon Web site around August, and sell out very quickly.

The year the National AIDS Marathon Training Program came to Chicago, their flyers papered the city and boldly proclaimed that if you joined, even if you'd never run a step before, program staffers could train you to run the Chicago Marathon. Several of Jim Pickett's friends signed up, and watching their accomplishments, their joy as they shared the camaraderie of their "pace groups," their elation as they pushed themselves week after week and added mile upon mile to their training runs, Jim's heart swelled with a feeling of . . .

. . . pity, really. Absolute pity. Clearly his friends weren't right in the head. Who ran 26.2 miles? What kind of insanity was that? Oh sure, it was for a good cause. Everyone who trained with the program had to raise at least $1,400, all of which would go to the AIDS Foundation of Chicago, a cause near and dear to Jim's heart. Not only is he HIV-positive himself, but he's also a staunch advocate for HIV prevention programs and for the rights of those afflicted with the disease. He's intimately aware of the gaps in this country's AIDS policy; the stigma still attached to the disease; the lack of quality health insurance, which leaves many unable to seek treatment; and, most of all, the woeful underfunding of prevention. So Jim was all for raising money for the AIDS Foundation of Chicago—but by running a marathon? Surely there were saner routes to altruism.

Still, Jim wanted to support his poor, deluded friends, so on race day he volunteered at the Frontrunners' aid station. When his friends approached, Jim was shocked. Not only didn't they seem miserable, but they absolutely radiated energy. And they weren't running—they were floating. They laughed, they smiled, they *glowed*. In that instant, Jim changed his mind: he wanted in. He decided to sign up for the next year's training program and run the Chicago Marathon.

As Jim began running with the National AIDS Marathon Training Program, he was impressed by the way it combined the very personal goal of running a marathon with the very global goal of fighting the battle against HIV and AIDS. Some people, like Jim, came to the program as established AIDS warriors. Others knew little about the disease but liked the idea of raising charitable funds as a quid pro quo for terrific training. With branches in Chicago, Los Angeles, San Francisco, and Washington, D.C., the program provides pace groups for runners of all speeds, from penguins to gazelles. For six months the groups congregate one day a week for a long run, which builds from 3 miles to the ultimate 26.2. In addition, members are encouraged to run on their own at least two additional days a week. Following this plan, 98% of runners who complete the program, regardless of their past running experience, also complete the marathon.

As a rule, Jim is fiercely independent. But within this program, he found the power of a team. He and his pace group worked together, encouraging and entertaining one another through difficult runs. And every donor became a member of his team, someone for whom Jim needed to deliver. Jim was also very aware of the people who would be on the receiving end of his fundraising—folks who needed and deserved his best efforts. All these people motivated Jim to get out of bed for every training run, bar none.

Then came the marathon itself, and yes, "The Glow." Though he admits there were moments around Mile 21 where he wasn't exactly glowing, on the whole he had the time of his life. Everyone running for charity seemed to get an added oomph from the spectators, especially the AIDS marathoners, whose bright yellow singlets made them impossible to miss. Jim's had his name emblazoned across the top, and for 26.2 miles he heard the crowd screaming for him. It was like being a rock star. He smiled and waved the whole way, and by the end he knew he was hooked: he'd do it again the next year. At this writing Jim had just completed his second Chicago Marathon and had raised more than $8,000 for the AIDS Foundation of Chicago, part of the more than $2 million the foundation has received through the National AIDS Marathon Training Program.

As I mentioned, even before his marathoning days, Jim was no stranger to HIV/AIDS patient advocacy, and he had found creative ways to reach people with his message. He's a phenomenal writer, both scathingly witty and searingly honest. (Google him and read some of his columns; you'll see what I mean.) After he was diagnosed positive in 1995, he began a column called "Sick" for a gay weekly. It was very personal—an unpacking of "the schizophrenia that is being positive; good, bad, and ugly." After that, Jim worked with the Chicago Department of Public Health to create *Faces of AIDS*, two books filled with stories of Midwesterners living with HIV. The books spawned a photo documentary of 100 portraits, which traveled around the country. Yet becoming a marathoner allowed Jim to reach people in new, surprisingly powerful ways.

Before long runs, all AIDS marathoners at a training site gather for announcements: some practical, some motivational, and some about HIV/

AIDS issues and why their fundraising efforts are so appreciated. During one of these sessions, Jim spoke about his experiences living with HIV. The revelation surprised many people; though they'd been running with him for a long time, many had no idea of his status, and the knowledge forced them to look at people living with HIV differently. One person listening to Jim speak that day wasn't a runner at all. He was a young kid; his boyfriend was running, and he had come to show support and volunteer. He had just tested HIV+ and was reeling—until he heard Jim speak. But it wasn't just Jim's words; the kid saw this guy, positive for many years, in shorts and a singlet, and about to run 26.2 miles. It gave the kid hope, and as Jim says, "You can't quantify how great that makes you feel."

Before he started training for the 2004 Chicago Marathon, Jim had never run more than 7 miles and even that was a stretch. So what would he tell anyone afraid they couldn't handle the miles? "You can do it, honey. You can absolutely do it. The [National AIDS Marathon Training] program is structured in such a way that if you follow it, you *will* do a marathon, and you'll be more than 90% likely to do it without injuries. Amazing people will support you along the way, and they'll make it fun. Yes, it's a time commitment, but you get back much more than you give. You get back something for your spirit, a sense of connection to humanity and your community. If you have an inkling to do it, come go for it." ■

Celebrate

After the race, head back to your room, shower, rest, and prepare to live it up at the fantastic post-race party from 6 PM to 11 PM. It's usually held at the Navy Pier and has live music, food and drink, and dancing. Every marathoner gets a free ticket to the party plus two complimentary drink tickets. Friends and family are welcome and can buy $15 entry tickets at the expo or at the door. Shuttle buses run from area hotels (check the marathon Web site for exact locations) to the party every 20 to 30 minutes between 5:30 and 7:30 PM, then begin service back to the hotels. Don't miss the chance to let loose, have fun, and savor your accomplishment with those who shared the experience.

BEYOND THE FINISH LINE

Replacing 2,620 Calories

Deep-dish pizza, decked-out dogs, creative caramel corn, haute cuisine—it's all here. Chicago's more than 7,000 restaurants include some of the country's finest (and priciest) eateries as well as simple storefront ethnic places and solid, unpretentious pubs.

The Loop

★ **GIORDANO'S.** It's the sauce that does it; no place else has a sauce this spicy, tangy, and delicious. The place serves thin-crust pizza, pasta dishes, and sandwiches, but the real reason to come is for the famous stuffed pizza. Toppings range from such basic favorites as pepperoni and mushrooms to more gourmet options like shrimp, broccoli, and pineapple. Expect to wait in line if you come at lunchtime; it's worth it. ⊠ 310 W. Randolph St., Loop ☎ 312/201-1441 ⊠ 223 W. Jackson Blvd., Loop ☎ 312/583-9400 ⊠ 730 N. Rush St., Near North ☎ 312/951-0747 ⊕ www.giordanos.com ♣ Reservations not accepted ▭ AE, DC, MC, V $.

GOLD COAST DOGS. What makes a dog a Chicago dog? First, the all-beef frankfurter snaps when you bite it, because of the natural casing (and here they're char-grilled as opposed to being steamed). Then there are the toppings: mustard, relish, onions, tomatoes, a pickle, peppers, and a shake of celery salt. If you're used to just meat and ketchup in a bun, you're in for a treat. ⊠ 159 N. Wabash St., Loop ☎ 312/917-1677 ▭ AE, D, MC, V ¢-$.

RUSSIAN TEA TIME. It's next to the Symphony Center and just steps from the Art Institute. Mahogany trim, samovars, and balalaika music set the stage for authentic dishes from Russia and neighboring republics (the owners hail from Uzbekistan). Highlights include Ukrainian borscht, blinis with caviar and salmon, lamb kebabs, and chicken-and-rice-stuffed cabbage. Top-quality caviars and ice-cold vodkas and champagnes entice the deep-pocketed. Afternoon tea is a welcome post-museum refresher. ⊠ 77 E. Adams St., Loop ☎ 312/360-0000 ⊕ www.russianteatime.com ♣ Reservations essential ▭ AE, D, MC, V $-$$$.

Near North

ADOBO GRILL. This lively Mexican restaurant perfects the basics and edges into more daring dishes. Guacamole is prepared table-side, a bit of culinary theater ensuring absolutely fresh dip at the spice level you prefer. Diners tend to linger over flavorful fare like grilled quail and red snapper Veracruzaná (deep-fried). The bar prepares better-than-average margaritas and stocks an impressive number of sipping tequilas—there's even a tequila sommelier to help with selection. ⊠ 1610 N. Wells St., Near North ☎ 312/266-7999 ⊕ www.adobogrill.com ⊟ AE, D, DC, MC, V ⊙ No lunch weekdays $-$$.

★ **BILLY GOAT TAVERN.** The late comedian John Belushi immortalized the Goat's short-order cooks on *Saturday Night Live* for barking, "No Coke! Pepsi!" and "No fries! Cheeps!" at customers. They still do the shtick at this subterranean hole-in-the-wall. Griddle-fried "cheezborgers" are the featured chow, and people-watching is the favored sport. ⊠ 430 N. Michigan Ave., lower level, Near North ☎ 312/222-1525 ⊕ www. billygoattavern.com ⊟ No credit cards ¢-$.

★ **GARRETT POPCORN SHOPS.** You might think popcorn is popcorn. Not true. Garrett's is beyond mouthwatering, which is why Chicagoans line up, sometimes out the door and down the street, to get a bag. You really can't go wrong with any flavor, but the cashew caramel crisp is so good it doesn't seem possible. ⊠ 670 N. Michigan Ave., Near North ⊠ 26 E. Randolph St., Loop ⊠ 4 E. Madison St., Loop ⊠ 2 W. Jackson Blvd., Downtown South ☎ 312/944-4730 ⊕ www.garrettpopcorn.com ⊟ AE, D, DC, MC, V ¢.

GIBSONS STEAKHOUSE. Gibsons is renowned for overwhelming portions, good service, and celebrity spotting. Generous steaks and chops center the menu, but there are plenty of fish options, including planked whitefish and massive Australian lobster tails. One dessert will feed a table of four. Reservations aren't required but are near essential given the many fans. ⊠ 1028 N. Rush St., Near North ☎ 312/266-8999 ⊕ www.gibsonssteakhouse.com ⚑ Reservations essential ⊟ AE, D, DC, MC, V $-$$$$.

GINO'S EAST. There are other good things on the menu, but the deep-dish pizza is so fresh, flavorful, and filling, that you'll want to get right to it. The cornmeal-dusted crust is particularly delicious. Graffiti from past diners covers nearly every surface in this place, which can get crowded. It's worth the wait to get in. ⊠ 633 N. Wells St., Near North ☎ 312/943-1124 ⊕ www.ginoseast.com ⚑ Reservations not accepted ⊟ AE, D, DC, MC, V $.

NOMI. NoMI's seventh-floor view—overlooking the Water Tower and Michigan Avenue beyond—is arguably the prettiest in town, and the food is equally special. There's a strong French influence, offset with Asian and Mediterranean accents. One must-try dish is the risotto, whether made with roasted beets and chanterelles or prosciutto and mascarpone cheese. ⊠ Park Hyatt Hotel, 800 N. Michigan Ave., Near North ☎ 312/239-4030 ⊕ www. nomirestaurant.com ⊟ AE, D, DC, MC, V $$$-$$$$.

SPIAGGIA. Refined Italian cooking dished alongside three-story views of Lake Michigan make Spiaggia one of the city's top eateries. Chef Tony Mantuano prepares elegantly simple, seasonal dishes such as ravioli filled with purple potatoes and leeks, grilled squab with truffle sauce, or Mediterranean bass with braised fennel. Oenophiles consider the wine list scholarly. For Spiaggia fare, minus the luxury ingredients, try lunch or dinner at the casual Cafe Spiaggia next door. ⊠ 980 N. Michigan Ave., Near North ☎ 312/280-2750

⊕ www.spiaggiarestaurant.com ⌁ Reservations essential ⛪ Jacket required ▤ AE, D, DC, MC, V ☺ No lunch $$–$$$$.

Far North Side

ARUN'S. The finest Thai restaurant in Chicago—some say in the country—is also the most expensive, with multicourse menus for a flat $85. Your meal might include intricate golden pastry baskets filled with diced shrimp and shiitake mushrooms, whole tamarind snapper, or veal medallions with ginger-lemongrass sauce. Expect the freshest ingredients and beautiful presentations. The quiet dining room has lots of natural wood, complemented by Thai art. Arun's out-of-the-way location in a residential neighborhood on the northwest side doesn't discourage its fans—locals and visiting foodies alike. ✉ 4156 N. Kedzie Ave., Irving Park ☎ 773/539-1909 ⊕ www.arunsthai.com ⌁ Reservations essential ▤ AE, D, DC, MC, V ☺ Closed Mon. No lunch $$$$.

Lincoln Park

★ CHARLIE TROTTER'S. Plan well in advance to dine at top toque Charlie Trotter's namesake. The experimental Trotter prepares his menus daily from the best of what's available globally. Past raves include antelope strudel with wild mushrooms and foie-gras ravioli with mango and lemongrass sauce. Menus follow a multicourse, $130 degustation format ($100 for the vegetarian version). For a worthwhile splurge order the wines-to-match option. ✉ 816 W. Armitage Ave., Lincoln Park ☎ 773/248-6228 ⊕ www.charlietrotters.com ⌁ Reservations essential ⛪ Jacket required ▤ AE, DC, MC, V ☺ Closed Sun. Sometimes open Mon. No lunch $$$$.

River North

BIN 36. This hip hybrid—fine restaurant, lively wine bar, and wineshop—pours wines by the bottle, glass, half glass, and as "flights" of multiple 1½-ounce tastings. The menu also encourages sampling, with lots of small-plate grazing choices. Contemporary entrées, such as braised lamb shank and peppercorn-crusted swordfish, are listed with two wine recommendations each. An all-glass west wall and 35-foot ceilings lend loft looks to the sprawling bar and dining room, which is open between standard mealtimes. ✉ 339 N. Dearborn St., River North ☎ 312/755-WINE ⊕ www.bin36.com ▤ AE, D, DC, MC, V $–$$.

★ FRONTERA GRILL. Devotees of chef-owner Rick Bayless queue up for his distinct fare at this casual restaurant, brightly trimmed in Mexican folk art. Bayless annually visits Mexico with his entire staff in tow. Servers, consequently, are highly knowledgeable about the food. Look for salmon in pumpkin-seed mole, pork in a pasilla-pepper sauce, and chiles rellenos. Since the restaurant accepts reservations only for large parties, arrive early or anticipate a two-margarita wait. ✉ 445 N. Clark St., River North ☎ 312/661-1434 ⊕ www.fronterakitchens.com ▤ AE, D, DC, MC, V ☺ Closed Sun. and Mon. $$–$$$.

MK. Foodies and fashionistas favor owner-chef Michael Kornick's ultrahip spot for its sleek look and elegant menu. Occupying a renovated warehouse, MK balances brick walls and soaring ceilings with fine linens, expensive flatware, and designer wine stems. Start with chilled oysters, or, if you're feeling indulgent, the sautéed veal sweetbreads with mushrooms and smoked bacon. Enjoy entrées like a whitefish/lobster combination. Imaginative desserts end the meal on a high note. ⊠ 868 N. Franklin St., River North ☎ 312/482–9179 ⊕ www.mkchicago.com ⊲ Reservations essential ☰ AE, DC, MC, V ⊘ No lunch $$-$$$$.

SHAW'S CRAB HOUSE AND BLUE CRAB LOUNGE. The city's chief specialist in bivalves nurtures a split personality, spanning a dressy main dining room in spiffed-up loft digs and a lively exposed-brick bar where shell shuckers work harder than the barkeeps. Preparations tend toward the simple and the classic; try the fried calamari, steamed blue mussels, and Maryland crab cakes for appetizers. Crab, lobster, and shrimp are menu standards, along with a half dozen varieties of fresh oysters. ⊠ 21 E. Hubbard St., River North ☎ 312/527-2722 ☰ AE, D, DC, MC, V $-$$$$.

★ **TOPOLOBAMPO.** Chef-owner Rick Bayless wrote the book on regional Mexican cuisine—several books, actually—and in Topolobampo he takes his faithfully regional food upscale. The menu showcases game, seasonal fruits and vegetables, and exotic preparations. Tequila-cured salmon and pheasant roasted in banana leaves are two examples. Good service and an interesting wine list add to the appeal. ⊠ 445 N. Clark St., River North ☎ 312/661-1434 ⊕ www.fronterakitchens.com ⊲ Reservations essential ☰ AE, D, DC, MC, V ⊘ Closed Sun. and Mon. No lunch Sat. $$-$$$$.

Sightseeing on (and off) Your Feet

Chicago's variety is dazzling. You'll find just about anything you want to see, from great architecture, to museums, to theater, to sports; there's even a beach scene. The only question is where to begin. And the answer? It all depends how you're feeling.

I Feel Great!

★ **FIELD MUSEUM.** More than 6 *acres* of exhibits fill this museum, which explores the world's cultures and environments. Shrink to the size of a bug to burrow beneath the surface of the soil in the Underground Adventure exhibit ($7 extra). You'll come face to face with a wolf spider twice your size and have other encounters with the life that teems under our feet. As part of Inside Ancient Egypt, the remarkable Mastaba complex includes a working canal, a living marsh where papyrus is grown, a shrine to the cat goddess Bastet, burial-ceremony artifacts, and 23 mummies. Don't miss the Life over Time: DNA to Dinosaurs exhibit, which traces the evolution of life on Earth from one-cell organisms to the great reptiles. Kids especially enjoy 65-million-year-old "Sue," the largest and most complete Tyrannosaurus rex fossil ever found. More than 600 other fossils are on exhibit, including gigantic posed dinosaur skeletons. The DinoStore sells a mind-boggling assortment of dinosaur-related merchandise. ⊠ 1400 S. Lake Shore Dr., Museum Campus ☎ 312/922-9410 ⊕ www.fieldmuseum.org ⊠ $12; free Mon. and Tues. in Jan., Feb., and Sept.–3rd wk of Dec. ⊘ Daily 9–5.

★ **FOLLOW THE BIKE PATH.** Chicago's 20-odd-mile lakefront bicycle path has fabulous views of both the lake and the skyline. If your legs are feeling strong, take in vistas by walking, biking, or skating the path. **Bike Chicago** (⊠ 600 E. Grand Ave., Near North (Navy Pier) ☎ 312/595-9600 ⊙ Apr.-Oct. ⊠ 239 E. Randolph St., Loop (Millennium Park) ☎ 888/BIKE-WAY ⊕ www.bikechicago.com) rents bikes and skates. Fees start at $8.75 an hour and $29 a day. The company also offers free maps outlining suggested rides and self-guided tours. **Londo Mondo** (⊠ 1100 N. Dearborn St., Near North ☎ 312/751-2794 ⊕ www.londomondo.com) rents and sells skates and accessories. Rentals are $7 an hour, $20 a day.

LINCOLN PARK ZOO. Begun in 1868, many of the big houses, such as the lion house, were built in the classical brick typical of 19th-century zoos. In the newer exhibits the animals' natural habitats are re-created. The zoo is noted for its great ape house, with 24 gorillas. Because the park participates in breeding programs, there are usually several babies about. The spectacular glass-dome Regenstein Small Mammal and Reptile House has simulated jungle, river, and forest environments for animal residents, including the much-loved koalas. The zoo has a large-mammal house (elephants, giraffes, black rhinos); a primate house; a bird house with a lush free-flight area and a waterfall; and a huge polar bear pool with two bears. For youngsters, there are the children's zoo, the Farm in the Zoo (farm animals and a learning center with films and demonstrations), and the Conservation Station, with hands-on activities. ⊠ 2001 N. Clark St., Lincoln Park ☎ 312/742-2000 ⊕ www.lpzoo.com ☜ Free ⊙ Mar.-Memorial Day and Labor Day-Nov., daily 9-6; Memorial Day-Labor Day weekdays 9-6, weekends 9-7; Nov.-Feb., daily 9-5.

I Feel Pretty Good

★ **ART INSTITUTE OF CHICAGO.** Some of the world's most famous art is here, including an incredibly strong collection of impressionist and postimpressionist paintings, with seminal works by Monet, Renoir, Gauguin, and Van Gogh, among others. The museum also has impressive collections of medieval, Renaissance, and modern art. Less well known are its fine holdings in Asian art and photography. The Thorne Miniature Rooms show interior decoration in every historical style; they'll entrance anyone who's ever furnished a dollhouse or built a model. Be sure to visit the Rubloff paperweight collection and the Stock Exchange Room, a reconstruction of the trading floor of the old Chicago Stock Exchange.

If you're with a child, make an early stop at the Kraft Education Center downstairs. Kids can choose from an assortment of 25 or so gallery games, some of which come with picture postcards. The museum store has an outstanding collection of art books, calendars, and merchandise related to current exhibits, as well as gift items. ⊠ 111 S. Michigan Ave., Loop ☎ 312/443-3600 ⊕ www.artic.edu ☜ $12, free Tues. ⊙ Mon.-Wed. and Fri. 10:30-4:30, Thurs. 10:30-8, weekends 10-5.

★ **MILLENNIUM PARK.** Built atop a rail yard at the northwest corner of Grant Park, the 24½-acre Millennium Park has turned an eyesore into another of the city's jewels. The showstopper here is Frank Gehry's stunning Jay Pritzker Pavilion. Dramatic ribbons of stainless steel stretching 40 feet into the sky look like petals wrapping the stage.

Spanish sculptor Jaume Plensa's Crown Fountain at the park's southwest corner has two 50-foot-high glass blocks displaying video images of people. Children squeal with delight under the sudden shoots of water as the faces on the fountain appear to spit on them. Cloud Gate, which graces the park between Washington and Madison streets, is Anish Kapoor's 60-foot-long, 30-foot-high elliptical sculpture of seamless polished steel, which has been likened to a giant jelly bean. In summer, the 3 acres of carefully manicured plantings bloom in the Lurie Garden; in winter, the McCormick Tribune Ice Rink is open for public skates. Stop by the **Welcome Center** (✉ 201 E. Randolph St. ☎ 312/742–2963 ⊙ Oct.–Mar., daily 10–4) for park maps and event information. ✉ Bounded by Michigan Ave., Columbus Dr., Randolph Dr., and Monroe St., Loop ⊕ www.millenniumpark.org ✎ Free ⊙ Daily 6 AM–11 PM.

★**NAVY PIER.** No matter the season, Navy Pier is a fun place to spend a few hours. Constructed in 1916 as a commercial-shipping pier, it was renamed in honor of the Navy in 1927 (the Army got Soldier Field). The once-deserted pier contains an outdoor landscaped area with gardens, a fountain, a carousel, a 15-story Ferris wheel, and an ice-skating rink. Also on the pier is Crystal Gardens, one of the country's largest indoor botanical parks; an IMAX theater; an outdoor beer garden; shopping promenades, restaurants, and bars; and the 57,000-square-foot Chicago Children's Museum, a hands-on environment where kids learn as they play. ⊕ www.navypier.com.

SEARS TOWER. In Chicago, size matters. This soaring 110-story skyscraper was once the world's tallest building. Enter on Jackson Boulevard to take the ear-popping ride to the 103rd-floor skydeck observatory. Video monitors make the 70-second elevator ride fun. On a clear day you can see to Michigan, Wisconsin, and Indiana. (Check on visibility ratings at the security desk before you ride up.) Interactive exhibits tell about Chicago's dreamers, schemers, architects, musicians, writers, and sports stars. Knee-High Chicago, a 4-foot-high exhibit which has cutouts of Chicago sports, history, and cultural icons at a child's-eye level, should entertain the kids. The lower level has a food court, some exhibits, and an eight-minute movie about the city. Don't miss the Calder mobile sculpture *The Universe* in the lobby on the Wacker Drive side. Security is very tight, so figure in a little extra time for your visit to the Skydeck. ✉ 233 S. Wacker Dr., Loop ☎ 312/875–9696 ⊕ www.theskydeck.com ✎ $11.95 ⊙ May–Sept., daily 10–10; Oct.–Apr., daily 10–8.

Let's Take It Slowly

★**ADLER PLANETARIUM & ASTRONOMY MUSEUM.** Opened in 1930 as the first such public structure in the Western Hemisphere, the Adler still has a traditional in-the-round Zeiss planetarium (called the Sky Theater) that shows constellations and planets in the night sky. There's also a Gateway to the Universe gallery where you feel like you're stepping into infinite space. Other galleries house special exhibits and astronomical artifacts. The high-tech Sky Pavilion, a glass structure that wraps around the old building, contains the interactive StarRider Theater. Through control buttons on your armrest, you can choose how you'd like to journey into space; what you see on the screen is based on the majority sentiment of the audience. (Part of the technology is based on aircraft flight simulators.) Also in this building are a telescope terrace and interactive exhibits that in-

WOO-HOO! I'M GONNA SEE OPRAH!

What could be more fitting than seeing *Oprah* when you're in Chicago for the marathon? Were it not for Ms. Winfrey, marathoning would be nowhere near as popular as it is today. For many, it was Oprah's success in tackling the Marine Corps Marathon that transformed the sport from an elite pursuit into something anyone could accomplish. We've all witnessed Oprah's struggles with weight over the years; we know she's not a born athlete. And yet in 1994, she completed her race in 4:29:15, proving that with the right amount of sweat and determination, anyone can run a marathon. Today, many first-timers are intimidated by the idea of 26.2 miles, but they grit their teeth and recite the mantra heard on treadmills and trails across the country: "If Oprah can do it, I can do it."

For free *Oprah* tickets, call **Harpo Studios** (✉ 1058 W. Washington Blvd., Near West Side ☎ 312/591–9222 ⊕ www.oprah.com) weekdays, 10–4 Central Time. The show books audiences only for the current and following month, so try in September for a marathon week taping. When you get through, a staffer will give you the taping schedule and a list of available dates. You can reserve up to four seats for any one taping (all attendees must be at least 18). If you can't get tickets in advance, check the Web site for occasional last-minute tickets via e-mail.

On show day, arrive at Harpo Studios' audience entrance (at the corner of Carpenter and Washington streets) between 7 and 7:30 for a morning taping, or between 11 and 11:30 for an afternoon taping. Tapings end at approximately 11 AM and 3 PM, respectively. If your show is canceled or requires a special audience, Audience Department staffers will let you know and try to reschedule you, though there's no guarantee they can do so during your Chicago visit. Seats are first-come, first-served, so arrive early to check in with your valid photo ID. Dress for the weather—you'll wait outside until the doors open. Upon entering be prepared for a security check: you'll leave cameras, recorders, cell phones, and pagers at the door.

Before or after your taping, grab a bite of decadent diner food with a Creole twist at **Wishbone** (✉ 1001 W. Washington Blvd., Near West Side ☎ 312/ 850–2663 ⊕ www.wishbonechicago.com), just a block from the studio. At breakfast, try shrimp and grits or the savory corn cakes. Lunch items include crawfish cakes and Hoppin' John (peas or beans on rice with cheese, scallions, and tomatoes).

clude 3-D computer animations of the Milky Way and of the birth of the solar system. Additional charges apply for planetarium and interactive shows. ⊠ 1300 S. Lake Shore Dr., Museum Campus ☎ 312/922-STAR ⊕ www.adlerplanetarium.org ⊠ $16 museum and 1 show, $20 museum and 2 shows. Free every Mon. and Tues. mid-Jan.–Feb. and mid-Sept.–3rd wk of Dec. ۞ Labor Day–Memorial Day: daily 9:30–4:30. Memorial Day–Labor Day: daily 9:30–6. Open 1st Fri. of month until 10 PM.

★ JOHN G. SHEDD AQUARIUM. Built in 1930, the Shedd houses more than 8,000 aquatic animals. Amazon Rising takes you on a journey along the banks of the Amazon River with an up-close look at many animals, including piranhas, snakes, and stingrays. You can walk through an underwater kingdom rich with marine biodiversity and coral reefs in the Wild Reef exhibit. Get up close and personal with the "demons of the deep" as dozens of sharks swim the 400,000-gallon habitat exploring one of the world's largest coral reefs. In the spectacular Oceanarium, pools seem to blend into Lake Michigan, which is visible through the huge glass wall. You can have a stare-down with one of the knobby-headed beluga whales (they love to people-watch), observe Pacific white-sided dolphins at play, and explore the simulated Pacific Northwest nature trail. An educational dolphin presentation, scheduled daily, shows natural behaviors, including vocalizing, breaching, and tail-walking. Be sure to check out the underwater viewing windows for the dolphins and whales and the information-packed, hands-on activities on the lower level. ⊠ 1200 S. Lake Shore Dr., Museum Campus ☎ 312/939-2438 ⊕ www.sheddaquarium.org ⊠ $23 all-access pass (main building and Oceanarium, Aquarium, and Wild Reef); $15 Mon. and Tues. mid-Sept.–Feb. ۞ Memorial Day–Labor Day, daily 9–6 (Thurs. until 10 PM); Labor Day–Memorial Day, weekdays 9–5, weekends 9–6.

Ow! No.

JOHN HANCOCK CENTER. The 94th floor has an observation deck, but you can enjoy the same view and avoid the entrance fee and long lines by buying an exorbitantly priced drink and resting your legs in the bar that adjoins the Signature Room at the 95th restaurant. Oddly, the best view is from inside the women's room on the 95th floor. ⊠ 875 N. Michigan Ave., Magnificent Mile ☎ 312/751-3681 ⊕ www.hancock-observatory.com ⊠ Observation deck $9.75 ۞ Daily 9 AM–11 PM.

PICNIC ON THE BEACH. Chicago has about 20 miles of lakefront, most of it sand or rock beach. It's far too cold in October to consider swimming, but if it's a particularly nice day, you might consider lounging on the beach, or bringing food for a picnic. The **North Avenue Beach** (⊠ Lincoln Park) attracts many athletes; its south end has plenty of lively volleyball action in summer and fall. Bathrooms are available. **Oak Street Beach** (⊠ Near North) probably rates as Chicago's most popular. To access it from the Magnificent Mile area, cross Oak Street in front of the Drake Hotel and take the underground passage. Bathrooms are available. The **12th Street Beach** (⊠ South of Adler Planetarium, Near South) is a nice place to relax, particularly after museum hopping. A cup of joe from the Windy City Coffee Stand won't hurt either.

TAKE IN A MATINEE. The **Gene Siskel Film Center** (⊠ 164 N. State St., Loop ☎ 312/846-2600 ⊕ www.siskelfilmcenter.org) specializes in unusual current films and revivals of rare classics. The program changes almost daily, and filmmakers may give lectures to accompany the films. Movies ($9) are shown at several times each day; check the Web

FORGET SIGHTSEEING. GET ME TO A SPA!

Though several Chicago hotels have excellent spas, these day spas are also quality choices.

KIVA. Aching feet? Try one of *six* spa pedicures ($55–$65), with the hot-stone massage version being particularly decadent. Massage options range from an intense deep-tissue sports (50–110 minutes, $98–$175) to a gentle aromatherapy (50–110 minutes, $90–$165). ✉ 196 E. Pearson St., Near North ☎ 312/840–8120 ⊕ www.kivakiva.com ☉ Sun. and Mon. 10–5, Tues. and Wed. 10–8, Thurs. 9–9, Fri. 9–8, Sat. 9–6 ▭ AE, D, MC, V.

SPASPACE. A sweet escape to calm and tranquility, the spa offers such body treatments as the deliciously luxurious pineapple-papaya body scrub followed by a kukui-coconut oil massage (90 minutes, $150). The runner's massage (60–90 minutes, $90–$130) can be tailored to pre-event, post-event, or ongoing conditioning. ✉ 161 N. Canal St., West Loop ☎ 312/466–9585 ⊕ www.spaspace.com ☉ Sun. 11–5, Mon. and Wed.–Fri. 10–8, Tues. noon–8, Sat. 9–6 ▭ AE, MC, V.

URBAN OASIS. Here they specialize in all kinds of massage. Before your appointment, slip into a kimono and sandals and enjoy complimentary beverages, or try any of their three showers: steam, European, or rain. The sports massage (30–90 minutes, $55–$130) can be geared towards pre- and post-event conditioning. ✉ 12 W. Maple St., Near North ☎ 312/587–3500 ⊕ www.urbanoasis.biz ☉ Mon. noon–8, Tues.–Thurs. 10–8, Fri. 9–7, Sat. 9–5, Sun. noon–5 ▭ AE, D, MC, V.

---

site for a schedule. The **Music Box Theatre** (✉3733 N. Southport Ave., Lake View ☎773/871-6604 ⊕ www.musicboxtheatre.com), a small, richly decorated 1920s movie palace, shows a mix of foreign flicks, classics, and outstanding recent films, emphasizing independent filmmakers. The organ is played between shows on weekends and as an accompaniment to silent films. Tickets for most showings are $9.25. The first show of the day Monday through Thursday is $8.25; weekend matinees cost $7.25.

Shop Around

Areas

THE LOOP. Two of the city's major department stores, Marshall Field's and Carson Pirie Scott, anchor State Street, which is striving to regain the stature it had when it was immortalized as "State Street, that great street." LaSalle Street, with its proximity to the Board of Trade, has several fine men's clothiers. The blocks surrounding the intersection of Wabash Avenue and Madison Street are designated as Jewelers Row; five high-rises cater to the wholesale trade, but many showrooms sell to the public at prices 25%–50% below retail. Note that several Loop stores are on upper floors of office buildings.

MAGNIFICENT MILE. Some of the most exclusive names in retail line this stretch of Michigan Avenue from the Chicago River to Oak Street. It's also home to four vertical malls. The block of Oak Street between North Michigan Avenue and Rush Street is Chicago's answer to Rodeo Drive. A slew of boutiques carry expensive clothing as well as fine jewelry, luxury linens, and stylish home accessories.

RIVER NORTH. Contained by the Chicago River on the south and west, Clark Street on the east, and Oak Street on the north, River North is home to art galleries, high-end antiques shops, home furnishings stores, and a few clothing boutiques. All have a distinctive style that fits in with this artsy area. It's also a wildly popular entertainment district; touristy theme restaurants such as Ed Debevic's and Rainforest Café peddle logo merchandise as aggressively as burgers.

BUCKTOWN & WICKER PARK. Artists and musicians were the first to claim this rundown area near the intersection of North, Damen, and Milwaukee avenues; trendy coffeehouses, nightclubs, and restaurants followed. Young, hip families were next, and shopping has since snowballed. Now scads of edgy clothing boutiques, art galleries, home design ateliers, alternative music stores, and antiques shops dot the area, making it a unique shopping destination. Many stores don't open until at least 11 AM, some shops are closed on Monday and Tuesday, and hours can be erratic. To get here from downtown on the El, take the Blue Line toward O'Hare and exit at Damen Avenue.

LINCOLN PARK. Armitage Avenue between Orchard Street and Racine Avenue is one of the city's best shopping areas for clothing, tableware, jewelry, and gifts. There are also great finds on Webster Avenue. On Halsted Street, between Armitage Avenue and Fullerton Parkway, look for chain stores geared to the young and the thin. The Clybourn Corridor section of this neighborhood, which runs along North Avenue and Clybourn Avenue, has standbys like J. Crew and Restoration Hardware. The star of the show, though, is Crate & Barrel. The area is easily reached by taking the Ravenswood (Brown Line) El to the Armitage stop.

LAKE VIEW. Lake View, just north of Lincoln Park, has spawned a number of worthwhile shopping strips. Clark Street between Diversey Avenue and Addison Street has myriad clothing boutiques and specialty stores. Farther north on Halsted Street between Belmont Avenue and Addison are more boutiques as well as a smattering of vintage-clothing and antiques stores. In West Lake View distinctive shops with trendy upscale fashions have sprung up. The Century Mall, in a former movie palace at Clark Street, Broadway, and Diversey Parkway, houses stores catering to a young and trendy crowd. To reach this neighborhood from downtown, take the 22 Clark Street Bus at Dearborn Street or the 36 Broadway Bus at State Street heading north. Or, take the Howard (Red Line) or Ravenswood (Brown Line) El north to the Belmont stop.

Department Stores

CARSON PIRIE SCOTT. Famed Chicago architect Louis Sullivan designed this longtime Chicago emporium; the building is worth visiting just to see the iron scrollwork on the northwest door, at the corner of State and Madison streets. The emphasis is on moderately priced goods, including clothing, housewares, accessories, and cosmetics. It's also a good place to pick up Chicago souvenirs. ✉ 1 S. State St., Loop ☎ 312/641–7000.

★ **MARSHALL FIELD'S.** Founder Marshall Field's motto was "Give the lady what she wants!" and for many years both ladies and gentlemen have found everything from fine clothing to stationery on one of the main branch's nine levels. The ground floor and lower level are set up with boutique areas occupied by such international companies as Yahoo, selling Internet service and computer equipment, and Yves St. Laurent, selling accessories, as well as local retailers like Merz Apothecary, a pharmacy that opened on the North Side of Chicago in 1875 and sells homeopathic remedies and European toiletries. The seventh-floor Walnut Room restaurant is a magical place to dine, and many consider Field's famous Frango mints to be Chicago's greatest edible souvenirs. The glossy Water Tower branch also stocks a fine selection of merchandise but lacks the old-world atmosphere. ✉ 111 N. State St., Loop ☎ 312/781–1000 ✉ Water Tower Place, 835 N. Michigan Ave., Magnificent Mile ☎ 312/335–7700.

Malls

CHICAGO PLACE. Saks Fifth Avenue is the big tenant here, and there's also a multilevel Ann Taylor. Several boutiques carry distinctive art for the table and home, including Chiaroscuro, Design Toscano, and Kasmir Handicrafts. An airy food court on the top floor has a fabulous view. ✉ 700 N. Michigan Ave., Magnificent Mile ☎ 312/642–4811.

900 NORTH MICHIGAN SHOPS. This slightly ritzier venue houses the Chicago branch of Bloomingdale's, along with dozens of smaller boutiques and specialty stores, such as Gucci, J. Crew, Coach, Club Monaco, Lalique, Williams-Sonoma, and Fogal. ✉ 900 N. Michigan Ave., Magnificent Mile ☎ 312/915–3916.

SHOPS AT NORTH BRIDGE. The newest mall on the block is anchored by Nordstrom. Chains like Sephora, Ann Taylor Loft, and Tommy Bahama share space with specialty stores like Vosges Haut-Chocolat, a local chocolatier with an international following. The third floor, dedicated to children's fashions and toys, includes the LEGO Store and adjacent LEGO Construction Zone play area, as well as Jordan Marie, a baby boutique selling limited-run designs. ✉ 520 N. Michigan Ave., Magnificent Mile ☎ 312/327–2300.

WATER TOWER PLACE. The most popular Mag Mile mall contains branches of Marshall Field's and Lord & Taylor, as well as seven floors of specialty stores. Many are standard mall stores, but there are quite a few more unusual shops, including Field of Dreams (sports collectibles), Calypso 968 (home decor), and Jacadi (children's wear). Foodlife, a step above the usual mall food court fare, is the best spot for a quick bite, quality takeout, or lunch with the kids. ✉ 835 N. Michigan Ave., Magnificent Mile ☎ 312/440–3165.

I Love the Nightlife

Bars & Lounges

CALIFORNIA CLIPPER. This bar just west of Wicker Park has a 1940s vintage look, including a curving 60-foot-long Brunswick bar and tiny booths lining the long room back-to-back like seats on a train. Alternative country acts and soul-gospel DJs are part of the eccentric musical lineup. ✉ 1002 N. California Ave., Humboldt Park ☎ 773/384-2547 ⊕ www.californiaclipper.com.

SIGNATURE LOUNGE AT THE 95TH. There's no competition when it comes to views. Perched on the 95th floor of the John Hancock Center—above even the tower's observation deck—the bar offers stunning vistas of the skyline and lake for only the cost of a pricey drink. ✉ 875 N. Michigan Ave., Near North ☎ 312/787-9596 ⊕ www.signatureroom.com.

SONOTHEQUE. With its tasteful, modern design and sparse, podlike seating, Sonotheque is one of Chicago's more progressive lounges. An impressive Scotch list, high-profile DJs, and down-to-earth service bring heavy crowds to West Town, a few blocks south of Wicker Park, on weekends. ✉ 1444 W. Chicago Ave., West Town ☎ 312/226-7600 ⊕ www.sonotheque.org.

Bowling

Rock out to live music while you roll in the 36 lanes at **DIVERSEY RIVER BOWL** (✉ 2211 W. Diversey Pkwy., Bucktown ☎ 773/227-5800 ⊕ www.drbowl.com). Light up the lanes or play pool at the superhip **SEVEN TEN LOUNGE** (✉ 2747 N. Lincoln Ave., Lincoln Park ☎ 773/549-2695) in fashionable Lincoln Park. **WAVELAND BOWL** (✉ 3700 N. Western Ave., Roscoe Village ☎ 773/472-5900 ⊕ www.wavelandbowl.com) offers 24-hour bowling with 40 lanes.

Dance Clubs

BERLIN. It's a multicultural, pansexual dance club near the Belmont El station. Look for progressive electronic dance music and fun theme nights, such as Prince Sunday, disco Wednesday, and male go-go dancer nights. The crowd tends to be predominantly gay on weeknights, mixed on weekends. ✉ 954 W. Belmont Ave., Lake View ☎ 773/348-4975 ⊕ www.berlinchicago.com.

CROBAR—THE NIGHTCLUB. The reigning Chicago nightclub has a South Beach feel, a glass-enclosed VIP lounge, and a booth-lined balcony. Top DJs spin house and techno over the enormous dance floor, which draws a mostly gay crowd, especially on the so-called Anthem Sundays. ✉ 1543 N. Kingsbury St., Near North ☎ 312/266-1900 ⊕ www.crobar.com.

Music Clubs

CAROL'S PUB. Carol's showcased country before it was ever cool. The house band at this urban honky-tonk plays country and country-rock tunes on weekends, and the popular karaoke night on Thursday draws from all walks of life, from preppie to punk. ✉ 4659 N. Clark St., Uptown ☎ 773/334-2402.

GREEN MILL. This Chicago institution, off the beaten track in untrendy Uptown, has been around since 1907. Deep leather banquettes and ornate wood paneling line the walls, and a photo of Al Capone occupies a place of honor on the piano behind the bar. The jazz entertainment is both excellent and contemporary—the club launched the careers of Kurt Elling and Patricia Barber—and the Uptown Poetry Slam, a competitive poetry reading, takes center stage on Sunday. ✉ 4802 N. Broadway, Uptown ☎ 773/878-5552 ⊕ www. greenmilljazz.com.

HOTHOUSE. It bills itself as "the center for international performance and exhibition," and delivers globe-spanning musical offerings—Spanish guitar one night, mambo the next—in a spacious venue that can be counted on to draw an interesting crowd. ✉ 31 E. Balbo Ave., Downtown South ☎ 312/362-9707 ⊕ www.hothouse.net.

Theater

Chicago's theater scene is vibrant and fueled by a multitude of small ensembles, some of which, like the Steppenwolf, have gained wide acclaim. Theater companies include the following:

BLACK ENSEMBLE THEATER. It has a penchant for long-running musicals based on popular African-American icons. Founder and executive producer Jackie Taylor has written and directed such hits as *The Jackie Wilson Story* and *The Other Cinderella.* ✉ 4520 N. Beacon St., Ravenswood ☎ 773/769-4451 ⊕ www.blackensembletheater.org.

TWO TICKETS, PLEASE

HOT TIX
(⊕ www.hottix.org).
•
METROMIX
(⊕ www.metromix.com).
•
TICKETMASTER
(☎ 312/902-1500
⊕ www.ticketmaster.com).

CHICAGO SHAKESPEARE THEATER. With three plays a year and considerable talents, it keeps the Bard's flame alive in Chicago. At its courtyard-style 525-seat theater on Navy Pier, no seat is farther than 28 feet from the thrust stage, and there are sparkling city views to appreciate during intermission. ✉ 800 E. Grand Ave., Near North ☎ 312/595-5600 ⊕ www.chicagoshakes.com.

GOODMAN THEATRE. One of Chicago's oldest theaters, it features polished performances of classic and contemporary works starring well-known actors. Its heart-of-the-Loop complex has two stages—including a studio for new works and one-act plays—and a retail-restaurant arcade. ✉ 170 N. Dearborn St., Loop ☎ 312/443-3800 ⊕ www. goodman-theatre.org.

LOOKINGGLASS THEATRE COMPANY. The Lookingglass creates a unique, acrobatic style of performance utilizing theater, dance, music, and circus arts. The ensemble, co-founded by David Schwimmer of *Friends* fame, produces physically—and artistically—daring works. The once-itinerant company now resides in the Chicago Water Works building, a befitting showcase for their often-fantastical productions. ✉ 821 N. Michigan Ave., Magnificent Mile ☎ 312/337-0665 ⊕ www.lookingglasstheatre.org.

SECOND CITY. This home for improv and sketch comedy has been a Chicago institution since 1959, and has served as a launching pad for some of the hottest comedians around. Alumni include Dan Aykroyd and the late John Belushi. Shows are presented on two stages, with a free improv set after the show every night but Friday. ✉ 1616 N. Wells St., Near North ☎ 312/337-3992 ⊕ www.secondcity.com.

STEPPENWOLF. It's committed to ensemble collaboration and artistic risk and has won national acclaim for its cutting-edge acting style and its consistently successful productions. Illustrious alumni include John Malkovich, Gary Sinise, Joan Allen, Martha Plimpton, and Laurie Metcalf. ✉ 1650 N. Halsted St., Lincoln Park ☏ 312/335-1650 ⊕ www. steppenwolf.org.

VICTORY GARDENS THEATER. The winner of the 2001 Regional Tony Award is known for its workshops and Chicago premieres. The theater sponsors works mainly by local playwrights on four stages. ✉ 2257 N. Lincoln Ave., Lincoln Park ☏ 773/871-3000 ⊕ www. victorygardens.org.

HELPFUL INFO

Air Travel

The city's major gateway, O'Hare International Airport, is 20 miles northwest of downtown. Midway Airport, which is about 7 miles southwest of downtown, primarily serves budget airlines. American Airlines is the Chicago Marathon's official carrier; check the marathon Web site for current discounts and codes.

🔳 **AIRLINE INFO American Airlines** ☏ 800/433-7300 ⊕ www.aa.com

🔳 **AIRPORTS Midway Airport** ☏ 773/838-0600 ⊕ www.ohare.com. **O'Hare International Airport** ☏ 773/686-2200 ⊕ www.ohare.com.

TRANSFERS

Shuttle buses run between O'Hare and Midway airports and various points in the city. Airport Express coaches provide service from both airports to major downtown and Near North hotels; call for reservations. The trip downtown from O'Hare can take a half hour or longer, depending on traffic and your destination; the fare is $21, $39 round-trip. The trip downtown from Midway takes about a half hour; the fare is $15, $27 round-trip.

Chicago Transit Authority (CTA) trains are the cheapest way to and from the airports; they can also be the most convenient. TRAINS TO CITY signs will guide you to the subway or elevated train line. In O'Hare the Blue Line station is in the underground concourse between terminals. Travel time to the city is about 45 minutes. Get off at the station closest to your hotel, or at the first stop in the Loop (Washington and Dearborn streets) and take a taxi. At Midway the Orange Line El runs to the Loop. The stop at Adams Street and Wabash Avenue is the closest to the hotels on South Michigan Avenue; for other hotels, get off anywhere in the Loop and hail a cab. Train fare is $1.75, and you'll need correct change. A fare card is another option.

Metered cabs to and from O'Hare incur a $1 surcharge. Expect to pay about $25-$35 plus tip from O'Hare to Near North and downtown locations, about $17-$27 plus tip from Midway. Some cabs, such as Checker Taxi and Yellow Cab, participate in a share-a-ride pro-

DISCOUNTS & DEALS

The Chicago CityPass costs $49.50 and admits you to the Art Institute of Chicago, the Field Museum, the Museum of Science and Industry, the Adler Planetarium, the Shedd Aquarium, and the Hancock Observatory. You can buy the pass at participating attractions or online (www.citypass.com); it's good for nine days from the first use.

Chicago Greeter and **InstaGreeter** (⌷ 77 E. Randolph St. ☎ 312/744–8000 ⊕ www.chicagogreeter.com) are two free services that match knowledgeable Chicagoans with visitors for tours. Chicago Greeter requires reservations. InstaGreeter is available Friday and Saturday 10–4 and Sunday 11–4. Look for package deals, itinerary ideas, and other specials on ⊕ **www.877chicago.com.** For half-price day-of-show theater tickets, try **Hot Tix** (⊕ www.hottix.org), which has several booths around town.

---

gram and carry up to four individual passengers going from the airport to downtown. The cost per person is $19 to or from O'Hare, $14 to or from Midway.

🚖 **TAXIS & SHUTTLES Airport Express** ☎ 312/454–7800 or 888/2THEVAN (284–3826) ⊕ www.airportexpress.com. **American United Cab Co.** ☎ 773/248–7600. **Checker Taxi** ☎ 312/243–2537. **Flash Cab** ☎ 773/561–1444. **Yellow Cab Co.** ☎ 312/829–4222.

🚖 **PUBLIC TRANSIT INFO CTA** ☎ 312/836–7000 ⊕ www.transitchicago.com.

Bus & Elevated Travel

Greyhound has nationwide service to its main terminal in the Loop and to neighborhood stations: at the 95th Street and Dan Ryan Expressway CTA station, and at the Cumberland CTA station near O'Hare Airport. The Harrison Street terminal is far from most hotels, so plan on another bus or a cab to your hotel.

The CTA operates the rapid transit trains (the El), city buses, and suburban buses (PACE). City buses generally stop on every other corner northbound and southbound (on State Street they stop at every corner). Eastbound and westbound buses generally stop on every corner. Those from the Loop generally run north–south. Principal transfer points are on Michigan Avenue at the north side of Randolph Street for northbound buses, Adams Street and Wabash Avenue for westbound buses and the El, and State and Lake streets for those southbound.

Each of the El's seven lines has a color name and a route name: Blue (O'Hare–Congress–Douglas), Brown (Ravenswood), Green (Lake–Englewood–Jackson Park), Orange (Midway), Purple (Evanston), Red (Howard–Dan Ryan), Yellow (Skokie–Swift). In general, the route names indicate the first and last stops. Most lines run 24 hours; some stations close at night. In general, late-night CTA travel is not recommended. Note that the Red and Blue lines are subways; the rest are elevated.

Exact fares ($1.75) must be paid in cash (dollar bills or coins) or by transit cards, which you can buy at machines at CTA train stations, Jewel and Dominicks grocery stores, currency exchange offices, and the CTA booth at the marathon expo. The $10 transit cards have $11 worth of rides; the $20 cards have $22 worth of rides. You can also buy transit cards of any denomination over $1.50.

Visitor passes, sold at transit card booths, hotels, museums, and the CTA booth at the marathon expo, are another option. For $5 a one-day Fun Pass offers 24 hours of unlimited CTA riding from the time you first use it. A two-day pass is $9, a three-day pass is $12, and a five-day pass is $18.

🚩 **CTA** ☎ 888/968–7282 or 312/836–7000 ⊕ www.transitchicago.com. **Greyhound Lines** ☎ 800/231–2222 or 312/408–5970 ⊕ www.greyhound.com.

Car Travel

Chicago's public transit system is so extensive and its taxis are so readily available that you really don't need a car. In fact, it's probably better that you don't have one: traffic is often heavy, on-street parking is nearly impossible to find, lots are expensive, and other drivers may be impatient with you if you don't know exactly where you're going.

GETTING AROUND

Pick up the free brochure "Downtown Transit Sightseeing Guide" for routes, hours, fares, and other pertinent information. It's available at transit booths and many other places around town.

That said, if you're planning to visit farther-flung suburbs, a car can come in handy. Major routes through the city include I–90, which runs from the northwest to the southeast, eventually traveling into Indiana. Through downtown Chicago, I–90 overlaps with I–94. After the two separate, I–94 also wends its way into Indiana. I–55 moves east–west through downtown Chicago around Chinatown, eventually ending at Lake Shore Drive, along Lake Michigan. Lake Shore Drive itself is also known as Highway 41, and cruises north–south, hugging Lake Michigan as it goes.

There are car rental agencies at the airports. The drive to and from O'Hare takes about an hour; to and from Midway, about 45 minutes. From O'Hare follow the signs to I–90 east (Kennedy Expressway), which merges with I–94 (Edens Expressway). Take the eastbound exit at Ohio Street for Near North locations, the Washington or Monroe Street exit for downtown. After you exit, continue east about a mile to reach Michigan Avenue. From Midway, follow the signs to I–55 east, which leads to I–90.

🚩 **RENTAL AGENCIES Alamo** ☎ 800/327–9633 ⊕ www.alamo.com. **Avis** ☎ 800/331–1212 ⊕ www.avis.com. **Budget** ☎ 800/527–0700 ⊕ www.budget.com. **Dollar** ☎ 800/800–4000 ⊕ www.dollar.com. **Enterprise** ☎ 800/867–4595 ⊕ www.enterprise.com. **Hertz** ☎ 800/654–3131 ⊕ www.hertz.com. **National Car Rental** ☎ 800/227–7368 ⊕ www.nationalcar.com.

PARKING

The majority of Chicago's streets have meters, most of which take quarters, buying as little as 15 minutes in high-traffic areas and up to an hour in less crowded neighborhoods. Some neighborhoods, such as Wrigleyville, enforce restricted parking and will tow cars without a permit. Many major thoroughfares restrict parking during peak travel hours. Read signs carefully to determine if a spot is legal or not.

Disabilities & Accessibility

In 2000, Easter Seals recognized Chicago as a model of excellence in its accessibility for people with disabilities. Most curbs are cut to accommodate wheelchairs, and most tourist attractions have high accessibility. For additional information, contact the Mayor's Office for People with Disabilities.

▓ **Mayor's Office for People with Disabilities** ☎ 312/744-4496 ⊕ www.cityofchicago. org.

Emergencies

▓ **HOSPITALS Northwestern Memorial Hospital** ✉ 251 E. Erie St., Near North ☎ 312/ 926-5188 ⊕ www.nmh.org. **Rush University Medical Center** ✉ 1653 W. Congress Pkwy., Loop ☎ 312/942-5000 ⊕ www.rush.edu.

▓ **24-HOUR PHARMACIES Osco** ☎ 800/539-3561 for nearest location ⊕ www.savon. com. **Walgreens** ⊕ www.walgreens.com.

Taxis

You can hail a cab on just about any busy street. Hotel doormen can hail one for you as well. Available taxis are indicated by an illuminated rooftop light. Chicago taxis are metered; fares start at $1.90 and then cost $1.60 for each mile. A charge of 50¢ is made for each additional passenger between the ages of 12 and 65. There's no extra baggage charge. Taxi drivers expect a 15% tip.

▓ **TAXI COMPANIES American United Cab Co.** ☎ 773/248-7600. **Checker Taxi** ☎ 312/ 243-2537. **Flash Cab** ☎ 773/561-1444. **Yellow Cab Co.** ☎ 312/829-4222.

Train Travel

Amtrak offers nationwide service to Chicago's Union Station, at 225 South Canal Street. Train schedules and payment options are available by calling Amtrak directly or consulting its Web site. Amtrak trains tend to fill up, so if you don't purchase a ticket in advance, at least make a reservation. The Metra commuter rail runs from Chicago's Union Station to many locations in northeast Illinois, including sights like casinos, Six Flags Great America, and all kinds of local attractions. Check the Metra Web site for fares and schedules.

▓ **TRAIN INFORMATION Amtrak** ☎ 800/872-7245 ⊕ www.amtrak.com. **Metra** ☎ 312/ 322-6777 weekdays 8-5, 312/836-7000 evenings and weekends ⊕ www.metrarail.com.

CHAPTER 11

NOVEMBER

ING New York City Marathon

When my friend Amy lived in New York, she had a marathon-day tradition: flip on the TV to watch the live broadcast of the start, then bundle up, slip out, and make her way to the 59th Street Bridge to see the elite athletes arrive in Manhattan. (It always amused her that they covered 13 miles in the time it took her to walk 20 blocks.) The area by the bridge was always packed, and as the elites came into view, the crowd would erupt into screams and cheers—a roar that began with the leaders and didn't end until the last marathoners pulled themselves by.

Though Amy has since left New York, her friends who live in the city still turn out to see the marathon every year, and each has her own traditional spot. They're not alone. New Yorkers are proud of their city. They're proud of its marathon, and they're proud of the people who tackle that marathon—so proud that they turn out in droves. When it began, the New York Marathon was just four loops through Central Park. But to celebrate the nation's bicentennial, the route was changed to include all five boroughs, taking runners through local neighborhoods, past favorite bars, over bridges traveled a million times a day, and all lined with New Yorkers—people from all walks of life who come together in honor of their town. *This*, the marathon seems to say, is New York.

So You're Running New York . . .

Although you'll be running through all five boroughs of New York City, there's only one in which you'll want to stay: Manhattan. Nothing against the other boroughs, but Manhattan is the hub of all marathon activity, and let's face it: when Sinatra sings about waking up in a city that doesn't sleep, he's not talking about Staten Island.

Walk Manhattan and you'll find a dizzying kaleidoscope of sights. Look up at the tops of skyscrapers, and you'll see a riot of mosaics, carvings, and ornaments. Peep down side streets, even in crowded Midtown, and you may find fountains, greenery, and sudden bursts of flowers. Turn the corner and find a gleaming gourmet market next to a dusty thrift shop next to a quaint town house. Neighborhoods change completely every few blocks, and the people-watching is unparalled.

Do *not* rent a car for this trip. There's no need. Manhattan is a walker's paradise. If you have the time (and your legs feel good), you can walk just about anywhere. Otherwise, the subway and buses are fantastic, and cabs are everywhere, except at the rush hour of 4:30–5 PM, when many are off duty and changing shifts.

Most of this 28-square-mile island is very easy to navigate. Above 14th Street, the streets form a grid. Numbered streets run east and west (crosstown), and broad avenues, many of them also numbered, run north (uptown) and south (downtown). The chief exceptions

THE OUTER BOROUGHS

When most people think of New York, they think of Manhattan, with Brooklyn, Queens, the Bronx, and Staten Island as one big peripheral blob—the sticky, brown caramel surrounding the real Big Apple. Although Manhattan admittedly contains most of the city's major sights, more than 80% of the city's population live outside Manhattan, in the "outer boroughs."

BROOKLYN. Brooklyn is full of impressive museums, spacious parks, excellent restaurants, and trendy neighborhoods. Williamsburg attracts stylish young people, and has a lively nightlife scene. DUMBO, full of galleries and residential lofts inside former warehouses, is likened to SoHo before the artists were priced out. Fort Greene, with the Brooklyn Academy of Music as its anchor, has become a performing arts hub. In Carroll Gardens, chefs trained at posh Manhattan restaurants have their own successful bistros. Brooklyn Heights, Cobble Hill, and Park Slope are favored by young families and professionals drawn by the dignified brownstone- and tree-lined streets.

THE BRONX. New York City's northernmost and only mainland borough (the others are all on islands) was the retreat of wealthy New Yorkers in the 19th century, when the area consisted of a picturesque patchwork of farms. In the 1920s the elevated subway line attracted an upwardly mobile population, and the Grand Concourse was fashioned as New York City's Champs-Elysées. Although the Bronx has a reputation as a gritty, down-and-out place, the borough is full of vital areas and cultural gems: the New York Botanical Garden, the Bronx Zoo, and, of course, Yankee Stadium, home of the celebrated Bronx Bombers.

QUEENS. Home of LaGuardia and JFK airports, Queens is seen by most visitors only from the window of an airplane and cab. Yet it accounts for a full third of the city's entire area, and its population of nearly 2,230,000 is the city's most diverse. Queens communities such as Astoria (Greek and Italian), Jackson Heights (Colombian, Mexican, and Indian), Sunnyside (Turkish and Romanian), Woodside (Irish), and Flushing (Korean and Chinese) are fascinating to explore, particularly if you want to try some of the city's tastiest—and least expensive—cuisine.

STATEN ISLAND. For many New Yorkers Staten Island seems like a distant suburb. Its inhabitants number about 450,000, yet share a space that's 2½ times the size of Manhattan. Locals, many of whom are second- or third-generation residents, feel a strong allegiance to their borough. Its small museums hold unexpected offerings, and its historic villages at Richmondtown and Snug Harbor give a sense of New York's past. Its Greenbelt, a chain of parks, forests, and nature preserves, dwarfs Manhattan's own Central Park.

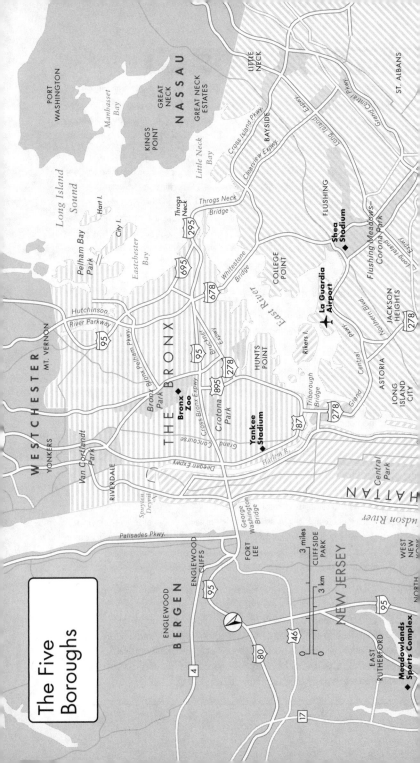

are Broadway and the thoroughfares that hug the shores of the Hudson and East rivers. Broadway runs the entire length of Manhattan. At its southernmost end it follows the city's north–south grid; at East 10th Street it turns and runs on a diagonal to West 86th Street, then at a lesser angle until West 107th Street, where it merges with West End Avenue.

Below 14th Street—in the oldest parts of Manhattan—the streets go catywampus. They may be aligned with the shoreline, or they may twist along what was once a cow path. Here you'll find West 4th Street intersecting West 11th Street, Greenwich Street running roughly parallel to Greenwich Avenue, and Leroy Street turning into St. Luke's Place for one block and then becoming Leroy again. There's an East Broadway and a West Broadway, both of which run north/south, and neither of which is an extension of plain old Broadway. Logic won't help you below 14th Street; only a good street map and good directions will.

To help you explore the city, here's an overview of its key neighborhoods:

DOWNTOWN

VISITOR INFO

NYC & Company

✉

810 7th Ave., between
W. 52nd and W. 53rd Sts.,
Midtown West

☎

212/484-1200

🌐

www.nycvisit.com

WALL STREET & THE BATTERY. In Battery Park, you can stroll along the water and look out on the confluence of the Hudson and East River estuaries. Wall Street dominates much of lower Manhattan, and is within sight of such enduring symbols of America as the Statue of Liberty. The World Trade Center once stood in this section of the city, and its absence creates not just a physical hole in the skyline, but a gaping emotional hole as well. Though so much was lost, lower Manhattan has made amazing progress in rebuilding itself, and will continue to do so in the years to come.

THE SEAPORT & THE COURTS. New York's role as a great port is easiest to understand downtown, with both the Hudson River and East River waterfronts within walking distance. The deeper Hudson River came into its own in the steamship era; the more sheltered waters of the East River saw most of the action in the 19th century, during the age of clipper ships. This era is preserved in the South Street Seaport restoration. Only a few blocks away you can visit another seat of New York history: the City Hall neighborhood, which includes Manhattan's court and government buildings.

LITTLE ITALY & CHINATOWN. The once sprawling Little Italy today is mostly contained to Mulberry Street. North of this is the area known as NoLita (*North of Little Italy*), home to trendy shops and restaurants. South of Little Italy lies Chinatown, home to about a quarter of the city's 400,000 Chinese residents. It's a lively, crowded district crammed with souvenir shops and markets bursting with fresh seafood and strangely shaped produce. Restaurants in funky pagoda-style buildings serve every imaginable type of Chinese cuisine: Hunan, Szechuan, Cantonese, Mandarin, and Shanghainese.

SOHO & TRIBECA. SoHo (*South of Houston* Street, roughly bounded by Lafayette, Canal Street, and 6th Avenue) and TriBeCa (the *Triangle Below Canal* Street, although in effect it goes no farther south than Murray Street and no farther east than West Broadway) are synonymous with a certain style—an amalgam of black-clad artists, hotshot investors, and media moguls darting between expansive loft apartments, chic boutiques, and packed-to-the-gills restaurants. It's all very urban, very cool, very now. Look for trendy galleries, shops, and cafés, together with marvelous cast-iron buildings and vintage Belgian-block pavements.

GREENWICH VILLAGE. Known as "the Village," this is where you'll find blocks that are almost pastoral, with brick town houses and low-rises, tiny green parks and hidden courtyards, and a crazy-quilt pattern of narrow, tree-lined streets. Block for block, the Village is one of the most vibrant parts of the city. Well-heeled professionals occupy high-rent apartments and town houses side by side with bohemian longtime residents and NYU students. Locals and visitors rub elbows at dozens of small restaurants, cafés spill out onto sidewalks, and an endless variety of small shops pleases everyone.

EAST VILLAGE & LOWER EAST SIDE. The East Village is bounded by East 14th Street on the north, 4th Avenue or the Bowery on the west, East Houston Street on the south, and the East River. The area is home to artistic types and members of Polish, Ukrainian, Slovene, Puerto Rican, Dominican, Japanese, and Filipino enclaves. The once sketchy Alphabet City (named for its Avenues A, B, C, and D) now seems like a walk in the park. Look for good restaurants, stylish bars, and funky shops. The Lower East Side is bounded by East Houston to the north, the Bowery to the west, and East Broadway to the south. Artists and young professionals have begun colonizing the area, which once had substantial Hispanic and Chinese communities. Storefronts here are a mix of trendy dress shops, Puerto Rican bodegas, chic eateries, Chinese produce markets, and kosher restaurants. At night the sidewalks belong to lounge lizards.

MURRAY HILL, FLATIRON DISTRICT & GRAMERCY. These neighborhoods, east of 6th Avenue roughly between 14th and 40th streets, have preserved much of their historic 19th-century charm. Murray Hill has brownstone mansions and town houses and the Empire State Building; the Flatiron District brims with boutique hotels and trendy bistros and is dotted with turn-of-the-20th-century skyscrapers, including the famous Flatiron Building; and Gramercy surrounds a leafy square that evokes those in London.

CHELSEA. The graceful row houses of this haven for artists, writers, and other creative spirits often contain art galleries. On 6th Avenue, you'll find "superstores" in restored historic cast-iron buildings. One-of-a-kind boutiques along 7th, 8th, and 9th avenues are sprinkled among unassuming grocery stores and other remnants of the neighborhood's immigrant past. Chelsea extends west of 5th Avenue from 14th to 29th streets.

MIDTOWN

42ND STREET. Few streets in America claim as many landmarks as Midtown Manhattan's central axis, from Times Square, Bryant Park, and the main branch of the New York Public Library on its western half to Grand Central Terminal and the United Nations on its eastern flank. Although the area went through a seedy period, today it's all about new shops, restaurants, and hotels, each more lavish than the last.

ROCKEFELLER CENTER & MIDTOWN SKYSCRAPERS. Conceived by John D. Rockefeller during the Great Depression, the Rock Center complex occupies nearly 22 acres of

Manhattan
Neighborhoods

MORNINGSIDE
HEIGHTS

HARLEM

Morningside
Park

W. 116th St.
E. 110th St.
E. 106th St.

Wards
Island

Henry Hudson Pkwy.
Riverside Dr.
Amsterdam Ave.
Broadway

W. 96th St.
E. 96th St.

UPPER
WEST SIDE

UPPER
EAST SIDE

Riverside
Park

W. 86th St.
E. 86th St.

Central Park West
West End Ave.
Columbus Ave.

Central
Park

Metropolitan
Museum of Art

E. 79th St.

American
Museum of
Natural
History

W. 72nd St.
E. 72nd St.

Park Ave.
Lexington Ave.
5th Ave.

E. 65th St.

FDR Dr.
Roosevelt Island

QUEENS

Lincoln
Center

Broadway

Queensboro
Bridge

W. 67th St.
E. 67th St.
E. 59th St.

1st Ave.

Rockefeller
Center

E. 50th St.

Grand
Central
Terminal

United
Nations

11th Ave.
10th Ave.
9th Ave.
8th Ave.
Madison Ave.

Times
Square

Queens-Midtown
Tunnel

Lincoln Tunnel

W. 42nd St.
E. 42nd

Port Authority
Bus Terminal

MIDTOWN

3rd Ave.
2nd Ave.

W. 34th St.

Broadway

Javits
Convention
Center

Madison
Square Garden

Empire State
Building

Ave. of the Americas

MURRAY HILL

W. 23rd St.
E. 23rd St.

Hudson River

CHELSEA

7th Ave.

Union
Sq.

GRAMERCY

W. 14th St.
E. 14th St.

GREENWICH
VILLAGE

West St.
West Side Hwy.

EAST
VILLAGE

Washington
Sq.

W. Houston
St.

E. Houston St.

Williamsburg Bridge

Broadway

NOLITA

LOWER
EAST SIDE

SOHO

LITTLE
ITALY

Holland Tunnel

Canal
St.

CHINA-
TOWN

Manhattan Bridge

TRIBECA

West St.

Chambers St.

Brooklyn Bridge

NEW
JERSEY

LOWER
MANHATTAN

World Trade
Center Site

South Street
Seaport

East River

Battery
Park

Brooklyn-Battery
Tunnel

BROOKLYN

prime real estate between 5th and 7th avenues and West 47th and 52nd streets. Plazas, concourses, and shops create a sense of community for the nearly quarter of a million people who use it daily. Here the mundane (shoe-repair shops, doctors' offices, barbershops, banks) sit side by side with the glamorous (NBC Studios—including the *Today* show's Studio 1A, Radio City Music Hall, the Rainbow Room). All parts of the complex are linked by underground passageways.

5TH AVENUE & 57TH STREET. International fashion firms make this stretch of 5th Avenue just north of Rockefeller Center (and, incongruously, St. Patrick's Cathedral) one of the world's great shopping districts. The rents and price tags rise even higher along East 57th Street, where there's a parade of exclusive boutiques and galleries.

UPTOWN

UPPER EAST SIDE. It's the epitome of high style and high society. Alongside Central Park, between 5th and Lexington avenues, up to about East 96th Street, the trappings of wealth are everywhere: tidy buildings, children in private-school uniforms, nannies wheeling baby carriages, dog walkers, limousines, and doormen in braided livery. Yet plenty of residents live modestly. The northeast section is more ethnically mixed, with a jumble of high and low buildings, old and young people. East of Lexington Avenue and between the 80s and 90s, young singles reign.

MUSEUM MILE. Once known as Millionaires' Row, the stretch of 5th Avenue between East 79th and 104th streets has been fittingly renamed Museum Mile, for it now contains New York's most distinguished cluster of cultural institutions. The connection is more than coincidental: many museums are in what used to be the great mansions of the 19th century's merchant princes and wealthy industrialists.

UPPER WEST SIDE. This haven for families has always had an earthy appeal. On weekends, stroller-pushing parents cram the sidewalks, and shoppers jam the gourmet food stores and fashion emporiums that line Broadway. In the evenings, the action moves inside to bars and restaurants along Columbus and Amsterdam avenues. Altogether, the neighborhood's lively thoroughfares, quiet tree-lined side streets, and leading cultural complexes afford a lot of things to see and do in a relatively compact area.

MORNINGSIDE HEIGHTS. On the high ridge north and west of Central Park, a cultural outpost grew up at the end of the 19th century, spearheaded by a triad of institutions: the relocated Columbia University, which developed the mind; St. Luke's Hospital, which cared for the body; and the Cathedral of St. John the Divine, which tended the soul. This is an uptown student neighborhood—friendly, fun, and intellectual.

HARLEM. The capital of African-American culture and life for nearly a century has seen tough times. Deserted buildings and yards of rubble still scar certain streets, but shining amid them are old jewels such as the Apollo Theatre, countless architecturally splendid churches, and cultural magnets such as the Studio Museum in Harlem. Black (and, increasingly, white—Bill Clinton's office is here) professionals and young families are also restoring many of Harlem's classic brownstone and limestone buildings, bringing new life to the community.

RACE BASICS

The first time my friend Jessica watched the marathon, it was to cheer on a friend. As she made her way from her Queens apartment to the finish line, she says, "I took my time getting there and wandered through the neighborhoods and watched the spectators. It was amazing. It was like a big block party everywhere I went along the route. After I had met up with [my friend] at the finish line, I walked home and saw the streets littered with orange peels and paper cups. It was like some big monster had wandered through the city leaving its waste in its wake. Then I realized that there *had* been a big monster; the New York City Marathon had snaked its way through the city for 26 miles."

To run New York is to become a New Yorker. You soak in all five boroughs, all the flavors of the varied communities along the way. You get to know the city intimately, earning your way in with your sweat and your grit. And as a reward, you're embraced by the residents, who come out in droves to welcome you into the fold with hollers and screams. Just like the city itself, the New York Marathon is larger than life.

With more than 34,000 finishers, New York is the world's largest marathon, and it could easily be still larger. More than *twice* as many people want to get in. This marathon is not flat; it's not simple. Many who have run it warn that unless you're among the elite, you shouldn't even think about getting a PR. The cold weather in the morning, the long wait before the race begins, the brutal hills innocuously called "bridges"—all of this can make New York a gut-checking challenge. But you simply won't find another race that so keenly makes you feel like you're part of something larger. Boston may be marathoning's Wimbledon, but New York is its Super Bowl. It's huge, it's raucous, it's wild, and no matter how you do, there's nothing in the world like being a part of it.

The Lottery (and Exceptions to It)

It might be an exaggeration to say that *everyone* wants to get into the New York Marathon, but only a slight one. In 2004, more than 75,000 people from all over the world tried to enter, yet there were only 35,000 slots. A few slots go to invited elite athletes. And the rest? They're mostly decided by lottery, although there are several groups that are guaranteed entry to the race:

INTERNATIONAL RUNNERS ON TOUR PACKAGES. International runners can buy a tour package plus guaranteed entry to the race from an authorized tour operator. You can go through an operator only in your home country. Check the marathon Web site (or call their office) for a list of authorized operators.

THOSE DENIED ENTRY THREE YEARS IN A ROW. If this happens to you, include a note with your application to let the race organizers know.

PEOPLE WHO CANCELED THE YEAR BEFORE. If you get in through the lottery but cancel, you'll be guaranteed entry in the next year's race. You can cancel by mail or online between early July and early November of your marathon year, or in person at the marathon expo. When you cancel, you won't get your registration fees back, and you can't change your mind and reenter the race. The next year, you'll get instructions on how to take advantage of your guaranteed entry, which you must do before the beginning of May. There's no limit to how many times you can cancel; each time you do, you'll be guaranteed a space in next year's race.

VETERANS OF 15 OR MORE NEW YORK MARATHONS. At that point, you've *earned* your spot in the race.

NEW YORK ROAD RUNNERS. Members of this club who have completed at least nine NYRR-scored, qualifying races during the calendar year before the race gain entry to the marathon. These runners must have been NYRR members since the end of January that year.

NYRR RACE WINNERS. Place first, or first in your age group, in an NYRR-scored and qualifying race in the year before the marathon, and you're guaranteed entry.

FASTER RUNNERS. If you have a qualifying marathon or half-marathon time between January 1 the year before the race and May 1 of the race year, you're in. Just include the race name and date on your application. At this writing, the New York Road Runners Club is in the process of changing its automatic-qualifying times; contact the race, or check the race Web site for details.

Wheelchair athletes and other athletes with disabilities need not apply through the lottery. Instead, they typically enter the race through the **ACHILLES TRACK CLUB** (⊕www.achillestrackclub.org).

Registration

Registration opens early in the calendar year, and the simplest way to apply for the marathon is online. The easy-to-navigate Web site is filled with useful information and is a great place to find training tools. As race day nears, the site swells with added tips, tools, and tidbits, so be sure to check it regularly. A particularly cool feature is the "Interactive Course Tour," which brings each mile to life with vivid pictures and descriptions, and gets you hungry to run the route and see it all for yourself.

If you're an international runner or a guaranteed-entry participant, you must have your registration in by May 1. If you're a U.S. resident, you can enter the lottery until midnight on June 1. Basic fees for U.S. residents are $70 for NYRR members and $80 for non-members. International participants (including those from Puerto Rico) pay $115. In addition, everyone is charged a $7 processing fee. If you don't own your own ChampionChip, you also must pay a $35 security deposit to use the race-provided chip (a fee that's processed only if you fail to return the chip within two weeks of the race). You'll also pay $15 for the bus to the starting line. Though this is technically optional, consider it mandatory. The buses are the best way to get from your Manhattan base to the Staten Island starting line. Buses leave from lower Manhattan, Midtown Manhattan, or New Jersey, and you'll be asked to choose which bus you want. I recommend you stay in Midtown, and choose the Midtown bus.

The official results magazine is the final optional fee on the registration form. It's free to NYRR members, $10 for U.S. residents, and $12 for international runners. This one is truly a personal choice. If you want the keepsake, order it, and it will be mailed to you after the race.

So the bottom-line registration fee will vary, but for a U.S. runner who's not an NYRR member, is taking the bus to the start, and is ordering a results magazine, we're talking $147, of which $35 will most likely be refunded. It's steep, but you do get a lot for your money: a marathon-eve pasta dinner, fireworks, a starting-line festival with food and entertainment, a phenomenally run and manned course, and tickets for you and a guest to the post-race party at a Manhattan club.

RACE CONTACT

ING New York City Marathon

✉
New York Road Runners,
9 E. 89th St.,
New York, NY 10128

☎
212/423-2249 (in U.S.)
or 212/423-2242
(outside the U.S.)

🌐
www.ingnycmarathon.org or
www.ingnycmarathon.com

DID I GET IN?

The results of the international lottery are posted online in mid-May, and the U.S. results are posted in mid-June. To see who got in, go to "Entrant Info" on the site, then click "Entrant Database" and start looking people up. If you're not online, you'll learn whether or not you got in via postcard. If you're denied entry, the only fee you'll pay is the $7 processing charge.

In the months before the race, look forward to e-mails from the NYRR about both the upcoming marathon and other NYRR events. Over the summer, you'll get an official participant handbook filled with comprehensive information: the expo hours, logistics at the starting and finish lines, discounted area hotels—everything you need to know. Don't forget to pack it—you'll want it with you marathon weekend. In early October you'll get your registration card, which you must bring to the expo to receive your bib number and goodie bag. And keep visiting the Web site for new updates and fun extras and activities, like voting for the official T-shirt design.

Hotels to Consider

The minute you know you got into the marathon, book your hotel. Ideally, you'll want to stay in Midtown, though other parts of the borough are only a walk, cab, or subway ride

WHY NEW YORKERS RULE

There's a myth that the New York Marathon lottery is biased against New Yorkers. It's not. I have been assured by the New York Road Runners that it's completely random. If anything, the race entry process is biased *in favor* of New Yorkers. They have a better chance than anyone to earn guaranteed entry, since all they have to do is join the Road Runners and participate in at least nine qualifying NYRR races in the calendar year before the race. This may sound like a lot, but the Road Runners offer several qualifying races each month. These races vary in length, and range in tone from your basic 10K in Central Park, to my personal favorite race, the **Nike Run Hit Wonder** (⊕ www. runhitwonder.com). It's a brilliant concept in which one-hit wonders like Tone Loc, Tommy Tutone, and Flock of Seagulls dot the 5 or 10K course. (Don't even think of a PR—it's all about stopping to rock out and sing along. Admit it, you know all the words.) Check www.nyrr.org for a full list of races, then start running to guarantee your spot in next year's New York Marathon.

---

away. Expect to spend money: Manhattan hotels are not cheap. You can, however, get amazing hotel discounts by booking through the New York City Marathon. Its list of headquarter and official discounted hotels (usually about 30 of them) is posted online around the time of the lottery.

Book headquarter hotels (the Hilton New York and the Sheraton New York Hotel and Towers) by contacting them directly and requesting marathon rates. Book official discounted hotels through **TOTAL TRAVEL MANAGEMENT** (☎ 516/222–9229). Either call, or fill out and fax or mail the room request form you'll find both on the race Web site and in your participant handbook. Note that many of the hotels listed below are affiliated with the marathon. Their price categories, however, are based on rack rates; check the marathon Web site and/or handbook for discounted rates.

Midtown West

BELVEDERE HOTEL. This affordable hotel has some fun with its art deco café and playful floor patterning, but the rooms are surprisingly conservative, with patterned bedspreads and curtains and traditional wooden headboards (an odd juxtaposition to the modern art prints on the walls). Still, the rooms are large enough for kitchenettes and have two full beds if you need them (you can also request a queen- or king-size bed). ⊠ 319 W. 48th St., between 8th and 9th Aves., Midtown West, 10036 ☎ 212/245–7000 or 888/468–3558 ⊕ www.belvederehotelnyc.com ⇌ 398 rooms, 2 suites ⚐ Restaurant, café, wake-up calls, coffeemakers, cable TV with movies and video games, in-room data ports, in-room safes, kitchenettes, microwaves, refrigerators, Wi-Fi (fee), 24-hr gym, shop, dry cleaning, laundry facilities, laundry service, concierge, business services, parking (fee) ⊟ AE, D, DC, MC, V Ⓜ C, E to 50th St. $–$$.

★ **BROADWAY INN.** In the heart of the theater district, this friendly B&B welcomes with a brick-walled reception room made charming by a humpback sofa, bentwood chairs, fresh flowers, and stocked bookshelves that encourage lingering. Impeccably clean neo-deco-style rooms with black-lacquer beds are basic, but cheerful. An extra $70 or $80 gets you a suite with a sofa bed and a kitchenette hidden by closet doors. ⊠ 264 W. 46th St., between Broadway and 8th Ave., Midtown West, 10036 ☎ 212/997-9200 or 800/826-6300 ⊕ www.broadwayinn.com ⤴ 28 rooms, 12 suites △ Wake-up calls, alarm clocks, cable TV, some in-room data ports, some kitchenettes, some microwaves, some refrigerators, concierge, parking (fee), no-smoking rooms ⊟ AE, D, DC, MC, V Ⓜ 1, 2, 3, 7, 9, N, Q, R, S, W to 42nd St./Times Sq. $-$$$.

DREAM HOTEL. A Kafkaesque dream by way of hotelier Vikram Chatwal, this Midtown scenester focuses more on style than comfort. The lobby oddly combines an awesome two-story cylindrical neon-lighted aquarium, an unsettling two-story photograph of a tattooed woman, and a copper sculpture of Catherine the Great. Step off the elevator onto your floor and you'll be met with a jarring neon photograph; rooms are almost as disquieting—stark white walls, black furniture, and light box desks that glow from within. Stay here if you love things modern: plasma TVs, complimentary iPod use, a Deepak Chopra spa, and a velvet-rope rooftop bar scene. ⊠ 210 W. 55th St., at Broadway, Midtown West, 10019 ☎ 212/247-2000 or 866/437-3266 ⊕ www.dreamny.com ⤴ 208 rooms, 20 suites △ Restaurant, room service, wake-up calls, alarm clocks, newspapers, robes, cable TV with movies, in-room data ports, in-room safes, minibars, 24-hr gym, spa, 3 bars, dry cleaning, laundry service, concierge, meeting rooms, parking (fee), some pets allowed (fee) ⊟ AE, D, DC, MC, V Ⓜ N, Q, R, W to 57th St. $$.

ESSEX HOUSE, A WESTIN HOTEL. The lobby of this stately Central Park South property is an art deco masterpiece, with inlaid marble floors and bas-relief elevator doors. Reproductions of Chippendale or Louis XV antiques adorn guest rooms. The top 20 floors of the hotel, called the St. Regis Club, provide even more lavish rooms—all with park views—as well as butler service. *Runner's World* maps with running routes from the hotel are available to guests. Post-race, enjoy a massage, steam, or sauna at the spa. ⊠ 160 Central Park S, between 6th and 7th Aves., Midtown West, 10019 ☎ 212/247-0300 or 800/937-8461 ⊕ www.essexhouse.com ⤴ 526 rooms, 79 suites △ 2 restaurants, 24-hr room service, wake-up calls, alarm clocks, robes, cable TV with movies and video games, in-room data ports, in-room fax, in-room safes, minibars, gym, spa, bar, shops, babysitting, dry cleaning, laundry service, concierge, business services, meeting rooms, parking (fee), no-smoking floors ⊟ AE, D, DC, MC, V Ⓜ F, N, R, Q, W to 57th St. $$$$.

FLATOTEL. Its name gives it away. This 46-story tower started life as British-built condominium apartments (flats) but has been transformed into a hotel full of spacious, minimalist rooms. At cocktail time, the contemporary leather couch–filled lobby lounge is a hub of genteel carousing. The beds are custom-designed with attached night-lights

NO MEANS NO . . . OR DOES IT?

So you raced to check online the day the lottery results were posted, all ready to start your training regimen for the New York Marathon—and you didn't get in. Guess you have to wait till next year, right?

Not necessarily. Even after the lottery, there are usually slots available to those who sign up with Team for Kids, a charity that supports running programs for underprivileged kids. It's a great cause, and participants get extra perks on marathon day, such as special buses to the race start and their own post-race party. To join this program, you must agree to raise $2,500 for the charity. You'll give the organization a credit card, and if you don't raise the full $2,500 by a couple of weeks after the race, your credit card will be charged the balance. If you're interested, contact Team for Kids at 212/423-2227 or foundation@nyr.org.

---

and anchored at their feet by built-in drawers, and fitted with goose-down duvets and luxe linens. Bathrooms have oversize marble hot tubs. ⊠ 135 W. 52nd St., between 6th and 7th Aves., Midtown West, 10019 ☎ 212/887-9400 or 800/352-8683 ⊕ www.flatotel.com ↝ 210 rooms, 70 suites ⌂ Restaurant, 24-hr room service, wake-up calls, alarm clocks, coffeemakers, newspapers weekdays, robes, cable TV with VCRs, in-room data ports, in-room safes, microwaves, refrigerators, gym, bar, concierge, business facilities, parking (fee) ⊟ AE, D, MC, V Ⓜ B, D, E to 7th Ave.; 1, 9 to 50th St.; N, R, W to 49th St. $$-$$$$.

⃗ HILTON NEW YORK. One of the marathon headquarter hotels, the Hilton has a Vegas-size range of business facilities, eating establishments, and shops, all designed for convenience. Considering the size of this property, guest rooms are well maintained. Room service and restaurant menus are adjusted to appeal to runners' needs. Take advantage of the 8,000-square-foot Atrium Fitness Center and Spa. ⊠ 1335 6th Ave., between W. 53rd and W. 54th Sts., Midtown West, 10019 ☎ 212/586-7000 or 800/445-8667 ⊕ www.newyorktowers.hilton.com ↝ 2,079 rooms, 2 penthouses, 5 suites ⌂ 2 restaurants, café, room service, wake-up calls, alarm clocks, coffeemakers, newspapers weekdays, cable TV, in-room data ports, in-room safes, minibars, gym, hair salon, hot tub, spa, 2 bars, sports bar, shops, babysitting, dry cleaning, laundry service, concierge, concierge floors, business services, parking (fee) ⊟AE, D, DC, MC, V Ⓜ B, D, F, V to 47th–50th Sts./Rockefeller Center $$-$$$$.

HOTEL QT. This hotel gives budget a good name. The unique lobby centers on a raised pool with peep-show-like windows that overlook the bar. Upstairs, rooms are modern and dorm-room in size, but they have upscale hotel touches such as feather-pillow-topped

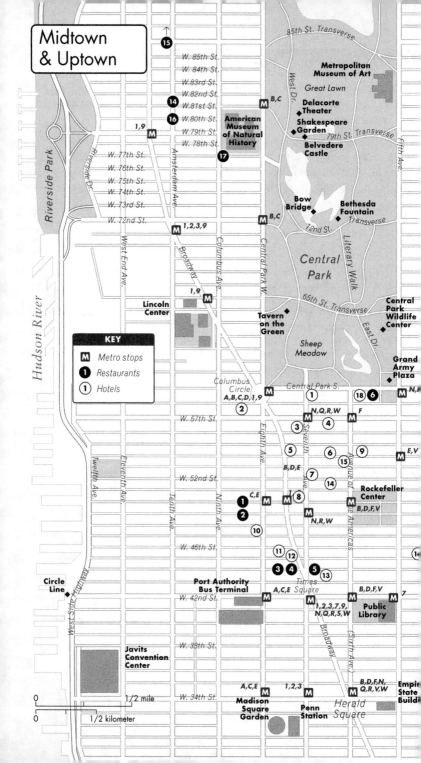

Midtown & Uptown

KEY
- **M** Metro stops
- **1** Restaurants (black circle)
- **1** Hotels (white circle)

W. 85th St.
W. 84th St.
W. 83rd St.
W. 82nd St.
W. 81st St.
W. 80th St.
W. 79th St.
W. 78th St.
W. 77th St.
W. 76th St.
W. 75th St.
W. 74th St.
W. 73rd St.
W. 72nd St.

W. 57th St.
W. 52nd St.
W. 46th St.
W. 42nd St.
W. 38th St.
W. 34th St.

Hudson River

Riverside Park

Riverside Dr.

West End Ave.

Amsterdam Ave.

Broadway

Columbus Ave.

Central Park W.

West Dr.

Fifth Ave.

Eleventh Ave.

Twelfth Ave.

Tenth Ave.

Ninth Ave.

Eighth Ave.

Seventh Ave.

Avenue of the Americas

(Sixth Ave.)

Broadway

85th St. Transverse

Metropolitan Museum of Art
Great Lawn
Delacorte Theater
Shakespeare Garden
79th St. Transverse
Belvedere Castle

American Museum of Natural History

Bow Bridge
Bethesda Fountain
72nd St. Transverse

Central Park

Literary Walk

65th St. Transverse

Central Park Wildlife Center

Tavern on the Green

Sheep Meadow

East Dr.

Grand Army Plaza

Lincoln Center

Columbus Circle
A,B,C,D,1,9

Central Park S.

West Side Highway

Circle Line

Port Authority Bus Terminal
A,C,E

Times Square
A,C,E

Javits Convention Center

Madison Square Garden
A,C,E

Penn Station
1,2,3

Herald Square

Public Library
B,D,F,V
7

Rockefeller Center
B,D,F,V

Empire State Building

Metro stops / letters:
B,C
1,9
1,2,3,9
1,9
A,B,C,D,1,9
N,Q,R,W
F
E,V
B,D,E
C,E
N,R,W
B,D,F,V
1,2,3,7,9, N,Q,R,S,W
B,D,F,V
B,D,F,N, Q,R,V,W
N,

Numbered markers:
15 14 16 17 18 6
1 2 3 4 5 6 7 8 9 10
11 12 15 14 13 16
3 4 5

0 ———— 1/2 mile
0 ———— 1/2 kilometer

Hotels

Restaurants

mattresses, rain-head showers, and DVD players to accompany the flat-screen TVs. There's no work space, no bathtubs, and double rooms have bunk beds sprouting out of the wall, but you can't beat the price—rooms start at just $125, including Continental breakfast— and the location is as central as they come. ⊠ 125 W. 45th St., between 5th and 6th Aves., Midtown West, 10036 ☎ 212/354-2323 ⊕ www.hotelqt.com ⤴ 140 rooms ♿ Wake-up calls, cable TV with movies, in-room data ports, in-room safes, refrigerators, free Wi-Fi, indoor pool, 24-hr gym, sauna, steam room, bar ⊟ AE, DC, MC, V Ⓜ B, D, F, V to 42nd St.; 7 to 5th Ave. $-$$$.

THE HUDSON. The Hudson is yet another extravaganza from the team of Ian Schrager and Philippe Starck. One thousand rooms are squeezed into 23 floors, some as small as 150 square feet, and service is at a minimum. Tight quarters are balanced by low (by Manhattan standards) rates, but if you're staying here, it's for the atmosphere, not the accommodations. Some bathrooms have see-through shower walls, and all have a supply of candles. The garden-lounge, which is like a posh living room, is one of the most coveted outdoor spaces in town. ⊠ 356 W. 58th St., between 8th and 9th Aves., Midtown West, 10019 ☎ 212/554-6000 ⊕ www.hudsonhotel.com ⤴ 1,000 rooms ♿ Restaurant, 24-hr room service, wake-up calls, alarm clocks, coffeemakers, cable TV with movies, in-room data ports, in-room safes, Wi-Fi (fee), 24-hr gym, massage, bar, library, laundry service, babysitting, concierge, business services, meeting rooms, parking (fee), no-smoking floors ⊟ AE, D, DC, MC, V Ⓜ 1, 9, A, B, C, D to 59th St./Columbus Circle $-$$$$.

MARRIOTT MARQUIS. With its own little city of restaurants, a sushi bar, shops, meeting rooms, and ballrooms—there's even a Broadway theater—it defines over-the-top. As at other Marriotts, all of the nearly 2,000 rooms here look alike and are pleasant and functional. Some have more dramatic urban views than others. The View, the revolving restaurant and bar on the 49th floor, provides one of the city's most spectacular panoramas, but it's open only in the evening. Make a reservation to get in. ⊠ 1535 Broadway, at W. 45th St., Midtown West, 10036 ☎ 212/398-1900 or 800/843-4898 ⊕ www.marriott.com ⤴ 1,886 rooms, 56 suites ♿ 3 restaurants, café, coffee shop, room service, wake-up calls, alarm clocks, coffeemakers, newspapers weekdays, cable TV with movies, in-room data ports, in-room safes, minibars, 24-hr gym, 3 bars, theater, babysitting, dry cleaning, laundry service, concierge, business services, meeting rooms, parking (fee), some pets allowed, no-smoking rooms ⊟ AE, D, DC, MC, V Ⓜ 1, 2, 3, 7, 9, S, N, Q, R, W to 42nd St./Times Sq. $$-$$$$.

LE PARKER MERIDIEN. This chic Midtown hotel provides two things that don't always come together in New York: sleek styling and top-of-the-line service. The lobby's striking atrium combines cherry paneling, hand-painted columns, and contemporary art. Crisp, modern rooms include low platform beds, rotating ceiling-to-floor entertainment units, Aeron chairs, CD players, and Central Park or skyline views. A 15,000-square-foot health club has a glass-enclosed rooftop pool and spa services. The discreetly hidden Burger Joint is a neighborhood favorite. Hotel menus "carb up" the day before the marathon and race day. ⊠ 118 W. 57th St., between 6th and 7th Aves., Midtown West, 10019 ☎ 212/245-5000 or 800/ 543-4300 ⊕ www.parkermeridien.com ⤴ 701 rooms, 249 suites ♿ 2 restaurants, 24-hr room service, wake-up calls, alarm clocks, newspapers weekdays, cable TV with DVD/VCR players, in-room data ports, in-room safes, minibars, microwaves, free Wi-Fi, indoor pool, gym, spa, basketball, racquetball, bar, babysitting, dry cleaning, laundry service, concierge, business services, meeting rooms, parking (fee), some pets allowed, no-smoking rooms, no-smoking floors ⊟AE, D, DC, MC, V Ⓜ B, D, E, N, Q, R, W to 57th St. $$$$.

RIHGA ROYAL. Manhattan's only luxury all-suites hotel has a loyal following among celebrities and business travelers. Each of its contemporary-style suites—many of them quite spacious—has a living room, bedroom, and large marble bath with glass-enclosed shower and separate tub. Some suites have French doors and bay windows. ⊠ 151 W. 54th St., between 6th and 7th Aves., Midtown West, 10019 ☎ 212/307-5000 or 800/937-5454 ⊕ www.rihgaroyalny.com ↩ 507 suites ⏅ Restaurant, 24-hr room service, wake-up calls, alarm clocks, robes, cable TV with movies and video games, in-room data ports, in-room fax, in-room safes, minibars, 24-hr gym, massage, sauna, bar, babysitting, dry cleaning, laundry service, concierge, business services, meeting rooms, parking (fee), some pets allowed, no-smoking floors ⊟AE, D, DC, MC, V Ⓜ B, D, E to 7th Ave.; N, Q, R, W to 57th St. $$$-$$$$.

★ **RITZ-CARLTON NEW YORK, CENTRAL PARK SOUTH.** This luxurious retreat with stellar views of Central Park is easily one of the top properties in the city. For a splurge, consider their exceptional marathon weekend package: a two-night stay in a park-view suite, two tickets to the finish-line banquet at Tavern on the Green, VIP Tiffany welcome gifts, Saturday morning breakfast at Tiffany's with a store tour, Saturday evening dinner at their Atelier restaurant, and a $200 Tiffany gift certificate, all for $2,125 per night (2005 package and price). All guests can enjoy morning complimentary bottled water by the entrance, and pampering in the La Prairie spa. ⊠ 50 Central Park S, at 6th Ave., Midtown West, 10019 ☎ 212/308-9100 or 800/241-3333 ⊕ www.ritzcarlton.com ↩ 213 rooms, 48 suites ⏅ Restaurant, 24-hr room service, wake-up calls, alarm clocks, newspapers, robes, cable TV with movies, in-room data ports, in-room safes, minibars, 24-hr gym, lounge, concierge, concierge floor, business services, meeting rooms, no-smoking floors, parking (fee), some pets allowed ⊟AE, D, DC, MC, V Ⓜ F, V to 57th St. $$$$.

THE ROYALTON. Each guest room has a low-lying, custom-made bed, tasteful lighting, and fresh flowers. Some of the rooms have working fireplaces, and all have CD players. Slate bathrooms with stainless-steel and glass fixtures may also include round, two-person tubs. In-room massages are available by request. ⊠ 44 W. 44th St., between 5th and 6th Aves., Midtown West, 10036 ☎ 212/869-4400 or 800/635-9013 ⊕ www.royaltonhotel.com ↩ 178 rooms, 27 suites ⏅ Restaurant, room service, wake-up calls, alarm clocks, newspapers weekdays, robes, cable TV with movies, in-room data ports, in-room safes, minibars, refrigerators, Wi-Fi (fee), 24-hr gym, massage, bar, babysitting, dry cleaning, laundry service, concierge, business services, meeting rooms, parking (fee), some pets allowed, no-smoking rooms ⊟AE, DC, MC, V Ⓜ B, D, F, V to 42nd St. $$$$.

SHERATON NEW YORK HOTEL AND TOWERS. One of the headquarter hotels, this spot gives you easy access to marathon weekend activities. Enjoy a steam, sauna, or massage in the health club or head across the street to the Sheraton Manhattan Hotel to use the indoor 50-foot swimming pool. Rooms vary in size, and some can be rather small, but all provide the comfort of the Sheraton "Sweet Sleeper" bed. ⊠ 811 7th Ave., between 52nd and 53rd Sts., Midtown West, 10019 ☎ 212/581-1000 or 888/625-5144 ⊕ www.starwoodhotels.com ↩ 1,719 rooms, 31 suites ⏅ Restaurant, café, 24-hr room service, wake-up calls, alarm clocks, coffeemakers, cable TV with movies and video games, in-room data ports, in-room safes, gym, massage, sauna, steam room, 2 bars, babysitting, dry cleaning, laundry service, concierge, concierge floor, business services, meeting rooms, parking (fee), some pets allowed, no-smoking floors ▬AE, D, DC, MC, V Ⓜ D, E to 7th Ave. $$$$.

TIME HOTEL. This spot half a block from the din of Times Square tempers trendiness with a touch of humor. A ridiculously futuristic glass elevator—eggshells line the bottom of the shaft—transports guests to the second-floor lobby. The smallish guest rooms, each themed on one of the primary colors—red, yellow, or blue—have mood lighting and even specific "color" aromas that create a unique, if contrived, hotel experience. ⊠ 224 W. 49th St., between Broadway and 8th Ave., Midtown West, 10019 ☎ 212/320-2900 or 877/846-3692 ⊕ www.thetimeny.com ⇆ 164 rooms, 29 suites ⚐ Restaurant, room service, wake-up calls, alarm clocks, coffeemakers, newspapers, robes, cable TV with movies, in-room data ports, in-room fax, in-room safes, minibars, refrigerators, 24-hr gym, bar, dry cleaning, laundry service, concierge, business services, meeting room, parking (fee), no-smoking floors ▬AE, D, DC, MC, V Ⓜ 1, 9, C, E to 50th St.; R, W to 49th St. $$$$.

★ WARWICK. Astonishingly, this palatial hotel was built by William Randolph Hearst in 1927 as a private hotel for his friends and family. The Midtown favorite is well placed for the Theater District and the marathon. Handsome, Regency-style rooms have soft pastel color schemes, mahogany armoires, and marble bathrooms. The Cary Grant suite was the actor's New York residence for 12 years and encapsulates a more refined moment in New York glamour. ⊠ 65 W. 54th St., at 6th Ave., Midtown West, 10019 ☎ 212/247-2700 or 800/203-3232 ⊕ www.warwickhotels.com ⇆ 359 rooms, 67 suites ⚐ Restaurant, 24-hr room service, wake-up calls, alarm clocks, cable TV with movies and video games, in-room data ports, in-room safes, minibars, Wi-Fi (fee), gym, bar, babysitting, dry cleaning, laundry service, concierge, business services, meeting rooms, parking (fee), no-smoking floors ▬AE, DC, MC, V Ⓜ E, V to 5th Ave.; N, Q, R, W to 57th St. $$$$.

WELLINGTON HOTEL. This large, old-fashioned property's main advantages are reasonable prices and its proximity to marathon activities. The lobby has an aura of faded glamour, from the lighted-up red awning outside to the chandeliers and ornate artwork inside. Rooms are small, baths are serviceable, and the staff is helpful. ⊠ 871 7th Ave., at W. 55th St., Midtown West, 10019 ☎ 212/247-3900 or 800/652-1212 ⊕ www.wellingtonhotel.com ⇆ 500 rooms, 100 suites ⚐ Restaurant, coffee shop, room service, wake-up calls, alarm clocks, cable TV with movies, some kitchenettes, Wi-Fi (fee), hair salon, shop, dry cleaning, laundry service, parking (fee), no-smoking floors ▬AE, D, DC, MC, V Ⓜ N, Q, R, W to 57th St. $-$$$.

Midtown East

THE BENTLEY. It's a little out of the way for marathon activities but a great find for budget-minded travelers. Although the lobby is minimal, the pocket-size library is inviting and has free cappuccino round-the-clock. Rooms are relatively large compared with other hotels in the same price category. Sheets are Belgian, toiletries are boutiquey—the whole place is reminiscent of a small European hotel. Noise can sometimes be a problem on the lowest floors, so request a high floor, preferably with a view of the East River. The 21st-floor restaurant has wonderful river and city vistas. ⊠ 500 E. 62nd St., at York Ave., Midtown East, 10021 ☎ 212/644-6000 or 888/664-6835 ⊕ www.nychotels.com ⇆ 200 rooms ⚐ Restaurant, room service, wake-up calls, alarm clocks, cable TV with movies, in-

Downtown

W.42nd St.   E.42nd St.   Queens-Midtown Tunnel

Bryant Park

E.38th St.
E.36th St.
E.34th St.

Empire State Building

W.31st St.   E.29th St.
                 E.27th St.

←TO LIBERTY HELICOPTER TOURS

Madison Sq.

W.23rd St.   E.23rd St.
                 E.21st St.

W. 20th St.   *Gramercy Park*
W. 18th St.   E. 19th St.
W. 16th St.
W. 15th St.   *Stuyvesant Sq.*
                 Union Sq.
W. 14th St.   E.14th St.
                 E. 13th St.
W. 12th St.   E. 12th St.
W. 10th St.   E. 11th St.
W. 8th St.   E. 10th St.
White Horse Tavern **Cedar Tavern**
                 E. 9th St.
                 E. 7th St.
                 E. 5th St. **Russian & Turkish Baths**
Waverly Pl.   E. 3rd St.
Washington Sq.

Minetta Tavern

Bleecker St.

W. Houston St.   E. Houston St.
                 Prince St.
                 Spring St.

Delancey St.
Broome St.
Grand St.

Holland Tunnel   Canal St.
                 Watts St.

Hudson River

Chambers St.

Columbus Park

Vesey St.

World Trade Center Site   **South Street Seaport Historic District**
Liberty St.

Wall St.

Battery Park

Ferry to Statue of Liberty/ Ellis Island

Brooklyn-Battery Tunnel

East River

East River Park

Williamsburg Bridge

Manhattan Bridge

Brooklyn Bridge

BROOKLYN

KEY

M *Metro stops*
① *Restaurants*
① *Hotels*

0 . . . . . 1/4 mile
0 . . . . . 1/4 kilometer

room data ports, Wi-Fi (fee), laundry service, no-smoking rooms ⊟ AE, D, DC, MC, V Ⓜ 4, 5, 6, F, N, R, W to 59th St./Lexington Ave. $.

★ **FOUR SEASONS.** Architect I. M. Pei designed this limestone-clad stepped spire amid the prime shops of 57th Street. Everything here comes in epic proportions—from the rooms averaging 600 square feet to the sky-high Grand Foyer, with French limestone pillars, marble, onyx, and acre upon acre of blond wood. The soundproof guest rooms have 10-foot-high ceilings, English sycamore walk-in closets, and blond-marble bathrooms with tubs that fill in 60 seconds. Post-race, enjoy the excellent spa, complete with massage, hot tub, sauna, steam room, and free fruit and juice. ⊠ 57 E. 57th St., between Park and Madison Aves., Midtown East, 10022 ☎ 212/758–5700 or 800/487–3769 ⊕ www.fourseasons.com ⤴ 303 rooms, 61 suites ♨ Restaurant, 24-hr room service, wake-up calls, alarm clocks, newspapers, robes, cable TV with movies, in-room data ports, in-room safes, minibars, 24-hr gym, sauna, spa, steam room, hot tub, bar, lobby lounge, babysitting, dry cleaning, laundry service, concierge, business services, meeting rooms, parking (fee), some pets allowed, no-smoking floors ⊟ AE, D, DC, MC, V Ⓜ 4, 5, 6, N, Q, R, W to 59th St./Lexington Ave. $$$$.

Lower Manhattan

EMBASSY SUITES HOTEL NEW YORK. It's directly across from the World Trade Center site, and closest to the Battery Park bus to the starting line. As the name suggests, every room is at least a one-bedroom suite, with a living area that includes a pullout sofa and other amenities that make the rooms ideal for families. Breakfast here is always complimentary; breads and beverages are set out especially early for runners on marathon morning. There's a complimentary cocktail reception from 5:30 PM to 7:30 PM every night. ⊠ 102 North End Ave., at Murray St., Lower Manhattan, 10281 ☎ 212/945–0100 or 800/ 362–2779 ⊕ www.embassysuites.com ⤴ 463 suites ♨ Restaurant, room service, wake-up calls, alarm clocks, coffeemakers, newspapers weekdays, cable TV with movies and video games, in-room data ports, in-room safes, minibars, microwaves, refrigerators, gym, bar, shop, playground, concierge, dry cleaning, laundry facilities, laundry service, business services, meeting rooms, some pets allowed (fee), parking (fee), no-smoking floors ⊟ AE, D, DC, MC, V $$–$$$.

AND YOU'RE OFF . . .

The Expo

The expo is held the Thursday, Friday, and Saturday before the race at the Javitz Center on 11th Avenue at 38th Street. Although there are evening hours on Thursday and Friday, bib number and goodie-bag pickup closes about an hour before the expo itself, so don't show up too late. Expect crowds no matter when you go, but try to hit it anytime Thursday or early Friday to avoid the thickest of the throngs.

Despite the huge number of runners, bib-number, chip, and goodie-bag pickup is incredibly well organized, and takes no time at all. Of note in your goodie bag are your prerace dinner and post-race party tickets, snacks and swag from sponsors, and an official marathon program, full of incredibly practical, detailed information about the marathon schedule, spectating, and how to prepare in those final prerace days.

The expo is huge—expect all kinds of vendors, tons of product samples, lots of official marathon merchandise. Many high-profile speakers are drawn to this expo; look online for a schedule of lectures and autograph signings. If you need extra tickets to the prerace pasta dinner or a spot on the bus to the starting line, you can buy them at the expo. Additionally, runners can sign up to join (for free) one of 10 ING pace teams that will finish the race at times between 3:15 and 5:30. These groups are a terrific way to stay on target despite your amped-up excitement at the marathon start.

Getting to the expo is simple: you can walk, take public buses, or take race shuttles. Public bus routes M34 (running along 34th Street) and M42 (running along 42nd Street) stop at the Javitz. The fare is $2, which you can pay with a MetroCard or exact change in coins. These buses are wheelchair accessible.

Free race shuttles travel on two loops. The transit-hub loop circles between the Javitz Center, Penn Station and Grand Central Terminal. Shuttles run roughly every 30 minutes early in the day, every 15 minutes later on. The hotel loop hits several Midtown hotels and runs about every 10 minutes. Check the marathon Web site and/or handbook for specific pickup and dropoff points.

SHOPPING TIP

The best expo purchase is a cheap, disposable, waterproof track suit. It will keep you dry during the long, cold, sometimes wet wait at the Staten Island starting area.

Race Day

The Starting Area

The best way to get to the starting area at Ft. Wadsworth, Staten Island, is on a marathon bus. These buses board continuously from 5 AM (in Midtown and lower Manhattan) or 5:30 AM (in Jersey) to 7 AM. Midtown buses leave from the New York Public Library. Enter at 42nd Street and 6th Avenue (a.k.a. Avenue of the Americas). Athletes with disabilities should enter on 5th Avenue between 36th and 39th. Lower Manhattan buses leave from Battery Place, between Church and West streets, in Battery Park's northern end. New Jersey-ites catch their bus at the Continental Airlines Arena, in the Meadowlands Sports Complex. Show your bib to board the buses, and expect lines, though they move quickly. To make sure you have plenty of time, the marathon suggests you arrive at the boarding spots by 6 AM.

"Wait," you might say, "I have to get to the bus by 6 AM for a race that doesn't start until 10:10 AM?! That's not 'plenty of time', that's an eternity!"

NIGHT-BEFORE PASTA DINNER (AND FIREWORKS!)

Whatever your prerace dinner plans, try to be in Central Park at 7:30 PM, when fireworks will explode right over the marathon finish line. Live music accompanies the show, a rousing official kickoff to the race festivities.

Of course, you may well already be in the park, if you're enjoying the prerace pasta dinner at Tavern on the Green. Every runner gets a ticket for the buffet at this New York icon, right in the middle of Central Park (Central Park West and 67th Street). Tickets are marked with a specific seating time between 4:30 PM and 9 PM; the only way to change your time is to swap with another marathoner. Extra tickets, good for any seating, will be sold at the expo for $20 each while supplies last. No matter what your seating time, expect a line to get in—the dinner is very popular. It includes a selection of pasta dishes (meat or vegetarian), bread, salad, fruit, beverages, and dessert. While you eat, enjoy live music and the company of other runners from around the world.

Alternatively, have your meal at an area restaurant. New York is filled with great places for a prerace carbo load; reserve well ahead.

CARMINE'S. Savvy New Yorkers line up early for the affordable family-style meals at this large, busy eatery. Portions are massive, so bring fellow runners and enjoy mountains of all kinds of pasta in a host of different sauces. Non-marathoners might go for popular, toothsome items such as fried calamari, linguine with white clam sauce, or chicken parmigiana. You'll inevitably order too much, but most of the food tastes just as wonderful the next day. My friend Erzsi recommends the Upper West Side location; it's far less touristy than the branch by Times Square. ✉ 200 W. 44th St., between 7th and 8th Aves., Midtown West ☎ 212/221-3800 Ⓜ N, Q, R, S, W, 1, 2, 3, 7 to 42nd St./Times Sq. ✉ 2450 Broadway, between 90th and 91st Sts., Upper West Side ☎ 212/362-2200 Ⓜ 1 to 86th St. or 1, 2, 3 to 96th St. ⊕ www. carminesnyc.com ▭ AE, D, DC, MC, V $-$$$$.

TONY'S DI NAPOLI. This is my friend (and New Yorker) Craig's favorite Italian restaurant, and it could have been created specifically for premarathon meals. Portions are enormous—large enough for two or three people (or one very hungry carbo loader)—and served family-style. There's a huge selection of excellent pasta dishes, everything from your basic spaghetti and linguine marinara or primavera to ravioli di Napoli (stuffed with cheese, covered with marinara and Parmesan, then glazed under the broiler). Craig says that the spaghetti and meatballs are incredible. Save room for the strawberry shortcake: it's both delicious and, of course, huge. ✉ 1606 2nd Ave., at 83rd St., Upper East Side ☎ 212/861-8686 Ⓜ 4, 5, 6 to 86th St. ✉ 147 W. 43rd St., between 6th and 7th Aves., Midtown West ☎ 212/221-0100 Ⓜ N, Q, R, S, W, 1, 2, 3, 7 to 42nd St./Times Sq. ⊕ www.tonysnyc.com ▭ AE, D, DC, MC, V $$-$$$$.

TRATTORIA BELVEDERE. Tucked away next to a Ramada Inn, this hidden gem has not only an excellent and extensive menu, but a "ridiculously long list of specials," as my friend Jessica says. "There's not a bad meal to be had here," she raves, and she says the gnocchi are particularly spectacular. Of course, as a true Italian, she frames her deepest compliment like so: "The marinara sauce tastes like my grandmother's, just as the lemon sorbet tastes like the lemon ice my grandfather used to make." ✉ 165 Lexington Ave., between 30th and 31st Sts., Midtown East ☎ 212/684–8805 ▭ AE, MC, V Ⓜ 6 to 28th St. $–$$.

Well, yes, it could seem that way, and that's why some runners opt for public transportation. You could, for example, hop the free Staten Island ferry, which departs from Manhattan every 30 minutes, and then take a $2 ride on the S51 bus to South Beach, just two blocks from the marathon staging area. Or from Brooklyn, you could catch the S53 bus at 86th Street and 4th Avenue, taking it to the first stop on Staten Island, the intersection of Fingerboard Road and the Staten Island Expressway. From there you'd follow signs to Ft. Wadsworth. You could even take a taxi or private vehicle.

Here's the rub: there's an X-factor to these other forms of transportation. You could have trouble catching a cab; there could be service delays with the MTA; you could mis-time your car trip and not make it across the Verrazano-Narrows Bridge before it closes at 7:30 AM. I'm not saying these things are likely to happen, but why do anything to add stress to marathon morning? The marathon buses will get you to Ft. Wadsworth in time. Take advantage of them.

The staging area itself is designed to make your long wait as entertaining and comfortable as possible. It's split into three athlete villages, color-coded orange, green, and blue to match the color coding on your bib number. Each village has its own portable toilets; baggage check; medical tent; photography; and a breakfast of coffee, water, sports drink, bananas, bagels, and yogurt. Complimentary five-minute massages are also available. Live entertainment begins at 6 AM and is broadcast over a Jumbotron.

Although your wait will be long, it doesn't have to be hard. Wear disposable outer layers to keep warm, enjoy the food and music, and talk to other runners; you'll be surrounded by people from every corner of the world, all with at least one huge, sprawling, 26.2-mile thing in common. Soak in that camaraderie; share your excitement and your nerves. It'll make the hours until the start fly by.

About a half hour before the race, everyone will head to the starting corrals, which correspond to bib numbers and lay out the field according to expected finish times. As a rule, you should line up in your proper corral. If, however, you want to start the race with a friend who's much faster or slower, you can; just go to the corral of whomever has the higher bib number. There's one exception: particularly speedy runners (in 2005 that meant all those with bib numbers below 18,000) *must* be in their proper corral or risk disqualification. So if you and your friend are both particularly speedy, and want to start together, check with race volunteers; there are many available to answer runner questions.

The Course

Several athletes get an early race start, including athletes with disabilities, wheelchair and handcycle athletes, and the elite women. In fact, in 2002 the New York City Marathon was the first major U.S. race to give the elite women a head start, so their finish would receive the attention it deserves, and not be muddied by the field of fast-but-not-elite men, as it is when the elite women begin with the rest of the field.

About a half hour after the professional women hit the course, the professional men and open field are off and zooming over the Verrazano-Narrows Bridge. Fireboats in the bay shoot spouts of water high into the air as you cross into Brooklyn. For the first 8 miles, the green, orange, and blue runner groups take slightly different paths, all racing through several ethnic communities, the denizens of which come out in force to showcase their culture. At Mile 4, for example, you hit Sunset Park, which has a rich Hispanic culture as well as Brooklyn's Chinatown. By Mile 9, you're in Bedford-Stuyvesant, home to the city's largest African-American community. Mile 10 is in Williamsburg, a major enclave of Hasidic Judaism.

WEATHER THE RUN

On average the race day low is about 47°F; race day high is 62°F.

By Mile 12, you've moved from Williamsburg into Greenpoint, home to New York's largest Polish community. As you reach the halfway point at the Pulaski Bridge and head into Queens, you'll catch a thrilling glimpse of Manhattan. After a couple of miles in Queens, brace yourself for the seemingly endless climb up the Queensboro Bridge. When you finally (mercifully) reach its peak and start to descend into Manhattan, listen. You'll hear it: a low, rumbling murmur that becomes a roar as you burst off the bridge into Manhattan, where the streets are packed with screaming spectators.

Their cheers will buoy you up 1st Avenue, through Harlem, then (over yet *another* bridge!) into the Bronx. You'll catch a glimpse of Yankee Stadium before returning to Manhattan and the homestretch at Mile 21. Funny thing about this part of the race: Fifth Avenue becomes a mountain. Slog through the steep uphill, then pour into Central Park, passing the statue of marathon founder Fred Lebow, who passed away in 1994. You'll see the Metropolitan Museum of Art at Mile 24, then briefly pop out of the park in the last mile before careering through the finish line at Tavern on the Green.

All along the course, race amenities are excellent. Water stations start at Mile 3 and appear every following mile. Sports drink is available every other mile between Miles 4 and 22, then every mile thereafter. The fluid stations stretch over several tables, and on both sides of the course. If the first table is crowded, move on to the next. The last table is marked with balloons.

At Mile 17 you'll run through a "hydration zone," two blocks themed to simulate a Maine forest. Expect music, plenty of water, and sponges soaked with water. If you'd like, keep a sponge with you—beginning at Mile 19, the last two water station tables will have pools in which you can resoak it. Mile 18 brings an energy gel station. Medical-aid stations appear every mile, starting at Mile 3; there are portable toilets about every 4 miles. More than 100 live bands play along the course, and shows on a large stage at Columbus Circle add extra inspiration for the final sprint to the finish, which remains open officially until eight hours after the race start.

Once you cross the finish line, someone will remove your ChampionChip, and you'll receive your medal, a Mylar blanket, water, and sports drink. You'll walk through the runner-refresh area seemingly forever, hitting baggage pickup and getting a bag of snacks along the way before finally exiting to the family reunion area. When you're ready to leave, either walk back to your hotel or hop the subway—trying to find a taxi amid the race day tumult would be an exercise in pure madness.

I literally ran this marathon for the first time two weeks ago, and I'm still awestruck by the experience. It is epic. And while the marathon's organization and amenities are excellent, and the sightseeing is terrific, it's truly the New Yorkers that make this race special. More than 2 million people turn out to watch the race, an almost unthinkable number. Some show up at official entertainment zones, others just hang outside their apartments or favorite bars, but they'll all give you a piece of themselves and pull you through.

My friend Amy walked the marathon in 2002 and remembers only one block that wasn't lined with people. By the time she got to Harlem the race had been going for five hours already, but people were still dancing in the streets. In some neighborhoods, she saw kids offering runners their extra Halloween candy; she saw Hasidic kids in Brooklyn asking everyone where they were from, and getting so excited when the answer was a foreign country; she saw Central Park South packed with countless screaming people as she reached the last mile, hours after the winners. And all along the course she heard words of encourage-

> **FOR SLOWER RUNNERS**
>
> If you think you'll finish in 6.5 hours or more, check your bag in the late family-reunion truck. Your stuff will be waiting for you at the finish from 4:45 PM to 7 PM.

ment: "Whaddaya doin' walking? Come on, run, you can do it!" Then, when she assured people she *meant* to walk the race, "Okay then. Great job! Go! Go!"

As my friend Jessica says about marathon day, "It's always a party. You cheer with your neighbors (even if you don't know their names) and you hand out orange slices or Hershey's Kisses or glasses of water and for one day a year you feel like you're a part of an enormous community. It's amazing to yell out someone's name and watch their head perk up as they realize you're cheering for them. It's like 364 days a year every New Yorker is on his own, but this one day, as silly as it sounds, you watch these people doing this extraordinary thing, pushing themselves in this crazy way, and you feel like you are a part of that extraordinary thing. You feel proud."

Run the New York Marathon and you become an intimate of the city; its streets, its neighborhoods, its people. Run it, and for at least that one day, you are a New Yorker.

Spectating

As you've probably gathered by now, this is a race in which spectating is as much an event as the marathon itself. So what's the best way to join in the fun?

One option is the finish-line banquet at Tavern on the Green. It's pricey, but it's a fabulously upscale way to enjoy the race. For $160 ($180 if you order your tickets after Sep-

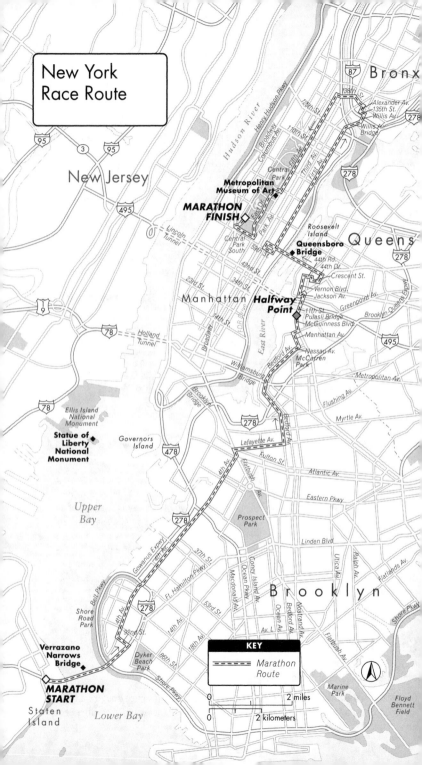

BREAKFAST SPOTS

Absolutely take time out for Sunday brunch before you watch the race. These excellent restaurants are in the ¢–$$ range.

EJ'S LUNCHEONETTE. A greasy-spoon diner without the grease. Don't let the wait stop you from enjoying huge portions of delicious breakfast favorites for a reasonable price. Service is speedy and reliable. Giant pancakes come with your choice of toppings, including bananas and pecans, chocolate chips, or blueberry compote. Crunchy French toast coats challah with almonds and corn-flakes. Splurge on a milk shake, and get it extra extra thick. ✉ 1271 3rd Ave., at 73rd St., Upper East Side ☎ 212/472–0600 ▬ No credit cards Ⓜ 6 to 77th St. ✉ 447 Amsterdam Ave., between 81st and 82nd Sts., Upper West Side ☎ 212/873–3444 ▬ No credit cards Ⓜ 1 to 79th St. ✉ 432 6th Ave., between 9th and 10th Sts., Greenwich Village ☎ 212/473–5555 ▬ AE Ⓜ A, E, D, F to W. 4th St.

ISABELLA'S. A wee bit pricey, super-trendy, and a little lacking in service, but both my friends Erzsi and Jessica swear the food is worth it. It's Jessica's favorite restaurant in Manhattan, and she says that "in all my nontrendiness, I have never felt out of place." Brunch starts at 10 and includes a cocktail or juice plus coffee or tea. The menu has great variety: enjoy lobster Benedict on lemon brioche, Bosc pear and cranberry crepes, or a burger and fries. ✉ 359 Columbus Ave., at 77th St., Upper West Side ☎ 212/724–2100 ⊕ www.brguestrestaurants.com ▬ AE, D, MC, V Ⓜ B, C to 86th St.

SARABETH'S. Whatever you order, make sure something in the dish works as a vehicle for preserves. A muffin, a scone, a waffle—doesn't matter, as long as you can slather it with Sarabeth's absolutely delectable spread. The atmosphere is sophisticated, as is the food. Omelets are fresh and delicious. For a sweet breakfast, try the pumpkin waffles. Don't miss the four flowers juice, a blend of banana, pineapple, orange, and pomegranate. ✉ 1295 Madison Ave., at 92nd St., Upper East Side ☎ 212/410–7335 Ⓜ 6 to 96th St. ✉ 945 Madison Ave., in The Whitney, at 75th St., Upper East Side ☎ 212/570–3670 ✪ Closed Mon. Ⓜ 6 to 77th St. ✉ 40 Central Park S, between 5th and 6th Aves., Midtown ☎ 212/826–5959 Ⓜ R to 5th Ave. ✉ 423 Amsterdam Ave. at 80th St., Upper West Side ☎ 212/496–6280 Ⓜ 1 to 79th St. ✉ 75 9th Ave., in Chelsea Market, at 15th St., Chelsea ☎ 212/989–2424 ✪ No dinner Ⓜ A, C, E, L to 14th St. ⊕ www.sarabeths.com ▬ AE, D, DC, MC, V.

tember 1), you get a gourmet breakfast and lunch, an open bar, access to computers that track the athletes along the course, and several TV screens that show local marathon coverage. Furthermore, you get outdoor VIP seats at the finish line, which is really the only way to get a good look at the runners as they cross. The banquet opens at 9:30 AM and stays open until 3 PM; your ticket allows you to enter at any time. This package sells out long before the race; buy tickets early.

If seeing the finish line is a priority but you're not interested in the banquet, consider buying tickets for the VIP seating only. For $55 ($65 if purchased after September 1), you get access to bleacher seating at the finish line, in clear view of the Jumbotron showing the local coverage. VIP seating opens at 9:30 AM and remains open until the race is over. To make sure you get a good seat, race officials suggest you arrive by 11:30 AM. To arrange for either of the VIP options, go through the marathon Web site or call 212/423–2276. VIP seating can also usually be purchased at the expo.

Of course, you don't have to spend any money at all to enjoy spectating. In Manhattan, 1st Avenue between 59th and 110th streets (just after Mile 16 through Mile 19) is a terrific place to stake out a spot. Watch on the west side of the street, then walk over to the east side of 5th Avenue, between 110th and 86th streets (about Mile 22.5 to about Mile 24). After your runner zooms by, head to the family reunion area, on Central Park West, between West 71st and West 60th streets.

Celebrate!

Don't crash too hard after the race, 'cause you've got plans for the evening: the official post-race celebration party, held at a Manhattan club. Every runner gets two tickets in their goodie bag, so bring a friend, let loose, and rejoice with a room full of people who share your euphoria. The gala runs from 7:30 PM to 1:30 AM and features video highlights of the race, live music, and a chance to loosen your muscles by dancing the night away.

The next morning, be sure to pick up the *New York Times*. All who finish in less than six hours get their names printed in a special marathon section. Monday morning is also a great time to get official marathon merchandise. Check the Web site for the location and time of the sale. Arrive early, since there are always crowds and items sell out.

BEYOND THE FINISH LINE

Replacing 2,620 Calories

Manhattan is filled with amazing, incredible restaurants—from the most famous high-end eateries to delicious dives. Although you can certainly just poke around the city and stumble into gustatory greatness, why risk settling for something that's just mediocre? After running 26.2 miles, you deserve something scrumptious. Here's where to find it:

Little Italy & Chinatown

DIM SUM GO GO. Dim sum gets a creative spin at this sleek red-and-white spot. Dumplings go beyond steamed shrimp and pork with combos such as duck skin and crab in a spinach wrapper. The stars that mark certain menu items denote the restaurant's specialties, not "hot and spicy." ⊠ 5 E. Broadway, at Chatham Sq., Chinatown ☎ 212/732–0797 ⊟ AE, MC, V Ⓜ F to East Broadway $–$$.

★ **LOMBARDI'S.** Brick walls, red-and-white check tablecloths, and the aroma of thin-crust pies emerging from the coal oven set the mood for some of the best pizza in Manhattan. Lombardi's has served pizza since 1905 (though not in the same location), and business has not died down a bit. The mozzarella is always fresh, resulting in an almost greaseless slice, and the toppings are all top quality. ⊠ 32 Spring St., between Mott and Mulberry Sts., Little Italy ☎ 212/941–7994 ⊕ www.lombardispizza.com ⊟ No credit cards Ⓜ 6 to Spring St.; F, V to Broadway–Lafayette St. $–$$.

SoHo & NoLita

BALTHAZAR. This grand brasserie's raw bar may be the best in town, with an outstanding selection of impossibly fresh crustaceans and bivalves. Nightly specials are classic French dishes: steak tartare, steak frites, duck shepherd's pie. Breakfast is a civilized affair, with croissants and pains au chocolat coming from the restaurant's own bakery (and you don't need to make reservations). ⊠ 80 Spring St., between Broadway and Crosby St., SoHo ☎ 212/965–1785 ⊕ www.balthazarny.com ⚑ Reservations essential ⊟ AE, MC, V Ⓜ 6 to Spring St.; N, R to Prince St. $$–$$$.

CAFÉ HABANA. The atmosphere is friendly and casual at this small neighborhood hangout, and the menu is Cuban-Latin: Cubano sandwiches, rice and beans, and *camarones al ajillo* (shrimp in garlic sauce), all at budget prices. Expect crowds. Some fans actually prefer Café Habana to Go around the corner, where the *tortas* and grilled corn (which my friend Erzsi says is a must, even for breakfast) are cheap and tasty. ⊠ 229 Elizabeth St., between Houston and Prince Sts., NoLita ☎ 212/625–2002, 212/625–2001 Habana to Go ⊟ AE, MC, V Ⓜ 6 to Spring St. $.

RICE. All meals are built on a bowl of rice at this dark, narrow storefront where you can sit on chairs or bar stools while you dine at small tables. Choose from basmati, brown, Thai black, or Bhutanese red, and create a meal by adding a savory topping such as Jamaican jerk chicken wings, warm lentil stew, or Indian chicken curry. The fresh, well-seasoned, budget-price menu affords a satisfying mix of multicultural cuisine and comfort food. ⊠ 227 Mott St., between Prince and Spring Sts., SoHo ☎ 212/226–5775 ⚑ Reservations not accepted Ⓜ 6 to Spring St. ⊠ 115 Lexington Ave., at 28th St., Gramercy ☎ 212/686–5400 ⚑ Reservations not accepted Ⓜ 6 to 28th St. ⊕ www.riceny.com ⊟ No credit cards $.

TriBeCa

★ **NOBU.** A curved wall of river-worn black pebbles, a hand-painted beech floor, bare wood tables, and sculptural birch trees set the stage for Nobu Matsuhisa's dramatic food: the paper-thin hamachi spiced up with jalapeño or sea bass topped with black truffle slivers. Put yourself in the hands of the chef by ordering the tasting menu, the *omakase*—

Edward Ines was tricked into doing his first marathon.

It was New Year's 1993, and he and a bunch of friends were kicking around when one tossed out the half-baked idea that, at some point, they should all run a marathon. They were all out of their 20s, out of grad school, and out of shape, and it sounded like a decent goal. Everyone murmured their assent, then immediately forgot about it.

Everyone, that is, except Ed's friend Max Yoshikawa, who went home and immediately signed up for the L.A. Marathon, their hometown race. He called each one of the group: "Ed, you want me to sign you up for the marathon? Al's doing it." "Monty, you want me to sign you up for the marathon? Ed's doing it." One by one, Max hoodwinked each friend into thinking the others were completely gung ho for this marathon thing, until he had signed up a group of about 13. They all started training January 2 for the early March race, with absolutely no idea what they were doing. "We didn't have a training plan," Ed says, "We just thought we'd run, run, run—like an hour or so every morning before work." On marathon day, Ed and his friends showed up at the starting line, raring to go. Ed wore cotton shorts and a T-shirt ("moisture wicking fabric" wasn't yet in his vocabulary); he had his house key safely pinned to his shorts and $5 tucked in his pocket, just in case he crashed and had to take the bus home.

As they waited for the starting gun, Ed and his friends imagined themselves all crossing the finish line together, a triumphant brotherhood. The race began, and they shot off excitedly . . . all except Ed, the tortoise to his friends' hares. But like the tortoise, the final satisfaction was Ed's, as one by one he passed most of his then-exhausted friends in the later miles. The whole group eventually finished: some in pain, some nauseous, some openly weeping, but all quite sure that they had done their dance with the marathon and had no need to ever revisit it again.

Ten years later in 2003, Ed had built a successful dental practice. He had an office in Beverly Hills, a full slate of loyal patients, and a lot of extra pounds on his frame. He knew he had to work out but just couldn't get motivated. He needed some kind of deadline. Then a patient mentioned the San Diego Rock 'n' Roll Marathon, and something clicked in Ed's head. A marathon. That's how he'd lose the weight. The race was only six weeks away, but that was plenty of time to train, right? He called Max, who agreed to join him, and they started training immediately.

Okay, "training" might be a misnomer. Ed didn't train so much as he just ran. A lot. About 8 miles at a stretch at least every other day. The good news was that in six weeks he lost 30 pounds. The bad news? By the time he reached the starting line in San Diego he was completely and utterly exhausted. And although he had been zealous about those 8-mile runs, he had never run beyond that distance, leaving 18.2 miles of uncharted territory. But as they waited for the starting gun to fire, Ed and Max made a pact: whatever happened, they weren't going to stop. And they didn't. They ran the entire way, finishing in 5:11. There bodies were thrashed, but unlike after their first race, Ed didn't feel completely done with 26.2. He liked the way the training had whipped him into shape, and he wanted to maintain it. He also enjoyed sightseeing along the route and wanted to experience other cities the same way.

Clearly there were more marathons in Ed's future, but now he wanted to do them properly. He found a training schedule online; he got a water belt; he bought some moisture-wicking clothes. He also got another runner to join Max and himself: that'd be Yours Truly. We decided we'd run the Las Vegas Marathon, and for the first time, Ed trained for a race by the book. He did everything right.

Then he got bit by a spider two days before the race.

Ed's knee inflated like a balloon; there was no way he could run. Though he was finally truly prepared to go the distance, he had to spend the race on the sidelines cheering for Max (I had discovered I was pregnant a week before the race, and was sidelined as well), who ran the race of his life, finishing in 4:10 before collapsing in exhaustion.

Despite being thwarted at Vegas, Ed refused to let his training go to waste, and two months later he and Max again ran the Los Angeles Marathon, finishing together in a triumphant 5:10. By now, of course, the marathon bug was firmly lodged under Ed's skin, and a year later he was again training regularly with Max and myself. In 2005 he ran both the New York City and Las Vegas Marathons within the span on a single month.

Before running the New York City Marathon, Ed had never been to Manhattan, and he was impressed by the differences between it and L.A. "It's such a vertical city," he says, "you feel like you're in shadows all the time." He said the marathon felt larger than life, and he was hard-pressed to pick out what he liked best about it. He and I ran that race together, and in the end, he said, it was all about the little moments: shedding our disposable layers too quickly in the starting corrals and giddily snatching up others' discarded sweats to warm up on the long walk to the starting line; losing his camera in Brooklyn and darting into a convenience store to buy another; the building roar of the crowd as we came down the 59th Street Bridge into Manhattan; the beauty of fall leaves sprinkling down on us as we slogged through Central Park in those last few torturous miles. Ed remembered feeling like he couldn't make it, and then seeing that sign—300 YARDS TO GO—and thinking, "You can do this. This is just a long par-three." He was sure he didn't have it in him for the B.O.S., the Burst of Speed with which Ed, Max, and I end all our training runs. As we neared those final yards, we just looked at one another . . . could we do it? We did. With the very last of our energy, Ed and I poured it on for a final burst, sprinting triumphantly across the finish line for a time of 5:42.

Though Ed fell into marathoning unwittingly, it has wormed its way inside him. Now it's an integral part of who he is. He loves the camaraderie of the weekly training runs with Man and myself; he loves the confidence that comes from doing something he once thought impossible; he loves the way marathoning keeps him in shape and gives him a hobby outside of his other obsession, golf. Yet for Ed, the most profound change that has come from marathoning is in his relationship to music. He used to relish listening to music, feeling all its nuances. But over time, that joy slipped away. He didn't have the patience for it. In retrospect he's sure he was depressed—working like crazy and making little time for himself. But he distinctly remembers one morning while training for that first Las Vegas Marathon. It was 4:30, and he loped out of his Manhattan Beach house, headphones on. He saw the moonlight shimmering on the ocean and although he doesn't even remember the song that was playing, he recalls that it came alive in his ears; moving him for the first time in years. Marathoning has given Ed the mental space in which to relax and drink in the music again, a gift for which he'll always be thankful. ■

specify how much you want to spend (the minimum is $80 per person) and the kitchen does the rest. Can't get reservations? Try your luck at the first-come, first-served sushi bar inside or at Next Door Nobu, with its less expensive menu. ✉ 105 Hudson St., at Franklin St., TriBeCa ☎ 212/219–0500, 212/219–8095 for same-day reservations ⊕ www.myriadrestaurantgroup.com ♠ Reservations essential ▤ AE, D, DC, MC, V ☺ No lunch weekends Ⓜ 1, 9 to Franklin St. $$–$$$.

Greenwich Village

★ **BABBO.** After one bite of the ethereal homemade pasta or the tender suckling pig, you'll understand why it's so hard to get reservations at Mario Batali's flagship restaurant. The menu includes such high points as spicy lamb sausage and fresh mint "love letters," and rich beef-cheek ravioli. There's something for everyone, from simple dishes like succulent whole fish baked in salt to custardy brain ravioli for the adventuresome eater. ✉ 110 Waverly Pl., between MacDougal St. and 6th Ave., Greenwich Village ☎ 212/777–0303 ⊕ www.babbonyc.com ♠ Reservations essential ▤ AE, DC, MC, V ☺ No lunch Ⓜ A, B, C, D, E, F, V to W. 4th St. $$–$$$.

FLORENT. When it's 4 AM and a slice of pizza just won't cut it, head to Florent. Open 24 hours, this brushed-steel-and-Formica diner is always a blast—expect loud music, drag queens, and members of every walk of city life. The simple French menu features treats like onion soup, mussels steamed in white wine, and pâté. From midnight on, you can also order from a full breakfast menu. ✉ 69 Gansevoort St., between Greenwich and Washington Sts., Greenwich Village ☎ 212/989–5779 ⊕ www.restaurantflorent.com ▤ No credit cards Ⓜ A, C, E to 14th St.; L to 8th Ave. $–$$.

> ## IN THE NOBU
>
> Unless you're Robert De Niro (he's a partner), you need to make reservations a month in advance at Nobu, New York's most famous Japanese restaurant.

GOTHAM BAR & GRILL. Celebrated chef Alfred Portale, who made the blueprint for architectural food, builds on a foundation of simple, clean flavors. People come to gorge on transcendent dishes: no rack of lamb is more tender, no scallop sweeter. A stellar 20,000-bottle cellar provides the perfect accompaniments—at a price. There's also a perfectly splendid three-course $25 prix-fixe lunch from noon to 2:30 weekdays. ✉ 12 E. 12th St., between 5th Ave. and University Pl., Greenwich Village ☎ 212/620–4020 ⊕ www.gothambarandgrill.com ♠ Reservations essential ▤ AE, DC, MC, V ☺ No lunch weekends Ⓜ L, N, Q, R, W, 4, 5, 6 to 14th St./Union Sq. $$$–$$$$.

MOUSTACHE. There's always a crowd waiting outside this appealing Middle Eastern restaurant. The focal point is the pita—the perfect vehicle for the tasty salads, lemony chickpea and spinach, and hearty lentil and bulgur among them. Also delicious is *lahmajun*, spicy ground lamb on a crispy flat crust. For entrées, try the leg of lamb or merguez sausage sandwiches. Although the service can be slow, it's always friendly. ✉ 90 Bedford St., between Barrow and Grove Sts., Greenwich Village ☎ 212/229–2220 ♠ Reservations not accepted ▤ No credit cards Ⓜ 1, 9 to Christopher St.–Sheridan Sq. ✉ 265 E. 10th St., between Ave. A and 1st Ave., East Village ☎ 212/228–2022 ♠ Reservations not accepted ▤ No credit cards Ⓜ 6 to Astor Pl. $.

East Village & Lower East Side

GNOCCO. Owners Pierluigi Palazzo and Rossella Tedesco named the place after a regional specialty—deep-fried dough, sort of like wontons, served with salami and prosciutto. Head to the roomy rear canopied garden for savory salads, house-made pastas (tagliatelle with sausage ragù is a winner), pizza, and hearty entrées like sliced beef tenderloin. Homesick expats come here for a dose of comfort. ✉ 337 E. 10th St., between Aves. A and B, East Village ☎ 212/677-1913 ⊕ www.gnocco.com ▭ No credit cards ⊙ No lunch weekdays Ⓜ L to 14th St. $–$$.

Murray Hill, Flatiron District & Gramercy

CRAFT. Crafting your ideal meal here is like choosing from a gourmand's well-stocked kitchen. The menu's bounty of simple yet intriguing starters and sides makes it easy to forget there are also main courses to partner them with. Seared scallops, braised veal, seasonal vegetables—just about everything is exceptionally prepared with little fuss. The serene dining room features burnished dark wood, custom tables, a curved leather wall, and a succession of dangling radiant bulbs. ✉ 43 E. 19th St., between Broadway and Park Ave. S, Flatiron District ☎ 212/780-0880 ⌳ Reservations essential ▭ AE, D, DC, MC, V ⊙ No lunch weekends Ⓜ R, W, 6 to 23rd St. $$–$$$$.

DOS CAMINOS. The array of 150 tequilas will put you in the right frame of mind for anything chefs Ivy Stark and Scott Linquist create. Kobe beef tacos are given searing heat by cascabel chilis, and slow-roasted pork ribs in chipotle barbecue sauce achieve quite a depth of flavor. Be forewarned: the noise level can be a problem. ✉ 373 Park Ave. S, between 26th and 27th Sts., Flatiron District ☎ 212/294-1000 Ⓜ 6 to 28th St. ✉ 475 W. Broadway, at Houston St., SoHo ☎ 212/277-4300 ⊕ www.brguestrestaurants.com ⌳ Reservations essential ▭ AE, DC, MC, V Ⓜ N, R to Prince St. $$–$$$.

Midtown West

ANGUS MCINDOE. "If people like the theater-district vibe," my friend Craig says, "Angus McIndoe has great food, and you'll often see Broadway folk there." He should know; his wife is a Broadway actress. The food at Angus McIndoe has an old-school sophistication, with classics like oysters on the half shell, roasted monkfish, and a grilled porterhouse steak for two. You can get fried or scrambled eggs all day, served with upscale tweaks like bourbon barbecued beans and warm potato scones. ✉ 258 W. 44th St., between 8th Ave. and Broadway, Midtown West ☎ 212/221-9222 ⊕ www.angusmcindoe.com ▭ AE, MC, V Ⓜ C, E, N, Q, R, S, W, 1, 2, 3, 7 to 42nd St./Port Authority $–$$$.

CHURRASCARIA PLATAFORMA. This sprawling, boisterous shrine to meat, with its all-you-can-eat prix-fixe menu, is best experienced with a group of ravenous friends. A caipirinha (sugarcane liquor and lime) will kick you off nicely; then hit the vast salad bar groaning with vegetables, meats, cheeses, and hot tureens of feijoada (beans, pork, greens and manioc). Next comes an ongoing parade of all manner of grilled meats and poultry brought to the table on long skewers until you beg for mercy. ✉ 316 W. 49th St., between 8th and 9th Aves., Midtown West ☎ 212/245-0505 ⌳ Reservations essential ▭ AE, DC MC, V Ⓜ C, E to 50th St. $$$$.

★ **RUBY ET VIOLETTE.** After running a marathon, you deserve what are by far the best cookies ever made: mouthwateringly fresh baked circles of chewy perfection in flavors ranging from Perfect Chocolate Chunk to Malted Milk to Kitchen Sink Chocolate Chunk. The store is closed weekends, so either stop by the counter to pick up your cookies Friday before the race, or treat yourself the Monday morning after. ⊠ 457 W. 50th St., between 9th and 10th Aves., Midtown West ☎ 212/582-6720 ⊕ www.rubyetviolette.com ⊟ AE, DC, MC, V ⊘ Closed weekends, except Sat. in Nov. Ⓜ C, E to 50th St. ¢.

VIRGIL'S REAL BBQ. Really want to indulge? Start with stuffed jalapeños, unbelievably succulent barbecue chicken wings, or "trainwreck fries," covered in two cheeses, bacon, scallions, pickled jalapeños, and ranch dressing. Then, what the hell: go for the "pig out"— a rack of pork ribs, Texas hot links, pulled pork, rack of lamb, chicken, and, of course, more. It's that kind of place. Enjoy domestic microbrews on tap, plus several top beers from around the world. ⊠ 152 W. 44th St., between 6th Ave. and Broadway, Midtown West ☎ 212/921-9494 ⊕ www.virgilsbbq.com ⚐ Reservations essential ⊟ AE, MC, V Ⓜ N, Q, R, S, W, 1, 2, 3, 7, 9 to 42nd St./Times Sq. $-$$.

Upper East Side

JG MELON. Though some complain about the portion size of both the food and drinks, most (like my cousin Sue) agree that the burgers are absolutely excellent. There are other entrées, like broiled fish and even steak tartare, but it's all about the burgers, fries, and drinks, both alcoholic and nonalcoholic, served in a fun atmosphere. ⊠ 1291 3rd Ave., at 74th St., Upper East Side ☎ 212/650-1310 ⊟ No credit cards Ⓜ N, R, W, 4, 5, 6 to 77th St./Lexington Ave. $-$$.

★ **MAYA.** Here you'll find some of the city's best Mexican food. Begin with a fresh mango margarita, then tuck into intensely delicious roasted corn soup, poblano pepper stuffed with seafood and Gouda cheese, and smoky butterflied beef tenderloin marinated in lime or ancho chili-crusted striped bass. Finish with crepes dribbled with goat milk *dulce de leche* and you'll leave wearing a great big grin. ⊠ 1191 1st Ave., at 64th St., Upper East Side ☎ 212/585-1818 ⊕ www.mayany.com ⚐ Reservations essential ⊟ AE, DC, MC, V ⊘ No lunch Ⓜ 6 to 68th St./Hunter College $$-$$$.

★ **SERENDIPITY 3.** It's one of my personal favorites. This fun ice-cream parlor bedecked with stained-glass lamps also dishes out excellent burgers, foot-long hot dogs, French toast, omelets, salads, and *the best sandwich ever* (in my opinion): a Summer Bries (turkey, sliced apples, melted Brie cheese, and alfalfa sprouts, on pumpernickel-raisin bread, served with Thousand Island dressing). Most people come for the huge, decadent sundaes, as well as Serendipity's most famous dessert—the frozen hot chocolate. If you have to wait for a table, scope out the tchotchkes in the foyer. ⊠ 225 E. 60th St., between 2nd and 3rd Aves., Upper East Side ☎ 212/838-3531 ⊕ www.serendipity3.com ⊟ AE, DC, MC, V Ⓜ N, R, W, 4, 5, 6 to 59th St./Lexington Ave. ¢-$$.

Sightseeing on (and off) Your Feet

Let's face it: there's no earthly way to take in all New York has to offer in one long weekend. Pick what appeals to you most, see how you're feeling after the race, and carve out your own slice of The Big Apple.

I Feel Great!

★ **CENTRAL PARK.** Without the park's 843 acres of meandering paths, tranquil lakes, ponds, and open meadows, New Yorkers might be a lot less sane. You'll see some of Central Park during the race, but if your legs are up for it, consider a stroll that takes in some or all of its highlights. If your legs are really sore, take a tour by horse-drawn carriage. Find one at Grand Army Plaza or any other major intersection of Central Park South at 59th Street between 5th Avenue and Columbus Circle. Rates are $34 for 20 minutes or $54 for 45 minutes for up to four people.

Start at Grand Army Plaza (59th St. and 5th Ave.) and walk more or less parallel to East Drive along the Pond. Just to the north is Wollman Memorial Rink, where you can watch skaters cut up the ice from October to April. Beyond the rink, walk uphill past the Dairy, cross the road, and veer a bit left to the Literary Walk, flanked at its start by statues of Sir Walter Scott and Robert Burns. A stroll north under a canopy of elms leads to the Mall, where it's easy to imagine yourself a 19th-century high-society New Yorker. Near the end of the Mall to your left is Skater's Circle, where you can watch the semiprofessional skate-dancers boogie to DJ-spun tunes.

At the end of the Mall, walk down the stairs to the Bethesda Fountain, a popular place to hang out on warm days. A path directly west of the fountain forks north and south: go north to stand on the wood-and-cast-iron Bow Bridge, overlooking the Lake. Walk south along the Lake to Cherry Hill to get a glimpse of the West Side skyline. From here, loop around the Lake all the way up to the Shakespeare Garden and, just beyond it, Belvedere Castle. Climb the castle to overlook the Delacorte Theater stage and the Great Lawn beyond. From here, walk east along the path and then turn north past Cleopatra's Needle. A left turn brings you to the Great Lawn, usually chock-full on warm days. Make your way across, minding the Frisbees and sidestepping the picnickers, or settle in for a little R&R yourself before following west-leading paths out to 81st Street and Central Park West, facing the Museum of Natural History.

Even a leisurely side trip to the small but delightful Central Park menagerie that is the **Central Park Wildlife Center** will take only about an hour. Don't miss the sea lion feedings, possibly the zoo's most popular attraction, daily at 11:30, 2, and 4. Clustered around the central Sea Lion Pool are separate exhibits for each of the Earth's major environments. Penguins and polar bears live at Polar Circle; the highlights of the open-air Temperate Territory are the chattering monkeys; and the Rain Forest contains the flora and fauna of the tropics. The Tisch Children's Zoo gives kids the opportunity to pet and feed sheep, goats, rabbits, cows, and pigs. The Enchanted Forest is a surreal place filled with "acorns" the size of Saint Bernards, a climbable "spiderweb," and hoppable "lily pads." ✉ Entrance at 5th Ave. and E. 64th St., Central Park ☎ 212/439-6500 ⊕ www.centralparkzoo.org ☞ $6 ☞ No children under 16 admitted without adult ⊙ Apr.–Oct., weekdays 10–5, weekend

10–5:30; Nov.–Mar., daily 10–4:30 Ⓜ 6 to 68th St./Hunter College; N, R, W to 5th Ave./59th St.; F to Lexington Ave./63rd St.

Allow two hours to complete this walk (excluding the wildlife center). If the weather's in your favor, though, consider making a half day of it, stopping to rest, eat, play, and really enjoy the attractions and scenery. Although the park has one of the lowest crime rates in the city, use common sense when you're in it: stay within sight of other park visitors, and don't wander around after dark. Directions, park maps, and events calendars can be obtained from volunteers at two 5th Avenue information booths, at East 60th Street and East 72nd Street. ☎ 212/360–2727 tours schedule ⊕ www.nycgovparks.org.

SOUTH STREET SEAPORT HISTORIC DISTRICT. Had it not been declared a historic district in 1967, this charming, cobblestone corner of New York with the city's largest concentration of early-19th-century commercial buildings would likely have been gobbled up by skyscrapers. Some area highlights include the *Titanic* Memorial and Bowne & Co. Stationers, a reconstructed working 19th-century print shop. The **South Street Seaport Museum** (☎ 212/748–8600 ☉ Apr.–Oct., Tues.–Sun. 10–6; Nov.–Mar., Fri.–Mon. 10–5) hosts walking tours, hands-on exhibits, and fantastic creative programs for children, all with a nautical theme. Cross South Street to Pier 16 to see historic ships, including the *Pioneer*, a 102-foot schooner built in 1885; the *Peking*, the second-largest sailing bark in existence; the iron-hulled *Wavertree*; and the lightship *Ambrose*. The Pier 16 ticket booth provides information and sells tickets to the museum, ships, tours, and exhibits. ✉ Visitor center: 211 Water St., South St. Seaport, Lower Manhattan ☎ 212/732–7678 for events and shopping information ⊕ www.southstseaport.org ✉ $8 to ships, galleries, walking tours, Maritime Crafts Center, films, and other seaport events Ⓜ 2, 3, 4, 5, J, Z, M to Fulton St.; A, C to Broadway/Nassau.

I Feel Pretty Good

★ **AMERICAN MUSEUM OF NATURAL HISTORY.** It has 45 exhibition halls and more than 32 million artifacts and specimens. Dinosaur mania begins in the massive, barrel-vaulted Theodore Roosevelt Rotunda, where a 50-foot-tall skeleton of a barosaurus rears on its hind legs, protecting its fossilized baby from an enormous marauding allosaurus. Three spectacular dinosaur halls on the fourth floor use real fossils and interactive computer stations to present interpretations of how dinosaurs and pterodactyls might have behaved. Other highlights include the 34-ton *Ahnighito*—the largest meteorite on display in the world; and the popular 94-foot blue whale model. The spectacular Hayden Planetarium is in a 90-foot aluminum-clad sphere that appears to float inside an enormous glass cube, which in turn is home to the Rose Center for Earth and Space. Films on the museum's 40-foot-high, 66-foot-wide **IMAX Theater** (☎ 212/769–5034 showtimes) screen are usually about nature and cost $19, including museum admission. ✉ Central Park W at W. 79th St., Upper West Side ☎ 212/769–5100 for general information, 212/769–5200 for event reservations ⊕ www.amnh.org ✉ $14 suggested donation, includes admission to Rose Center; museum and planetarium show combination ticket $22. Prices vary for special exhibitions ☉ Daily 10–5:45 Ⓜ B, C to 81st St.

LITERARY PUB CRAWL. Where there are academics, writers, and artists, there are pubs and bars nearby in which to swill away the pain of procrastination and lament the limits of creativity. A literary lot has long frequented the West Village's "think tanks," and a tour of a few makes for a sophisticated pub crusade rather than a crawl. Especially since 10-minute walks separate each.

The most famous '50s watering hole is the **White Horse Tavern** (✉ 567 Hudson St., at 11th St., Greenwich Village ☎ 212/989-3956), where poet Dylan Thomas did not go gentle into that good night as much as he drank himself into the state. He died at 39 of alcoholism in 1953 after a last drink here.

Walk east one block along 11th Street to Bleecker and take a right. It's a good 10-minute walk southeast on Bleecker, past many mediocre NYU bars, to MacDougal Street, which is one block east of 6th Avenue. Take a left when you reach it. At **Minetta Tavern** (✉ 113 MacDougal St., between Bleecker and W. 3rd Sts., Greenwich Village ☎ 212/475-3850) Italian fare is now served in the venerable Village watering hole that dates to Prohibition. During those years, the tavern was called the Black Rabbit, some say for the scandalous 1890s sex shows held here. In 1923, De Witt Wallace printed his first copies of the simply named *Reader's Digest* in the basement. Suffice it to say that Wallace and his wife became benefactors of the Met. More recently poets and lit lions, including Nobel Prize-winning poet Seamus Heaney, have been regulars here.

Take a sobering walk north to Washington Square Park, cross it to Washington Square East, and take a left, walking north on University Place, heading for 11th Street. During the '40s and '50s abstract expressionist Jackson Pollock practiced the *non*dribble method when lifting drink to mouth at the **Cedar Tavern** (✉ 82 University Pl., between 11th and 12th Sts., Greenwich Village ☎ 212/929-9089). Willem de Kooning and his wife, Elaine, regularly processed their marital troubles from the captain's-chair bar stools during the same time, and rumor has it that beat writer Jack Kerouac, a regular, lost his drinking privileges here for emptying his bladder in an ashtray. Complete any necessary business of this kind in the traditional WC before waving down a cab for your hotel.

★**METROPOLITAN MUSEUM OF ART.** The Western Hemisphere's largest art museum (spanning four blocks, it encompasses 2 million square feet and has a permanent collection of nearly 3 million works from all over the world), the Met is one of the city's supreme cultural institutions. Past the admission booths, a wide marble staircase leads to the European paintings galleries, whose 2,500 works include Botticelli's *The Last Communion of St. Jerome* (circa 1490), Pieter Brueghel's *The Harvesters* (1565), Johannes Vermeer's *Young Woman with a Water Jug* (circa 1660), Velázquez's *Juan de Pareja* (1648), and Rembrandt's *Aristotle with a Bust of Homer* (1653). The arcaded European Sculpture Court includes Auguste Rodin's massive bronze *The Burghers of Calais* (1884–95).

To the left of the Great Hall on the first floor are the Greek and Roman Galleries. Grecian urns and mythological marble statuary are displayed beneath a skylighted, barrel-vaulted stone ceiling. An indoor courtyard holds Roman sculpture, and on the walls are a collection of rare wall paintings excavated from the lava of Mt. Vesuvius. The Met's awesome Egyptian collection, spanning some 4,000 years, is on the first floor, directly to the right of the Great Hall. Also on the first floor are the Medieval Galleries. To the north of the Medieval Galleries is the Arms & Armor exhibit, which is full of chain mail, swords, shields, and fancy firearms. On the lower level, the Costume Institute has changing exhibits of clothing and fashion spanning seven centuries. ✉ 1000 5th Ave at 82nd St., Upper East Side ☎ 212/535-7710 ⊕ www.metmuseum.org ✉ $15 suggested donation ⊙ Tues.-Thurs. and Sun. 9:30-5:30, Fri. and Sat. 9:30-9 Ⓜ 4, 5, 6 to 86th St.

Let's Take It Slowly

★ **ELLIS ISLAND AND THE STATUE OF LIBERTY.** A trip to the Statue of Liberty and Ellis Island takes up the better part of a day, and more often than not it requires a good dose of patience to deal with large crowds and rigorous security checks. But it's worth the effort. It's no overstatement to say that these two sights have played defining roles in American culture. They're both well run and eminently satisfying to visit.

Unless time constraints dictate otherwise, it makes sense to see both sights in one trip. Ferries leaving from Battery Park every half hour take you to both islands. (Note that large packages and oversize bags and backpacks aren't permitted on board.) There's no admission fee for either sight, but the ferry ride costs $11.50. It's worth the additional $1.75 charge to reserve tickets in advance—you'll still have to wait in line, both to pick up the tickets and to board the ferry, but you'll be able to reserve a spot on the Statue of Liberty observatory tour, which will make your experience significantly richer.

Between 1892 and 1924, approximately 12 million men, women, and children first set foot on U.S. soil at the Ellis Island federal immigration facility. By the time the facility closed in 1954, it had processed ancestors of more than 40% of Americans living today. The island's main building, now a national monument, reopened in 1990 as the **Ellis Island Immigration Museum,** containing more than 30 galleries of artifacts, photographs, and taped oral histories. The centerpiece of the museum is the white-tile Registry Room (also known as the Great Hall). While you're here, take a look out the Registry Room's tall, arched windows and try to imagine what passed through immigrants' minds as they viewed lower Manhattan's skyline to one side and the Statue of Liberty to the other. ⊠ Lower Manhattan ☎ 212/363-3200 ⊕ www.nps.gov/elis ⊙ Daily 9:30-5:15.

For millions of immigrants, the first glimpse of America was the **Statue of Liberty.** You get a taste of the thrill they must have experienced as you approach Liberty Island on the ferry from Battery Park. *Liberty Enlightening the World,* as the statue is officially named, was presented to the United States in 1886 as a gift from France. The 152-foot-tall figure was sculpted by Frederic-Auguste Bartholdi and erected around an iron skeleton engineered by Gustav Eiffel. It stands atop an 89-foot pedestal designed by Richard Morris Hunt, with Emma Lazarus's sonnet "The New Colossus" ("Give me your tired, your poor, your huddled masses...") inscribed on a bronze plaque at the base. Over time, the statue has become precisely what its creators dreamed it would be: a powerful symbol of American ideals. Inside the statue's pedestal is a museum whose highlights include the original flame (which was replaced because of water damage), full-scale replicas of Lady Liberty's face and one of her feet, Bartholdi's alternative designs for the statue, and a model of Eiffel's intricate framework. ⊠ Liberty Island, Lower Manhattan ☎ 212/363-3200 or 866/782-8834 ferry info/ticket reservations ⊕ www.nps.gov/stli, www.statuereservations. com for reservations ⊙ Daily 9:30-5.

EMPIRE STATE BUILDING. This art deco behemoth opened on May 1, 1931, after a mere 13 months of construction; the framework rose at a rate of 4½ stories per week, making it the fastest-rising skyscraper ever built. In 1951 a TV transmittal tower was added to the top, raising the total height to 1,472 feet. Ever since the 1976 American bicentennial celebration, the top 30 stories have been spotlighted at night with colors honoring different holidays and events. Tickets are sold on the concourse level and on the building's Web site (a good way to avoid the considerable line). The 86th-floor observatory (1,050 feet high) is open to the air and circles the building; on clear days you can see up to 80 miles. Time your visit for early or late in the day (morning is the least-crowded time), when the sun is low on the horizon and the shadows are deep across the city.

On the **New York Skyride** (☎ 212/279-9777 or 888/759-7433 ⊕ www.skyride.com 🖃 $25; $32 for Skyride and Observatory ⊙ Daily 10–10) a Comedy Central video presentation on the virtues of New York precedes a rough-and-tumble motion-simulator ride above and around some of the city's top attractions, which are projected on a two-story-tall screen. Since it's part helicopter video and part roller-coaster ride, children love it. ✉ 350 5th Ave., at E. 34th St., Murray Hill ☎ 212/736-3100 or 877/692-8439 ⊕ www. esbnyc.com 🖃 $16 ⊙ Daily 8 AM–midnight; last elevator up leaves at 11:15 PM Ⓜ B, D, F, N, Q, R, V, W to 34th St./Herald Sq.

WORLD TRADE CENTER SITE. On September 11, 2001, terrorist hijackers steered two commercial jets into the World Trade Center's 110-story towers, demolishing them and five outlying buildings and killing nearly 3,000 people. Dubbed Ground Zero, the fenced-in 16-acre work site that emerged from the rubble has come to symbolize the personal and historical impact of the attack. In an attempt to grasp the reality of the destruction, to pray, or simply to witness history, visitors come to glimpse the site, clustering at the two-story see-through fence surrounding it. Temporary panels listing the names of those who died in the attacks and recounting the history of the twin towers have been mounted along the fence on the west side of Church Street and the north side of Liberty Street. ✉ Lower Manhattan Ⓜ R, W to Cortlandt St.

Ow! No.

RIDE THE WATERWAYS. During the three-hour **Circle Line** (✉ Pier 83 at W. 42nd St., Midtown West ☎ 212/563-3200 ⊕ www.circleline42.com) cruise that circumnavigates Manhattan, the narrations are as interesting and individual as the guides who deliver them. Circle Line operates daily (except for Tuesday and Wednesday in January and February and Tuesday in March), and the price is $28. Semi-Circle cruises, more limited tours of two hours, cost $23. Circle Line also runs 75-minute, $18 sightseeing tours of New York Harbor and lower Manhattan.

The free 20- to 30-minute **Staten Island Ferry** (✉ State and South Sts., Lower Manhattan ☎ 718/390-5253 ⊕ www.siferry.com) ride across New York Harbor provides great views of the Manhattan skyline, the Statue of Liberty, the Verrazano-Narrows Bridge, and the New Jersey coast. On weekend mornings until 7:30 AM, ferries leave the southern tip of Manhattan at Whitehall Terminal every hour on the half hour; from 7:30 AM until 7:30 PM, they run every half hour, then go back to every hour.

RUSSIAN & TURKISH BATHS. It's clear from the older Soviet types devouring blintzes and Baltika beer served in the lobby that this is no 5th Avenue spa. But the three-story

RUNNING FOR THEIR LIVES

In the weeks after the tragedy of September 11, 2001, the New York Road Runners had to pause in their grief to consider a question. The New York City Marathon was scheduled to occur in less than two months. Should it go on as planned? Would it be appropriate? Would it be safe? Would anyone actually come?

Despite these worries, the call was made to hold the race as planned, albeit with heightened security. Some accepted entrants dropped out; other runners took the opportunity to jump in. On the morning of November 4, 2001, there were 30,574 runners at the starting area, even more than the year before. They came from all over the world to show their support for this great city in its most heartbreaking time. They came to prove that New York still had hope; it still had life. Runners dressed in red, white, and blue; they carried American flags; they painted "FDNY" across their stomachs.

As the field tore across the Verrazano-Narrows Bridge to start the race, a silence settled over them. It was impossible not to look out at the Manhattan skyline and see what wasn't there. That vast absence, filled only by the thrum of police and press helicopters.

But as the athletes pounded into Brooklyn, that thrum was overwhelmed by a roar of spectators. Once again, the people of New York had come out to cheer the marathoners, but this year they were cheering for so much more. For the first time since the unfathomable had occurred, the city had a reason to celebrate, and they did so in force. More than 2 million New Yorkers came out to prove that life there would go on, that they would not be cowed in fear, that they would feel joy again, even in the face of utter devastation.

---

public bathhouse, which dates to 1892, isn't about pampering as much as getting a practical, hearty cleansing. There's a eucalyptus steam room, a redwood sauna, pull-chain showers, and an ice-cold plunge pool (45 degrees), and you're encouraged to alternate cooking in the hot rooms with plunges in the cold pool to stimulate circulation. Traditional treatments are offered without appointment, such as the detoxifying Platza Oak Leaf ($30), in which a Russian strongman or woman swats your soapy skin with an oak-leaf broom. Except for a few single-sex hours per week, the baths are coed. ✉ 268 E. 10th St., between 1st Ave. and Ave. A, East Village ☎ 212/674-9250 or 212/473-8806 ⊕ www.russianturkishbaths.com ✉ $25 🕐 Mon., Tues., Thurs., and Fri. 11 AM–10 PM, Wed. 9 AM–10 PM, weekends 7:30 AM–10 PM Ⓜ L to 1st Ave.

TAKE TO THE SKIES. Liberty Helicopter Tours (✉ Heliport, W. 30th St. at 12th Ave., Midtown West ☎ 212/967-6464 ⊕ www.libertyhelicopters.com) has six pilot-narrated tours from $30 per person for a two-minute sneak peek, up to $849 to reserve the whole helicopter for a 15-minute ride. Some tours depart from Pier 6 in Lower Manhattan.

Shop Around

Shopping in Manhattan is an event. For every bursting department store, there's an echoing, minimalist boutique; for every nationally familiar brand, there's a local favorite. There are also myriad opportunities for bargains: hawkers of not-so-real Rolex watches and Kate Spade bags are stationed at street corners, and there are uptown thrift shops where socialites send their castoffs, and downtown spots where the fashion crowd turns in last week's must-haves. The following is a basic guide to Manhattan's shopping neighborhoods and what you'll find in each.

CHELSEA, THE FLATIRON DISTRICT & THE MEATPACKING DISTRICT. Fifth Avenue south of 23rd Street, along with the streets fanning east and west, nurses a lively downtown shopping scene. You'll find a mix of the hip, such as Emporio Armani, Intermix, and Paul Smith, and the hard core, such as the mega-discounter Loehmann's on 7th Avenue. Broadway has the richly overstuffed ABC Carpet & Home and the comprehensive Paragon Sporting Goods. Farther south, the Meatpacking District has become chic, thanks to high-fashion temple Jeffrey; the two mega-Mcs, Stella McCartney and Alexander McQueen; a few fresh galleries; and a slew of restaurants-of-the-moment.

5TH AVENUE. Fifth Avenue from Rockefeller Center to Central Park South still wavers between the money-is-no-object crowd and an influx of more accessible stores. The flag-bedecked Saks Fifth Avenue faces Rockefeller Center, which harbors branches of Banana Republic and J. Crew. Then there are the perennial favorites: Cartier jewelers and Salvatore Ferragamo, at 52nd Street; Takashimaya, at 54th Street; Henri Bendel, at 56th Street; Tiffany and Bulgari jewelers, at 57th Street; and Bergdorf Goodman at 58th Street. Exclusive design houses such as Versace, Prada, and Gucci are a stone's throw from the über-chain Gap and a souped-up branch of Brooks Brothers.

57TH STREET. Luxury houses stake their claims here. Louis Vuitton wraps the northeast corner of 5th Avenue, with Yves Saint Laurent as its neighbor. Christian Dior is in the area as well. These glamazons are surrounded by other swank flagships such as Burberry and Chanel. The block isn't limited to top-echelon shopping; a NikeTown sits cheek by jowl with the couture houses. To the west of 5th Avenue are less monolithic shops, such as Smythson of Bond Street and Rizzoli bookstore.

LOWER EAST SIDE & THE EAST VILLAGE. The Lower East Side is a great place to find bargains, and home to edgy boutiques, particularly in the first block south of East Houston Street, where places like DDC Lab and Seven New York show newly hatched clothing concepts. Among the Orchard Street veterans are Fine & Klein for handbags and Klein's of Monticello for deals on dressy clothes. Note that many Orchard Street stores are closed Saturday in observance of the Jewish Sabbath. Ludlow Street, one block east of Orchard, buzzes with storefronts selling hipster gear like electric guitars, vintage '60s and '70s furniture, and clothing and accessories from local designers. To the north, the East Village offers diverse, offbeat specialty stops, plenty of collectible kitsch, and some great vintage-clothing boutiques, especially along East 7th and East 9th streets.

MADISON AVENUE. Madison Avenue from East 57th to about East 79th streets can satisfy almost any couture craving. Giorgio Armani, Dolce & Gabbana, Valentino, Gianni Versace, and Prada are among the avenue's Italian compatriots. French houses assert

FORGET SIGHTSEEING. GET ME TO A SPA!

Some of Manhattan's finest hotels have equally luxurious spas. Among the best are those in the Mandarin Oriental, the Peninsula, and the Four Seasons. You can try to get into one on marathon weekend, but it could prove difficult unless you're a hotel guest. The following day spas are also good choices:

GRACEFUL SPA. Named "Best Massage on a Budget" by *New York* magazine, Graceful offers a 60-minute massage for just $80, an unbelievable price in Manhattan. Given the deal, you might want to opt for 90 minutes or add a facial massage. The Graceful massage is a combination of Qi-Gong Tui-Na, deep tissue, Swedish, and shiatsu. It aims to rid you of pain by balancing your energy, or "Qi," leaving you both relaxed and powerfully energized. ⊠ 205 W. 14th St., Chelsea ☎ 212/675-5145 ⊕ www.gracefulspa.com Ⓜ 1, 2, 3 to 14th St. ⊠ 1097 2nd Ave., between 57th and 58th St., Midtown East ☎ 212/593-9904 ⊕ www.gracefulservices.com Ⓜ 4, 5, 6 to 59th St. ⊟ AE, MC, V ⊗ Daily 10–10.

OASIS DAY SPA. This spa has three locations (not including the one in the Jet-Blue terminal at JFK), and promises a peaceful, beautiful environment as well as luxurious spa treatments. Founded by a husband and wife, these spas understand how to cater perfectly to both men's and women's needs. Try the Muscle Meltdown (30–90 minutes, $70–$130), a sports massage combined with a moist heat treatment to melt the miles away. ⊠ 1 Park Ave., between 32nd and 33rd Sts., Midtown East Ⓜ 6 to 33rd St. ⊠ 108 E. 16th St., 2nd fl., between Union Sq. E and Irving Pl., Gramercy Ⓜ L, N, R, 4, 5, 6 to 14th St. ⊠ 150 E. 34th St., 2nd fl., between Lexington and 3rd Aves., Midtown East Ⓜ 6 to 33rd St. ☎ 212/254-7722 ⊕ www.oasisdayspanyc.com ⊟ AE, D, MC, V ⊗ Weekdays 10–10, weekends 9–9.

THE SPA AT CHELSEA PIERS. The cocoonlike atmosphere will make you forget you're in a huge sports complex. Indulge in a sports massage (50–80 minutes, $105–$135), or consider the $230 Athlete's State of Zen: an exercise class of your choice (yoga, Pilates, etc.), a 50-minute sports massage, a 25-minute reflexology session, and a mineral salt or sugar scrub. They even throw in a protein smoothie. Spend at least $75 on a treatment and you get free access to the sports center, including its six-lane, 25-yard pool and oversize whirlpool spa. ⊠ Pier 60, 23rd St. and the Hudson River, Chelsea ☎ 212/336-6780 ⊕ www.chelseapiers.com ⊗ Weekdays 10–9, weekends 10–7 ⊟ AE, D, MC, V Ⓜ C, E to 8th Ave.

themselves with Yves Saint Laurent, Rive Gauche, Hermès, Jean Paul Gaultier, and a pair of Chanel specialty boutiques. New York's Donna Karan posts both DKNY and Donna Karan collections. The full-fledged department store Barneys fits right in. A couple of marvelous bookstores, several outstanding antiques dealers, a branch of the foodie haven Dean & Deluca, and numerous art galleries are here as well.

NOLITA. Tiny, one-of-a-kind boutiques sprout here like mushrooms after rain. A cache of stylish shops—such as Mayle, Tracy Feith, Seize sur Vingt, and the various Calypsos—will start your sartorial engines running. Accessories are hardly neglected; Jamin Puech provides swish purses, and spots like Coclico, Geraldine, and Hollywould play to women's shoe cravings. Sigerson Morrison covers both bases with smart shoes and handbags. Meanwhile, Me + Ro and Femmegems beckon with jewelry.

SOHO. Its cobbled streets are packed with high-rent boutiques and national chains. Look for big fashion guns such as Louis Vuitton, Chanel, Burberry, and Prada, along with secondary-line designer outposts such as D&G, DKNY, and Miu Miu. Unique stores include Dean & Deluca, a gourmet food emporium; Moss, full of well-designed home furnishings and gifts; and the Enchanted Forest toy store. There are the two Kates as well: Kate's Paperie, for paper products, and Kate Spade, for handbags and accessories. On Lafayette Street below East Houston, a fashionable strip includes shops outside the mainstream, dealing in urban street wear and vintage 20th-century furniture.

TIMES SQUARE. C'mon, who doesn't want cheap souvenirs? You'll find them here, but you'll also find behemoth stores like the Virgin Megastore and Toys R Us, which has not only a full-size Ferris wheel on which you can ride with characters like E. T., but also a giant T-Rex that blows smoke and roars. When you're not shopping, gaze up and be wowed by the ubiquity and enormity of the signs: two-story-high cups of coffee that actually steam; a 42-foot-tall bottle of Coca-Cola; mammoth, superfast digital displays of world news and stock quotes; on-location network studios; and countless other technologically sophisticated allurements. Zoning now actually *requires* that buildings be decked out with ads, as they have been for nearly a century.

I Love the Nightlife

Bars & Lounges

★ **CAMPBELL APARTMENT.** One of Manhattan's more beautiful rooms, this restored space inside Grand Central Terminal dates to the 1920s, when it was the private office of an executive named John W. Campbell. He knew how to live, and you can enjoy his good taste from an overstuffed chair. ✉ 15 Vanderbilt Ave. entrance, Midtown East ☎ 212/953-0409 Ⓜ 4, 5, 6, 7, S to 42nd St./Grand Central.

★ **THE CARLYLE.** The hotel's discreetly sophisticated Café Carlyle hosts such top performers such as Bette Buckley, Elaine Stritch, Barbara Cook, and Ute Lemper. Stop by on a Monday night and take in Woody Allen, who swings on the clarinet with his New Orleans Jazz Band. Bemelmans Bar, with murals by the author of the Madeline books, features a rotating cast of pianist-singers. ✉ 35 E. 76th St., between Madison and Park Aves., Upper East Side ☎ 212/744-1600 ⊕ www.thecarlyle.com Ⓜ 6 to 77th St.

CHUMLEY'S. There's no sign to help you find this place—they took it down during its days as a speakeasy—but when you reach the corner of Bedford and Barrow, you're very close (just head a little north on Barrow and duck into the doorway on the east side of the street). A fireplace warms the relaxed dining room, where the burgers are hearty and the clientele is collegiate. ⊠ 86 Bedford St., between Barrow and Grove Sts., Greenwich Village ☎ 212/675-4449 Ⓜ 1, 9 to Christopher St./Sheridan Sq.

CORNELIA STREET CAFÉ. Share a bottle of merlot at a street-side table on a quaint West Village lane. Downstairs, groove to live jazz, catch a poetry reading, or take in the "Entertaining Science" evenings hosted by the Nobel laureate chemist Roald Hoffmann. ⊠ 29 Cornelia St., between W. 4th and Bleecker Sts., Greenwich Village ☎ 212/989-9319 ⊕ www.corneliastreetcafe.com Ⓜ A, C, E, B, D, F, V to W. 4th St.

FLATIRON LOUNGE. Soft lighting and smart leather banquettes distinguish this art deco hideout where guest mixologists, a seasonal drink menu, and owner Julie Reiner's daily "flights" of fanciful mini-martinis elevate bartending to an art form. ⊠ 37 W. 19th St., between 5th and 6th Aves., Chelsea ☎ 212/727-7741 ⊕ www.flatironlounge.com Ⓜ F, V to 23rd St.

JOE'S PUB. Wood paneling, red-velvet walls, and comfy sofas make a lush setting for top-notch performers and the A-list celebrities who come to see them. There's not a bad seat in the house, but if you want to sit, arrive at least a half hour early and enjoy the Italian dinner menu. ⊠ 425 Lafayette St., between E. 4th St. and Astor Pl., East Village ☎ 212/539-8770 for info, 212/539-8778 for reservations ⊕ http://web.joespub.com Ⓜ 6 to Astor Pl.

MERCBAR. A chic local crowd comes to this dark, nondescript bar for the wonderful martinis. Its street number is barely visible—look for the French doors, which stay open in summer. ⊠ 151 Mercer St., between Prince and W. Houston Sts., SoHo ☎ 212/966-2727 ⊕ www.mercbar.com Ⓜ R, N, W to Prince St.

P. J. CLARKE'S. Mirrors and polished wood adorn New York's most famous Irish bar, where scenes from the 1945 movie *Lost Weekend* were shot. The after-work crowd that unwinds here seems to appreciate the old-fashioned flair. ⊠ 915 3rd Ave., at E. 55th St., Midtown East ☎ 212/317-1616 ⊕ www.pjclarkes.com Ⓜ 4, 5, 6 to 59th St.

★ **PRAVDA.** Cocktails are the rule at this Eastern European–style bar. Choose from more than 70 brands of vodka, including house infusions, and nearly as many types of martinis. The cellarlike space, with an atmospheric vaulted ceiling, is illuminated with candles. Reserve a table for the Russian-inspired fare, especially on weekends. ⊠ 281 Lafayette St., between Prince and Houston Sts., SoHo ☎ 212/226-4944 ⊕ www.pravdany.com Ⓜ B, F to Broadway/Lafayette St.

★ **ROYALTON.** Check out both the large lobby bar furnished with armchairs and chaise longues, and the banquette-lined Round Bar. In a circular room to your right as you enter, it's the place to sip vodka and champagne. The hotel entrance is hard to find (look for the curved silver railings). ⊠ 44 W. 44th St., between 5th and 6th Aves., Midtown West ☎ 212/869-4400 ⊕ www.royaltonhotel.com Ⓜ B, D, F, V to 42nd St.

★ **SPICE MARKET.** Asian street fare accompanies Spice Market's exotic cocktails. An open space with slowly rotating fans, and sheer flowing curtains lends an aura of calm to this hot celebrity hangout. ⊠ 403 W. 13th St., at 9th Ave., Meatpacking District ☎ 212/675-2322 Ⓜ A, C, E to 14th St.; L to 8th Ave.

Bowling

Bowl to dance tunes at the funky **BOWLMOR LANES** (✉ 110 University Pl., between E. 12th and E. 13th Sts., Greenwich Village ☎ 212/255-8188 ⊕ www.bowlmor.com Ⓜ 4, 5, 6, N, R, Q, W to 14th St./Union Sq.), a 42-lane bi-level operation that can have a two-hour wait for a lane on weekend nights. If you're lucky, you can stay inside with a beeper so you can eat, drink at the bar, or wander upstairs to the pool tables while you wait. After 6 PM it's strictly 21 and over.

Dance Clubs

★ **CLUB SHELTER.** A warehouselike space is home to this low-key attitude club with some of the best dancing in the city. ✉ 20 W. 39th St., between 5th and 6th Aves., Midtown West ☎ 212/719-4479 ⊕ www.clubshelter.com Ⓜ B, D, F, V to 42nd St.

EXIT. This extravagant multilevel club has everything from a massive dance floor to an outdoor patio. A-list DJs spin for an enthusiastic crowd that often includes a hip-hop star or two. ✉ 610 W. 56th St., between 11th and 12th Aves., Midtown West ☎ 212/582-8282 ⊕ www.exit2nightclub.com Ⓜ 1, 9, A, B, C, D to 59th St.

Jazz Clubs

BLUE NOTE. Considered by many to be the jazz capital of the world, the Blue Note could see in an average month Spyro Gyra, Ron Carter, and Jon Hendricks. Expect a steep cover charge except on Monday, when record labels promote their artists' recent releases for an average ticket price of less than $20. ✉ 131 W. 3rd St., near 6th Ave., Greenwich Village ☎ 212/475-8592 ⊕ www.bluenote.net Ⓜ A, C, E, F, V to W. 4th St.

★ **VILLAGE VANGUARD.** This prototypical jazz club, tucked into a cellar in Greenwich Village, has been the haunt of legends like Thelonious Monk. Today you might hear jams from the likes of Wynton Marsalis and Roy Hargrove, among others. ✉ 178 7th Ave. S, between W. 11th and Perry Sts., Greenwich Village ☎ 212/255-4037 ⊕ www.villagevanguard.net Ⓜ 1, 2, 3 to 14th St.

Rock Clubs

★ **BOWERY BALLROOM.** This theater with art deco accents is the city's top midsize concert venue. You can grab one of the tables on the balcony or stand on the main floor. There's a comfortable bar in the basement. ✉ 6 Delancey St., near the Bowery, Lower East Side ☎ 212/533-2111 ⊕ www.boweryballroom.com Ⓜ J, M to Bowery.

IRVING PLAZA. This two-story venue has a near monopoly on the hottest bills in town, from Erasure to Norah Jones. The good sound system and ample sight lines don't hurt, either. ✉ 17 Irving Pl., at E. 15th St., Gramercy ☎ 212/777-6800 ⊕ www.irvingplaza.com Ⓜ 4, 5, 6, L, N, Q, R, W to 14th St./Union Sq.

KNITTING FACTORY. This art-rock club is one of the city's most enjoyable performance spaces—the 400-capacity room never gets overcrowded, the sound system is superb, and the front-room bar is a convivial retreat when your eardrums need a break. Indie-rock darlings, Japanese hard-core legends, and avant-garde noise bands are common sights on

TICKET TAKES

For Broadway shows, off-Broadway shows, and other big-ticket events, you can order tickets well in advance through **Telecharge** (☎ 212/239–6200 ⊕ www.telecharge.com) and **Ticketmaster** (☎ 212/307–4100 ⊕ www. ticketmaster.com). For off-Broadway shows, try **SmartTix** (☎ 212/868–4444 ⊕ www.smarttix.com) or **Ticket Central** (✉ 416 W. 42nd St., between 9th and 10th Aves., Midtown West ☎ 212/279–4200 ⊕ www.ticketcentral.org Ⓜ A, C, E to 42nd St.)

For tickets at 25% to 50% off the usual price, head to **TKTS** (✉ Duffy Sq., W. 47th St. and Broadway, Midtown West Ⓜ N, R, W to 49th St.; 1, 9 to 50th St. ✉ South St. Seaport, at Front and John Sts., Lower Manhattan Ⓜ 2, 3 to Fulton St.). There's usually a good selection of shows available, but don't expect to see the latest hits. The kiosks accept cash and traveler's checks—no credit cards. The Times Square location is open Monday–Saturday 3–8 and Sunday 11–7:30, as well as Wednesday and Saturday at 10–2 for matinee shows. South Street Seaport hours are weekdays 11–6, Saturday 11–7, and Sunday 11–4.

Online deals can be found at **TheaterMania** (⊕ www.theatermania.com) and **Playbill** (⊕ www.playbill.com). For long-running shows, including popular hits like *Phantom of the Opera,* numerous vendors offer discount ticket vouchers. Exchange them at the box office for an actual ticket. The **Broadway Ticket Center** (✉ 1560 Broadway, between W. 46th and W. 47th Sts., Midtown West ☎ No phone Ⓜ R, W to 49th St.), inside the Times Square Visitors Center, is open Monday–Saturday 10–6 and Sunday 10–3.

Need to see the hottest show, no matter what it costs? **Continental Guest Services** (☎ 212/944–8910 or 800/BWY–TKTS (299–8587) ⊕ www. intercharge.com) is one of the best-known ticket brokers in Manhattan. Be warned: tickets can be double the usual price. Order "VIP tickets" from **Broadway Inner Circle** (☎ 866/847–8587 ⊕ www.broadwayinnercircle.com).

---

the main stage; quieter and more obscure performers prevail in the two smaller rooms on the lower levels. ✉ 74 Leonard St., between Broadway and Church St., TriBeCa ☎ 212/219-3132 Ⓜ 1, 9 to Franklin St.

Theater

To most people, New York theater is Broadway, meaning the region roughly bounded by West 41st and West 52nd streets, between 6th and 9th avenues. The names of the many theaters read like a roll call of American theater history: Edwin Booth, the Barrymores (Ethel, John, and Lionel), Eugene O'Neill, George Gershwin, Alfred Lunt and Lynn Fontanne, Helen Hayes, Richard Rodgers, Neil Simon, and now renowned theatrical illustrator Al Hirschfeld (after whom the Martin Beck was renamed in 2003).

Even so, the best theater can often be found far from Times Square. Off- and off-off-Broadway houses are where you can find showcases for emerging playwrights, classic plays performed with new twists, and crowd-pleasers like *Blue Man Group* and *Stomp*. The venues themselves are often found in clusters around the city—in Greenwich Village, the East Village, and the Lower East Side, as well as in Brooklyn neighborhoods like DUMBO and Williamsburg.

Among the 40-odd Broadway theaters are some old playhouses as interesting for their history as for their current offerings. The handsomely renovated Selwyn is now known as the **AMERICAN AIRLINES THEATRE** (✉ 227 W. 42nd St., between 7th and 8th Aves., Midtown West ☎ 212/719-1300 ⊕ www.roundabouttheatre.org Ⓜ A, C, E to 42nd St.). After various reincarnations as a burlesque hall and pornographic movie house, this Venetian-style theater is now home to the Roundabout Theatre Company, which is acclaimed for its revivals of classic musicals and plays. The lavish **HILTON THEATRE** (✉ 214 W. 43rd St., between 7th and 8th Aves., Midtown West ☎ 212/307-4100 Ⓜ A, C, E to 42nd St.) is an 1,839-seat house that combines two classic auditoriums, the Lyric and the Apollo. It incorporates architectural elements from both, adding state-of-the-art sound and lighting equipment.

Disney refurbished the art nouveau **NEW AMSTERDAM THEATER** (✉ 214 W. 42nd St., between 7th and 8th Aves., Midtown West ☎ 212/282-2907 Ⓜ A, C, E to 42nd St.), where Eddie Cantor, Will Rogers, Fanny Brice, and the Ziegfeld Follies once drew crowds. Today it's the long-running den of *The Lion King*. The **ST. JAMES** (✉ 246 W. 44th St., between Broadway and 8th Ave., Midtown West ☎ 212/239-6200 Ⓜ A, C, E to 42nd St.), current home of Mel Brooks's juggernaut *The Producers*, is where Lauren Bacall was an usherette in the '40s and where a little show called *Oklahoma!* changed musicals forever.

HELPFUL INFO

Airports

The major air gateways to New York City are LaGuardia Airport (LGA) and JFK International Airport (JFK) in the borough of Queens, and Newark Liberty International Airport (EWR) in New Jersey. Although all major airlines service the city, Continental Airlines is the official marathon airline, and offers discounts. Check the race Web site or your participant handbook for discount details and codes.

🚹 AIRPORT INFORMATION JFK International Airport ☎ 718/244-4444 ⊕ www.kennedyairport.com. LaGuardia Airport ☎ 718/533-3400 ⊕ www.laguardiaairport.com. Newark Liberty International Airport ☎ 973/961-6000 or 888/397-4636 ⊕ www.newarkairport.com.

🚹 OFFICIAL AIRLINE Continental Airlines ☎ 800/523-3273 ⊕ www.continental.com.

Airport Transfers

Air-Ride provides detailed, up-to-the-minute recorded information on how to reach your destination from any of New York's airports. Note that if you arrive after midnight at any airport, you may wait a long time for a taxi. Consider calling a car service, as there's no shuttle service at that time.

🛈 TRANSFER INFORMATION Air-Ride ☎ 800/247-7433 (800/AIR-RIDE).

TAXIS & CAR SERVICES

Outside the baggage-claim area at each of New York's major airports are taxi stands where a uniformed dispatcher helps passengers find taxis. Cabs can't pick up fares anywhere else in the arrivals area, so if you want a taxi, take your place in line.

Car services can be a great deal because the driver will often meet you on the concourse or in the baggage-claim area and help you with your luggage. The flat rates and tolls are often comparable to taxi fares, but some car services will charge for parking and waiting time at the airport. To eliminate these expenses, other car services require that you phone their dispatcher when you land so they can send the next available car to pick you up. New York City Taxi and Limousine Commission rules require that all car services be licensed and pick up riders only by prior arrangement; if possible, reserve 24 hours in advance. Drivers of nonlicensed vehicles ("gypsy cabs") often solicit fares outside the terminal and in baggage claim areas. Don't take them: even if you do have a safe ride, you'll pay more than the going rate.

From JFK, taxis charge a flat fee of $45 plus tolls (which may be as much as $6) to Manhattan only, and take 35–60 minutes. Prices are roughly $16–$55 for trips to most other locations in New York City. You should also tip the driver. From LaGuardia, taxis cost $20–$30 plus tip and tolls (again as high as $6) to most destinations in New York City, and take at least 20–40 minutes. Taxis to Manhattan from Newark cost $40–$65 plus tip and tolls ($5) and take 20–45 minutes. "Share and Save" group rates are available for up to four passengers between 8 AM and midnight—make arrangements with the airport's taxi dispatcher. If you're heading to Newark from Manhattan, a $15 surcharge applies to the normal taxi rates and the $5 toll.

SHUTTLES

Shuttles generally pick up from a designated spot along the curb. New York Airport Service runs buses between JFK and LaGuardia airports, and buses from those airports to Grand Central Terminal, Port Authority Bus Terminal, Penn Station, Bryant Park, and hotels between 31st and 60th streets in Manhattan. Fares are $12–$15. Buses operate from 6:15 AM to 11:10 PM from the airport; between 5 AM and 10 PM to the airport.

SuperShuttle vans travel to and from Manhattan to JFK, LaGuardia, and Newark. They will stop at your home, office, or hotel. Courtesy phones are at the airports. For travel to the airport, give 24-hour notice. Fares range from $15 to $19 per person.

AirTrain JFK links to the A subway line's Howard Beach station, and to Long Island Railroad's (LIRR) Jamaica Station, which is adjacent to the Sutphin Boulevard/Archer Avenue E/J/Z subway station, with connections to Manhattan. The light-rail system runs 24 hours, leaving from the Howard Beach and the LIRR stations every 4–8 minutes during peak times and every 12 minutes during low traffic times. From Midtown Manhattan, the longest trip to JFK is via the A train, a trip of less than an hour that costs $2 in subway fare in addition to $5 for the AirTrain. The quickest trip is with the Long Island Railroad (about 30 minutes), for a total cost of about $12. When traveling to the Howard Beach station, be sure to take the A train marked FAR ROCKAWAY or ROCKAWAY PARK, not LEFFERTS BOULEVARD.

AirTrain Newark is an elevated light-rail system that connects to New Jersey Transit and Amtrak trains at the Newark Liberty International Airport Station. Total travel time to Penn Station in Manhattan is approximately 20 minutes and costs $11.55 if you connect to a New Jersey train (it costs significantly more to connect to an Amtrak train). AirTrain runs from 5 AM to 2 AM daily. Before heading to Manhattan, the AirTrain stops at Newark's Penn Station. The five-minute ride here costs $6.80. From Newark Penn Station you can catch PATH trains, which run to Manhattan 24 hours a day. PATH trains run every 10 minutes on weekdays, every 15 to 30 minutes on weeknights, and every 20 to 30 minutes on weekends. After stopping at Christopher Street, one line travels along 6th Avenue, making stops at West 9th Street, West 14th Street, West 23rd Street, and West 33rd Street. Other PATH trains connect Newark Penn Station with the World Trade Center site. PATH train fare is $1.50.

For $2 you can ride the M-60 public bus (there are no luggage facilities on this bus) from LaGuardia to 116th Street and Broadway, across from Columbia University on Manhattan's Upper West Side. From there, you can transfer to the No. 1 subway to Midtown. Alternatively, you can take Bus Q-48 to the Main Street subway station in Flushing, where you can transfer to the No. 7 train. Allow at least 90 minutes for the entire trip to Midtown. Olympia Trails buses leave Newark for Grand Central Terminal and Penn Station in Manhattan about every 20 minutes until midnight. The trip takes roughly 45 minutes, and the fare is $12. Between the Port Authority or Grand Central Terminal and Newark, buses run every 20 to 30 minutes. The fare is $12.

🚌 SHUTTLE SERVICE AirTrain JFK ⊕ www.airtrainjfk.com. **AirTrain Newark** ☎888/397-4636 ⊕ www.airtrainnewark.com. **Long Island Railroad** Jamaica Station ✉ 146 Archer Ave., at Sutphin Blvd. ☎718/217-5477. **Metropolitan Transit Authority (MTA) Travel Information Line** ☎718/330-1234, 718/330-4847 for non-English speakers ⊕www.mta.nyc.ny.us. **MTA Status information hotline** ☎718/243-7777, updated hourly. **New York Airport Service** ☎718/875-8200 ⊕ www.nyairportservice.com. **Olympia Trails** ☎212/964-6233 or 877/894-9155 ⊕ www.olympiabus.com. **PATH Trains** ☎800/234-7284 ⊕ www.pathrail.com. **SuperShuttle** ☎212/258-3826 ⊕ www.supershuttle.com.

Bus Travel

Most long-haul and commuter bus lines feed into the Port Authority Bus Terminal, on 8th Avenue between West 40th and 42nd streets. You must purchase your ticket at a ticket counter, not from the bus driver. Six bus lines, serving northern New Jersey and Rockland County, New York, make daily stops at the George Washington Bridge Bus Station from 5 AM to 1 AM. The station is connected to the 175th Street Station on the A line of the subway, which travels down the West Side of Manhattan.

City bus routes go up or down the north-south avenues, or east and west on the major two-way crosstown streets: 96th, 86th, 79th, 72nd, 57th, 42nd, 34th, 23rd, and 14th. Most bus routes operate 24 hours, but service is infrequent late at night. Certain bus routes pro-

METROCARD BASICS

You pay for mass transit with a MetroCard, a plastic card with a magnetic strip. After you swipe the card through a subway turnstile or insert it in a bus's card reader, the cost of the fare is automatically deducted. With that same Metro-Card, you have up to two hours to transfer free from bus to subway, subway to bus, or bus to bus.

MetroCards are sold at all subway stations and at some stores—look for an "Authorized Sales Agent" sign. There are two kinds of cards: unlimited ride and pay-per-ride. Seven-day unlimited-ride MetroCards ($24) allow bus and subway travel for a week. If you will ride more than 13 times, this is the card to get. The one-day unlimited-ride Fun Pass ($7) is good from the day of purchase through 3 AM the following day. It's sold only by neighborhood MetroCard merchants and MetroCard vending machines at stations (not through the station agent).

When you purchase a pay-per-ride card worth $10 or more, you get a 20% bonus—six rides for the price of five. Unlike unlimited-ride cards, pay-per-ride MetroCards can be shared between riders; unlimited-ride MetroCards can be used only once at the same station or bus route in an 18-minute period.

You can buy or add money to an existing MetroCard at a MetroCard vending machine, available at most subway station entrances (usually near the station booth). The machines accept major credit cards and ATM or debit cards. Many also accept cash, but note that the maximum amount of change they will return is $6.

vide limited-stop service during weekday rush hours. A sign posted at the front of the bus indicates it has limited service; ask the driver whether the bus stops near where you want to go before boarding.

To find a bus stop, look for a light-blue sign (green for a limited bus) on a green pole; bus numbers and routes are listed, with the stop's name underneath. Route maps and schedules are posted at many bus stops in Manhattan and at major stops throughout the other boroughs. Each of the five boroughs of New York has a separate bus map; the best places to obtain them are the MTA booth in the Times Square Information Center, or the information kiosks in Grand Central Terminal and Penn Station.

Bus fare is the same as subway fare: $2. MetroCards allow you one free transfer between buses or from bus to subway; when using a token or cash, you can ask the driver for a free transfer coupon, good for one change to an intersecting route. Legal transfer points are listed on the back of the slip. Transfers generally have time limits of two hours. You can't use the transfer to enter the subway system.

🚌 BUS INFORMATION Adirondack, Pine Hill, and New York Trailways ☎800/225-6815 ⊕ www.trailways.com. Bonanza Bus Lines ☎888/751-8800 ⊕ www.bonanzabus. com. Greyhound Lines Inc. ☎800/231-2222 ⊕ www.greyhound.com. New Jersey

Transit ☎ 800/772-2222 ⊕ www.njtransit.com. **Peter Pan Trailways** ☎ 413/781-2900 or 800/237-8747 ⊕ www.peterpanbus.com. **Shortline** ☎ 800/631-8405 ⊕ www. shortlinebus.com. **Vermont Transit** ☎ 800/552-8737 ⊕ www.vermonttransit.com.

🚌 BUS STATIONS **George Washington Bridge Bus Station** ✉ 4211 Broadway, between 178th and 179th Sts., Washington Heights ☎ 800/221-9903 ⊕ www.panynj.gov. **Port Authority Bus Terminal** ✉ 625 8th Ave., at 42nd St., Midtown West ☎ 212/564-8484 ⊕ www.panynj.gov.

🚌 CITY BUS INFORMATION **Metropolitan Transit Authority (MTA) Travel Information Line** ☎ 718/330-1234, 718/330-4847 for non-English speakers ⊕ www.mta.nyc.ny. us. **MTA Status information hotline** ☎ 718/243-7777, updated hourly.

Car Travel

Drive into Manhattan only if you must, and use your car sparingly. Park it in a guarded garage for at least several hours; rates decrease somewhat if a car is left for a significant amount of time. All over town, lots charge exorbitant prices—as much as $23 for two hours (this includes an impressive sales tax of 18.625%). Free parking is difficult to find in Midtown, and violators can be towed away literally within minutes. If you find a spot on the street, be sure to check parking signs carefully. Rules differ from block to block, and they're nearly all confusing.

Try to avoid the morning and evening rush hours (a problem at the crossings into Manhattan) and lunch hour. Streets are in generally good condition, although there are enough potholes and bad patch jobs to make driving a little rough in places. Heavy rains can cause street flooding in some areas, most notoriously on the Franklin Delano Roosevelt Drive (known as the FDR or East River Drive), where the heavy traffic can grind to a halt when lakes suddenly appear on the road. The deterioration of the bridges to Manhattan, especially those spanning the East River, means lots of repair work. Listen to traffic reports on the radio before you set off, and don't be surprised if a bridge is partially or entirely closed.

Driving within Manhattan can be a nightmare of gridlocked streets, obnoxious drivers and bicyclists, and seemingly suicidal jaywalkers. Narrow and one-way streets are common, particularly downtown, and can make driving even more difficult. The most congested streets of the city lie between 14th and 59th streets and 3rd and 8th avenues. If after all that you still feel the need to rent a car, Avis is a marathon partner, and offers discounts. Check the race Web site or your participant handbook for details and codes.

🚗 CAR RENTAL AGENCY **Avis** ☎ 800/230-4898 ⊕ www.avis.com.

Disabilities & Accessibility

At most street corners, curb cuts allow wheelchairs to roll along unimpeded. Many restaurants, shops, and movie theaters with step-up entrances have wheelchair ramps. And though some New Yorkers may rush past those in need of assistance, you'll find plenty of people who are more than happy to help you get around.

Hospital Audiences maintains a Web site with information on the accessibility of many landmarks and attractions. A similar list, "Tourist and Cultural Information for the Disabled," is available from New York City's Web site. Big Apple Greeters has tours of New York City tailored to visitors' personal preferences.

🔟 LOCAL RESOURCES Big Apple Greeters ⊠ 1 Centre St., Suite 2035, Lower Manhattan, New York, NY 10007 ☎ 212/669–2896 ⊕ www.bigapplegreeter.org. Hospital Audiences ☎ 212/575–7676 ⊕ www.hospaud.org. New York City ☎ 311 in New York City, 212/639–9675 (212/NEW–YORK) outside of New York ⊕ www.nyc.gov.

Emergencies

🔟 HOSPITALS Bellevue ⊠ 462 1st Ave., at E. 27th St., Gramercy ☎ 212/562–4141. Lenox Hill Hospital ⊠ 100 E. 77th St., between Lexington and Park Aves., Upper East Side ☎ 212/434–2000. New York Presbyterian Hospital ⊠ 525 E. 68th St., at York Ave., Upper East Side ☎ 212/746–5454. NYU Hospital Downtown ⊠ 170 William St., between Beekman and Spruce Sts., Lower Manhattan ☎ 212/312–5000. NYU Medical Center ⊠ 530 1st Ave., at E. 32nd St., Murray Hill ☎ 212/263–7300. St. Luke's–Roosevelt Hospital ⊠ 10th Ave. at 59th St., Midtown West ☎ 212/523–4000. St. Vincent's Hospital ⊠ 7th Ave. and W. 12th St., Greenwich Village ☎ 212/604–7000.

🔟 24-HOUR PHARMACIES CVS ⊕ www.cvs.com. Rite-Aid ⊕ www.riteaid.com.

Subway Travel

The 714-mile subway system operates 24 hours a day and serves nearly all the places you're likely to visit. It's cheaper than a cab, and during the workweek it's often faster than either taxis or buses. The trains are clean, well lighted, and air-conditioned. Still, the New York subway is hardly problem free. Many trains are crowded, and the older ones are noisy. Homeless people sometimes take refuge from the elements by riding the trains, and panhandlers head there for a captive audience. Although trains usually run frequently, especially during rush hours, you never know when some incident somewhere on the line may stall traffic. In addition, subway construction sometimes causes delays or limitation of service, especially on weekends.

Most subway entrances are at street corners and are marked by lampposts with an illuminated MTA logo or globe-shape green or red lights—green means the station is open 24 hours, and red means the station closes at night (though colors don't always correspond to reality). Subway lines are designated by numbers and letters, such as the 3 line or the A line. Some lines run express and skip stops, and others are locals and make all stops. Each station entrance has a sign indicating the lines that run through the station. Some entrances are also marked "uptown only" or "downtown only." One of the most frequent mistakes visitors make is taking the train in the wrong direction.

Maps of the full subway system are posted in every train car and usually on the subway platform (though these are sometimes out-of-date). You can usually pick up free maps at station booths. For the most up-to-date information on subway lines, call the MTA's Travel Information Center or visit its Web site. The Web site HopStop can help you find the best line to take to reach your destination. Alternatively, ask a station agent.

Subway fare is the same as bus fare: $2. You can transfer between subway lines an unlimited number of times at any of the numerous stations where lines intersect. If you use a MetroCard to pay your fare, you can also transfer to intersecting MTA bus routes for free. Such transfers generally have time limits of two hours. Pay your subway fare at the turnstile, using a MetroCard bought at the station booth or from a vending machine.

⊠ SUBWAY INFORMATION Hopstop ⊕ www.hopstop.com. **MTA Travel Information Line** ☎ 718/330-1234, 718/330-4847 for non-English speakers ⊕ www.mta.nyc.ny.us. **MTA Lost Property Office** ☎ 212/712-4500. **MTA Status information hotline** ☎ 718/243-7777.

Taxis & Car Services

There are several differences between taxis (cabs) and car services, also known as livery cabs. Taxis run on a meter, whereas car services charge a flat fee. And by law, car services can't pick up passengers unless you call for one first.

Since taxis can be hard to find in the outer buroughs, you may have no choice but to call a car service. Determine the fee beforehand; a 10%–15% tip is customary above that.

Yellow cabs are everywhere in Manhattan, and usually easy to hail on the street or from a cab stand in front of major hotels, though finding one at rush hour or in the rain can take some time. Even so, never put yourself in danger by accepting a ride from a gypsy cab.

You can see if a taxi is available by checking its rooftop light; if the center panel is lighted and the side panels are dark, it's available. Fares cost $2.50 for the first $1/5$ mile, 40¢ for each $1/5$ mile thereafter, and 20¢ for each minute not in motion. A $1 surcharge is added to rides begun 4–8 PM, and a 50¢ surcharge is added between 8 PM and 6 AM.

One taxi can hold a maximum of four passengers (an additional passenger under the age of seven is allowed if the child sits on someone's lap). There's no charge for extra passengers. You must pay any bridge or tunnel tolls incurred during your trip (a driver will usually pay the toll himself to keep moving quickly, but that amount will be added to the fare when the ride is over). Taxi drivers expect a 15% to 20% tip.

⊠ CAR RESERVATIONS Carmel Car Service ☎ 212/666-6666 or 800/922-7635 ⊕ www. carmelcarservice.com. **London Towncars** ☎ 212/988-9700 or 800/221-4009 ⊕ www. londontowncars.com. **Tel Aviv Car and Limousine Service** ☎ 212/777-7777 or 800/222-9888 ⊕ www.telavivlimo.com.

CHAPTER 12

DECEMBER

Honolulu Marathon

Let's just start with the obvious: the race is in Hawai'i, and it's in December. It could be the world's lousiest marathon, and I, for one, would still go. As it happens, the Honolulu Marathon is a spectacular 26.2-mile jaunt through paradise. Further, it's organized by the nonprofit Honolulu Marathon Association, whose members actively coax the aloha spirit into every aspect of their race. Everyone is made to feel special. The marathon board, the staff, elite athletes, and other guests are treated to a lavish buffet several nights before the run; sponsors and race officials are feted with a sumptuous post-race cookout; runners and their guests are energized at a massive prerace lū'au and concert. No matter how you participate, you'll feel attended to, appreciated, embraced.

And did I mention it's in Hawai'i in December? Just sayin'.

So You're Running Honolulu . . .

Ahhh, Hawai'i. If you've never been, you're in for a treat. There's a very specific feel to the air. It's often humid, with moisture that you can practically touch, but it's not the least bit stifling. It's actually refreshing, like you just sprayed your face with a replenishing mist. And the air smells different in Hawai'i—floral, organic, alive.

I can't help it. I wax rhapsodic when I talk about Hawai'i. It's that amazing.

Several islands actually comprise Hawai'i: the Big Island, O'ahu, Maui, Kaua'i, Lāna'i, and Moloka'i. For this marathon, you'll travel to O'ahu and make your way to Waikīkī Beach in Honolulu. Want a sense of Waikīkī? Picture the Vegas Strip. Get rid of the casinos and the neon. Now pick the whole thing up and plop it down on a gorgeous crescent of sand that ends at a stunning 760-foot-high volcanic crater.

Can't get the image? Let me explain. The main drag of Waikīkī is Kalākaua Avenue, which runs down Waikīkī's 2½-mile length. Kalākaua's east side teems with tourists at all hours. Hotels, stores, and malls line the street; vendors stand on the sidewalk handing out coupons and incentives for tours, lū'au, and other (often cheesy) attractions; in the evening street performers ply their craft on every block. Cross the street, though, and you're on the beach: a tranquil oasis by night; a surfer, swimmer, and sunbather playground by day. This dichotomy is what makes Waikīkī so unique and fun. Although you'll spend a lot of time in this area, there are plenty of other places to explore.

KAPI'OLANI PARK & DIAMOND HEAD. At Waikīkī Beach's south end and within walking distance of all its hotels, Kapi'olani Park is marathon central, home to the prerace lū'au and concert, gear check, shuttles to the starting line, and the finish line. Established in the late 1800s by King Kalākaua and named after his queen, the 500-acre park sits in the shadow of Diamond Head Crater, named by sailors who thought they had found precious gems on its slopes. The "diamonds" proved to be volcanic refuse.

DOWNTOWN HONOLULU. Buildings here tell the story of Hawai'i's history through architecture, from the Chinatown buildings of the late 1800s, to the 1926 Aloha Tower, to the 21st-century First Hawaiian Building. Washington Place, built in 1846, was the home of Queen Lili'uokalani until her death in 1917, and until 2003 it served as the residence for Hawai'i's governors.

SOUTHEAST O'AHU. At once historic and contemporary, serene and active, the east end of O'ahu holds within its relatively small area remarkable variety and picture-perfect scenery of windswept cliffs and wave-dashed shores. Here you'll find one of O'ahu's most famous snorkeling destinations, the Hanauma Bay Nature Preserve.

NORTH SHORE & WINDWARD O'AHU. O'ahu's North Shore is about an hour's drive from Waikīkī, but it may as well be a world away. Here, bumper-to-bumper traffic and chorus lines of hotels give way to funky surf shops, suburban living, and some of the world's tallest winter waves. Windward O'ahu is only a 15-minute drive from busy Honolulu, yet has a relatively low profile (just the way its residents like it).

CENTRAL O'AHU. Between the Ko'olau and Wai'anae mountain ranges is the central plain that stretches from Pearl Harbor to the residential towns of Mililani and Wahiawā. Central O'ahu isn't as congested as Honolulu but is more developed than the North Shore. Once carpeted in pineapple and sugarcane plantations, the land is now home to ranches, banana farms, and fields of exotic flowers and coffee grown for export. Sights here include Pearl Harbor, the Dole Plantation, and the Aloha Stadium.

VISITOR INFO

Hawai'i Visitors and Convention Bureau

☎

800/GO-HAWAII

🌐

www.gohawaii.com

•

O'ahu Visitors Bureau

☎

800/672-6124

🌐

www.visit-oahu.com

RACE BASICS

The marathon is held on the second Sunday of December, a perfect time to escape the cold settling into most of the continental United States. Yet Americans aren't the only ones who flock to this marathon: 40 different countries were represented in 2004, with 61% of the runners coming from Japan.

Since its inception in 1973, the Honolulu Marathon has grown from a local affair attracting 167 entrants to the world's sixth-largest marathon. Its festivities include not only the big race, but also a 5K run a few days before

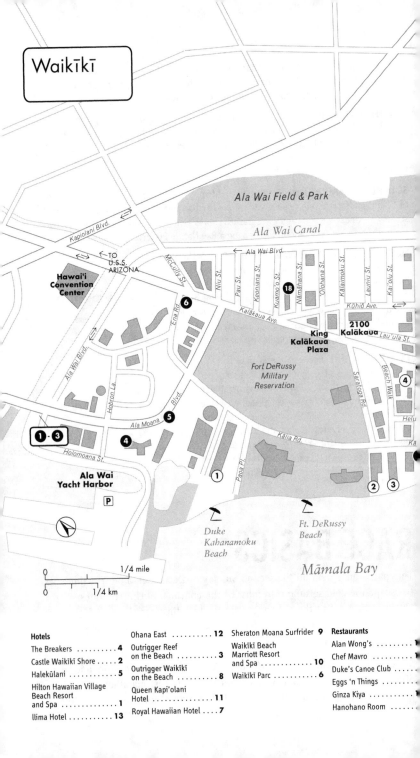

Waikīkī

Ala Wai Field & Park

Ala Wai Canal

Kapiolani Blvd.

← TO
U.S.S.
ARIZONA

Hawai'i
Convention
Center

Ala Wai Blvd. →

McCully St.

Niu St.
Pau St.
Keoniana St.
Kuamo'o St.
Nāmāhana St.
Olohana St.
Kālaimoku St.
Launiu St.
Ka'iolu St.

18

Kalākaua Ave.

Kūhiō Ave.

6

Ena Rd.

**2100
Kalākaua**

Lau'ula St.

King
Kalākaua
Plaza

Fort DeRussy
Military
Reservation

Ala Wai Blvd.

Hobron La.

Beach Walk

Saratoga Rd.

4

Helu

Ala Moana

5

Kālia Rd.

1 · 3

4

Holomoana St.

Paoa Pl.

1

Ka

2

3

**Ala Wai
Yacht Harbor**

P

Duke
Kahanamoku
Beach

Ft. DeRussy
Beach

Māmala Bay

1/4 mile

1/4 km

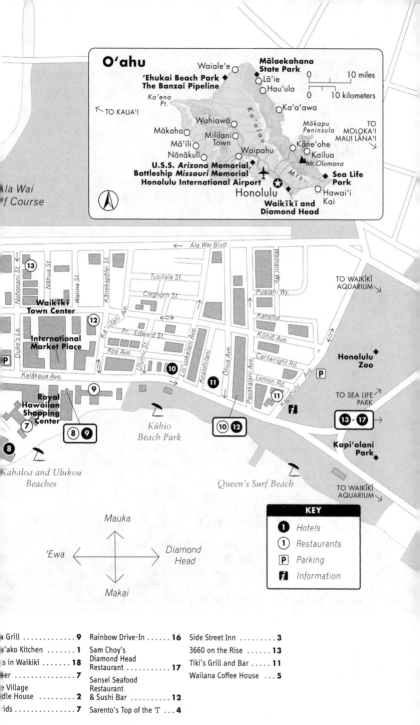

and a race-day 10K walk. Despite the growth, race quality hasn't suffered in the least, and organizers do their best to ensure that every single runner has a positive experience.

Registration

Registration opens in late January for locals and early February for the rest of the world. Fees are $95 before the end of October ($60 for Hawai'i residents), $105 between the end of October and mid-November, and $125 between mid-November and the race. There's no cap on the number of entrants.

You can register online through the end of November and by mail or fax through mid-November. After that, you can only register at the marathon expo. All who sign up before the end of October receive a confirmation card in the mail. When you register you can also buy tickets ($25 each) for the prerace lū'au and concert. Do so. The event is fantastic.

RACE CONTACT

Honolulu Marathon Office

✉

3435 Waialae Ave., Suite 208m, Honolulu, HI 96816

📠

808/734-7200

🌐

www.honolulumarathon.org

The marathon Web site is remarkably simple to navigate and filled with pertinent info. Many of the pages can be translated into other languages with just a click. Another standout feature is the course tour with pictures of 49 points along the route. Though the site lacks comprehensive travel and training resources, it has something else that sets it apart: the human touch. In 2005, for example, there were "Endorphin Man" running cartoons created by race director Jim Barahal and John Pritchett; a comic essay by Barahal called "How to Set Your P.W. (Personal Worst)", a heartfelt article from HMA member Jeanette Chun, sharing why she's passionate about this marathon; plus trivia, games, and other diversions to put a smile on your face and start the spirit of aloha flowing.

Hotels to Consider

You can't go wrong with the hotels or condos along Waikīkī Beach, all within walking distance of Kapi'olani Park. Both the Outrigger and Ohana hotels work with the marathon and the Outrigger Reef is the official race hotel. For the best deals, contact hotels directly or work with one of two race-affiliated agencies: **Pleasant Holidays** (☎ 800/536-4032 🌐 www.pleasantholidays.com) or **Marathon Tours** (☎ 800/444-4097 🌐 www.marathontours.com).

Hotels

★ **HALEKŪLANI.** It's absolutely the best. Spacious, marble- and wood-appointed rooms have ocean views. Just before the beach is a freshwater pool with an orchid mosaic created from more than 1.2 million glass tiles. A stay here gets you complimentary tickets to the Honolulu Symphony, Contemporary Art Museum, and Honolulu Academy of Arts. Room service offers carbo-loading dinners before the race and boxed Continental breakfasts race morning (order them by midnight). Post-marathon, enjoy the decadence of the spa. ✉ 2199 Kālia Rd., Waikīkī, 96815 ☎ 808/923-2311 or 800/367-2343 ⊕ www.halekulani.com ➴412 rooms, 43 suites ♨3 restaurants, 24-hr room service, wake-up calls, alarm clocks, newspapers, robes, cable TV with movies, in-room data ports, minibars, in-room safes, free Wi-Fi, pool, gym, hair salon, spa, beach, 3 bars, shops, dry cleaning, concierge, business services, meeting room, parking (fee); no smoking ▭AE, DC, MC, V $$$$.

HILTON HAWAIIAN VILLAGE BEACH RESORT AND SPA. The HHV is a bit far from Kapi'olani Park, but it has a lot to offer. Its five towers sit amid lavish gardens, pools, waterfalls, and koi ponds on 22 *acres* along Waikīkī's widest stretch. There are many free activities: lei making, poolside hula shows, fireworks. The full-service Mandara Spa is also on property. ✉2005 Kālia Rd., Waikīkī, 96815 ☎808/949-4321 or 800/221-2424 ⊕www.hiltonhawaiianvillage.com ➴3,432 rooms, 365 suites, 264 condominiums ♨ 20 restaurants, room service, wake-up calls, alarm clocks, coffeemakers, cable TV, in-room data ports, minibars, refrigerators, in-room safes, Wi-Fi (fee), 5 pools, hot tub, gym, spa, beach, 8 bars, shops, concierge, babysitting, children's programs (ages 5-12), dry cleaning, laundry service, business services, meeting rooms, car rental, parking (fee), no-smoking floors ▭AE, D, DC, MC, V $$-$$$$.

OHANA EAST. It's only two blocks from the beach and a 20-minute stroll from Kapi'olani Park. Among its offerings are 14 no-smoking floors and in-room Nintendo systems for restless kids. Although you can arrange for in-room massages, a stay here also gets you privileges at Outrigger's Serenity Spa in the Outrigger Reef on the Beach. ✉ 150 Kaiulani Ave., Waikīkī, 96815 ☎808/922-5353 or 800/462-6262 ⊕www.ohanahotels.com ➴423 rooms, 17 suites ♨ 3 restaurants, coffee shop, refrigerators, room service, wake-up calls, alarm clocks, coffeemakers, newspapers, cable TV with movies and video games, in-room data ports, some kitchenettes, in-room safes, free Wi-Fi, pool, hot tub, gym, hair salon, 4 bars, video game room, laundry facilities, dry cleaning, business services, meeting rooms, car rental, parking (fee), no-smoking floors ▭AE, D, DC, MC, V $-$$.

⚘ **OUTRIGGER REEF ON THE BEACH.** In the oceanfront or ocean-view rooms at the marathon's official hotel, you can see Diamond Head from your lānai. Most rooms have just a shower; ask if you want a shower/tub. Aloha Friday sees this hotel brimming with lei makers, entertainers, and artisans sharing their talents. Restaurants have marathon specials, and the hotel offers marathon rates. Post-race, take advantage of the Serenity Spa. ✉ 2169 Kālia Rd., Waikīkī, 96815 ☎ 808/923-3111 or 800/688-7444 ⊕ www.outrigger.com ➴804 rooms, 44 suites ♨3 restaurants, coffee shop, room service, wake-up calls, alarm clocks, coffeemakers, cable TV with movies and video games, refrigerators, in-room safes, pool, hot tub, gym, beach, 4 bars, shops, concierge, laundry facilities, babysitting, business services, meeting rooms, parking (fee), no-smoking floors ▭AE, D, DC, MC, V $-$$$$.

⚘ **OUTRIGGER WAIKĪKĪ ON THE BEACH.** A bit more expensive than the official race hotel, this 16-story resort also offers marathon rates, and is much closer to Kapi'olani Park. Rooms evoke plantation-style living, with rich dark-wood furnishings and Hawaiian artwork. For a night out on the town, the main showroom has the "Society of Seven" Las Vegas–style revue. Duke's Canoe Club has beachfront concerts under the stars. For post-race aches, try the Waikīkī Plantation Spa. ⊠ 2335 Kalākaua Ave., Waikīkī, 96815 ☎ 808/923-0711 or 800/688-7444 ⊕ www.outrigger.com ⬂ 500 rooms, 24 suites ⚄ 3 restaurants, coffee shop, snack bar, room service, wake-up calls, alarm clocks, coffeemakers, cable TV with movies and video games, in-room data ports, minibars, refrigerators, in-room safes, pool, beach, gym, hot tub, 4 bars, theater, shops, babysitting, dry cleaning, laundry facilities, business services, meeting rooms, parking (fee), no-smoking floors ▭ AE, D, DC, MC, V $$-$$$$.

QUEEN KAPI'OLANI HOTEL. It's a half block from the beach and very close to Kapi'olani Park. Accommodations include everything from standard hotel rooms to studios with kitchenettes to one-bedroom suites. Rates won't break the bank. ⊠ 150 Kapahulu Ave., Waikīkī, 96815 ☎ 808/922-1941 or 800/367-2317 ⊕ www.queenkapiolani.com ⬂ 308 rooms, 7 suites ⚄ Restaurant, wake-up calls, coffeemakers, cable TV with movies and video games, in-room data ports, some kitchenettes, refrigerators, in-room safes, pool, shop, dry cleaning, laundry facilities, no-smoking floors ▭ AE, D, DC, MC, V $-$$.

SURF'S UP!

Many Waikīkī hotels offer surf lessons, catamaran rides, kayak rentals, and other water activities. Call your concierge or front desk for details.

ROYAL HAWAIIAN HOTEL. The Pink Palace of the Pacific, so named for its cotton-candy color, was built in 1927. A modern tower has since been added, but the historic wing is more romantic thanks to canopy beds, Queen Anne–style desks, and the planet's pinkest phones. The hotel has private sands on a wide, central swatch of Waikīkī. Post-race, consider some pampering in Abhasa Spa's outdoor treatment cabanas. The high-octane mai tais at this resort's outdoor bar made the drink famous. ⊠ 2259 Kalākaua Ave., Waikīkī, 96815 ☎ 808/923-7311 or 866/716-8109 ⊕ www.royal-hawaiian.com ⬂ 475 rooms, 53 suites ⚄ 2 restaurants, 24-hr room service, wake-up calls, alarm clocks, some coffeemakers, robes, cable TV with Web TV (fee), in-room data ports, minibars, pool, hair salon, gym, spa, beach, bar, shops, children's programs (ages 5–12), concierge, business services, parking (fee), no-smoking floors ▭ AE, D, DC, MC, V $$$$.

SHERATON MOANA SURFRIDER. Opened in 1901, the Moana is still a wedding and honeymoon favorite with its sweeping main staircase and period furnishings in its historic main wing. You can even renew your vows at the Promise Me Again ceremony, held Saturday evening underneath the stars. The hotel feels like a step back in time, especially during classic high tea on the Banyan Veranda or while sipping a cocktail at sunset. You can relax on the private beach or in a poolside cabana. Massages can be arranged. ⊠ 2365 Kalākaua Ave., Waikīkī 96815 ☎ 808/922-3111 or 866/716-8109 ⊕ www.moana-surfrider.com ⬂ 793 rooms, 46 suites ⚄ 3 restaurants, snack bar, 24-hr room service, wake-up calls, alarm clocks, coffeemakers, robes, cable TV with Web TV, in-room data ports, in-room safes, pool, salon, beach, bar, concierge, shops, children's programs (ages 5–12), business services, meeting rooms, no-smoking floors ▭ AE, DC, MC, V $$$-$$$$.

WAIKĪKĪ BEACH MARRIOTT RESORT AND SPA. Very close to Kapi'olani Park, this hotel is very convenient for marathoners. Some hotel restaurants add pasta specials during race weekend. Deep Hawaiian woods and bold tropical colors fill its two towers, which have ample courtyards and public areas open to ocean breezes and sunlight. Rooms in

IT'S BEGINNING TO LOOK A LOT LIKE . . .

Hey, look! It's Santa, riding a sleigh pulled by eight tiny rein . . . *fish?!* That's part of the beauty of December in Waikīkī: tons of Christmas decorations—from the traditional to the aquatic. Be sure to wander through the Royal Hawaiian: the Pink Palace of the Pacific has Christmas trees festooned in pink lights. The lobbies of the Sheraton Moana Surfrider and the Sheraton Princess Kaiulani display stunning gingerbread villages. The charm and detail will fill you with awe; the scent will fill you with hunger. Drive into town to experience Honolulu City Lights (nightly till about 11), an annual tradition of over-the-top decorations whose focal point is Honolulu Hale (city hall). Enjoy the 50-foot Christmas tree and all the wreaths from an annual competition, and then drive down King Street to take in all the lighted displays and scenes—ever seen Santa kicking back and giving a *shaka* (hang loose sign)?

---

the Kealohilani Tower are among Waikīkī's largest; some of the Paokalani Tower's rooms offer breathtaking views of Diamond Head crater and Kapi'olani Park. The outdoor Moana Terrace features Hawaiian music in the early evening. Post-race, take advantage of Spa Olakino. ⊠ 2552 Kalākaua Ave., Waikīkī, 96815 ☎ 808/922–6611 or 800/367–5370 ⊕ www.marriottwaikiki.com ➫ 1,297 rooms, 13 suites ♿ 5 restaurants, coffee shop, room service, wake-up calls, alarm clocks, coffeemakers, cable TV with Web TV and movies and video games, in-room data ports, in-room safes, minibars, refrigerators, free Wi-Fi, 2 pools, 24-hr gym, spa, bar, nightclub, shops, laundry services, concierge, business services, meeting rooms, car rental, parking (fee), no-smoking floors ☰ AE, D, DC, MC, V $–$$$.

WAIKĪKĪ PARC. One of Waikīkī's best-kept secrets is this boutique hotel owned by the same group as the Halekūlani. It offers the same impeccable service, but is just off the beach and more reasonably priced. You have access to all the facilities of the Halekūlani except the pool, as this property has its own on the eighth floor. Guest rooms have plantation-style shutters that open out to the lānai, sitting areas, writing desks, and flat-screen TVs. A full breakfast buffet is included in the rates. ⊠ 2233 Helumoa Rd., Waikīkī, 96815 ☎ 808/921–7272 or 800/422–0450 ⊕ www.waikikiparc.com ➫ 297 rooms ♿ 2 restaurants, room service, wake-up calls, alarm clocks, coffeemakers, in-room data ports, in-room safes, minibars, refrigerators, cable TV with movies, pool, gym, concierge, babysitting, laundry facilities, business services, parking (fee), no-smoking floors ☰ AE, D, DC, MC, V $$–$$$.

Waikīkī Condos

THE BREAKERS. For a taste of '60s Hawai'i, try this low-rise a half block from Waikīkī Beach. The six two-story buildings surround a pool and overlook gardens. Head to the poolside bar for one of the Breaker Cafe's legendary grilled hamburgers. Guest rooms have Japanese-style shoji doors that open to the lānai, kitchenettes, and bathrooms with showers only. The toughest part of your visit just might be finding an available room, as guests return here year after year. ✉ 250 Beach Walk, Waikīkī, 96815 ☎ 808/923–3181 or 800/426–0494 ⊕ www.breakers-hawaii.com ⇆ 64 units ♿ Restaurant, wake-up calls, in-room safes, kitchenettes, pool, bar, free parking ▭ AE, D, DC, MC, V ¢–$.

CASTLE WAIKĪKĪ SHORE. The only condo right on Waikīkī Beach is between Ft. DeRussy Beach Park and the Outrigger Reef on the Beach. The studios and one- and two-bedroom suites have panoramic ocean views. Many units have full kitchens, some only kitchenettes; inquire when booking. Some love this place for its spaciousness, others for its quiet location. ✉ 2161 Kālia Rd., Waikīkī, 96815 ☎ 808/952–4500 or 800/367–5004 ⊕ www.castleresorts.com ⇆ 168 units ♿ Wake-up calls, alarm clocks, coffeemakers, cable TV with movies, in-room data ports, some kitchens, some kitchenettes, beach, laundry facilities, parking (fee) ▭ AE, D, DC, MC, V $$–$$$$.

ILIMA HOTEL. On a residential side street near the Ala Wai Canal, this 17-story condominium-style hotel is a gem. The glass-wall lobby with koa-wood furnishings, original artwork, and friendly staff create a Hawaiian home away from home. Rates are decent for the spacious studios with kitchenettes as well as the one- and two-bedroom suites with full kitchens, Jacuzzi baths, cable TV with free HBO and Disney channels, multiple phones, and spacious lānai. It's a three-block walk to Waikīkī Beach and Kalākaua Avenue. ✉ 445 Nohonani St., Waikīkī, 96815 ☎ 808/923–1877 or 888/864–5462 ⊕ www.ilima.com ⇆ 99 units ♿ Wake-up calls, alarm clocks, coffeemakers, cable TV, in-room data ports, in-room safes, kitchens, newspapers (except Sunday), pool, gym, sauna, laundry facilities, meeting room, free parking ▭ AE, D, DC, MC, V $–$$$.

PRE-RACE FUEL

Many ABC Stores (the ubiquitous Hawaiian convenience store) open early on marathon morning. Check schedules posted in store windows.

AND YOU'RE OFF . . .

The Expo

The expo is held Wednesday through Saturday at the Hawai'i Convention Center. It's a very doable walk from Waikīkī hotels, plus courtesy shuttles run regularly between the convention center and several Waikīkī locations (check marathon Web site for specifics). At the expo, you'll find all the usual running gear and official marathon merchandise, plus booths with Hawaiian beauty products and displays by Hawaiian artisans. You can also take in running seminars, meet with Hollywood celebrities, and enjoy Hawaiian arts-and-crafts demonstrations.

There's one other prerace stop you might need to make. This marathon has no race-day gear check, so if you want to check post-race clothes, drop them at the tent in Kapi'olani Park on the Friday or Saturday before the race.

NIGHT-BEFORE PASTA DINNER

The Honolulu Marathon kicks off the festivities good and early; instead of a night-before pasta dinner, it sponsors a huge lū'au and concert at the Waikīkī Shell (amphitheater) starting at 4 PM *two days* before the race. The tickets are well worth $25. Though it's called a lū'au, don't expect hula girls, fire twirlers, and a whole roast pig. *Do* expect a massive all-you-can-eat buffet, beverages, and hours of great music. Local entertainers play until 7 PM, when the main acts take the stage. Past headliners have included *Riders on the Storm,* featuring original members of The Doors, and Brian Wilson of Beach Boys fame.

The lū'au/concert is a great way to get psyched for the marathon, but leaves you without plans for a night-before pasta dinner. Luckily, Honolulu's restaurants can fill the void.

GINZA KIYA. Want to go a different route for a pre-race carb-up? This unfancy Tokyo-style noodle spot has rich broth and fresh *udon* (wheat) and *soba* (buckwheat) noodles. Hot noodle soup, cold noodles with dipping sauce, and *donburi* (rice bowls), are offered, plus such specialties as *hiya yakko* (cold tofu topped with ginger and soy sauce) and Western-style green salad on noodles with sesame dressing. ✉ Aston Waikīkī Circle Hotel, 2464 Kalākaua Ave., Waikīkī ☎ 808/923–8840 ⚄ Reservations not accepted ▤ No credit cards $.

SARENTO'S TOP OF THE "I." Among the best view restaurants in the city, looking toward both the Ko'olau Mountains and the South Shore, 30th-floor Sarento's specializes in regional Italian cuisine. The lobster ravioli and osso buco are local favorites; the wine cellar contains some gems, and prices are reasonable. ✉ Renaissance 'Ilikai Waikīkī Hotel, 1777 Ala Moana, top fl., Waikīkī ☎ 808/955–5559 ⚄ Reservations essential ▤ AE, D, DC, MC, V ☉ No lunch $$–$$$$.

Race Day

The Course

The Honolulu Marathon begins at 5 AM at Ala Moana Boulevard and Queen Street. Shuttles run continuously between the Honolulu Zoo (at Kapi'olani Park) and the start from 2 AM to 4 AM. Other options include taxis (make arrangements in advance) or walking. The starting line is less than a mile from most Waikīkī hotels. Once there, you'll find portable toilets and water fountains, plus music that carries across the whole starting field. There are no official starting corrals; expected finishing times are posted, and you're trusted to line up accordingly.

It's still dark at 5 AM—perfect for the fireworks that kick off the race. You cruise through downtown for the first 4 miles, passing landmarks like the Aloha Tower, a clock tower that was once Hawai'i's tallest building; 'Iolani Palace, notable as the only royal palace in the United States; a gilded statue of King Kamehaha, who united the Hawaiian Islands; and Honolulu Hale (city hall). Soon after Mile 4 you hit Waikīkī, where you zoom down Kalākaua Avenue, catching great beach views. You pass Kapi'olani Park, move toward Diamond Head, and encounter a major climb around Mile 8. Concentrate on the stunning views, not your aching legs.

Next up are several suburban areas, including Hawai'i Kai, through which you'll loop between Miles 15 and 18. Look for Koko Crater towering up above. After the Hawai'i Kai loop, you head for home, passing beach parks and the Waialae Country Club, home of the Hawaiian Open PGA Golf Tournament. At Mile 24 you again maneuver past Diamond Head, but this time closer to the ocean; keep an eye out for the lighthouse. Finally, you emerge back onto Kalākaua Avenue, and soar toward triumph at the finish line in Kapi'olani Park.

Despite its popularity, this is not a major spectator marathon, save for the start, finish, and Waikīkī Beach hotel district. Local cheerleading squads move around the course, and several bands dot the route, but for much of the race your major motivator will be the beautiful scenery. Sixteen aid stations offer water, sports drinks, medical assistance, portable toilets, and cold sponges.

When you cross the finish line to the cheers of the crowd, don't worry about getting your ChampionChip removed. Unlike those at most marathons, Honolulu's single-use chips are meant to be kept as souvenirs. Receive your finishers' lei, then proceed to a true Honolulu Marathon perk: outdoor showers. Linger in their spray, then take in postrace Kapi'olani Park: one tent offers apples, oatmeal cookies, and water to marathoners; another hands out official finisher medals and T-shirts; still another provides free shiatsu massage. Finisher certificates are available at the park the day after the race; if you don't pick yours up, it will be mailed around February.

The Honolulu Marathon is open to all who want to tackle its 26.2-mile course, regardless of speed. There's no course time limit; the last aid station doesn't close until 4:30 PM, 11½ hours after the start. Although the finish line arch and timing mats are dismantled around 3 PM, the official marathon clock continues to run. And no matter how long it takes (the final finisher in 2004 completed the race in 15 hours, 8 minutes), a race official will be there when the last person finishes.

Spectating

Waikīkī has two great viewing options. First, you can walk, hop a cab, or, if there's room, take the marathon shuttle to the start. Thrill to the fireworks and the energy of the pack as it bursts onto the course, then travel down Ala Moana Boulevard in the opposite direction from the marathon. It's just a short walk to Ala Moana and Piikoi, where you can catch the pack around Mile 3.5. Once they've passed, grab some breakfast and maybe hit the beach before heading to Kapi'olani Park to watch your runner finish.

Alternatively, sleep in a bit and wait for the field to run through Waikīkī. Two of the most comfortable specator spots are the Wailana Coffee House (1860 Ala Moana Boulevard,

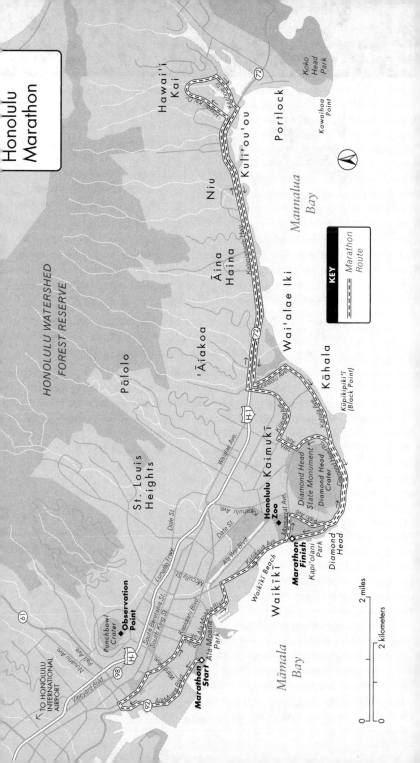

Honolulu Marathon

KEY

‑ ‑ ‑ ‑ *Marathon Route*

Honolulu International Airport • Marathon Start • Marathon Finish • Honolulu Zoo • Observation Point

Punchbowl Crater • St. Louis Heights • Pālolo • 'Āiakoa • HONOLULU WATERSHED FOREST RESERVE

Waikīkī • Kaimukī • Kāhala • Wai'alae Iki • 'Āina Haina • Niu • Kuli'ou'ou • Hawai'i Kai • Portlock

Mōʻiliʻili • Ala Moana Park • Kapiʻolani Park • Waikīkī Beach • Diamond Head • Diamond Head Crater • Diamond Head State Monument • Kūpikipikiʻi (Black Point)

Māmala Bay • Maunalua Bay • Koko Head Park • Kawaihoa Point

Nuʻuanu Ave • Pali Hwy • Vineyard Blvd • Ala Moana Blvd • Lunalilo Frwy • McCully St • South King St • South Beretania St • Kapiʻolani Blvd • Wilder Ave • Dole St • Date St • Ala Wai Blvd • Kalākaua Ave • Monsarrat Ave • Pākī Ave • Kapahulu Ave • Waiʻalae Ave • Kīlauea Ave • Kealaolu Ave • Kahala Ave • Kalanianaole Hwy • Hawaiʻi Kai Dr • Keahole St

H-1 • H-3 • 92 • 98 • 61 • 72

0   2 miles
0   2 kilometers

In 2004, a celebrity ran the Honolulu Marathon.

She had to be a celebrity; it was the only explanation. She came with an entourage, and all along the route people cheered for her by name. They begged for pictures with her, and she graciously obliged. Even other runners paused in their marathon quest to pay their respects to this racing luminary.

Her name was Glady Burrill or "Glady," as it was emblazoned on her T-shirt. Her entourage wore "Team Glady" shirts, but many of her screaming fans preferred the moniker given to her by a local newspaper: The Gladyator. "Gladyator, go!" they cried, as she coursed through Honolulu. Glady always acknowledged their support with a smile or a wave.

Who was this woman who had so captured the collective imagination of the Honolulu Marathon? One way to find out was to ask Glady's family. Her husband, for example. Or her children, grandchildren, or *great*-grandchildren.

Glady Burrill was an 86-year-old first-time marathoner. That certainly isn't the most common age to take up marathoning, but then again there has never been anything common about Glady. She was born into a very poor family, the youngest of six children. Her father knew he was dying when she was born, and named her Glady in hopes that she'd bring joy to her family, which she did. Despite the poverty and a case of polio at age 11, Glady has always kept an infectious positive attitude. This and her faith in God let her accomplish any goal she sets, from climbing Mt. Hood six weeks after giving birth to a daughter, to becoming a pilot at age 50.

Though she was an avid walker, the idea of tackling a marathon never entered her mind. Then one year she was at her condo at marathon time and saw the start of the race: the fireworks, the emotion, and the energy all moved her, and immediately she knew she had to be a part of it. She signed up right away and started preparing on January 1, 2004, by hiking in the Arizona desert. Over the course of seven weeks, Glady walked 300 miles; shorter jaunts during the week, longer ones on the weekends. No matter where she and her husband traveled that year, Glady stuck with her training. Not even the Arctic Circle deterred her: she struck out from their motor home to get in her miles, only pausing when she heard the crush of brush beside the trail. It was a mama black bear with her cubs. That day's walk quickly became a run.

Back in Honolulu, meanwhile, word was spreading about the 86-year-old who had signed up for the marathon. Local newspapers both in Honolulu

and her home state of Oregon featured her in their pages. Glady was surprised. She had no idea everyone would learn her age, nor did she think it
would be such a big deal. After all, she certainly didn't feel old; she was
just another person eager to test her mettle against the marathon. But her
story was clearly touching people. The phone kept ringing with people offering their support. Neighbors in Honolulu would approach to wish her luck.

By race day, Glady was ready. She and her entourage took a limo to the
starting line. Her husband and daughter Gina cheered her on; her son
Mike and his son Mike Jr. joined her on the course. As the race began, the
sight of those fireworks gave her chills; their power was even greater now
that she was a marathoner. She started strong, buoyed by all her fans. Her
goal was to finish in about 7 hours, but along the way a foot bruise she
suffered during training acted up, and the pain was terrible. Her son told
her she didn't have to finish the race. But Glady thought of all the people
she had inspired and refused to stop. This quest had become bigger; dropping out wasn't an option. She fought through the ache, praying for
strength, and within 5 miles the pain disappeared.

Crowds cheered as Glady ran toward the finish line. "Go, Mom!" she heard
from the throng. She smiled when she saw Gina and her husband. But they
weren't alone. Cheering with them were Glady's four other daughters who
had flown in to surprise her. Glady stopped in her tracks, her hands flying up
to her face. "Go, Mom, go!" her daughters laughed. "You're not at the finish
line!" Moved beyond words, Glady lunged forward, finishing the race with a
chip time of 9:09:33. She felt wonderful until the second she crossed the finish line, when the physical and emotional toll of the race caught up with her,
leaving her sick. Happily, it was nothing that couldn't be helped with post-
race oatmeal cookies and water, and by that night she felt fantastic.

Two days later, Glady was back on the streets of Honolulu, getting in a 7-
mile walk. She loved the Honolulu Marathon, but there's one thing that still
eats at her: her finishing time. She knows she can do better, and at this
writing she's nearing the end of her training for the 2005 race, which she's
sure she can finish in closer to 7 hours. She'll be 87.

And what comes after the marathon? Glady isn't sure, but she has toyed
with the idea of skydiving. Her grandson, Mike Jr., wants to tandem jump
with her. Glady's tempted, but says she'd better stick to her walking—for
now. Which brings us to another of Glady's dreams: to be a spokesperson
for Nike. Glady loves that company. Not only does she have about a
dozen pairs of Nike running shoes, she practically lives in the brand's
clothes when she trains and races. So if you're out there, Nike-Powers-That-
Be, give it some thought. There's surely no one who better embodies the
spirit of "Just Do It" than Glady Burrill. ■

and the Honolulu Coffee Company (in the Sheraton Moana Surfrider Hotel, 2365 Kalākaua Avenue), both between Miles 4 and 5. Another option is to position yourself along Kalākaua Avenue from about Mile 4.5 to about Mile 6. Depending on where you're staying, this could be as easy as stepping outside your hotel or padding onto your lānai. Once the crowd passes, surf, lounge, eat, or otherwise bask in the joy that is Hawai'i before heading to Kapi'olani Park for the finish and the reunion with your favorite runner.

BEYOND THE FINISH LINE
Replacing 2,620 Calories

Honolulu has everything from island fusion dishes served up by celebrity chefs to low-key (but just as tasty) plate-lunch joints and small ethnic eateries. Many excellent dining choices are right in Waikīkī and within walking distance of your hotel. Others are well worth a drive or ride into other parts of Honolulu.

Waikīkī

DUKE'S CANOE CLUB. Duke's is both an open-air bar and a very popular steak-and-seafood grill. It's known for its Big Island pork ribs, *huli-huli* (rotisserie) chicken, and grilled catch of the day, as well as for a simple, economical Sunday brunch. A drawback is that it's often loud and crowded, and the live contemporary Hawaiian music often stymies conversation. ⊠ Outrigger Waikīkī on the Beach, 2335 Kalākaua Ave., Waikīkī ☎ 808/922-2268 ⊕ www.dukeswaikiki.com ⚓ Reservations essential ☰ AE, DC, MC, V $$–$$$.

HANOHANO ROOM. It's all about the spectacle here, from the astounding views to the astounding desserts flambé. The restaurant sits 30 stories above Waikīkī Beach, and sunset vistas are phenomenal. Live entertainment plays from 8:30 PM to 11:30 PM. This plus the formal attire and gourmet entrées (say, prime rib encrusted with Hawaiian salt, rosemary, and crushed pepper) evoke old-school sophistication. ⊠ Sheraton Waikīkī, 225 Kalākaua Ave., Waikīkī ☎ 808/922-4422 ⊕ www.sheraton-waikiki.com ⚓ Reservation essential ⚲ Jacket and tie ☰ AE, DC, MC, V $$$–$$$$.

KEO'S IN WAIKĪKĪ. Many islanders—and Hollywood stars—got their first taste of pad thai noodles, lemongrass, and coconut milk curry at one of Keo Sananikone's restaurants. This one, at the entrance to Waikīkī, characterizes his formula: a bright, clean space awash in flowers with intriguing menu titles and reasonable prices. Evil Jungle Prince, a stir-fry redolent of Thai basil, flecked with chilies, and rich with coconut milk, is a classic. ⊠ 2028 Kūhiō Ave., Waikīkī ☎ 808/951-9355 ☰ AE, D, DC, MC, V $$–$$$$.

LA MER. La Mer, like the hotel in which it's housed (Halekūlani, "House Befitting Heaven") is pretty much heavenly. Windows in the softly lighted, low-ceiling room are open to the breeze, the perfectly framed vista of Diamond Head, and the faint sound of music from a courtyard below. The food captures the rich and yet sunny flavors of the south of France

BREAKFAST SPOTS

The following breakfast spots are terrific options. All are in the ¢ to $$ category and all are conveniently located in Waikīkī.

EGGS 'N THINGS. A local favorite for its late hours (11 PM to 2 PM daily) and excellent food, this restaurant has a hearty, country-style menu with a few island touches (tropical pancake syrups, fresh grilled fish) and a permanent line out front. Pancakes are deliciously decadent; some come with towers of whipped cream. ⊠ 1911–B Kalākaua Ave., Waikīkī ☎ 808/949–0820 ⊕ www.eggsnthings.com ⊟ No credit cards ⊗ No dinner.

HULA GRILL. Beginning at 6:30 AM, enjoy upscale breakfast fare in an open venue decorated in plantation-period kitsch, with a fabulous view of Diamond Head. The banana-and-macadamia nut pancakes are unbelievable. Return for dinner, and a spicy-sweet dipping oil that's beyond addictive. ⊠ Outrigger Waikīkī on the Beach, 2335 Kalākaua Ave., Waikīkī ☎ 808/923–4852 ⊕ www.hulagrillwaikiki.com ⟆ Reservations essential ⊟ AE, D, DC, MC, V ⊗ No lunch.

WAILANA COFFEE HOUSE. It's open and serves breakfast 24 hours a day. Enjoy all your basic comfort foods, including a host of pancake options, such as pineapple, banana, and macadamia nut. Service is friendly, and portions are generous. ⊠ 1860 Ala Moana Blvd., Waikīkī ☎ 808/955–1764 ⊟ AE, D, DC, MC, V.

---

n one tiny, exquisite course after another. Try the degustation menu; place yourself in the sommelier's hands for wine choices from the hotel's exceptional cellar. ⊠ Halekūlani, 2199 Kālia Rd., Waikīkī ☎ 808/923–2311 ⊕ www.halekulani.com ⟆ Reservations essential ⑯ Jacket required ⊟ AE, DC, MC, V ⊗ No lunch $$$–$$$$.

★ **ORCHIDS.** Along the seawall at historic Gray's Beach, Orchids is open to the breezes and has plenty of its namesake to lend splashes of color. The seafood is perfectly prepared, and the wine list intriguing. Consider the seafood curry, exploding with complex flavors. Finish with the signature coconut layer cake, which tastes so delicate and light, you'll swear t's good for you. ⊠ Halekūlani, 2199 Kālia Rd., Waikīkī ☎ 808/923–2311 ⟆ Reservations essential ⊟ AE, D, DC, MC, V $$–$$$$.

★ **SANSEI SEAFOOD RESTAURANT & SUSHI BAR.** I could eat here every single night for the rest of my life and never get bored. D. K. Kodama's Japanese-based Pacific Rim cuisine is not to be missed. My husband and I have vivid, drooling fantasies about the mango-crab rolls and the Matsuhisa-style miso cod. We've been working our way through the entire menu, and have yet to find a single dish that isn't incredible. Bargain hunters will love early-bird dinners (from 5 PM) or discounted late-night dining (until 1 AM, with karaoke). Absolutely leave room for the hot apple tart à la mode. ⊠ Waikīkī Beach Marriott Resort and Spa, 2552 Kalākaua Ave., Waikīkī ☎ 808/931–6286 ⊕ www.dkrestaurants. om ⊟ AE, D, MC, V $–$$$$.

TIKI'S GRILL AND BAR. Tiki's is the kind of place people come to Waikīkī for. It's a retro-South Pacific spot with a back-of-the-bar faux volcano, an open-air lounge with live local-style music, indoor-outdoor dining, and a view of the beach. The menu is contemporary island cuisine (Japanese seven-spice salmon, plate-lunch standards reinterpreted in sophisticated ways), with exceptional desserts and a late-night bar menu. ⊠ Aston Waikīkī Beach Hotel, 2570 Kalākaua Ave., Waikīkī ☎ 808/923–TIKI ⊕ www.tikisgrill.com ⓐ Reservations essential ▭ AE, D, DC, MC, V $-$$$.

Ala Moana, Downtown & Chinatown

KAKA'AKO KITCHEN. Russell Siu was the first of the local-boy fine-dining chefs to open a place of the sort he enjoys when he's off duty, serving high-quality plate lunches. The "two scoops of rice" can be either white or brown; there's green salad instead of the usual macaroni salad; and there are vegetarian options as well as grilled fresh fish specials. Breakfast is especially good with combos like corned beef hash and eggs and exceptional goods such as *poi* bread. ⊠ Ward Centre, 1200 Ala Moana Blvd., Kaka'ako ☎ 808/596-7488 ⓐ Reservations not accepted ▭ AE, DC, MC, V $.

LITTLE VILLAGE NOODLE HOUSE. Unassuming and budget-friendly, Little Village sets a standard of friendly and attentive service to which every Chinese restaurant should aspire. Dishes across the large, pan-China menu are excellent, and include shredded beef, spinach with garlic, Shanghai noodles, honey-walnut shrimp, and orange chicken with actual oranges. ⊠ 1113 Smith St., Chinatown ☎ 808/545–3008 ⊕ www.littlevillagehawaii.com ▭ AE, D, MC, V $-$$.

SIDE STREET INN. It's famous as a place where celebrity chefs gather after hours. If you can ignore annoying smoke and sometimes surly staff, you'll find some of the world's best darned pork chops and fried rice. Local-style bar food comes in huge, share-plate portions. Come to nosh all night, watch sports on TV, and sing karaoke until they boot you out. Enjoy pūpū (in portions so large as to be dinner) from 4 PM to 12:30 AM daily. ⊠ 1225 Hopaka St., Ala Moana ☎ 808/591-0253 ▭ AE, D, DC, MC, V ⊗ No lunch weekends $.

East & Diamond Head

ALAN WONG'S. At Alan Wong's the aloha spirit is evident in the skilled but unstarched service and the playful interpretations of island cuisine. Try Da Bag (seafood steamed in a Mylar pouch), Chinatown roast duck nachos, and Poki Pines (rice-studded seafood wonton appetizers). With a view of the Koolau Mountains, warm tones of koa wood, and lauhala grass weaving, you'll forget you're on the third floor of an office building. ⊠ McCully Court, 1857 S. King St., Mō'ili'ili ☎ 808/949-2526 ⊕ www.alanwongs.com ▭ AE, DC, MC, V ⊗ No lunch $$$-$$$$.

CHEF MAVRO. Chef George Mavrothalassitis draws out the truest and most concentrated flavors, tracks down the freshest fish, and creates one-of-a-kind wine pairings. The menu changes quarterly; every dish (including dessert) is matched with a select wine. Order anything with shrimp from the aquafarms of the North Shore's Kahuku area; the Keahole lobster from the Big Island is also good. The atmosphere is serene with starched white tablecloths, fresh flowers, wood floors, and contemporary island art. ⊠ 1969 S. King St.,

ISLAND-GROWN GOODNESS

For terrific, island-grown produce and other foodstuffs, check out the **KCC Farmers Market** (⊠ Kapi'olani Community College, 4303 Diamond Head Rd. ☉ Sat. 8–noon). The atmosphere is relaxed; many islanders bring their dogs and linger over coffee as they peruse the fresh flowers, prepared meals, and island crafts. Come for breakfast: every week, a Waikīkī restaurateur offers up a special dish at a discount price.

Mō'ili'ili ☎ 808/944–4714 ⊕ www.chefmavro.com ⚠ Reservations essential ▭ AE, DC, MC, V ☉ Closed Mon. No lunch $$$–$$$$.

★ **RAINBOW DRIVE-IN.** It's local, cheap, and delicious. Wait in line to grab a plate lunch of teriyaki beef, boneless chicken, curry served with rice, macaroni salad, a burger, or a sandwich, then snag one of the five or so outdoor tables or take your food to go. Crowds are a given, but turnover is fast. Portions are generous. ⊠ 3308 Kanaina Ave., Diamond Head ☎ 808/737–0177 ⚠ Reservations not accepted ▭ No credit cards ¢–$.

SAM CHOY'S DIAMOND HEAD RESTAURANT. It's home to Sam Choy's TV cooking show and Hawaiian regional cuisine. Creative options include the seafood *laulau* (made with steamed mahimahi, shrimp, scallops, and vegetables). Sunday brunch sees a seemingly endless variety of food, including fish, omelets, a carving station, and a table of decadent desserts. ⊠ 449 Kapahulu Ave., Diamond Head ☎ 808/944–4714 ⊕ www.samchoy. com ⚠ Reservations essential ▭ AE, DC, MC, V ☉ No lunch $$–$$$$.

3660 ON THE RISE. This casual but stylish eatery is a 10-minute drive from Waikīkī. Sample Chef Russell Siu's crab cakes, or the signature 'ahi *katsu* wrapped in seaweed and deep-fried with a wasabi-ginger butter sauce. Siu combines a deep understanding of local flavors with a sophisticated palate, making this place especially popular with homegrown gourmands. The dining room can feel snug when it's full; go early or late. ⊠ 3660 Wai'alae Ave., Kaimukī ☎ 808/737–1177 ⊕ www.3660.com ▭ AE, D, DC, MC, V ☉ Closed Mon. $$–$$$$.

Sightseeing on (and off) Your Feet

Honolulu is filled with things to do, including several lovely cultural institutions. But let's be honest: the best part is the outdoors. And though you experience a lot of it on the marathon route, there's much, much more. What's the perfect way to soak it in? It all depends on how you feel.

I Feel Great!

BIKE ALONG A TRAIL. There's beautiful biking along the **'Aiea Loop Trail** (⊠ Central O'ahu, just past Kea'iwa Heiau State Park, at end of 'Aiea Heights Dr.), which has a little bit of everything you might expect to find in Hawai'i—wild pigs crossing your path, an ancient Hawaiian *heiau* (holy ground), and the remains of a World War II airplane. There are campsites and picnic tables along the way. Enjoy the foliage change from bamboo to

Norfolk pine in your climb along this 4½-mile track. For information concerning trails, permits, and state laws, contact the **Honolulu City and County Bike Coordinator** (☎ 808/527–5044).

For a serious ride, rent at **Boca Hawai'i LLC** (⊠ 330 Cooke St., Waikīkī ☎ 808/591–9839 ⊕ www.bocahawaii.com) for full-suspension bikes at $35 a day. Call ahead; supplies are limited. **Blue Sky Rentals & Sports Center** (⊠ 1920 Ala Moana Blvd., across from Hilton Hawaiian Village, Waikīkī ☎ 808/947–0101) has bicycles for $15 for 4 hours, $20 for 8 hours, $25 for 24 hours, and $75 per week. Prices include a bike, helmet, lock, and water bottle.

HANG 10. Perhaps no activity is more associated with Hawai'i than surfing, and O'ahu has plenty of famous spots. Banzai Pipeline, Waimea Bay, Kaiser Bowls, and Sunset Beach resonate in surfers' hearts the world over. The attraction comes with a price: competition for those waves. If you're a new or nervous surfer, avoid these hot spots.

Waikīkī Beach attracts surfers who are just learning, many taking lessons through their hotels. White Plains Beach, at the former Kolaeloa Military Installation, attracts novice to intermediate surfers. Poplars is a break about a half-mile paddle out from the Waikīkī Beach, in front of the Royal Hawaiian Hotel. It's friendly to rookies and veterans and rarely overcrowded. Diamond Head Beach and Cliffs, at the base of the cliffs off Diamond Head, lets you watch the Diamond Head lighthouse as you surf right into the base of the dormant volcano.

> **NEED A BREAK?**
>
> If you head to the North Shore, stop at **Matsumoto Shave Ice** (⊠ 66-087 Kamehameha Hwy., Hale'iwa ☎ 808/637–4827 ⊕ www.matsumotoshaveice. com), a legendary local joint that's been patronized by actor Tom Hanks, sumo wrestler Konishiki, and ice-skater Kristi Yamaguchi.

At **C&K Beach Service,** on the beach fronting the Hilton Hawaiian Village, rentals cost $10 to $15 per hour, depending on board size. If you head to the North Shore, rent a short board for $5 an hour or a long board for $7 an hour ($24 and $30 for full-day rentals) at **Surf-N-Sea** (⊠ 62-595 Kamehameha Hwy., Haleiwa ☎ 808/637–9887 or 800/899–7873). The shop also rents water bikes, pedal boats, and kayaks.

Surf-lesson outfits abound in Waikīkī, but if you want the best, there's only one option: **Hawaiian Fire, Inc.** (⊠ 3318 Campbell Ave., Honolulu ☎ 808/737–FIRE or 888/955–7873 ⊕ www.hawaiianfire.com). Off-duty firefighters pick you up at your Waikīkī hotel and whisk you off to a secluded beach. The instructors are fantastic: total smart-asses who get you laughing and enjoying yourself the minute you hop in the van. They're also consummate professionals, and geniuses at getting even the most uncoordinated klutz (that'd be me) to successfully ride a wave. Expect 45 minutes of beach-time training, all the equipment you need, and an hour and a quarter in the water. It's a workout. Afterward, you're rewarded with a snack, a T-shirt, water, pictures available for purchase, and some great memories. It costs $119 for a premium lesson (3:1 student/teacher ratio) or $169 for a private lesson.

PADDLE THE WAVES. Kayaking on the ocean allows you a vantage point not afforded by swimming and surfing. Just don't travel too far away from shore, especially if you're inexperienced. Many hotels and other outfits along Waikīkī Beach rent kayaks. Alternatively, visit Lanikai Beach, past Kailua Beach Park. Its still waters and onshore winds make it perfect amateur territory, and there are many kayak rental companies right up the street in Kailua (cost: about $49–$59 a day). For something a little different, try Kahana River, which empties into Kahana Bay, 8 miles east of Kāne'ohe. The Ko'olau Mountains, with waterfalls aplenty when it's raining, are a magnificent backdrop to this 2-mile round-trip jaunt. Just bring bug repellent; mosquitoes will want to join the ride.

RIDE LIKE THE WIND. How sore are you? Want to get even sorer? 'Cause hanging on while windsurfing or kiteboarding can turn your arms to spaghetti in no time. Of the two, kiteboarding is far more extreme; the kite will sometimes take you in the air for hundreds of feet. To rent equipment or take lessons, try **Kailua Sailboard and Kayaks Company** (⊠ 130 Kailua Rd., Kailua ☎ 808/262-2555 ⊕ www.kailuasailboards.com), which offers both beginner and high-performance gear as well as lessons ($69 for a three-hour group lesson or $35 for a one-hour individual lesson; minimum rental is for a half-day and starts at $39). At **Naish Hawai'i** (⊠ 155A Hamakua Dr., Kailua ☎ 808/261-6067 ⊕ www.naish.com) a three-hour windsurfing rental package, including 90 minutes of instruction, costs $75. A beginner kiteboarding lesson runs $125 for 90 minutes.

I Feel Pretty Good

EXPLORE THE DEPTHS. There are literally hundreds of species of fish and marine life here, as well as fascinating wrecks. If you want to scuba dive, save your vacation time and get certified before leaving home. Snorkeling requires no certification: if you can swim, you can snorkel. Snuba is the marriage of the two: you're hooked up to a standard air tank via a 20-foot air hose attached to a raft, and you can swim down as far as 15 feet.

At Maunalua Bay, east of Diamond Head, scuba divers enjoy Turtle Canyon, with lava-flow ridges and sandy canyons teeming with green sea turtles of all sizes; *Kāhala Barge*, a penetrable, 200-foot sunken vessel; Big Eel Reef, with many varieties of moray eels; and Fantasy Reef, a series of lava ledges and archways populated with barracuda and eels. There's also the sunken Corsair—it's not much for sea life, but there *is* something to be said about sitting in the cockpit of a plane 100 feet below the ocean's surface.

Snorkelers can explore China Walls on Maunalua Bay's east side. It's a drift dive—park at the end of Portlock Road, jump off the rocks, and let the current take you down to the beach as you check out the fish and occasional monk seal. Those who don't want to leave Waikīkī Beach can snorkel in Queen's Surf, a marine reserve between Waikīkī's break wall and the Queen's pier. Look for colorful reef fish and the occasional sea turtle just yards from shore.

To rent or buy snorkel equipment, learn about the best spots of the day, or schedule dolphin excursions, cruises or other tours, head for **Snorkel Bob's** (⊠ 700 Kapahulu Ave., Honolulu ☎ 808/735-7944 ⊕ www.snorkelbobs.com). Scuba dive packages are available through many companies, including **Captain Bruce's Hawai'i** (☎ 808/373-3590 or 800/535-2487 ⊕ www.captainbruce.com), whose outings range from $95 to $110.

The best place for underwater activities is the **Hanauma Bay Nature Preserve** (⊠ 7455 Kalaniana'ole Hwy. ☎ 808/396-4229 ☜ $5; parking $1; tram from parking lot to beach $1.50 ⊙ Wed.–Mon. 6–6, until 10 PM 2nd Sat. every month). Fish here are more like family pets than skittish marine life. An old volcanic crater has created a haven from the waves where the coral has thrived. There's an educational center where you must watch a nine-minute video about the preserve before being allowed down to the bay. Try to come early (around 7); it can be difficult to park later in the day. You can rent a mask, snorkel, and fins for $8. **Hanauma Bay Dive Tours** (☎ 808/256–8956 or 800/505–8956) runs snorkeling ($56), snuba ($87), and scuba ($89) tours to Hanauma Bay with transportation from Waikīkī hotels.

HOOF IT—ONE WAY OR ANOTHER. If you're up for it, cap off the marathon with a hike. Contact the **Hawai'i State Department of Land and Natural Resources** (⌂ 1151 Punchbowl St., Room 130, Honolulu 96813 ☎ 808/587–0300 ⊕ www.hawaii.gov) for a free O'ahu recreation map outlining 33 major trails, including Mānoa Falls, an excellent hike. The **City and County of Honolulu Trails and Access Manager** (☎ 808/973–9782) offers a free hiking-safety guide. Ask for a copy of "Hiking on O'ahu: The Official Guide."

Kualoa Ranch (✉ 49-560 Kamehameha Hwy., Ka'a'awa ☎ 808/237–8515 ⊕ www.kualoa.com) leads horseback trail rides in beautiful Ka'a'awa Valley. Rides cost between $59 and $99. Kualoa offers other activities such as ATV rides and kayaking. **Happy Trails Hawai'i** (✉ 59-231 Pupukea Rd., North Shore ☎ 808/638–RIDE ⊕ www.happytrailshawaii.com) offers guided horseback rides through the verdant Waimea Valley. Expect panoramic views from Kaena Point to the famous North Shore surfing spots. Rates vary depending on duration and skill level.

SAIL ABOVE IT ALL. Wearing a parachute while attached to a boat by a really long leash, parasailing basically turns you into a human kite, flying around 500 feet off the water. **Hawai'i X-Treme Parasailing** (✉ Kewalo Basin Harbor, Honolulu ⊕ www.hawaiiactive.com (click "O'ahu", then "O'ahu Ocean Excursions" and scroll down) is reputed to be the highest parasail ride on O'hu, pulling people as high as 1,200 feet for 15 minutes. It offers pickups from Waikīkī, and rates run from $40 to $78.

Let's Take It Slowly

GO FISH. Go deep-sea fishing for yellowfin tuna, spearfish, mahimahi, and Pacific blue marlin, among others. The magnificent 50-foot *Pacifica* fishing yacht from **Magic Sportfishing** (☎ 808/596–2998 ⊕ www.magicsportfishing.com) is built for comfort and can accommodate up to six. Contact them for rates.

HONOLULU ZOO. There are bigger and better zoos, but this one is lovely and conveniently located in Waikīkī. At the petting zoo kids can pet a llama and meet Abbey, the resident monitor lizard. ✉ 151 Kapahulu Ave., Waikīkī ☎ 808/971–7171 ⊕ www.honoluluzoo.org ≋ $6 ☉ Daily 9–4:30.

★ **SEA LIFE PARK.** The amount of animal interaction will delight you. Kids will especially enjoy feeding turtles and seals. For an extra fee, try a behind-the-scenes tour; a Hawaiian Ray encounter; an underwater photo safari in which you enter the Hawaiian Reef Tank to interact with fish, rays, and a sea turtle; or Dolphin Adventures, not to be missed. It's a deepwater encounter with the dolphins, including touching them, learning to train them, and swimming with them. I got to do a lot of incredible things while researching this book. Cuddling with a dolphin? Far and away the best. ✉ 41-202 Kalaniana'ole Hwy., Waimānalo ☎ 808/259–7933 ≋ $26 ☉ Daily 9:30–5.

WAIKĪKĪ FOR FREE

Waikīkī has many ways to separate you from your money. Yet there's also a staggering number of terrific activities that cost nothing at all, including tours of historic hotels, ukulele lessons, musical performances, fireworks—even sunset movies on the beach. For a full calendar of free events visit the **Waikīkī Improvement Association** (⊕ www.waikikiimprovement.com) Web site.

★ **USS *ARIZONA* MEMORIAL.** A simple, gleaming white structure shields the hulk of the USS *Arizona,* which sank with 1,102 men aboard when the Japanese attacked Pearl Harbor on December 7, 1941. The tour includes a 23-minute documentary with actual news footage from the day of the attack and a shuttle-boat ride to the memorial. Appropriate dress is required (no bathing suits, flip-flops, or bare feet). ⊠ National Park Service, Pearl Harbor ☎ 808/422-0561 or 808/423-2263 ⊕ www.nps.gov/usar ☞ Free ⊙ Daily 8–3.

WAIKĪKĪ AQUARIUM. This amazing little attraction harbors more than 420 species of Hawaiian and South Pacific marine life, endangered Hawaiian monk seals, sharks, and the only chambered nautilus living in captivity. The Edge of the Reef exhibit showcases five types of reef environments found along Hawai'i's shorelines. Check out the Sea Visions Theater, the biodiversity exhibit, and the self-guided audio tour, included with admission. ⊠ 2777 Kalākaua Ave., Waikīkī ☎ 808/923-9741 ⊕ www.waquarium.org ☞ $9 ⊙ Daily 9–4:30.

Ow! No.

FLY AROUND. Island Seaplane Service (⊠ 85 Lagoon Dr., Honolulu ☎ 808/836-6273 ⊕ www.islandseaplane.com) takes off from Ke'ehi Lagoon (transportation to/from Waikīkī hotels is provided). Flight options are either a half-hour O'ahu shoreline tour or an hour island circle tour. Rates are $99–$179. **Original Glider Rides** (⊠ Dillingham Airfield, Mokulē'ia ☎ 808/637-0207 ⊕ www.honolulusoaring.com) offers piloted rides for one or two passengers in sleek, bubble-top, motorless aircraft. You'll get aerial views of mountains, shoreline, coral pools, and, in winter, humpback whales. Reservations are recommended; prices vary depending on number of people and duration. **Makani Kai Helicopters** (⊠ 110 Kapalulu Pl., Honolulu ☎ 808/834-5813 or 877/255-8532 ⊕ www.makanikai.com) offers day flights plus a Waikīkī by Night excursion that soars over the city lights. Tours range from $79 to $206.

HIT THE BEACH. Since you're staying in **Waikīkī,** why not stick around and enjoy its beach? Sunning, swimming, surfing, people-watching—it's all here.

In southeast O'ahu, **Halona Cove** (⊠ Below Halona Blow Hole Lookout parking lot ⚿ No facilities) is never crowded, because of the treacherous little climb down to the sand. But what a treat it is for the intrepid. It's in a break in the ocean cliffs, and surrounding crags provide protection from the wind. Turtles seek respite here from the otherwise blustery coast. Pack a lunch and hole up for the day. In windward O'ahu, **Makapu'u Beach** (⊠ Across from Sea Life Park on Kalaniana'ole Hwy., 2 mi south of Waimānalo ⚿ Lifeguard, toilets, showers, picnic tables, grills) is magnificent. Hang gliders circle above the beach; body boarders fill the water. Just off the coast you can see Bird Island, a sanctuary for aquatic fowl.

Lanikai Beach Park (✉ Past Kailua Beach Park; street parking on Mokulua Dr. for various public access points to beach ⚲ Lifeguard, showers) seems like the beach you've been seeing in commercials: peaceful blue waters, soft sands, families and dogs frolicking gleefully. It's a perfect spot to camp out with a book, or to watch wind- and kite surfers. The North Shore's **Waimea Bay** (✉ Across from Waimea Valley, 3 mi north of Hale'iwa on Kamehameha Hwy. ⚲ Lifeguard, toilets, showers, picnic tables, parking lot) is a slice of big-wave heaven, home to king-size 25- to 30-foot winter waves.

LAY BACK AND CRUISE. Sprawl out on a catamaran, grab a drink, and relax. Seven catamarans dotting Waikīkī Beach offer 60-minute day sails ($15–$25) and 90-minute sunset excursions ($20–$30). Some provide free drinks, some charge for them, and some let you pack your own. The fast, sleek **Mai'Tai Catamaran** (☎ 808/922-5665) takes off from between the Halekulani and Sheraton Waikīkī hotels. **Na Hoku II Catamaran** (☎ 808/239-3900 ⊕ www.nahokuii.com) is the Animal House of cats, with reggae music and free drinks. It's beached in front of Duke's Barefoot Bar at the Outrigger Waikīkī Hotel, and sails five times daily.

Paradise Cruises (✉ Pier 8, Aloha Tower MarketPl. ☎ 808/983-STAR (7827) or 800/334-6191 ⊕ www.paradisecruises.com) offers a little of everything: day tours around Diamond Head with snorkeling, kayaking, and windsurfing; fine dining night cruises with lobster and live entertainment; Hawaiian cultural cruises with lei making and hula lessons. Prices vary.

Want to go underwater without getting wet? Try **Atlantis Submarines** (✉ Hilton Hawaiian Village Beach Resort and Spa, 2005 Kālia Rd., Waikīkī ☎ 808/973-1296 or 800/548-6262 ⊕ www.atlantisadventures.com). Its 64-passenger vessel cruises past shipwrecks, turtle breeding-grounds, and coral reefs galore. The tours, which leave from the pier at the Hilton Hawaiian Village, are available in several languages and cost $69 to $115.

Shop Around

Waikīkī

DFS GALLERIA WAIKĪKĪ. Hermès, Cartier, Calvin Klein, and Hawai'i's largest cosmetics store are among the shops at this mall. An exclusive boutique floor caters to duty-free shoppers. The Waikīkī Walk offers authentic fashions, arts and crafts, and gifts of the Hawaiian Islands. ✉ 330 Royal Hawaiian Ave., Waikīkī ☎ 808/931-2655 ⊕ www.dfsgalleria.com.

KING KALĀKAUA PLAZA. Fashionable and relatively new, the open-air King Kalākaua Plaza has flagship Banana Republic and Nike Town stores. ✉ 2080 Kalākaua Ave., Waikīkī ☎ 808/955-2878.

KING'S VILLAGE. It looks like a Hollywood stage set of monarchy-era Honolulu, complete with a changing-of-the-guard ceremony every evening at 6:15. Shops include Hawaiian Island Creations Jewelry, Swim City USA Swimwear, and Island Motor Sports. ✉ 131 Ka'iulani Ave., Waikīkī.

ROYAL HAWAIIAN SHOPPING CENTER. It fronts the Royal Hawaiian and Sheraton Waikīkī hotels and has more than 100 stores on four airy levels. Shops range from the

FORGET SIGHTSEEING. GET ME TO A SPA!

Waikīkī is filled with luxurious hotel spas, but the following stand out.

NĀ HŌʻOLA AT THE HYATT WAIKĪKĪ. Along with your treatment, enjoy jet baths, Vichy showers, and cushy robes. Go for the La Stone massage, in which hot and cold stones work in conjunction with Swedish strokes to melt your aches away. ⊠ Hyatt Regency Waikīkī Resort and Spa, 2424 Kalākaua Ave., Waikīkī ☎ 808/921–6097 ⊕ www.hyattwaikiki.com ⊟ AE, D, DC, MC, V ⊙ Daily 8–6.

SPA OLAKINO AT THE WAIKĪKĪ BEACH MARRIOTT. Lush Hawaiian foliage, sleek Balinese teak furnishings, and the scents of ylang-ylang and nutmeg inspire relaxation. The signature Magic Island Massage (80 minutes, $140) fuses Thai, shiatsu, lomi lomi, and reflexology into one ultimate session. ⊠ Waikīkī Beach Marriott Resort and Spa, 2552 Kalākaua Ave., Waikīkī ☎ 808/922–6611 ⊕ www.marriottwaikiki.com ⊟ AE, D, DC, MC, V ⊙ Daily 8–8.

SPAHALEKULANI. Signature massages include the invigorating Japanese Ton Ton Amma and the relaxing Polynesian Nonu, which utilizes warm stones and healing nonu gel. Both are $180–$255 for 75–120 minutes. ⊠ Halekūlani Hotel, 2199 Kālia Rd., Waikīkī ☎ 808/931–5322 ⊕ www.halekulani.com ⊟ AE, D, DC, MC, V ⊙ Daily 9–8.

Hawaiian Heirloom Jewelry Collection by Philip Rickard, which also has a museum with Victorian pieces, to Harley-Davidson Motor Clothes and Collectibles Boutique. The center often hosts hula, ukulele, or lei-making sessions. ⊠ 2201 Kalākaua Ave., Waikīkī ☎ 808/922–0588 ⊕ www.shopwaikiki.com.

2100 KALĀKAUA. Tenants of this three-story, town house–style center include Chanel, Coach, Tiffany & Co., Yves Saint Laurent, Gucci, and Tod and Bocheron. ⊠ 2100 Kalākaua Ave., Waikīkī ⊕ www.2100kalakaua.com.

WAIKĪKĪ SHOPPING PLAZA. This five-floor shopping center is across the street from the Royal Hawaiian Shopping Center. Walden Books, Guess, Clio Blue jewelers, and Tanaka of Tokyo Restaurant are some of its 50 shops and restaurants. Hawaiian cultural classes are offered daily. ⊠ 2270 Kalākaua Ave., Waikīkī ☎ 808/923-1191.

WAIKĪKĪ TOWN CENTER. Free hula shows liven up this open-air complex on Monday, Wednesday, Friday, and Saturday at 7 PM. Shops sell fashions and jewelry. ⊠ 2301 Kūhiō Ave., Waikīkī ☎ 808/922-2724.

Honolulu: Ala Moana & Downtown

ALA MOANA SHOPPING CENTER. One of the nation's largest open-air malls is five minutes from Waikīkī on Bus 8, 19, or 20 or the Waikīkī Trolley's pink line. More than 240 stores and 60 restaurants make up this 50-acre complex. Look for such designer shops as Gucci, Louis Vuitton, Gianni Versace, and Emporio Armani. Major department stores include Neiman Marcus, Sears, and Macy's. ⊠ 1450 Ala Moana Blvd., Ala Moana ☎ 808/955-9517 ⊕ www.alamoana.com.

ALOHA TOWER MARKETPLACE. This festival marketplace cozies up to Honolulu Harbor. Along with restaurants and entertainment venues, it has 80 shops and kiosks selling expensive sunglasses, local artwork, and souvenir magnets. From Waikīkī, take Bus 19, 20, 2, or 13. ⊠ 1 Aloha Tower Dr., Downtown Honolulu ☎ 808/528-5700 ⊕ www.alohatower.com.

VICTORIA WARD CENTERS. Take Bus 19 or 20 or the Waikīkī Trolley yellow line to get to these five distinct shopping-complex areas with more than 120 specialty shops and 20 restaurants. A "shopping concierge" can help you navigate. ⊠ 1050–1200 Ala Moana Blvd., Ala Moana ☎ 808/591-8411 ⊕ www.victoriaward.com.

West O'ahu

ALOHA STADIUM SWAP MEET. This outdoor bazaar attracts hundreds of vendors and even more bargain hunters. Every Hawaiian souvenir imaginable can be found here, from coral shell necklaces to bikinis, as well as a variety of ethnic wares, from Chinese brocade dresses to Japanese pottery. There are also ethnic foods, silk flowers, and luggage in aloha floral prints. Wear comfortable shoes, use sunscreen, and bring bottled water. The flea market takes place in the Aloha Stadium parking lot on Wednesday and weekends from 6 to 3; the $6 admission fee includes round-trip shuttle service from Waikīkī. ⊠ 99-500 Salt Lake Blvd., Honolulu ☎ 808/486-6704.

WAIKELE PREMIUM OUTLETS. Anne Klein Factory, Donna Karan Company Store, Kenneth Cole, and Saks Fifth Avenue Outlet anchor this discount destination. ⊠ 94-790 Lumiaina St, Waipahu ☎ 808/676-5656.

I Love the Nightlife

With no post-race party, you'll be looking for a great way to celebrate. Happily, Waikīkī doesn't disappoint, with its variety of ways to let loose and play.

Bars & Clubs

BANYAN VERANDA. It's steeped in history. From this location the radio program *Hawai'i Calls* first broadcast the sounds of Hawaiian music and the rolling surf to a U.S. mainland audience in 1935. Today, a variety of Hawaiian entertainment continues to provide the perfect accompaniment to waves. ⊠ Sheraton Moana Surfrider, 2365 Kalākaua Ave., Waikīkī ☎ 808/922-3111 ⊕ www.moana-surfrider.com.

★ **COBALT LOUNGE.** Take the glass elevator up 30 stories to dance or just enjoy the sunset in this lounge in the center of the Hanohano Room. Floor-to-ceiling windows offer breathtaking views of Diamond Head and the Waikīkī shoreline. On the first and third Saturday of each month, the lounge becomes "Skyline," a DJ nightclub with a $10 cover charge. ⊠ Sheraton Waikīkī, 2255 Kalākaua Ave., Waikīkī ☎ 808/922-4422.

★ **DUKE'S CANOE CLUB.** Making the most of its oceanfront spot, Duke's presents "Concerts on the Beach" every Friday, Saturday, and Sunday with contemporary Hawaiian musicians. At Duke's Barefoot Bar, solo Hawaiian musicians take the stage nightly. ✉ Outrigger Waikīkī, 2335 Kalākaua Ave., Waikīkī ☎ 808/922-2268 ⊕ www.dukeswaikiki.com.

FORMAGGIO WINE AND CHEESE BAR. Only people in the know, know where Formaggio is. There's no flashy signage for this establishment on the outskirts of Waikīkī—only the word "Formaggio" painted on the tinted door. It cloaks a dimly lighted bar, where young professionals and baby boomers enjoy live jazz nightly. There are more than 40 wines by the glass and a Mediterranean menu with everything from pizzas to paninis. ✉ Market City Shopping Center, 2919 Kapi'olani Blvd., lower level, Waikīkī ☎ 808/739-7719.

HULA'S BAR AND LEI STAND. Hawai'i's oldest and best-known gay-friendly nightspot offers calming panoramic views of Diamond Head and the ocean by day and a high-energy club scene by night. Check out the soundproof, glassed-in dance floor. ✉ Waikīkī Grand Hotel, 134 Kapahulu Ave., 2nd fl., Waikīkī ☎ 808/923-0669 ⊕ http://hulas.com.

MAI TAI BAR AT THE ROYAL HAWAIIAN. This bar created the namesake drink, and they make 'em good and strong. The pink, umbrella-covered tables at the outdoor bar are front-row seating for Waikīkī sunsets and an unobstructed view of Diamond Head. Contemporary Hawaiian music is usually on stage. ✉ Royal Hawaiian Hotel, 2259 Kalākaua Ave., Waikīkī ☎ 808/923-7311 ⊕ www.royal-hawaiian.com.

MOANA TERRACE. Three floors up from Waikīkī Beach, this open-air terrace is the home of Aunty Genoa Keawe, the "First Lady of Hawaiian Music." Her falsetto sessions include jams with the finest Hawaiian musicians. ✉ Waikīkī Beach Marriott Resort and Spa, 2552 Kalākaua Ave., Waikīkī ☎ 808/922-6611 ⊕ www.marriottwaikiki.com.

NASHVILLE WAIKĪKĪ. Country music in the tropics? You bet! Put on your *paniolo* (Hawaiian cowboy) duds and mosey on out to the giant dance floor. Enjoy pool tables, dartboards, line dancing, and free dance lessons (Wednesday at 6:30 PM). Expect wall-to-wall crowds on the weekend. ✉ Ohana Waikīkī West Hotel, 2330 Kūhiō Ave., Waikīkī ☎ 808/926-7911 ⊕ www.ohanahotels.com.

SCRUPLES BEACH CLUB. After the sun goes down, the beach party moves from the sand to this discotheque right off Waikīkī's strip. Dance to the latest alternative, house, and Top 40 music with a clientele that is as diverse as all Hawai'i. ✉ 2310 Kuhio Ave., Waikīkī ☎ 808/923-9530.

WONDER LOUNGE AT THE W DIAMOND HEAD. The hotel's Diamond Head Grill restaurant is also an after-hours nightclub, full of hip, young professionals who enjoy martinis and not-so-serious networking. Look for a younger group on Saturday. Enjoy fantastic (though pricey) eats until midnight, and dance until 2 AM. ✉ W Honolulu—Diamond Head, 2885 Kalākaua Ave., Waikīkī ☎ 808/922-1700.

Lū'au

Everyone should experience a lū'au. Today's events combine traditional food and entertainment with contemporary flair. With most, you can even watch the roasted pig being carried out of its 'imu, a hole in the ground used for cooking meat with heated stones.

Lū'au cost anywhere from $58 to $110. Most that are held outside of Waikīkī offer shuttle service. Reservations are essential.

GERMAINE'S LŪ'AU. It's billed as being "100 years away from Waikīkī," though it's really only 35 minutes away, on a private beach. Expect a lively crowd on the bus. The food is the usual multicourse, all-you-can-eat buffet, but it's very tasty. It's a good lū'au for first timers. ☎808/949–6626 or 800/367–5655 ⊕ www.germainesluau.com ⊙ Daily at 6.

PARADISE COVE LŪ'AU. The scenery here is almost as unbelievable as the sunsets. Watch Mother Nature's special-effects show on a remote beachfront estate beside a picturesque cove, a good 27 miles from the bustle of Waikīkī. The food isn't bad, and the show features a fire-knife dancer, singing emcee, and both traditional and contemporary hula. Get your money's worth by experiencing an array of traditional island games, arts and crafts, and canoe rides in the cove. ☎808/842–5911 ⊕ www.paradisecovehawaii.com ⊙ Daily at 5:30.

★**POLYNESIAN CULTURAL CENTER ALI'I LŪ'AU.** The most traditional, and perhaps the most elaborate, of all the lū'au is an hour's drive from Honolulu on the North Shore. It's set amid seven re-created Polynesian villages. Go for a whole-day excursion; package deals include admission and dinner, which is an all-you-can-eat buffet with traditional lū'au food such as *kālua* pig and lomi lomi salmon. It's all followed by a revue. ☎808/ 293–3333 or 800/367–7060 ⊕ www.polynesia.com ⊙ Mon.–Sat. center opens at noon; lū'au starts at 5.

ROYAL HAWAIIAN LŪ'AU. For those who don't want to travel too far from the South Shore, Waikīkī's only oceanfront lū'au is exotic and upscale. You won't get to see the 'imu ceremony here because Waikīkī law forbids it. You will, however, get a great view of the setting sun, Diamond Head, the Pacific Ocean, and the legendary Pink Palace. ☎808/931– 8383 ⊕ www.royal-hawaiian.com ⊙ Mon. at 6.

HELPFUL INFO

Air Travel

Most nonstop flights to Honolulu International Airport originate in Los Angeles or San Francisco. Flying time from the West Coast is 4½ to 5 hours. Some hotels have their own airport pickup service; check when you book. There are taxis at the airport baggage-claim exit. The fare to Waikīkī will run approximately $25, plus tip. Drivers are also allowed to charge 30¢ per suitcase. Roberts Hawai'i runs an airport shuttle ($8 one way, $14 round-trip) to and from Waikīkī. Look for a representative at the baggage claim. TheBus, the municipal bus, will take you into Waikīkī for only $2, but you're allowed only one bag, and it must fit on your lap.

There are several car rental companies at the airport. If you rent a car, you'll get to Waikīkī by taking Interstate H1 E to Exit 23, Punahou Street. Make a right onto Punahou, a quick right onto S. Beretania Street, and an even quicker left onto Kalākaua Avenue, the main drag. The drive (sans traffic) takes about 15 minutes.

🔳 **Honolulu International Airport** ✉ 300 Rodgers Blvd., Honolulu ☎ 808/836–6411 🌐 www.hawaii.gov/dot/airports. **Roberts Hawai'i** ☎ 808/539–9400 or 800/831–5541 🌐 www.robertshawaii.com.

🔳 **RENTAL CARS Avis** ☎ 808/834–5536 or 800/321–3712 🌐 www.avis.com. **Budget** ☎ 808/836–1700 or 800/527–7000 🌐 www.budget.com. **Dollar** ☎ 808/831–2331 or 800/800–4000 🌐 www.dollar.com. **Hertz** ☎ 808/831–3500 or 800/654–3131 🌐 www.hertz.com. **National Car Rental** ☎ 808/831–3800 or 800/227–7368 🌐 www.nationalcar.com.

Bus & Trolley Travel

You can go all around the island or just down Kalākaua Avenue for $2 on Honolulu's municipal transportation system, affectionately known as TheBus. You get one free transfer per fare if you ask for it when boarding. Exact change in coins and/or bills is required. A four-day pass costs $20 and is available at ABC convenience stores in Waikīkī. Monthly passes cost $40. There are no official bus-route maps, but you can find privately published booklets at most drug and convenience stores. The important buses for Waikīkī are 2, 4, 8, 19, 20, and 58.

The Waikīkī Trolley has four lines and about 40 stops that allow you to design your own itinerary. The Red Line cruises around Waikīkī, Ala Moana, and downtown. The Yellow Line hits major shopping centers and restaurant locations. The Blue Line provides a tour of O'ahu's southeastern coast, including Hanauma Bay and Sea Life Park. The Pink Line is the Ala Moana Shopping Shuttle Line. Trolleys depart from the Royal Hawaiian Shopping Center in Waikīkī every 15 minutes daily from 8 to 4:30. A one-day unlimited ride pass is $25, a four-day unlimited ride pass is $45 (single trips to Ala Moana are $2 each way).

🔳 **TheBus** ☎ 808/848–5555 🌐 www.thebus.org. **Waikīkī Trolley** ☎ 808/591–2561 or 800/824–8804 🌐 www.waikikitrolley.com.

Car Travel

Waikīkī is only 2½ miles long and ½ mile wide, which means you can usually walk to wherever you're going. If you plan to venture outside of Waikīkī, however, a car is essential. Roads and streets are well marked, though in Honolulu many are one-way. The two main highways are the Nimitz Highway (Hawai'i 92), running from Pearl Harbor to Waikīkī, passing the airport along the way; and Interstate H1, which works its way across the southern portion of O'ahu and heads into Honolulu.

Driving in Honolulu's rush-hour traffic (6:30–8:30 AM and 3:30–5:30 PM) can be exasperating, because left turns are prohibited at many intersections and many roads turn into contraflow lanes. Parking along many streets is curtailed during these hours, and towing is strictly enforced. Read the curbside parking signs before leaving your vehicle, even at a meter. And don't leave valuables in your car; rentals are often targets for thieves.

Disabilities & Accessibility

Access Aloha Travel is a terrific resource for travelers with disabilities. This agency's Web site is loaded with vital information, including the best places to get beach wheelchairs, accessible Waikīkī hotel rooms, and island transportation.

↗ Access Aloha Travel ☎808/545-1143 or 800/480-1143 ⊕www.accessalohatravel.com.

Emergencies

↗ DOCTORS Doctors on Call ⊠Sheraton Princess Kaiulani Hotel, 120 Kaiulani Ave., Waikīkī ☎808/971-6000.

↗ HOSPITALS Queen's Medical Center ⊠1301 Punchbowl St., Downtown Honolulu, Honolulu ☎808/538-9011. **Straub Clinic** ⊠888 S. King St., Downtown Honolulu, Honolulu ☎808/522-4000.

↗ PHARMACIES Kūhiō Pharmacy ⊠Ohana Waikīkī West, 2330 Kūhiō Ave., Waikīkī ☎808/923-4466. **Longs Drugs** ⊠Ala Moana Shopping Center, 1450 Ala Moana Blvd., 2nd level, Ala Moana ☎808/949-4010.

Taxis

You can usually get a taxi right outside your hotel. Most restaurants will call a taxi for you. Rates are $1.50 at the drop of the flag, plus $2.50 per mile. Flat fees can also be negotiated for many destinations—just ask your driver. For transportation throughout the island, try Charley's Taxi & Tours.

↗ Charley's Taxi & Tours ☎808/531-1333.

ACKNOWLEDGMENTS

This book has been an absolute joy to research and write, and it wouldn't have been possible without the help of a great many people, most notably Laura Kidder, the best editor in the entire known universe. Laura, you're not only staggeringly brilliant at your job, but you've also been a wonderful friend and supporter. I owe you many, many thanks, and I look forward to a long and happy partnership. Thanks also to the many people at Fodor's who worked on this book's production and to the excellent Fodor's writers who have worked on previous guides for my marathon cities. Some of your reviews appear in this book; others helped guide me in my own research.

I met many incredible people while researching this book, but I'd be remiss if I didn't single out two particular groups. First, the race directors and marathon public-relations people: Laura Cianciolo, Jon Hughes, and Ann Perez, who were so helpful with the Disney World Marathon; Mike Cambre and later Bill Burke with the Mardi Gras Marathon; Karen Kalen and Cher Cox with Devine Racing and the L.A. Marathon; Jack Fleming with the Boston Marathon; Iris Simpson-Bush with the Flying Pig Marathon, who made me feel like a Very Important Pig; Bruce Durkee with the Newport Marathon, who has been so supportive and encouraging; Bob Wood with the *Deseret Morning News* Marathon, who clearly doesn't read his own press, since he has no idea how impressive he is; David Hirschfeld with the Grizzly Marathon, whose delightful family (human, canine, and bovine) it was my extreme pleasure to meet; Peter Wright with the Stowe Marathon; Amy Berner with the Chicago Marathon; Maeve Mullally with the New York City Marathon; and Pat Bigold and Jeanette Chun with the Honolulu Marathon, whose gracious hospitality enveloped my whole family in the spirit of aloha.

I also want to specifically thank all my "Anyone Can Run a Marathon" profile and other interview subjects. You've made me laugh, gasp in awe, and often go completely slack-jawed with amazement, but most of all you've touched and inspired me with your insights not only on the marathon, but on life. Shymeka, Paula, Scott, Jeremy, Michael, Bob, Cynthia, Debi, Pam, Sean, David, Jim, Ed, and Glady, thank you for letting me into your lives and sharing your stories.

Jeanette Lundgren, my fabulous agent, I appreciate everything you've done. Debbie McMahon, this whole marathon thing is your fault. Thanks for reading the book and giving me your insights; I value both your opinion and your friendship beyond words. Amy Wolfram, Jessica Ammirati, Erzsi Karkus, Sue Goldberg, and Craig Shemin, your help with the New York City Marathon chapter was invaluable. Bob Lundgren and Allison Victoria Harrison Kinsey, Esq., through you I found two of my wonderful profiles—thank you. Thanks to Michelle Westin for her fantastic work on www.travelingmarathoner.com. To Aaron Chapin and to my running partners, Edward Ines and Max Yoshikawa, I don't know that I'd be such an avid marathoner if it weren't for you. And a huge thank-you to Helen Vitaris for being so wonderful and loving with my daughter Madeline while I work.

Finally to my family: Mom-Mom Eva, Pop-Pop Irv (very much alive in my heart), Mom and Jim, Stephanie (Loaf!), Rob and Fran, Eden Sarah Nellis and Everett Matthew Nellis, Jen and Marty, Sid and Betty, Mom-Mom Sylvia and Pop-Pop Nate, Dad and Linda, Michael, Linda, Lauren, and Sue and the rest of the crew, I love you so much. Special thanks to my mom, Ina Lentz, who traveled to New Orleans and Disney World with Maddie and me; to my Dad, Larry Allen, who joined us in Stowe and Choteau; to my sister Stephanie Jacobs, who accompanied us in Stowe and Chicago; and to my aunt and uncle, Linda and Michael Goldberg, who housed us in New York City. And as for Riley, you're the best pooch in the world, the best big brother, and a constant source of love, support, and chicken. And you're very hungry. I think you need a treat.

Most of all, all my thanks, all my love, and all my heart go to my husband, Randy Nellis. It couldn't have been easy watching your increasingly pregnant wife jet around the country, and I'm sure it didn't get easier when I started dragging our infant daughter around with me (which I never would have had the courage to do if you hadn't come along on our first trip, to Honolulu). Your love and support mean everything to me, and I can never thank you enough. To our daughter Madeline Rose: Maddie, you hold my heart. You're the best traveling partner anyone could want, and I'm the luckiest mommy in the world to have you.

INDEX